lonely planet

Costa Rica

Arenal & Northern Lowlands
p241

Northwestern Costa Rica
p191

Central Valley & Highlands
p103

Caribbean Coast
p138

Península de Nicoya
p285

San José
p62

Central Pacific Coast
p347

Southern Costa Rica & Península de Osa
p405

ND RESEARCHED BY

arrell, Anna Kaminski

JUL 2017

Contents

OXCART WHEEL, SARCHÍ
P114

Contents

ON THE ROAD

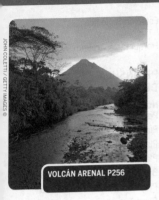

VOLCÁN ARENAL P256

Contents

UNDERSTAND

PARQUE NACIONAL CORCOVADO P439

SURVIVAL GUIDE

SPECIAL FEATURES

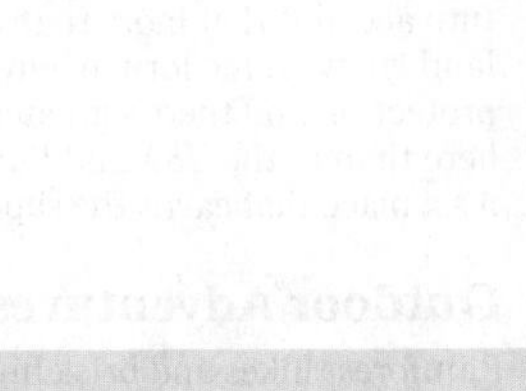

Welcome to Costa Rica

All trails lead to waterfalls, misty crater lakes or jungle-fringed, deserted beaches. Explored by horseback, foot or kayak, Costa Rica is a tropical choose-your-own-adventure land.

Peaceful Soul

As the eco- and adventure-tourism capital of Central America, Costa Rica has a worthy place in the cubicle daydreams of travelers around the world. With world-class infrastructure, visionary sustainability initiatives and no standing army since 1948 (when the country redirected its defense funds toward education, healthcare and the environment), Costa Rica is a peaceful green jewel of the region. Taking into account that more than a fourth of the land enjoys some form of environmental protection and there's greater biodiversity here than in the USA and Europe combined, it's a place that earns the superlatives.

Outdoor Adventures

Rainforest hikes and brisk high-altitude trails, rushing white-water rapids and world-class surfing: Costa Rica offers a dizzying suite of adventures in every shape and size – from the rush of a canopy zip line to a sun-dazed afternoon at the beach. National parks allow visitors to glimpse life in the tropical rainforest and cloud forest, simmering volcanoes offer otherworldly vistas, and reliable surf breaks are suited to beginners and experts alike. Can't decide? Don't worry, you won't have to. Given the country's diminutive size, it's possible to plan a relatively short trip that includes it all.

Wild Life

Such wildlife abounds in Costa Rica as to seem almost cartoonish: keel-billed toucans ogle you from treetops and scarlet macaws raucously announce their flight paths. A keen eye will discern a sloth on a branch or the eyes and snout of a caiman breaking the surface of a mangrove swamp, while alert ears will catch rustling leaves signaling a troop of white-faced capuchins or the haunting call of a howler monkey. Blue morpho butterflies flit amid orchid-festooned trees, while colorful tropical fish, sharks, rays, dolphins and whales thrive offshore – all as if in a conservationist's dream.

Pure Life

And then there are the people. Costa Ricans, or Ticos as they prefer to call themselves, are proud of their little slice of paradise, welcoming guests to sink into the easygoing rhythms of the *pura vida* (pure life). The greeting, farewell, catchy motto and enduring mantra gets to the heart of Costa Rica's appeal – its simple yet profound ability to let people relax and enjoy their time. With the highest quality of life in Central America, all the perfect waves, perfect sunsets and perfect beaches seem like the *pura vida* indeed.

Why I Love Costa Rica

By Ashley Harrell, Writer

The night I moved to Costa an expat in a bar congratulated me. 'The best part,' she said, 'is you can do anything here.' She wasn't talking about traveling the entire country, undertaking extreme adventures or attending a Christmas party in a bikini (but yeah, done all that). She meant that people here have the time, freedom and permission to truly live. Want to sleep in a shack and surf constantly? Do it. Want to rescue baby sloths? Somebody has to. I wanted to travel, study wildlife, write and feel alive. Now I do. *Pura vida*.

For more about our writers, see p544.

Above: Red-eyed tree frog peeking through a hole in a leaf

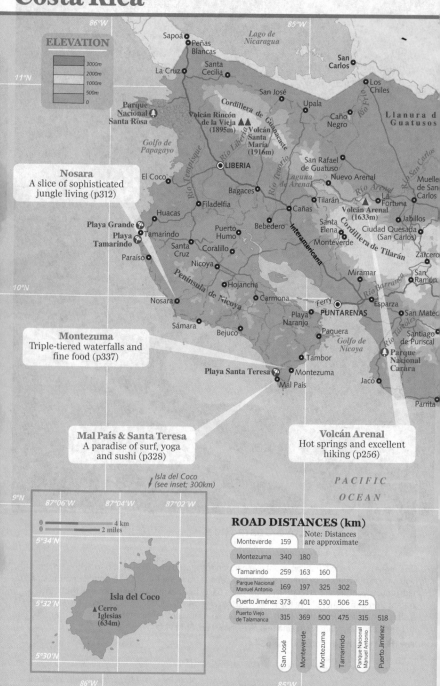

Costa Rica

ELEVATION

3000m
2000m
1000m
500m
0

Nosara
A slice of sophisticated jungle living (p312)

Montezuma
Triple-tiered waterfalls and fine food (p337)

Mal País & Santa Teresa
A paradise of surf, yoga and sushi (p328)

Volcán Arenal
Hot springs and excellent hiking (p256)

Isla del Coco
(see inset; 300km)

PACIFIC OCEAN

Isla del Coco

▲ Cerro Iglesias (634m)

0 — 4 km
0 — 2 miles

ROAD DISTANCES (km)

Note: Distances are approximate

	San José	Monteverde	Montezuma	Tamarindo	Parque Nacional Manuel Antonio	Puerto Jiménez
Monteverde	159					
Montezuma	340	180				
Tamarindo	259	163	160			
Parque Nacional Manuel Antonio	169	197	325	302		
Puerto Jiménez	373	401	530	506	215	
Puerto Viejo de Talamanca	315	369	500	475	315	518

Sarapiquí Valley
A paddling paradise with excellent ecolodges (p276)

CARIBBEAN SEA

Poás Region
Cloud forest hikes and misty volcanic craters (p111)

NICARAGUA

Parque Nacional Tortuguero
Glide on waterways past nesting turtles (p152)

San José
Dig into Costa Rican culture and cuisine (p62)

Southern Caribbean Coast
Mix of indigenous, Tico and Afro-Carribean cultures (p163)

Cerro Chirripó
Icy lakes, windswept heights and rugged hiking (p416)

Parque Nacional Manuel Antonio
Accessible rainforest and beautiful beaches (p383)

PANAMA

Parque Nacional Corcovado
The country's premier wilderness experience (p439)

Río San Juan

Boca Tapada

Barra del Colorado

Llanura de San Carlos

Pital

Llanura de Tortuguero

Tortuguero

Puerto Viejo de Sarapiquí

Cariari

Parque Nacional Tortuguero

San Miguel

Parque Nacional Volcán Poás

Llanura de Santa Clara

Guácimo

Parismina

Volcán Poás (2704m)

Guápiles

Siquirres

ALAJUELA

HEREDIA

Volcán Irazú (3432m)

Lajas

PUERTO LIMÓN

Ciudad Colón

SAN JOSÉ

CARTAGO

Pacayas

San Ignacio de Acosta

Paraíso

Turrialba

Moravia

Pandora

Cahuita

San Marcos de Tarrazú

Santa María de Dota

Tapantí

Puerto Viejo de Talamanca

Valle de Parrita

Parque Nacional Chirripó

Bribrí

Shiroles

Sixaola

Quepos

Savegre

Parque Nacional Los Quetzales

Rivas

Cerro Chirripó (3820m)

Amubri

Guabito

Changuinola

San Isidro de El General

Reserva Biológica Durika

Cordillera de Talamanca

Bocas del Toro

Parque Nacional Manuel Antonio

Dominical

Ujarrás

Almirante

Uvita

Buenos Aires

Bahía de Coronado

Valle del General

Paso Real

Potrero Grande

Río Cotón

PANAMA

Ciudad Cortés

Palmar Norte

Valle de Coto Brus

Santa Elena

Interamericana

Fila Costeña

San Vito

Sabalito

Sierpe

Agua Buena

Río Sereno

Boquete

Rincón

Golfo Dulce

Golfito

Río Claro

Neily

Parque Nacional Corcovado

Península de Osa

Puerto Jiménez

Ferry

Paso Canoas

Concepción

Laguna Corcovado

Playa Zancudo

Valle de Coto Colorado

David

Carate

Puerto Armuelles

Costa Rica's
Top 20

White-Water Rafting

1 So many rivers, so little time. But the dedicated adrenaline junkie could easily cover some heart-pounding river miles in the span of a few days in this compact little country. For those without the drive to do them all, pick a river, any river: Pacuare (p132), Reventazón, Sarapiquí. Any of the three are fun runs (though we're partial to the Pacuare), with rapids ranging from Class II to Class V, and all have stretches of smooth water that allow rafters to take in the luscious jungle scenery surrounding these river gorges. Below: Río Pacuare (p132)

Volcán Arenal & Hot Springs

2 While the molten night views are gone, this mighty, perfectly conical giant (p256) is still considered active and worthy of a pilgrimage. There are several beautiful trails to explore, especially the magnificent climb to Cerro Chato. At its base, you are just a short drive away from her many hot springs. Some of these springs are free, and any local can point the way. Others are, shall we say, embellished, dressed up, luxuriated – dip your toes into the romantic Eco Termales, for starters.

KEVIN SCHAFER / GETTY IMAGES ©

NICK LEDGER / GETTY IMAGES ©

Southern Caribbean Coast

3 By day, lounge in a hammock, cruise by bike to snorkel off uncrowded beaches, hike to waterfall-fed pools and visit the remote indigenous territories of the Bribrí and Kéköldi. By night, dip into zesty Caribbean cooking and sway to reggaetón at open-air bars cooled by ocean breezes. The villages of Cahuita, Puerto Viejo de Talamanca and Manzanillo, all outposts of this unique mix of Afro-Caribbean, Tico and indigenous culture, are the perfect, laid-back home bases for such adventures on the Caribbean's southern coast (p163).

Wildlife-Watching

4 Monkeys and crocs, toucans and iguanas: Costa Rica's menagerie is a thrill. World-class parks, long-standing dedication to environmental protection and mind-boggling biodiversity enable the country to harbor scores of rare and endangered species. It's one of the best wildlife-watching destinations on the globe. In fact, visitors hardly have to make an effort; no matter where you travel, the branches overhead are alive with critters. And if there's an animal you happen to miss, the country is replete with rescue centers like the Jaguar Centro de Rescate (p181). Bottom: Keel-billed toucan (p495)

KRYSIA CAMPOS / GETTY IMAGES ©

CHRISTER FREDRIKSSON / GETTY IMAGES ©

Poás Region

5 An hour northwest of the capital, Poás (p111) is a fairy-tale land of verdant mountains, hydrangea-lined roadsides and the largest and most accessible volcanic crater on the isthmus. Although a 6.2 earthquake rocked the region in 2009, the area's most intriguing attractions endured. The windy drive past strawberry farms and coffee plantations still culminates with the smoking volcano and emerald-green crater lake. And over at La Paz Waterfall Gardens, visitors hike to storybook waterfalls and encounter rescued monkeys, tropical birds and wild cats, including three jaguars. Above: Volcán Poás (p111)

Mal País & Santa Teresa

6 In the rugged little surf towns of Mal País and Santa Teresa (p328), the sea is alive with marine wildlife and the waves are near-ideal in shape, color and temperature. The hills are lush and the coastline long, providing an ideal backdrop for the pink and orange sunsets. The road may be rutted, but it is also dotted with stylish boutique sleeps and ends in an authentic Tico fishing hamlet. Here you can feel sort of like a castaway but still score a dinner worthy of royalty. Top right: Playa El Carmen (p328), Santa Teresa

Parque Nacional Tortuguero

7 Canoeing the canals of Parque Nacional Tortuguero (p152) is a boat-borne safari, where thick jungle meets the water and you can get up close with shy caimans, river turtles, crowned night herons, monkeys and sloths. In the right season, under the cover of darkness, watch the awesome, millennia-old ritual of turtles building nests and laying their eggs on the black-sand beaches. Sandwiched between extravagantly green wetlands and the wild Caribbean Sea, this is among the premier places in Costa Rica to watch wildlife.

Parque Nacional Corcovado

8 Muddy, muggy and intense, the vast, largely untouched rainforest of Parque Nacional Corcovado (p439) is anything but a walk in the park. Here travelers with a flexible agenda and a sturdy pair of rubber boots thrust themselves into the unknown and come out the other side with the story of a lifetime. And the further into the jungle you go, the better it gets: the country's best wildlife-watching, most desolate beaches and most vivid adventures lie down Corcovado's seldom-trodden trails.

Top: Scarlet macaw (p495)

Montezuma

9 If you dig artsy-rootsy beach culture, enjoy rubbing shoulders with neo-Rastas and yoga fiends, or have always wanted to spin fire, study Spanish or lounge on sugar-white coves, find your way to Montezuma (p337). Strolling this intoxicating town and rugged coastline, you're never far from the rhythm of the sea. From here you'll also have easy access to the famed Cabo Blanco reserve, and can take the tremendous hike to a triple-tiered waterfall. Oh, and when your stomach growls, the town has some of the best restaurants in the country.

Parque Nacional Manuel Antonio

10 Although droves of visitors pack Parque Nacional Manuel Antonio (p383) – the country's most popular (and smallest) national park – it remains an absolute gem. Capuchin monkeys scurry across its idyllic beaches, brown pelicans dive-bomb its clear waters and sloths watch over its accessible trails. It's a perfect place to introduce youngsters to the wonders of the rainforest, and splashing around in the waves you're likely to feel like a kid yourself. There's not much by way of privacy, but it's so lovely that you won't mind sharing.

Bosque Nuboso Monteverde

11 A pristine expanse of virginal forest totaling 105 sq km, Monteverde Cloud Forest (p209) owes much of its impressive natural beauty to Quaker settlers, who left the US in the 1950s to protest the Korean War and helped foster conservationist principles with Ticos of the region. But as fascinating as the history is, the real romance of Monteverde is in nature itself: a mysterious Neverland shrouded in mist, dangling with mossy vines, sprouting with ferns and bromeliads, gushing with creeks, blooming with life and nurturing rivulets of evolution.

Surfing

12 Costa Rica's Caribbean coast may move to the terminally laid-back reggae groove, but the country's best year-round surfing is on the Pacific side. It's home to a number of seaside villages where the day's agenda rarely gets more complicated than a scrupulous study of the surf report, a healthy application of sunblock and a few cold Imperials. With plenty of good breaks for beginners, and the country's most reliable rides – including what may be the world's second-longest left-hand break, in Pavones (p457) – Costa Rica has inexhaustible potential for surfers. Below: Pavones (p457)

Sarapiquí Valley

13 Sarapiquí (p276) rose to fame as a principal port in the nefarious old days of United Fruit dominance, before it meandered into agricultural anonymity, only to be reborn as a paddler's mecca thanks to the frothing serpentine mocha magic of its namesake river. These days it's still a paddling paradise, and it's also dotted with fantastic ecolodges and private forest preserves that will educate you about pre-Columbian life, get you into that steaming, looming, muddy jungle, and bring you up close to local wildlife. Right: Poison-dart frog (p497)

NIKPAL / GETTY IMAGES ©

ROB FRANCIS / ROBERTHARDING / GETTY IMAGES ©

Nosara

14 Nosara (p312) is a cocktail of international surf culture, jungled microclimes and yoga bliss, where three stunning beaches are stitched together by a network of swerving, rutted earth roads that meander over coastal hills. Visitors can stay in the alluring surf enclave of Playa Guiones – where there are some fabulous restaurants and a drop-dead-gorgeous beach – or in Playa Pelada, which is as romantic as it is rugged and removed. One resident described the area as 'sophisticated jungle living,' and who wouldn't want more of that in their life? Left: Playa Guiones (p312)

17

Quetzal-Spotting

15 Once considered divine by pre-Columbian cultures of Central America, the strikingly beautiful, re-splendent quetzal was sought after for its long, iridescent-green tail feath-ers, which adorned the headdresses of royalty. This unusual, jewel-toned bird remains a coveted find in modern times, but now as a bucket-list sighting for bird-watchers. Fortunately, though the quetzal's con-servation status is listed as near-threatened, it is commonly sighted in San Gerardo de Dota (p409) and at lodges like Mirador de Quetzales, especially during its breeding season in April and May.

Playa Sámara

16 Some expat residents call Playa Sámara (p320) the black hole of happiness, which has something to do with that crescent of sand spanning two rocky head-lands, the opportunity to learn to surf, stand-up paddle board, surf cast or fly above migrating whales in an ultra-light, and the plethora of nearby all-natural beaches and coves. All of it is easy to access on foot or via pub-lic transportation, which is why it's becoming so popular with families, who enjoy Sámara's palpable ease and tranquillity.

Cerro Chirripó

17 The view from the rugged peak of Cer-ro Chirripó (p416), Costa Rica's highest summit – of windswept rocks and icy lakes – may not resemble the Costa Rica of the post-cards, but the two-day hike above the clouds is one of the country's most satisfy-ing excursions. A pre-dawn expedition rewards hardy hikers with the real prize: a chance to catch the fiery sunrise and see both the Caribbean Sea and the Pacific Ocean in a full and glorious panoramic view from 3820m high.

18

San José

18 The heart of Tico culture lives in San José (p62), as do university students, intellectuals, artists and politicians. While not the most attractive capital in Central America, it does have some graceful neoclassical and Spanish-colonial architecture, leafy neighborhoods, museums housing pre-Columbian jade and gold, nightlife that goes on until dawn, and some of the most sophisticated restaurants in the country. Street art – of both officially sanctioned and guerrilla varieties – add unexpected pops of color and public discourse to the cityscape. For the seasoned traveler, Chepe, as it is affectionately known, has its charms.

Zip-Lining through the Rainforest Canopy

19 The wild-eyed, whoop-de-whoop happiness of a canopy tour is self-evident. Few things are more purely joyful than clipping into a high-speed cable that's laced above and through the teeming jungle. This is where kids become little daredevils and adults become kids. Invented in Monteverde, zip-line outfits quickly multiplied, cropping up in all corners of Costa Rica. The best place to sample the lines is still Monteverde (p199), where the forest is alive, the mist fine and swirling, and the afterglow worth savoring.

Coffee Plantations

20 Take a little country drive on the scenic, curvy back roads of the Central Valley, where the hillsides are a patchwork of varied agriculture and coffee shrubbery. If you're curious about the magical brew that for many makes life worth living, tour one of the coffee plantations and learn all about how Costa Rica's golden bean goes from plant to cup. A couple of the best places for a tour are Finca Cristina (p128) in the Orosi Valley and Café Britt Finca near Barva.

Bottom right: Coffee plantation in the Valle de Orosi (p128)

Need to Know

For more information, see Survival Guide (p503)

Currency
Costa Rican colón (₡)

Language
Spanish, English

Visas
Generally not required for stays of up to 90 days.

Money
Both US dollars and Costa Rican colones are accepted everywhere and dispensed from ATMs across the country. Except for the smallest towns and shops in rural areas, credit cards are accepted.

Cell Phones
➡ 3G and 4G systems available, but those compatible with US plans require expensive international roaming.

➡ Prepaid SIM cards are cheap and widely available.

➡ Of the four cellular providers (Claro, Kolbi, Movistar, TuYo), Kolbi has the best coverage in remote areas and Movistar has the worst.

Time
Central Standard Time (GMT/UTC minus six hours)

When to Go

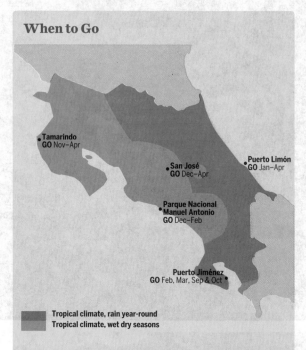

- Tamarindo **GO** Nov–Apr
- San José **GO** Dec–Apr
- Puerto Limón **GO** Jan–Apr
- Parque Nacional Manuel Antonio **GO** Dec–Feb
- Puerto Jiménez **GO** Feb, Mar, Sep & Oct

Tropical climate, rain year-round
Tropical climate, wet dry seasons

High Season
(Dec–Apr)

➡ 'Dry' season still sees some rain; beach towns fill with domestic tourists.

➡ Accommodations should be booked well in advance; some places enforce two- or three-day minimum stays.

Shoulder
(May–Jul & Nov)

➡ Rain picks up and the stream of tourists starts to taper off.

➡ Roads are muddy and rivers begin to rise, making off-the-beaten-track travel more challenging.

Low Season
(Aug–Oct)

➡ Rainfall is highest, but storms bring swells to the Pacific, and the best surfing conditions.

➡ Rural roads can be impassable due to river crossings.

➡ Accommodations prices lower significantly.

Useful Websites

Anywhere Costa Rica (www.anywherecostarica.com) Excellent overviews of local destinations; run by a tour agency that gets good reviews.

Essential Costa Rica (www.visitcostarica.com) The Costa Rica Tourism Board (ICT) website has general travel information, as well as planning tips and destination details.

The Tico Times (www.ticotimes.net) Costa Rica's English-language newspaper's website; its searchable archives can be helpful for trip planning around specific destinations.

Lonely Planet (www.lonelyplanet.com/costa-rica) Destination information, hotel bookings, traveler forum and more.

Important Numbers

Country code	506
International access code	011
International operator	00
Emergency	911
Costa Rica Tourism Board	1-800-868-7476

Exchange Rates

Australia	A$1	₡374
Canada	C$1	₡375
Euro zone	€1	₡581
Japan	¥100	₡453
New Zealand	NZ$1	₡372
UK	£1	₡761
USA	US$1	₡534

For current exchange rates, see www.xe.com.

Daily Costs

Budget:
Less than US$40

➡ Dorm bed: US$8–15

➡ Meal at a *soda* (inexpensive eatery): US$3–7

➡ DIY hikes without a guide: free

➡ Travel via local bus: US$1 or less

Midrange:
US$40–100

➡ Basic room with private bathroom: US$20–50 per day

➡ Meal at a restaurant geared toward travelers: US$5–12

➡ Travel on an efficient 1st-class bus company such as Interbus: US$50–60

Top End:
More than US$100

➡ Luxurious beachside lodges and boutique hotels: from US$80

➡ Meal at an international fusion restaurant: from US$15

➡ Guided wildlife-watching excursion: from US$30

➡ Short domestic flight: US$50–100

➡ 4WD rental for local travel: from US$60 per day

Opening Hours

Banks 9am to 4pm Monday to Friday, sometimes 9am to noon Saturday.

Bars & clubs 8pm to 2am.

Government offices 8am and 5pm Monday to Friday. Often closed between 11:30am and 1:30pm.

Restaurants 7am to 9pm. Upscale places may open only for dinner. In remote areas, even the small *sodas* (inexpensive eateries) might open only at specific meal times.

Shops 8am to 6pm Monday to Saturday.

Arriving in Costa Rica

Aeropuerto Internacional Juan Santamaría (San José) Alajuela–San José buses (US$1.10) from the airport to central San José run from 5am to 10pm. Taxis charge US$25 to US$30 and depart from the official stand; the trip takes 20 minutes to an hour. Interbus (p99) runs between the airport and San José accommodations (US$15 per adult, US$7 per child under 12).

Aeropuerto Internacional Daniel Oduber Quirós (Liberia) Buses run to the Mercado Municipal (30 minutes, hourly) from 6am to 7pm, Monday through Friday only. Taxis from Liberia to the airport are about US$20. There are no car-rental desks at the airport; make reservations in advance and your company will meet you at the airport with a car.

Getting Around

Air Inexpensive domestic flights between San José and popular destinations such as Puerto Jiménez, Quepos and Tortuguero will save you driving time.

Bus Very reasonably priced, with extensive coverage of the country, though travel can be slow and some destinations have infrequent service.

Private shuttle For door-to-door service between popular destinations, private and shared shuttles like Interbus or Gray Line can save time by allowing you to schedule to your needs.

Car Renting a car lets you access destinations that are not served by buses. Cars can be rented in most towns. Renting a 4WD vehicle is advantageous (and essential in some parts of the country); avoid driving at night.

For much more on **getting around**, see p519

First Time Costa Rica

For more information, see Survival Guide (p503)

Checklist

➡ Check the validity of your passport

➡ Check the visa situation and government travel advisories

➡ Organize travel insurance

➡ Check flight restrictions on luggage and camping or outdoors equipment

➡ Check your immunization history

➡ Contact car-insurance provider about foreign coverage

➡ If you plan to rent a car, bring your driver's license and a copy of your current insurance policy

What to Pack

➡ Bathing suit

➡ Camera; binoculars

➡ Flip-flops and hiking boots

➡ Sunglasses

➡ Sunscreen – it's expensive in Costa Rica

➡ Refillable water bottle

➡ Bug repellent with DEET

➡ Flashlight or headlamp

➡ Poncho

➡ First-aid kit

➡ A small day pack

Top Tips for Your Trip

➡ In Costa Rica, things have a way of taking longer than expected – Tico time is in effect. Make space for leisurely meals, learn to relax into delays and take these as opportunities to get to know the locals.

➡ Avoid driving at night – pedestrians, animals and huge potholes are difficult to see on Costa Rica's largely unlit roads. Also keep an eye out for impatient drivers passing slower traffic on two-lane roads.

➡ If you need directions, ask a few different people before setting out. Ticos like to seem helpful even when they can't be.

➡ Although credit cards are widely accepted, it's often cash only in more remote areas. It's good to have a stash of colones or dollars.

➡ Ticos use quite a lot of local slang, so even experienced Spanish speakers might need to adjust to the regional vocabulary.

What to Wear

Although the coastal areas are hot and humid, calling for shorts and short sleeves, you'll want to pack a sweater and lightweight jacket for popular high-elevation destinations such as Volcán Irazú and Monteverde. If you plan to hike up Chirripó, bring lots of layers and a hat and gloves. Additionally, while hiking through the rainforest is often a hot and sweaty exercise, long sleeves and lightweight, quick-drying pants help keep the bugs away.

Sleeping

If you're visiting during high season, it's best to book ahead; this is especially important during the Christmas, New Year and Easter (Semana Santa) holidays.

➡ **Hotels** Range from small, family-run affairs to boutique and larger establishments, catering to all budgets and needs.

➡ **B&Bs** There's a variety of B&Bs throughout the country, reflecting the diversity of the landscape as well as the individual proprietors.

➡ **Hostels** You'll find a great bunch of hostels in the more popular locales, most providing dorms, wi-fi, communal kitchens and excellent travel information.

➡ **Apartments & villas** Those seeking better deals and more privacy are well served with all levels of short-term rental apartments and villas.

Money

Both US dollars and Costa Rican colones are accepted everywhere and dispensed from ATMs across the country. With the exception of the smallest towns and shops in rural areas, credit cards are accepted.

For more information, see p510.

Bargaining

In markets and in arranging informal tours or transport, it's common to haggle before settling on a price. Otherwise, expect to pay the stated price.

Tipping

➡ **Restaurants** Your bill at many restaurants will usually include a 10% service charge. If not, you might leave a small tip to show your appreciation, but it is not required.

➡ **Hotels** It is customary to tip the bellhop/porter (US$1 to US$5 per service) and the housekeeper (US$1 to US$2 per day) in top-end hotels, less in budget places.

➡ **Taxis** Taxi drivers are not usually tipped unless some special service is provided.

➡ **Guides** On guided tours, tip the guide US$5 to US$15 per person per day. Tip the tour driver about half of what you tip the guide. Naturally, tips depend upon quality of service.

Language

Spanish is the national language of Costa Rica, and knowing some very basic phrases is not only courteous but also essential, particularly when navigating through rural areas. That said, a long history of North American tourists has made English the country's unofficial second language. With the exception of basic *sodas* (inexpensive eateries), local buses, and shops catering exclusively to locals, travelers can expect bilingual menus, signs and brochures.

See Language (p525) for more information.

Etiquette

While Ticos are very laid-back as a people, they are also very conscientious about being *bien educado* (polite). A greeting when you make eye contact with someone, or more generally maintaining a respectful demeanor and a smile, will go a long way.

➡ **Asking for help** Say *disculpe* to get someone's attention, *perdón* to ask for an apology.

➡ **Visiting indigenous communities** Ask permission to take photos, particularly of children, and dress more modestly than beachwear.

➡ **Surfing** Novices should learn the etiquette of the lineup, not drop in on other surfers, and be aware of swimmers in their path.

➡ **Hitchhiking** Picking up hitchhikers in rural areas is common. If you get a ride from a local, offer a small tip.

➡ **Topless sunbathing** It isn't appropriate for women to sunbathe topless in public; respect local customs by resisting the urge.

What's New

New San José Restaurants

A food and drink revolution is taking place in Costa Rica's capital, with new restaurants and cafes emphasizing innovative, artisanal and farm-to-table fare. Leading the way are La Ventanita Meraki (p83), Al Mercat (p89) and Café Miel (p86).

Really Experience Community

A nonprofit started the country's first slum tour of El Triángulo, a squatter development of 2000 people north of San José. The respectful tour introduces guests to community entrepreneurs. (p73)

Las Tablillas Border Crossing

The new border crossing at Las Tablillas, 6km north of Los Chiles, opened in May 2015. A new bridge over the Río San Juan means you don't have to take a boat to Nicaragua anymore. (p517)

Improvements to the Interamericana

Between Cañas and Liberia, the Interamericana is now four lanes instead of two. By 2017, the road, overpasses and ramps should all be complete.

Diamante Eco Adventure Park

Near Playa Matapalo on the Península de Nicoya, this new oceanfront adventure park offers ATV tours, hiking, biking, horseback riding, kayaking, scuba diving, stand-up paddleboarding, surfing, zip lining and more. (p293)

Caminos de Osa

A new sustainable tourism initiative that takes visitors on multiday hikes through villages on Costa Rica's wildest peninsula, introducing them to the locals and the history. (p450)

Parque Nacional Corcovado's New Trail & Ranger Station

Sirena ranger station has been rebuilt. There's also a new seven-hour loop trail into the park that starts from the Dos Brasos ranger station. (p442)

Changes at Cerro Chirripó

Crestones Base Lodge, Chirripó's base camp, has been upgraded by its new owners, a private consortium. Dorm bed prices have risen to US$39 but include bedding and three meals a day. Booking remains a challenge. (p419)

Alturas Animal Sanctuary

This wildife rescue in Dominical has opened to take in orphaned and injured animals and illegal pets. The animals are rehabilitated when possible, and the rest are looked after indefinitely. (p391)

Paddle 9

A new tour company is the first and only outfit to offer stand-up paddleboarding in Quepos. It does day tours of the Pacific coast, combining an intro to SUP with waterfall swims. (p370)

Finca 6

In 2014 the pre-Columbian stone spheres found around Sierpe and in its Finca 6 museum were granted Unesco World Heritage status. The spheres' attraction is expanding to bring attention to this overlooked part of Costa Rica. (p427)

For more recommendations and reviews, see lonelyplanet.com/costa-rica

If You Like...

Beaches

Playa Manuel Antonio With mischievous monkeys, perfect sand and turquoise water, this beach is worth the park fee. (p384)

Playa Grande This seemingly endless beach is good for strolling and frequented by leatherback turtles and surfers. (p298)

Playa Guiones Backed by lush vegetation, these gentle waves are ideal for swimming, surfing or just frolicking. (p312)

Playa Negra Cahuita's wild black-sand beach doesn't draw many surfers, making it ideal for swimming. (p164)

Parque Nacional Marino Ballena The long, rugged, coconut-strewn beaches of Ballena feel like an isolated desert island. (p399)

White-Water Rafting & Kayaking

With Costa Rica's ample waterways and excellent operators, the opportunities for rushing down frothing white-water rapids and coasting through mangrove channels will satisfy even the greatest thirst for adventure.

Río Pacuare Take on runs of Class II to IV rapids on the country's best white water. (p132)

Río Sarapiquí This less-frequented river is a great place to raft or learn how to kayak. (p277)

Golfo Dulce Lucky kayakers can paddle out with dolphins and explore sea caves. (p453)

Canales de Tortuguero Excellent for kayaking through canals to get close to birds and wildlife. (p152)

Río Savegre Gentle rapids that pick up in the rainy season serve as a great introduction to rafting; trips depart from Quepos. (p370)

Surfing

Salsa Brava This Caribbean break has the country's biggest surf – in December waves get up to 7m. (p173)

Pavones One of the longest left-hand breaks on Earth draws the goofy-footed from near and far. (p457)

Dominical Countless foreigners show up here to surf, and can't bring themselves to leave. (p391)

Playa Guiones The best beach break in the Central Peninsula, especially when there's an offshore wind. (p312)

Playa Grande Costa Rica's most reliable break draws hordes – luckily it's so big it never seems crowded. (p299)

Playa Hermosa Several beautiful beach breaks for pros, a stone's throw from Jacó's beginner breaks. (p365)

Wildlife-Watching

Even for those who don't know their snowy-bellied emerald from their gray-breasted wood wren, Costa Rica's birds are a thrill. Nearly 900 bird species fill Costa Rica's skies – more than in the entire US and Canada combined.

Rancho Naturalista More than 250 species of bird have been seen from the balcony of this avian-crazy lodge. (p134)

Wilson Botanical Garden This private reserve attracts many specialty birds of southern Costa Rica, including rare high-altitude species. (p424)

Península de Osa Although they're rare in the country, scarlet macaws frequent the skies around Parque Nacional Corcovado. (p405)

Parque Nacional Los Quetzales Named for its banner attraction, the flamboyantly colored ceremonial bird of the Maya. (p411)

Monteverde & Santa Elena
Keep your eyes peeled for the keel-billed toucan, three-wattled bellbirds and motmots. (p193)

Parque Nacional Tortuguero
Herons, kites, ospreys, kingfishers, macaws: the bird list is a mile long at this wildlife-rich park. (p152)

Hiking

Rainforest trails and endless strolls down the beach, high-altitude mountains and cloud forest: the only way to see it all in Costa Rica is to don some boots and hit the trail.

Parque Nacional Chirripó Up and up: the trail to the top of Costa Rica is a thrilling (chilly) adventure. (p416)

Parque Nacional Corcovado
These challenging trails provide a supreme look at the wonders of the rainforest. (p439)

Monteverde Cloud Forest
Utterly fantastic for day hikes, with walks through cloud-forest gorges among plant and animal life. (p209)

Parque Nacional Volcán Tenorio
The trails circumnavigate volcanoes and misty waterfalls, with frequent blue morpho butterfly sightings. (p218)

Volcán Barva A little tough to get to, but the trip is worth the reward: crater lakes and quiet cloud forest. (p142)

Luxury Spas & Resorts

Long gone are Costa Rica's rough-and-tumble days; nowadays travelers enjoy this country in the lap of luxury. These plush comforts are scattered throughout the country and many

Top: Hiker in Bosque Nuboso Monteverde (p209)
Bottom: White-water rafting on the Río Sarapiquí (p278)

espouse standard-setting sustainability practices.

El Silencio Hanging at the edge of a canyon amid endless acres of rolling green, this place is a sumptuous slice of Zen in the cloud forest. (p118)

La Paloma Lodge A posh delight in Costa Rica's wildest corner, this chic jungle lodge is far off the grid. (p433)

Hotel Villa Caletas Guests enjoy seclusion, personalized service and breathtaking sunsets atop a Pacific cliff just north of Playa Herradura. (p358)

Peace Lodge Surrounded by trails near the Volcán Poás, this storybook resort and rescue center enchants. (p112)

Ecolodges

Although Costa Rica's amazing natural resources are at risk of being loved to death, the wealth of top ecolodges give visitors an opportunity to make a minimal impact without sacrificing creature comforts.

Casa Corcovado Jungle Lodge Osa's first top-certified ecolodge is removed from civilization, near the wilds of Corcovado. (p438)

Villa Blanca Cloud Forest Hotel & Nature Reserve With the highest sustainability rating, Villa Blanca offers plush ecological digs. (p119)

Pacuare Lodge This posh, riverfront lodge transcends the need for electricity with high style and adventure. (p145)

Arenas del Mar The best ecolodge near Manuel Antonio, this architectural stunner has private Jacuzzis overlooking the coast. (p377)

Ecolodge San Luis One of the highest rated ecolodges of the region, with Monteverde just outside the door. (p204)

Diving & Snorkeling

Costa Rica's many small islands, caves and coastal rock formations are excellent for underwater exploration, although visibility varies greatly with the season and climate.

Isla del Coco The only world-class dive spot in Costa Rica, the waters surrounding this island are filled with hammerheads. (p403)

Isla del Caño Reliable visibility, sea turtles, barracudas and, if you're lucky, humpback whales. (p438)

Isla Murciélago Manta rays, bull sharks and even humpback whales migrate through these waters. (p289)

Playa Manzanillo In September and October this Caribbean beach has the best snorkeling in the country. (p328)

Fishing

A venture into the open sea can be a pricey proposition, but very possibly worth it: Costa Rica's sportfishing is the stuff of legend.

Golfo Dulce Boats from little Puerto Jiménez and Golfito often return with fish that challenge world records. (p453)

Caño Negro An abundant population of tarpon and no-frills fishing ventures make this a low-key Northern Lowlands option. (p268)

Quepos Plenty of captains lead fishing ventures into the waters off Quepos, which offer a shot at marlin and sailfish. (p370)

San Gerardo de Dota Trout-fishing in the clear upper regions of the Río Savegre is excellent. (p409)

Playa Grande Epic surf casting brings in big fish from rocks that get thrashed with waves. (p298)

Month by Month

January

Every year opens with a rush, as North American and domestic tourists flood beach towns to celebrate. January sees dry days and occasional afternoon showers.

✵ Fiesta de la Santa Cruz

Held in Santa Cruz in the second week of January, this festival centers on a rodeo and bullfights. It also includes the requisite religious procession, music, dances and a beauty pageant.

☆ Jungle Jam

The biggest musical event to hit Jacó, Jungle Jam stretches over several days and venues outside of the main event, which is set in the jungle just outside of town. Held in mid-January. (p360)

✵ Las Fiestas de Palmares

Ten days of beer drinking, horse shows and other carnival events take over the tiny town of Palmares in the second half of the month (www.fiestaspalm ares.com). There's also a running of the bulls.

February

February is the perfect month, with ideal weather and no holiday surcharges. The skies above Nicoya are particularly clear, and it's peak season for turtle-nesting.

☆ Envision Festival

Held in Uvita in late February, this is a festival with a consciousness-raising, transformational bent, bringing together fire dancers and performance artists of all stripes, yoga, music and spiritual workshops. Also takes place during the first week of March in Dominical. (p397)

✵ Fiesta Cívica de Liberia

A beauty pageant and a carnival atmosphere complete with games and typical food enliven Liberia at the end of February.

March

Excellent weather continues through the early part of March, though prices shoot up during Semana Santa, the week leading up to Easter (and North American spring break).

✵ Feria de la Mascarada

During the Feria de la Mascarada, people don massive colorful masks (some of which weigh up to 20kg) and gather to dance and parade around the town square of Barva. Usually held during the last week of March. (p123)

✵ Día del Boyero

A colorful parade, held in Escazú on the second Sunday in March, honors oxcart drivers and includes a blessing of the animals. (p75)

April

Easter and Semana Santa can fall early in April, which means beaches crowd and prices spike. Nicoya and Guanacaste are dry and hot, with little rain.

🌟 Día de Juan Santamaría

Commemorating Costa Rica's national hero, who died in battle against American colonist William Walker's troops in 1856, this weeklong celebration includes parades, concerts and dances.

☆ FIA (Festival de las Artes)

This multidisciplinary arts festival descends upon venues all across San José in alternating years during April (or March). (p75)

May

Attention budget travelers: wetter weather patterns begin to sweep across the country in May, which begins the country's low season. So although the weather is decent, prices drop.

✖ Día de San Isidro Labrador

Visitors can taste the bounty of San Isidro and other villages of Costa Rica during the nation's largest agricultural fairs, on May 15.

June

The Pacific Coast gets fairly wet during June, though this makes for good surfing. The beginning of the so-called green season, this time of year has lots of discounted rates.

🌟 Día de San Pedro & San Pablo

Celebrations with religious processions are held in villages of the same name on June 29.

July

July is mostly wet, particularly on the Caribbean coast, but the month also occasionally enjoys a brief dry period that Ticos call *veranillo* (summer). You can expect rain, particularly late in the day.

🌟 Fiesta de La Virgen del Mar

Held in Puntarenas and Playa del Coco on the Saturday closest to July 16, the Festival of the Virgin of the Sea involves colorful, brightly lit regattas and boat parades.

🌟 Día de Guanacaste

Celebrates the annexation of Guanacaste from Nicaragua. There's also a rodeo in Santa Cruz. It takes place on July 25.

August

The middle of the rainy season doesn't mean that mornings aren't bright and sunny. Travelers who don't mind some rain will find great hotel and tour deals.

🌟 La Virgen de los Ángeles

The patron saint of Costa Rica is celebrated with an important religious procession from San José to Cartago on August 2.

September

The Península de Osa gets utterly soaked during September, which is in the heart of the rainy season and what Ticos refer to as the *temporales del Pacífico*. It's the cheapest time of year to visit the Pacific.

🌟 Independence Day

The center of the Independence Day action is the relay race that passes a 'Freedom Torch' from Guatemala to Costa Rica. The torch arrives at Cartago on the evening of the 14th, when the nation breaks into the national anthem.

October

Many roads become impassable as rivers swell and rain continues to fall in one of the wettest months in Costa Rica. Lodges and tour operators are sometimes closed until November.

🌟 Día de la Raza

Columbus' historic landing on Isla Uvita has traditionally inspired a small carnival in Puerto Limón on October 12, with street parades, live music and dancing.

November

The weather can go either way in November. Access to Parque Nacional Corcovado is difficult after several months of rain, though by the month's end the skies clear up.

⭐ Día de los Muertos

Families visit graveyards and have religious parades in honor of the dead – a lovely and picturesque festival on November 2.

December

Although the beginning of the month is a great time to visit – with clearer skies and relatively uncrowded attractions – things ramp up toward Christmas and advance reservations become crucial.

⭐ Las Fiestas de Zapote

In San José between Christmas and New Year's Eve, this weeklong celebration of all things Costa Rican (rodeos, cowboys, carnival rides, fried food and booze) draws tens of thousands of Ticos to the bullring in the suburb of Zapote every day. (p75)

⭐ Fiesta de los Diablitos

Men booze up and don wooden devil masks and burlap sacks, then re-enact the fight between the indigenous and the Spanish. (In this rendition, Spain loses.) Held in Boruca from December 30 to January 2 and in Curré from February 5 to February 8. (p421)

Top: Costumed reveler in Boruca for Fiesta de los Diablitos

Bottom: Locals don elaborately carved wooden masks during Fiesta de los Diablitos

Itineraries

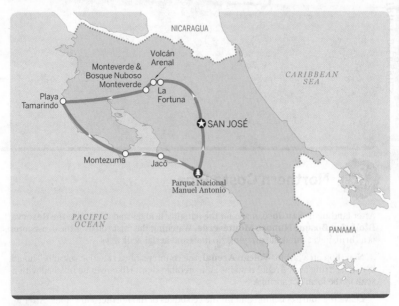

2 WEEKS Essential Costa Rica

This is the trip you've been dreaming about: a romp through paradise with seething volcanoes, tropical parks and ghostly cloud forests.

From **San José**, beeline north to **La Fortuna**. After a refreshing forest hike on the flanks of **Volcán Arenal**, soak in the country's best hot springs. Then catch a boat across Laguna de Arenal, and a bus to **Monteverde**, where you might encounter the elusive quetzal on a stroll through the **Reserva Biológica Bosque Nuboso Monteverde**.

Next: beach time. Head west to the biggest party town in Guanacaste, **Playa Tamarindo**, and enjoy the ideal surf, top-notch restaurants and rowdy nightlife.

Continuing south, visit waterfalls and linger a bit in chilled-out **Montezuma**, where you can connect via jet boat to **Jacó**, another town with equal affection for surfing and partying. Spend half a day busing to Quepos, the gateway to **Parque Nacional Manuel Antonio**. A full day in the park starts with some jungle hikes and wildlife-watching and ends with a picnic and a dip in the park's perfect waters.

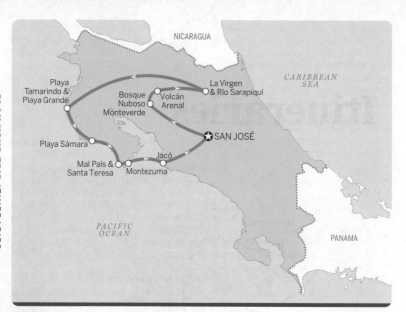

2 WEEKS Northern Costa Rica

After landing in **San José**, make for the hanging bridges and scenery of the **Reserva Biológica Bosque Nuboso Monteverde**. Watching the mist roll over the dense forests is a thrill, never mind the dizzying zip lines and aerial walkways.

Now, hop on a bus for **Volcán Arenal**, the country's biggest active volcano. Though it's not spitting lava, Arenal remains an incredible sight. Hikes can be finished with a soak in the local hot springs.

Leave the tourists behind and hit the ecolodges of the northern lowlands. After a couple days of connecting with easygoing Ticos, make for **La Virgen** to raft the white water of **Río Sarapiquí**.

Devote at least a few days to the beach. First stop: **Playa Tamarindo**, to party, sample some of the country's best cuisine and learn to surf. During turtle season, **Playa Grande** will be hosting a horde of nesting leatherbacks, and the humans often offer equally illuminating displays.

Stay put or take a bus south to enjoy the sand and contemporary cuisine at **Playa Sámara** or swells at **Mal País & Santa Teresa**. Wind down your trip with yoga in **Montezuma** and head back by boat and bus to San José via **Jacó**, where you can catch some last rays of sunshine and a decadent meal.

Pacific Coast Explorer

2 WEEKS

Kick things off with **Parque Nacional Carara**, home to enchanting scarlet macaws, and spend a few hours hiking up and down the coast. Then head south to **Quepos**, a convenient base for the country's most popular national park, **Parque Nacional Manuel Antonio**. Here the rainforest sweeps down to meet the sea, providing refuge for rare animals, including the endangered squirrel monkey.

Continue south, stopping to sample the roadside *ceviche* stands, and visit **Hacienda Barú National Wildlife Refuge** for some sloth-spotting, or keep heading south to **Dominical** in search of waves. For deserted beach wandering, continue on to **Uvita**, where you can look for whales spouting offshore at **Parque Nacional Marino Ballena**.

From Uvita, continue to the **Península de Osa**, where you'll set out on journeys through the country's top national park for wildlife-viewing. Emerge at the northern end in remote **Bahía Drake**, where you'll swim in paradisiacal coves. Return to civilization via ferry through Central America's longest stretch of mangroves to **Sierpe**, home of the ancient stone spheres.

Southern Costa Rica & Osa

2 WEEKS

Hands down the best itinerary for adventurers, this is the wilder side of Costa Rica.

Either head down the Pacific coast or fly into **Puerto Jiménez**, gateway to Península de Osa. Here you can spend a day or so kayaking the mangroves and soaking up the charm.

The undisputed highlight of the Osa is **Parque Nacional Corcovado**, the crown jewel of the country's national parks. Spend a few days exploring jungle and beach trails with a local guide, whose expert eyes will spot tapirs and rare birds; trekkers willing to get down and dirty can tackle a through-hike of the park.

Return to Puerto Jiménez and travel up the Pacific Costanera Sur to **Uvita**, where you can wander empty beaches, surf and snorkel at **Parque Nacional Marino Ballena**. Then it's off to the mountains. Link together buses for **San Gerardo de Rivas**, where you can spend a day acclimating to the altitude and hiking through the **Cloudbridge Nature Reserve**. End the trip with an exhilarating two-day adventure to the top of **Cerro Chirripó**, Costa Rica's highest peak.

 10 DAYS Caribbean Coast

Latin beats change to Caribbean rhythms as you explore the 'other Costa Rica.'

Hop on the first eastbound bus out of **San José** for Cahuita, capital of Afro-Caribbean culture and gateway to **Parque Nacional Cahuita**. Decompress in this mellow village before moving on to **Puerto Viejo de Talamanca**, the Caribbean's center for nightlife, cuisine and all-round positive vibes.

From Puerto Viejo, rent a bicycle and ride to Manzanillo, jumping-off point for snorkeling, kayaking and hiking in **Refugio Nacional de Vida Silvestre Gandoca-Manzanillo**.

To fall further off the map, grab a boat from Moín to travel up the canal-ribboned coast to **Tortuguero**, where you can watch nesting turtles. But the real reason you're here is to canoe the mangrove-lined canals of **Parque Nacional Tortuguero**, Costa Rica's mini-Amazon. After spotting your fill of wildlife, head back to San José via water taxi and bus through the tiny town of Cariari and then **Guápiles**, an ideal base for gazing at open farmland and exploring **Parque Nacional Braulio Carrillo**.

 10 DAYS Central Valley

The Central Valley circuit is all about (lightly) sleeping volcanoes, strong cups of coffee and the spiritual core of the country – all sans the madding crowds. Begin the scenic route of volcanoes by hiking the volcanic lakes and trails surrounding **Volcán Poás**, one of Costa Rica's most accessible glimpses into an active crater.

Move on to **San Isidro de Heredia** for a close encounter with rescued baby sloths and toucans and a taste of the region's chocolate history. With the geological and culinary wonders complete, raft the **Río Pacuare**, one of the country's best white-water runs and providing some of Central America's most scenic rafting.

Move on to **Monumento Nacional Arqueológico Guayabo**, the country's only significant archaeological site, protecting ancient petroglyphs and aqueducts. Finally, swing south into the heart of the **Valle de Orosi**, Costa Rican coffee country, and take the caffeinated 32km loop passing the country's oldest church and endless green hills. End on a spiritual note at the country's grandest colonial-era temple, the Basílica de Nuestra Señora de Los Ángeles in **Cartago**.

Above: Refugio Nacional de Vida Silvestre Gandoca-Manzanillo (p186)

Right: Valle de Orosi (p128)

SATHISH JOTHIKUMAR / GETTY IMAGES ©

Off the Beaten Track: Costa Rica

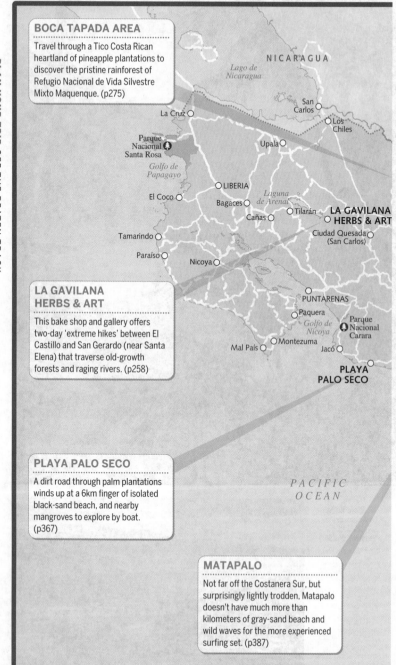

BOCA TAPADA AREA

Travel through a Tico Costa Rican heartland of pineapple plantations to discover the pristine rainforest of Refugio Nacional de Vida Silvestre Mixto Maquenque. (p275)

LA GAVILANA HERBS & ART

This bake shop and gallery offers two-day 'extreme hikes' between El Castillo and San Gerardo (near Santa Elena) that traverse old-growth forests and raging rivers. (p258)

PLAYA PALO SECO

A dirt road through palm plantations winds up at a 6km finger of isolated black-sand beach, and nearby mangroves to explore by boat. (p367)

MATAPALO

Not far off the Costanera Sur, but surprisingly lightly trodden, Matapalo doesn't have much more than kilometers of gray-sand beach and wild waves for the more experienced surfing set. (p387)

NICARAGUA

Lago de Nicaragua

San Carlos

Los Chiles

La Cruz

Parque Nacional Santa Rosa

Golfo de Papagayo

Upala

LIBERIA

Laguna de Arenal

El Coco

Bagaces

Cañas

Tilarán

LA GAVILANA HERBS & ART

Tamarindo

Ciudad Quesada (San Carlos)

Paraíso

Nicoya

PUNTARENAS

Paquera

Golfo de Nicoya

Parque Nacional Carara

Mal País

Montezuma

Jacó

PLAYA PALO SECO

PACIFIC OCEAN

PARISMINA

This far-flung spit of sand between canal and Caribbean Sea has only the barest bones of tourist-oriented infrastructure and not a lot of action besides turtle conservation and kayaking the local canals. (p151)

SELVA BANANITO

One of the country's most secluded and delightful ecolodges offers wildlife encounters, delicious meals and comfy cabins made from recycled hardwood atop Caribbean-style stilts. (p168)

PARQUE INTERNACIONAL LA AMISTAD

The country's deepest, most impenetrable wilderness lies in this vast park that spans both Costa Rica and Panama. Encompassing numerous life zones, the forest's diversity is truly awesome. (p425)

LUNA LODGE

Up a winding road into the mountains, this remote ecolodge borders Parque Nacional Corcovado and is run by an infectiously passionate conservationist. (p443)

Map labels

TRINIDAD

BOCA TAPADA AREA
Trinidad
Barra del Colorado

Puerto Viejo de Sarapiquí
Cariari
Tortuguero
Parque Nacional Tortuguero
PARISMINA

Parque Nacional Volcán Poás

ALAJUELA
HEREDIA
SAN JOSÉ
CARTAGO
Turrialba
Siquirres
PUERTO LIMÓN
SELVA BANANITO

Cahuita
Puerto Viejo de Talamanca
Sixaola

CARIBBEAN SEA

Parque Nacional Los Quetzales
Parque Nacional Chirripó
PARQUE INTERNACIONAL LA AMISTAD
Quepos
San Isidro de El General
MATAPALO

Bahía de Coronado
Palmar Norte
Paso Real
Río Claro
Golfito
Neily
Golfo Dulce
Parque Nacional Corcovado
Puerto Jiménez
Paso Canoas
David
PANAMA
LUNA LODGE

Playa Guiones (p312), Nosara

Plan Your Trip
Activities Guide

Miles of shoreline, endless warm water and a diverse array of national parks and reserves provide an inviting playground for active travelers. Whether it's the solitude of absolute wilderness, hiking and rafting adventures kids can enjoy, or surfing and jungle trekking you seek, Costa Rica offers fun to suit everyone.

Best Activities

Best Beginner Surf Beaches

Playas Tamarindo, Jacó and Sámara

Best Epic Hikes

Cerro Chirripó, Corcovado Through-Hike

Best Dive Sites

Isla del Coco, Isla del Caño

Best Wildlife-Watching

Parque Nacional Corcovado

Best Rainforest for Families

Parque Nacional Manuel Antonio

Best White Water

Río Pacuare

Hiking & Trekking

Hiking opportunities around Costa Rica are seemingly endless. With extensive mountains, canyons, dense jungles, cloud forests and two coastlines, this is one of Central America's best and most varied hiking destinations.

Hikes come in an enormous spectrum of difficulty. At tourist-packed destinations such as Monteverde, trails are clearly marked and sometimes paved. This is fantastic if you're traveling with kids or aren't confident about route-finding. For long-distance trekking, there are many more options in the remote corners of the country.

Opportunities for moderate hiking are typically plentiful in most parks and reserves. For the most part, you can rely on signs and maps for orientation, though it helps to have some navigational experience. Good hiking shoes, plenty of water and confidence in your abilities will enable you to combine several shorter day hikes into a lengthier expedition. Tourist-information centers at park entrances are great resources for planning your intended route.

If you're properly equipped with camping essentials, the country's longer and more arduous multiday treks are at your disposal. Costa Rica's top challenges are scaling Cerro Chirripó, traversing Corcovado and penetrating deep into the heart of La Amistad. While Chirripó can be undertaken independently, local guides are required for much of La Amistad and for all of Corcovado.

How to Make it Happen

If you're planning your trip around long-distance trekking, it's best to visit during the dry season (December to April). Outside this window, rivers become impassable and trails are prone to flooding. In the highlands, journeys become more taxing in the rain, and the bare landscape offers little protection.

Costa Rica is hot and humid: hiking in these tropical conditions, harassed by mosquitoes, can really take it out of you. Remember to wear light clothing that will dry quickly. Overheating and dehydration are the main sources of misery on the trails, so be sure to bring plenty of water and take rest stops. Make sure you have sturdy, comfortable footwear and a lightweight rain jacket.

Unfortunately there are occasional stories of people getting robbed while on some of the more remote hiking trails. Although this rarely happens, it is always advisable to hike in a group for added safety. Hiring a local guide is another excellent way to enhance your experience, avoid getting lost and learn an enormous amount about the flora and fauna around you.

Some of the local park offices have maps, but this is the exception rather than the rule. If you are planning to do independent hiking on long-distance

THESE BOOTS WERE MADE FOR WALKING

Some suggestions for sturdier tropical-hiking footwear, to supplement the flip-flops.

Rubber boots Pick these up at any hardware store (approximately US$6). They're indestructible, protect you from creepy-crawlies and can be hosed off at day's end. Downsides: not super-comfortable, and if they fill up with water or mud, your feet are wet for the rest of the day.

Sport sandals Chacos, Tevas or Crocs are great for rafting and river crossings, though they offer minimal foot protection.

Waterproof hiking boots If you are planning a serious trek in the mountains, it's best to invest in a pair of solid, waterproof hiking boots.

trails, be sure to purchase your maps in San José in advance.

A number of companies offer trekking tours in Costa Rica:

➡ **Osa Wild** (p445) Offers a huge variety of hikes in the Osa, in partnership with a sustainability organization.

➡ **Costa Rica Trekking Adventures** (p419) Offers multiday treks in Chirripó, Corcovado and Tapantí.

➡ **Osa Aventura** (p447) Specializes in treks through Corcovado.

Surfing

Point and beach breaks, lefts and rights, reefs and river mouths, warm water and year-round waves make Costa Rica a favorite surfing destination. For the most part, the Pacific coast has bigger swells and better waves during the latter part of the rainy season, but the Caribbean cooks from November to May. Basically, there is a wave waiting to be surfed at any time of year.

For the uninitiated, lessons are available at almost all of the major surfing destinations – especially popular towns include Jacó, Dominical and Tamarindo on the Pacific coast. Surfing definitely has a steep learning curve, and can be potentially dangerous if the currents are strong. With that said, the sport is accessible to children and novices, though it's advisable to start with a lesson and always inquire locally about conditions before you paddle out.

Throughout Costa Rica, waves are big (though not massive), and many offer hollow and fast rides that are perfect for intermediates. As a bonus, Costa Rica is one of the few places on the planet where you can surf two different oceans in the same day. Advanced surfers with plenty of experience can contend with some of the world's most famous waves. The top ones include Ollie's Point and Witch's Rock, off the coast of the Santa Rosa sector of the Área de Conservación Guanacaste; Mal País and Santa Teresa, with a groovy scene to match the powerful waves; Playa Hermosa, whose bigger, faster curls attract a more determined (and experienced) crew of wave-chasers; Pavones, a legendary long left across the sweet waters of the Golfo Dulce; and the infamous Salsa Brava in Puerto Viejo de Talamanca, for experts only.

How to Make it Happen

Most international airlines accept surfboards (they must be properly packed in a padded board bag) as one of the two pieces of checked luggage, though this is getting harder and pricier in the age of higher fuel tariffs. Domestic airlines offer more of a challenge; they will accept surfboards for an extra charge, but the board must be under 2.1m in length. On full flights, there's a chance your board won't make it on because of weight restrictions.

An alternative is to buy a new or used board in Costa Rica and then sell it before you leave. Great places to start your search include Jacó, Mal País and Santa Teresa, and Tamarindo. It's usually possible to buy a cheap longboard for about US$250 to US$300, and a cheap shortboard for about US$150 to US$200. Many surf shops will buy back your board for about 50% of the price you paid.

Outfitters in many of the popular surf towns rent all kinds of boards, fix dings, give classes and organize excursions. Jacó, Tamarindo, Pavones and Puerto Viejo de Talamanca are good for these types of activities.

Surfer's Map

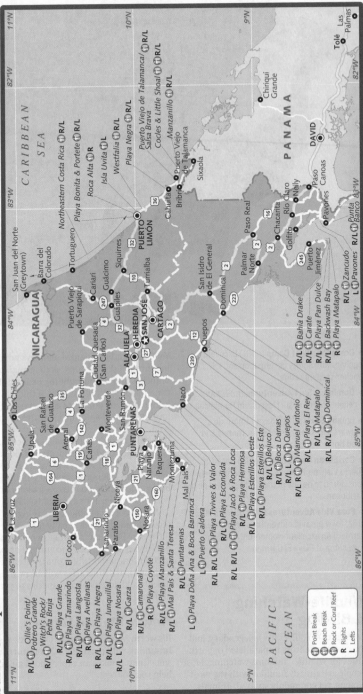

Scarlet macaw (p495)

➡ **Costa Rica Surf Camp** (p391) Excellent teachers with safety certification and low teacher-student ratios.

➡ **Dominical Surf Adventures** (p392) An excellent source of surf lessons in Dominical.

➡ **Iguana Surf** (p301) Playa Tamarindo's stalwart surf shop has lessons, rentals and good tips.

➡ **Caribbean Surf School** (p173) Based in Puerto Viejo de Talamanca, Hershel is widely considered to be one of the best teachers on the Caribbean.

➡ **Pura Vida Adventures** (☎in USA 415-465-2162; www.puravidaadventures.com; Playa del Carmen) An excellent women-only surf-and-yoga camp at Playa El Carmen.

Wildlife-Watching & Birding

Costa Rica's biodiversity is legendary, and the country delivers unparalleled opportunities for wildlife- and bird-watching. Most people are already familiar with the most famous, yet commonly spotted, animals.

You'll instantly recognize monkeys bounding through the treetops, sloths clinging to branches and toucans gliding beneath the canopy. Young children, even if they have been to the zoo dozens of times, typically love the thrill of spotting creatures in the wild.

For the slightly older, keeping checklists is a fun way to add an educational element to your travels. If you really want to know what you're looking at, pick up wildlife and bird guides before your trip – look for ones with color plates for easy positive IDs.

A quality pair of binoculars is highly recommended and can really make the difference between far-off movement and a veritable face-to-face encounter. For expert birders, a spotting scope is essential, and multipark itineraries will allow you to quickly add dozens of new species to your all-time list.

How to Make it Happen

It's worth pointing out that Costa Rica is brimming with avian life at every turn, but sometimes it takes an experienced guide to help you notice it.

Sloths, Parque Nacional Cahuita (p170)

➡ **Aratinga Tours** (☎2574-2319; www.aratinga-tours.com) ✆ Some of the best bird tours in the country are led by Belgian ornithologist Pieter Westra.

➡ **Tropical Feathers** (www.costaricabirding tours.com; cnr Barrio Laboratorio & Calle Mariposa) Local owner and guide Noel Ureña has over 16 years' experience leading birding tours.

➡ **Bird Treks** (☎in USA 717-548-3303; www.birdtreks.com) An international bird-tour company with highly entertaining and qualified guides in Costa Rica.

Windsurfing & Kitesurfing

Laguna de Arenal is the nation's undisputed windsurfing (and kitesurfing) center. From December to April winds are strong and steady, averaging 20 knots in the dry season, often with maximum winds of 30 knots, and windless days are a rarity. The lake has a year-round water temperature of 18°C (64°F) to 21°C (70°F) with 1m-high swells. For warmer water (but more inconsistent winds), try Puerto Soley in the Bahía Salinas.

White-Water Rafting & Kayaking

White-water rafting has remained one of Costa Rica's top outdoor pursuits since the '80s. Ranging from family-friendly Class I riffles to nearly unnavigable Class V rapids, the country's rivers offer highly varied white-water experiences.

First-time runners are catered for year-round, while seasoned enthusiasts arrive en masse during the wildest months from June to October. There is also much regional variation, with gentler rivers located near Manuel Antonio along the central Pacific coast, and world-class runs along the Río Pacuare in the Central Valley. Since all white-water rafting in Costa Rica requires the presence of a certified guide, you will need to book trips through a reputable tour agency.

River kayaking has its fair share of loyal fans. The tiny village of La Virgen in the northern lowlands is the unofficial

---

TOP SPOTS TO WATCH WILDLIFE

➡ **Parque Nacional Corcovado** (p439) At the heart of the Península de Osa, this is the country's richest wildlife area.

➡ **Área de Conservación Guanacaste, Santa Rosa Sector** (p233) The tropical dry forest along the Pacific coast harbors a unique ecosystem.

➡ **Parque Nacional Tortuguero** (p152) Canals and waterways provide excellent bird-watching.

➡ **Refugio Nacional de Vida Silvestre Caño Negro** (p268) Expansive wetlands provide a refuge for reptiles and avians.

➡ **Monteverde & Santa Elena** (p193) These reserves provide unique insight into the cloud-forest ecosystem.

FRANCESSO RICCARDO IACOMINO / GETTY IMAGES ©

Above: Rafting on the
Río Sarapiquí (p278)
Left: Kayaking in
Parque Nacional
Tortuguero (p152)

kayaking capital of Costa Rica and the best spot to hook up with other paddlers. The Río Sarapiquí has an impressive variety of runs that cater to all ages and skill levels.

With 1228km of coastline, two gulfs and plentiful mangrove estuaries, Costa Rica is also an ideal destination for sea kayaking. This is a great way for paddlers to access remote areas and catch glimpses of rare birds and wildlife. Difficulty of access varies considerably, and is largely dependent on tides and currents.

How to Make it Happen

June to October are considered peak season for river rafting and kayaking, though some rivers offer good runs all year. Government regulation of outfitters is shoddy, so ask lots of questions about your guide's water-safety, emergency and medical training. If you suspect they're bluffing, move along – there are plenty of legit outfits.

River kayaking can be organized in conjunction with white-water rafting trips if you are experienced; sea kayaking is popular year-round.

➡ **Aguas Bravas** (p249) In La Virgen, this is the best outfitter on Costa Rica's best white water.

➡ **Exploradores Outdoors** (p173) This outfit offers one- and two-day trips on the Ríos Pacuare, Reventazón and Sarapiquí.

➡ **Pineapple Kayak Tours** (p391) Exciting half-day kayak trips go through caves and mangrove channels.

➡ **H2O Adventures** (p371) Arranges two- and five-day adventures on the Río Savegre.

➡ **Ríos Tropicales** (☏2233-6455, in USA 866-722-8273; www.riostropicales.com) Multiday adventures on the Río Pacuare and two days of kayaking in Tortuguero.

➡ **Costa Rica Expeditions** (☏2521-6099; www.costaricaexpeditions.com) This outfitter handles small groups and offers rafting trips that cater to foodies.

➡ **Gulf Islands Kayaking** (☏in Canada 250-539-2442; www.seakayak.ca) Tours on offer include five days of sea kayaking in Corcovado.

Canopy Tours

The most vibrant life in the rainforest takes place at canopy level, but with trees extending 30m to 60m in height, the average human has a hard time getting a

TOP SPOTS FOR WHITE WATER

➡ **Turrialba** (p132) Home to the country's most popular rafting rivers, the Pacuare and Reventazón.

➡ **La Virgen** (p278) The base town for rafting and kayaking on the Río Sarapiquí.

➡ **Parque Nacional Manuel Antonio** (p383) A tourist mecca that offers family-friendly rafting year-round.

➡ **Parque Nacional Tortuguero** (p152) Boasts 310 sq km of wildlife-rich and kayak-friendly lagoons and canals.

➡ **Bahía Drake** (p430) Extensive mangrove patches are optimally explored by kayak.

look at what's going on up there. You will find canopy tours everywhere in Costa Rica, and many of them will also have a zip line or two to whiz along for a small additional charge. The most elaborate facilities also have Superman cables (which allow you to fly like the Man of Steel) and Tarzan swings.

Some companies have built elevated walkways through the trees. SkyTrek (p199) near Monteverde and Rainmaker (p371) near Quepos are two of the most established operations. A somewhat newer operation is Diamante Eco Adventure Park (p293) in Guanacaste, which offers dual zip lines allowing guests to ride side by side.

You can also take a ski lift–style ride through the tree tops on aerial trams run by Rainforest Adventures (p514) near Braulio Carrillo or Veragua Rainforest Research & Adventure Park (p147) near Límon.

Diving & Snorkeling

The good news is that Costa Rica offers body-temperature water with few humans and abundant marine life. The bad news is that visibility is low because of silt and plankton, and soft corals and sponges are dominant.

However, if you're looking for fine opportunities to see massive schools of fish,

Rainforest Aerial Tram (p142)

as well as larger marine animals such as turtles, sharks, dolphins and whales, then jump right in. It's also worth pointing out that there are few places in the world where you could feasibly dive in the Caribbean and the Pacific on the same day, though why not take your time?

The Caribbean Sea is better for novice divers and snorkelers, with the beach towns of Manzanillo and Cahuita particularly well suited to youngsters. Puerto Viejo lays claim to a few decent sites that can be explored on a discovery dive. Along the Pacific, Isla del Caño ups the ante for those with solid diving experience.

Isla del Coco is the exception to the rule – this remote island floating in the deep Pacific is regarded by veteran divers as one of the best spots on the planet. To dive the wonderland of Coco, you'll need to visit on a liveaboard and have logged some serious time underwater.

How to Make it Happen

Generally visibility isn't great during the rainy months, when rivers swell and their outflow clouds the ocean. At this time, boats to offshore locations offer better viewing opportunities.

The water is warm – around 24°C (75°F) to 29°C (84°F) at the surface, with a thermocline at around 20m below the surface where it drops to 23°C (73°F). If you're keeping it shallow, you can skin-dive.

If you're interested in diving but aren't certified, you can usually do a one-day introductory course that will allow you to do one or two accompanied dives. If you love it, which most people do, certification courses take three to four days and cost around US$350 to US$500.

To plan a trip to Isla del Coco, get in touch with the liveaboard operation Undersea Hunter (p403).

Horseback Riding

Though horseback-riding trips are ubiquitous throughout Costa Rica, quality and care for the horses vary. Rates range from US$25 for an hour or two to more than US$100 for a full day. Overnight trips with pack horses can also be arranged and are a popular way of accessing remote destinations in the national parks. Riders weighing more than 100kg (220lb) cannot be carried by small local horses.

Horseback riding on Playa Carrillo (p324)

Mountain-biking in Parque Nacional Volcán Irazú (p127)

Reliable outfitters with healthy horses include Discovery Horseback Tours (p359) and **Serendipity Adventures** (📞2556-2222, in USA & Canada 877-507-1358; www.serendipity-adventures.com).

Mountain Biking & Cycling

Although the winding, pot-holed roads and aggressive drivers can be a challenge, cycling is on the rise in Costa Rica. Numerous less-trafficked roads offer plenty of adventure – from scenic mountain paths with sweeping views to rugged trails that take riders through streams and past volcanoes.

The best long-distance rides are along the Pacific coast's Interamericana, which has a decent shoulder and is relatively flat, and on the road from Montezuma to the Reserva Natural Absoluta Cabo Blanco on the southern Península de Nicoya.

Mountain biking has taken off in recent years and there are good networks of trails around Corcovado and Arenal, as well as more rides in the central mountains.

How to Make it Happen

Most international airlines will fly your bike as a piece of checked baggage for an extra fee. Pad it well, because the box is liable to be roughly handled.

Alternatively, you can rent mountain bikes in almost any tourist town, but the condition of the equipment varies greatly. For a monthly fee, **Trail Source** (www.trailsource.com) can provide you with information on trails all over Costa Rica and the world.

Outfitters in Costa Rica and the US can organize multiday mountain-biking trips. If you want to tour Costa Rica by bicycle, be forewarned that the country's cycling shops are decidedly more geared toward utilitarian concerns. Bring any specialized equipment (including a serious lock) from home.

Companies organizing bike tours in Costa Rica include **Backroads** (📞in USA 800-462-2848, in USA 510-527-1555; www.backroads.com), **Coast to Coast Adventures** (📞2280-8054; www.ctocadventures.com), Costa Rica Expeditions (p47), **Lava Tours** (📞2281-2458; www.lava-tours.com) and Serendipity Adventures.

Children crossing a suspension bridge in lush forest

Plan Your Trip
Travel with Children

In a land of such dizzying adventure and close encounters with wildlife, waves, jungle zip lines and enticing mud puddles, it can be challenging to choose where to go. Fortunately, your options aren't limited by region, and kids will find epic fun in this accessible paradise (that parents will enjoy too).

Best Regions for Kids

Península de Nicoya

Excellent beaches and family-friendly resorts make this an ideal destination for families. This is a great place for kids (and their folks) to take surfing lessons.

Northwestern Costa Rica

The mysterious and ghostly cloud forests of Monteverde pique children's imaginations about the creatures that live there, while the area's specialty sanctuaries let them see bats, frogs, butterflies and reptiles up close.

Central Pacific Coast

Easy trails lead past spider monkeys and sloths to great swimming beaches at Parque Nacional Manuel Antonio, a busy but beautiful piece of coastal rainforest.

Caribbean Coast

The whole family can snorkel all day at the relatively tranquil waters of Manzanillo or Cahuita and set out on a night adventure to see nesting turtles.

Costa Rica for Kids

Mischievous monkeys and steaming volcanoes, mysterious rainforests and palm-lined beaches – Costa Rica sometimes seems like a comic-book reality. The perfect place for family travel, it is a safe, exhilarating tropical playground that will make a huge impression on younger travelers. The country's myriad adventure possibilities cover the spectrum of age-appropriate intensity levels – and for no intensity at all, some kids might like the idea of getting their hair braided and beaded by a beachside stylist in Puerto Viejo de Talamanca. Whatever you do, the warm, family-friendly culture is extremely welcoming of little ones.

In addition to amazing the kids, this small, peaceful country has all of the practicalities that rank high with parents, such as great country-wide transportation infrastructure, a low crime rate and an excellent health-care system. But the reason to bring the whole family is the opportunity to share unforgettable experiences such as spotting a dolphin or a sloth, slowly paddling a kayak through mangrove channels, or taking a night hike in search of tropical frogs.

Children's Highlights
Wildlife-Watching

You can't not spot wildlife in Costa Rica – coatis cause regular traffic jams around Laguna de Arenal and scarlet macaws loudly squawk in tropical-almond trees down the central Pacific coast. Stay a day or two at a jungle lodge, and the wildlife will come to you.

➜ **Parque Nacional Manuel Antonio** (p383) Tiny and easily accessible; a walk through this park usually yields sightings of squirrel monkeys, stripy iguanas and coatis.

➜ **Parque Nacional Cahuita** (p170) Seeing white-faced capuchins is practically assured along the beach trail; go with a guide and you'll probably also see sloths.

➜ **Parque Nacional Tortuguero** (p152) Boat tours through Tortuguero canals uncover wildlife all around, but staying in any jungle lodge outside the village will reveal the same.

➜ **Chilamate Rainforest Eco Retreat** (p280) In the steamy rainforest of the Sarapiquí Valley, this family-friendly lodge has miles of trails for easy wildlife-spotting hikes.

➜ **Turtle-Watching** On both the Pacific and Caribbean coasts, one of Costa Rica's truly magical experiences is watching sea turtles lay their eggs under the cover of night.

Animal Sanctuaries

Animal encounters are guaranteed at wildlife sanctuaries or animal refuges. Many of these organizations rescue and rehabilitate orphaned or injured animals for release or lifetime care.

➜ **Sloth Sanctuary of Costa Rica** (p164) With their slow-mo locomotion and Mona Lisa smiles, baby sloths might be the cutest creatures on the planet – and this sanctuary is the best place to meet some.

➡ **Fundacion Santuario Silvestre de Osa** (p453) This boat-accessible sanctuary rehabilitates whatever injured and orphaned animals come their way. Friendly monkeys roam freely.

➡ **Frog's Heaven** (p283) A frog-lover's heaven, this tropical garden is filled with all sorts of brightly colored (and transparent!) amphibians.

➡ **Ecocentro Danaus** (p245) Walk the trails to look for monkeys and sloths, visit a pond with caimans and turtles, delight in the butterfly garden and ogle frogs in the ranarium (frog pond).

➡ **Jaguar Centro de Rescate** (p181) No jaguars here, but you may get to hold a howler monkey or a baby sloth. You'll also see colorful snakes (in terrariums), raptors and frogs.

➡ **Alturas Animal Sanctuary** (p391) Meet various rescued critters here, from macaws and monkeys to Bubba the famous coatimundi.

Beaches

➡ **Playa Ocotal** (p292) Placid, wooded gray-sand beach on the quiet northern end of Península de Nicoya.

➡ **Playa Pelada** (p313) In the Nosara area, this low-key beach has little wave action and big, intriguing boulders.

➡ **Playa Carrillo** (p324) South of family-friendly Sámara, this beach can be all yours during the week and convivially crowded with Tico families on the weekends.

➡ **Parque Nacional Manuel Antonio** (p383) Beach visits are usually enlivened by monkeys, coatis and iguanas.

➡ **Parque Nacional Marino Ballena** (p399) A stretch of white-sand, jungle-fringed beach, a sand spit shaped like a whale's tail at low tide, and the chance to see whales spouting offshore.

➡ **Playa Negra** (p164) This black-sand, blue-flag beach (meeting Costa Rica's highest ecological standards) has plenty of space to plant your own flag.

➡ **Playa Manzanillo** (p328) Beautiful, jungle-backed beach from here to Punta Mona (about as far south as you can go before you have to start bushwhacking).

Adventures

➡ **Mangrove tours** Kayaking or canoeing through the still waters of mangrove canals can turn up waterbirds, caimans, sleeping bats and sloths. Try Parque Nacional Marino Ballena (p399), around Puerto Jiménez and Tortuguero.

➡ **Surfing lessons** For surfing lessons tailored to kids, check out One Love (p173) on the Caribbean coast; kids' lessons are also offered at beginner beaches in Jacó and Tamarindo.

Boys enjoying a dip near Volcán Miravalles (p220)

➡ **White-water rafting** Family-friendly rafting and 'safari trips' happen year-round on Ríos Sarapiquí, Savegre and Pejibaye.

➡ **Parque Nacional Volcán Poás** (p514) Has a stroller-friendly walkway along the observation area, one of the few national parks accessible in this way.

Planning

Although Costa Rica is in the heart of Central America, it's a relatively easy place for family travel, making the nature of pre-departure planning more similar to North America or Europe than, say, Honduras.

Getting There & Away

➡ Children under the age of 12 receive a 25% discount on domestic-airline flights, while children under two fly free (provided they sit on a parent's lap).

➡ Children (except for those under the age of three) pay full fare on buses.

➡ Car seats for infants are not always available at car-rental agencies, so bring your own or make sure you double check with the agency in advance.

Gallo pinto (p55) with accompaniments

Plan Your Trip

Eat & Drink Like a Local

Traditional Costa Rica fare, for the most part, is comfort food. The diet consists largely of beans and rice, fried plantains and the occasional slab of chicken, fish or beef. But in the last few years, locals have started to experiment more with the country's fresh, exotic and plentiful produce. The results have been inspiring and delicious.

The Year in Food

Food festivals are concentrated at the end of the rainy season, but the tropical Eden that is Costa Rica produces exotic and incredible fruits and vegetables and vends them in farmers markets year-round.

Rainy season (Oct & Nov)

Deliciously ripe mangoes and *mamon chino* (rambutan), plus agricultural celebrations such as the Fiesta del Maíz (Festival of Corn) and the Feria Nacional de Pejibaye (National Peach Palm Market).

Christmas (Dec)

Tamales, prepared with masa, pork, potatoes and garlic and steamed in banana leaves, become a very big deal at this time of year.

Coffee harvest (Sep–Jan)

Many seasonal laborers from Nicaragua head down to pick *grano de oro* (golden bean).

Food Experiences

Meals of a Lifetime

➡ **Hotel Quelitales** (p131) The chef here looks like a Tico Richard Gere, and cooks up the creamiest pejibaye soup imaginable. The fish with heart of palm sauce is also exquisite.

➡ **Cool & Calm Cafe** (p186) Best lobster Caribeño around, ensnared and prepared by a one-legged wonder. And fruit drinks will hydrate your soul.

➡ **Park Café** (p88) Fine dining among antiques from around the world, with a chef who once studied under Joël Robuchon. Get the tuna filet with carpaccio of red snapper.

➡ **Graffiti** (p363) The famous cacao-and-coffee-encrusted filet mignon is exceptional, complemented by the likes of macadamia-and-passionfruit catch of the day, decadent cheesecake and creative cocktails.

➡ **Xandari** (p110) Nails a mix of Costa Rican and international, while serving vegetarians well and utilizing the resort's homegrown organic produce.

Cheap Treats

➡ **Guanabana** Also known as soursop, this sweet and sticky fruit should be purchased wherever found, and eaten with the hands.

➡ **Patí** A flaky, Caribbean-style turnover filled with meat, onions, garlic and spicy goodness.

➡ **Street mango** Sold in plastic bags with salt, lime juice and sometimes chili powder, this is the ultimate refreshment.

Dare to Try

➡ **Museo de Insectos** (p72) This bug museum has its own kitchen, where guests are served meal worms and crickets with lots of salt and oregano.

➡ **Mondongo** Tripe intestines are a *campesino* (farmers) favorite in Costa Rica, and they are served surprisingly spicy, oftentimes at (illegal) cockfights.

➡ **Meat on a stick** Is it pork? Chicken? Beef? Who cares. On roadsides and at local fiestas, this mysterious Tico delicacy is just as good as it smells, even after the vendor uses a paint brush to apply spicy sauce.

Green Treats

➡ **Sibu Chocolate** (p124) In San Isidro de Heredia, the history of chocolate illuminates and satisfies.

➡ **Feria Verde de Aranjuez** (p95) San José's 'green market,' and an all-around winner for breakfast, produce, smoothies, everything.

➡ **Punta Mona** (p188) The sprawling garden at this secluded eco-retreat has one of the world's largest collections of edible tropical plants.

What to Eat & Drink

Breakfast for Ticos is usually *gallo pinto* (literally 'spotted rooster'), a stir-fry of last night's rice and beans. When combined, the rice gets colored by the beans, and the mix obtains a speckled appearance. Served with eggs, cheese or *natilla* (sour cream), *gallo pinto* is generally cheap, filling and sometimes downright tasty. If you plan to spend the whole day surfing or hiking, you'll find that *gallo pinto* is great energy food. If you aren't keen on rice and beans, many hotels offer a tropical-style continental breakfast, usually consisting of toast with butter and jam, accompanied by fresh fruit. American-style breakfasts are also available in many eateries and are, needless to say, heavy on the fried foods and fatty meats.

Most restaurants offer a set meal at lunch and dinner called a *casado* (literally 'married'), a cheap, well-balanced plate of rice, beans, meat, salad and sometimes *plátanos maduros* (fried sweet plantains) or *patacones* (twice-fried plantains), which taste something like french fries.

Food is not heavily spiced, unless you're having traditional Caribbean-style cuisine. Most local restaurants will lay out a bottle of Tabasco-style sauce, homemade salsa or Salsa Lizano, the Tico version of Worcestershire sauce and the 'secret' ingredient of *gallo pinto*.

Specialties

Considering the extent of the coastline, it is no surprise that seafood is plentiful, and fish dishes are usually fresh and delicious. While not traditional Tico fare, *ceviche* (seafood marinated in lemon or lime juice, garlic and seasonings) is on most menus, usually made from *pargo* (red snapper), *dorado* (mahi-mahi), octopus or tilapia. Raw fish is marinated in lime juice

Café con leche

MELANIE ACEVEDO/ GETTY IMAGES ©

THE GALLO PINTO CONTROVERSY

No other dish in Costa Rica inspires Ticos quite like their national dish of *gallo pinto*, that ubiquitous medley of rice, beans and spices. You might even hear Costa Ricans refer to themselves as *'más Tico que gallo pinto'* (literally, 'more Costa Rican than *gallo pinto*'). Exactly what type and amount of this holy trinity makes up authentic *gallo pinto* is the subject of intense debate, especially since it is also the national dish of neighboring Nicaragua.

Both countries claim that *gallo pinto* originated on their soil. Costa Rican lore holds that the dish and its iconic name were coined in 1930 in the neighborhood of San Sebastián, on the southern outskirts of San José. Nicaraguans claim that it was brought to the Caribbean coast of their country by Afro-Latinos long before it graced the palate of any Costa Rican.

The battle for the rights to this humble dish doesn't stop here, especially since the two countries can't even agree on the standard recipe. Nicaraguans traditionally prepare it with small red beans, whereas Costa Ricans swear by black beans. And let's not even get into the subtle complexities of balancing cilantro, salt and pepper.

Nicaragua officially holds the world record for making the biggest-ever pot of *gallo pinto*. On September 15, 2007, a seething vat of it fed 22,000 people, which firmly entrenched Nicaragua's name next to *gallo pinto* in the *Guinness Book of World Records*. Costa Rica responded in 2009 by cooking an even more massive avalanche of the stuff, feeding a small crowd of 50,000. Though the event was not officially recognized as setting any records, that day's vat of *gallo pinto* warmed the hearts and bellies of many a proud Tico.

Casado (p55)

with some combination of chilis, onions, tomatoes and herbs. Served chilled, it is a delectable way to enjoy fresh seafood. Emphasis is on 'fresh' here – it's raw fish, so if you have reason to believe it is not fresh, don't risk eating it.

Most bars also offer the country's most popular *boca* (snack), *chifrijo*, which derives its name from two main ingredients: *chicharrón* (fried pork) and frijoles (beans). Diced tomatoes, spices, rice, tortilla chips and avocado are also thrown in for good measure. Fun fact about *chifrijo:* in 2014 a restaurant owner named Miguel Cordero claimed he officially invented it. He brought lawsuits against 49 businesses and demanded a cool US$15 million in damages. So far he has not been able to collect.

Caribbean cuisine is the most distinctive in Costa Rica, having been steeped in indigenous, *criollo* (Creole) and Afro-Caribbean flavors. It's a welcome cultural change of pace after seemingly endless *casados*. Regional specialties include *rondón* (whose moniker comes from 'rundown,' meaning whatever the chef can run down), a spicy seafood gumbo; Caribbean-style rice and beans, made with red beans,

coconut milk and curry spices; and *patí,* the Caribbean version of an *empanada* (savory turnover), the best street food, bus-ride snack and picnic treat.

Drinks

Coffee is probably the most popular beverage in the country and, wherever you go, someone is likely to offer you a *cafecito*. Traditionally, it is served strong and mixed with hot milk to taste, also known as *café con leche*. Purists can get *café negro* (black coffee); if you want a little milk, ask for *leche al lado* (milk on the side).

For a refresher, nothing beats *batidos*. These fresh fruit shakes are made either *al agua* (with water) or *con leche* (with milk).

The array of available tropical fruit can be intoxicating and includes everything from mango and papaya to carambola (starfruit) and guanabana (soursop or cherimoya).

The most popular alcoholic drink is *cerveza* (beer; aka *birra* locally), and there are several national brands. Imperial is the most popular – either for its smooth flavor or for the ubiquitous merchandise emblazoned with the eagle-crest logo. Pilsen, which has a higher alcohol content,

Where to Eat

The most popular eating establishment in Costa Rica is the *soda*. These are small, informal lunch counters dishing up a few daily *casados*. Other popular cheapies include the omnipresent fried- and rotisserie-chicken stands.

A regular *restaurante* is usually higher on the price scale and has slightly more atmosphere. Many *restaurantes* serve *casados,* while the fancier places refer to the set lunch as the *almuerzo ejecutivo* (literally 'executive lunch').

For something smaller, *pastelerías* and *panaderías* are shops that sell pastries and bread, while many bars serve *bocas.*

Vegetarians & Vegans

If you don't mind rice and beans, Costa Rica is a relatively comfortable place for vegetarians to travel.

Most restaurants will make veggie *casados* on request and many are now including them on the menu. They usually include rice and beans, cabbage salad and one or two selections of variously prepared vegetables or legumes.

With the high influx of tourism, there are also many specialty vegetarian restaurants or restaurants with a veggie menu in San José and tourist towns. Lodges in remote areas that offer all-inclusive meal plans can accommodate vegetarians with advance notice.

Vegans, macrobiotic and raw food–only travelers will have a tougher time, as there are fewer outlets accommodating those diets, although this is slowly changing. If you intend to keep to your diet, it's best to choose a lodging where you can prepare food yourself. Many towns have *macrobióticas* (health-food stores), but selection varies. Fresh vegetables can be hard to come by in isolated areas and will often be quite expensive, although farmers markets are cropping up throughout the country.

Habits & Customs

When you sit down to eat in a restaurant, it is polite to say *buenos días* (good morning), *buenas tardes* (good afternoon) or *buenas noches* (good evening) to the waitstaff and any people you might be sharing a table with – and it's generally good form to acknowledge everyone in the room this way. It is also polite to say *buen provecho,* which is the equivalent of *bon appetit,* at the start of the meal.

Guanabana (soursop) is a popular juice

is known for its saucy calendars featuring *las chicas Pilsen* (the Pilsen girls).

After beer, the poison of choice is *guaro,* which is a colorless alcohol distilled from sugarcane and usually consumed by the shot, though you can order it as a sour.

Local rums are inexpensive and worthwhile, especially the Ron Centenario.

How to Eat & Drink

When to Eat

Breakfast for Ticos is taken in the early morning, usually from 6am to 8am, and consists of *gallo pinto.*

A midday lunch (served between 11:30am and 2:30pm) at most *sodas* usually involves a *casado* or *patacones.*

For dinner (6pm to 9pm), upscale Tico establishments may serve *lomito* (a lean cut of steak) and dishes like *pescado en salsa palmito* (fish in heart of palm sauce). Some of the more forward-thinking eateries in San José may drop an experimental vegetable plate in front of you.

Regions at a Glance

Where will your passion take you? Wildlife-watchers will be in heaven here, with a vast array of life zones supporting a multitude of colorful species, including the quetzal, the elusive jaguar and nesting sea turtles. Surfers will need no intro to the country, whose plentiful and varied surf spots are open secrets, and novices will find plenty of beginner breaks. Hikers can traverse the thick, humid jungle of remote Corcovado, summit the country's highest peak, Cerro Chirripó, or just meander through cloud forests, around the rims of steaming volcanoes and along beachside trails on day hikes.

San José

Museums
Music
Food

Old Gold & Upstart Art

Gritty, no-nonsense San José doesn't offer much in the way of architectural beauty, but it's the innards that count. In all of Costa Rica, this is the only place with a dense concentration of museums, exhibiting everything from pre-Columbian gold frogs to the hottest multimedia installations by local artists.

Música en Vivo

As the cultural capital of Costa Rica, this is where you come to catch chamber music, international touring bands and up-and-coming local talent. The National Theater is a solid place to start.

Cuisine Scene

Argentinian, vegetarian, Asian-fusion and classic French cuisine shine in superb San José venues. Some of the country's finest restaurants reside here, bringing welcome diversity.

p62

Central Valley & Highlands

Volcanoes
Rapids
Highland Countryside

Volcanic Action

Volcanoes in this region range from the wild and moderately active (Turrialba) to the heavily trafficked (Poás), showing off ultramarine crater lakes and desolate, misty moonscapes.

White Water

World-class white water awaits on the Río Pacuare – well worth a run for its cascade of thrilling rapids through a stunningly beauteous jungle gorge.

Wind & Dine

The highland countryside of Costa Rica is often overlooked in favor of its beaches. But here cows nibble contentedly along twisting mountain roads, and villages boast organic farmers markets and parks with psychedelic topiaries – perfect places for picnics with local produce.

p103

Caribbean Coast

Culture
Wildlife
Turtles

Afro-Caribbean Flavor

Set apart geographically and culturally from the rest of Costa Rica, the Caribbean coast has a distinct Afro-Caribbean flavor all of its own. Taste it in the coconut rice, hear it in the local patois and live it in superchill Cahuita.

Wildlife

The waterlogged coast along the Caribbean teems with sloths, three of Costa Rica's four monkey species, crocodiles, caimans, poison-dart frogs, manatees, tucuxi dolphins and over 375 species of bird.

Turtle Life

On this wild coast, turtle nesting is serious business. In Parismina and Tortuguero, the leatherback, green and hawksbill turtles return to their natal beaches to nest – a breathtaking experience.

p138

Northwestern Costa Rica

Forests
Ecolodges
Water

Canopy Views

Northwestern forests birthed the ubiquitous canopy tour. Studded with cathedral trees, which sprout dozens of species and shelter valuable watersheds, you'll be in awe of forests on volcanic slopes, along the wild coast and leering over the continental divide.

Unique Sleeps

The sheer number of groovy, independently owned and operated ecolodges means you can choose from cute B&Bs to spectacular working *fincas* (farms) or biological stations ensconced in natural forest.

Rafting, Surfing & More

Lose yourself in aquamarine rivers, ride perfect lefts that crash on wilderness beaches, or ride the wind on the most epic bay you've never heard of.

p191

Arenal & Northern Lowlands

Local Perspective
Birds
Water

Community Tourism

This is where you'll discover real-life Costa Rica – on working *finca* homestays, tours through rainforest preserves, and inky lagoons or mocha rivers with lifelong resident guides.

Birder's Paradise

The humid swamps and, yes, hills of these lowlands are thick with forests and teeming with hundreds of species of bird, from storks and egrets to toucans and great green macaws.

Kayaking & Fishing

Whether you plan on paddling frothing white water shadowed by looming forest, wish to carve inland lakes by kayak, or just want to hop a motorboat to spot caimans or reel in tarpon, this is your Neverland.

p241

Península de Nicoya

Surfing
Diving
Food

Perfect Breaks

It's almost impossible to believe that there are so many waves on one spectacular, rugged peninsula. But, from the bottom to the top, there are countless perfect breaks to meet your needs.

Undersea Life

Don't expect Caribbean clarity or bathwater warmth, but if you do stride into the water you can expect mantas, bull sharks and schools of pelagics that will bend your brain.

Creative Local Eats

The creative kitchens that dot this intrepid coast source ingredients from local *fincas* and fishermen, and the dishes are prepared with passion and skill.

p285

Central Pacific Coast

Surfing
National Park
Beaches

Surf for All

From the pros-only Playa Hermosa to the beginner-friendly Dominical, the famous breaks of the Pacific coast bring blissful swells and tons of variety.

Small Packages

Manuel Antonio, Costa Rica's smallest and most popular national park, is a kid-friendly, beach-lined delight. Sure, there are crowds of people, but at times they're outnumbered by monkeys, coatis and tropical birds.

Deserted Beaches

It's a bit of a hike to get to Parque Nacional Marino Ballena, but those lucky few who find themselves on its empty beaches can scan the sparkling horizon for migrating whales.

p347

Southern Costa Rica & Península de Osa

Mountain Peak
Hiking
Culture

Reach the Peak

Scaling the peak of Chirripó is an adventure into a wholly different Costa Rica from that of the postcards. The view at sunrise from above the clouds is the highlight of this three-day excursion.

Go Wild

Jaguars, jungle trails and wild beaches galore: this is among the world's most biologically intense patches of green, representing a whopping 2.5% of the planet's biodiversity. Hiking Corcovado is a sublime trip into untamed tropical rainforest.

Indigenous Communities

Traveling deep into Costa Rica's mountains or the jungle of the Osa allows you to meet some of Costa Rica's diverse indigenous citizens and learn about ancient traditions.

p405

On the Road

Arenal & Northern Lowlands
p241

Northwestern Costa Rica
p191

Central Valley & Highlands
p103

Caribbean Coast
p138

Península de Nicoya
p285

San José
p62

Central Pacific Coast
p347

Southern Costa Rica & Península de Osa
p405

San José

POP OVER 1.5 MILLION / AREA 2366 SQ KM / ELEV 1170M

Best Places to Eat

➡ Park Café (p88)

➡ La Esquina de Buenos Aires (p87)

➡ Sofía Mediterráneo (p89)

➡ Saúl Bistro (p90)

➡ Café de los Deseos (p83)

Best Places to Drink

➡ Club Vertigo (p92)

➡ 8ctavo Rooftop (p94)

➡ Hoxton Pub (p92)

➡ Stiefel (p91)

➡ Calle la Amargura (p92)

Why Go?

Chances are San José wasn't the top destination on your list when you started planning your Costa Rica trip, but give this city a chance and you just might be pleasantly surprised. It's true that Chepe – as San José is affectionately known – doesn't make a great first impression, with its unremarkable concrete structures and honking traffic, but it's well worth digging deeper to discover the city's charms.

Take your time poking around historic neighborhoods such as Barrio Amón, where colonial mansions have been converted into contemporary art galleries, restaurants and boutique hotels. Stroll with Saturday shoppers at the farmers market, join the Sunday crowds in Parque La Sabana, dance the night away to live music at one of the city's vibrant clubs, or visit the museums of gold, jade, art and natural history, and you'll begin to understand the multidimensional appeal of Costa Rica's largest city and cultural capital.

When to Go

➡ Rainy season usually lasts from mid-April through December, and is therefore a great time to look for deals and beat the crowds. Beware of October, which usually sees heavy rains for days at a time.

➡ The city's climate is considerably cooler than on the coasts, especially at night; daytime temps generally vary between 21°C and 27°C (70°F to 80°F).

➡ The best time to visit is around the Christmas holidays, when the Ticos' festive cheer reaches its height with the Festival de la Luz and Las Fiestas de Zapote.

➡ Any season is good for exploring the capital's cultural attractions.

San José Highlights

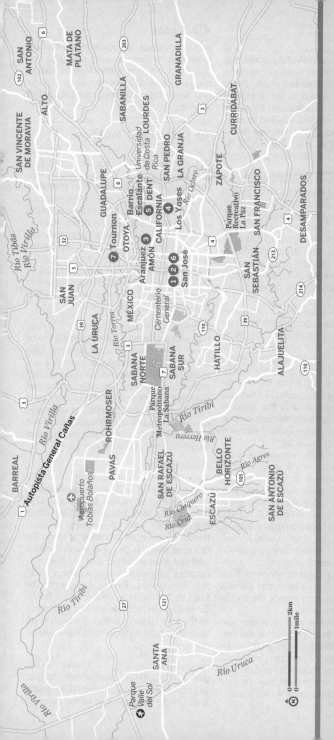

1 Admiring Costa Rica's artistic traditions, past and present at the **Museo de Oro** (p64).

2 Savoring classical music and dance performances amid the beaux-arts interior of the **Teatro Nacional** (p94).

3 Poking around the lively **Feria Verde de Aranjuez** (p95) farmers market in search of locally grown and gourmet treats.

4 Grooving to live bands and DJs at **Hoxton Pub** (p92).

5 Indulging your taste buds at the fun bars and fine eateries of **Barrio Escalante** (p88).

6 Exploring the vast universe of carved stone and ceramic treasures at the **Museo de Jade** (p65).

7 Learning about the struggles of less fortunate city residents on a respectful and engaging tour of a slum with **Really Experience Community** (p73).

History

For much of the colonial period, San José played second fiddle to the bigger and relatively more established Cartago, a city whose origins date back to 1563 and which, during the colonial era, served as the provincial capital. Villanueva de la Boca del Monte del Valle de Abra – as San José was first known – was not founded until 1737, when the Catholic Church issued an edict that forced the populace to settle near churches (attendance was down).

The city remained a backwater for decades, though it did experience some growth as a stop in the tobacco trading route during the late 18th century. Following independence in 1821, rival factions in Cartago and San José each attempted to assert regional supremacy. The struggle ended in 1823 when the two sides faced off at the Battle of Ochomongo. San José emerged the victor and subsequently declared itself capital.

Despite its new status, the city remained a quiet agricultural center into the 20th century. The calm was shattered in the 1940s, when parts of San José served as a battlefield in the civil war of 1948, one of the bloodiest conflicts in the country's history. Out of that clash, José Figueres Ferrer of the Partido de Liberación Nacional (National Liberation Party) emerged as the country's interim leader – signing a declaration that abolished the army at the armory that now serves as the Museo Nacional.

The rest of the 20th century would see the expansion of the city from diminutive coffee-trading outpost to sprawling urban center. In the 1940s San José had only 70,000 residents. Today, the greater metro population stands at almost 1.6 million. Recent years have been marked by massive urban migration as Ticos (Costa Ricans) and, increasingly, Nicaraguans have moved to the capital in search of economic opportunity. As part of this, shantytowns have mushroomed on the outskirts, and crime is increasingly becoming a part of life for the city's poorest inhabitants.

The city remains a vital economic and arts hub, home to important banks, museums and universities – as well as the everyday outposts of culture: live-music spaces, art centers, bookstores and the corner restaurants where *josefinos* (people from San José) gather to chew over ideas.

◉ Sights

San José is small and best explored on foot, joining locals along teeming sidewalks and pedestrian boulevards that lead to vintage theaters, crowded cafes, tree-shaded parks and some of the finest museums in Central America.

◉ Central San José East

Catedral Metropolitana CATHEDRAL
(Map p70; Avs 2 & 4 btwn Calles Central & 1) East of Parque Central, the Renaissance-style Catedral Metropolitana was built in 1871 after the previous cathedral was destroyed in an earthquake. The graceful neoclassical interior has colorful Spanish-tile floors, stained-glass windows, and a Christ figure that was produced by a Guatemalan workshop in the late 17th century. On the north side of the nave, a recumbent Christ that dates back to 1878 draws devout Ticos, who arrive here to pray and deposit pleas scribbled on small slips of paper.

Plaza de la Cultura PLAZA
(Map p70; Avs Central & 2 btwn Calles 3 & 5) For many Ticos, Costa Rica begins here. This architecturally unremarkable concrete plaza in the heart of downtown is usually packed with locals slurping ice-cream cones and admiring the wide gamut of San José street life: juggling clowns, itinerant vendors and cruising teenagers. It is perhaps one of the safest spots in the city since there's a police tower stationed at one corner.

Museo de Oro
Precolombino y Numismática MUSEUM
(Map p70; ☑ 2243-4202; www.museosdelbanco-central.org; Plaza de la Cultura, Avs Central & 2 btwn Calles 3 & 5; adult/student/child US$11/8/free; ⊙ 9:15am-5pm) This three-in-one museum houses an extensive collection of Costa Rica's most priceless pieces of pre-Columbian gold and other artifacts, including historical currency and some contemporary regional art. The museum, located underneath the Plaza de la Cultura, is owned by the Banco Central and its architecture brings to mind all the warmth and comfort of a bank vault. Security is tight; visitors must leave bags at the door.

★ Teatro Nacional NOTABLE BUILDING
(Map p70; ☑ 2010-1110; www.teatronacional.go.cr; Av 2 btwn Calles 3 & 5; admission US$10; ⊙ 9am-7pm) On the southern side of the Plaza de

la Cultura resides the Teatro Nacional, San José's most revered building. Constructed in 1897, it features a columned neoclassical facade that is flanked by statues of Beethoven and famous 17th-century Spanish dramatist Calderón de la Barca. The lavish marble lobby and auditorium are lined with paintings depicting various facets of 19th-century life. The hourly tours (p74) here are fantastic, and if you're looking to rest your feet, there's also an excellent onsite cafe (p83).

The theater's most famous painting is *Alegoría al café y el banano,* an idyllic canvas showing coffee and banana harvests. The painting was produced in Italy and shipped to Costa Rica for installation in the theater, and the image was reproduced on the old ₡5 note (now out of circulation). It seems clear that the painter never witnessed a banana harvest because of the way the man in the center is awkwardly grasping a bunch (actual banana workers hoist the stems onto their shoulders).

Museo Nacional de Costa Rica   MUSEUM
(Map p66; ☑ 2257-1433; www.museocostarica. go.cr; Calle 17 btwn Avs Central & 2; adult/child US$8/4; ☺ 8:30am-4:30pm Tue-Sat, 9am-4:30pm Sun) Entered via a beautiful glassed-in atrium housing an exotic butterfly garden, this museum provides a quick survey of Costa Rican history. Exhibits of pre-Columbian pieces from ongoing digs, as well as artifacts from the colony and the early republic, are all housed inside the old Bellavista Fortress, which served historically as the army headquarters and saw fierce fighting (hence the pockmarks) in the 1948 civil war.

It was here that President José Figueres Ferrer announced, in 1949, that he was abolishing the country's military. Among the museum's many notable pieces is the fountain pen that Figueres used to sign the 1949 constitution.

Don't miss the period galleries in the northeast corner, which feature turn-of-the-20th-century furnishings and decor from when these rooms served as the private residences of the fort's various commanders.

★ Museo de Jade   MUSEUM
(Map p70; ☑ 2521-6610; www.museodeljade.ins-cr. com; Plaza de la Democracia; adult/child US$15/5; ☺ 10am-5pm) Reopened in its brand-new home in mid-2014, this museum houses the world's largest collection of American jade (pronounced 'ha-day' in Spanish). The ample new exhibition space (five floors offer six exhibits) allows the public greater access to the museum's varied collection. There are nearly 7000 finely crafted, well-conserved pieces, from translucent jade carvings depicting fertility goddesses, shamans, frogs and snakes to incredible ceramics (some reflecting Maya influences), including a highly unusual ceramic head displaying a row of serrated teeth. Children under 10 may enter at no cost.

SAN JOSÉ IN...

One Day
Begin with a peek inside the city's most beautiful building, the 19th-century **Teatro Nacional** (p64). Enjoy an espresso at the theater's atmospheric **cafe** (p83) before heading into the nearby **Museo de Oro Precolombino y Numismática** (p64) to peruse its trove of pre-Columbian gold treasures.

Take lunch in an eatery of the up-and-coming Barrio Escalante, either on the terrace of **Kalú Café & Food Shop** (p90) or among the vertical gardens of **Al Mercat** (p89). Afterwards, browse the shops of historic Barrio Amón, such as **Galería Namu** (p95) and **eÑe** (p96), then end your afternoon sampling Costa Rican microbrews at **Stiefel** (p91) or enjoying a cocktail at the artsy **Café de los Deseos** (p83).

Two Days
Start your second day in town with a primer on Costa Rican history at the **Museo Nacional de Costa Rica** (p65), then cross Plaza de la Democracia to the newly relocated and expanded **Museo de Jade** (p65). After a stroll through the neighboring **Mercado Artesanal** (p96) for handicrafts, head northwest to the **Mercado Central** (p71) to shop for Costa Rican coffee, cigars and cheap snacks.

In the evening, grab dinner at the city's top restaurant, **Park Café** (p88), then venture east to Los Yoses and San Pedro, where you'll find a rollicking nightlife scene. Don't miss the wildly popular **Hoxton Pub** (p92), particularly if it's Tuesday.

San José

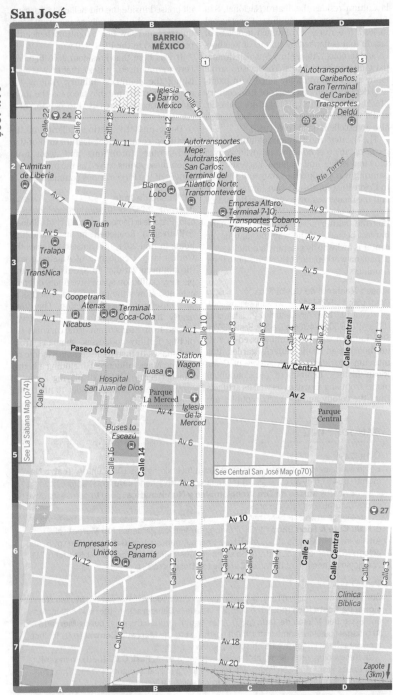

BARRIO MÉXICO

Iglesia Barrio México

Autotransportes Caribeños; Gran Terminal del Caribe; Transportes Deldú

Pulmitan de Liberia

Autotransportes Mepe; Autotransportes San Carlos; Terminal del Atlántico Norte; Transmonteverde

Blanco Lobo

Empresa Alfaro; Terminal 7-10; Transportes Cobano; Transportes Jacó

Río Torres

Tuan

Tralapa

TransNica

Coopetrans Atenas

Terminal Coca-Cola

Nicabus

Paseo Colón

Station Wagon

Av Central

Tuasa

Hospital San Juan de Dios

Parque La Merced

Iglesia de la Merced

Parque Central

Buses to Escazú

See La Sabana Map (p74)

See Central San José Map (p70)

Empresarios Unidos

Expreso Panamá

Clínica Bíblica

Zapote (3km)

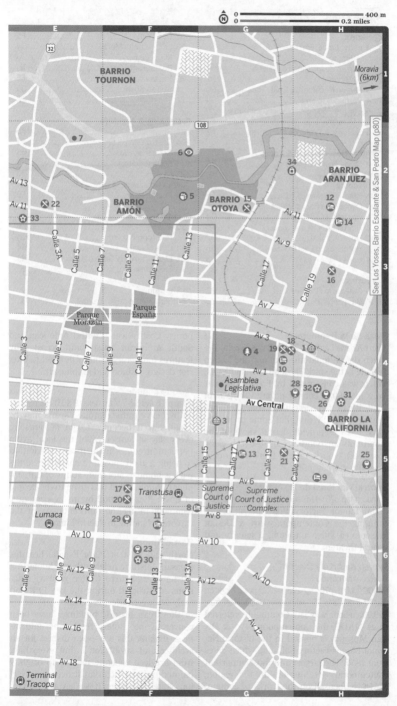

San José

Plaza de la Democracia   PLAZA
(Map p70; Avs Central & 2 btwn Calles 13 & 15) Between the national museum and the Museo de Jade is the stark Plaza de la Democracia, which was constructed by President Oscar Arias in 1989 to commemorate 100 years of Costa Rican democracy. The concrete plaza is architecturally dull, but some of its elevated terraces provide decent views of the mountains surrounding San José (especially at sunset). On its western flank is an open-air crafts market (p96).

Central Nacional de la Cultura   LANDMARK
(Cenac; Map p70) Housed in the historic National Liquor Factory, this cultural center contains the Contemporary Art & Design Museum, a video museum, a gallery and several theaters.

**Museo de Arte y Diseño
Contemporáneo**   MUSEUM
(MADC; Map p70; ☑ 2257-7202; www.madc.cr; cnr Av 3 & Calle 15; admission US$3, Mon free; ⊙9:30am-5pm Mon-Sat) Commonly referred to as MADC, the Contemporary Art & Design Museum is housed in the historic National Liquor Factory building, which dates from 1856. The largest and most important contemporary-art museum in the region, MADC is focused on the works of contem-

porary Costa Rican, Central American and South American artists, and occasionally features temporary exhibits devoted to interior design, fashion and graphic art.

Parque España   PARK
(Map p70; Avs 3 & 7 btwn Calles 9 & 11) Surrounded by heavy traffic, Parque España may be small, but it becomes a riot of birdsong every day at sunset when the local avian population comes in to roost. In addition to being a good spot for a shady break, the park is home to an ornate statue of Christopher Columbus that was given to the people of Costa Rica in 2002 by his descendants, commemorating the quincentenary of the explorer's landing in Puerto Limón.

Barrio Amón   AREA
North and west of Plaza España lies this pleasant, historic neighborhood, home to a cluster of *cafetalero* (coffee grower) mansions constructed during the late 19th and early 20th centuries. In recent years, many of the area's historic buildings have been converted into hotels, restaurants and offices, making this a popular district for an architectural stroll. You'll find everything from art-deco concrete manses to brightly painted tropical Victorian structures in various states of upkeep. It is a key arts center.

Parque Morazán   PARK

(Map p70; Avs 3 & 5 btwn Calles 5 & 9) To the southwest of the Parque España is Parque Morazán, named for Francisco Morazán, the 19th-century general who attempted to unite the Central American nations under a single flag. Once a notorious center of prostitution, the park is now beautifully illuminated in the evenings. At its center is the Templo de Música, a concrete bandstand that serves as an unofficial symbol of San José.

Edificio Metálico   LANDMARK

(Map p70; cnr Av 5 & Calle 9) One of downtown San José's most striking buildings, this century-old, two-story metal edifice on Parque España's western edge was prefabricated in Belgium, then shipped piece by piece to San José. Today it functions as a school and local landmark.

Casa Amarilla   HISTORIC BUILDING

(Map p70; Av 7 btwn Calles 11 & 13) On Parque España's northeast corner, this elegant colonial-style yellow mansion (closed to the public) houses the ministry of foreign affairs. The ceiba tree in front was planted by John F Kennedy during his 1963 visit to Costa Rica. If you walk around to the property's northeast corner, you can see a graffiti-covered slab of the Berlin Wall standing in the rear garden.

TEOR/éTica   GALLERY

(Map p70; ☑2221-1051; www.teoretica.org; cnr Calle 7 & Av 11; ☉9am-5pm Mon, Tue & Thu, to 6pm Wed, to noon Fri, 10am-4pm Sat) **FREE** This contemporary-art museum is the bricks-and-mortar gathering space for the TEOR/éTica Foundation, a nonprofit organization that supports Central American art and culture. Housed in a pair of vintage mansions across the street from one another, each of its elegant rooms exhibits cutting-edge works by established and emerging figures from Latin America and the world.

Parque Zoológico Nacional Simón Bolívar   ZOO

(Map p66; ☑2233-6701; www.fundazoo.org; Av 11 btwn Calles 7 & 9; adult/child US$5/3.50; ☉8am-3:30pm Mon-Fri, 9am-4:30pm Sat & Sun; ⊕) It may seem ironic to visit a zoo in one of the most biologically rich countries in the world, but this is a popular spot with local families who pour in on weekends to peek at the animals. It's rough around the edges – the cages are cramped and a few travelers have complained of the animals' filthy living spaces – but for small children it can serve as a basic primer on the area's wildlife.

If you have time for a day trip, a much better option is Zoo Ave (p111) outside Alajuela.

Spirogyra Jardín de Mariposas   GARDENS

(Map p66; ☑2222-2937; www.butterflygardencr. com; Barrio Amón; adult/child US$7/5; ☉9am-2pm Mon-Fri, to 3pm Sat & Sun; ⊕; ☐to El Pueblo) Housing more than 30 species of butterfly (including the luminescent blue morpho) in plant-filled enclosures, this small butterfly garden is a great spot for kids. Visit in the morning to see plenty of fluttering.

SAN JOSÉ FOR KIDS

Chances are if you're in Costa Rica on a short vacation you'll be headed out to the countryside fairly quickly. But if for some reason you're going to be hanging out in San José for a day – or two or three – with your kids, know that it's not a particularly kid-friendly destination. There is lots of traffic and the sidewalks are crowded and cracked, making it difficult to push strollers or drag toddlers around. Although the city offers relatively few things specifically for children, here are a few activities they will likely enjoy.

Near Parque La Sabana, the Museo de Ciencias Naturales (p72) will impress youngsters with its astounding array of skeletons and endless cases full of stuffed animals, while the Museo de los Niños (p71) is a sure hit for children who just can't keep their hands off the exhibits. Young nature-lovers will enjoy getting up close and personal with butterflies at the Spirogyra Jardín de Mariposas (p69) or checking out the exotic animals at the Parque Zoológico Nacional Simón Bolívar (p69). Just a little further afield (an easy day trip from San José) is the wonderful zoo and wildlife-rescue center Zoo Ave (p111), where you can enjoy native birds and monkeys in a more naturalistic setting.

If you're spending more than a week in the city, note that many Spanish-language academies offer special custom-made lessons for teens.

Central San José

Av 7

Buses to Heredia

BARRIO AMÓN

Calle 3

29

33

22

Calle 3A

Calle 5

Av 5

Calle Central

28

48

51

Calle 8

Calle 6

Calle 4

Calle 2

Calle 1

30

13

Av 3

8

Banco Nacional

Av 1

37

7

Banco Central

Av Central

49 38

Banco de Costa Rica

39

16

52

Av 2

Teatro Nacional

i 20

14 10

26

Calle 8

Calle 6

Calle 4

Av 4

11

4

Metrópoli

Calle 2

Calle Central

Calle 1

Calle 3

19

Calle 5

Calle 7

Av 6

The garden is 150m east and 150m south of Centro Comercial El Pueblo, which can be reached on foot (about a 20- to 30-minute walk from downtown), by taxi or by bus.

Parque Nacional PARK
(Map p66; Avs 1 & 3 btwn Calles 15 & 19) One of San José's nicest green spaces, this shady spot lures in retirees to read newspapers and young couples to smooch coyly on concrete benches. At its center is the Monumento Nacional, a dramatic 1953 statue that depicts the Central American nations driving out American filibuster William Walker. The park is dotted with myriad monuments devoted to Latin American historical figures, including Cuban poet, essayist and revolutionary José Martí, Mexican independence figure Miguel Hidalgo and 18th-century Venezuelan humanist Andrés Bello.

Across the street, to the south, stands the Asamblea Legislativa, which also bears an important statue: this one a depiction of Juan Santamaría – the young man who helped kick the pesky Walker out of Costa Rica – in full flame-throwing action.

**Estación del
Ferrocarril de Costa Rica** HISTORIC BUILDING
(Map p66; cnr Av 3 & Calle 21) Less than a block to the east of the Parque Nacional is San José's historic train station to the Atlantic, which was built in 1908. Nowadays offering weekday train service to Heredia and Cartago, it's a remarkable example of tropical architecture, with swirling art nouveau–inspired beams and elaborate stonework all along the roofline.

⊙ Central San José West

Parque Central PARK
(Map p70; Avs 2 & 4 btwn Calles Central & 2) The city's central park is more of a run-down plaza than a park. At its center is a grandiose bandstand that looks as if it was

lined with vendors hawking everything from spices and coffee beans to *pura vida* souvenir T-shirts made in China. It's all super cheap, and likely made in China or Nicaragua.

In December Mercado Central is also open on Sundays.

Mercado Central Annex MARKET

(Map p70; Avs 1 & 3 btwn Calles 6 & 8; ⏰6am-6pm Mon-Sat) The Mercado Central Annex is less touristy than Mercado Central, and is crowded with butchers, fishmongers and informal counters dishing out typical Costa Rican *casados* (a set meal of rice, beans and cabbage slaw served with chicken, fish or meat).

Museo de los Niños & Galería Nacional MUSEUM

(Map p66; ☎2258-4929; www.museocr.org; Calle 4, north of Av 9; adult/child US$4.20/3.80; ⏰8am-4:30pm Tue-Fri, 9:30am-5pm Sat & Sun; ♿) If you were wondering how to get your young kids interested in art and science, this unusual museum – actually two museums in one – is an excellent place to start. Housed in an old penitentiary built in 1909, it is part children's museum and part art gallery. Small children will love the hands-on exhibits related to science, geography and natural history, while grown-ups will enjoy the unusual juxtaposition of contemporary art in abandoned prison cells.

⊙ La Sabana

West of downtown, the bustle of the city's congested center gives way to private homes, condo towers and shopping areas chock-full of Ticos. At the heart of this district lies the sprawling Parque Metropolitano La Sabana, a popular recreation center – and a welcome patch of green amid the concrete of the capital.

Parque Metropolitano La Sabana PARK

(Map p74) Once the site of San José's main airport, this 72-hectare green space at the west end of Paseo Colón is home to a museum, a lagoon and various sporting facilities – most notably Costa Rica's national soccer stadium (p95). During the day, the park's paths make a relaxing place for a stroll, a jog or a picnic.

Museo de Arte Costarricense MUSEUM

(Map p74; ☎2256-1281; www.musarco.go.cr; east entrance of Parque La Sabana; ⏰9am-4pm Tue-Sun;

designed by Mussolini: massive concrete arches support a florid roof capped with a ball-shaped decorative knob.

Teatro Melico Salazar HISTORIC BUILDING

(Map p70; ☎2295-6032; www.teatromelico.go.cr; Av 2 btwn Calles Central & 2) On the north side of Parque Central is this theatre, which was built in 1928 in a beaux-arts style. It is named after the well-known Costa Rican tenor Melico Salazar (1887–1950), who performed internationally (among other places, he sang at the Metropolitan Opera in New York City). The theater was the site of the 2002 presidential inauguration, and regularly hosts fine-arts engagements.

Mercado Central MARKET

(Map p70; Avs Central & 1 btwn Calles 6 & 8; ⏰6am-6pm Mon-Sat) Though *josefinos* mainly do their shopping at chain supermarkets, San José's crowded indoor markets retain an old-world feel. This is the main market,

Central San José

(✈) This Spanish-style structure served as San José's main airport terminal until 1955. The newly remodeled museum features regional art and other exhibits.

**Museo de Ciencias
Naturales La Salle** MUSEUM
(☏ 2232-1306; www.museolasalle.ed.cr; Sabana Sur; adult/child US$2/1.60; ⊙8am-4pm Mon-Sat, 9am-5pm Sun; ✈) Ever wanted to see a spider-monkey skeleton or a herd of stuffed tapirs? This natural-history museum near Parque La Sabana's southwest corner has an extensive collection of taxidermic animals and birds from Costa Rica and far beyond, alongside animal skeletons, minerals, preserved specimens and a vast new collection of butterflies. Kids in particular will appreciate this place.

◎ Los Yoses, Barrio Escalante & San Pedro

Museo de Insectos MUSEUM
(Insect Museum; Map p80; ☏ 2511-5318; www.mi-ucr.ucr.ac.cr; San Pedro; admission US$2; ⊙8am-noon & 1-5pm Mon-Fri) Reputedly Central America's largest insect museum, this place has an extensive collection assembled by the Facultad de Agronomía at the Universidad de Costa Rica. After viewing the specimens, visitors are invited to a room with a kitchen to sample meal worms, scarabs and crickets. A little salt and oregano does wonders.

Curiously, the museum is housed in the basement of the music building (Facultad de Artes Musicales), a brutalist structure painted an incongruous shade of Barbie pink.

Activities

If you want to swim with the kiddies and your hotel doesn't have a pool, head to the Ojo de Agua Springs (p106) in San Antonio de Belén, a popular swimming spot for Tico families.

Parque Metropolitano La Sabana (p71) has a variety of sporting facilities, including tennis courts, volleyball, basketball and baseball areas, jogging paths and soccer pitches. Pickup soccer games can be had on most days, though you'd better be good: Ticos can sink a drop shot by age seven. There is also an Olympic-size swimming **pool** (Map p74; US$3; ☉9am-7pm) for serious lap swimmers.

 Courses

Merecumbé Escazú　　　COURSE
(Map p82; ☑8884-7553, 2289-4774; cnr Av 26 & Calle Cortés) Improve your dance moves at Merecumbé, a chain of studios that will get you grooving to everything from salsa to waltz. Most courses are for locals, but some sessions are geared to foreign travelers. Schedules vary; call ahead. The company has various studios, including another one in **San Pedro** (☑2224-3531; 100m south & 25m west of the Banco Popular) (though, unfortunately, nothing downtown).

 Tours

The city is small and easily navigable. If you're looking for a walking tour that will guide you to key sites, there are plenty on offer.

★**Really Experience Community**　　TOUR
(Triángulo de la Solidaridad Slum Tour; ☑2297-7058; elninoylabolacr.org; per person US$12-25) Nonprofit Boy with a Ball wants to be clear: this is a slum tour. It may seem exploitative, but visiting El Triángulo, a squatter development of 2000 people north of San José, is anything but. Promising young residents lead the tours, introducing guests to neighbors and community entrepreneurs. No cameras are allowed, but the conversations make a lasting impression.

Barrio Bird Walking Tours　　WALKING TOUR
(☑6280-6169; www.toursanjosecostarica.com; tours from US$29) Knowledgeable and engaging guides show visitors San José's famous and not-so-famous sights, providing history and insight on the city's architecture, markets and urban art. Specialized tours also cater to foodies as well as LGBT enthusiasts.

ChepeCletas　　TOUR
(☑8849-8316, 2222-7548; www.chepecletas.com) This dynamic Tico-run company offers cultural walking tours and free cycling tours of San José (tips accepted), a foodie-oriented exploration of the Mercado Central, a bar-hopping tour focused on traditional downtown *cantinas* (canteens), and a guided visit to San José's parks and green spaces. They also offer a nighttime biking tour once a week and group rides every Sunday morning.

SAN JOSÉ ACTIVITIES

TALK LIKE A TICO

San José is loaded with schools that offer Spanish lessons (either privately or in groups) and provide long-term visitors to the country with everything from dance lessons to volunteer opportunities. Well-established options include the following:

Amerispan Study Abroad (☑in USA & Canada 800-511-0179, worldwide 215-531-7917; www.amerispan.com; from US$380/225)

Costa Rican Language Academy (Map p80; ☑2280-5834, in USA 866-230-6361; www.crlang.co.cr; Calle Ronda, Barrio Dent)

Institute for Central American Development Studies (ICADS; ☑2225-0508; www.icads.org; Curridabat; month-long courses with homestay/without homestay US$1990/915)

Personalized Spanish (☑2278-3254, in USA 786-245-4124; www.personalizedspanish.com; Tres Ríos)

Already speak Spanish? To truly talk like a Tico, check out the **Costa Rica Idioms** app, available for iOS and Android. It's quite basic but defines local lingo and uses each term in a sentence. *Tuanis, mae!* (Cool, dude!)

La Sabana

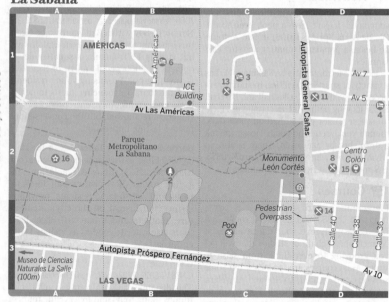

La Sabana

Teatro Nacional CULTURAL TOUR
(Map p70; ☑ 2010-1143; www.teatronacional.go.cr/
Visitenos/turismo; Av 2 btwn Calles 3 & 5; tours
US$10; ⊗ 9am-5pm) On this fascinating tour,
guests are regaled with stories of the art,
architecture and people behind Costa Rica's
crown jewel, the national theater. The best
part is a peek into otherwise off-limits areas,
such as the Smoking Room, which feature
famous paintings, lavish antique furnishings
and ornate gold trim.

Tours are offered every hour on the hour
in Spanish and English, to a maximum of 15
people. Children under 12 are free.

Costa Rica Art Tour TOUR
(☑ 8359-5571, in USA 877-394-6113; www.costa
ricaarttour.com; per person US$150) This small
outfit run by Molly Keeler conducts private
day tours that offer an intimate look at artists in their studios, where you can view
(and buy) the work of local painters, sculp-
tors, printmakers, ceramicists and jewel-
ers. Lunch and San José city hotel pickup
is included in the price. Reserve at least a
week in advance. Discounts are available for
groups.

Festival de las Artes PERFORMING ARTS
(FIA; ☑2248-3240; www.festivaldelasartes.go.cr)
About every other year, San José becomes
host to this biennial citywide arts showcase
that features theater, music, dance and film.
It's held for two weeks in March or April.
Keep an eye out for information in the daily
newspapers.

Desfile de los Boyeros CULTURAL
(Oxcart Parade; ☉Nov) This parade of oxcarts
down Paseo Colón is a celebration of the
country's agricultural heritage.

Festival de la Luz RELIGIOUS
(Festival of Light; www.festivaldelaluz.cr; ☉Dec)
December brings San José's big Christmas
parade, marked by elaborate costumes and
floats, and an absurd amount of plastic
'snow.'

Las Fiestas de Zapote CULTURAL
(www.fiestaszapote.com; ☉late Dec–early Jan) Between Christmas and New Year's, this week-
long holiday celebration of all things Costa
Rican (namely rodeos, cowboys, carnival
rides, fried food and booze) annually draws
in tens of thousands of Ticos to the bullring
in the suburb of Zapote, just southeast of
San José.

🛏 Sleeping

Accommodations in San José run the gamut
from simple but homey hostels to luxurious
boutique retreats. If you're flying into or
out of Costa Rica from here, it may be more
convenient to stay in Alajuela, as the town is
minutes from the international airport.

Reservations are recommended in the
high season (December through April), in
particular the two weeks around Christmas
and Semana Santa (Holy Week, the week
preceding Easter).

You'll find the cheapest sleeps in the city
center, with nicer midrange and top-end
spots clustered in more well-to-do districts
such as Barrio Amón and La Sabana. Also
worthwhile for their charm, safety and serenity are the adjacent neighborhoods of
Los Yoses and San Pedro, which lie within
walking distance of downtown. For tonier
options, the upscale suburb of Escazú – a
20-minute bus ride away – is a good choice.

🛏 Central San José East

Most of downtown's better sleeping options
are located east of Calle Central, many of
them in historic Victorian and art-deco

Carpe Chepe TOUR
(☑8326-6142; www.carpechepe.com; guided
pub crawls US$20; ☉7pm Thu & Sat) For an
insider's look at Chepe's nightlife, join one
of these lively Thursday- and Saturday-
evening guided pub crawls, led by an
enthusiastic group of young locals. A free
welcome shot is included at each of the four
bars visited. Online bookings receive a 20%
discount.

Swiss Travel Service WALKING TOUR
(Map p66; ☑2282-4898; www.swisstravelcr.com)
This long-standing agency offers a four-
hour afternoon city tour of San José that
hits all the key sites.

⛪ Festivals & Events

Día del Boyero CULTURAL
(☉Mar) On the second Sunday of March,
Escazú holds this popular event honoring
Costa Rica's *boyeros* (oxcart drivers). Dozens
of attendees from all over the country decorate traditional, brightly painted carts and
form a colorful (if slow) parade.

Día de San José RELIGIOUS
(St Joseph's Day; ☉19 Mar) San José marks the
day of its patron saint with mass in some
churches.

mansions. Many of the top-end hotels accept credit cards.

★ **Hostel Pangea** HOSTEL $
(Map p70; ☑ 2221-1992; www.hostelpangea.com; Av 7 btwn Calles 3 & 3A, Barrio Amón; dm US$14, d with/without bathroom US$55/35, ste from US$70; P @ 🛜 🌊) This industrial-strength hostel – 25 dorm beds and 25 private rooms – has been a popular 20-something backpacker hangout for years. It's not difficult to see why: it's smack in the middle of the city and comes stocked with a pool and a rooftop restaurant-lounge with stellar views. Needless to say, it's a party spot.

Rooms are tidy, mattresses firm and the shared bathrooms enormous and clean. The hostel's five suites have king-size beds and flat-screen TVs. Other perks include free internet, luggage storage and 24-hour airport shuttles (from US$12).

★ **Hostel Casa del Parque** HOSTEL $
(Map p66; ☑ 2233-3437; www.hostelcasadelparque.com; Calle 19 btwn Avs 1 & 3; dm US$14, d with/without bathroom US$49/39; 🛜) A vintage art-deco manse from 1936 houses this cozy and welcoming spot on the northeastern edge of Parque Nacional. Five large, basic private rooms (two with private bathroom), a new five-bed dormitory and an older 10-bed dormitory upstairs have parquet floors and simple furnishings. Take some sun on the plant-festooned outdoor patio and take advantage of the shared kitchen.

The bilingual young owner is a good source of local dining information.

Costa Rica Backpackers HOSTEL $
(Map p66; ☑ 2223-2406, 2221-6191; www.costaricabackpackers.com; Av 6 near Calle 21; dm US$12-16, d without bathroom US$35; P @ 🛜 🌊) This popular hostel has 17 basic but clean dormitories and 14 doubles with shared bathrooms surrounding a spacious hammock-filled garden and a free-form pool. Two bars, a restaurant and ambient chillout music enhance the inviting, laid-back atmosphere. Other benefits include a communal kitchen and TV lounge, free luggage storage, internet access, an onsite travel agency and low-cost airport transfers ($26).

Hostel Shakti HOSTEL $
(Map p66; www.hostelshakti.com; cnr Av 8 & Calle 13; dm/s/d/tr US$18/30/40/60; P ✳ @ 🛜) This lovely little guesthouse uses bold colors and natural materials to create an oasis of calm and comfort amid the chaos

of San José. Three dorms and four private rooms are dressed up with eclectic furnishings and colorful bedding. There is a fully equipped kitchen, but you might not need it, as the onsite restaurant is healthy, fresh and amazing.

Casa Ridgway GUESTHOUSE $
(Map p66; ☑ 2222-1400, 2233-6168; www.casaridgwayhostel.com; cnr Calle 15 & Av 6A; incl breakfast dm US$17, s/d without bathroom US$24/38; P ⊜ 🛜) This small, peaceful guesthouse on a quiet side street is run by the adjacent Friends' Peace Center, a Quaker organization promoting social justice and human rights. There is a small lounge, a communal kitchen and a lending library filled with books about Central American politics and society. No smoking or alcohol is allowed, with quiet hours from 10pm to 6am.

★ **Hotel Aranjuez** HOTEL $$
(Map p66; ☑ 2256-1825; www.hotelaranjuez.com; Calle 19 btwn Avs 11 & 13; incl breakfast s US$28-55, d US$48-65, s/d without bathroom US$22/38; P @ 🛜) This hotel in Barrio Aranjuez consists of five nicely maintained vintage homes that have been strung together with a labyrinth of gardens and connecting walkways. The 36 spotless rooms come in various configurations, all with lockbox and cable TV. The hotel's best attribute, however, is the lush garden patio, where a legendary breakfast buffet is served every morning.

Though the architecture can be a bit creaky and the walls thin, the service is efficient and the hotel is a solid, family-friendly option. Rooms in the new apartment-building annex half a block away lack the charm and sense of community of the main hotel, but annex guests still have access to the bounteous breakfast and pleasant common areas across the street.

Luz de Luna BOUTIQUE HOTEL $$
(Map p80; ☑ 2225-4919; luzdelunahotelboutique.com; Calle 33 btwn Avs 3 & 5; r US$50-80; 🛜) A converted old mansion, this new boutique hotel, restaurant and cafe is in a prime location: the heart of Barrio Escalante's Paseo Gastronómico La Luz district and its up-and-coming restaurants. Foodies who like to relax will appreciate this sanctuary and self-described 'lunar complex' for its lush gardens, hardwood floors and occasional pre-Columbian statue.

VOLUNTEERING IN SAN JOSÉ

For travelers who want an experience beyond vacation, there are dozens of not-for-profit organizations in San José that gladly accept volunteers.

Boy with a Ball (☑2297-7058; elninoylabolacr.org) This nonprofit offers volunteer opportunities and runs tours to El Triángulo (p73).

Central American Service Expeditions (☑8839-0515; www.serviceexpeditions.com) A Costa Rican nonprofit that creates custom volunteer opportunities for families and teens focused on sustainability.

GeoVisions (☑203-453-5838, in USA 855-875-6837; www.geovisions.org) An international nonprofit that places volunteers in a Costa Rican children's hospital.

Educational Travel Adventures (☑in USA & Canada 866-273-2500; www.etadventures. com) Arranges a wide variety of volunteer trips, conservation projects and service learning opportunities.

United Planet (☑1-617-267-7763; www.unitedplanet.org) Places volunteers in programs on global health, education and the environment.

Hotel Posada del Museo　　　GUESTHOUSE **$$**
(Map p66; ☑2258-1027; www.hotelposadadel museo.com; cnr Calle 17 & Av 2; s US$50-80, d US$70-90; @🖥) Managed by an amiable, multilingual couple, this architecturally intriguing, 1928-vintage inn is diagonally across from the Museo Nacional. French doors line the entrances to each of the rooms, no two of which are alike. Some rooms accommodate up to four people, making this a family-friendly option. Light sleepers, take note: the hotel is adjacent to the train tracks.

Kaps Place　　　GUESTHOUSE **$$**
(Map p66; ☑2221-1169; www.kapsplace.com; Calle 19 btwn Avs 11 & 13; incl breakfast s US$35-45, d/ tr US$55/65, apt US$100-140; P@🖥) On a residential street in Barrio Aranjuez, this homey guesthouse has 21 rooms of various configurations spread over two buildings. Guests have access to patios decorated in colorful mosaics, three shared kitchens, a games room with ping-pong, pool and foosball tables, a big-screen TV lounge with huge DVD library, and free phone calls to 60 countries.

Hotel Santo Tomás　　　HOTEL **$$**
(Map p70; ☑2255-0448; www.hotelsantotomas. com; Av 7 btwn Calles 3 & 5; r incl breakfast US$59-116; P🌀@🖥🏊) A Barrio Amón landmark that once belonged to the Salazar family of *cafetaleros* (coffee growers), this stately early-20th-century colonial-style mansion oozes history. Slightly frayed rooms with high ceilings and period furnishings occupy the mansion itself, while a back annex offers more modern amenities. The garden courtyard contains a swimming pool with tiled waterslide, Jacuzzi and small open-air gym.

Hemingway Inn　　　HOTEL **$$**
(Map p70; ☑2221-1804, 2257-8630; www.hemingwayinn.com; cnr Calle 9 & Av 9; incl breakfast s US$40-68, d US$57-85; 🖥🏊) This family-owned, funky little spot in Barrio Amón offers 17 simple, comfortable and unique rooms in a rambling *cafetalero* house dating to the 1920s. The garden, shared kitchen and wall murals lend the inn a relaxed and friendly ambiance, and room prices include a full made-to-order breakfast. As a rare perk, pets can be accommodated with prior notice.

Bells' Home Hospitality　　　HOMESTAY **$$**
(☑2225-4752; www.homestay-thebells.com; s/d incl breakfast US$35/60, dinner US$10) This recommended agency is run by the bilingual Marcela Bell, who has operated the business for more than 20 years. She can arrange stays in more than a dozen homes around San José, each of which has been personally inspected and all of which are close to public transportation. Airport pickup is also available.

Hotel Colonial　　　HOTEL **$$**
(Map p70; ☑2223-0109; www.hotelcolonialcr. com; Calle 11 btwn Avs 2 & 6; s/d/ste incl breakfast US$68/80/113; P🌀@🖥🏊) An intricately carved baroque-style carriage door and an arched poolside promenade usher guests into this 1940s Spanish-style inn. The 16 rooms and one suite are either whitewashed or painted an earthy mustard-yellow color,

with dark wood furnishings and bright bedspreads. Those on higher floors have sweeping views of the city and outlying mountains, while three ground-level rooms are wheelchair-accessible.

Hotel Rincón de San José HOTEL **$$**

(Map p70; ☎2221-9702; www.hotelrinconde sanjose.com; cnr Av 9 & Calle 15; s/d/tr/q incl breakfast from US$60/70/90/115; @📶) Comprising three houses of varying ages in Barrio Otoya, this tidy spot has 40 guest rooms – ranging from rather faded older units to modern ones with bright linens and ceramic tile. Breakfast is served in an attractive interior garden courtyard, and there's a small sun terrace with nice views of surrounding houses and distant mountains.

Casa Alfi HOTEL **$$**

(Map p70; ☎2222-2817; www.casaalfihotel.com; Calle 3 btwn Avs 4 & 6; s/d/tr incl breakfast US$45/60/75; @📶) Steps from the Teatro Nacional, this simple two-story structure comprises nine guest rooms – each with TV, telephone, private bathroom and lockbox – surrounding a covered courtyard. Friendly and well-traveled owner Alfi offers guests three breakfast choices: continental, tropical or traditional Costa Rican.

Laundry service available; both a restaurant and spa were in the works at the time of research.

Hotel Fleur de Lys HOTEL **$$**

(Map p70; ☎2223-1206; www.hotelfleurdelys.com; Calle 13 btwn Avs 2 & 6; incl breakfast s US$78-98, d US$86-106, junior/master ste US$126/156; P⊖@📶) Impeccably maintained, this century-old, bright-pink Victorian mansion houses 30 spotless wood-paneled rooms with firm beds, ceiling fans and wicker furnishings. A small onsite bar provides a welcome cocktail or smoothie, and on Fridays there is live music. The staff are attentive and the location central (note the proximity of the train tracks). German, French and English are spoken; credit cards accepted.

Hotel Presidente BOUTIQUE HOTEL **$$$**

(Map p70; ☎2010-0000, in USA 1-877-540-1790; www.hotel-presidente.com; Av Central; r US$107-160; P❄📶) 🍃 A revamp in 2015 turned this formerly drab hotel into a glorious boutique stay. The new lobby offers tons of inlaid brick, antique adornments and a red spiral staircase to a rooftop garden. The central location remains ideal, as do the 74 well-appointed rooms, the best of which feature Jacuzzis and stunning city views.

Gran Hotel Costa Rica HOTEL **$$$**

(Map p70; ☎2221-4000; www.granhotelcosta rica.com; Calle 3 btwn Avs Central & 2; incl breakfast d standard/superior/deluxe US$102/124/146, ste master/presidential US$175/225; ⊖❄@📶) 🍃 Constructed in 1930 the city's first prominent hotel is recognized as a national landmark (John F Kennedy and soccer legend Pelé both stayed here). Frequent renovations keep the 107 rooms modern and comfortable, though they retain period touches such as brass bed frames and wood furnishings. The popular terrace bar-restaurant out front features live piano music on weekday evenings.

Some rooms have wonderful views of the Teatro Nacional, and here and there are subtle architectural reminders of the hotel's history: exposed beams, molded ceilings and the dramatic entrance hall lined with vintage photographs of San José.

Hotel Don Carlos HOTEL **$$$**

(Map p70; ☎2221-6707; www.doncarloshotel.com; Calle 9 btwn Avs 7 & 9; incl breakfast s/d US$80/91, ste s/d US$91/102; P@📶🏊) Built around an early-20th-century house that once belonged to President Tomás Guardia, this welcoming Barrio Amón inn exudes a slightly campy colonial-era vibe. Thirty rooms are nestled around a faux-pre-Columbian sculpture garden with a sundeck and small kiddie-depth pool. All rooms have cable TV, lockbox and hair dryer; upstairs units are generally nicer than the mustier ones downstairs.

Don't miss the Spanish-tile mural, just outside the onsite restaurant, which beautifully depicts central San José in the 1930s. Credit cards accepted.

La Sabana & Around

You'll find everything from hostels to vintage B&Bs in the neighborhoods that surround Parque Metropolitano La Sabana.

Gaudy's HOSTEL **$**

(Map p74; ☎2248-0086; www.backpacker.co.cr; Av 5 btwn Calles 36 & 38; dm US$13, r with/without bathroom US$39/32; P@📶) Popular among shoestring travelers for years, this homey hostel inside a sprawling modernist house northeast of Parque La Sabana has 13 private rooms and two dormitories. The owners keep the design scheme minimalist and the vibe mellow, with professional service and well-maintained rooms. There's a communal kitchen, a TV lounge, a pool table and a courtyard strung with hammocks.

Mi Casa Hostel
HOSTEL $

(Map p74; ☑ 2231-4700; www.micasahostel.com; incl breakfast dm US$15, r with/without bathroom from US$38/27; P@�) This converted modernist home in La Sabana has polished-wood floors, vintage furnishings and 14 eclectic guest rooms to choose from, including one 10-person dorm and another room that's wheelchair-accessible. Mellow communal areas are comfortably furnished, and the shared kitchen is clean and roomy. There is a pleasant garden, a pool table, free internet, and laundry service.

Rosa del Paseo
HOTEL $$

(Map p74; ☑ 2257-3225; www.rosadelpaseo. com; Paseo Colón btwn Calles 28 & 30; s/d/ste from US$75/85/90; P@�) ✐ Don't let the Paseo Colón location and the small facade fool you: this sprawling Victorian-Caribbean mansion (built in 1910 by the Montealegre family of coffee exporters) has 18 rooms reaching way back into an interior courtyard far from the city noise. The hotel still maintains the original tile floors and other historic details, including antique oil paintings and sculptures.

Rooms are simple, with polished-wood floors and period-style furnishings. There's a wonderful front sitting room where guests can listen to vintage vinyl discs on the phonograph, and the garden, where breakfast is served each morning, is filled with heliconias and bougainvilleas. Credit cards accepted.

Colours Oasis Resort
HOTEL $$

(☑ 2296-1880, in USA & Canada 866-517-4390; www.coloursoasis.com; cnr Triángulo de Pavas & Blvr Rohrmoser; r US$55-200; �✹) This long-time LGBT-friendly hotel occupies a sprawling Spanish colonial–style complex in the elegant Rohrmoser district (northwest of La Sabana). Rooms and mini-apartments have modern furnishings and impeccable bathrooms. Facilities include TV lounge, mini-gym, pool, sundeck and Jacuzzi, as well as a new international restaurant, ideal for evening cocktails.

Apartotel La Sabana
HOTEL $$

(Map p74; ☑ 2220-2422; www.apartotel-lasabana. com; d/apt/f incl breakfast from US$85/101/141; P✳@�✹) This lovely, well-maintained apartment complex 150m north of Rosti-pollos has 32 units in various configurations that draw long-term business travelers as well as families. Apartments (with or without kitchen) are accented with wood furnishings and folk art. The interior courtyard has a nice pool, and free shuttle service is offered both from and to the airport. Special rates are available for weekly and monthly stays.

★Hotel Grano de Oro
BOUTIQUE HOTEL $$$

(Map p74; ☑ 2255-3322; www.hotelgranodeoro. com; Calle 30 btwn Avs 2 & 4; d US$187-356, ste US$362-593; P⊖@�) It's easy to see why honeymooners love it here. Built around a sprawling early-20th-century Victorian mansion, this elegant inn has 39 demure 'Tropical Victorian' rooms furnished with wrought-iron beds and rich brocade linens. Some rooms boast private courtyards with gurgling fountains, and a rooftop garden terrace offers two bubbling Jacuzzis. The whole place sparkles with tropical flowers and polished-wood accents.

If you want to experience the Costa Rica of a gilded age, this would be the place to do it.

🛏 Los Yoses, Barrio Escalante & San Pedro

Locals use several prominent landmarks when giving directions, including Spoon restaurant, the Fuente de la Hispanidad fountain and Más x Menos supermarket.

★Hostel Bekuo
HOSTEL $

(Map p80; ☑ 2234-1091, in USA 1-813-750-8572; www.hostelbekuo.com; dm US$11-13, d from US$30; �) For pure positive energy, you won't find a nicer hostel anywhere in San José. This restful spot, in a hip area of Los Yoses just a block south of Av Central, feels extremely homey, thanks to frequent backyard BBQs, spontaneous pitchers of free sangria, a living room with piano and guitar, and a kitchen equipped with good knives, appliances and an inviting central work space.

The airy modernist structure has nine unique and colorful rooms with high-quality beds and mattresses (including four dormitories, one reserved especially for women), along with large tiled bathrooms, an expansive TV lounge dotted with beanbags, and an interior courtyard slung with hammocks. Well-traveled owner Brian Van Fleet and his staff go the extra mile for

Los Yoses, Barrio Escalante & San Pedro

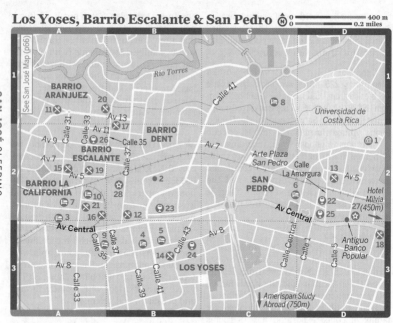

Los Yoses, Barrio Escalante & San Pedro

guests, with colorful and well-conceived information displays and evening outings designed to show visitors the best of San José's nightlife. Yet this remains a place where you can get a good night's sleep; quiet time is respected from 11pm on.

Hostel Urbano HOSTEL $
(Map p80; ☎ 2281-0707; www.hostelurbano. com; dm US$12-14, d with/without bathroom US$38/32) Within easy walking distance of the university and its associated nightlife, yet right on the bus line into downtown San José, this immaculate new hostel is in

a 1950s home, opposite Parque Kennedy in San Pedro. Guests feel instantly welcome, with its open floor plan, spacious backyard, pool table, modern internet facilities and kitchen-dining area that's nice enough to host a dinner party.

Smaller rooms, which are often rented out as private doubles, are also ideal for groups of three or four friends traveling together. Even the larger 12- and 16-bed dorms manage not to feel claustrophobic, thanks to the thoughtful placement of well-constructed modern bunks.

Hostel Casa Yoses   HOSTEL $

(Map p80; ☑ 2234-5486; www.casayoses.com; Av 8, Los Yoses; incl breakfast dm US$11-15, d US$42; P @ 🛜) A mellow spot, this Spanish Revival–style house from 1949 is perched on a hill that offers lovely views of the valley from the front garden. Here you'll find 10 rooms (four of them dorms) of varying decor and style, all of which are spotless, with wood floors and tiled hallways.

There is a shared kitchen, an attached bar, La Sospecha, with a pool table and foosball, and even an area for BBQs. The young owners speak Spanish, English and French.

Hostel Backpackers San José   HOSTEL $

(Map p80; ☑ 2234-8186; Av Central btwn Calles 29 & 33, Los Yoses; dm/r without bathroom US$14/40, s/d/tr/q with bathroom US$40/55/69/80; P @ 🛜 ✈) This graceful neoclassical home once belonged to José Figueres Ferrer, the Costa Rican president who abolished the army and granted women the right to vote. While the hostel contains five dormitories, it feels much more like an inn, with seven large private rooms with modern bathrooms, sofas, wi-fi and flat-screen TVs. The owners recently opened a bar facing the street.

Hotel Milvia   B&B $$

(☑ 2225-4543; www.hotelmilvia.com; s/d/tr incl breakfast US$67/78/85; @ 🛜) Owned by a well-known Costa Rican artist and former museum director, this lovely Caribbean-style building offers a homey retreat from the city. Nine eclectic rooms, all dotted with bright artwork, surround a pleasant courtyard with a trickling fountain. An upstairs terrace provides views of the mountains. It's in San Pedro, 100m north of Más x Menos.

Hotel Ave del Paraíso   HOTEL $$

(Map p80; ☑ 2225-8515, 2283-6017; hotelave delparaiso.com; s/d incl breakfast US$68/79;

@ 🛜) 🖉 Decorated with beautiful mosaic tiles, this hotel run by an artsy family is set back from the busy street just far enough to permit a good night's sleep. There's a bubbling outdoor Jacuzzi tub on the property and a wonderful restaurant and bar, Café Kracovia (p88), owned by the same family. The university is just a two-minute walk north.

Hotel 1492 Jade y Oro   B&B $$

(Map p80; ☑ 2280-6265, 2225-3752; www.hotel 1492.com; Av 1 btwn Calles 29 & 33; s/d/tr incl breakfast US$50/108/138; P 🛜) On a quiet Barrio Escalante side street you'll find this 10-room B&B in a Spanish-style house built in the 1940s by the Volio family. The rooms vary in size, but all are nicely accented, with Portuguese tile work and some original furnishings. Breakfast is served in a charming rear garden.

Hotel Le Bergerac   BOUTIQUE HOTEL $$$

(Map p80; ☑ 2234-7850; www.bergerachotel.com; Calle 35 btwn Avs Central & 8; d standard/superior/deluxe/grande incl breakfast US$109/132/160/177; P @ 🛜) This Los Yoses standard-bearer features 25 rooms, most with private garden patio, in a whitewashed building tranquilly removed from the main street. Though sizes and configurations vary, all rooms are comfortable and sunny, accented with wood floors and floral bedspreads, and equipped with immaculate bathroom, cable TV, telephone and safe. There is an onsite restaurant with a full bar.

🛏 Escazú

Escazú is a stylish area with accommodations ranging from sleek boutique inns to homey B&Bs – but there's not much for the budget traveler. Street addresses aren't always given; call directly or check hotel websites for directions (which are invariably complicated).

Three kilometers west of Escazú is the affluent expat suburb of Santa Ana. On the road between the two, you'll find a few out-of-the-way spots to stay and eat.

★ Posada El Quijote   B&B $$

(☑ 2289-8401; www.quijote.cr; Calle del Llano; d standard/superior/deluxe/studio apt incl breakfast US$85/95/105/115; P ⊖ ❋ 🛜) This Spanish-style hillside *posada* (guesthouse) in Bello Horizonte rates as one of the area's top B&Bs. Homey standard rooms have wood floors, throw rugs, cable TV and hot-water

Escazú

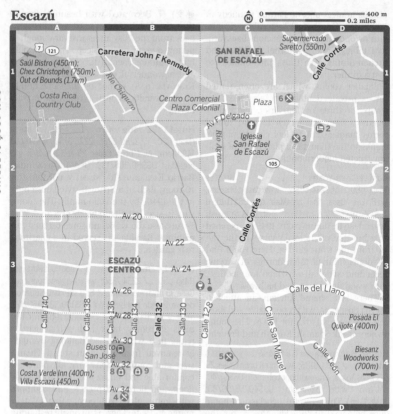

Escazú

✪ Activities, Courses & Tours
1 Merecumbé Escazú C3

🛏 Sleeping
2 Casa de las Tías D2

🍴 Eating
3 Automercado D2
4 Buena Tierra B4
5 La Posada de las Brujas C4
6 Más X Menos C1

🍷 Drinking & Nightlife
7 Pub C3

🛍 Shopping
8 Escazú farmers markets B4
9 Sin Domicilio Fijo B4

bathrooms; superior and deluxe units have a patio or a private terrace. Guests are invited to take a nip at the honor bar, then soak up sweeping Central Valley views on the patio. A backyard swing set and trampoline make this place especially fun for families with kids.

Costa Verde Inn   INN **$$**
(☑ 2228-4080, in USA 1-800-773-5013; www. costaverdeinn.com; Escazú; s/d/tr incl breakfast US$60/70/80, d apt from US$90; 🅿 @ 🛜 🌊) This homey stone inn is surrounded by gardens that contain a hot tub, a mosaic-tile swimming pool, a BBQ area and a sundeck with wi-fi. Fourteen rooms of various sizes have king-size beds, comfy rocking chairs and folk-art accents. Five apartments come with fully equipped kitchen. A generous Tico breakfast is served on the outdoor terrace. Weekly rates are available.

Villa Escazú   B&B **$$**
(☑ 2289-7971; www.hotels.co.cr/villaescazu; d incl breakfast US$50-65; 🅿 🛜) This wooden chalet with wraparound veranda is surrounded

by gardens and fruit trees. The two quaint, wood-paneled rooms feature local artwork, comfy couches and a shared bathroom. Breakfast is served on the outdoor balcony.

Two-night minimum stay; reserve well in advance. It's 900m west of Banco Nacional.

Hotel Mirador Pico Blanco HOTEL $$
(☑2289-6197, 2228-1908; www.hotelpicoblanco. com; Calle Salitrillos; d standard/ste US$40/50; 🅿) A sleepy stone inn located high in the hills, Pico Blanco is perched on a ridge 3km southeast of central Escazú. The hotel has seen better days, but the 15 rooms are comfortable, with tile floors, cable TV and clean, if slightly worn, bathrooms. For the money, you won't find more extravagant metropolitan views. There is a small onsite restaurant, which cooks up traditional meals. Credit cards accepted.

★Casa de las Tías B&B $$$
(Map p82; ☑2289-5517; www.casadelastias.com; US$90-110; 🅿😀🛜) In a quiet area of San Rafael, this yellow-and-turquoise Cape Cod–style house (complete with picket fence) has five immaculate, individually decorated rooms, all with private bathrooms. The house is adorned with crafts that friendly, helpful owners Xavier and Pilar have picked up on their travels in Latin America, lending the place a cozy, intimate feel.

Hotel Alta Las Palomas HOTEL $$$
(☑2282-4160, in USA 888-388-2582; www.thealta- hotel.com; Old Rd, btwn Santa Ana & Escazú; d/ste from US$203/277, extra person US$20; 🅿❄@ 🛜🏊) This graceful Mediterranean-style villa has 23 whitewashed rooms decked out in terracotta tiles, contemporary wood furnishings and expansive bathrooms equipped with hair dryers and robes. Upstairs balconies offer stunning views of the surrounding hills, and the onsite restaurant, La Luz, serves up fresh Mediterranean fare in an elegant setting. An upstairs parlor often hosts classical music performances.

× Eating

From humble corner stands dishing out gut-filling *casados* (set meals) to contemporary bistros serving fusion everything, in cosmopolitan San José you will find the country's best restaurant scene. Dedicated foodies should also check out the dining options in Los Yoses, San Pedro and Escazú.

Top-end restaurants tend to get busy on weekend evenings; make a reservation.

× Central San José East

Long-standing neighborhood *sodas* (lunch counters) mix effortlessly with contemporary cafes and Asian-fusion eateries on San José's eclectic east side.

★Café de los Deseos CAFE $
(Map p66; ☑2222-0496; www.facebook.com/ Cafedelosdeseos; Calle 15 btwn Avs 9 & 11; mains US$5-12; ⏰2-10pm Tue-Sat; 🛜) Abuzz with artsy young bohemians, this cozy, colorful Barrio Otoya cafe makes a romantic spot for drinks (from wine to cocktails to smoothies), *bocas* (handmade tortillas with Turrialba cheese, salads, teriyaki chicken, individual pizzas), and tempting desserts. Walls are hung with the work of local artists and rooms are adorned with hand-painted tables, beaded curtains and branches entwined with fairy lights.

La Ventanita Meraki FAST FOOD $
(Map p66; ☑4034-2655; www.facebook.com/ laventanitameraki; Av 3 & Calle 21, in front of the train station; mains US$5-8; ⏰noon-9pm Tue-Thu, to 2am Fri, 6pm-2am Sat) Ventanita means 'little window' in Spanish and Meraki means 'artistry' in Greek. Put them together and it's an accurate moniker for this new fusion hole-in-the-wall, a to-go window in front of downtown's train station that serves innovative street food. Expect elaborate spins on typical fare, along with sandwiches like pumpkin butter cheese madness, and Twinkie *frito* (fried Twinkie) for dessert.

Café Té Ría CAFE $
(Map p70; ☑2222-8272; www.facebook.com/ CafeTeRiaenAmon; cnr Av 7 & Calle 13; mains US$6, cakes US$1.50-3; ⏰10:30am-7:30pm Mon-Fri, noon-7:30 Sat; 🛜🐾🏊) This petite, pet-friendly cafe in Barrio Amón is adorned with local art and replete with homey goodness. It's a perfect place to work over a few cups of morning coffee, then stay for lunch. Specials often include a mouth-watering baked trout with capers and a fresh salad. Sandwiches and pastries are also a big hit, and vegetarians are well-served.

Alma de Café CAFE $
(Map p70; ☑2010-1119; www.almadecafe.net; Teatro Nacional; mains US$6-11; ⏰9am-7pm Mon-Sat, to 6pm Sun) One of the most beautiful cafes in the city, this atmospheric spot evokes early-20th-century Vienna. In other words, a perfect place to sip cappuccino, enjoy a crepe or quiche and take in the lovely ceiling

ALFONSE PAGANO / GETTY IMAGES ©

1. Outdoor markets (p95)
San José's many markets offer everything from fresh fruit and vegetables to hammocks and souvenirs.

2. Museo Nacional de Costa Rica (p65)
This former fortress houses pre-Columbian artifacts and colonial relics.

3. Catedral Metropolitana (p64)
Dating from 1871, the cathedral boasts a colourful neoclassical interior.

4. Teatro Nacional (p64)
The theater's most famous painting depicts coffee and banana harvests.

frescoes and rotating art exhibitions. The elaborate coffee cocktails are an excellent midday indulgence.

Talentum
CAFE $

(Map p66; ☑ 2256-6346; www.galeriatalentum.com; Av 11 btwn Calles 3 & 3A; lunch specials US$8-10; ⊙ 11am-7pm Mon-Tue, to 8pm Wed-Fri) This vibrant, quirky cultural space in a renovated mansion runs the gamut from cafe to art gallery. Sporting local artwork inside and out, with cozy seating on vintage couches and an outdoor deck, it's a fun place for a midday break. The ever-changing cultural agenda includes book signings, films, anatomical drawing classes and occasional live music.

Café Miel
CAFE $

(Map p70; www.facebook.com/cafemielcostarica; Av 9 btwn Calle 11 & 13; coffee US$1-5, pastries US$2; ⊙ 9am-6pm Mon-Fri, 2-6pm Sat) This tiny cafe opened to such wild success in 2014 that the owners opened another one right down the street. What's their secret? In addition to adorable and homey interiors, the artisanal products from the cafes' chefs and bakers. The mushroom *empanadas* are divine, as is the locally sourced coffee.

Zero Army
CAFE $

(Map p70; ☑ 2248-2401; www.facebook.com/zeroarmycr; Calle 9 & Av 9; smoothies US$3-4; ⊙ 6:30am-5:15pm Mon-Fri, 9am-2pm Sat) Named for Costa Rica's nonexistent army, this new smoothie and juice bar in the center of Barrio Amón serves fresh fruit drinks in reusable glass bottles. The smoothies are all-natural, highly refreshing and named for Costa Rican destinations. Breakfast wraps are highly recommended.

Café Rojo
CAFE $

(Map p70; ☑ 2221-2425; cnr Av 7 & Calle 3; mains US$7-10, coffee US$1.50-4; ⊙ noon-7pm Mon-Thu, to 8pm Fri & Sat, 10am-7pm Sun; ☑) This quaint new cafe with a towering cactus out front uses the fresh produce of Costa Rica to create innovative lunch specials, such as green plantain balls and pickled beets with chayote pureé. Vegans will find plenty to like here, as will coffee enthusiasts. All the flavorings and syrups for drinks are homemade, and the iced ginger coffee is divine.

Maza Bistro
BISTRO $

(Map p66; ☑ 7293-9082; www.facebook.com/Mazacostarica; Calle 19, on Parque Nacional; mains US$8; ⊙ 10am-7pm Mon-Fri; ☑) The furniture here is disorganized, making it tough to get in the door. But maybe the owners are focused on food? Each day, the menu is written on scrolls, often including whatever is organic, fresh and local. Think bowls of veggies and cured trout, homemade honey wine and *tortas* of kale. Terrariums and mini-records as coasters lend some charm.

Restaurante La Criollita
COSTA RICAN $

(Map p70; ☑ 2256-6511; Av 7 btwn Calles 7 & 9; breakfast from US$6, casados US$8-10; ⊙ 6:30am-9pm Mon-Fri, to 4pm Sat, 8am-5pm Sun) This homey local spot, popular with office types, dishes out a changing menu of simple Costa Rican specialties, such as stewed chicken or grilled fish. The setting is pleasant and the service efficient, and you can accompany your meal with a glass of Chilean or Spanish wine (US$4).

Restaurante Shakti
VEGETARIAN $

(Map p66; ☑ 2222-4475; cnr Av 8 & Calle 13; mains US$5-10; ⊙ 7:30am-7pm Mon-Fri, 8am-6pm Sat; ☑) This informal neighborhood health-food outpost has simple, organic-focused cooking and freshly baked goods. Favorites include veggie burgers, along with various fish and chicken dishes, but most people come for the vegetarian *plato del día* (meal of the day) – only US$6 for soup, salad, main course and fruit drink (or US$8 with coffee and dessert thrown in)!

Café del Barista
CAFE $

(Map p66; www.cafedelbarista.com; Av 9 btwn Calles 19 & 21; ⊙ 7am-7pm Mon-Fri, 1pm-6pm Sat) This corrugated-roofed, warehouse-like space in Barrio Aranjuez brews up a great cup of gourmet coffee (and makes a halfway decent cinnamon roll too).

Perimercado
SUPERMARKET $

(Map p70; ☑ 2222-2252; Calle 3 btwn Avs Central & 1; ⊙ 6:30am-8:30pm Mon-Thu, to 9:30pm Fri-Sat, 9am-6pm Sun) An economical chain, conveniently located downtown.

Automercado
SUPERMARKET $

(Map p70; ☑ 2233-5511; www.automercado.co.cr; cnr Calle 3 & Av 3; ⊙ 6:30am-9pm Mon-Sat, 9am-6pm Sun) Pricey with a good selection of cheeses, produce, liquor, coffee and chocolate.

Alma de Amón
LATIN AMERICAN $$

(Map p70; ☑ 2222-3232; www.facebook.com/AlmadeAmon/; Calle 5 btwn Avs 9 & 11; small plates US$6-9; ⊙ 11am-10pm Mon-Wed, to midnight

Thu-Sat) With entrées from nearly a dozen Latin countries and considerable Caribbean influence, this new restaurant is raising the bar in Barrio Amón. Popular menu items include *mofongo* (a Puerto Rican dish with fried plantains) and *coxinhas* (Brazilian croquettes with chicken). The mixologist whips up spicy and delicious cocktails; El Chapulin has tequila, ginger beer, lime and sugar-cane syrup.

Café Mundo ITALIAN $$
(Map p70; ☎2222-6190; cnr Av 9 & Calle 15; mains US$8-36; ⊘11am-10pm Mon-Wed, to 10:30pm Thu, 5pm-11:30 Sat; ✐) This longtime Italian cafe and expat favorite is set on a sprawling terrace in a vintage Barrio Otoya mansion. It's a perfect spot to enjoy a glass of wine and good (if not earth-shattering) pizzas and pastas within sight of a splashing outdoor fountain. At lunchtime on weekdays, don't miss the good-value *plato del día* (US$8).

Lubnan LEBANESE $$
(Map p74; ☎2257-6071; www.facebook.com/lubnancostarica; Paseo Colón btwn Calles 22 & 24; mains US$8-25; ⊘11am-3pm & 6pm-midnight Tue-Fri, noon-4pm & 6pm-midnight Sat, 11am-5pm Sun; P) This atmospheric Lebanese place is a great date spot, with creamy hummus, flavorful tabbouleh and an array of succulent meats – some cooked, some deliciously raw. Waiters wear fezzes and a live belly-dancing performance goes down every Thursday at 8:30pm.

El Patio del Balmoral INTERNATIONAL $$
(Map p70; ☎2221-1700; www.elpatiodelbalmoral.com; Av Central btwn Calles 7 & 9; mains US$8-27; ⊘6am-10pm, terrace bar 4-10pm Mon-Thu, to 11pm Fri, noon-11pm Sat) Filled with chattering gringos and suited Ticos, this all-purpose cafe-restaurant is a good place to chill out while taking in the pedestrian action on Av Central. Bonus: on sunny days the restaurant opens its retractable roof. The upstairs terrace bar hosts live bands on Wednesday, Thursday and Friday nights.

Don Wang CHINESE $$
(Map p66; ☎2223-5925, 2233-6484; www.donwangrestaurant.com; Calle 11 btwn Avs 6 & 8; mains US$8-18; ⊘11am-3:30pm & 5:30-10pm Mon-Thu, to 11pm Fri, 11am-11pm Sat, 11am-10pm Sun; ✐⊛) This hopping Chinese gourmet eatery is an ideal place for dim sum – served all day every day – as well as a long list of Chinese, Japanese and Thai specialties, from stir-fried shrimp with cashews, to a la carte hot pot, to Peking duck.

Stereo Sushi SUSHI $$
(Map p66; ☎7293-9738, 7106-5174; ss.cr; Av 2 btwn Calles 19 & 21; rolls US$10-13, tempura US$13; ⊘3pm-2am Tue-Sat) There's better sushi in San José, but nowhere else to eat it so high up. Stereo Sushi opened in 2015 on the 9th floor of an otherwise quiet apartment building, and quickly developed a reputation among university students as a 'sky club,' illuminated in fluorescent blue light with DJs nightly. Sushi rolls and tempura are served until 11pm.

★**La Esquina de Buenos Aires** ARGENTINE $$$
(Map p70; ☎2223-1909; laesquinadebuenosaires.com; cnr Calle 11 & Av 4; mains US$15-29; ⊘11:30am-3pm & 6-10:30pm Mon-Thu, 11:30am-11pm Fri, 12:30pm-11pm Sat, noon-10pm Sun; ✐) White linens and the sound of old tango evoke the atmospheric bistros of San Telmo, as does the menu, featuring grilled Argentine cuts of steak, house-made *empanadas* and an extensive selection of fresh pastas in exquisite sauces. The excellent South American-centric wine list, attentive service and flickering candlelight make this an ideal place for a date. Reservations recommended.

Restaurante Tin-Jo ASIAN $$$
(Map p66; ☎2221-7605; www.tinjo.com; Calle 11 btwn Avs 6 & 8; mains US$11-19; ⊘11:30am-2:30pm & 6-10pm Mon-Thu, noon-2:30pm & 6-11pm Fri & Sat, noon-9pm Sun; ✐) The interiors of this popular Asian standard-bearer are a riot of pan-Asian everything, just like the menu. Expect a wide range of fare from various regions – from *kung pao* shrimp to spicy tuna *maki* to pad thai – as well as an extensive vegetarian menu.

✖ **Central San José West**

The city's hectic commercial heart has some of the cheapest eats in town. One of the best places for a budget-priced lunch is the Mercado Central (p71), where you'll find a variety of *sodas* serving *casados*, tamales, seafood and everything in between.

La Sorbetera de Lolo Mora DESSERTS $
(Map p70; ☎2256-5000; Mercado Central; desserts US$2-5; ⊘9:30am-5:45pm Mon-Sat) Head to the main market for dessert at this century-old local favorite that serves up fresh sorbet and cinnamon-laced frozen

custard. Do as the locals do and order *barquillos* (cylindrical sugar cookies that are perfect for dipping).

Q Café
CAFE $$

(Map p70; ☑4056-5604; 2nd fl, cnr Av Central & Calle 2; mains US$8-20; ⊙9am-9pm Mon-Sat,10am-8pm Sun) A sleek, monochromatic cafe with excellent views of the ornate Correo Central building, this modern 2nd-story spot near the heart of San José's pedestrian zone is perfect for coffee drinks (including delicious iced mochas) and pastries. Try the *empanadas*, which go well with the cafe's homemade hot sauce.

La Sabana & Around

Supermarkets include **Más X Menos** (Map p74; ☑2248-0968; www.masxmenos.co.cr; cnr Autopista General Cañas & Av 5; ⊙7am-midnight Mon-Sat, to 10pm Sun; ℗) and **Palí** (Map p74; ☑2256-5887; www.pali.co.cr; Paseo Colón btwn Calles 24 & 26; ⊙8am-7pm Mon-Thu, to 8pm Fri & Sat, to 5pm Sun; ℗).

Soda Tapia
SODA $

(Map p74; ☑2222-6734; www.sodatapia.com; cnr Av 2 & Calle 42; mains US$4-10, desserts US$2-7; ⊙6am-2am Sun-Thu, 24hr Fri & Sat; ℗⊛) An unpretentious '50s-style diner with garish red-and-white decor, this place is perpetually filled with couples and families noshing on grilled sandwiches and generous *casados*. If you have the nerve, try the monstrous 'El Gordo,' a pile of steak, onions, cheese, lettuce and tomato served on Spanish bread. Save room for dessert: ice-cream and fruit sundaes are a specialty here.

Machu Picchu
PERUVIAN $$

(Map p74; ☑2255-1717; www.restaurantemachupicchu.com; Calle 32 btwn Avs 1 & 3; mains US$9-22; ⊙11am-10pm Mon-Sat, to 6pm Sun; ℗⊚⊛) This locally renowned Peruvian restaurant does Andean right. A popular spot for a leisurely Sunday lunch, it has an encyclopedic menu featuring Peruvian classics such as *pulpo al olivo* (octopus in olive sauce), *ají de gallina* (a nutty chicken stew) and *causa* (chilled potato terrines stuffed with shrimp and avocado). The pisco sours here are deliciously powerful.

Las Mañanitas
MEXICAN $$

(Map p74; ☑2248-1593; Calle 40 btwn Paseo Colón & Av 3; mains US$6-17; ⊙11:30am-10pm Mon-Sat) At this authentic Mexican place near the park, well-rendered specialties include tacos in sets of four – corn tortillas accompanied by chicken, steak, sea bass or *carne al pastor* (spiced pork). Fans of *mole poblano* (central Mexico's famous chili and chocolate sauce) will also want to try it here, as the restaurant's owner hails from Puebla.

★ Park Café
EUROPEAN $$$

(Map p74; ☑2290-6324; parkcafecostarica.blogspot.com; tapas US$6-15; ⊙5-9:15pm Tue-Sat) At this felicitous fusion of antique shop and French restaurant, Michelin-starred chef Richard Neat offers an exquisite degustation menu featuring smaller sampling plates (Spanish tapas–style) and a carefully curated wine list. The romantic, candlelit courtyard is eclectically decorated with Asian antiques imported by Neat's partner, Louise French. It's near Parque La Sabana's northeast corner (100m north of Rostipollos restaurant).

The tantalizing menu includes classic flavor combinations – carpaccio of beef with mustard dressing – alongside innovative offerings such as crab ravioli with asparagus and ginger cappuccino, crispy leg of duck with cucumber-mint salad or Gorgonzola gnocchi with prune-stuffed pork fillet, all prepared with passion and flair by Neat himself. An eight-table limit enhances the intimate atmosphere.

Restaurante Grano de Oro
FUSION $$$

(Map p74; ☑2255-3322; www.hotelgranodeoro.com; Calle 30 btwn Avs 2 & 4; lunch mains US$15-29, dinner mains US$19-42; ⊙7am-10pm) Known for its Costa Rican–fusion cuisine, this stately, flower-filled restaurant is one of San José's top dining destinations. The menu is laced with unique specialties such as sea bass breaded with toasted macadamia nuts or seared duck crowned with caramelized figs, and there's an encyclopedic international wine list. For dessert, don't miss the coffee cream mousse. Dinner reservations recommended.

Los Yoses, Barrio Escalante & San Pedro

Succulent Turkish sandwiches, Caribbean-style *rondón* (seafood gumbo), wood-fired pizzas – you can find every type of cuisine imaginable in this corner of the city. Just north of Los Yoses, Calles 33 and 35 in Barrio Escalante are prime foodie destinations, boasting several fine restaurants within a few city blocks.

Café Kracovia
CAFE $

(Map p80; ☑ 2253-9093; www.cafekracovia.com; snacks US$4-10, mains US$8-14; ⊙ 10:30am-9pm Mon, to 11pm Tue-Sat; 🐾) With several distinct spaces, from a low-lit, intimate downstairs to an outdoor garden courtyard, this hip cafe has something for everyone. Contemporary artwork and a distinct university vibe create an appealing ambiance for lunching on crepes, wraps, salads, daily specials and craft beer. It's 500m north of the Fuente de la Hispanidad traffic circle, where San Pedro and Los Yoses converge.

Automercado
SUPERMARKET $

(Map p80; ☑ 2225-0361; Av Central btwn Calles 39 & 41; ⊙ 7am-9pm Mon-Sat, 8am-8pm Sun) A pricey but well-stocked grocery store near Los Yoses. Has a good selection of healthy items, including veggie burgers.

Más X Menos
SUPERMARKET $

(Map p80; ☑ 2225-0636; Av Central; ⊙ 7am-midnight Mon-Sat, to 9pm Sun) Large, modern grocery store in San Pedro.

★ Al Mercat
GASTRONOMY $$

(Map p80; ☑ 2221-0783; almercat.com; Barrio Escalante; US$13-25; ⊙ noon-3pm Mon-Fri, 7:30pm-midnight Thu-Sat; 🐾) This exquisite new Barrio Escalante restaurant serves whatever is fresh from the market. Family-style courses of items like grilled avocado and hummus with chickpeas and peach palm fruit are fresh and flavorful. And although vegetarians are well served, meat eaters will appreciate the fine cuts of meat. The service here is impeccable, and the atmosphere is enlivened by vertical gardens.

★ Olio
MEDITERRANEAN $$

(Map p80; ☑ 2281-0541; www.facebook.com/Restaurante.olio; cnr Calle 33 & Av 3; tapas from US$7, dishes US$12-22; ⊙ noon-midnight Mon-Fri, from 6pm Sat; 🐾) This cozy, Mediterranean-flavored gastropub in a century-old brick building in Barrio Escalante serves a long list of tempting tapas, including divine stuffed mushrooms, goat-cheese croquettes, and house-made pastas. The enticing drinks list includes homemade sangria and a decent selection of beers and wine. It's a romantic spot for a date, with imaginative, conversation-worthy quirks of decor and beautiful patrons.

★ Sofia Mediterráneo
MEDITERRANEAN $$

(Map p80; ☑ 2224-5050; www.facebook.com/SofiaMediterraneo; cnr Calle 33 & Av 1; mains US$8-22; ⊙ 6pm-11pm Tue-Fri, noon-11pm Sat, noon-5pm & 6:30-9pm Sun; 🐾) This Barrio Escalante gem serves a superb mix of authentic Mediterranean specialties, including house-made hummus, tortellini, grilled lamb and a rotating selection of daily specials, accompanied by sweet, delicate baklava for dessert. The restaurant doubles as a community cultural center where owner Mehmet Onuralp hosts occasional theme dinners featuring musicians, chefs and speakers from around the world.

Rávi Gastropub
PUB FOOD $$

(Map p80; ☑ 2253-3771; www.facebook.com/ravicostarica; cnr Calle 33 & Av 5; mains US$9-18; ⊙ 3pm-midnight Tue-Sat) This cool corner pub in Barrio Escalante is awash in bright murals, with seating in funky red booths, intimate back rooms or at the convivial bar stools up front. A menu of *bocas*, sandwiches, pizzas and more is served with craft brew on tap and homemade tropical-fruit sodas served in cute little bell jars.

At lunchtime, pick from the rotating menu of nine appetizers and nine main dishes and throw in a homemade soda, all for US$10.

Él Porton Rojo
PIZZA $$

(Map p80; ☑ 2224-4872; www.facebook.com/PizzaElPortonRojo; Av 10 & Calle 43; pizza small US$8-10, large US$16-18; ⊙ noon-3pm & 6-11:30pm Mon-Sat) Serving up some of the best pizza and sangria in the Los Yoses area, this hip restaurant doubles as a gallery. Funky local art sells right off the walls, and a steady influx of customers from Hostel Bekuo (p79) keeps things lively.

Mantras
VEGETARIAN $$

(Map p80; ☑ 2253-6715; www.facebook.com/mantrasveggiecafe; Calle 35 btwn Avs 11 & 13; mains US$8-10; ⊙ 8:30am-5pm; 🐾) Widely recognized as the best vegetarian restaurant in San José (if not all of Costa Rica), Mantras draws rave reviews from across the foodie spectrum for meatless main dishes, salads and desserts so delicious that it's easy to forget you're eating healthily. It's in Barrio Escalante, and for Sunday brunch, the line often stretches out the door.

Lolo's
PIZZA $$

(Map p80; ☑ 2283-9627; pizzas US$14-24; ⊙ 6pm-midnight Mon-Sat) Fans of bohemian chic will appreciate this quirky pizzeria, hidden in a mustard-yellow house (No 3396) along the railroad tracks north of Av Central in Barrio Escalante. The vibrantly colorful, low-lit interior, hung with an eclectic collection of plates and other knickknacks, creates an artsy, romantic setting for sangria and pizzas fired up in the bright-red oven out back.

El Buho
VEGETARIAN $$

(Map p80; ☑ 2224-6293; www.facebook.com/El-BuhoVegetariano; Av 5, 25m east of Calle 3; mains US$10-18; ⊙ 11:30am-8pm Mon-Fri; ☑) Drawing health-food devotees from the nearby university and much further afield, this buzzing San Pedro eatery just off Calle de la Amargura serves a variety of vegan, vegetarian and gluten-free treats, from eggplant croquettes to stir-fries, mushroom casseroles to passion-fruit cookies.

Restaurant Whapin
CARIBBEAN $$

(Map p80; ☑ 2283-1480; cnr Calle 35 & Av 13; mains US$10-28; ⊙ 11:30am-10pm Mon-Sat, to 5pm Sun) For a taste of the Caribbean without leaving San José, try this corner spot in Barrio Escalante painted Rasta red, yellow and green. Steamy bowls of *rondón* (seafood gumbo), rice and red beans, and fish simmered in spicy coconut sauce go well with *agua de sapo*, a zesty sweet ginger drink. Don't forget the fried plantains and, in season, the crisp breadfruit.

★ Kalú Café & Food Shop
INTERNATIONAL $$$

(Map p80; ☑ 2253-8426, 2253-8367; www.kalu.co.cr; cnr Calle 31 & Av 5; mains US$15-21; ⊙ noon-10pm Tue-Fri, 9am-10pm Sat, 9am-4pm Sun; ☑) Sharing a sleek space with Kiosco SJO (p95) in Barrio Escalante, chef Camille Ratton's exceptional back-patio cafe serves a global fusion menu of soups, salads, sandwiches, pastas and unconventional delights such as the fish taco trio filled with mango-glazed salmon, red curry prawns and macadamia-crusted tuna. Don't miss the mind-meltingly delicious passion-fruit pie.

✗ Escazú

On Saturday, head down to the **farmers market** (Map p82) that's held along Av 2, just south of the park in Escazú Centro. There's also an organic farmers market on Wednesday, featuring produce as well as delectables such as cheese, honey and fish. Find it 1km south of Paco, across from the Red Cross building.

Self-caterers will find plenty of choice in Escazú's supermarkets. The best is the gigantic **Automercado** (Map p82; ☑ 2588-1812;

Atlantis Plaza, Calle Cortés, San Rafael; ⊙ 7am-10pm Mon-Sat, 8am-9pm Sun), but there's also **Más X Menos** (Map p82; ☑ 2228-2230; Centro Comercial Escazú, Carretera John F Kennedy, San Rafael; ⊙ 6:30am-midnight Mon-Sat, to 10:30pm Sun) and **Supermercado Saretto** (☑ 7209-2862; www.saretto.cr; San Rafael; ⊙ 8am-9pm Mon-Sat, to 8pm Sun).

Buena Tierra
ORGANIC $

(Map p82; ☑ 2288-0342; www.facebook.com/Cafe-OrganicoBuenaTierra; cnr Calle 134 & Av 34; mains US$6-8; ⊙ 9am-5:30pm Mon-Fri, to 2pm Sat; ☑) With tree-trunk tabletops and huge windows, this friendly organic cafe in Escazú Centro is a good place to detox. The cured trout sandwiches are sublime, and delicious *batidos* (fruit shakes) are made with water, milk, goat's milk, yogurt or almond milk. The cafe organizes a Wednesday-morning organic farmers market and has opened an adjacent health food store – Abarrotes Buena Tierra.

Chez Christophe
BAKERY $

(☑ 2228-2512; pastries US$2-5; ⊙ 7am-7pm Tue-Sat, 8am-7pm Sun) If you have a hankering for a coffee éclair, croque monsieur or plain (but transcendent) croissant, linger here awhile. French *tostadas* are reserved for Sunday, but every other day this authentic French bakery offers freshly baked breads and pastries, as well as espresso and a full breakfast and lunch menu. It's just south of Centro Comerical El Paco in San Rafael.

★ Saúl Bistro
MEDITERRANEAN $$

(☑ 2228-8685; www.facebook.com/SaulBistroCostaRica; Centro Commercial 7 Bancas, on Old Rd to Santa Ana; appetizers US$10-16, mains US$11-25; ⊙ 7am-10pm Sun-Thu, to midnight Fri & Sat) There are life-sized plastic zebras in the dining room at this snazzy open-air restaurant that appeared (and became a sensation) in 2015. An extension of Saúl Mendez, the Guatemala-based empire of men's fashion, the restaurant is adorned with curious art, bubbling fountains and vertical gardens, and serves delicious Mediterranean cuisine, savory crepes, fine wine and exquisite cocktails. Quite the scene.

★ Maxi's By Ricky
CARIBBEAN $$

(☑ 2282-8619; Santa Ana; appetizers US$1.50-8, mains US$9-30; ⊙ noon-midnight) If you can't make it to Costa Rica's Caribbean Coast, this restaurant is a good substitute. Owner Ricky is a native of Manzanillo; he transported himself and his lip-smacking restaurant to the Central Valley in 2014. The secret is out, and everybody is showing up to feast on the traditional rice and beans, Caribbean chicken and *rondón* soup. Seriously. It's amazing. It's tricky to find: ask locally for directions.

★ **La Posada de las Brujas** COSTA RICAN $$
(Map p82; 2228-1645; www.posadadelabruja. com; off Av 30, btwn Calles San Miguel & 128; mains US$6-24; ⊙ 11am-1am Tue-Sat, to 10pm Sun; [P] [🔥])
In 2013, this open-air steak house became Escazú's finest family option. Spacious indoor and outdoor seating accommodates large groups, and big eaters are well-served with heaping plates of rice, beans, fried plantains and a savory meat of their choice. An onsite menagerie (think goats, rabbits, a donkey and tropical birds) and two trampolines will be big hits with kids.

Tiquicia COSTA RICAN $$
(2289-7330; www.tiquiciacr.com; bocas US$5-17, mains US$13-23; ⊙ noon-11pm Tue-Thu, to midnight Fri & Sat, to 9pm Sun) This long-running hilltop restaurant 5km south of Escazú Centro serves up bounteous platters, along with live folk music on weekends. Yes, the food is only so-so, but you're not here to eat, you're here to admire the extravagant views of the Central Valley. It's tricky to find; call for directions or check the website for a map.

🍷 Drinking & Nightlife

Whatever your poison, San José has plenty of venues to keep you lubricated.

San José has a thriving club scene. From thumping electronica and hip-hop to salsa, merengue and reggaetón, Chepe's clubs offer a galaxy of musical styles to help you get your groove on. Most spots open at around 10pm, and don't truly get going until after midnight. Admission charges vary depending on the location, the DJ and the night; they're generally US$5 to US$10. Places come and go with alarming regularity, so ask around before heading out.

🍷 Central San José East

On weekends, these streets between downtown and Los Yoses are packed with 20-something revelers puffing cigarettes and pondering where to head for the next *chili guaro* (an increasingly popular shot with sugar-cane liquor, hot sauce and lime juice). Popular bars in this hood include **La Concha de la Lora** (Map p66; 2222-0130; www.facebook.com/laconchalora; Calle 21 btwn

---

Avs Central & 1; ⊙ 8:30pm-3am Thu-Sat), **El Observatorio** (Map p66; 2223-0725; www.elobservatorio.tv; Calle 23 btwn Avs Central & 1; ⊙ 6pm-1am Mon-Sat), **Craic Irish Pub** (Map p66; cnr Av 2 & Calle 25A; ⊙ 6pm-2am) and El Cuartel de la Boca del Monte (p94).

★ **Stiefel** PUB
(Map p70; www.facebook.com/StiefelPub; ⊙ 6pm-2am Mon-Sat) Two dozen-plus Costa Rican microbrews on tap and an appealing setting in a historic building create a convivial buzz at this pub half a block from Plaza España. Grab a pint of Pelona or Maldita Vida, Malinche or Chichemel; better yet, order a flight of four miniature sampler glasses and try 'em all!

Chubbs SPORTS BAR
(Map p70; 2222-4622; 2nd fl, Calle 9 btwn Avs 1 & 3) Decidedly local, in the heart of the San José tourist belt, this humble little sports bar has reasonably priced drinks, tasty burgers, a stack of TVs displaying the game and a supersized mural of dogs playing poker. Awesome.

Chelle's BAR
(Map p70; 2221-1369; cnr Av Central & Calle 9; ⊙ 24hr) If you're drinking the night away with Ticos, you might find yourself here at 4am, clutching a cold one and professing your love for recent acquaintances. This venerable 24-hour *soda* doubles as one of Chepe's most atmospheric spots for a nightcap, with surly service and big buses careening around the corner outside, looking perilously close to crashing through the window.

🍷 Central San José West

Castro's CLUB
(Map p66; 2256-8789; cnr Av 13 & Calle 22; ⊙ 6pm-3am Sun-Thu, 5pm-4:30am Fri & Sat) Chepe's oldest dance club, this classic Latin American disco in Barrio México draws crowds of locals and tourists to its large dance floor with a dependable mix of salsa, cumbia and merengue.

🍷 La Sabana & Around

Rapsodia LOUNGE
(Map p74; ☑2248-1720; www.rapsodiacr.com; cnr Paseo Colón & Calle 40; ⊗9:30pm-3:30am Fri, to 6am Sat) This hyper-chic, see-and-be-seen club clad in white and gold has an extensive list of cocktails and a menu of Mediterranean-inspired dishes and snacks. Guest DJs set the mood with a mix of electronica and other sounds every Friday and Saturday.

Club Vertigo CLUB
(Map p74; ☑2257-8424; www.vertigocr.com; Paseo Colón btwn Calles 38 & 40; cover US$6-15; ⊗10pm-dawn) Located on the ground floor of the nondescript Centro Colón office tower, the city's premier club packs in Chepe's beautiful people with a mix of house, trance and electronica. Downstairs is an 850-person-capacity sweat-box of a dance floor; upstairs is a chill-out lounge lined with red sofas. Dress to the nines and expect admission charges to skyrocket on guest-DJ nights.

🍷 Los Yoses, Barrio Escalante & San Pedro

Calle La Amargura (Sorrow St) is the more poetic name for Calle 3, north of Av Central. However, it should be called Calle de la Cruda (Street of Hangovers) because it has the highest concentration of bars of any single street in town, and many of these are packed with customers (mainly university students) even during daylight hours. Places come and go, but **Terra U** (Map p80; ☑2283-7728; www.facebook.com/Terra

---

WHERE TO DRINK

Chepe's artsiest, most sophisticated drinking venues are concentrated north and east of the center, in places like Barrio Amón and Barrio Escalante. For a rowdier, younger scene, head to Barrio la California (p91), the UCR university district, or Calle la Amargura.

Good spots for people-watching over a beer or a coffee include Café 1930 at the Gran Hotel Costa Rica (p78), with unbeatable views of Teatro Nacional; the upstairs terrace at El Patio del Balmoral (p87), overlooking the pedestrian walkway on Av Central; and Café de los Deseos (p83) in Barrio Otoya.

USanPedro; Calle La Amargura; ⊗10am-2:30am Mon-Sat, 3pm-2:30am Sun) and **Caccio's** (Map p80; www.caccios.com; Calle La Amargura; ⊗10am-2am Mon-Thu, 2:30pm-1am Fri & Sat) are longtime party spots. The area gets rowdy in the wee hours: watch out for drunks and pickpockets.

Wilk BREWERY
(Map p80; www.facebook.com/wilkcraftbeer; Calle 33 & Av 9; ⊗4pm-1am Tue-Sat) This new pub in Barrio Escalante attracts a mixed crowd of Ticos and gringos who share an appreciation for craft brews and seriously delicious burgers (veggie included). The wide selection of craft beer includes all of the inventive concoctions of Costa Rica Craft Brewing, which is a partner in the pub.

Hoxton Pub PUB
(Map p80; ☑7168-1083; www.facebook.com/hoxtonstag; ⊗9pm-4am Tue-Sat) Good cocktails, great music and a lively dance floor in a cool old Los Yoses mansion just east of Subaru. The place often holds theme nights and brings in good DJs on the weekend. Tuesday's ladies night is the biggest party in town, with ladies paying no cover and drinking free until midnight. Hundreds show up to rage til dawn.

Roots Reggae Bar BAR
(Map p80; ☑2253-1953; www.facebook.com/rootscoolandcalm; Av 8; ⊗8pm-2:30am Tue-Sun) The dreadlocked set crowds this cool Los Yoses lounge bar, which brings in DJs from as far afield as Puerto Viejo on the Caribbean coast. It's a sweet spot to get a beer and hang with reggae-loving locals. Find it between Calle 43 and Av 8.

🍷 Escazú

If you're looking for a spicy cocktail and some house music, 8ctavo Rooftop (p94) is where the beautiful people partake. And just a short drive west you'll find the country's premier brewery, Costa Rica Craft Brewing, along with its popular tasting room.

Escazú also has a few dive bars sprinkled around its main plaza, but none are particularly appealing.

★**Costa Rica Craft Brewing** BREWERY
(☑2249-0919; www.facebook.com/craftbeercosta rica; Ciudad Colón; ⊗9am-5pm Mon, to 11pm Tue & Wed, to midnight Thu, noon-5pm Fri, 1pm-midnight Sat, noon-6pm Sun) Just when everyone thought it would be Imperial and Pilsen

GAY & LESBIAN VENUES

The city is home to Central America's most thriving gay and lesbian scene. As with other spots, admission charges vary depending on the night and location (from US$5 to US$10). Some clubs close on various nights of the week (usually Sunday to Tuesday) and others host women- or men-only nights; inquire ahead or check individual club websites for listings.

Many clubs are on the south side of town, which can get rough after dark. Take a taxi.

La Avispa (Map p66; ☑ 2223-5343; www.laavispa.com; Calle 1 btwn Avs 8 & 10; ☻8pm-6am Thu-Sat, 5pm-6am Sun) A lesbian disco bar that has been in operation for more than three decades, La Avispa (the Wasp) has a bar, pool tables and a boisterous dance floor that's highly recommended by travelers.

Bochinche (Map p66; ☑ 2221-0500; cnr Calle 11 & Av 10; ☻8pm-5am Wed-Sat) A club that features everything from classic disco to electronica, as well as special themed nights. As this club is on the south side of town, it can get rough after dark.

Pucho's Bar (Map p66; ☑ 2256-1147; cnr Calle 11 & Av 8; ☻8pm-2am Mon-Sat) This gay male outpost is more low-rent (and significantly raunchier) than some; it features scantily clad go-go boys and over-the-top drag shows.

---

forever, this artisanal brew pub paved the way for craft beer in Costa Rica. The brewery's new location in Ciudad Colón offers facility tours and tastings of its fine products, which include staple ales such as Libertas and Segua, along with more experimental drinks such as barley wines and Russian Imperil stouts.

It's out of town; ask locally for directions.

Pub BAR
(Map p82; ☑ 2288-3062; www.facebook.com/the-pubcr; Av 26 btwn Calles 128 & 130; ☻4pm-2am Sun-Fri, 1pm-2am Sat) This small, friendly expat pub has a list of more than two dozen international beers, more than a dozen local brews and a selection of shots. Well-priced happy-hour drink specials keep things hopping, and a greasy bar menu is available to soak up the damage.

☆ Entertainment

Pick up *La Nación* on Thursday for listings (in Spanish) of the coming week's attractions. The *Tico Times* 'Weekend' section (in English) has a calendar of theater, music and museum events. The free publication GAM Cultural (www.gamcultural.com) and the website San José Volando (www.sanjosevolando.com) are also helpful guides to nightlife and cultural events.

Cinema

Many cinemas show recent Hollywood films with Spanish subtitles and an English soundtrack. Occasionally, films are dubbed over in Spanish (*doblado* or *hablado en es-*

pañol) rather than subtitled; ask before buying a ticket. Movie tickets cost about US$4 to US$5, and generally Wednesday is cheaper. Check newspaper listings or individual theater websites for schedules.

There are bigger multiplexes in Los Yoses and San Pedro, while the most modern theaters are in Escazú.

Centro de Cine CINEMA
(Map p70; ☑ 2242-5200; www.centrodecine.go.cr; cnr Calle 11 & Av 9) This pink Victorian mansion houses the government-run film center and its vast archive of national and international flicks. Festivals, lectures and events are held here and in outside venues; check the site for current events.

Sala Garbo CINEMA
(Map p74; ☑ 2222-1034; www.salagarbocr.com; cnr Av 2 & Calle 28) Art-house and classic films.

Cine Magaly CINEMA
(Map p66; ☑ 2222-7116; www.facebook.com/Cine-Magaly; Calle 23 btwn Avs Central & 1) Screens the latest releases in a large theater, along with independent films in English.

Live Music

The best spots to see live, local music in San José are El Lobo Estepario, Hoxton Pub and El Sótano (p94). Internationally renowne~~ DJs frequently appear at Club Vertig~ 8ctavo (p94).

El Lobo Estepario
(Map p70; ☑ 2256-3934; www.loboesteparioc; Av 2, corner opposit~

ANDE; ◎ 4pm-12:45am Sun-Thu, to 2am Fri & Sat, closed Mon) This artsy dive attracts some of the top local talent for live music gigs.

8ctavo Rooftop
LIVE MUSIC

(☑ 4055-0588; www.facebook.com/8voRooftop; Hotel Sheraton San José) See and be seen at this swanky rooftop lounge, where international DJs regularly perform. If you want to show up early and dine first, this place is also a hit for the city views, the eclectic menu and the spicy cocktails.

It's right off Hwy 27 on the west side of Escazú.

Jazz Café
LIVE MUSIC

(Map p80; ☑ 2253-8933; www.jazzcafecosta rica.com; Av Central; cover US$5-10; ◎ 6pm-2am Mon-Sat) This intimate San Pedro venue presents a different band every night. Countless performers have taken to the stage here, including legendary Cuban bandleader Chucho Valdés and Colombian pop star Juanes. Its sister club in **Escazú** (☑ 2288-4740; Autopista Próspero Fernández, north side; cover US$5-10; ◎ 6pm-2am) features a similar mix of local and international bands.

El Sótano
LIVE MUSIC

(Map p66; ☑ 2221-2302; www.facebook.com/ sotanocr; cnr Calle 3 & Av 11; ◎ 7pm-2:30am Mon, noon-2:30am Tue-Sat, 2-6pm Sun) One of Chepe's most atmospheric nightspots, Sótano is named for its cellar jazz club, where people crowd in for frequent performances including intimate Tuesday jam sessions. Upstairs, a cluster of elegant high-ceilinged rooms in the same mansion have been converted to a gallery space, stage, and dance floor where an eclectic mix of groups play live gigs.

Arenas Skate Park
LIVE MUSIC

(Map p66; Calle 11 btwn Avs 10 & 12; ◎ 1-11pm Tue-Thu, to 2:30am Fri & Sat, 11am-7pm Sun) On Friday and Saturday nights, punk shows are all the rage at this skate park in Barrio Soledad.

Auditorio Nacional
CONCERT VENUE

(Map p66; ☑ 2222-7647; www.museocr.org; Museo de los Niños, Calle 4) A grand stage for concerts, dance, theater and plays, affiliated with the Centro Costarricense de Ciencia y Cultura.

El Cuartel de la Boca del Monte
LIVE MUSIC

(Map p66; ☑ 2221-0327; www.facebook.com/ lcuartelcr; Av 1 btwn Calles 21 & 23; ◎ 11:30am- n Mon-Fri, 6pm-midnight daily) This atmos- ric old Barrio La California bar has long drawn cheek-by-jowl crowds for live bands. Friday is a good night to visit, as is Monday, when women get free admission and the band cranks out a crazy mix of calypso, salsa, reggae and rock. It's popular with university students, who indulge in flirting, drinking and various combinations thereof.

Theater

There is a wide variety of theatrical options in San José, including some in English. Local newspapers, including the *Tico Times,* list current shows. Most theaters are not very large, so performances tend to sell out; get tickets as early as possible.

★ Teatro Nacional
THEATER

(Map p70; ☑ 2010-1111; www.teatronacional.go.cr; Calles 3 & 5 btwn Avs Central & 2) Costa Rica's most important theater stages plays, dance, opera, symphony, Latin American music and other major events. The main season runs from March to November, but there are performances throughout the year.

Teatro Melico Salazar
THEATER

(Map p70; ☑ 2295-6032; www.teatromelico.go.cr; Av 2 btwn Calles Central & 2) The restored 1920s theater has regular fine-arts performances, including music, theater, ballet and other dance.

Little Theatre Group
THEATER

(☑ 8858-1446; www.littletheatregroup.org) This English-language performance troupe has been around since the 1950s and presents several plays a year; call or go online to find out when and where the works will be shown.

Teatro Eugene O'Neill
THEATER

(Map p80; ☑ 2207-7554; www.centrocultural.cr; Calle 37) Has performances sponsored by the Centro Cultural Costarricense Norteamericano, a cultural center that promotes ties between Costa Rica and the United States. It's north of Av Central, in San Pedro.

Sport

Bullfighting is popular and fights are held seasonally in the southern suburb of Zapote over the Christmas period. Members of the public (usually drunk) are encouraged to participate in the action. The bull isn't killed in the Costa Rican version of the sport; however, many bulls are taunted, kicked and otherwise injured as a result of the fights, and animal welfare groups are keen to see the fights stopped.

Estadio Nacional de Costa Rica   STADIUM
(Map p74; Parque Metropolitano La Sabana) Costa Rica's graceful, modernist 35,000-seat national soccer stadium, constructed with funding from the Chinese government and opened to the public in 2011, is the venue for international and national Division-1 *fútbol* (soccer) games. Its predecessor, dating to 1924 and located in the same spot in Parque Metropolitano La Sabana, hosted everyone from Pope John Paul II to soccer legend Pelé to Bruce Springsteen over its 84-year history.

Casino

Gamblers will find casinos in several of the larger hotels. Most of these are fairly casual, but in the nicer spots it's advisable to ditch the T-shirts in favor of a button-down shirt as there may be a dress code. Gents: be advised that casinos are frequented by prostitutes, so be wary if you're suddenly the most desirable person in the room.

Casino Club Colonial   CASINO
(Map p70; ☑ 2258-2807; www.casinoclubcoloni al.com; Av 1 btwn Calles 9 & 11; ☉ 24hr) San José's most elegant casino.

🔒 Shopping

Whether you're looking for indigenous carvings, high-end furnishings or a stuffed sloth, San José has no shortage of shops, running the gamut from artsy boutiques to tourist traps stocked full of tropical everything. Haggling is not tolerated in stores (markets are the exception).

In touristy shops, keep watch for 'authentic' woodwork pieces that have 'Made in Indonesia' stamped on the bottom. For the country's finest woodcrafts, it is absolutely worth the trip to Biesanz Woodworks.

★ Feria Verde de Aranjuez   MARKET
(Map p66; www.feriaverde.org; ☉ 7am-noon Sat) For a foodie-friendly cultural experience, don't miss this fabulous Saturday farmers market, a weekly meeting place for San José's artists and organic growers since 2010. You'll find organic coffee, artisanal chocolate, tropical-fruit ice blocks, fresh produce, baked goods, leather, jewelry and more at the long rows of booths set up in the park at the north end of Barrio Aranjuez.

Sin Domicilio Fijo   HANDICRAFTS
(Map p82; ☑ 2289-9461; www.facebook.com/ sindomiciliofijo; ☉ 10am-6pm Mon-Sat, 11am-4pm Sun) In downtown Escazú, this art and design shop opened recently in a historic,

WORTH A TRIP

BIESANZ WOODWORKS

Located in the hills of Bello Horizonte in Escazú, the workshop of **Biesanz Woodworks** (☑ 2289-4337; www.biesanz. com; ☉ 8am-5pm Mon-Fri, 9am-2pm Sat) can be difficult to find, but the effort will be well worth it. This shop is one of the finest woodcrafting studios in the nation, run by celebrated artisan Barry Biesanz.

His bowls and other decorative containers are exquisite and take their inspiration from pre-Columbian techniques, in which the natural lines and forms of the wood determine the shape and size of the bowl. The pieces are expensive (from US$45 for a palm-size bowl), but they are unique – and so delicately crafted that they wouldn't be out of place in a museum.

150-year-old house with adobe walls, near the southwest corner of Escazú's church. The place is full of unique handicrafts that make ideal gifts, from dainty footwear to kitchen adornments. There's also a lovely open-air cafe that serves up fresh coffee and a delicious Saturday brunch.

Galería Namu   HANDICRAFTS
(Map p70; ☑ 2256-3412, in USA 800-616-4322; www.galerianamu.com; Av 7 btwn Calles 5 & 7; ☉ 9am-6:30pm Mon-Sat year-round, plus 1-4pm Sun Dec-Apr) This fair-trade gallery brings together artwork and cultural objects from a diverse population of regional ethnicities, including Boruca masks, finely woven Wounaan baskets, Guaymí dolls, Bribrí canoes, Chorotega ceramics, traditional Huetar reed mats, and contemporary urban and Afro-Caribbean crafts. It can also help arrange visits to remote indigenous territories in different parts of Costa Rica.

Kiosco SJO   HANDICRAFTS
(Map p80; ☑ 2253-8426; www.kioscosjo.com; cnr Calle 31 & Av 5; ☉ noon-10pm Tue-Fri, 9am-10pm Sat, 9am-4pm Sun) With a focus on sustainable design by Latin American artisans, this sleek shop in Barrio Escalante stocks handmade jewelry, hand-tooled leather boots and bags, original photography, artisanal chocolates, fashion and contemporary home decor by established regional designers. It's pricey, but rest assured that everything you find here will be of exceptional quality.

eÑe
HANDICRAFTS

(Map p70; ☑2222-7681; laesquina13y7@gmail. com; cnr Av 7 & Calle 13; ⊘10am-6:30pm Mon-Sat) This hip little design shop across from Casa Amarilla sells all manner of pieces crafted by Costa Rican designers and artists, including clothing, jewelry, handbags, picture frames, zines and works of graphic art.

Mora Books
BOOKS

(Map p70; ☑8383-8385; www.morabooks.com; Calle 5 btwn Avs 5 & 7; ⊘11am-7pm) Dog-eared paperbacks in English, Spanish, French and German teeter in precarious towers atop crammed shelves at this chaotic jumble of a used bookstore. The best place in town for stocking up on reading material for the road. Hours are hit and miss.

Mercado Artesanal
MARKET

(Crafts Market; Map p70; Plaza de la Democracia, Avs Central & 2 btwn Calles 13 & 15; ⊘8:30am-5pm) A touristy open-air market that sells everything from handcrafted jewelry and Bob Marley T-shirts to elaborate woodwork and Guatemalan sarongs.

Librería Lehmann
BOOKS

(Map p70; ☑2522-4848; www.librerialehmann. com; Av Central btwn Calles 1 & 3; ⊘8am-6:30pm Mon-Fri, 9am-5pm Sat, 11am-4pm Sun) Good selection of English-language books, maps and guidebooks (including Lonely Planet).

Rincón del Habano
SOUVENIRS

(Map p70; Calle 7 btwn Avs Central & 1; ⊘9am-6:30pm Mon-Sat, to 5:30pm Sun) You'll find a wide selection of cigars in this tiny shop. The international array of stogies includes brands from Costa Rica, the Dominican Republic, Nicaragua and Cuba.

❶ Orientation

San José's center is arranged in a grid with *avenidas* (avenues) running east to west and *calles* (streets) running north to south. Av Central is the nucleus of the downtown area and is a pedestrian mall between Calles 6 and 9. The downtown has several loosely defined *barrios* (neighborhoods); those of greatest interest to tourists are north and east of Plaza de la Cultura, including Barrio Amón, Barrio Otoya, Barrio Aranjuez and Barrio La California. The central area is home to innumerable businesses, hotels and cultural sites, while the area immediately west of downtown is home to San José's central market and many of its bus terminals.

Slightly further west of downtown is La Sabana, named for its huge and popular park where many *josefinos* spend their weekends jogging, swimming, picnicking or attending soccer matches.

A few kilometers southwest is the affluent outer suburb of Escazú, really three neighborhoods in one: Escazú Centro with its peaceful central plaza and unhurried Tico ambiance; the USA expatriate enclave of San Rafael, dotted with strip malls, top-end car dealerships, tract housing and chain restaurants; and San Antonio, a hillside mix of humble rural homes, sprawling estates and spectacular views.

East (and within walking distance) of the center are the contiguous neighborhoods of Los Yoses and San Pedro, the former a low-key residential area with some nice accommodations, the latter home to the tree-lined campus of the UCR, the country's most prestigious university. Marking the dividing line between Los Yoses and San Pedro is a traffic roundabout graced by a large fountain known as the Fuente de la Hispanidad (a frequently referenced local landmark). North of Los Yoses is Barrio Escalante, home to some of San José's trendiest bars and restaurants.

You can pick up a free map of the city at the tourist office.

❶ Information

DANGERS & ANNOYANCES

Though Costa Rica has the lowest crime rate of any Central American country, crime in urban centers such as San José is a problem. The most common offense is opportunistic theft (eg pickpocketing and mugging). Keep a streetwise attitude and follow the tips below.

➡ Do not wear flashy jewelry.

➡ Keep your camera in your bag when you are not using it.

➡ Carry only as much cash as you'll need for the day.

➡ Unless you think you'll need it for official business, leave your passport in the hotel safe; a photocopy will do for most purposes.

➡ Be wary of pickpockets at crowded events and the areas around bus stops.

➡ Never put your bag in the overhead racks on a bus.

➡ Do not walk around alone at night, and stick to licensed taxis.

➡ If you are renting a car, always park it in a secure, guarded lot, and never leave anything in it.

➡ Men should be aware that prostitutes are known for their sleight-of-hand abilities, and that they often work in pairs.

Neighborhoods covered by Lonely Planet are generally safe during the day, though you should be especially careful around the Coca-Cola bus terminal and the red-light district south of Parque Central, particularly at night. Be advised that adjacent neighborhoods can vary greatly in terms of safety; inquire locally before setting out.

Gridlocked traffic, gigantic potholes, noise and smog are unavoidable components of the San José experience. Most central hotels are subject to street noise, no matter how nice they are. Be skeptical of touts and taxi drivers who try to sell you tours or tell you that the hotel you've booked is a crime-infested bordello. Many of these folks will say anything to steer you to the places that pay them commissions.

EMERGENCY

Fire	☑ 118
Red Cross	☑ 128
Traffic Police	☑ 2222-9245, 2222-9330

INTERNET ACCESS

Most accommodations offer free wi-fi and/or guest computers. You'll also find plenty of cyber cafes, charging US$0.50 to US$1 per hour.

MEDICAL SERVICES

For serious medical emergencies, head to **Hospital CIMA** (☑ 2208-1000; www.hospitalcima.com; Los Laureles) in San Rafael de Escazú, whose facilities are the most modern in the greater San José area.

Clínica Bíblica (☑ 2522-1000; www.clinicabiblica.com; Av 14 btwn Calles Central & 1; ⊙ 24hr) The top private clinic downtown has a 24-hour emergency room; doctors speak English, French and German.

Hospital Calderón Guardia (☑ 2212-1000; cnr Calle 17 btwn Avs 7 & 9) A public hospital in central San José.

Hospital La Católica (☑ 2246-3000; www.hospitallacatolica.com; Guadalupe) Pricey private clinic geared toward medical-tourism patients from abroad.

Hospital San Juan de Dios (☑ 2547-8000; cnr Paseo Colón & Calle 14) Free public hospital open 24 hours; expect long waits.

POST

Correo Central (Central Post Office; Map p70; ☑ 2223-9766; www.correos.go.cr; Calle 2 btwn Avs 1 & 3; ⊙ 6:30am-6pm Mon-Fri, to noon Sat) In a gorgeous historic building near the center of town. Express and overnight services.

TOURIST INFORMATION

Canatur (Cámara Nacional de Turismo; ☑ 2234-6222, 2440-1676; www.canatur.org; Aeropuerto Internacional Juan Santamaría; ⊙ 7am-10pm) The Costa Rican National Chamber of Tourism provides information on member services from a small stand next to international baggage claim.

ⓘ TOURIST POLICE

The establishment in 2007 of the *policía turística* (tourist police; you'll see them patrolling in pairs around San José, on foot, bicycle and even horseback) has helped prevent petty crimes against foreigners. These officers can be helpful in the event of an emergency since most of them speak at least some English.

If you find yourself the victim of a crime, you'll have to file a report in person at the **Organismo de Investigacíon Judicial** (☑ 2222-1365, 2295-3643; Calle 17 btwn Avs 6 & 8; ⊙ 24hr) in the Supreme Court of Justice building on the south side of downtown.

Instituto Costarricense de Turismo (ICT; Map p70; ☑ 2222-1090, in USA & Canada 866-267-8274; www.visitcostarica.com; Edificio de las Academias, Av Central btwn Calles 1 & 3; ⊙ 8am-5pm Mon-Fri) The government tourism office provides handy intercity bus schedules and free maps of San José and Costa Rica.

ⓘ Getting There & Away

San José is the country's transportation hub, and it's likely that you'll pass through the capital a number of times throughout your travels (whether you want to or not).

AIR

All international flights leave from Juan Santamaría (SJO) airport outside Alajuela.

Aeropuerto Internacional Juan Santamaría (☑ 2437-2400; fly2sanjose.com) Handles all international flights and **NatureAir** (☑ 2299-6000, in USA 1-800-235-9272; www.natureair.com) domestic flights in its main terminal. Domestic flights on **Sansa** (☑ 2290-4100; www.flysansa.com) depart from the Sansa terminal.

Aeropuerto Tobías Bolaños (☑ 2232-2820; Pavas) In the San José suburb of Pavas; services private charter and a few national flights.

BUS

Bus transportation in San José can be bewildering. There is no public bus system and no central terminal. Instead, dozens of private companies operate out of stops scattered throughout the city. Many bus companies have no more than a stop (in this case pay the driver directly); some have a tiny office with a window on the street; others operate from bigger terminals servicing entire regions.

Note that bus schedules and prices change regularly. Pick up a copy of the free (but not always up-to-date) booklet *Itinerario de Buses*

SAN JOSÉ GETTING THERE & AWAY

ⓘ TAXI/HOTEL SCAM

Note that many taxi drivers in San José are commissioned by hotels to bring them customers, and the hotel scene is so competitive that drivers will say just about anything to steer you to the places they represent. Among other things, they will 'call' your hotel and a voice on the other end will tell you that they're fully booked. Be skeptical. Tell drivers firmly where it is you would like to go. And if you have concerns about where you have chosen to stay, ask to see a room before settling in for the night.

from San José's downtown tourist office, or download a PDF version from www.visitcosta rica.com (most easily located in your search engine by typing 'Costa Rica Itinerario de Buses'). Buses are crowded on Friday evening and Saturday morning and packed to the gills at Christmas and Easter.

For buses that run infrequently, it is advisable to buy tickets in advance.

Bus Terminals

Collectively, the following five San José terminals serve Costa Rica's most popular destinations. Chances are you'll be passing through one or more of them during your trip. Be aware that thefts are common in many bus terminals. Stay alert, keep your valuables close to you and don't stow anything important (such as passports and money) in the overhead racks or luggage compartment of a bus.

Gran Terminal del Caribe (Calle Central) A roomy station north of Av 13; serves destinations on the Caribbean slope, with connections to Tortuguero.

Terminal 7-10 (☑ 2519-9740; www.terminal7-10. com; 7th Ave & Calle 10) A brand new bus terminal serving Nicoya, Nosara, Sámara, Santa Cruz, Tamarindo, Jacó, Cóbano and a few other places. The four-story facility has a food court, shopping center and parking lot. Although it's located in the *zona roja*, historically a dangerous area of the city, police have stepped up patrols to reduce crime.

Terminal Coca-Cola (Map p66; Av 1 btwn Calles 16 & 18) A well-known, labyrinthine landmark; buses leave from the terminal and the four-block radius around it to points all over Costa Rica, including the Central Valley and the Pacific coast.

Terminal del Atlántico Norte (cnr Av 9 & Calle 12) A small, rather decrepit terminal serving Monteverde, La Fortuna and southern Caribbean coastal destinations.

Terminal Tracopa (Map p66; ☑ 2221-4214; www.tracopacr.com; Calle 5 btwn Avs 18 & 20) On the south end of town; serves southern and southwestern destinations including Golfito, Quepos/Manuel Antonio, and Paso Canoas on the Panama border.

Domestic Bus Companies

Autotransportes Caribeños (☑ 2222-0610; www.grupocaribenos.com; Gran Terminal del Caribe, Calle Central) Northeastern destinations including Puerto Limón, Guápiles, Cariari, Siquirres and Puerto Viejo de Sarapiquí; the Caribeños group encompasses several smaller companies (Empresarios Guapileños, Líneas del Atlántico etc), all of which share the same terminal and customer-service phone number.

Autotransportes Mepe (☑ 2758-1572, 2257-8129; www.mepecr.com; Terminal del Atlántico Norte) Southern Caribbean destinations including Cahuita, Puerto Viejo de Talamanca, Manzanillo, Bribrí and Sixaola.

Autotransportes San Carlos (☑ 2255-4300; Terminal del Atlántico Norte) La Fortuna, Ciudad Quesada and Los Chiles.

Blanco Lobo (Map p66; ☑ 2257-4121; Calle 12 btwn Avs 7 & 9) Puerto Jiménez.

Coopetrans Atenas (Map p66; ☑ 2446-5767; www.coopetransatenas.com; Terminal Coca-Cola) Atenas.

Empresa Alfaro (☑ 2222-2666; www.empresa alfaro.com; Terminal 7-10) Nicoya, Nosara, Sámara, Santa Cruz and Tamarindo.

Empresarios Unidos (Map p66; ☑ 2222-8231; cnr Av 12 & Calle 16) San Ramón and Puntarenas.

Lumaca (Map p66; ☑ 2552-5280, 2537-2320; Av 10 btwn Calles 5 & 7) Cartago.

Metrópoli (Map p70; ☑ 2530-1064; Av 2 btwn Calles 1 & 3) Volcán Irazú.

Pulmitan de Liberia (Map p66; ☑ 2222-0610; Calle 24 btwn Avs 5 & 7) Northwestern destinations including Cañas, Liberia, Playa del Coco and Tilarán; the Pulmitan group encompasses the smaller companies of Empresa La Cañera and Autotransportes Tilarán, both of which use Pulmitan's terminal.

Station Wagon (Map p66; ☑ 2441-1181; Av 2 btwn Calles 10 & 12) Alajuela and the airport.

Tracopa (Map p66; ☑ 2221-4214; www.traco pacr.com; Calle 5 btwn Avs 18 & 20) Southwestern destinations including Ciudad Neily, Dominical, Golfito, Manuel Antonio, Palmar Norte, Paso Canoas, Quepos, San Isidro del General, San Vito and Uvita; Tracopa encompasses the smaller companies Delio Morales and Unidos La Costanera, which now share Tracopa's terminal.

Tralapa (Map p66; ☑ 2248-1925; Av 5 btwn Calles 20 & 22) Several Península de Nicoya destinations, including Playa Flamingo, Playa Hermosa, Playa Tamarindo and Santa Cruz.

Transmonteverde (☎ 2645-7447; www.face
book.com/Transmonteverde; Terminal del Atlántico Norte, cnr Av 9 & Calle 12) Monteverde.

Transportes Cobano (☎ 2221-7479; trans
portescobano@gmail.com; Terminal 7-10)
Montezuma and Mal País.

Transportes Deldú (Gran Terminal de Caribe)
Peñas Blancas (Nicaraguan border).

Transportes Jacó (☎ 2290-2922, 2290-7920;
www.transportesjacoruta655.com; Terminal
7-10) Jacó.

Transtusa (Map p66; ☎ 2222-4464; www.
transtusacr.com; Calle 13A btwn Avs 6 & 8)
Cartago and Turrialba.

Tuan (Map p66; ☎ 2494-2139, 2258-2004; cnr
Av 5 & Calle 18A) Grecia.

Tuasa (Map p66; ☎ 2442-6900; Av 2 btwn
Calles 12 & 14) Alajuela and the airport.

International Bus Companies

International buses get booked up fast. Buy your
tickets in advance – and take your passport.

Expreso Panamá (Map p66; ☎ 2221-7694;
www.expresopanama.com; Terminal Empresarios Unidos, cnr Av 12 & Calle 16) Panama City
(Panama).

Nicabus (Map p66; ☎ 2221-2581; cnr Av 1 &
Calle 20) Managua (Nicaragua).

Tica Bus (Map p74; ☎ 2296-9788; www.tica-
bus.com; cnr Transversal 26 & Av 3) Nicaragua,
Panama, El Salvador and Guatemala.

TransNica (Map p66; ☎ 2223-4242; www.
transnica.com; Calle 22 btwn Avs 3 & 5) Nicaragua and Honduras.

Shuttle Buses

Grayline (☎ 2220-2126; www.graylinecostar-
ica.com) and **Interbus** (☎ 4100-0888; www.
interbusonline.com) shuttle passengers in
air-conditioned minivans from San José to a

long list of popular destinations around Costa
Rica. They are more expensive than the standard bus services, but they offer door-to-door
service and can get you there faster.

ⓘ Getting Around

Central San José frequently resembles a parking
lot – narrow streets, heavy traffic and a complicated one-way system mean that it is often
quicker to walk than to take the bus. The same
applies to driving: if you rent a car, try to avoid
downtown. If you're in a real hurry to get somewhere that's more than 1km away, take a taxi.

If traveling by bus, you'll arrive at one of several international bus terminals sprinkled around
the western and southern parts of downtown.
Some of this area is walkable provided you aren't
hauling a lot of luggage and are staying nearby.
But, if you're arriving at night, take a taxi, since
most terminals are in dodgy areas.

TO & FROM THE AIRPORT

International flights arrive at **Aeropuerto Internacional Juan Santamaría** (p97) in nearby
Alajuela.

In normal traffic, an official taxi from the airport to downtown San José should cost around
US$30, as measured on the meter. You can
reserve a pickup with **Taxi Aeropuerto** (☎ 2221-
6865). Plan on spending extra for wait time
during periods of heavy traffic.

Interbus (p99) runs shuttles in both directions between the airport and San José hotels
(US$15 per adult, US$7 per child under 12) –
good value if you're traveling alone.

Even cheaper are the public buses (US$1.10)
operated by **Tuasa** (Map p66; ☎ 2442-6900; Av
2 btwn Calles 12 & 14) and **Station Wagon** (p98),
which pick up passengers at a stop on the main
road in front of the airport. Make sure to verify

INTERNATIONAL BUSES FROM SAN JOSÉ

DESTINATION	BUS COMPANY	COST (US$)	DURATION (HR)	FREQUENCY
David (Panama)	Tracopa	21	8	7:30am, noon
Guatemala City (Guatemala)	Tica Bus	105	48	3am
Managua (Nicaragua)	Tica Bus	29-42	9	3am, 6am, 7:30am, 12:30pm
Managua (Nicaragua)	TransNica	29-38	8-9	4am, 5am, 9am, noon
Managua (Nicaragua)	Nicabus	29	8	5:30am, 9:30am
Panama City (Panama)	Expreso Panamá	40	14	noon
Panama City (Panama)	Tica Bus	42-58	16	noon, 11:45pm
San Salvador (El Salvador)	Tica Bus	84	20	3am
Tegucigalpa (Honduras)	TransNica	57	18	4am

the destination before boarding, as some buses from this stop go to Alajuela, others to San José. On the return trip, board at the Tuasa or Station Wagon terminal in downtown San José (both opposite Iglesia de La Merced near the corner of Av 2 and Calle 12) and be sure to tell the driver that you are getting off at the airport *(Voy al aeropuerto, por favor)*. Most hotels can also arrange for private airport pickup at reasonable rates.

From downtown, the drive to the airport can take anywhere from 20 minutes to an hour (more if you take the bus) – and vice versa. Plan accordingly.

BUS

Local buses are useful to get you into the suburbs and surrounding villages, or to the airport. Most buses run between 5am and 10pm and cost between US$0.40 and US$1.10.

La Sabana To catch a bus heading west from San José towards La Sabana (US$0.40), head for the convenient downtown stop at the southeast corner of Av 3 and Calle 3. Buses returning from Parque La Sabana to downtown follow Paseo Colón, then go over to Av 2 at the San Juan de Dios hospital. They then go three different ways through town before eventually heading back to La Sabana. Buses are marked Sabana–Estadio, Sabana–Cementerio or Cementerio–Estadio. These buses are a good bet for a cheap city tour.

Los Yoses & San Pedro Catch eastbound buses to Los Yoses and San Pedro (US$0.50) from the northeast corner of **Calle Central and Av 9** (Map p70). These buses run east along Av 2 and then switch over to Av Central at Calle 29. (Many are easily identifiable by the big sign that says 'Mall San Pedro' on the front window.)

DOMESTIC BUSES FROM SAN JOSÉ

DESTINATION	BUS COMPANY	COST (US$)	DURATION (HR)	FREQUENCY
Cahuita	Mepe	8.95	4	6am, 10am, noon, 2pm, 4pm
Cañas	Pulmitan	5.43	3½	11:40am, 1:30pm, 3:30pm
Cariari	Caribeños	3.25	2½	6:30am, 9am, 10:30am, 1pm, 3pm, 4:30pm, 6pm, 7pm, 10:30pm
Cartago	Lumaca	1.08	1	every 15min
Ciudad Neily	Tracopa	13.80	8	5am, 7:40am, 10:15am, 1:05pm, 2pm, 3:30pm, 6:30pm, 8:30pm
Ciudad Quesada	San Carlos	3.34	3	hourly
Dominical & Uvita	Tracopa	10.86	4½-5½	6am, 6:30am, 3pm
Golfito	Tracopa	13.85	7	6:30am, 7am, 3:30pm
Grecia	Tuan	1.88	1	half-hourly
Guápiles	Caribeños	2.75	1¼	half-hourly
Jacó	Transportes Jacó	4.45	2½	every 2hr 7am-7pm
La Fortuna	San Carlos	4.70	4	6:15am, 8:40am, 11:30am
Liberia	Pulmitan	7.30	4½	hourly
Los Chiles	San Carlos	4.50	5	5:30am, 3pm
Manzanillo	Mepe	11.70	5	noon
Monteverde/Santa Elena	Transmonteverde	5.23	4½	6:30am, 2:30pm
Montezuma/Mal País	Cobano	15.10	5½-6	6am, 2pm
Nicoya	Alfaro	7.13	5	7:30am, 10am, 1pm, 3pm, 5pm
Palmar Norte	Tracopa	10.86	4½	5am, 7am, 10am, 1pm, 6:30pm
Paso Canoas	Tracopa	15.40	6½	5am, 11am, 1pm, 6:30pm
Peñas Blancas	Deldú	8.62	6	9 daily
Playa del Coco	Pulmitan	8.70	5½	8am, 2pm, 4pm
Playa Flamingo	Tralapa	11.34	6	8am, 10:30am, 3pm

Escazú Buses southwest to Escazú (US$0.65 to US$0.80, 15 to 25 minutes) leave from two different locations: **Av 6** (Map p66) between Calles 14 and 16 (south of the Hospital San Juan de Dios), and Calle 16 between Avs 1 and 3 (near the Coca-Cola terminal). Buses labeled 'San Antonio de Escazú' climb the hill south of Escazú and end near the Iglesia San Antonio de Escazú; those labeled 'Escazú Centro' end in Escazú's **main plaza** (Map p82); others, labeled 'Guachipelín', go west on the Carretera John F Kennedy and pass the Costa Rica Country Club. All go through San Rafael.

Heredia Regular **buses** (Map p70) leave from Calle 1 between Avs 7 and 9.

CAR

It is not advisable to rent a car just to drive around San José. The traffic is heavy, the streets are narrow and the meter-deep curbside gutters make parking nerve-wracking. In addition, break-ins are frequent, and leaving a car – even in a guarded lot – might result in a smashed window and stolen belongings.

If you are renting a car to travel throughout Costa Rica, there are more than 50 car-rental agencies – including many of the global brands – in and around San José. Travel agencies and up-market hotels can arrange rentals; you can also arrange rentals online and at the airport. Note: If you book a rental car online and the low cost seems too good to be true, it is. Rental agencies are notorious for tacking on hundreds of dollars in mandatory insurance when you arrive. They are also known to lie about this over the phone.

One excellent local option is **Wild Rider** (☏2258-4604; www.wild-rider.com; Paseo Colón btwn Calles 30 & 32; ⊙8am-6pm). They have a fleet of more than 60 very reasonably priced 4WD vehicles (from US$380 per week in

SAN JOSÉ GETTING AROUND

DESTINATION	BUS COMPANY	COST (US$)	DURATION (HR)	FREQUENCY
Playa Hermosa	Tralapa	10.90	5	3:30pm, 5pm
Playa Nosara	Alfaro	9	6	5:30am
Playa Sámara	Alfaro	8.26	5	noon
Playa Tamarindo	Alfaro	10.50	5	11:30am, 3:30pm
Playa Tamarindo	Tralapa	12	5	7am, 4pm
Puerto Jiménez	Blanco Lobo	13	8	8am, noon
Puerto Limón	Caribeños	5.95	3	hourly
Puerto Viejo de Sarapiquí	Caribeños	4.71	2½	13 daily
Puerto Viejo de Talamanca	Mepe	10.60	4½	6am, 10am, noon, 2pm, 4pm
Puntarenas	Empresarios Unidos	5.10	2½	hourly
Quepos/Manuel Antonio	Tracopa	7.60	3½	every 1-2hr
San Isidro de El General	Tracopa	5.75	3	hourly
San Vito	Tracopa	12.70	7	6am, 8:15am, noon, 2:15pm, 4pm
Santa Cruz	Alfaro	10.59	5	7 daily
Santa Cruz	Tralapa	9.90	5	7am, 10:30am, noon, 2pm, 4pm, 6pm
Sarchí	Tuan	2.15	1½	12:15pm, 5:30pm, 6pm Mon-Fri
Siquirres	Caribeños	3	2	hourly
Sixaola	Mepe	13	5½	6am, 10am, 2pm, 4pm
Tilarán	Pulmitan	7.48	4	7:30am, 9:30am, 12:45pm, 3:45pm, 6:30pm
Turrialba	Transtusa	2.75	2	hourly
Volcán Irazú	Metrópoli	9 (round trip)	2	8am

high season, including all mandatory insurance coverage). Long-term rentals (four weeks or more) allow a discount of up to 40%. Reserve well in advance.

MOTORCYCLE

Wild Rider (p101) rents sports bikes such as the Honda XR-250 or the Suzuki DRZ-400S. Prices start at US$420 per week in high season (including insurance, taxes and helmets).

TAXI

Red taxis can be hailed on the street day or night, or you can have your hotel call one for you.

Marías (meters) are generally used, though a few drivers will tell you they're broken and try to charge you more – especially if you don't speak Spanish. Not using a meter is illegal. The rate for the first kilometer should automatically appear when the meter starts up (at the time of research, the correct starting amount was 610 colones). Make sure the maría is operating when you get in, or negotiate the fare up front. Short rides downtown cost US$2 to US$4. There's a 20% surcharge after 10pm that may not appear on the maría.

You can hire a taxi and a driver for half a day or longer if you want to do some touring around the area; for such trips, it is best to negotiate a flat fee in advance. Uber has also become a popular form of transport in the city.

Central Valley & Highlands

Best Places to Eat

➜ Xandari (p110)

➜ Hotel Quelitales (p131)

➜ Jalapeños Central (p109)

➜ Colbert Restaurant (p112)

➜ Bromelias Del Río (p125)

Best Places to Sleep

➜ Wagelia Espino Blanco Lodge (p134)

➜ Vista Atenas B&B (p113)

➜ Hotel Quelitales (p131)

➜ Peace Lodge (p112)

➜ Bosque de Paz (p118)

Why Go?

It is on the coffee-cultivated hillsides of the Central Valley that you'll find Costa Rica's heart and soul. This is not only the geographical center of the country, but also its cultural and spiritual core. It is here that the Spanish first settled, here that coffee built a prosperous nation, here that picturesque highland villages still gather for centuries-old fiestas. It is also here that you'll get to fully appreciate Costa Rica's country cooking: artisanal cheeses, steamy corn cakes and freshly caught river trout.

Curvy mountain roads force travelers to slow their roll. Quaint and quirky agricultural towns invite leisurely detours to farmers markets and church processions, a refreshing break from the tourist-industrial complex on the coasts. But it's not all cows and coffee – world-class rapids, resplendent quetzals and close encounters with active volcanoes all show off the rich landscape in which Costa Rica's character is rooted.

When to Go

➜ During high season (December to March), an elevated altitude and landlocked location mean perfect weather.

➜ Afternoon showers are not uncommon during 'green' season (June to December), but so too are bargains.

➜ The rainy months from June to October are great for white-water rafting.

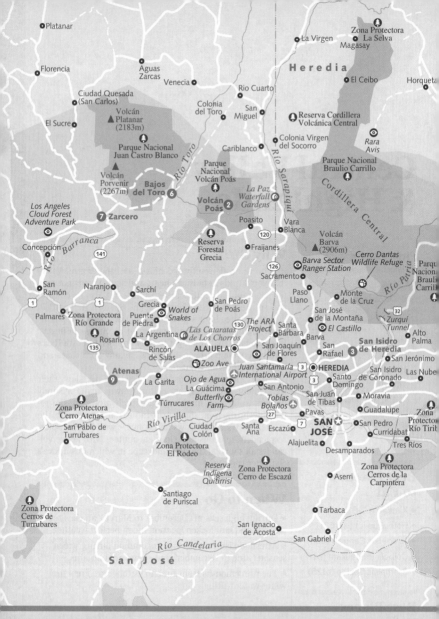

Central Valley & Highlands Highlights

1 Paddling for your life down the cascading rapids of the **Río Pacuare** (p132) near Turrialba.

2 Peering into mammoth craters and volcanic lakes at **Volcán Irazú** (p127) and **Volcán Poás** (p111).

3 Learning the history of chocolate, and meeting rescued toucans and sloths in **San Isidro de Heredia** (p124).

4 Contemplating the aqueducts and petroglyphs at Costa Rica's largest archaeological site, **Monumento Nacional Arqueológico Guayabo** (p135).

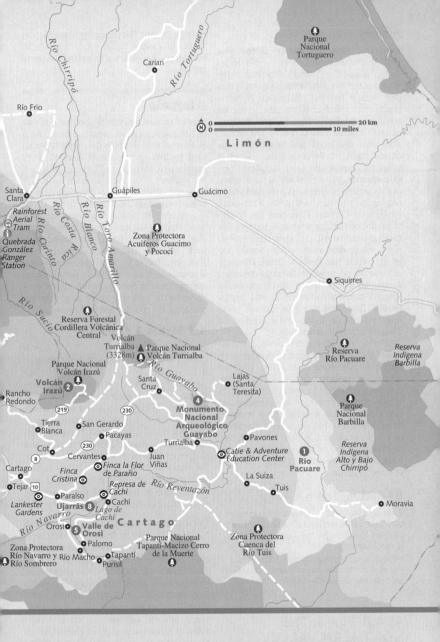

Cariari

Río Chirripó

Río Tortuguero

Parque Nacional Tortuguero

Río Frío

Limón

Santa Clara

Rainforest Aerial Tram

Quebrada González Ranger Station

Guápiles

Guácimo

Río Costa Rica

Río Blanco

Río Toro Amarillo

Río Corinto

Zona Protectora Acuíferos Guácimo y Pococí

Siquirres

Río Sucio

Reserva Forestal Cordillera Volcánica Central

Volcán Turrialba (3328m)

Parque Nacional Volcán Turrialba

Reserva Río Pacuare

Reserva Indígena Barbilla

Parque Nacional Volcán Irazú

Volcán Irazú 2

Río Guayabo

Santa Cruz

Lajas (Santa Teresita)

Rancho Redondo

219

230

Monumento Nacional Arqueológico Guayabo 4

Parque Nacional Barbilla

Tierra Blanca

San Gerardo

Pacayas

Turrialba

Pavones

Reserva Indígena Alto y Bajo Chirripó

Cot

8

230

Cartago

Cervantes

Juan Viñas

Catie & Adventure Education Center

Río Pacuare 1

Tejar

10

Finca Cristina

Finca la Flor de Paraíso

La Suiza

Tuis

Lankester Gardens

Paraíso

Represa de Cachí

Río Reventazón

Río Navarro

Ujarrás 8

Cachí

Lago de Cachí

Cartago

Moravia

Orosí 5

Valle de Orosí

Zona Protectora Río Navarro y Río Macho

Palomo

Parque Nacional Tapantí-Macizo Cerro de la Muerte

Zona Protectora Cuenca del Río Tuis

Río Sombrero

Tapantí

Purisil

N

0   20 km
0   10 miles

5 Exploring the wilderness, culture and coffee *fincas* of **Valle de Orosí** (p128).

6 Bird-watching beside a rushing river or hiking in **Bajos del Toro** (p115).

7 Winding along scenic mountain roads to **Zarcero** (p115), the home of trippy topiary and organic farming.

8 Sharing a lazy Sunday afternoon in the park with Tico families beside the 17th-century church ruins in **Ujarrás** (p131).

9 Relaxing by the square and breathing the clean mountain air in **Atenas** (p113).

History

As in other parts of the country, there is little in the historical record about the ethnicities that inhabited the Central Valley prior to the arrival of the Spanish. What is known is that the people of the area – largely the Huetar – practiced an animist religion, produced stone sculpture and clay pottery, and communicated in a Chibchan dialect that is now extinct. They also developed and maintained the ancient highland city of Guayabo – which is today the biggest and most significant pre-Columbian archaeological site in the country.

European settlement in Costa Rica would not begin in earnest until 1563, when Juan Vásquez de Coronado founded the colonial capital of Cartago – what is today Costa Rica's oldest Spanish city. Over the next two centuries, Spanish communities would pop up in Heredia, San José and Orosi. Throughout this period, however, the area remained a colonial backwater, a checkerboard of Spanish farming communities and *indios bravos* (fierce Indians) who had not come under colonial dominion, and who practiced a largely itinerant agriculture.

It was only after independence, in the 1830s, that the area began to prosper with the expanded cultivation of coffee. The *grano de oro* (golden bean) transformed the country, providing the revenue to invest in urban infrastructure such as electricity and pavements, not to mention many baronial mansions. Coffee has since been overtaken as a key agricultural export by pineapples and bananas, but its legacy lives on, reflected in the culture, architecture and traditions of many highland towns.

ⓘ Getting There & Away

While all of the towns in this area are connected by regular buses, renting a car makes sense if you want to explore the many worthwhile hard-to-reach corners.

Locals occasionally wave down passing cars. If you want to hitchhike yourself, beware that there are risks, and always offer to help with gas costs.

ALAJUELA & THE NORTHERN VALLEY

Volcanoes shrouded in mist, undulating coffee *fincas* (plantations), bustling agricultural centers: the area around the provincial capital of Alajuela, 18km northwest of San José, seems to have it all – including Juan Santamaría International Airport, just 3km

outside the city. The proximity to the airport makes this area a highly convenient transit point if you are entering or leaving the country here.

Alajuela

Costa Rica's second city is also home to one of the country's most famous figures: Juan Santamaría, the humble drummer boy who died putting an end to William Walker's campaign to turn Central America into slaving territory in the Battle of Rivas in 1856. A busy agricultural hub, it is here that farmers bring their products to market.

Alajuela is by no means a tourist 'destination.' Much of the architecture is unremarkable, the streets are often jammed and there isn't a lot to see. But it's an inherently Costa Rican city, and, in its more relaxed moments, it reveals itself as such, where families have leisurely Sunday lunches and teenagers steal kisses in the park. It's also a good base for exploring the countryside to the north.

◉ Sights & Activities

Museo Juan Santamaría   MUSEUM
(☑2441-4775; www.museojuansantamaria.go.cr; Av 1 btwn Calles Central & 2; ☺10am-5:30pm Tue-Sun) FREE Situated in a century-old structure that has served as both a jail and an armory, this museum chronicles Costa Rican history from early European settlement through the 19th century, with special emphasis on the life and history of Juan Santamaría and the pivotal mid-1850s battles of Santa Rosa, Sardinal and Rivas. Exhibits include videos, vintage maps, paintings and historical artifacts related to the conflict that ultimately safeguarded Costa Rica's independence.

Ojo de Agua Springs   SWIMMING
(☑2441-0655; www.facebook.com/ojodeaguacr?-fref=ts; San Antonio de Belén; admission US$3, under 3yr free; ☺7:30am-4:30pm; ⊞) About 6km south of Alajuela, this picturesque working-class water park gets packed with local families on weekends. Approximately 20,000L of water gushes from the spring every minute, powering a small waterfall and filling various pools (including an Olympic-size lap pool complete with diving tower) and an artificial boating lake.

Half-hourly buses to the springs depart from the main terminal area on Alajuela's southwestern edge. From San José, drivers can take the San Antonio de Belén exit off the Interamericana.

Courses

Intensa LANGUAGE COURSE

(☎ 2442-3843, in USA & Canada 866-277-1352; www.intensa.com; US$325/470) Schools in Alajuela and Heredia teach everything from medical to business Spanish. One week of classes, which includes four lessons of an hour each per day, costs US$325. With homestay included the weekly rate is US$470. Prices drop when students study for longer periods.

✾ Festivals & Events

In the town that gave birth to Juan Santamaría, it would be expected that the anniversary of the **Battle of Rivas**, on April 11, would be particularly well celebrated. This momentous event is commemorated with civic events, including a parade and lots of firecrackers.

🛏 Sleeping

Since Alajuela is so close to the international airport, most hotels and B&Bs can arrange airport transfers for a small fee (or for free). If you're driving your own car, note that many places in the city center don't have dedicated parking, but there are many guarded lots available. Street noise is a fact of life.

A few budget hotels also offer dorm rooms. All top-end hotels accept credit cards, as do most midrange places.

Hotel Pacandé B&B $

(☎ 2443-8481; www.hotelpacande.com; Av 5 btwn Calles 2 & 4; incl breakfast r US$50-60, without bathroom US$35; P@🖥) This popular, locally run option is spotlessly clean throughout, offering 10 large rooms with wood furnishings, folk-art touches and cable TV. Less expensive rooms share bathrooms. The bright and sunny breakfast nook is a great spot for a morning brew.

Hostel Maleku HOSTEL $

(☎ 2430-4304; www.malekuhostel.com; incl breakfast dm US$15, s/d without bathroom US$25/38; @🖥) This super-friendly, family-run backpackers' abode has five spick-and-span rooms tucked into a vintage home between the airport and downtown Alajuela (opposite Hospital San Rafael). There's a communal kitchen, plus free storage for items brought from home that you don't need while in Costa Rica (winter coats, bike boxes). Free airport drop-off service is available hourly between 5am and 5pm.

A BEACON FOR BOOK LOVERS

Goodlight Books (☎ 2430-4083; www.goodlightbooks.com; Av 3 btwn Calles 1 & 3; ⊙10am-6pm Mon-Sat), managed by Alajuelense Rosa Carballo, offers a selection of over 20,000 well-organized books (both used and new). She also keeps a worthwhile stock of difficult-to-find books on Costa Rica, a growing supply of Spanish-language titles and a sizable array of volumes in other European languages.

Alajuela Backpackers Boutique Hostel HOTEL $

(☎ 2441-7149; www.alajuelabackpackers.com; cnr Av 4 & Calle 4; dm/r/ste US$19/55/70; ❄@🖥) This four-story place with cookie-cutter rooms may feel a tad institutional at first glance, but dig deeper and you'll discover some big pluses: free shuttles to and from the airport, air-conditioned dorms and doubles with en suite bathrooms and a super-cool 4th-floor bar terrace where you can sip beers while watching planes take off in the distance.

Hotel Los Volcanes GUESTHOUSE $$

(☎ 2441-0525; www.hotellosvolcanes.com; Av 3 btwn Calles Central & 2; incl breakfast s/d without bathroom US$40/52, with bathroom US$52/68, with air-con US$72/84; P⊙❄@🖥) Tranquil and centrally located, this welcoming place in a refurbished 1920s mansion has 15 rooms, from vintage units with period-style furniture and clean, shared bathrooms, to contemporary rooms with flat-screen TV, air-con and safe. There's an enjoyable courtyard in the back, complete with gurgling fountain. The helpful owners arrange free airport drop-off at the end of your stay.

Villa Pacandé GUESTHOUSE $$

(☎ 2441-6795; www.villapacande.com; Rd to Volcán Poás; d/tr/q from US$40/50/60, all incl breakfast; P@🖥🐾) 🌿 Located 3km north of Alajuela center, this Spanish-style home is set on gorgeous grounds, festooned with blooms and buzzing with hummingbirds. The nine rooms are simple and comfortable, some offering a lovely view of the garden. This is a perfect choice for your first or last night if you're not interested in exploring the charms of Alajuela.

Alajuela

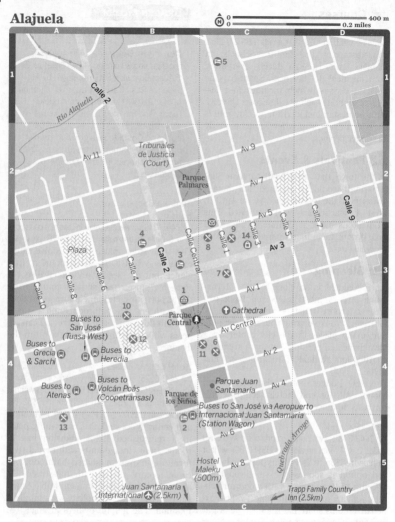

Alajuela

◎ Sights
1 Museo Juan Santamaría B3

🛏 Sleeping
2 Alajuela Backpackers Boutique
   Hostel B5
3 Hotel Los Volcanes B3
4 Hotel Pacandé B3
5 Vida Tropical B&B C1

🍴 Eating
6 Balcón Mansarda C4
7 Coffee Dreams Café C3

8 El Chante Vegano C3
9 Jalapeños Central C3
10 Más X Menos B3
11 MegaSuper C4
12 Mercado Central B4
13 Palí Supermarket A5
   Puntalitos de Manuela .... (see 1)

🛍 Shopping
14 Goodlight Books C3

At the time of research, the hotel was about to open a new restaurant serving Spanish cuisine.

Vida Tropical B&B
B&B **$$**

(☑ 2443-9576; www.vidatropical.com; Calle 3; incl breakfast s/d US$45/65, without bathroom US$35/50; P@🛜🐕) In a quiet residential neighborhood a five-minute walk north of downtown Alajuela, this friendly house has seven snug, simple guest rooms awash in bright murals; two share a bathroom. The well-tended backyard is perfect for catching some sun in a hammock, and laundry service is available. Owners can help arrange airport pickup (US$8) at any hour.

In the backyard, kids will enjoy a worm farm and two playful pet bunny rabbits.

★ Xandari Resort Hotel & Spa
HOTEL **$$$**

(☑ 2443-2020, in USA 1-866-363-3212; www.xandari.com; d villa US$300-418, q villa US$644; P🌐❄🛜🐕) 🏊 With spectacular bird's-eye views of the Central Valley, this romantic spot is the fanciful creation of an architect–designer couple. Spacious individual villas, tastefully but playfully decorated in vibrant tropical colors and hand-woven textiles include garden-view shower and sitting area. The grounds offer 4km of trails, five waterfalls, three pools, two Jacuzzis, a ping-pong table, a spa and an organic-foods restaurant.

Tacacori Ecolodge
BUNGALOW **$$$**

(☑ 2430-5846; www.tacacori.com; d incl breakfast US$120, extra person US$20) Expat owners Nadine, Patrick and their two sheepdogs run this peaceful retreat high above Alajuela. Four spacious bungalows with ultra-modern fixtures and abundant ecofriendly touches (solar hot water, LED lighting, dual-flush toilets) sit astride a verdant hillside. Attractively priced 'Hello-Goodbye' packages and 15-minute airport transfers (US$18 uphill, US$12 downhill) provide incentive to begin and end your travels here.

Trapp Family Country Inn
INN **$$$**

(☑ 2431-0776; www.trappfam.com; incl breakfast r US$122, additional person US$30, child 5-11yr US$25; P@🛜🐕) The most attractive option you'll find so close to the airport landing strip, this hacienda-style country inn houses eight terra-cotta-tiled rooms with comfortable beds. The best units have balconies overlooking the inviting turquoise pool and verdant garden laced with bougainvillea and fig trees. Despite its rural feel, it's only 2km

from the international airport; free airport transfers are provided.

Hotel Buena Vista
HOTEL **$$$**

(☑ 2442-8595, in USA 1-800-506-2304; www.hotel buenavistacr.com; incl breakfast d standard/deluxe/junior ste/villa US$157/169/188/236; P🌐@🛜🐕) 🏊 About 5km north of Alajuela, this white-washed Mediterranean-style hotel, perched on a mountaintop, has panoramic views of the nearby volcanoes. The best of the tastefully decorated rooms have private balconies with valley views; five villas offer private balconies along with wood-beamed ceilings and minibar. A small trail leads down through a coffee *finca* to the main road.

✖ Eating & Drinking

For the cheapest meals, head to the enclosed **Mercado Central** (Calles 4 & 6 btwn Avs 1 & Central; ⊗8am-6pm Mon-Sat). Self-caterers can stock up on groceries at the **Palí** (cnr Av 2 & Calle 10; ⊗8am-8pm), **MegaSuper** (Av Central btwn Calles Central & 2; ⊗8am-9pm Mon-Sat, to 8pm Sun) or **Más X Menos** (Av 1 btwn Calles 4 & 6; ⊗7am-9pm Mon-Sat, to 8pm Sun) supermarkets.

For beer and *bocas* (appetizers), the relaxed 4th-floor terrace bar at Alajuela Backpackers Boutique Hostel (p107) is the airiest spot in town, although it may be closed in low season. There's no shortage of dive bars and karaoke, if that's more your style.

★ Jalapeños Central
MEXICAN **$**

(☑ 2430-4027; Calle 1 btwn Avs 3 & 5; mains US$4-8; ⊗11:30am-9pm Mon-Sat, to 8pm Sun) Offering the best Tex-Mex in the country, this popular, 11-table spot will introduce some much-needed spice into your diet. The simple and fresh burritos, chimichangas and enchiladas come in a meal deal or on their own, and regardless should be devoured alongside a salty margarita.

The devoted staff caters to the whims of customers – lick that guac bowl clean and don't be surprised if a second one lands in front of you!

El Chante Vegano
VEGETARIAN **$**

(☑ 2440-3528, 8911-4787; www.elchantevegano.com; mains US$7-10; ⊗11am-8pm Tue-Sun; 🖉) Two brothers, their mom and a girlfriend run this eatery specializing in healthy, organic food. Vegan treats are served on an open-air, street-facing patio, including garbanzo and portobello-mushroom burgers, falafel, textured-soy-protein nachos, pasta, pizza and sandwiches like the Veggie Lú (grilled veggies, avocado and sprouts on homemade bread).

Puntalitos de Manuela   CAFE $
(☑ 8855-8650; Museo Juan Santamaría; daily specials US$6; ⊘ 11am-5:30pm Tue-Sat) Tranquilly tucked into the courtyard of Alajuela's historic museum, this simple cafe with comfy booths and cushioned chairs makes a good spot to relax over sweet and savory snacks or the well-priced *plato del día* (daily special).

Coffee Dreams Café   CAFE $
(☑ 2430-3970; cnr Calle 1 & Av 3; mains US$5-9; ⊘ 8am-8pm Mon-Sat, 9am-6pm Sun; ☑) For breakfast, *bocas* (appetizers) and a variety of *típico* (traditional Costa Rican) dishes, this centrally located cafe is a reliably good place to dine or enjoy a coffee accompanied by one of its rich desserts.

Balcón Mansarda   COSTA RICAN $$
(☑ 2441-4390; 2nd fl, Calle Central btwn Avs Central & 2; mains US$5-16; ⊘ 11am-11pm) Grilled fish and chicken dishes are the specialty at this casual balcony restaurant overlooking the street. The *casados* (set meals) are also large

and tasty, but save room for the *flan de coco* (coconut flan) or, better yet, a belt of Flor de Caña rum.

★ Xandari   INTERNATIONAL $$$
(☑ 2443-2020; www.xandari.com; Xandari Resort Hotel & Spa; mains US$9-26; ⊘ 7am-9pm; ☑)
🍃 If you want to impress a date, you can't go wrong at this elegant restaurant with incredible views. The menu is a mix of Costa Rican and international, with plenty of vegetarian options. The restaurant utilizes the resort's homegrown organic produce, supplemented by locally grown organic produce whenever possible – making for tasty *and* feel-good gourmet meals.

ℹ Information

Citibank (cnr Calle 2 & Av 6; ⊘ 9am-5pm Mon-Fri, to noon Sat) Near the bus terminals; has ATMs dispensing dollars and colones.

Hospital San Rafael (☑ 2436-1000; www.hospitalsanrafael.sa.cr; Calle 4) Alajuela's hospital, housed in a three-story complex 300m south of Av 10.

Post Office (☑ 2443-2653; cnr Av 5 & Calle 1; ⊘ 8am-5:30pm Mon-Fri, to noon Sat)

BUSES FROM ALAJUELA

Taxis charge between US$6 and US$8 (depending on destination) for the five- to 10-minute drive from Juan Santamaría International Airport into Alajuela.

There is no central bus terminal; instead, a number of small terminals and bus stops dot the southwestern part of the city. Note that there are two Tuasa terminals – **east** (☑ 2442-6900; Calle 8 btwn Avs Central & 1) and **west** (Calle 8 btwn Avs Central & 1) – right across the street from each other. From there, **buses to Grecia & Sarchí** (cnr Calle 10 & Av 1) are a block west; **buses to Atenas** (Calle 10 btwn Avs Central & 2) are one block west and one block south; and **buses to Volcán Poás** (☑ 2442-6900; Calle 8 btwn Avs Central & 2) are a block south. **Buses to San José via Aeropuerto Internacional Juan Santamaría** (Av 4 btwn Calles 2 & 4) leave from in front of the Parque de los Niños, on the opposite side of the street.

DESTINATION	COMPANY	COST (US$)	DURATION (MIN)	FREQUENCY
Atenas	Coopetransatenas	1.40	45	every 30-90min 7am-10:30pm Mon-Sat (less frequent Sun)
Grecia	Transportes Tuan	1.40	45	half-hourly 6am-10pm (hourly 8am-10pm Sat & Sun)
Sarchí	Transportes Tuan	1.65	80	half-hourly 6am-10pm (hourly 8am-10pm Sat & Sun)
Heredia	Tuasa East	1.05	30	every 15min 4am-10pm
San José via Juan Santamaría International Airport	Station Wagon	1.10	45	every 10min 4am-11:30pm
San José	Tuasa West	1.10	45	every 10min 5am-11pm
Volcán Poás	Coopetransasi	4.65 round trip	90 each way	departs 9am, returns 2:30pm

Parque Nacional Volcán Poás

Just 37km north of Alajuela by a winding and scenic road is **Parque Nacional Volcán Poás** (☎2482-1226; admission US$15; ⏱8am-3:30pm), the most heavily trafficked national park in Costa Rica. It's ideal for those who want to peer into an active volcano without the hardship of hiking one. The centerpiece is Volcán Poás (2704m), which had its last blowout in 1953, forming the enormous crater measuring 1.3km across and 300m deep.

Poás offers the wonderful opportunity to watch the bubbling, steaming cauldron belch sulfurous mud and water hundreds of meters into the air. There are three craters, one of which contains a sapphire-blue lake ringed by high-altitude forest.

The main crater at Poás continues to be active to varying degrees. In fact, the park was briefly closed in May 1989 after a minor eruption sent volcanic ash spouting more than 1km into the air, and lesser activity closed the park intermittently in 1995. In recent years, however, Poás has posed no imminent threat, though scientists still monitor it closely.

About 10km before the entrance to the national park, a winding, paved road heads east through Poasito, crossing through bucolic high pastureland en route to the village of Vara Blanca, where it turns north toward La Paz Waterfall Gardens. This is scenic, uncluttered countryside – ideal for a pleasant drive or to spend the night.

Some 250,000 people visit the park annually; weekends get especially jammed. The best time to go is on a weekday in the dry season. In particular, arrive early in the morning before the clouds obscure the view. If the summit is cloudy, hike to the other craters and return to the cauldron later – winds shift and sometimes the cloud cover is blown away.

Be advised that overnight temperatures can drop below freezing, and it may be windy and cold during the day. Also, Poás receives almost 4000mm of rainfall each year; dress accordingly.

🏃 Activities

From the visitors center there is a paved, wheelchair-accessible 600m path that leads to a crater lookout. Visitors are prohibited from descending into the crater because of

ZOO AVE

About 10km west of Alajuela, you'll find **Zoo Ave** (☎2433-8989; www.rescateanimalzooave.org; La Garita; adult/child US$15/5; ⏱9am-5pm; P ♿), a well-designed animal park sheltering more than 115 species of birds on colorful, squawking display in a relaxing 14-hectare setting. The zoo houses all four species of Costa Rican monkey, wild cats, reptiles and other native critters, many of which are rescues. Though technically a zoo, it is also an important animal-breeding center that aims to reintroduce native species into the wild; admission fees fund wildlife rescue, rehabilitation, release and conservation programs.

The park recently opened both a restaurant and a canopy tour with four platforms. Adults can zip-line for US$21, kids for US$15.

the toxic sulfuric-acid fumes that are emitted from the cauldron.

Upon leaving the lookout, you can simply retrace your steps to the parking lot, or continue touring the park on a series of trails that collectively make a 3.6km loop back to the main path. For the longer loop, head east from the crater lookout onto **Sendero Botos**, a 1.4km, 30-minute trail that takes you through dwarf cloud forest, which is the product of acidic air and freezing temperatures. Here you can wander about looking at bromeliads, lichens and mosses clinging to the curiously shaped and twisted trees growing in the volcanic soil. Birds abound, especially the magnificent fiery-throated hummingbird, a high-altitude specialty of Costa Rica. The trail ends at **Laguna Botos**, a peculiar cold-water lake that has filled in one of the extinct craters.

From here, continue south on **Sendero Canto de Aves**, a 1.8km, 45-minute trail through taller forest, which gets significantly less traffic than the other parts of the park and is ideal for bird-watching. Species to look for include the sooty robin, black guan, screech owl and even the odd quetzal (especially from February to April). Although mammals are infrequently sighted in the park, coyotes and the endemic montane squirrel are present.

CENTRAL VALLEY & HIGHLANDS PARQUE NACIONAL VOLCÁN POÁS

LA PAZ WATERFALL GARDENS

A storybook garden complex just east of Volcán Poás, **La Paz Waterfall Gardens** (☑2482-2720, reservations 2482-2100; www.waterfallgardens.com; adult/under 13yr US$40/24, package tours from San José adult/child US$88/78; ☺8am-5pm; ℗🚻) offers the most enchanting day trip in the Central Valley. Guests walk 3.5km of trails to five scenic waterfalls, and can also wander around a butterfly conservatory, hand-feed hummingbirds and toucans, tour a serpentarium and ranarium (frog garden), and witness wild cat's meals (three baby jaguars were born here in 2015).

It's an ideal spot for families, and you can stay on-site at the Peace Lodge.

Return to the main path via the 400m, 10-minute **Sendero Escalonia**, which will drop you at the restrooms just north of the visitors center.

🛏 Sleeping

There are no accommodations inside the park itself (camping included), but the area offers a range of options for all tastes and budgets.

Lagunillas Lodge — LODGE $

(☑2448-5837, 8959-0119; www.lagunillaslodge.com; d US$35-40, cabinas US$55) Run by a charming local family, this rustic lodge and farm 3km below the park entrance is the closest accommodation to Poás. Hillside log *cabinas* offer stellar views; basic lodge rooms cost less. Amenities include trails, horseback rides (from US$15), breakfast (US$6) and dinners (US$10 to US$12) featuring fresh-caught trout. A 4WD is indispensable for navigating the treacherously steep 1km driveway.

Poás Lodge — B&B $$

(☑2482-1091; www.poaslodge.com; d incl breakfast US$85-95; ℗🛜) Expat brothers Stephan and Jimmie have amped up the cozy, welcoming vibe at this roadside hotel perched high on Poás's slopes 4km south of the park entrance. The upstairs restaurant's wraparound windows offer gorgeous sunset perspectives, while a roaring fireplace invites convivial pre- and post-dinner conversation. Downstairs, four comfortable, contemporary rooms have satellite TV, wi-fi and stunning views. Children under 7 are not allowed.

★ Peace Lodge — LODGE $$$

(☑2482-2720; www.waterfallgardens.com; d standard/deluxe/villa US$410/485/675, additional adult/child US$40/20; ℗🛜🏊) Guests feel they've stepped into a fairy tale at this over-the-top lodge, with its exquisite villas boasting majestic valley views, private decks with Jacuzzis, fireplaces and huge bathrooms with waterfall showers. There's an animal-rescue center, hiking trails, five giant waterfalls and a trout pond where you can fish for your own lunch. This highly imaginative setting, with its multiple pools and interactive animal experiences (toucan and hummingbird feeding), will have kids over the moon. Worth the splurge.

Poás Volcano Lodge — LODGE $$$

(☑2482-2194; www.poasvolcanolodge.com; Vara Blanca; incl breakfast junior ste US$184, master ste US$220-333; ℗@🛜) For contemporary class in an idyllic rural setting, visit this high-altitude dairy farm, whose 11 suites combine rusticity and elegance; the best have balcony and private garden and/or fireplace. Spacious common areas include a game room and a library. More than 3km of hiking trails offer quetzal sightings and views of the volcano (and even Nicaragua!) on clear days.

🍴 Eating

The road up to the park is lined with stands selling fruit (especially local strawberries), cheese and snacks – as well as countless touristy spots serving typical Tico fare – so you won't go hungry. Bring your own bottled water, though, as the tap water is undrinkable.

Freddo Fresas — BREAKFAST $

(☑2482-2800; breakfast US$3-7, lunch US$6-10; ☺7am-4pm) This homey brunch spot looks like it was built from oversize Lincoln logs. It's known for heavenly strawberry smoothies (milky ones beat watery ones) and large, piping hot breakfasts that fuel some serious volcano hikes. For those returning from Volcan Poás, a wide soup selection warms the soul. Find Freddo's a couple blocks north of the cemetery.

★ Colbert Restaurant — FRENCH $$

(☑2482-2776; www.colbert.co.cr; Vara Blanca; mains US$9-26; ☺noon-8pm Fri-Tue) At this charming restaurant 6km east of Poasito, the toque-clad, mustachioed French chef Joël Suire looks like he's straight out of central casting. Naturally, the menu is loaded with traditional French items such as onion soup, house-made pâté and rabbit with beer sauce. A good wine list (bottles from US$17) is strong on vintages from South America and France.

❶ Information

Near the park entrance there's a visitors center with a souvenir shop, a cafe, a small museum and informative videos that play hourly between 9am and 3pm.

❶ Getting There & Away

Numerous local companies offer daily tours to the volcano (US$40 to US$100). However, it's much cheaper and nearly as easy to visit the volcano on the daily Coopetransasi bus from Alajuela. The downside to both of these options is that they typically reach the summit at around 10am – right when the clouds start rolling in.

To beat the clouds and crowds, your best bet is to hire a car (per day from US$40) or a taxi (around US$30 from Alajuela, US$50 from San José) and arrive up top near the park's 8am opening time. If you're driving, the road from Alajuela to the volcano is well signed.

Coopetransasi (☑ 2449-5141) runs a daily bus to the summit (round trip US$4.60, 1½ hours each way), leaving Alajuela at 9am and returning from the mountaintop at 2:30pm. If you're coming from San José, catch a local Tuasa bus (US$1.10, 45 minutes) no later than 8:15am from Tuasa's terminal on Av 2 between Calles 12 and 14, then upon arrival in Alajuela walk one block south to the Volcán Poás bus stop.

Atenas

This small village, on the historic *camino de carretas* (oxcart trail) that once carried coffee beans as far as Puntarenas, is best known as having the most pleasant climate in the world, at least according to a 1994 issue of *National Geographic*. It's not too heavy on sights, but springtime is always in the air, and the sizable expat community gives the town a cosmopolitan feel.

⌨ Sleeping & Eating

★**Vista Atenas B&B**   B&B **$$**
(☑ 2446-4272; www.vistaatenas.com; r incl breakfast US$75-85, cabina/casita without breakfast US$75/95; ❄❄) Ⓟ Five minutes west of town (and straight up!), this is a bright and peaceful hillside oasis where the mix of comfy rooms and self-catering cabins is enhanced by spectacular valley views from the swimming-pool terrace. Expat owner Vera has lovingly enhanced

the property with ecofriendly touches. Multilingual manager Jonathan goes out of his way to make guests feel welcome.

Restaurant La
Trocha del Boyero   COSTA RICAN **$$**
(☑ 2446-0533; casados US$9, mains US$9-18; ❍ 11:30am-8:30pm Thu-Tue; ❄) Tico families pour into the pleasant outdoor deck on weekends for the variety of *casados* on offer, fresh trout (in season) and heaping bowls of *chifrijo* (rice and beans with fried pork, corn chips and fresh tomato salsa). It's located on the main road to Alajuela, 300m east of the gas station, and 100m to the south. Look for a sign at the turnoff.

❶ Getting There & Away

Hourly buses run to Atenas from Alajuela (US$1.40, 45 minutes) and San José (US$1.95, 1¼ hours) throughout the day. The area is quite spread out, however, and best navigated by car.

Grecia

The village of Grecia – once named the 'Cleanest Little Town in Latin America' – is centered on pleasant **Parque Central** (Central Plaza), anchored by one of the most charming churches in Costa Rica.

◉ Sights

Catedral de la Mercedes   CHURCH
At the heart of town you'll find the incredibly quaint Catedral de la Mercedes, a red metal structure that was prefabricated in Belgium and shipped to Costa Rica in 1897 – and resembles a gingerbread church. It has an airy nave, bright Spanish-tile floors and a Gothic-style altar covered in marble.

Las Cataratas de Los Chorros   WATERFALL
(☑ 7091-2554; admission US$6; ❍ 8am-4pm Tue-Sun) About 7km southeast of Grecia, toward Flores and Tacares, are two gorgeous waterfalls and a swimming hole surrounded by picnic tables. It's a popular spot for weekending couples. Get detailed directions before setting out.

⌨ Sleeping & Eating

A **Palí supermarket** (☑ 2444-6696; ❍ 8am-8:30pm Mon-Sat, to 6pm Sun) sits to the southeast of the church. Cheap eats can be found at the lunch counters and shops in the bus station, and a farmers market takes place north of town on Friday afternoon and Saturday morning.

CENTRAL VALLEY & HIGHLANDS ATENAS

Mangífera Hostel   HOSTEL **$**

(✆ 2494-6065; www.mangiferahostel.com; dm/s/d US$10/34/38, s without bathroom US$20; P 🛜) This cozy hostel on the north side of Parque Central feels instantly welcoming, with its wood floors and friendly ambience. It has eight rooms, three of which are dorms. There's a shared kitchen and small garden in the back. Laundry service is available.

ⓘ Getting There & Away

Buses for San José and Sarchí stop at the TUAN bus terminal, 150m north of Grecia's central plaza.

San José US$3.15, one hour, departs at least half-hourly from 5am to 8:30pm.

Sarchí, connecting to Naranjo US$1, 20 minutes, departs half-hourly from 5:50am to 10:15pm.

Sarchí

Welcome to Costa Rica's most famous crafts center, where artisans produce the ornately painted oxcarts and leather-and-wood furnishings for which the Central Valley is known. You'll know you've arrived because just about everything is covered in the signature geometric designs – even city hall. Yes, it's a tourist trap, but it's a pretty one. The town is stretched out along a road that weaves through hilly countryside.

Most people come in for an afternoon of shopping and call it a day, but if you have time on your hands, it is possible to meet different artisans and custom order a creation.

In Sarchí Norte, you'll find the heart of the village, including a twin-towered church, some restaurants and *pulperías* (corner stores), and what is purported to be the world's largest oxcart (photo op!).

⊙ Sights

Jardín Botánico Else Kientzler   GARDENS

(✆ 2454-2070; www.elsegarden.com; Sarchí Norte; adult/child US$6/5; ⊗8am-4pm; 🛝) This well-tended botanical garden 1.4km north of Sarchí Norte's soccer field has 2km of trails winding through more than 2000 types of clearly labeled plants, including succulents, fruit trees, palms, heliconias and orchids. There's also a picnic area and an excellent playground, outfitted with sturdy multilevel climbing structures and three zip lines.

🛏 Sleeping & Eating

A great farmers market is held on Friday behind Fábrica de Carretas Eloy Alfaro, where you can grab homemade snacks, *queso palmito* (a local cheese) and lots of produce.

Hotel Paraíso Río Verde   BUNGALOW **$$**

(✆ 2454-3003; www.hotelparaisorioverde.com; San Pedro de Sarchí; r US$45, bungalow from US$60; P 🛜🏊) A worthwhile 3.4km detour northeast of Sarchí, this spot in the highland village of San Pedro enjoys nice panoramic vistas of coffee plantations and volcanoes Poás, Barva and Irazú. Two inexpensive doubles (including one with prime morning perspectives on the valley) are complemented

---

SHOPPING SARCHÍ

Most travelers come to Sarchí for one thing only: *carretas*, the elaborate, colorfully painted oxcarts that are the unofficial souvenir of Costa Rica – and official symbol of the Costa Rican worker. In Sarchí, these come ready for the road (oxen sold separately) or in scaled-down versions. But the area produces plenty of other curios as well: leatherand-wood furniture (including those incredible rocking chairs that collapse for shipping), wooden tableware and trinkets emblazoned with the colorful mandala design popularized by *carretas*.

There are more than 200 vendors, and prices and quality vary, so it pays to shop around. Workshops are usually open from 8am to 5pm daily; they accept credit cards and US dollars, and can arrange international shipping for you. These are two of the most respected and popular spots:

Fábrica de Carretas Eloy Alfaro (✆ 2454-4131; Sarchí Norte; ⊗8am-5pm) Just west of the town center (100m north of the Palí supermarket); produced the massive oxcart in Sarchí's main plaza.

Fábrica de Carretas Joaquín Chaverri (✆ 2454-4411; Sarchí Sur; ⊗8am-5pm) Sarchí's oldest and best-known factory, 1.5km southeast of the plaza; watch artisans doing their meticulous work in the small studio in the back.

by a pair of spacious four-person bungalows with kitchenette. Optional breakfast costs US$8 per person.

❶ Getting There & Away

If you're driving from San José, from the Interamericana take the signed exit to Grecia and from there follow the road north to Sarchí. If you're coming from the west, take the turnoff north to Naranjo, then head east to Sarchí.

Buses arrive and depart from Sarchí Norte.

Alajuela US$1.65, 1¼ hours, departs half-hourly from 6am to 10pm.

Grecia US$1, 20 minutes, departs half-hourly from 5am to 8:30pm.

San José US$2.25, 1½ hours, three direct buses daily; otherwise make connections in Grecia.

Zarcero

North of Naranjo, the road winds for 20km until it reaches Zarcero's 1736m perch at the western end of the Cordillera Central. This is a gorgeous location: the mountains look as if they've been lifted from landscape paintings and the climate is famously fresh. But the real reason you're here is to see the country's most surreal shrubbery.

Parque Francisco Alvarado, in front of the blue Iglesia de San Rafael (built 1895), was just a normal plaza until the 1960s, when a gardener named Evangelisto Blanco suddenly became inspired to shave the ordinary, mild-mannered topiary into a bizarre series of drippy, abstract shapes. Over the years, these have morphed into fanciful chimeras, blobby dancing creatures and a double tunnel of melting arches. In other words, bring your camera.

🛏️ Sleeping & Eating

A couple of blocks up from the church is **Hotel Zarcero** (☑2463-4141; s/d/tr/q US$24/30/40/50), the only accommodation in town. There are 15 basic rooms with locally made furnishings. Stay here if you must, but for a real treat, check out the dreamy horse farm Rancho Amalia just 10 minutes south of town.

★**Rancho Amalia**   FARMSTAY **$$**
(☑2463-2401; www.ranchoamalia.com/en; cabin US$90) Attention horse people: this family-owned, mountaintop ranch just 10 minutes south of Zarcero is your dream. The premises includes four charming and well-

constructed cabins with fireplaces and full kitchens, a dining hall and elegant stables. The property's 10 horses carry guests across the hillside, through forests and over scenic pastureland surrounded by wild flowers and views of the Central Valley.

Note that the *rancho* is only open from December to May, although groups may rent it out year-round.

Hereford Steak House   STEAK **$$**
(☑2463-4309; meals US$7-33; ⊙11am-midnight Sun-Thu, to 2am Fri & Sat) When in cowboy country, hit the steak house. With plenty of steer horns and tack lining the walls, this longtime favorite grills up New York strips, filet mignon and plenty of other mouth-watering cuts. For the less carnivorous, there are sandwiches, pastas and pizzas. Open-mike nights are a hoot here on the weekends.

❶ Getting There & Away

Transportes Zarcero (☑2451-4080) runs daily direct buses to San José (US$2.25, two hours) at 9:15am, 12:15pm, 4:15pm, 5:15pm and 6:15pm. Hourly buses traveling between San José and Ciudad Quesada also stop in Zarcero, but may be full, particularly on weekends. There are also buses to/from Alajuela, San Ramón and Grecia. All buses stop along the main street below the square.

Bajos del Toro

A gorgeous road snakes northeast out of Zarcero, climbing steeply through hillsides dotted with family dairy farms, then plunging abruptly into the stunning valley of the Río Toro, surrounded by the lower reaches

ALFREDO MAIQUEZ / GETTY IMAGES ©

1. Parque Nacional Volcán Irazú (p127)
The dramatic principal crater of Volcán Irazú is 1050m in diameter and 300m deep.

2. Parque Nacional Juan Castro Blanco (p118)
Take in stunning waterfalls at this national park, home to the headwaters of five major rivers.

3. Volcán Poás (p111)
Although it last erupted in 1953, the volcano's main crater is still active.

4. Ruins of Ujarrás (p131)
Wander among the crumbling walls of Iglesia de Nuestra Señora de la Limpia Concepción, dating back to 1693.

PARQUE NACIONAL JUAN CASTRO BLANCO

This 143-sq-km **national park** (admission by donation) was created to protect the slopes of Volcán Platanar (2183m) and Volcán Porvenir (2267m) from logging and mining. The headwaters for five major rivers originate here, making this one of the most important watersheds in the country.

While federally protected, much of the park is still privately owned by plantation families – only those parts that have already been purchased by the government are technically open to travelers.

From the **visitors center** (☑ 8815-7094; apanajuca@gmail.com) a 1.5km trail climbs through pastureland, then descends to **Pozo Verde**, a green lake surrounded by mountains. A rougher trail continues 3.5km to **Las Minas**, an abandoned mine site.

The park is popular among anglers as the five rivers are brimming with trout. The limited infrastructure and tourist traffic means your chances of spotting rare wildlife (quetzals, black guans, curassow) are higher than average. Guides can be arranged through tour agencies and hotels in the area.

Sleeping & Eating

Albergue Ecológico Pozo Verde (☑ 8872-9808; d incl breakfast US$50-70; ☎) A kilometer before the park entrance, these charming accommodations include six spotless cabins, some with fireplaces and front porches. The owners are friendly locals with a penchant for golden retrievers (they've got four), who also know a great deal about the park. Hours here are irregular; call ahead to make sure the place is open.

Restaurante El Congo (☑ 8872-9808; mains US$11; ☉ 9am-5pm Sat & Sun; ☎) With its own trout ponds, this log-cabin restaurant serves up the freshest of catches, along with delicious blackberry juice. Call ahead to be sure it's open.

Getting There & Away

The park entrance is located at the end of a rough 10km road from El Sucre, 20km north of Zarcero. The road is passable for 2WD vehicles until the final descent; if you don't have a 4WD, park on the hilltop 300m before the visitors center.

---

of the area's cloud-forest ecosystem. If you were looking for a little piece of Costa Rica where everybody knows everybody, then look no further. This 275-person town (full name: Bajos del Toro Amarillo) is rural idyll at its finest. There are no banks and only one tiny internet cafe. Bring all the cash you need.

🛏 Sleeping & Eating

There are only three hotels in the area, and they are very popular. Be sure to show up with a reservation.

Catarata del Toro   CABINA **$$**
(☑ 8399-7476, 2476-0800; www.catarata-del-toro.com; r US$55-65) At this roadside spot 6km north of Bajos del Toro, three rustic wood-paneled rooms are tucked under A-frame-style eaves. However, the real attraction is the adjacent waterfall, a 90m-tall beauty that cascades dramatically into an ancient volcanic crater, reached by a steep but well-maintained trail (admission US$10). There's also a restaurant where hummingbirds flock to feed alongside the humans.

★ **Bosque de Paz Rain/Cloud Forest Lodge & Biological Reserve**   LODGE **$$$**
(☑ 2234-6676; www.bosquedepaz.com; incl 3 meals s US$163-225, d US$246-346; ⓟ ☎) 🅿 A birdwatcher's paradise, this 10-sq-km reserve straddles an important wilderness corridor between Parque Nacional Volcán Poás and Parque Nacional Juan Castro Blanco, with more than 22km of trails in old-growth forest and an orchid garden. The dozen spacious, terracotta-tiled rooms, within earshot of a rushing river, feature large windows with forest views. Vegan diets can be accommodated. Advance reservations recommended.

El Silencio   LODGE **$$$**
(☑ 2476-0303, reservations 2231-6122; www.elsilenciolodge.com; ste/villa incl breakfast & guided hike US$406/777; ⓟ ☉ ☎) 🅿 Secluded outside of town, this upscale lodge comprises

16 luxuriously designed *cabina* suites with private deck, rocking chairs, Jacuzzi and fine mountain views, plus two six-person villas with gas fireplaces and full kitchens. Additional amenities include a spa, 8km worth of trails (leading to stunning waterfalls) and a health-conscious restaurant whose meals (US$30 to US$40) feature organic produce grown on site.

❶ Getting There & Away

Driving north from the Interamericana through Zarcero, take a right immediately after the church and continue northeast about 15km. Alternatively, take the road due north from Sarchí's central plaza. Both roads are almost entirely paved but involve steep climbs and hairpin turns; a 4WD is helpful but not obligatory. There are a couple of daily buses from Sarchí (US$2, one hour).

San Ramón

The colonial town of San Ramón is no wallflower in the pageant of Costa Rican history. The 'City of Presidents and Poets' has sent five men to the country's highest office, including ex-president Rodrigo Carazo, who built a tourist lodge a few kilometers to the north.

Another of Costa Rica's beloved presidents, José Figueres Ferrer, is paid respect in an edifying culture and history culture center just north of the city's central park.

◉ Sights

José Figueres Ferrer Center for Culture & History ARTS CENTER

(☎2447-2178; http://centrojosefigueres.org; ⊙10am-6pm Tue-Sat) FREE This museum and cultural center celebrates all things José Figueres, the three-time Costa Rican president best known for abolishing the country's army in 1948. The museum has historical exhibits and artistic representations of Figueres on display, and also contains art and music classrooms and performance spaces.

🛏 Sleeping

The options in town are decent, and surrounding hills contain some truly inspiring and unique stays, particularly Tierras Enamoradas and Villa Blanca Cloud Forest Hotel & Nature Reserve.

Hotel La Posada INN $$

(☎2445-7359; www.posadahotel.net; s/d US$45/60, incl breakfast US$50/70; P❄@⊛) Well-maintained rooms surround a lush, plant-filled courtyard at this pleasant inn, 400m north of the church. Rooms are somewhat baroque-looking, outfitted with massive, handcrafted beds that lie somewhere on the design continuum between Louis XIV and African safari. All have mini-fridge and cable TV; more expensive units come with Jacuzzis. Some are wheelchair-accessible, and a few have air-conditioning.

Casa Amanecer B&B $$

(☎2445-2100; www.casa-amanecer-cr.com; s/d incl breakfast US$75/85; P⊛) A 10-minute drive northeast of San Ramón, this sleekly designed B&B, owned by former Habitat for Humanity volunteers, offers five graceful contemporary rooms with polished-concrete floors and orthopedic beds. Tasty veggie breakfasts are served on the breezy shared terrace. Additional meals and airport transfers (US$75 for up to four people) can be arranged with advance reservation.

★Villa Blanca Cloud Forest Hotel & Nature Reserve LODGE $$$

(☎2461-0300, in USA & Canada 1-877-256-8399; www.villablanca-costarica.com; d superior/deluxe/honeymoon US$205/230/255, additional person US$50, child under 6yr free; P@⊛) 🐾 Occupying a cloud-forest aerie, this private reserve, 18km north of San Ramón, is centered on a lodge and dairy ranch once owned by ex-president Rodrigo Carazo. Its 35 free-standing *casitas* (little houses) come with wi-fi, private terraces and minibar but deliberately eschew TVs. Additional facilities include a restaurant, a spa, a yoga center and a movie theater screening films nightly.

The surrounding 800 hectares of primary and secondary cloud forest offer excellent wildlife-spotting opportunities. Bilingual naturalist guides are available for morning and evening cloud-forest walks (US$26), and bird-watching (US$26) and quetzal-spotting (US$72) tours. Certified at the highest level of sustainability, the lodge practices composting, recycling and energy-efficient practices. For kids, there's an arcade and game room, and child-care services are available for a fee.

The turnoff is well signposted from the Interamericana. A taxi from San Ramón costs about US$25.

Tierras Enamoradas LODGE $$$

(Lands in Love; ☎2447-9331, in USA 1-408-215-1000; www.landsinlove.com; Hwy 702; d incl breakfast US$132, additional person US$27;

WORTH A TRIP

FIESTAS DE PALMARES

If you're around in mid-January, be sure to detour through Palmares for the rowdy annual **Fiestas de Palmares** (www.fiestaspalmares.com). The 13-day, beer-soaked extravaganza features carnival rides, a *tope* (horse parade), fireworks, big-name bands, small-name bands, exotic dancers, fried food, *guaro* (local firewater made with sugarcane) tents and the densest population of merry Ticos you've ever seen. It is one of the biggest events in the country – crowds can reach upwards of 10,000. For the rest of the year, Palmares is a tumbleweed town, where life is centered on the ornate stained-glass church in the attractive, palm-fringed main plaza.

P 🛜 🌊 🐾) 🅿 Midway between San Ramón and La Fortuna, this well-signposted vegetarian lodge has eclectic rooms with bright floral motifs, a lounge, an outdoor swimming pool and Jacuzzi, a pet hotel (US$40 per night) and a plethora of adventure activities, from a canopy tour to canyoning to horseback riding. The restaurant serves an international mix of delicious vegetarian and vegan dishes.

🍴 Eating

A decent number of expats call San Ramón home, which has paved the way for plenty of international restaurants. You'll also find the requisite *sodas*, steak houses and health-food outposts.

Mi Choza   COSTA RICAN **$$**
(☑2445-1286; Calle 7 & Av 10; mains US$8-20; ⊙11am-11pm) On the southeastern end of town, this lively *cantina* is decked out in mounted steer horns, soccer jerseys and flat-screen TVs. Even better, the steak cuts are large and the service is friendly.

El Rincón Poeta   COSTA RICAN **$$**
(☑2447-3942; Calle 1; mains US$7-18; ⊙11am-10pm) Hidden away off the main street and decorated with historical black-and-white photos of San Ramón, this locally popular spot serves up big platters of *típico* meat, seafood and rice dishes in a dining room filled with sturdy tree-trunk tables or on the

pleasant vine-shaded gravel patio up front. It's 150m southeast of the church.

ℹ️ Information

Banco de Costa Rica (⊙9am-4pm Mon-Fri) Has an ATM; 300m west of Parque Central.
Banco Nacional (⊙8:30am-5pm Mon-Fri) Has an ATM that also dispenses US dollars; 100m south of the southwest corner of the church.

ℹ️ Getting There & Away

San Ramón is served by hourly buses (US$2.60, 1¼ hours) from San José's Empresarios Unidos terminal (p98). Frequent buses also head north to Ciudad Quesada via Zarcero. Bus stops are just northwest of Parque Central.

HEREDIA AREA

Until recently, microchips produced in Heredia were one of Costa Rica's most important exports. Although Intel has closed its plant here, the region remains a vital coffee producer and a gateway to one of Costa Rica's largest swaths of highland forest, Parque Nacional Braulio Carrillo.

Heredia

During the 19th century, La Ciudad de las Flores (the City of the Flowers) was home to a *cafetalero* (coffee grower) aristocracy that made its fortune exporting Costa Rica's premium blend. Today the historic center retains some of this well-bred air, with a leafy main square, and low-lying buildings reflecting Spanish-colonial architectural style.

Although only 11km from San José, Heredia is – in personality – removed from the grit and grime of the capital. Universidad Nacional (National University) keeps things a touch bohemian, and on any afternoon you're bound to find local bars and cafes abuzz with young folk idling away their time.

Heredia is also the most convenient base from which to explore the little-visited Volcán Barva, within the Parque Nacional Braulio Carrillo.

⦿ Sights

El Fortín   TOWER
This tower, constructed in 1876 by order of Heredia's provincial governor, is the official

symbol of Heredia. It was declared a national historic monument in 1974, but because of its fragile state, it remains closed to the public.

Casa de la Cultura
MUSEUM

(📞 2261-4485; cnr Calle Central & Av Central; ⊙8am-5pm Mon-Fri) **FREE** Occupying a privileged position on the corner of the plaza just above the church, this low-lying Spanish structure dates back to the late 18th century. It served at one point as the residence of President Alfredo González Flores, who governed from 1913 to 1917. It is beautifully maintained and now houses permanent historical displays as well as rotating art exhibits.

INBioparque
GARDENS

(📞 2507-8107; www.inbioparque.com/en; Santo Domingo; adult/student/child US$25/19/15, serpentarium admission adult/child US$3/2; ⊙9am-3pm Fri, 9am-4pm Sat & Sun; 🚹) 🌿 At this excellent, wheelchair-accessible botanical garden, run by the nonprofit National Biodiversity Institute (INBio), visitors can admire the country's native plants and animals in miniature habitats. Other attractions include farm animals, a butterfly garden, a serpentarium and a model sustainable home. Children's theater and multimedia shows run throughout the day. It's 4km south of Heredia. See the website for directions.

Guided walking tours take place Friday through Sunday at 9am, 11am and 2pm. Reservations recommended.

Heredia

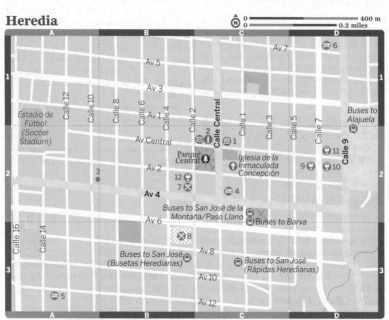

Heredia

◎ Sights
1 Casa de la Cultura................................C2
2 El Fortín..C2

✦ Activities, Courses & Tours
3 Intercultura...A2

🛏 Sleeping
4 Hotel América.....................................C2
5 Hotel Las Flores..................................A3
6 Hotel Valladolid..................................D1

✕ Eating
7 Espigas..B2
8 Mercado Municipal...............................B3

🍷 Drinking & Nightlife
9 El Bulevar Relax..................................D2
10 El Rancho de Fofo..............................D2
11 La Choza...D2
12 Miraflores Discotheque.....................B2

📚 Courses

Centro Panamericano
de Idiomas
LANGUAGE COURSE

(CPI; ☑2265-6306, in USA 1-877-373-3116; www.cpi-edu.com; 20 hrs of classes and homestay incl breakfast & dinner US$660) Based in San Joaquín de Flores, just outside of Heredia, this popular school also has a teen camp. There's a maximum of four students per class.

Intercultura
LANGUAGE COURSE

(☑2260-8480, in USA & Canada 866-978-6668; www.interculturacostarica.com; weekly rates with/without homestay from US$420/275) This school in Heredia also arranges volunteer opportunities and offers cooking and dance classes.

🛏 Sleeping

Hotel Las Flores
HOTEL $

(☑2261-8147; www.hotel-lasflores.com; Av 12 btwn Calles 12 & 14; s/d/tr US$17/32/44; P 🖥) A bit of a walk from the action, this spotless family-run place has 29 basic, brightly painted rooms with hot-water shower and TV. The attached *soda* serves breakfast and lunch.

Hotel Valladolid
HOTEL $$

(☑2260-2912, 2260-2905; www.hotelvalladolid.net; cnr Calle 7 & Av 7; s/d incl breakfast US$75/87; P ✴ @ 🖥) This business hotel on a quiet street has 12 bright, clean and business-like tiled rooms with microwave, mini-fridge, cable TV and private bathroom with hot water. Credit cards accepted.

Hotel América
HOTEL $$

(☑2260-9292; www.hotelamericacr.com; Calle Central btwn Avs 2 & 4; s/d/tr incl breakfast US$45/55/75; @ 🖥) Of the four hotels in this local chain, this is the best deal. It is centrally located just south of the church, and though unspectacular in design, it's clean and comfortable. Tile-floor rooms come equipped with solar hot water, cable TV, safe and fan.

Hotel Chalet Tirol
INN $$$

(☑2267-6222; www.hotelchaleteltirol.com; r US$110; P 🖥 ✷) Northeast of Heredia (3km north of Castillo Country Club), this charming hotel channels the gingerbread quaintness of the Alps. (It once served as a backdrop for a German beer advert.) The 15 suites and 20 chalets have cable TV, room service and a gorgeous mountain setting; some also have Jacuzzis, fireplaces or wheelchair-accessible facilities. The in-house restaurant hosts live music on weekends.

Although pets are allowed, a non-refundable deposit of US$100 is required.

Hotel Bougainvillea
HOTEL $$$

(☑2244-1414; www.hb.co.cr; Santo Domingo; d incl breakfast US$143-173; P 🖨 @ 🖥 ✖) 🖉 Set on

---

BUSES FROM HEREDIA

There is no central bus terminal; buses leave from stops scattered between the university and the Mercado Central.

The **San José–bound Rápidas Heredianas bus** (Av 8 btwn Calles Central & 1) is the best option if you're transferring to a Caribbean-bound bus, as it drops you near San José's Terminal Caribeña. The other bus to San José can be found two blocks **west** (Av 8 btwn Calle 2 & 4). **Buses to Barva** (Calle 1 btwn Avs 4 & 6), as well as **buses to San José de la Montana/Paso Llano** (Calle 1 btwn Avs 4 & 6), can be found due north of the San José Rápidas Heredianas buses near the main drag, Av 4. **Buses to Alajuela** (cnr Av 1 & Calle 9) are on the northeast side of town.

DESTINATION	COMPANY	COST (US$)	DURATION (MIN)	FREQUENCY
Alajuela	Tuasa	1	45	every 15min 5am-11pm
Barva	Transportes Barveños LTDA	0.40	10	every 15min 4:45am-10:45pm
San José	Busetas Heredianas	0.78	20	every 5min 5am-11pm
San José	Rápidas Heredianas	0.90	20	at least every 15min 4:40am-11pm
San José de la Montaña/Paso Llano for Volcán Barva	Transportes del Norte	1.40	60	5:25am & 6:25am Mon-Fri; 6:40am Sat; 6:45am Sun

four hectares about 6km outside of town, this efficient hotel is surrounded by an expansive, well-manicured garden dotted with old-growth trees, stunning flowers and plenty of statuary. The 81 crisp, whitewashed rooms have balconies with views of mountains or city, and several private trails wind by the swimming pool and tennis courts, through forest and orchards. Credit cards accepted.

It's located in a safe, quiet neighborhood and offers child care for a surcharge. Cribs are complimentary.

Eating

Mercado Municipal   MARKET $

(Calle 2 btwn Avs 6 & 8; ⊘6am-6pm) You can fill up for a couple of thousand colones at the Mercado Municipal, which has *sodas* to spare and plenty of very fresh groceries.

Espigas   COSTA RICAN $

(☑2237-3275; cnr Av 2 & Calle 2; meals US$8; ⊘7am-9pm) One of the only eateries open on Sunday, Espigas is the go-to cafe for traditional *casados* and breakfasts, with views of the main plaza diagonally across the street. Order sit-down meals at the counter, stop by the front window to pick up fresh *batidos* (fruit shakes) or pop in for a look at the tantalizing pastry case.

Drinking & Nightlife

With a thriving student body, there's no shortage of live music and cultural events. Stay aware: downtown Heredia can get a bit dodgy at nighttime.

The university district is hopping most nights of the week. La Choza (Av Central btwn Calles 7 & 9; ⊘11am-late), El Bulevar Relax (cnr Calle 7 & Av Central; ⊘11am-1am) and El Rancho de Fofo (www.ranchofofo.com; Av Central btwn Calles 7 & 9; ⊘11am-1:30am) are three long-running watering holes clustered together one block west of the university. At the Miraflores Discotheque (cnr Av 2 & Calle 2; ⊘8pm-6am Thu-Sun) locals groove to a mix of international beats.

ℹ️ Information

BCR (☑2284-6600; cnr Av 6 & Calle 1; ⊘9am-4pm Mon-Fri) The ATM gives both dollars and colones and is open from 5am to 10pm.

Hospital San Vicente de Paul (☑2562-8100; Calle 12) Modern hospital south of Av 14.

Barva

Surrounded by picturesque mountains only 2.5km north of Heredia is the historic town of Barva, a settlement dating back to 1561 that's been declared a national monument. The town center is dotted with low-lying 19th-century buildings and is centered on the towering Iglesia San Bartolomé, constructed in 1893. The surrounding area was once popular with the Costa Rican elite: Cleto González Víquez (1858–1937), twice president of Costa Rica (he built the original National Library), was born and raised here. It's a perfect spot for a lazy afternoon stroll.

This little town is all about coffee. Costa Rica's most famous coffee roaster Café Britt offers a bilingual tour here, as does the renowned Finca Rosa Blanca (p124).

◎ Sights & Activities

Museo de Cultura Popular   MUSEUM

(☑2260-1619; Santa Lucía; ⊘10am-5pm Sun) **FREE** Housed in a restored 19th-century farmhouse 1.5km southeast of Barva and 3km north of Heredia, this tiny museum surrounded by well-labeled gardens is run by the Universidad Nacional. Visitors can tour rooms full of antique furniture, textiles, ceramics and other period pieces. On Sunday the on-site restaurant La Fonda serves *casados* (US$8) on its pleasant open-air terrace.

The museum is also open by reservation only for groups of 10 or more people between Monday and Friday from 8am to 4pm. Admission on these days is US$10 per person.

Café Britt Finca   TOUR

(☑2277-1600; www.coffeetour.com; with/without lunch adult US$37/22, student US$30/17; ⊘tours 11am year-round, plus 3pm seasonally) Costa Rica's most famous coffee roaster offers a 90-minute bilingual tour of its plantation that includes coffee tasting and a comedic stage play about the history of coffee (kids will likely dig it). More in-depth tours are available, as are packages including transport from San José; reserve ahead. Drivers won't be able to miss the *many* signs between Heredia and Barva.

✨ Festivals & Events

Feria de la Mascarada   CULTURAL

Several times a year, the city hosts the Feria de la Mascarada, a tradition with roots in the colonial era, in which people don massive colorful masks (some weighing 20kg), and gather to dance and parade around the town square. Demons and devils are frequent subjects, but celebrities and politicians also feature (you haven't lived until you've seen a 6m-tall Celia Cruz).

It's sometimes held during the last week of March, but dates vary from one year to the next; inquire locally.

🛏 Sleeping

★ **Finca Rosa Blanca**   INN $$$
(📞2269-9392, in USA 305-395-3042; www.finca rosablanca.com; Santa Bárbara; d incl breakfast US$345-569; 🅿@🛜🐾) 🍴 Set amid a stunning hillside coffee plantation 6km northwest of Barva, this honeymoon-ready, Gaudí-esque confection of suites and villas is cloaked in fruit trees that shade private trails. The 14 sparkling-white adobe rooms with wood-beamed ceilings and private balconies are lavishly appointed; one tops a tower with 360-degree views, reached by a winding staircase made from a tree trunk.

Shower in an artificial waterfall, take a moonlit dip in the pool, have an organic citrus-coffee bath soak at the spa – or, better yet, dip into a very romantic dinner at the hotel's recommended restaurant, which serves Costa Rican fusion dishes such as queen sea bass encrusted in homemade chorizo. Credit cards accepted.

At 9am and 1pm, Finca Rosa Blanca offers a 2½-hour tour of its picturesque, 12-hectare organic coffee plantation, processing plant and roasting house. Guests hike the fields, learn the process and taste the delicious results.

ⓘ Getting There & Away

Buses travel about every 15 minutes between Heredia and Barva (US$0.40, 10 minutes), picking up and dropping off in front of Barva's church.

San Isidro de Heredia

This scenic, agrarian town to the northeast of San José offers all the lush greenery of the neighboring Parque Nacional Braulio Carillo, along with undulating drives over the countryside and a couple of the Central Valley's most enjoyable tours.

Light afternoon showers nearly every day make San Isidro de Heredia the rainbow capital of Costa Rica, and a fantastic place to grow (and eat) just about anything.

◉ Sights & Activities

Toucan Rescue Ranch   BIRD SANCTUARY
(📞2268-4041; http://toucanrescueranch.org; donation requested adult/6-10yr US$30/15, under 6 free; ⊙8am, 9am and 2pm tours by appointment only) A decade ago, expat Leslie Howle and her husband Jorge Murillo started taking in sick and injured toucans. The couple found it hard to turn any animal away, though, and eventually ended up with owls, sloths, monkeys, an otter, an oncilla, an anteater and more. Guests tour the picturesque grounds in the hills of San Isidro de Heredia.

The owners prefer that their location not be listed because it could endanger some of the (rather valuable) exotic animals. Call for directions or to inquire about volunteer opportunities.

★ **Sibu Chocolate**   TOUR, FOOD
(📞2268-1335; http://sibuchocolate.com; per person US$27; ⊙ tours at 10am Tue-Sat, restaurant open 11am-6pm Tue-Sat) 🍴 This divine chocolate tour educates guests on the culture and history surrounding Costa Rica's most decadent export. The clever tour guides will bring cacao's story to life as guests sample pre-Columbian-inspired hot chocolate and other intriguing treats. Lunch is available

---

COOL SPOTS FOR TOTS IN THE CENTRAL VALLEY

Family-friendly attractions abound in the Central Valley. Here are a few spots guaranteed to please kids and adults alike.

Parque Francisco Alvarado, Zarcero (p115) Kids will love zigzagging through rows of bushes sculpted into stegosauruses and other fantastic shapes in these topiary gardens.

Río Pejibaye (p133) Turrialba outfitters lead rafting trips on this Class I–II river that's plenty scenic but not too rough.

Zoo Ave, La Garita (p111) Stroll the grounds alongside peacocks and giant lizards, visit with monkeys or take the canopy tour at this zoo and animal-rescue center.

Parque Nacional Tapantí-Macizo Cerro de la Muerte (p130) Easy hiking trails lead down to sandy beaches where kids can splash in a boulder-strewn river.

on the outdoor terrace surrounded by lush gardens. Foodies and history buffs will really appreciate Sibu.

This storybook restaurant and chocolate operation is located just 20 minutes north of downtown San José, around 1.5km off the highway to Guápiles.

🛏 Sleeping & Eating

Options are limited. Try the Toucan Rescue Ranch or settle for a day trip.

Toucan Rescue Ranch   B&B $$$
(☑ 2268-4041; http://toucanrescueranch.org; d US$150, extra person US$25; ☑ ☎) This animal-rescue center also provides the best lodgings in town, with two adorable and well-constructed guesthouses just a short walk from the owls, sloths, toucans and other exotic, recovering creatures. It's an incredibly serene setting, with a backdrop of rainforest and rolling hills, and is conveniently located just 35 minutes from San José's international airport.

★ Bromelias del Río   CAFETERIA $$
(☑ 2268-8445; specialty coffee drinks US$7, mains US$9-20; ⊙ 7am-7pm) Ensconced in a tropical garden by a mountain stream, this bakery/restaurant wins for its spiked coffee drinks (hot mocha with Baileys and chocolate syrup) and decadent sandwiches, some piled high with *lomito* (steak), heart of palm, avocado and gravy. Share a main and save room for a sweet crepe for dessert. It's 50m off Hwy 32 at the Santa Elena exit to San Isidro.

A second Bromelias del Río bakery can be found in the center of town in San Isidro de Heredia. The third and newest outpost is further down Hwy 27, 500m north of the San Miguel exit.

Casa Azul   SPANISH $$
(☑ 2268-6908, 8376-6493; San Josécito, just off Hwy 32; mains US$9-26; ⊙ 5-10pm Wed-Fri, from noon Sat, noon-3pm Sun) Tucked away in a quaint little house adorned in blue curtains and multicolored lights, this Spanish–Costa Rican fusion restaurant is one of the Central Valley's most romantic spots. Popular dishes include paella, trout for two, and mouthwatering medallions of *lomito* that pair well with a bottle of cabernet.

❶ Getting There & Away

Buses for San José (Transportes Arnoldo Ocampo, SA) leave from a stop 100m east of San Isidro de Heredia's central plaza. Buses for Heredia leave from in front of the MegaSuper supermarket, 100m east of the Catholic church.

San José US$0.70, 20 minutes, departs roughly half-hourly from 4:50am to 9:45pm.

Heredia US$0.48, 15 minutes, departs every 20 minutes or less from 4:50am to 10:15pm.

CARTAGO AREA

The riverbank setting of the city of Cartago was handpicked by Spanish governor Juan Vásquez de Coronado, who said that he had 'never seen a more beautiful valley.' Cartago was founded as Costa Rica's first capital in 1563, and Coronado's successors endowed the city with fine colonial architecture. However, the city was destroyed during a 1723 eruption of the Volcán Irazú. Any remaining landmarks were toppled by earthquakes in 1841 and 1910.

Although the city was relegated to backwater status when the seat of government moved to San José in 1823, the surrounding area, particularly the Orosi Valley, flourished during the days of the coffee trade. Today much of the region continues to be devoted to coffee production, among other agricultural products. Although Cartago no longer has the prestige of a national capital, it nonetheless remains a vital commercial hub – not to mention the site of the country's most important religious monument.

Cartago

After the earthquake rubble was cleared, in the early 20th century, nobody bothered to rebuild Cartago to its former quaint specifications. As in other commercial towns, expect plenty of functional concrete structures. One exception is the bright white Basílica de Nuestra Señora de los Ángeles, which is visible from many parts of the city, standing out like a snowcapped mountain above a plain of one-story edifices.

The city is thrown briefly into the spotlight every August, when pilgrims from every corner of the country descend on the basilica to say their most serious prayers. The remainder of the year, Cartago exists mainly as a commercial and residential center, though the beauty of the surrounding mountains helps take the edge off modern life.

CENTRAL VALLEY & HIGHLANDS CARTAGO

◉ Sights

Basílica de Nuestra
Señora de Los Ángeles CHURCH
(Calle 15 btwn Avs 0 & 1) Cartago's most important site, and Costa Rica's most venerated religious shrine, this basilica exudes Byzantine grace, with fine stained-glass windows, hand-painted interiors and ornate side chapels featuring carved-wood altars. First built in 1635, the structure's central relic remains unharmed: La Negrita (the Black Virgin), a small representation of the Virgin Mary, found on this spot on August 2, 1635.

As the story goes, when the woman who discovered the statuette tried to take it with her, it miraculously reappeared back where she'd found it. Twice. So the townspeople built a shrine around her. In 1824, she was declared Costa Rica's patron Virgin. She now resides on a gold, jewel-studded platform at the main altar. Each August 2, on the anniversary of the statuette's miraculous discovery, pilgrims from every corner of the country (and beyond) walk the 22km from San José to the basilica. Many of the penitent complete the last few hundred meters of the pilgrimage on their knees.

Las Ruinas de la Parroquia RUIN
(Iglesia del Convento; Calle 0 btwn Avs 0 & 2) This now-ruined church was built in 1575 as a shrine to St James the Apostle. It was destroyed by the 1841 earthquake, rebuilt a few years later and then destroyed again in the 1910 earthquake. Today only the outer walls remain, and 'the Ruins' are a pleasant spot for people-watching. Legend has it that the ghost of a headless priest wanders here.

> **SPANISH SCHOOLS IN THE CENTRAL VALLEY**
>
> Unless otherwise noted, prices are given for five four-hour days of instruction, with/without a week's homestay. Prices include two meals a day.
>
> ➜ Adventure Education Center (p133)
> ➜ Amerispan Study Abroad (p514)
> ➜ Centro Panamericano de Idiomas (p122)
> ➜ Intensa (p107)
> ➜ Intercultura (p122)
> ➜ Spanish by the River (p133)

🏃 Activities

Finca La Flor de Paraíso VOLUNTEERING
(☑ 2534-8003; www.la-flor.org) Immerse yourself in the Central Valley's rural culture with a stay at Finca La Flor de Paraíso, outside Cartago. This not-for-profit organic farm operated by the Association for the Development of Environmental and Human Consciousness (Asodecah) has a volunteer-work program that will allow you to get your hands dirty on projects related to agriculture, reforestation, animal husbandry and medicinal-herb cultivation.

The cost of the volunteer-work programs, including room and board (in simple wood *cabinas* and dormitories), is US$28 per day. Vacationers can arrange guided visits (per person US$10) or overnight stays (per person with breakfast US$35, with three meals US$50). Family rates are available; advance reservations necessary.

🛏 Sleeping & Eating

For an atmospheric, authentically local eating experience, pull up a seat at one of the *sodas* inside the Mercado Central, or browse the aisles for fresh produce. You'll also find plenty of bakeries and other eateries along Avs 0 and 1 in the heart of town.

Los Ángeles Lodge B&B $$
(☑ 2551-0957, 2591-4169; hotel.los.angeles@hotmail.com; Av 1 btwn Calles 13 & 15; incl breakfast s US$35-40, d US$50-65; ❊ 🛜) With its balconies overlooking the Plaza de la Basílica, this decent B&B stands out with spacious and comfortable rooms, hot showers and breakfast made to order.

ℹ Information

Banco Nacional (cnr Calle 4 & Av 0; ⊙ 8:30am-3:45pm Mon-Fri) Has a 24-hour ATM.
Hospital Max Peralta (☑ 2550-1999; www.hmp.sa.cr; Av 6 btwn Calles 2 & 4) Emergency and medical services.

ℹ Getting There & Away

BUS
Bus stops are scattered around town.
Orosi (Autotransportes Mata Irola) US$0.95, 35 minutes, departs every 20 minutes between 5:30am and 10:25pm, from Calle 3 between Avs 2 and 4.
San José (Lumaca) US$1.10, 55 minutes, departs every 15 minutes between 5am and 11pm, from the terminal on Calle 6 between Avs 3 and 5.

Turrialba (Transtusa) US$1.60, 1½ hours, departs every 30 minutes from 5:45am to 10:40pm weekdays (less frequently on weekends), from Av 4 between Calles 5 and 7.

TRAIN

Train service runs between San José's Estación del Pacífico and Cartago's downtown **station** (Av 3 btwn Calles 4 & 6). The one-hour trip costs US$1.05. Trains run Monday to Friday only, with a schedule weighted toward morning and afternoon commute hours.

Parque Nacional Volcán Irazú

Looming on the horizon 19km (as the crow flies) northeast of Cartago, Irazú, which derives its name from the indigenous word *ara-tzu* (thunder-point), is the largest and highest (3432m) active volcano in Costa Rica. In 1723 the Spanish governor of the area, Diego de la Haya Fernández, watched helplessly as the volcano unleashed its destruction on the city of Cartago (one of the craters is named in his honor). Since the 18th century, 15 major eruptions have been recorded. At the time of research, the volcano was slumbering peacefully, aside from a few hissing fumaroles.

The summit is a bare landscape of volcanic-ash craters. The principal crater is 1050m in diameter and 300m deep; the adjacent Diego de la Haya Crater is 690m in diameter and 80m deep; and the shallowest, Playa Hermosa Crater, is being colonized by sparse vegetation. There is also a pyroclastic cone, consisting of rocks fragmented by volcanic activity.

Hotels in San José and Orosi provide a good base for this day trip.

Activities

Note that cloud cover starts thickening, even under the best conditions, by about 10am, around the same time the bus rolls in. If you're on one of those buses, do yourself a favor and head straight for the craters. If you have a car, make an effort to arrive early and you'll likely be rewarded with the best possible views and an uncrowded observation area. The park is busiest on Sunday and holidays, when a line of cars up to 1km long queues at the entrance.

At the summit it's theoretically possible to see both the Pacific Ocean and the Caribbean Sea, but it is rarely clear enough. The best chance for a clear view is in the very early morning during the dry season (January to April). It tends to be cold and windy up here and there's an annual rainfall of 2160mm – come prepared with warm, rainproof clothes.

From the parking lot, a 200m trail leads to a viewpoint over the main crater. Wooden railings prevent visitors from getting too close to the edge, but you're welcome to leave the paved trail and wander the volcanic sands of the adjacent Playa Hermosa Crater. About 300m above the main parking lot, a rutted 1km side road allows walkers and intrepid drivers to climb to Irazú's summit. While hiking, be on the lookout for high-altitude bird species, such as the volcano junco.

Tours

Tours are arranged by a variety of San José operators and cost US$40 to US$60 for a half-day, and up to US$100 for a full day combined with lunch and visits to sights such as the Lankester Gardens (p128) or the Orosi Valley.

Tours from hotels in Orosi (US$25 to US$40) can also be arranged – these may include lunch and visits to the basilica in Cartago or sights around the Orosi Valley.

Eating

Restaurant 1910 COSTA RICAN **$$**
(☎2536-6063; www.restaurant1910.com; mains US$9-24; ⊙11:30am-9pm Mon-Thu, to 10pm Fri & Sat, to 6:30pm Sun; P 📶) On the road to Irazú, 300m north of the Christ statue marking the Guayabo turnoff, is this homey spot with a glass-walled front deck. It's worth a stop just to see its collection of old photographs documenting the 1910 earthquake that completed the destruction of colonial Cartago. Expect a long list of Tico specialties, and a sumptuous Sunday buffet (adult/child US$24/12).

Information

Ranger Station (☎2200-5025, in Cartago 2551-9398; pnvolcanirazu@accvc.org; park admission US$15, parking US$2.20; ⊙8am-3:30pm) Pay admission and parking fees at the ranger station at the park's entrance, 1.5km before the summit.

Getting There & Away

A daily bus to Irazú (US$9) departs from San José at 8am and arrives at the summit around 10am. The bus departs from Irazú at 12:20pm.

A round-trip taxi from Cartago to the summit will cost about US$45; drivers usually allow you one hour to explore up top.

If you're in a group, renting a car is the best deal, as you can get to the park early, before the skies cloud over and the crowds arrive. Take Hwy 8 from Cartago, which begins at the northeast corner of the plaza and continues 31km to the summit. The road is well signed.

Valle de Orosi

This straight-out-of-a-storybook river valley is famous for mountain vistas, a lake formed by a hydroelectric facility, a truly wild national park and coffee – lots and lots of coffee. A well-paved 32km scenic loop winds through a landscape of rolling hills terraced with coffee plantations and valleys dotted with pastoral villages, all set against the backdrop of two volcanoes, Irazú and Turrialba. If you have a rental car (or a good bicycle), you're in for a treat, though it's still possible to navigate most of the loop via public buses.

The loop road starts 8km southeast of Cartago in Paraíso, heads south to Orosi, then doubles back northeast and west around the artificial Lago de Cachí, passing the historic church at Ujarrás en route back to Paraíso. Alternatively, from Orosi you can branch south into Parque Nacional Tapantí-Macizo Cerro de la Muerte, an end-of-the-road national park with superb river and mountain scenery.

Paraíso Area

Though the village of Paraíso isn't all that its name implies, it does lead to the wonderful Valle de Orosi beyond.

About 5km west of Paraíso on the road to Cartago (look for a blue sign with an image of an orchid), the University of Costa Rica runs the tranquil 11-hectare **Lankester Gardens** (☑ 2511-7939; www.jbl.ucr.ac.cr; adult/student US$10/7.50; ☺ 8:30am-4:30pm). Orchids are the big draw here, with more than 1000 species at their showiest from March to May. Other attractions along the meandering loop trail include a Japanese garden, a bamboo tunnel and sections dedicated to palms, ferns, cacti and bromeliads. This is one of the few places in the country where foreigners can legally purchase orchids to take home. Guided tours in English and Spanish can be arranged with prior reservation. The garden is wheelchair-accessible.

Heading south from Paraíso toward Orosi, you'll hit **Mirador Orosi** (☺ 6am-5pm) **FREE**, a scenic overlook complete with toilets, secure parking lot, and ample photo and picnic opportunities.

Finca Cristina   TOUR
(☑ 2574-6426, in US 203-549-1945; www.cafe cristina.com; guided tour per person US$15; ☺ by appointment only) Finca Cristina, 2km east of Paraíso on the road to Turrialba, is an organic coffee farm. Linda and Ernie have been farming in Costa Rica since 1977, and a 90-minute tour of their *microbeneficio* (miniprocessing plant) is a fantastic introduction to the processes of organic-coffee growing, harvesting and roasting.

ℹ Getting There & Away

Autotransportes Mata Irola (☑ 2533-1916) runs buses (US$0.95) back and forth between Orosi and Paraíso every 30 minutes. The trip is about 20 minutes and involves multiple stops.

Orosi

Named for a Huetar chief who lived here at the time of the conquest, Orosi charmed Spanish colonists in the 18th century with its perfect climate, rich soil and wealth of water – from lazy hot springs to bracing waterfalls. So, in the typical fashion of the day, they decided to take the property off Orosi's hands. Today the area remains picturesque – and is a good spot to revel in beautiful scenery and a small-town atmosphere.

◉ Sights

Iglesia de San José Orosi   CHURCH
Orosi is one of the few colonial-era towns to survive Costa Rica's frequent earthquakes, which have thankfully spared the photogenic village church. Built in 1743, it is the oldest religious site still in use in Costa Rica. The roof of the church is a combination of thatched cane and ceramic tiling, while the carved-wood altar is adorned with religious paintings of Mexican origin.

Museo de San José Orosi   MUSEUM
(☑ 2533-3051; admission US$1; ☺ 1-5pm Tue-Sat, 9am-5pm Sun) Adjacent to Orosi's church, this small museum displays interesting examples of Spanish-colonial religious art and artifacts, some of which date back to the 17th century.

☂ Activities

The town is a perfect base from which to explore Parque Nacional Tapantí-Macizo Cerro de la Muerte, which offers excellent bird-watching and some lovely hikes, or to rock climb in nearby Cachí.

On Orosi's main street, the Swiss bakery Panadería Suiza rents out motorcycles and scooters.

Monte Sky   HIKING
(☎8382-7502, 2228-0010; www.facebook.com/MonteSkyME; day use US$8) About 5km south of Orosi, high in the hills off the road to Tapantí, this 536-hectare private reserve teems with 290 bird species and offers hiking trails with jaw-dropping vistas. Call for directions; the folks at OTIAC (p130) in Orosi can also help arrange a visit.

Aventuras Orosi   RAFTING
(☎2533-4000; www.aventurasorosicr.com; ⊗9am-4pm) Operated by the charming Luis, who served as a guide for the venerable Ríos Tropicales rafting company for years, this small outfit operates out of the Don José restaurant. Luis organizes canopy tours and rafting expeditions (US$75 each, US$130 for both), as well as custom itineraries.

Thermal Springs

Being in a volcanic region means that Orosi has the perks of thermal springs. Though not nearly on the scale of the steaming-hot waters found near Fortuna, Orosi does offer a pair of warm-water pool complexes. **Balneario de Águas Termales Orosi** (☎2533-2156; www.balnearioaguastermalesorosi.com; admission US$5; ⊗7:30am-4pm Wed-Mon) is the more centrally located of the two, with four pools of varying sizes flanked by grassy expanses and a shaded bar-restaurant terrace. **Los Patios** (☎2533-3009; admission US$5; ⊗8am-4pm Tue-Sun) is a larger complex 1.5km south of town, whose waters include a 43°C (110°F) therapeutic pool suitable for adults only.

🛏 Sleeping

Montaña Linda   HOSTEL $
(☎2533-3640; www.montanalinda.com; dm US$9, s/d/tr without bathroom US$15/22/30, guesthouse s/d/tr US$30/30/35; P@) A short walk southwest of the bus stop, this welcoming, chilled-out budget option has three tidy dorms and eight private rooms surrounding a homey terrace with flowers, hammocks and a wood-heated hot tub. All share a guest kitchen and six bathrooms with hot showers. Owners provide an exceptional information packet highlighting local attractions, including hot springs, waterfalls and more.

★ Orosi Lodge   INN $$
(☎2533-3578; www.orosilodge.com; d/tr US$66/77, chalet d/tr/q US$107/124/141; P☎) This quiet haven, run by a friendly couple, has six bright rooms with wood-beamed ceilings, tile floors, minibar, coffeemaker and free organic coffee. Most rooms face a lovely garden courtyard with a fountain, and one is wheelchair-accessible. Delicious, wholesome breakfasts cost US$8 at the colorfully decorated on-site cafe with scenic balcony seating.

Rancho Río Perlas   RESORT $$$
(☎2533-3341; www.hotelrioperlascr.com; d US$130, incl meals US$228; P☎⚹) With trout-filled lakes, a system of thermal waters and 2km of hiking trails, this picturesque mountain resort is a top sanctuary for locals and visitors looking to escape city life. Nicer rooms offer artificial fireplaces and Jacuzzi tubs, and a conference center and wedding chapel make this a popular spot for weddings and other events.

🍴 Eating & Drinking

There aren't too many options around these parts, but the meals are huge and flavorful at Restaurante Coto. Also, the breakfast at Orosi Lodge is one of the best in the country.

Panadería Suiza   BAKERY $
(☎8706-6777; www.costarica-moto.com/caf-y-panaderia-suiza; pastries from US$1, breakfast US$6-7; ⊗6am-5pm Tue-Sat, to 3pm Sun) Starting at the crack of dawn, ebullient expat Franzisca serves healthy breakfasts and snacks at her main-street bakery, 100m south of Banco Nacional, including sweet and savory pastries, wholegrain breads and lunch packets for outdoors enthusiasts. She also rents out two charming cabins (US$40 to US$70), motorcycles (US$55 to US$85 per day) and scooters ($50 per day).

Restaurante Coto   COSTA RICAN $$
(☎2533-3032; mains US$7-15; ⊗8:30am-9pm) Established in 1952, this family-run eatery on the north side of the soccer field dishes out good *típico* food, particularly the whole fried fish, in a wood-beamed dining room with open-air seating. It's a great place to

enjoy mountain views and the goings-on about town.

Batidos La Uchuva JUICE BAR
(☑ 8802-9925; batidos US$2-4; ☺ 9am-5pm Tue-Sun) At this simple stall 100m south of Banco Nacional, owner André whips up flavorful *batidos* (fruit shakes) made with milk, water or yogurt. Choose from his long list of creative combinations, or invent your own.

ℹ Information

Find more information on the area via the village website (www.orosivalley.com).

Banco Nacional Has an ATM and changes money; 300m south of the park.

OTIAC (Orosi Tourist Information & Arts Café; ☑ 2533-3640; ☺ 8am-6pm Mon-Fri, 10:30am-5pm Sun; 🖥) Run by multilingual long-term residents Toine and Sara, this exceptionally helpful organization functions as an information center, cafe, cultural hall and book exchange. It can help arrange tours and is a good source of information about volunteer and teaching opportunities. Find it 200m south of the park and one block west of the main road.

ℹ Getting There & Away

Autotransportes Mata Irola (p128) runs buses (US$0.95) every 30 minutes to Paraíso (20 minutes) and Cartago (40 minutes) from multiple stops along Orosi's main street. Transfer in Paraíso for buses to Ujarrás and Cachí (US$1.15).

Parque Nacional Tapantí-Macizo Cerro de la Muerte

Protecting the lush northern slopes of the Cordillera de Talamanca, this 580-sq-km **national park** (adult/6-12yr US$10/5; ☺ 8am-4pm) is the wettest in Costa Rica, receiving an average of 8000mm of precipitation per year. Known simply as Tapantí, the park protects wild and mossy country that's fed by literally hundreds of rivers. Waterfalls abound, vegetation is thick and the wildlife is prolific, though not always easy to see because of the rugged terrain. In 2000 the park was expanded to include the infamous Cerro de la Muerte ('Mountain of Death'), a precipitous peak that marks the highest point on the Interamericana and the northernmost extent of *páramo,* a highland shrub and tussock-grass habitat – most commonly found in the Andes – that shelters a variety of rare bird species.

🏃 Activities

Rain gear is advisable year-round.

Hiking

Visitors receive a simple trail map upon paying fees at the park entrance, which doubles as the **Information Center** (☑ 2206-5615; ☺ 8am-4pm).

A well-graded dirt road, popular with mountain bikers, runs 4km into the park from the information center, dead-ending at a *mirador* (viewing platform) that affords broad views across the valley. Three signed trails branch off from this road: the 1.2km **Sendero Oropéndola** heads downhill to a picnic area, then follows the banks of the Río Grande de Orosi for a few hundred meters before looping back uphill; **Sendero La Pava** (0.4km) and **Sendero La Catarata** (0.9km) both descend from a common trailhead to boulder-strewn river beaches, the latter affording excellent views of a dramatic waterfall across the valley; the 2km **Sendero Natural Árboles Caídos** climbs steeply uphill from the main road before descending to rejoin it further west. Tapantí is not open to backcountry hiking.

Wildlife-Watching

More than 300 bird species have been recorded in the park, including hummingbirds, parrots, toucans, trogons and eagles. The bird-watching opportunities here are legendary, as it's possible to spot a large variety in a small area. Though rarely sighted due to the thick vegetation, monkeys, coatis, pacas, tayras and even pumas, ocelots and oncillas are also present.

Fishing

Fishing is allowed in season (April to October; permit required), but the 'dry' season (January to April) is generally considered the best time to visit.

🛏 Sleeping

Kiri Mountain Lodge LODGE $
(☑ 2533-2272, 8488-4085; www.kirilodge.net; s/d incl breakfast US$35/45; 🅿 🖥) About 2km before the park entrance, Kiri has six rustic *cabinas* with intermittent wi-fi and hot water, surrounded by 50 mossy hectares of land. Trails wind into the nearby Reserva Forestal Río Macho, and the lodge's **restaurant** (casados US$8-12; ☺ 7am-8pm) specializes in trout.

❶ Getting There & Away

With your own car, you can drive the 11km from Orosi to the park entrance; about halfway along, near the town of Purisil, the route becomes a bumpy gravel road (a 4WD recommended but not required).

Renting a bike in Orosi is another good option; the ride to the park takes about an hour. Buses only make it as far as Purisil, 5km from the entrance. Taxis charge about US$20 one way from Orosi to the park.

Cachí & Ujarrás

From Orosi, a scenic loop circles the artificial Lago de Cachí. The lake was created following the construction of the Represa de Cachí (Cachí Dam), which supplies San José and the majority of the Central Valley with electricity.

About 3km past the dam, you'll find the town of Ujarrás at the foot of a long, steep hill. To reach the old village, which was damaged by an 1833 flood and abandoned, turn left off the main road at the 'Ujarrás' sign and wind about 1km gently downhill, passing the well-signposted Restaurant La Pipiola en route.

◉ Sights & Activities

Casa del Soñador   GALLERY

(Dreamer's House; ☑ 2577-1186; ⊗ 8am-6pm) **FREE** This artisanal woodworking studio is run by Hermes and Miguel Quesada, sons of renowned Tico carver Macedonio Quesada. The brothers maintain the *campesino* (peasant farmer) tradition of whittling gnarled coffee-wood branches into ornate religious figures and whimsical characters. Their workshop displays sculptures of all sizes, with pieces available for purchase.

Ruins of Ujarrás   RUIN

(⊗ 8am-4:30pm) **FREE** Only the crumbling walls remain of Iglesia de Nuestra Señora de la Limpia Concepción, a 1693 stone church that was home to a miraculous painting of the Virgin discovered by a fisherman. According to lore, the relic refused to be moved, forcing clerics to build the church around it. In return the Virgin helped locals defeat a group of marauding British pirates. After floods and earthquakes, however, the painting conceded to move to Paraíso, leaving the ruins to deteriorate photogenically in a rambling park.

Every year, usually on the Sunday closest to April 14, there is a procession from Paraíso to the ruins, where Mass, food and music help celebrate the day of La Virgen de Ujarrás. The church's grassy grounds are a popular picnicking spot on Sunday afternoons – but go in the middle of the week and chances are that you will have them all to yourself.

Escalada Cachí   ROCK CLIMBING

(☑ 8867-8259; rockclimbingcachi@hotmail.com; ⊗ 8am-4pm Sat & Sun, by appointment only with 4-person minimum Mon-Fri) The road to Tucurrique forks off the main lake loop toward Escalada Cachí, a sport-climbing spot with routes of varying difficulty. A US$20 fee includes equipment rental, as much climbing on the 39 routes as you can crank out, and a soak in its lovely river-diverted pool afterwards. Call ahead and bring your own food (no restaurant).

Heed the roadside sign that recommends 4WD – if you don't think you or your rental can negotiate a supersteep track covered in marbles, park and hike down (and don't leave anything in your car).

🛏 Sleeping & Eating

Cabañas de Montaña
Piedras Albas   CABINA $$

(☑ 8883-6449; www.hotelpiedrasalbas.com; cabinas US$60; ℗) Across the main road from La Casona del Cafetal is the turnoff to these fully equipped *cabinas* in the hills beyond Cachí – a great place if you're here to really slow down. Bright wood *cabinas* come with kitchen, cable TV, and private deck with views, and there are trails for hiking. Ideal for families who want to get away; private transportation is a must.

★ Hotel Quelitales   BUNGALOW $$$

(☑ 2577-2222; www.hotelquelitales.com; d US$101-210; 🛜) This idyllically sited collection of six contemporary-chic bungalows features spacious rooms with wood floors, ultra-comfy mattresses, indoor and outdoor showers, private decks (some with waterfall views) and large canvases depicting the hummingbirds, ladybugs, toucans and other critters for whom the cabins are named. The delicious on-site restaurant (open to non-guests on weekends only) serves trout and other Tico specialties.

La Casona del Cafetal   COSTA RICAN $$

(☑ 2577-1515, 2577-1414; www.lacasonadelcafetal. com; mains US$8-29; ⊗ 11:30am-5pm; 🅿) This charming lakeside restaurant is situated in the middle of a coffee plantation and is especially popular with local families on buffet Sundays ($25). Specialties include fresh river trout and coffee-laced desserts. There is a small playground, as well as short trails and a lagoon with paddleboats for rent (in high season).

❶ Getting There & Away

Buses run from Orosi to the dam and nearby ruins, though this stretch is best explored by car or bicycle – and it's worth exploring as this is beautiful countryside. After Ujarrás, the route continues west for a few more kilometers to rejoin the main road at Paraíso.

TURRIALBA AREA

In the vicinity of Turrialba, at an elevation of 650m above sea level, the Río Reventazón gouges a mountain pass through the Cordillera Central. In the 1880s this geological quirk allowed the 'Jungle Train' between San José and Puerto Limón to roll through, and the mountain village of Turrialba grew prosperous from the coffee trade. Later, the first highway linking the capital to the coast exploited this same quirk. Turrialba thrived.

However, things changed by the early 1990s when the straighter, smoother Hwy 32 through Guápiles was completed and an earthquake shut down the railway for good. Suddenly, Turrialba found itself off the beaten path. Even so, the area remains a key agricultural center, renowned for its strong coffee, ubiquitous cheese and Central America's best white-water rafting. To the north, the area is home to two important sites: the majestic Volcán Turrialba and the archaeological site of Guayabo.

Turrialba

When the railway shut down in 1991, commerce slowed down, but Turrialba nonetheless remained a regional agricultural center, where local coffee planters could bring their crops to market. And with tourism on the rise in the 1990s, this modest mountain town soon became known as the gateway to some of the best white-water rafting on the planet. By the early 2000s, Turrialba was a hotbed of international rafters looking for Class-V thrills. For now, the Río Pacuare runs on, but its future is uncertain.

⊙ Sights

Catie (Centro Agronómico Tropical de Investigación) GARDENS
(Center for Tropical Agronomy Research & Education; ☑ 2556-2700; www.catie.ac.cr; adult/student/youth US$10/8/6, guided tours US$25-50; ⊙ 7am-4pm Mon-Fri, 8am-4pm Sat & Sun) Catie's sprawling grounds, 2km east of Turrialba, encompass 10 sq km dedicated to tropical agricultural research and education. Agron-

---

WHITE WATER IN THE CENTRAL VALLEY

The Turrialba area is a major center for white-water rafting. Traditionally the two most popular rafting rivers have been the **Río Reventazón** and the **Río Pacuare**, but the former has been dramatically impacted by a series of hydroelectric projects, including a huge 305-megawatt dam currently under construction.

As a result, most organized expeditions from Turrialba now head for the Río Pacuare, which arguably offers the most scenic rafting in Central America. The river plunges down the Caribbean slope through a series of spectacular canyons clothed in virgin rainforest, through runs named for their fury and separated by calm stretches that enable you to stare at near-vertical green walls towering hundreds of meters above.

Lower Pacuare With Class II–IV rapids, this is the more accessible run: 28km through rocky gorges, past an indigenous village and untamed jungle.

Upper Pacuare Classified as Class III–IV, but a few sections can go to Class V, depending on conditions. It's about a two-hour drive to the put-in, after which you'll have the prettiest jungle cruise on earth all to yourself.

The Pacuare can be run year-round, though June to October are considered the best months. The highest water is from October to December, when the river runs fast with huge waves. March and April are when the river is at its lowest, though it is still challenging.

omists from all over the world recognize this as one of the most important centers in the tropics. You'll need to make reservations for one of several guided tours through laboratories, greenhouses, a seed bank, experimental plots and one of the most extensive libraries of tropical-agriculture literature in the world. Alternatively, pick up a map and take a self-guided walk.

Activities & Tours

Plenty of local operators offer either kayaking or rafting in the area.

Ecoaventuras   OUTDOORS
(www.ecoaventuras.co.cr) An outdoor adventure company that offers white-water rafting in the Pacuare and Pejibaye rivers, along with horseriding, mountain biking and canopy tours. A three-day rafting experience with all meals, accommodations, equipment and an included zip-line tour costs US$360 per person. It's 100m north and 100m west of the Rawlings Factory.

Locos   RAFTING
(✆2556-6035, in USA 707-703-5935; www.whiteh2o.com) Loco's takes guests on wild rides of varying difficulty down the Ríos Pacuare and Reventazón. The outfit also runs a more relaxing trip down the Río Pejibaye. A day of rafting is typically around US$85 per person (depending on the size of the group).

Explornatura   RAFTING
(✆2556-0111, in USA & Canada 866-571-2443; www.explornatura.com; Av 4 btwn Calles 2 & 4) Does rafting, mountain-biking and horseriding tours. A rafting day trip on the Pacuare is US$85 per person, horseriding is US$68 per person and mountain biking costs US$60 per person.

Costa Rica Ríos   RAFTING
(✆2556-8664, in USA & Canada 888-434-0776; www.costaricarios.com; Calle 1, near Av 6) Offers week-long rafting trips that must be booked in advance. An 8-day adventure-tour package costs US$1899 per person with double occupancy.

Courses

Adventure Education Center   LANGUAGE COURSE
(✆in USA 800-237-2730; www.adventurespanishschool.com; US$485/325) Combine Spanish classes and white-water rafting at this Turrialba school that also offers medical Spanish. A group language lesson for a week with 20

hours of lessons is US$325 (with homestay it's US$485).

Spanish by the River   LANGUAGE COURSE
(✆2556-7380, in USA 1-877-268-3730; www.spanishatlocations.com; 5-day course with/without homestay US$315/225) A 5-minute bus ride from Turrialba, this school offers homestays or hostel beds along with weekly Spanish classes of varying levels.

Sleeping

In town, you'll find a solid mix of budget hostels and midrange hotels.

Around the Turrialba area there are some stellar hotels that bring guests close to nature. All can arrange tours and rafting trips.

In Turrialba

★**Casa de Lis Hostel**   HOSTEL $
(✆2556-4933; www.hostelcasadelis.com; Av Central near Calle 2; dm US$14, s/d/tr/q US$40/45/60/68, without bathroom US$36/36/48/56; ⊛) Hands down Turrialba's best value, this sweet, centrally located eight-room place is a traveler's dream come true. Spotless dorms and doubles with comfy mattresses and individual reading lamps are complemented by a fully equipped kitchen, volcano-view roof terrace, pretty back garden, fantastic information displays and a distinctly friendly atmosphere. Laundry service (US$8 per load) is available.

Hotel Interamericano   HOTEL $
(✆2556-0142; www.hotelinteramericano.com; Av 1 near Calle 1; s/d/tr/q US$25/35/45/55, without bathroom US$12/20/30/40; P⊛) On the south side of the old train tracks is this basic 20-room hotel, traditionally regarded by rafters as *the* meeting place in Turrialba. The collection of basic rooms includes some with private bathrooms, some without and many that combine bunks with regular beds. The friendly owner provides day care for children who are too young to go rafting.

Hotel Wagelia   HOTEL $$
(✆2556-1566; www.hotelwageliaturrialba.com; Av 4 btwn Calles 2 & 4; s/d incl breakfast US$55/80; P⊛) Simple, modern and clean rooms come with cable TV and face a quiet interior courtyard. A restaurant serves Tico specialties, and the pleasant terrace bar is a good place for a drink and wi-fi.

DAMNING THE RIVERS?

Considered one of the most beautiful white-water-rafting rivers in the world, the wild **Río Pacuare** became the first federally protected river in Central America in 1985. Within two years, however, Costa Rica's national power company, the Instituto Costarricense de Electricidad (ICE), unveiled plans to build a 200m gravity dam at the conveniently narrow and screamingly scenic ravine of Dos Montañas.

The dam would be the cornerstone of the massive Siquirres Hydroelectric Project, which would include four dams in total, linked by a 10km-long tunnel. If built, rising waters on the lower Pacuare would not only flood 12km of rapids up to the Tres Equis put-in, but also parts of the Reserva Indígena Awari and a huge swath of primary rainforest where some 800 animal species have been recorded.

The project was intended to help ICE keep up with the country's rapidly increasing power demands. But as the proposal moved from speculation to construction, a coalition of local landowners, indigenous leaders, conservation groups and, yep, white-water-rafting outfits organized against it. (Rafael Gallo, of the Fundación Ríos Tropicales, the charitable arm of the venerable rafting company, was a key figure in this fight.)

The group filed for the first Environmental Impact Assessment (EIA) in the region's history – and won. The move required ICE to seek an independent study of the dam's environmental impact and economic feasibility, effectively stalling its construction. In the meantime, organizers were able to draw international attention to the situation. In 2005 residents of the Turrialba area held a plebiscite on the issue of the dam. Of the 10,000 residents polled, 97% gave the project a thumbs down – a resounding 'No.'

Although the nearby Río Reventazón lost a third of its Class-V rapids due to the construction of dams, the Pacuare recently saw its greatest victory. On August 29, 2015, President Luis Guillermo Solís signed a decree banning hydroelectric projects of 500 kilowatts or more from the river for the next 25 years. Although the Pacuare seems safe for the meantime, another decree by a future president could again leave it unprotected. The takeaway for travelers is clear: raft now!

🛏 Around Turrialba

⭐ **Wagelia Espino Blanco Lodge** LODGE $$
(📞2556-0616; www.wageliaespinoblancolodge. com; r incl breakfast US$85, extra person US$15; 🅿) ⚑ Located high above Turrialba, this 10-bungalow ecolodge sits on 30 hectares of forestland. The quaint and well-constructed cabins are without electricity, TVs or anything else to distract from the serenity of the place, which also features a small amphitheater, a poets' corner, a charming restaurant and seven hiking trails of varying difficulty.

From Turrialba, it's about a 20-minute drive north up winding Hwy 230. The roads can be tricky – call for directions.

Turrialtico Lodge LODGE $$
(📞2538-1111; www.turrialtico.com; d incl breakfast US$58-75; 🅿🛜) Commanding dramatic, sweeping views of the Río Reventazón valley, this Tico-run lodge in an old farmhouse 9km east of Turrialba (off the highway to Siquirres) offers 18 attractive, polished-wood-panel rooms decorated with local artwork. Rooms in the reception building share a large terrace and sitting area, and a pleasant open-air restaurant (mains US$8 to US$20) serves up country cooking.

Rancho Naturalista LODGE $$$
(📞8704-3217; www.ranchonaturalista.net; r per person incl 3 meals US$180; 🅿@) About 1.3km south of Tuis and 900m above sea level, this small lodge on 50 hectares of land is a must-do for bird-watchers, who have recorded more than 450 species in the area (more than 250 from the lodge balcony alone). The 14 homey rooms in the lodge are complemented by a cluster of private *casitas,* surrounded by pretty landscaped grounds.

Meals include organic beef and pork from the cows and pigs raised on-site.

Casa Turire HOTEL $$$
(📞2531-1111; www.hotelcasaturire.com; d standard/ste/master ste incl breakfast US$164/255/400, additional person US$25-35, child under 6yr free; 🅿❄@🛜⊠) ⚑ This elegant three-story plantation inn has 16 graceful, well-appointed

rooms with high ceilings, wood floors and wrought-iron beds; a massive master suite comes with a Jacuzzi and excellent views of the coffee and macadamia-nut plantations in the distance. Adding icing to the cake are spa services, a restaurant and bar, horseback riding, bird-watching and kayaking on the on-site lake. A kiddie pool and an on-site playground will please the rug rats.

Take the La Suiza/Tuis turnoff from Hwy 10, head south for 2.3km, then follow signs an additional 1.4km down a dirt road to the hotel.

✖ Eating

For cheap meals, stroll along Calle 1, where you'll find *sodas*, pizzerias and roast-chicken places galore. Self-caterers can find supplies at the well-stocked **MegaSuper** (cnr Calle 3 & Av 2; ⊙7am-9pm).

★ **Maracuyá**   CAFE $
(☑2556-2021; Calle 2 north of Av 10; frozen coffee US$4, mains US$6; ⊙2-10pm Wed-Mon; ☑) This bright-walled cafe serves up one of the best coffee treats in the country – a frozen caffeine concoction with gooey *maracuyá* (passion fruit) syrup and crunchy seeds. Dishes include veggie wraps, creative salads and Latin American favorites such as patacones (fried plantains).

La Feria   COSTA RICAN $
(☑2556-5550; Calle 6 north of Av 4; mains US$6-15; ⊙11am-10pm Wed-Mon, to 3pm Tue; ☑) This unremarkable-looking eatery has friendly service and excellent, reasonably priced home cooking. Sometimes the kitchen gets a bit backed up, but the hearty *casados* (typical dishes with beans, rice, a small salad and a choice of protein) are well worth the wait.

Wok & Roll   ASIAN $
(☑2556-6756; Calle 1; mains US$7-19; ⊙11am-10pm Wed-Mon) Pan-Asian cuisine, from Singapore-style noodles to Chinese steamed buns, fills the menu at this new eatery near Turrialba's main square. OK, perhaps they're overdoing the fusion thing with the Turri Volcano Roll (made with avocado, cucumber and yes, Turrialba cheese!), but nobody can argue with tempura ice cream for dessert. Don't miss the homemade mint lemonade and honey-sweetened jasmine tea.

Avenida 6   BAR
(☑2556-1165; www.facebook.com/avenida6turrialba; Av 6, north of Parque Central; ⊙11:30am-11pm Sun-Thu, to midnight Fri & Sat) A popular bar for

the après-rafting crowd, and a good spot to check out live music.

ℹ Information

Banco de Costa Rica (cnr Av Central & Calle 3; ⊙9am-4pm Mon-Fri) Has a 24-hour ATM that dispenses dollars and colones.

ℹ Getting There & Away

A modern bus terminal is located on the western edge of town off Hwy 10.

San José via Paraíso and Cartago US$2.70, 1¾ hours, departs hourly from 4am to 9pm.

Siquirres, for transfer to Puerto Limón US$2.25, 1½ hours, departs every 60 to 90 minutes from 5:30am to 6:30pm. Schedules vary slightly on weekends.

Monumento Nacional Arqueológico Guayabo

Nestled into a patch of stunning hillside forest 19km northeast of Turrialba is **Monumento Nacional Arqueológico Guayabo** (☑2559-1220; US$5; ⊙8am-3:30pm), the largest and most important archaeological site in the country.

Guayabo is composed of the remains of a pre-Columbian city that was thought to have peaked at some point in AD 800. The site occupies 232 hectares, most of which remains unexcavated. Although Guayabo is not nearly as breathtaking as Mayan and Aztec archaeological sites, excavations have unearthed sophisticated infrastructure and mysterious petroglyphs. Polychromatic pottery and gold artifacts found here are also exhibited at the Museo Nacional in San José.

The site, which may have been occupied as early as 1000 BC, was mysteriously abandoned by AD 1400 – the Spanish conquistadors, explorers and settlers left no record of having found the ruins. For centuries, the city lay largely untouched under the cover of the area's thick highland forest. But in 1968, archaeologist Carlos Aguilar Piedra of the University of Costa Rica began systematic excavations of Guayabo. Though underfunded, archaeologists continue to hypothesize about Guayabo's significance, most believe it was an important cultural, religious and political center.

In 1973, as the site's importance became evident, Guayabo was declared a national monument, with further protections set forth in 1980.

The most impressive find at Guayabo is the aqueduct system, which may have served more than 20,000 people in AD 800, the height of the city's prominence. It uses enormous stones hauled in from far-off Río Reventazón along an 8km road that's in pretty good shape (by Costa Rican standards). The extra effort was worth it – the cisterns still work and (theoretically) potable water remains available on-site, which you can enjoy among various unearthed structures and unexcavated mounds.

Bilingual interpretive signs are placed at regular intervals along the well-maintained loop trail that runs through the ruins and surrounding forest; featured stops include the central mound where the city's largest dwelling once stood, the remains of an aqueduct and retaining pool, a viewpoint overlooking the entire site and a two-sided petroglyph depicting a jaguar and a lizard.

Average annual rainfall is about 3500mm, making dry season (January to April) the best time to visit – though it might still rain. Bring insect repellent; it gets mighty buggy.

🏃 Activities & Tours

The site currently protects the last remaining pre-montane forest in the province of Cartago, and although mammals are limited to squirrels, armadillos and coatis, there are good bird-watching opportunities here. Particularly noteworthy among the avifauna are the oropendolas, which colonize the monument by building sacklike nests in the trees. Other birds include toucans and brown jays – the latter are unique among jays in that they have a small, inflatable sac in their chest, which causes the popping sound that is heard at the beginning of their loud and raucous calls.

Asociación de Guías U-Suré   WALKING TOUR
(☑ 8534-1063; guided tour for 1-3 people US$20, for 4-9 US$35, for 10-20 US$50) To hire a guide for Guayabo, call at least eight days in advance.

ℹ️ Getting There & Away

By car, head north out of Turrialba and make a right after the metal bridge. The road is well signed from there, and all but the last 3km is paved; a 4WD is recommended, though not required, for the final rough section.

Buses from Turrialba (US$0.95, one hour) depart at 6am, 10:30am, 3pm, 6pm Monday through Friday and at 10:30am, 3pm and 6pm on Saturday and Sunday. Buses return from Guayabo to Turrialba at 7am, 12:30pm and 4pm daily. You can also take a taxi from Turrialba (about US$30 round trip, with one hour to explore the park).

Parque Nacional Volcán Turrialba

This rarely visited active volcano (3328m) was named Torre Alba (White Tower) by early Spanish settlers, who observed plumes of smoke pouring from its summit.

Turrialba was declared a national park in 1955, and protects a 2km radius around the volcano. Below the summit, the park consists of mountain rainforest and cloud forest, dripping with moisture and mosses, full of ferns, bromeliads and even stands of bamboo. Although small, these protected habitats shelter 84 species of bird and 11 species of mammal.

Turrialba's last major eruption was in 1866, but a century and a half later, the slumbering giant has begun showing sustained signs of life. Since 2010 it has regularly been belching forth quantities of sulfuric gas and ash, damaging the road to the summit, killing off trees and other vegetation and displacing small farming communities from the volcano's western slopes.

At the time of research, it was only possible to drive as far as Volcán Turrialba Lodge, about 6km shy of the summit; the park itself is closed due to access issues. For more details, contact park **headquarters** (☑ 2557-6262, 8704-2432; pnvolcanturrialba@gmail.com; ⊙ 8am-3:30pm).

🛏️ Sleeping

Volcán Turrialba Lodge   LODGE $
(☑ 8383-6084, 2273-4335; www.facebook.com/turrialbalodge; cabinas per person incl breakfast US$45; P 🐾) Reached by a tortuous, rugged road (4WD recommended), this working sheep and cattle ranch 14km northwest of Santa Cruz truly gets you away from it all. Tidy, lemon-yellow *cabinas* come with wood stoves and full kitchens, and many offer fantastic views of Volcán Turrialba. The staff organizes hikes and horseriding, and will provide food for US$8 per meal.

ℹ️ Information

Because of the recent volcanic activity, it's imperative to inquire locally about conditions in the national park before attempting a visit. For up-to-the-minute details on the volcano's status, contact park headquarters.

If and when the summit reopens, bear in mind that the average temperature is only about 15°C (59°F), so dress accordingly.

❶ Getting There & Away

The volcano is only about 15km northwest of Turrialba as the crow flies, but more than twice that far by car. From the village of Santa Cruz (13km from Turrialba and connected via public buses), an 18km road climbs to the top of the volcano. At the time of research, it was only possible to drive as far as Volcán Turrialba Lodge, about 6km shy of the summit; the park itself remained closed due to access issues.

Caribbean Coast

Best Places to Eat

➡ Sobre Las Olas (p169)

➡ Soda El Patty (p147)

➡ Selvin's Restaurant (p184)

➡ La Pecora Nera (p185)

➡ Cool & Calm Cafe (p186)

Best Off the Beaten Track

➡ Selva Bananito (p168)

➡ La Danta Salvaje (p144)

➡ Punta Mona (p188)

➡ Turtle Beach Lodge (p159)

➡ Aiko-logi (p172)

Why Go?

While the sunny climate and easy accessibility of the Pacific have paved the way (literally) for development on that rich coast, the Caribbean side has languished in comparison. The same rain-drenched malarial wildness that thwarted the first 16th-century Spaniards from settling here also isolated this region for centuries afterward. Thus, its culture – influenced by indigenous peoples and West Indian immigrants – blended slowly and organically and is distinctly different from that of the rest of Costa Rica.

It still takes a little more effort to travel here to see the nesting turtles of Tortuguero, raft the Río Pacuare or dive the reefs of Manzanillo. Life is more rugged and rustic on this coast, allowing wildlife to thrive. And it's well worth tasting its unique flavors: the *rondón* (spicy seafood gumbo), the lilt of patois, and the uncrowded stretches of palm-lined beaches.

When to Go

➡ From December to March, the biggest swells hit the southern Caribbean and the surfers descend.

➡ Turtle-nesting season from March to October means egg-laying and hatching spectacles in Tortuguero.

➡ The best times for sportfishing are from January to June and September to December, although fishing is good year-round in the northern Caribbean.

History

In 1502 Christopher Columbus spent a total of 17 days anchored off the coast of Puerto Limón on what would be his fourth and final voyage to the New World. He dropped anchor at an isle he baptized La Huerta (today known as Isla Uvita), loaded up on fresh water, and never returned.

For Costa Rica's Caribbean coast, this brief encounter foreshadowed the colonization that was to come. But it would be centuries before Europeans would fully dominate the area. Because of the difficult nature of the terrain (croc-filled swamps and steep mountain slopes) and the malaria delivered by relentless fleets of mosquitoes, the Spanish steadfastly avoided it. For hundreds of years, in fact, the area remained the province of indigenous ethnicities – the Miskito in the north and the Cabécar, Bribrí and Kèköldi in the south – along with a mix of itinerant Afro-Caribbean turtle hunters from Panama and Colombia.

It was the building of the railroad, beginning in 1871, that solidified the area's West Indian accent, with the arrival of thousands of former Jamaican slaves in search of employment. The plan was to build a port at the site of a grand old lemon tree (hence the name, Puerto Limón) on the Caribbean Sea, so that coffee barons in the Central Valley could more easily export their crops to Europe. The railway was intended to unify the country, but it was a source of segregation as well. Blacks were not allowed to vote or travel freely around Costa Rica until 1949. Out of isolation, however, sprung an independent culture, with its own musical and gastronomic traditions, and even its own unique language, a Creole called Mekatelyu – which is still spoken today.

Parks & Reserves

Many refuges and parks line the Caribbean coast. These are some of the most popular.

Parque Nacional Cahuita (p170) A patch of coastal jungle is home to armadillos, monkeys and sloths, while the protected reef is one of the most important on the coast.

Parque Nacional Tortuguero (p152) Jungle canals obscure snoozing caimans, while howler, spider and capuchin monkeys traipse overhead. The star attraction, however, is the sea turtles, which nest here from March to October.

Refugio Nacional de Vida Silvestre Barra del Colorado (p162) A remote park that draws fishing enthusiasts who come to hook species such as snook, tarpon and gar.

Refugio Nacional de Vida Silvestre Gandoca-Manzanillo (p186) A rich rainforest and wetland tucked away along the country's southeastern border, with rivers full of manatees, caimans and crocodiles.

❶ Getting There & Away

When traveling to Puerto Limón and the southern Caribbean, it's easy enough to hop on any of the regular buses from San José. Buses also connect most towns along the coast, from Sixaola, on the Panamanian border, to Puerto Limón. The roads are in good condition, so driving is also an option.

The north is a little trickier. Much of the area is only linked up by waterways, making boats the sole means of transport. Puerto Limón, Tortuguero, Parismina and Barra del Colorado all have landing strips, but only Tortuguero has daily commercial flights.

THE ATLANTIC SLOPE

The idea was simple: build a port on the Caribbean coast and connect it to the Central Valley by railroad, thereby opening up important shipping routes for the country's soaring coffee production. Construction began in 1871, through 150km of dense jungles and muddy mountainsides along the Atlantic slope. It took almost two decades to build the railroad, and the first 30km reportedly cost 4000 men their lives. But when the last piece of track was laid down in 1890, the economic forces it unleashed permanently changed Costa Rica (and the rest of Central America, for that matter). It was the dawn of the banana boom, an industry that would dominate life, politics and the environment in the region for almost a century.

Today, the railroad is no longer. Likewise, banana production is not as mighty as it once was, supplanted in many areas by pineapples and African oil palms.

Parque Nacional Braulio Carrillo

Enter this under-explored **national park** (✆2206-5500; adult/child $12/5; ⊗8am-3:30pm) and you will have an idea of what Costa Rica looked like prior to the 1950s, when 75% of

Caribbean Coast Highlights

1 Sliding silently through jungle canals in search of wildlife or volunteering to protect endangered sea turtles in **Tortuguero** (p152).

2 Riding the **Río Pacuare** (p173), the country's most extreme river.

3 Surfing, sampling the culinary scene, lazing on the beach and partying in **Puerto Viejo de Talamanca** (p171).

4 Chilling out in rustic bliss in **Cahuita** (p170) and soaking up the Caribbean Creole culture.

5 Snorkeling the teeming reefs and adventuring through the dripping jungle in **Manzanillo** (p186).

6 Witnessing the dramatic meeting of the murky Río Sucio and the crystal-clear Río Honduras in **Parque Nacional Braulio Carrillo** (p139).

7 Visiting cacao farms and indigenous villages around **Bribrí** (p188).

N

0 _____ 40 km
0 _____ 20 miles

CARIBBEAN
SEA

Parismina
Caño Blanco

San
Rafael

Reserva
Pacuare-
Matina

atán   Matina

Río Matina

22

Portete   PUERTO
LIMÓN

Moín

Liverpool

Isla
Uvita

Veragua Rainforest
Research &
Adventure Park

Río Bananito

Selva Bananito

Zona Protectora
Cuenca del
Río Banano

Sloth
Sanctuary
of Costa Rica

eserva Indígena Alto
y Bajo Chirripó

Valle de la Estrella

Penshurst

Río Estrella

Pandora

4 Cahuita

Parque
Nacional
Cahuita

Reserva
Indígena
Tayní

Puerto
Viejo de
Talamanca

Playa
Chiquita

Parque
Internacional
La Amistad

Reserva Biológica
Hitoy-Cerere

Bribrí

3

Punta
Uva

Punta
Mona

5 Manzanillo

Reserva Indígena
Cocles/Kèköldi

7

Río Teliré

Shiroles

Refugio Nacional
de Vida Silvestre
Gandoca-Manzanillo

Reserva
Indígena
Telire

Bratsi

Reserva Indígena
Talamanca Cabécar

Río Sixaola

Amubri

Reserva
Indígena
Yorkín

Sixaola

rdillera de
Talamanca

Reserva Indígena
Talamanca Bribrí

PANAMA

Guabito

the country's surface area was still covered in forest: steep hills cloaked in impossibly tall trees are interrupted only by cascading rivers and canyons. It has extraordinary biodiversity due to the range of altitudes, from steamy 2906m cloud forest alongside Volcán Barva to lush, humid lowlands on the Caribbean slope. Its most incredible feature, however, is that this massive park is only 30 minutes north of San José.

History

Founded in the 1970s, Braulio Carrillo's creation was the result of a unique compromise between conservationists and developers. At the time, the government had announced a plan to build a new highway that would connect the capital to Puerto Limón. Back then, San José's only link to its most important port was via a crumbling railroad or a slow rural road through Cartago and Turrialba. The only feasible route for the new thoroughfare was along a low pass between the Barva and Irazú volcanoes – an area covered in primary forest. Conservationists were deeply worried about putting a road (and any attendant development) in an area that served as San José's watershed. So a plan was hatched: the road would be built, but the 475 sq km of land to either side of it would be set aside as a national park. Thus, in 1978, Parque Nacional Braulio Carrillo was born.

🏃 Activities

Bird-watching in the park is excellent, and commonly sighted species include parrots, toucans and hummingbirds; quetzals can be seen at higher elevations, primarily in the Barva sector. Other rare but sighted birds include eagles and umbrella birds.

Mammals are difficult to spot due to the lush vegetation, though deer, monkeys and *tepezcuintle* (paca, the park's mascot) are frequently seen. Jaguars and ocelots are present but rare.

🏃 Quebrada González Sector

Three easy to moderate trails fan out from the **Quebrada González ranger station** (📞 2206-5500; ⏱ 8am-4pm) between Guápiles and San José. On the north side of Hwy 32, the mostly flat, gravel-paved 1km **Sendero El Ceibo** is the easiest of the three, passing a giant ceibo tree, a scenic overlook and seven other marked points of interest before looping back to the ranger station. Proximity to the highway creates some distracting traffic noise here.

Sendero Botarrama, a slightly more rugged spur trail (expect mud and exposed roots) branches off Sendero El Ceibo and continues another 1km to the junction of the crystal-clear Río Honduras with the Río Sucio (Dirty River), the yellow waters of which carry volcanic minerals.

Back on the south side of Hwy 32, the 1.6km, gravel-paved **Sendero Las Palmas** is another loop trail that climbs moderately into dense rainforest – prime territory for bird-watching.

🏃 Barva Sector

Volcán Barva   VOLCANO
Climbing Volcán Barva is a strenuous adventure along a remote but reasonably well-maintained trail. Because of its relative inaccessibility, there is a good chance you will be alone.

Begin from the western entrance of the park, north of Heredia. From there a 2.5km signed track climbs to the summit. Trails are often muddy, and you should be prepared for rain at any time of the year.

Near the volcano's summit are two lagoons – Lagos Barva and Copey – the prime destinations on a network of four trails that also leads to waterfalls and other scenic spots along the way.

👉 Tours

Rainforest Adventures   ECOTOUR
(📞 2257-5961, in USA 1-866-759-8726; www.rainforestadventure.com; adult/student & child tram US$60/30, zip line US$50/35; ♿) Rainforest Adventures and its aerial tram are a worthwhile splurge if you fancy visiting the heights of the forest canopy in a gondola. The 2.6km ride takes 40 minutes each way, affording unusual plant-spotting and bird-watching opportunities. The fee includes a knowledgeable guide, which is helpful since the

density of the vegetation can make observing animals difficult. Book online or in its **San José office** (Map p70; ☑ 2257-5961; Av 7 btwn Calles 5 & 7; ☺ 9am-5pm Mon-Fri).

A variety of other tours, as well as zip lining, are also available.

ⓘ Information

The park's three most accessible hiking trails originate at Quebrada González ranger station in the park's northeast corner, 21km past the Zurquí tunnel on the south side of the San José–Guápiles highway. Here, you'll find safe parking, toilets, drinking water and a ranger-staffed info booth. For security reasons, don't leave your car parked anywhere along the main highway.

People who want to climb Volcán Barva on a day trip or camp overnight can stop by the **Barva Sector ranger station** (☑ 2266-1883, 2266-1892; ☺ 8am-3:30pm), in the southwest of the park, 3km north of Sacramento.

ⓘ Getting There & Away

Frequent buses between San José and Guápiles can drop you off at the Quebrada González station, but the return trip is more challenging. While it's possible to flag a bus down on busy Hwy 32, your luck will depend on the driver's discretion and how full the bus is.

Drivers can reach the Barva station by following the decent paved road north from Heredia through Barva village to San José de la Montaña, Paso Llano and Sacramento. From Sacramento, a signed, 4WD-only trail leads 3km north to the entrance. It is not advisable to drive this stretch in the rainy season as the road is a mess of car-swallowing potholes. Public buses from Heredia will only get you as far as Paso Llano, 7km from the park entrance. For a day trip without your own vehicle, you'll need to take an early bus from Heredia. Make sure you're catching a bus that goes all the way to Paso Llano, or you'll be left more than 15km from the park's entrance.

Guápiles & Around

A pleasant and decidedly nontouristy (if not terribly scenic) lowland agricultural town, Guápiles lies at the base of the northern foothills of the Cordillera Central. It serves as a transportation center for the Río Frío banana-growing region and also makes a convenient base from which to explore Parque Nacional Braulio Carrillo – a 20-minute drive away – or to organize excursions to Tortuguero.

The center of town is about 1km north of Hwy 32, reached by a pair of well-marked

---

OFF THE BEATEN TRACK

LA DANTE SALVAJE

West of Guápiles, a 45-minute 4WD trip and three-hour hike leads to a fabulous 410-hectare rainforest reserve (altitude 800m) in a critical buffer zone adjoining Parque Nacional Braulio Carrillo. The rustic **La Danta Salvaje** (☑ 2750-0012; www.ladantasalvaje.com; 3-night packages per person US$250) lodge hosts small groups for four days of jungle hiking, wildlife-spotting and splashing around in idyllic swimming holes. Prices include guided hikes and three meals daily. Reserve ahead.

Transport from Guápiles is an extra US$10 each way.

---

turnoffs on either side of Taco Bell. Guápiles' two major streets are one way, running parallel to each other east and west. Most of the services are on the loop that these streets make through the busy downtown.

🛏 Sleeping

Hotel Irdama   CABIN $
(☑ 2710-7034; hotel.cabinas.irdama@gmail.com; r with fan/air-con US$30/36; ❄) This well-tended motel-like structure near the center of town offers 22 clean rooms and a small attached **restaurant** (meals US$6; ☺ 6am-8:30pm) serving breakfast and *casados*. Look for it 50m north of the Más x Menos supermarket (about 1km northeast of the bus terminal).

Casa Río Blanco B&B   B&B $$
(☑ 8570-8294, 2710-4124; www.casarioblanco. com; s/d/tr/q incl breakfast US$65/85/100/115; 🅿 🛜) 🌿 One of Costa Rica's original ecolodges, this welcoming place offers four cabins on a 2-hectare hillside above the Río Blanco. Devoid of cable TV and air-con, it's a throwback to earlier days when ecotourism was all about unplugging. Croaking frogs and flickering lightning bugs provide late-night entertainment, while daytime diversions include visits to the spectacular nearby swimming hole.

🍴 Eating

Restaurante El Yugo de Mi Tata   COSTA RICAN $
(☑ 2711-0090; mains US$5-10; ☺ 24hr) If there's a Costa Rican truck-stop heaven, it must look something like this. Strategically placed just below Hwy 32's tortuous climb into

BUSES FROM GUÁPILES

Guapiles' modern bus terminal, complete with eateries and a **BCR** (☑ 2211-1111; ⊙ 11am-1:30pm & 2:30-6pm Tue-Fri, 8:30am-noon & 1-3:30pm Sat) with an ATM, is 800m north of the main highway from the western Taco Bell turnoff.

DESTINATION	COST (US$)	DURATION (HRS)	FREQUENCY
Cariari (Coopetraca)	0.95	1	every 15 minutes, 6am-10pm
Puerto Limón via Guácimo & Siquirres (Tracasa)	5	2	hourly 7am-4pm, later on weekends
Puerto Viejo de Sarapiquí (Guapileños)	2.40	1	5:30am, 8am, 9am, 10:30am, noon, 1:15pm, 2:30pm, 4pm, 5pm & 6:30pm
San José (Guapileños)	2.60	1¼	every 30mins, 5am-7pm

Parque Nacional Braulio Carrillo (13km west of Guápiles), it's the perfect spot to brace yourself for the road ahead or recuperate from the harrowing descent. A fabulous array of tasty, affordable cafeteria-style food is available 24/7.

El Rubio
COSTA RICAN $

(☑ 2711-1118; mains US$5-12; ⊙ 11am-11pm) The clutter of pick-up trucks out front is a clue that you've stumbled on to this popular family eatery serving grilled fish, roasted meats and *bocas* (savory bar snacks). Our favorite is *chifrijo*, rice and beans studded with fried pork, tomato salsa and chips. Head north 250m on the paved road just east of Taco Bell, then turn east and continue on for another 250m.

❶ Orientation

The center of town is about 1km north of Hwy 32, reached by a pair of well-marked turnoffs on either side of Taco Bell. Guápiles' two major streets are one way, running parallel to each other east and west. Most of the services are on the loop that these streets make through the busy downtown.

Siquirres

The steamy lowland town of Siquirres has long served as an important transportation hub. It sits at the intersection of Hwy 32 (the main road that crosses the Atlantic slope to Puerto Limón) and Hwy 10, the old road that connects San José with Puerto Limón via Turrialba.

There is little reason to stop in Siquirres, unless you're heading to Parismina – in which case this is a good spot to find banking, internet and telephone services.

(Tip: buy phonecards here; they aren't sold in Parismina.) For purposes of orientation, the Siquirres church – a highly recognizable, round, red-domed building – is located to the west side of the soccer field.

History

Even before the highways bisecting the town were built, Siquirres was a significant location – for it was in Siquirres in the early 20th century that the lines of segregation were drawn. At the time, blacks were barred from traveling west of here without special permission. So any train making its way from Limón to San José was required to stop here and change its crew: black conductors and engineers would change places with their Spanish counterparts and the train would continue on its route to the capital. This ended in 1949, when a new constitution outlawed racial discrimination.

Today Siquirres still marks the place where Costa Rica takes a dip into the Caribbean – and not just geographically. This is where Costa Rican *casados* give way to West Indian *rondón*, where Spanish guitar is replaced with the strains of calypso, and where Costa Rica's inherently *mestizo* (mixed ancestry) race gives way to Afro-Caribbean features.

🛏 Sleeping

Centro Turístico Las Tilapias
CABINA $$

(☑ 2768-9293; d with fan/air-con US$45/50; 🅿 ❄ 🛜 ⊠) This charming, rustic option consists of 20 *cabinas* perched above a lagoon and thriving canal system. The owner Chito, a naturalist who built the canal, is famous for befriending, training and performing with a 12ft crocodile named Pocho who lived on the premises. The croc died in 2011, and the government outlawed crocodile training. Now Chito runs a canal tour.

There is also a very tasty restaurant and bar here. Take a taxi or ask locals for careful directions, as it's tricky to find.

Pacuare Lodge LODGE $$$
(📱4033-0060, in USA & Canada 1-800-963-1195; www.pacuarelodge.com; on the Río Pacuare; 2-night all-inclusive packages s/d from US$1173/1838) 🍃 This dream of an ecolodge is a trek, but worth it for nature lovers and rafting enthusiasts. Rather than using traditional transport, guests can raft to and from the lodge, where elegant, private bungalows with hardwood floors and solar-heated showers perch along the river. Bungalows have no electricity or walls, only screens, all the better to enjoy nature.

Package deals include transportation from San José, a bilingual guide, a rafting tour or ground transportation to the lodge, equipment, meals, most drinks (not mixed), a hike, and the return trip to San José.

ℹ Information

Banco de Costa Rica, 100m north of the park, has a 24-hour ATM.

Puerto Limón

The biggest city on Costa Rica's Caribbean coast, the birthplace of United Fruit and capital of Limón Province, this hardworking port city sits removed from the rest of the country. Cruise ships deposit dazed-looking passengers between October and May. Around here, business is measured by truckloads of fruit, not busloads of tourists, so don't expect any pampering.

A general lack of political and financial support from the federal government means that Limón is not a city that has aged gracefully. It is a grid of dilapidated buildings, overgrown parks and sidewalks choked with street vendors. Crime is a problem: the city, distressingly, has as many homicides annually as San José – even though San José has five times the population. It's worth noting, however, that most of this violence is related to organized crime and does not affect travelers. Despite its shortcomings, Limón can be a compelling destination for adventurous urban explorers.

History

Until the 1850s, the most frequent visitors to Limón were pirates, who used the area's natural deep-water bays as hideouts. At the time, the country's main port was in Puntarenas, on the Pacific, but when the railroad arrived in the late 19th century, Limón blossomed into a full-blown trade hub. The city ultimately served as the key export point for the country's newest agribusiness: bananas.

Beginning in 1913, a series of blights shut down many Caribbean *fincas* (farms) and a large portion of the area's banana production moved to the southern Pacific coast. Afro-Caribbean workers, however, couldn't follow the jobs, as they were forbidden to leave the province. Stranded in the least-developed part of Costa Rica, many turned to subsistence farming, fishing or managing small-scale cacao plantations. Others organized and staged bloody strikes against United Fruit. Fed up with the status quo, Limón provided key support to José Figueres (a Costa Rican revolutionary) during the 1948 civil war. This act was rewarded the

BUSES FROM SIQUIRRES

Siquirres has two main bus terminals. The one on the southeast corner of the park serves the first three destinations listed below. Buses for Turrialba leave from a separate terminal on the north side of the park.

DESTINATION	BUS COMPANY	COST (US$)	DURATION	FREQUENCY
Guápiles	Tracasa	1.75	45mins	hourly, 5:45am-7:50pm
Limón	Tracasa	2.30	1hr	almost hourly, 6:45am-6:55pm
San José	Autotransportes Caribeños	3.20	2hr	almost hourly, 4:30am-7pm
Turrialba	Transtusa	2.35	1½hr	almost hourly, 5:30am-7pm

Puerto Limón

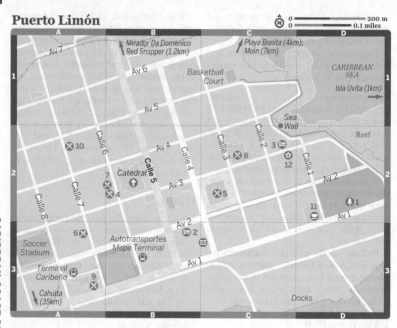

following year when the new president enacted a constitution that granted blacks full citizenship and the right to work and travel freely throughout Costa Rica.

Even though segregation was officially dismantled, Limón continues to live with its legacy. The province was the last to get paved roads and the last to get electricity (areas to the south of the city weren't on the grid until the late 1970s), and the region has chronically higher crime and unemployment rates than the rest of the country.

While two major new infrastructure developments have been announced in recent years – the construction of a US$1-billion container port in Moín by the multinational corporation APM and a Chinese-financed

US$221 million initiative to widen Hwy 32 to four lanes – it is unclear whether the economic benefits of these projects will be shared by the local population. Indeed, plans for the container port have sparked massive protests by dockworkers' union members in Limón and Moín who fear that privatization of the port will undermine, rather than improve, their standard of living.

◎ Sights

Parque Vargas　　　　　　　　　PARK
The city's waterfront centerpiece won't ever win best in show, but its decrepit bandstand, paths and greenery are surprisingly appealing, all shaded by palms and facing the docks.

Playa Bonita
BEACH

There are no beaches for swimming or surfing in Limón. If you are keen on getting in the water, Playa Bonita, 4km northwest of town, has a pleasant, sandy beach.

🎎 Festivals & Events

Día de la Raza
CULTURAL

(Columbus Day; ☉ Oct 12) When the city can afford it, Puerto Limón celebrates Día de la Raza with a boisterous week of Carnaval festivities, including live music, dancing and a big Saturday parade. During this time, book hotels in advance.

Festival Flores de la Diáspora Africana
CULTURAL

(www.festivaldiasporacr.org; ☉ late Oct) A celebration of Afro-Caribbean culture. While it is centered on Puerto Limón, the festival sponsors events showcasing African heritage throughout the province and San José.

👉 Tours

Veragua Rainforest Research & Adventure Park
ECOTOUR

(☑ 4000-0949; www.veraguarainforest.com; adult with/without zip-line tour US$99/66, child with/without zip-line tour US$75/55; 🚼) 🚺 In Las Brisas de Veragua, this bells-and-whistles rainforest adventure park is nestled into the foothills of the Cordillera de Talamanca. A sprawling complex, it has guided tours of the forest along elevated walkways, as well as attractions such as an aerial tram, a reptile vivarium, an insectarium, and hummingbird and butterfly gardens. During research, the park was converting to solar power.

There is also a zip-line canopy tour, available at an extra charge. Installations include a cafeteria and gift shop. Many of the attractions are wheelchair-accessible – a good way of exploring nature if traveling with an elderly person or small children.

To get here, take the signed turnoff south from Hwy 32 at Liverpool, 12km west of Puerto Limón.

🛏 Sleeping

Limón offers nothing remotely upscale; for something nicer, head to nearby Playa Bonita.

Hotel Miami
HOTEL $

(☑ 2758-0490; hmiamilimon@yahoo.com; Av 2 btwn Calles 4 & 5; s/d/tr US$27/37/42, with air-con US$41/58/67; 🅿 ❄ @) For its location on the main drag, this clean, mint-green place feels surprisingly serene, especially in the rooms

in back. All 34 tidy rooms are equipped with cable TV and fan. Rooms with air-conditioning have hot water. Welcoming staff, common balconies overlooking the street and a secure setup add up to the best value in town.

Oasys del Caribe
BUNGALOW $

(☑ 2795-0024; oasysdelcaribe@ice.co.cr; s/d/f US$35/49/70, without air-con US$45/59/78; 🅿 ❄ 🏊) About 3km northwest of Limón, on the inland side of the road, these cozy pink bungalows are decorated with lace curtains and bamboo furniture. The small pool is a huge perk, as this place does not have beach access.

Hotel Playa Bonita
HOTEL $$

(☑ 2795-1010; www.hotelplayabonita.com; s/d standard US$57/80, executive US$66/90, all incl breakfast; 🅿 ❄ 🛜 🏊) This seaside hotel has simple, whitewashed rooms and a breezy, ocean-view restaurant that serves everything from burgers to jumbo shrimp. It's about 5km from downtown Puerto Limón and 2.5km from the entrance to the docks at Moín.

Park Hotel
HOTEL $$$

(☑ 2798-0555; www.parkhotellimon.com; Av 3 btwn Calles 1 & 2; d incl breakfast US$130; 🅿 ❄ @ 🛜) Downtown Limón's most attractive hotel has 32 rooms in a faded yellow building that faces the ocean. Tiled rooms are tidy and sport clean bathrooms with hot water; superior and deluxe units come with ocean views and balconies. The hotel also houses the swankiest restaurant in the town center.

🍴 Eating

Find cheap eats at the *sodas* in the **central market** (Av 2 btwn Calles 3 & 4; ☉ 6am-8pm Mon-Fri). You can get groceries at the large **Más X Menos** (cnr Av 3 & Calle 3; ☉ 6:30am-10pm), or at the **Palí** (cnr Calle 7 & Av 1; ☉ 7am-9pm Mon-Fri, 8am-7:30pm Sat & Sun) next to the Terminal Caribeño.

⭐ Soda El Patty
CARIBBEAN $

(☑ 2798-3407; cnr Av 5 & Calle 7; patí US$1.50, mains US$4-5; ☉ 7am-7pm) This beloved nine-table Caribbean eatery serves up delicious *patí* – flaky beef turnovers stuffed with onion, spices, and Panamanian peppers – along with sweet plantain tarts and heaping plates of rice-n-beans (the spicier, more flavorful version of the country's traditional *casado*). On Fridays, the chef prepares a special, piping-hot cauldron of *rondón* soup.

THE BANANA LEGACY

The banana. Nothing embodies the tumultuous history of Latin America – and its complicated relationship to the United States – quite like this common yellow fruit. It is the crop that has determined the path of current affairs in more than one Central American nation. It is the sobriquet used to describe corrupt, dictatorial regimes – 'the banana republic.' Bananas are a symbol of frivolity, the raw material for Carmen Miranda hats and Busby Berkeley dance numbers. (Want to blow your mind? Look up 'The Lady with the Tutti Frutti Hat' from the 1942 musical flick *The Gang's All Here* – it's a hallucinogenic panorama of dancing bananas.)

It was in Costa Rica, interestingly, that the idea of bananas as an industry was born. Imported from the Canary Islands by sailors during the colonial period, the fruit had long been a basic foodstuff in the Caribbean islands. But it was 19th-century railroad baron Minor Keith who turned it into a booming international business. After building the railroad between San José and Limón, Keith proceeded to carpet vast swaths of Central America in bananas. Over the course of the 20th century, the company he founded – United Fruit – would become an integral part of the region's economies and a behind-the-scenes puppet master in its political systems. (For a highly readable history on this topic, pick up *Bananas: How the United Fruit Company Shaped the World*, by journalist Peter Chapman.)

Part of the reason bananas became a continent-wide crop boils down to profit and biology. Bananas – a fruit afflicted with a high rate of spoilage – require a vast economy of scale (and cheap labor) to be profitable. It's also an inordinately delicate fruit to cultivate, partly because bananas are clones. The fruit doesn't grow from seeds; its propagation requires that a cutting be taken from an existing plant and put into the ground. This makes them incredibly vulnerable to illness – what kills one banana kills all bananas. Entire networks of plantations can be devastated by fungus, such as the diseases that swept through Costa Rica's southern Caribbean coast in the 1910s and '20s.

Over the years, this weakness has led growers to turn to a veritable arsenal of chemicals to protect their crops. This, in turn, has taken a toll on both the environment and the workers who spray them, some of whom have been rendered sterile by powerful fungicides such as DBCP (now banned). Groups of workers in various countries have filed numerous lawsuits against fruit companies and chemical manufacturers – and won – but these victories are generally short-lived. Even when Central American courts rule in workers' favor, it is practically impossible for plaintiffs to secure payouts.

There have been some attempts at growing bananas organically, but according to some experts, those efforts will never be enough to replace the intense agribusiness that currently supplies the world with its fourth major foodstuff, after rice, wheat and milk. Costa Rica is sometimes thought of as a country of coffee producers, a nation built on the work of humble, independent farmers. But the fact is that bananas remain the country's number-one agricultural export – as they have been for decades. They are an inextricable part of the country's DNA. And, unless everyone suddenly starts putting sliced apples into their cereal, that likely won't change any time soon.

Macrobiótica Bionatura VEGETARIAN $
(☑2798-2020; Calle 6 btwn Avs 3 & 4; ☺8am-6:15pm Mon-Fri, to 5:15pm Sat; ✐) This macrobiotic grocery store sells healthy vegetarian foods, vitamins, and all things made of soy.

Fruit & Veggie Land VEGETARIAN $
(☑2758-4142; Calle 7 btwn Avs 2 & 3; smoothies from US$2; ☺9am-7pm; ✐) This great breakfast and lunch spot squeezes fresh fruit and blends it into smoothies of every color and flavor.

Mirador Da Domenico
Red Snapper CARIBBEAN $$
(☑2758-7613; mains US$9-35; ☺11:30am-midnight; ⊞) Head honchos for Limón's new port project often lunch at this scenic half-Italian half-Caribbean restaurant perched on a mountainside overlooking the city and coastline. The open-air dining room has a bunch of TVs and a convivial vibe, making it an ideal spot to catch a soccer game and devour a whole fried fish.

Caribbean Kalisi Coffee Shop   CARIBBEAN $$

(2758-3249; Calle 6 btwn Avs 3 & 4; mains from US$10; ⊙7am-8pm Mon-Fri, 8am-7:30pm Sat, 8am-5pm Sun) Belly up to the cafeteria-style counter at this friendly family spot and cobble together a plate of coconut rice, red beans and whatever Caribbean meat and veggie dishes are cooking today. Also recommended in the mornings for its affordable à la carte breakfasts and excellent *café con leche*.

Reina's   SEAFOOD $$

(2795-0879; mains US$9-15; ⊙10am-10pm) On the beach at Playa Bonita, Reina's has loud music, good vibes and plenty of *mariscos* (seafood) and *cerveza* (beer) on the menu.

Drinking & Nightlife

Bars by Parque Vargas and a few blocks west are popular hangouts for coastal characters: banana workers, sailors, ladies of the night, entrepreneurs, boozers, losers and everyone else. Tsunami Sushi is a good spot for live music.

The standard warnings for solo women travelers go double here; if you feel like having a beer, hit a restaurant. This is a lousy town for getting drunk in – keep your wits about you.

El Crucero   CAFE

(2758-7003; cnr Calle 1 & Av 1; ⊙7:30am-6pm Mon-Sat) Kick back with a smoothie, an empanada or an iced espresso and let the cross-breeze cool you at this corner cafe facing Parque Vargas and the docks.

Tsunami Sushi   LIVE MUSIC

(Av 3 btwn Calles 1 & 2; ⊙11am-2am) The bar gets packed here on Saturday nights, when reggae artists and DJs take the stage. Patrons also feast on sushi rolls and down *mangua-ro* shots (the sugar cane liquor *guaro* with mango).

ⓘ Information

DANGERS & ANNOYANCES

Though police presence has ramped up noticeably, pickpockets can be a problem, particularly in the market and along the sea wall. In addition, people do get mugged here, so stick to well-lit main streets at night, avoiding the sea wall and Parque Vargas. If driving, park in a guarded lot and remove everything from the car.

INTERNET ACCESS

There's an internet cafe in the Autotransportes Mepe Terminal.

MEDICAL SERVICES

Hospital Tony Facio (2758-2222) Serves the entire province. It's northeast of the center.

BUSES FROM PUERTO LIMÓN

Buses from all points west arrive at **Terminal Caribeño** (Av 2 btwn Calles 7 & 8), just west of the baseball stadium. Buses to all points south depart from **Autotransportes Mepe Terminal** (2758-1572; Calle 6 btwn Avs 1 & 2), on the east side of the stadium.

DESTINATION	COST (US$)	DURATION (HR)	TERMINAL	FREQUENCY
Bribrí	4.60	2	Autotransportes Mepe Terminal	hourly, 5am-7pm
Cahuita	2.40	1	Autotransportes Mepe Terminal	every 1-2hrs, 7:30am-4:30pm
Guápiles (Tracasa)	4.30	2	Terminal Caribeño	hourly, 6am-6pm
Manzanillo	4.90	2	Autotransportes Mepe Terminal	every 1-2hrs, 5:30am-6:30pm
Puerto Viejo de Talamanca	3.70	1.5	Autotransportes Mepe Terminal	every 1-2hrs, 7:30am-4:30pm
San José (Autotransportes Caribeños)	7	3	Terminal Caribeño	every 30mins, 4:30am-9:30am, then every hour to 4:30pm; later buses on weekends
Siquirres (Tracasa)	2.30	1	Terminal Caribeño	hourly, 6am-6pm
Sixaola	5.25	3	Autotransportes Mepe Terminal	hourly, 5am-7pm

MONEY

If you're traveling onward to Parismina or Tortuguero, Limón will be your last opportunity to get cash (and phonecards, for the Parismina-bound).

Banco de Costa Rica (☑ 2758-3166; cnr Av 2 & Calle 1) Exchanges US dollars and has an ATM.

Scotiabank (cnr Av 3 & Calle 2; ⊙ 9am-5pm Mon-Fri, to 1pm Sat) Exchanges cash and has a 24-hour ATM that dispenses US dollars.

POST

Post Office (Calle 4 btwn Avs 1 & 2; ⊙ 9am-4pm)

ⓘ Getting There & Away

Puerto Limón is the transportation hub of the Caribbean coast.

Cruise ships dock in Limón, but smaller passenger boats bound for Parismina and Tortuguero use the port at Moín, about 7km west of town.

If driving in Puerto Limón, leave your car in a guarded lot.

Moín

Just 8km northwest of Puerto Limón, this is the town's main transportation dock, where you can catch a boat to Parismina or Tortuguero.

ⓖ Tours

All Rankin's Tours   BOAT TOUR
(☑ 2709-8101, 2758-4160; www.greencoast.com/allrankin) These tours by longtime local resident Willis Rankin are also ideal for leisurely rides to Tortuguero. Rankin also offers package deals including accommodation in his rustic lodge near Tortuguero's airstrip.

Tortuguero Wildlife Tour & Transportation   BOAT TOUR
(William Guerrero, TUCA; ☑ 8371-2323, 2798-7027; www.tortuguero-wildlife.com) A small, well-recommended company run by master sloth-spotter William Guerrero and his wife. It's ideal if you want to book a leisurely ride to Tortuguero, with plenty of pit stops to see wildlife.

ⓘ Getting There & Away

BOAT

The journey by boat from Moín to Tortuguero can take anywhere from three to five hours, depending on how often the boat stops to observe wildlife (many tours also stop for lunch). Indeed, it is worth taking your time. As you wind through these jungle canals, you're likely to spot howler monkeys, crocodiles, two- and three-toed sloths and an amazing array of wading birds, including roseate spoonbills.

Tourist boat schedules exist in theory only and change frequently depending on demand. If you're feeling lucky, you can just show up in Moín in the morning and try to get on one of the outgoing tour boats (there's often at least one departure at 10am). But you're better off reserving in advance, particularly during slower seasons when boats don't travel the route on a daily basis. If the canal becomes blocked by water hyacinths or logjams, the route might be closed altogether. Call ahead for departure times and reservations.

One-way fares generally run between US$30 and US$40 to Tortuguero, or between US$25 and US$30 to Parismina. **ABACAT** (Asociación de Boteros de los Canales de Tortuguero; ☑ 8360-7325) arranges transport on various boats. Try Tortuguero (p161) for additional operators.

TURTLE BEACH TRAGEDY

The Caribbean's turtle-conservation community suffered a devastating blow on the night of May 30, 2013, when 26-year-old Costa Rican environmentalist Jairo Mora Sandoval was murdered while patrolling a stretch of Moín beach near Puerto Limón. The tragedy shines a light on the challenges facing turtle conservationists. While many communities along the coast have successfully engaged former poachers in guiding and conservation work, turtle eggs continue to be prized on the black market for their supposed aphrodisiac qualities. The remote section of beach where Mora was working, near Costa Rica's biggest Caribbean port, is frequented by drug runners, some armed with semiautomatic weapons.

Mora's death sparked strong international and domestic protest, with calls for a beefed-up police presence and stronger conservation measures. Although seven suspects were taken into custody, they were all acquitted after evidence went missing and investigators botched the case. Then they were called back for a retrial in early 2015. The saga has been devastating to Costa Rica's sea turtle conservation movement, but some bold activists still patrol the beaches on the Caribbean coast.

BUS

Tracasa buses to Moín from Puerto Limón (US$0.60, 20 minutes) depart from Terminal Caribeño hourly from 5:30am to 6:30pm (less frequently on Saturday and Sunday). Get off the bus before it goes over the bridge.

Tropical Wind (🖉8327-0317, 8313-7164) operates almost-daily shuttles between Tortuguero and Moín in high season.

NORTHERN CARIBBEAN

This is the wettest region in Costa Rica, a network of rivers and canals that is home to diminutive fishing villages and slick sportfishing camps, raw rainforest and all-inclusive resorts – not to mention plenty of wading birds and sleepy sloths.

Most significantly, the area's long, wild beaches serve as the protected nesting grounds for three kinds of sea turtle. In fact, more green turtles are born here than anywhere else in the world.

Parismina

For a sense of what Costa Rica's Caribbean coast was like prior to the arrival of mass tourism, jump ship in this sleepy coastal fishing village, wedged between the Canales de Tortuguero and the Caribbean Sea. Bereft of zip lines, it's the sort of spot where old men play dominoes on porches and kids splash around in mud puddles.

For those intrepid enough to make the journey, Parismina is also a great place to view turtles and aid in their conservation, without the crowds of Tortuguero. Leatherbacks nest between late February and early October, with the peak season in April and May. Green turtles begin nesting in June, with a peak in August and September. Hawksbills are sometimes seen between February and September.

Sportfishing is the other traditional tourist draw. The top tarpon season is from January to mid-May, while snook are caught from September to November.

🏃 Activities & Tours

Río Parismina Lodge (p152) organizes package sportfishing expeditions from the USA.

Asociación Salvemos
Las Tortugas de Parismina VOLUNTEERING
(ASTOP, Save the Turtles of Parismina; 🖉2798-2220; www.parisminaturtles.org; ⊙by arrange-

ment Mar-Sep) 🖉 Directed by 37-year resident and former Peace Corps volunteer Vicky Taylor, this grassroots turtle-protection organization with strong community support employs former poachers as 'turtle guides' and maintains a guarded turtle hatchery. Travelers can volunteer as guards to patrol the beaches alongside local turtle guides. Volunteers (five-night minimum commitment) pay a one-time US$35 registration fee.

ASTOP also organizes homestays (per night with three meals US$30), offers internet access free for volunteers, and can arrange horseback-riding trips, bike rentals, turtle-watching tours (per person US$25), wildlife-viewing excursions by boat, and farm and heliconia-garden tours in Caño Blanco.

Barrita SWIMMING
A 35-minute walk south of town brings you to the jungle-fringed freshwater lagoon called Barrita. From the Catholic church, head toward the beach and hang a right at the airstrip, then follow the path until it opens out on to the beach and lagoon.

🛏 Sleeping

There are some small, basic hotels that may or may not be open. At the hardware store, about 300m north of the dock, don Alex has camping and basic huts (US$7; high season only), with access to showers, bathrooms and a shared kitchen.

Green Gold Ecolodge LODGE **$**
(🖉8647-0691, 8697-2322; dm adult/child US$20/10, incl 3 meals US$50/30) 🖉 About 3km south of the dock, this simple solar- and generator-powered retreat, steps from the beach and surrounded by 36 hectares of jungle, is an authentic rainforest hideaway. Run by the charming (and bilingual) Jason and Juliana, its rustic but comfortable facilities include dorm beds in screened-in upstairs rooms, a shared open-air kitchen and shared bathrooms.

Jason leads tours of all kinds, and the area is rife with as much wildlife as Tortuguero, but hardly any people. Walk in from the village, or arrange for a truck ride from town (US$10 one way); advance reservations recommended.

Carefree Ranch CABINA **$**
(🖉8744-6403; r per person US$10) Opposite the Catholic church at the southern end of town, this clapboard house – bright yellow with green trim – has eight tidy rooms and

an inviting, broad front porch. It's about as quaint as things get in Parismina.

Tasty home-cooked *casados* (US$6) are also available.

Río Parismina Lodge   LODGE $$$
(☑in USA 210-824-4442, in USA 800-338-5688; www.riop.com; rates by arrangement; 🌀🐟) Top-of-the line spot, with swimming pool, Jacuzzi, English-speaking guides, daily laundry service and both river and ocean boats.

Soda Rancho La Palma   SODA $
(☑8550-7243; casados US$6; ⏰5am-9pm Mon-Sat) Right next to the dock, no-nonsense doña Amelia serves up fresh and tasty *casados*. She also keeps the small plaster statue of the Virgin that is paraded during an annual boat procession in July.

ⓘ Information

There are no banks or post offices in Parismina, and credit cards are not accepted, so make sure you bring enough cash.

You can find internet access (per hour US$2) at ASTOP (p151).

While the village has a couple of pay phones, no one in town sells phonecards – bring your own.

ⓘ Getting There & Away

Parismina is only accessible by boat or chartered flight.

The only scheduled boat service is to Caño Blanco (for transfer to Siquirres). Water taxis (US$2, 10 minutes) leave from the Parismina dock at 5:30am, 1:30pm and 4:30pm on weekdays, and at 5:30am, 9am, 1:30pm and 4:30pm on weekends. A bus will be waiting at Caño Blanco's dock to continue the journey to Siquirres (US$2.20, two hours), where you can find onward transport.

For travel to Tortuguero or Puerto Limón (via Moín), it's possible to reserve a seat on one of the tourist boats that travel between the two destinations, but advance planning is essential. Note that it may take 24 to 48 hours to secure transportation (around US$25 to either destination), as Parismina is not a regular stop. Call one of the boat companies in Moín or Tortuguero directly, or ask doña Amelia at Soda Rancho La Palma to help you book.

Parque Nacional Tortuguero

'Humid' is the driest word that could truthfully be used to describe 311-sq-km **Parque Nacional Tortuguero** (US$15; ⏰6-7am, 7:30am-noon & 1-4pm). With annual rainfall of up to 6000mm in the northern part of the park, it is one of the wettest areas in the country. In addition, the protected area extends into the Caribbean Sea, covering about 5200 hectares of marine habitat. In other words, plan on spending quality time in a boat.

The famed **Canales de Tortuguero** are the introduction to this park. Created to connect a series of lagoons and meandering rivers in 1974, this engineering marvel allowed inland navigation between Limón and coastal villages in something sturdier than a dugout canoe. Regular flights service the village of Tortuguero – but if you fly, you'll be missing half the fun. The leisurely taxi-boat ride, through banana plantations and wild jungle, is equal parts recreation and transportation.

Referred to as the 'mini-Amazon,' Parque Nacional Tortuguero's intense biodiversity includes over 400 bird species, 60 known species of frog, 30 species of freshwater fish and three monkey species, as well as the threatened West Indian manatee.

Caimans and crocodiles can be seen lounging on river banks, while freshwater turtles bask on logs.

Over 120,000 visitors a year come to boat the canals and see the wildlife, particularly to watch turtles lay eggs. This is the most important Caribbean breeding site of the green sea turtle, 40,000 of which arrive every season to nest. Of the eight species of marine turtle in the world, six nest in Costa Rica, and four nest in Tortuguero. Various volunteer organizations address the problem of poaching with vigilant turtle patrols.

Park headquarters is at **Cuatro Esquinas** (☑2709-8086; ⏰6-7am, 7:30am-noon & 1-4pm), just south of Tortuguero village.

Sharks and strong currents make the beaches unsuitable for swimming.

🏃 Activities

Most visitors come to watch sea turtles lay eggs on the wild beaches. The area, however, is more than just turtles: Tortuguero teems with wildlife. You'll find sloths and howler monkeys in the treetops, tiny frogs and green iguanas scurrying among buttress roots, and mighty tarpons and endangered manatees swimming in the waters.

Turtle-Watching

The area attracts four of the world's eight species of sea turtle, making it a crucial habitat for these massive reptiles. It will come as little surprise, then, that these hatching grounds gave birth to the sea-turtle-conservation movement. The Caribbean Conservation Corporation, the first program of its kind in the world, has continuously monitored turtle populations here since 1955. Today green sea turtles are increasing in numbers along this coast, but the leatherback, hawksbill and loggerhead are in decline.

Most female turtles share a nesting instinct that drives them to return to the beach of their birth (their natal beach) in order to lay their eggs. (Only the leatherback returns to a more general region, instead of a specific beach.) During their lifetimes, they will usually nest every two to three years and, depending on the species, may come ashore to lay eggs 10 times in one season. Often, a turtle's ability to successfully reproduce depends on the ecological health of this original habitat.

The female turtle digs a perfect cylindrical cavity in the sand using her flippers, and then lays 80 to 120 eggs. She diligently covers the nest with sand to protect the eggs, and she may even create a false nest in another location in an attempt to confuse predators. She then makes her way back to sea – after which the eggs are on their own. Incubation ranges from 45 to 70 days, after which hatchlings – no bigger than the size of your palm – break out of their shells using a caruncle, a temporary tooth. They crawl to the ocean in small groups, moving as quickly as possible to avoid dehydration and predators. Once they reach the surf, they must swim for at least 24 hours to get to deeper water, away from land-based predators.

Because of the sensitive nature of the habitat and the critically endangered status of some species, tours to see this activity are highly regulated. So as to not alarm turtles as they come to shore (a frightened turtle will return to the ocean and dump her eggs), tour groups gather in shelter sites close to the beach and a spotter relays a turtle's location via radio once she has safely crossed the high-tide mark and built her nest. At this time, visitors can then go to the beach and watch the turtle lay her eggs, cover her nest and return to the ocean. Seeing a turtle is not guaranteed, but licensed guides will still make your tour worthwhile with the wealth of turtle information they'll share. By law, tours can only take place between 8am and midnight. Some guides will offer tours after midnight; these are illegal.

Visitors should wear closed-toe shoes and rain gear. Tours cost US$25. This rate includes the purchase of a US$5 sticker that pays for the patrols that help protect the nesting sites from scavengers and looters. Nesting season runs from March to October, with July and August being prime time. The next best time is April, when leatherback turtles nest in small numbers. Flashlights and cameras are not allowed on the beach.

Other Wildlife-Watching
More than 400 bird species, both resident and migratory, have been recorded in Tortuguero – a bird-watchers' paradise. Due to the wet habitat, the park is especially rich in waders, including egrets, jacanas and 14 different types of heron, as well as species such as kingfishers, toucans and the great curassow (a type of jungle peacock known locally as the *pavón*). The great green macaw is a highlight, most common from December to April, when the almond trees are fruiting. In September and October, look for flocks of migratory species such as eastern kingbird, barn swallows and purple martins. The Sea Turtle Conservancy conducts a biannual monitoring program, in which volunteers can help scientists take inventory of local and migratory species.

Certain species of mammal are particularly evident in Tortuguero, especially mantled howler monkeys, the Central American spider monkey and the white-faced capuchin. If you've got a good pair of binoculars and a good guide, you can usually see both two- and three-toed sloths. In addition, normally shy neotropical river otters are reasonably habituated to boats. Harder to spot are timid West Indian manatees. The park is also home to big cats such as jaguars and ocelots, but these are savvy, nocturnal animals – sightings are very rare.

Turtles of the Caribbean

One of the most moving experiences for visitors to the Caribbean coast is turtle-watching on its wild beaches. Witnessing the return of a massive turtle to its natal beach and its laborious nesting ritual feels both solemn and magical. Four species of sea turtle nest along the Caribbean coast – green, leatherback, hawksbill and loggerhead – all of which are endangered or threatened.

A Population in Peril

Since it takes many years for sea turtles to mature and reproduce, their populations are quite vulnerable to environmental hazards such as pollution and poaching. Thus, conservation efforts are crucial to their survival – these efforts include guarding hatchlings from predators and providing incentives for local communities to protect turtles and their eggs. Volunteer opportunities are plentiful along the Caribbean coast, with tasks ranging from beach patrols, data collection and tagging to moving eggs to hatcheries and hatchling release.

Planning a Tour

Because of the sensitive habitat and critically endangered status of some species, turtle-nesting tours are highly regulated. Groups must be accompanied by licensed guides, who ensure that the turtles are able to lay their eggs in peace and that other nests are left undisturbed. Nesting season runs from March to October, with July and August being the most active period for green turtles. April is another good month, when leatherback turtles arrive.

1. Studying turtle eggs **2.** Leatherback-turtle hatchlings **3.** Baby leatherback turtle crawling to the surf

Depending on when you visit, you may find yourself watching a newly arrived mother hauling herself onto the beach, laboriously digging a nest with her flippers and hatching dozens of ping pong ball–sized eggs, or a parade of new hatchlings on their slow, determined and endearingly clumsy crawl back to the sea.

Turtle-watching tours can be arranged through Asociación Salvemos Las Tortugas de Parismina (ASTOP; p151) in Parismina and by licensed guides in Tortuguero village.

Doing Time for the Turtles

There are many opportunities for volunteers to help protect sea turtles and the many other creatures that inhabit the Caribbean coast. In most cases, organizations require a minimum commitment of a week. A few options:

Asociación Widecast (p171) Grassroots NGO that has volunteer opportunities in Cahuita and north of the Río Pacuare river mouth.

ASTOP (p151) Small, locally run group in Parismina.

Canadian Organization for Tropical Education & Rainforest Conservation (p157) Canadian not-for-profit with a research station in Tortuguero.

Sea Turtle Conservancy (p157) Long-time organization with a research station in Tortuguero.

Around Tortuguero

N
0 ————— 1 km
0 ————— 0.5 miles

Turtle Beach Lodge (1.5km)
Canadian Organization for Tropical Education & Rainforest Conservation
Caño La Palma
Cerro Tortuguero (119m)
CARIBBEAN SEA
Isla Chica
Tortuga Lodge & Gardens
Airstrip
Laguna Penitencia
Lagunas del Tortuguero
Laguna Lodge
Parque Nacional Tortuguero
La Baula Lodge
Hotel Aninga & Spa
Pachira Lodge
Evergreen Lodge
Mawamba Lodge
Rana Roja
Toucan & Tarpon Lodge
Wild Ginger
Sea Turtle Conservancy
TORTUGUERO VILLAGE
Caño Chiquero
Caño Mora
Isla Cuatro Esquinas
Cuatro Esquinas
Río Tortuguero
Lagunas del Tortuguero
Caño Haroldas

Most wildlife-watching tours are done by boat. To get the best from Tortuguero, be on the water early or go out following a heavy rain, when all the wildlife comes out to sunbathe. It is also highly recommended to take tours by canoe or kayak – these smaller, si-

lent craft will allow you to get into the park's less trafficked nooks and crannies.

Boating

Four aquatic trails wind their way through Parque Nacional Tortuguero, inviting waterborne exploration. **Río Tortuguero** acts as the entrance way to the network of trails. This wide, beautiful river is often covered with water lilies and is frequented by aquatic birds such as herons, kingfishers and anhingas – the latter of which is known as the snakebird for the way its slim, winding neck pokes out of the water when it swims.

Caño Chiquero and **Cañõ Mora** are two narrower waterways with good wildlife-spotting opportunities. According to park regulation, only kayaks, canoes and silent electric boats are allowed in these areas. Caño Chiquero is thick with vegetation, especially red guácimo trees and epiphytes. Black turtles and green iguanas like to hang out here. Caño Mora is about 3km long but only 10m wide, so it feels as if it's straight out of *The Jungle Book*. **Caño Harold** is actually an artificially constructed canal, but that doesn't stop the creatures – such as Jesus Christ lizards and caimans – from inhabiting its tranquil waters.

Canoe rental and boat tours are available in Tortuguero village.

Hiking

Behind Cuatro Esquinas ranger station, the park currently has just one trail on solid ground. Visitors can hike the muddy, 2km out-and-back trail that traverses the tropical humid forest and parallels a stretch of beach. Green parrots and several species of monkey are commonly sighted here. The short trail is well marked. Rubber boots are required and are available for rent at hotels and near the park entrance.

At the time of research, the park was preparing to open a second hiking option, Cerro Tortuguero Trail. To reach the trailhead, guests will take boats to the town of San Francisco, north of Tortuguero village, where they will disembark at a new ranger station and buy a ticket (prices TBD). The trail then takes visitors 1.8km up a hill for a view of the surrounding lagoon, forest and ocean.

⊙ Information

Park headquarters is at Cuatro Esquinas (p152), just south of Tortuguero village. This is a helpful ranger station, with maps and info. For canoe tours from this station, new rules limit the number of boats and the amount of time they spend on the canals. Boats are permitted in the park from 6am to 6:30am, 8:30am to 9am, 11am to 11:30am and 2:30pm to 3pm. The early morning and afternoon tours are best for encountering wildlife and beating the heat. Reserve early for the canal tour, especially in high season.

Jalova Station (⊙6-7am, 7:30am-noon & 1-4pm) is on the canal at the south entrance to the national park, accessible from Parismina by boat. Although tourists rarely stop here, there's a small visitor's center, a short nature trail and a bathroom.

🛈 Getting There & Away

The park is a short walk south of the village of Tortuguero (the most common entry point) and also accessible by boat from Parismina.

Tortuguero Village

Located within the confines of Parque Nacional Tortuguero, accessible only by air or water, this bustling little village with strong Afro-Caribbean roots is best known for attracting hordes of sea turtles (the name Tortuguero means 'turtle catcher') – and the hordes of tourists who want to see them. While the peak turtle season is in July and August, the park and village have begun to attract travelers year-round. Even in October, when the turtles have pretty much returned to the sea, caravans of families and adventure travelers arrive to go on jungle hikes and to canoe the area's lush canals.

🏃 Activities

Canadian Organization for Tropical Education & Rainforest Conservation   VOLUNTEERING
(COTERC; ☑2709-8052; www.coterc.org) This not-for-profit organization operates the Estación Biológica Caño Palma, 8km north of Tortuguero village. This small biological research station runs a volunteer program in which visitors can assist with upkeep of the station and ongoing research projects, including sea-turtle and bird monitoring, mammal, caiman and snake monitoring, and also a community program.

Volunteer fees start at US$250 per week and include accommodations in dormitory buildings and three meals per day. The minimum age for participation is 18, and a two-week minimum commitment is required. Call ahead to arrange a visit.

Sea Turtle Conservancy   VOLUNTEERING
(STC, formerly Caribbean Conservation Corporation; ☑2297-5510, in USA 352-373-6441; www.conserveturtles.org; museum admission US$2; ⊙10am-noon & 2-5pm) About 200m north of the village, Tortuguero's original turtle-conservation organization operates a research station, visitor center and museum. Exhibits focus on all things turtle-related, including a 20-minute video about the history of local turtle conservation. STC also runs a highly reputable environmental volunteer program.

During nesting season, volunteers can observe turtle tagging and assist with egg counts and biometric data collection. During bird-migration seasons, they help with mist-netting and point-counts. Volunteer fees (starting at US$1524) include accommodations, meals and transport to and from San José.

☞ Tours

Guides have posted signs all over town advertising their services for canal tours and turtle walks. The two most convenient places to arrange tours are at local hotels and at the official Asociación de Guías de Tortuguero (p158) kiosk.

Leonardo Tours   OUTDOORS
(☑8577-1685; www.leonardotours.wordpress.com) With nine years of experience guiding tours in the area, Leonardo Estrada brings extensive knowledge and infectious enthusiasm to his turtle, canoeing, kayaking and hiking tours.

Ballard Excursions   TOUR
(www.tortuguerovillage.com/ballardexcursions) Ross Ballard, a Canadian with deep local roots, leads 3½-hour walking tours focusing on the biology and ecology of the species-rich rainforest at the foot of Cerro Tortuguero, the region's tallest hill.

Tinamon Tours   TOUR
(☑8842-6561, 2709-8004; www.tinamontours.de) Trained zoologist and 20-plus-year Tortuguero resident Barbara Hartung offers hiking, canoeing, cultural and turtle tours in German, English, French or Spanish.

Castor Hunter Thomas   TOUR
(☑8870-8634; castorhunter.blogspot.com) Excellent local guide and 42-year Tortuguero resident who has led hikes, turtle tours and canoe tours for over 20 years.

Riverboat Francesca Nature Tours TOUR
(☑2226-0986; www.tortuguerocanals.com) A highly recommended company run by Modesto and Fran Watson, Riverboat Francesca offers sportfishing – two-day packages from US$165.

Asociación de Guías de Tortuguero TOUR
(☑2767-0836; www.asoprotur.com) The most convenient place to arrange tours is at the official Asociación de Guías de Tortuguero kiosk by the boat landing. Made up of scores of local guides, the association offers tours in English, French, German and other languages. Although guides are all certified to lead tours in the park, the quality of the tours can vary.

Rates at the time of research were US$20 per person for a two-hour turtle tour and US$40 for a three-hour boat tour. Other options include two-hour walking (US$20), bird-watching (US$35) and fishing (US$15) tours. Tours also involve a US$15 admission fee to the park (not required for the fishing tour).

Don Chico Tours TOUR
(☑2709-8033) The son of long-time local guide Chico offers both hiking and canoe tours; look for his sign just beyond Miss Miriam's restaurant (towards the beach on the north side of the soccer field).

🛏 Sleeping

🛏 In Tortuguero Village

In addition to a number of more upscale lodges and *cabinas*, Tortuguero village has a number of more basic *cabinas* charging US$18 and up for a double room.

★Aracari Garden Hostel HOSTEL $
(☑2767-2246; www.facebook.com/aracarigarden; dm US$10, r US$25-30; ☎) This newly renovated, tangerine-colored hostel on the south side of the soccer field has eight sparkling rooms, relaxing shared spaces and a resident kinkajou that dangles from the property's fruit trees. A stay comes with free coffee, a shared open-air kitchen, laundry ($3 per kg), and all the requisite camaraderie of an intimate, well-run hostel. The ocean is 50m away.

Cabinas Tortuguero CABINA $
(☑8839-1200, 2709-8114; www.cabinas-tortuguero. com; r $14-30; ☎) Down a side street between the boat landing and the park entrance, you'll find eight quaint bungalows surrounding a tidy garden at this popular budget spot. Under new ownership since 2015, the property also features hammocks for lounging, a shared kitchen and laundry service.

La Casona CABINA $
(☑2709-8092; lacasonadetortuguero@yahoo.com; s/d US$18/25, d with kitchenette US$35; ☎) Eleven cute rooms with rustic touches surround a lovely garden at this family-run spot. The entire place is adorned in art created from recycled materials and driftwood, and a waterfall on the property is home to several baby iguanas. It's on the north side of the soccer field.

El Icaco HOTEL $
(☑2709-8044; www.hotelelicaco.com; s/d/tr/q US$20/30/35/40; ☎🍴) This simple oceanfront lodging offers clean, brightly painted rooms and friendly service. The beachfront location is ideal, and there are plenty of hammocks from which to enjoy it. The hotel also offers access to an offsite swimming pool along with rental housing for groups and families. Cash only.

Cabinas Balcon del Mar CABINA $
(☑2709-8124, 2767-7412; s & d US$30, without bathroom s/d US$12/25; ☎) This beachfront option is super quiet, thanks to its prime location on the edge of town and next to the national park. Perks include comfortable beds, hot-water showers, a clean communal kitchen and lots of hammocks.

★Hotel Miss Junie CABINA $$
(☑2709-8029; www.iguanaverdetours.com; s/d standard US$50/55, superior US$65/75, all incl breakfast; ☎) Tortuguero's longest-established lodging, Miss Junie's place is set on spacious, palm-shaded grounds strewn with hammocks and wooden armchairs. Spotless, wood-paneled rooms in a tropical plantation–style building are tastefully decorated with wood accents and bright bedspreads. Upstairs rooms share a breezy balcony overlooking the canal; the restaurant (p160) downstairs is delicious. It's at the northern end of the town's main street.

Casa Marbella B&B $$
(☑8833-0827, 2709-8011; casamarbella.tripod. com; r incl breakfast US$35-65, extra person US$10; @☎) In the heart of the village, with a spacious and delightful canal-side deck, this B&B owned by naturalist Daryl Loth is one

of Tortuguero's most appealing in-town options. Ten simple, well-lit rooms come with ceiling fans, superclean bathrooms and hearty breakfasts served overlooking the water.

Street-side rooms pick up some noise from Tortuguero's village bustle during daylight hours; reserve ahead for the three popular upstairs rooms (one facing the river). It's a two-minute walk north (left) from the village boat landing.

🛏 North of Tortuguero Village

Most of the lodges north and west of the village cater to high-end travelers on package deals, though most will accept walk-ins (er, boat-ins) if they aren't full. Multinight packages typically include accommodation, three meals daily, boat and walking tours and transport to/from San José. Note that Mawamba Lodge and Laguna Lodge are on the same peninsula as Tortuguero village, so you can walk or boat into town. Other lodges lie across the canal and are only accessible by boat or water taxi.

★ Rana Roja　　　　　　LODGE $$
(☑ 2709-8260, 2223-1926; www.tortuguerorana roja.com; r/cabins per person incl breakfast US$55/70, r per person incl 3 meals US$70; @🗼🏊) ⚲ This jungle hideaway is one of Tortuguero's best-value options, especially for solo travelers. Fifteen immaculate rooms and 12 cabins with private terraces and rockers are connected by elevated walkways; all have tile floors, hot showers and awesome views of nature. Free kayaks are available onsite, and guests can make use of the pool at the adjacent Evergreen Lodge.

Toucan & Tarpon Lodge　　　CABINA $$
(☑ 8408-4239; www.toucanandtarpon.com; d incl breakfast US$60) Just across the river from Tortuguero village, this place was opened in late 2013. Three simple *cabinas* with solar electricity and Guatemalan textiles sleep between two and four. Other amenities include delicious homemade breakfasts, a communal kitchen with well-stocked spice cabinet, a ping-pong table, free canoe use and excellent wildlife-spotting (monkeys, sloths, toucans) in the surrounding trees.

La Baula Lodge　　　　　LODGE $$
(☑ 2711-3030; www.labaulalodge.com; s/d/tr/q incl breakfast US$50/70/80/90, incl full board US$80/130/170/210; @🗼🏊) Located north of town and across the river, this laid-back,

long-running lodge has an unpretentious atmosphere, though it could stand a minor makeover, and customer service can be rather lackadaisical. The outdoor dining area features live marimba and guitar music at mealtimes.

Turtle Beach Lodge　　　　LODGE $$$
(☑ 2241-1419, after hours 8837-6969; www.turtle beachlodge.com; 2-night all-inclusive packages per person s/d/tr/q/child US$278/239/220/204/85; @🗼🏊) ⚲ Surrounded by 70 hectares of tropical gardens and rainforest, Tortuguero's northernmost lodge (8km outside the village) is flanked by beach and river. Spacious wood cabins have tile floors, hardwood furniture and huge screened windows. Guests can explore the onsite network of jungle trails, kayak the adjacent canal, or lounge around the turtle-shaped pool or thatch-roofed hammock hut. Rates include transport.

Tortuga Lodge & Gardens　　LODGE $$$
(☑ 2709-8136, 2257-0766; www.tortugalodge. com; r US$74-223, 2-night packages per 2 adults/ child US$656/348; 🗼🏊) This elegant lodge, operated by Costa Rica Expeditions, is set amid 20 serene hectares of private gardens, directly across the canal from Tortuguero's airstrip. The 27 demure rooms channel a 19th-century safari vibe, with creamy linens, handmade textiles, vintage photos and broad terraces that invite lounging. The grounds come equipped with private trails and a riverside pool, bar and restaurant.

Evergreen Lodge　　　　　LODGE $$$
(☑ 2222-6841; evergreentortuguero.com; 2-night packages per person s/d US$279/229; 🗼🏊) One of three hotels operated by the Pachira group, this pleasant place has a more rustic, less resorty feel than its counterparts, with 55 rooms and private bungalows surrounded by jungle greenery. Guests have access to a sunny pool area, Tortuguero's only canopy tour (US$30), free use of kayaks and an upstairs bar overlooking the river.

Laguna Lodge　　　　　　LODGE $$$
(☑ 2272-4943, in USA 888-259-5615; www.laguna tortuguero.com; 2-night all-inclusive packages s/d/ tr US$308/556/744; 🗼🏊) This expansive lodge, liberally decorated with gorgeous mosaic art and trim, has 106 graceful rooms with high ceilings and wide decks lined with Sarchí-made leather rocking chairs. It also has a restaurant, two bars (canal-side and poolside), a massage room, a soccer pitch and a Gaudí-esque reception area.

Hotel Aninga & Spa LODGE $$$
(📞2222-6840, 2222-6841; www.aningalodge tortuguero.com; 2-night packages per person s/d US$249/209; 🛜❄) One of the trio of lodges run by the Pachira Group, this place 1km north of the village has similar grounds and facilities to the adjacent Pachira Lodge, along with Tortuguero's only spa. Nonguests can make appointments for massages (US$60 to US$95) and other treatments here.

Mawamba Lodge LODGE $$$
(📞2293-8181, 2709-8181; www.mawamba.com; 2-night all-inclusive packages s/d/tr US$345/642/ 792; 🛜❄) With pool tables, foosball, a mosaic swimming pool, and butterfly and frog gardens, this lodge sits between the canal and Tortuguero's main turtle nesting beach, within walking distance of town. Simple, wood-paneled rooms have firm beds, good fans and spacious bathrooms with hot water. All are fronted by wide verandas with hammocks and rocking chairs.

Pachira Lodge LODGE $$$
(📞2257-2242, 2256-7078; www.pachiralodge.com; 2-night packages per adult/child US$339/170; 🛜❄) A sprawling compound set on 14 hectares of land, this 88-room hotel with turtle-shaped pool is a popular family spot. Pristine, brightly painted clapboard bungalows with shared terraces house blocks of rooms that sleep up to four. Cribs and children's beds are available.

🍴 Eating

One of Tortuguero's unsung pleasures is the cuisine: the homey restaurants lure you in from the rain with steaming platters of Caribbean-style food.

★Taylor's Place CARIBBEAN $
(📞8319-5627; mains US$7-14; ⊙6-10pm) Low-key atmosphere and high-quality cooking come together beautifully at this backstreet eatery southwest of the soccer field. The inviting garden setting, with chirping insects and picnic benches spread under colorful paper lanterns, is rivaled only by friendly chef Ray Taylor's culinary artistry. House specialties include beef in tamarind sauce, grilled fish in garlic sauce, and fruit drinks both alcoholic and otherwise.

Fresh Foods CARIBBEAN $
(📞2767-1063; mains US$7-12, smoothies US$3-4) Next to the Morpho grocery store in the commercial center of the village, this family-owned food stand opened in 2013 to offer breakfast, solid Caribbean meals and giant, delicious smoothies in fishbowl glasses. And after a long day on the canals, a tasty Caribbean-style filet and a passion-fruit drink really nails it.

Dorling Bakery BAKERY $
(📞2767-0444; pastries US$2, breakfast US$4-5; ⊙5am-8:30pm Mon-Sat, to noon Sun) Thanks to its predawn opening time, this is a good spot to pick up homemade banana bread, lemon and orange cake or cinnamon rolls before an early-morning flight or canal tour.

Sunrise Restaurant CARIBBEAN $
(mains US$4-10; ⊙9:30am-9pm Wed-Mon) Between the boat dock and the national park, this cozy log cabin–like place will lure you in with the delicious smoky aroma of its grilled chicken and pork ribs. It also serves breakfast and a full Caribbean menu at lunch and dinnertime, at some of the best prices in town.

Soda Doña María SODA $
(📞8870-8634; dishes US$5-8; ⊙11am-7:30pm) Recover from a hike in the park at this riverside *soda,* serving *jugos* (juices), burgers and *casados.* It's about 200m north of the park entrance.

★Miss Junie's CARIBBEAN $$
(📞2709-8029; mains US$13-20; ⊙7-9am, noon-2pm & 6-9pm) Over the years, Tortuguero's best-known and most delicious Caribbean eatery has grown from a personal kitchen to a full-blown restaurant. Prices have climbed accordingly, but the menu remains true to its roots: chicken, fish and whole lobster cooked in flavorful Caribbean sauces, with coconut rice and beans. It's at the northern end of the main street.

Tutti's Restaurant STEAK $$
(📞2767-2218; ⊙9am-9:30pm Tue-Sun) This colorful, open-air surf-n-turf establishment opened up next to Super Las Tortugas in 2014. Hummingbirds zip by and calypso music fills the air as guests feast on juicy steaks, fresh seafood, and mouthwatering coconut flan for dessert. Cash only.

Wild Ginger FUSION $$
(📞2709-8240; www.wildgingercr.com; mains US$12-22; ⊙noon-3pm & 5:30-9pm; 🛜) This low-lit spot near the beach north of town specializes in fusion cuisine incorporating fresh local ingredients, such as lobster and mango *ceviche* (seafood marinated in lemon

or lime juice, garlic and seasonings), Caribbean beef stew and passion-fruit crème brûlée. It's 150m north of the elementary school.

Budda Cafe EUROPEAN $$
(2709-8084; www.buddacafe.com; mains US$10-18, pizzas US$7-9; ⊙noon-9pm; ♪) Ambient club music and stenciled 'om' symbols impart a hipster vibe to this cafe between the main road and the river. It's a pleasant setting for pizzas, cocktails and crepes (savory and sweet). Grab a table outside for a prime view of the yellow-bellied flycatchers zipping across the water.

Drinking & Nightlife

La Taberna Punto de Encuentro BAR
(⊙11am-11pm) Adjacent to the Super Bambú *pulpería,* this popular tavern is mellow in the afternoons but draws the party people after dark with cold beer and blaring reggaetón. The highlight, however, is the life-size statue of Jar Jar Binks.

La Culebra CLUB
(⊙8pm-close) Next to the public dock in the center of town, this bright-purple nightclub – Tortuguero's one and only – plays thumping music and serves beer and *bocas* right on the canal.

ⓘ Information

The community's website, Tortuguero Village (www.tortuguerovillage.com), is a solid source of information, listing local businesses and providing comprehensive directions on how to get to Tortuguero.

Immediately to the left of the boat landing, the local tour guides' association (p158) is a good source of tourist information, as is the **Tortuguero Info Center** (2709-8055; tortuguero info.tripod.com; ⊙8am-6pm).

Several local accommodations have internet connections, but these can be iffy, especially during heavy rains.

ⓘ Getting There & Away

If you're coming from San José, the two most convenient ways to get to Tortuguero are by air or all-inclusive bus-boat shuttles – though budget travelers can save money by taking public transportation.

If coming from the southern Caribbean, your best bets are the private boat operators from Moín (just outside Puerto Limón) or shuttle deals from Cahuita and Puerto Viejo.

ⓘ CASH IS KING

There are no banks or ATMs in town and only a few businesses accept credit cards, so bring all the cash you'll need.

AIR

The small airstrip is 4km north of Tortuguero village. **NatureAir** (2299-6000; www.natureair. com) has early-morning flights daily to/from San José and twice weekly to La Fortuna. Charter flights land here regularly as well.

BUS & BOAT

The classic public-transit route to Tortuguero is by bus from San José to Cariari to La Pavona, then by boat from La Pavona to Tortuguero. Alternatively, Tortuguero is accessible by private boat from Moín, near Puerto Limón on the Caribbean coast.

From San José & Cariari

From San José, take the 6:10am, 9am or 10:30am bus to Cariari (US$3.50, three hours) from Gran Terminal del Caribe. In Cariari, you will arrive at a bus station at the south end of town (known as the *estación nueva*). From here, walk or take a taxi 500m north to the *estación vieja* (old station), otherwise referred to as the Terminal Caribeño. Here you can catch a local **Coopetraca** (2767-7590) bus (US$2.20, 6am, 9am, 11:30am and 3pm) to La Pavona, where you'll transfer onto the boat (US$3.20 to US$4) to Tortuguero.

On the return trip, boats leave Tortuguero for La Pavona daily at 5:30am, 9am, 11am and 2:45pm, connecting with Cariari-bound buses at the La Pavona dock.

From Moín

Moín–Tortuguero is primarily a tourist route. While there isn't a scheduled service, boats do ply these canals frequently. When running, boats typically depart at 10am in either direction, charging US$30 to US$40 for the three- to five-hour trip. With advance notice, these same boats can stop in Parismina (one way from either Tortuguero or Moín US$25). Bear in mind that it may take 24 to 48 hours to secure transportation – especially in the low season. For onward transportation beyond Moín, catch a local bus (US$0.60, 20 minutes) to Puerto Limón's bus terminal.

Tropical Wind (2798-6059, 8327-0317) is a Tortuguero-based agency that makes the run regularly. Alternatively, you can make arrangements with companies operating out of Puerto Limón.

SHUTTLE SERVICES

If you prefer to leave the planning to someone else, convenient shuttle services can whisk you to Tortuguero from San José, Arenal-La Fortuna or the southern Caribbean coast in just a few hours. Shuttle companies typically offer minivan service to La Pavona or Moín, where waiting boats take you the rest of the way to Tortuguero. This is a relatively inexpensive, hassle-free option, as you only have to buy a single ticket, and guides help you negotiate the van-to-boat transfer.

Caribe Shuttle (☑2750-0626; caribeshuttle. com) Shuttles from Puerto Viejo (US$75, five hours) and Arenal-La Fortuna (US$60, six hours).

Exploradores Outdoors (p173) More expensive package deals that include transport from San José, Puerto Viejo or Arenal-La Fortuna, a mid-journey Río Pacuare rafting trip, and accommodations in Tortuguero.

Jungle Tom Safaris (☑2221-7878; www. jungletomsafaris.com) Offers one-way shuttles between Tortuguero and San José (US$45). All-inclusive one- and two-night packages (US$99 to US$152) can also include shuttles from Cahuita (US$60), Puerto Viejo (US$60) and Arenal-La Fortuna (US$60), as well as optional tours.

Pleasure Ride (☑2750-2113) Shuttles from Puerto Viejo and Cahuita (US$70 each).

Ride CR (☑2469-2525; www.ridecr.com) Shuttles from Arenal-La Fortuna (US$55).

Riverboat Francesca Nature Tours (p158) Shuttles from San José to Tortuguero via Moín (US$75, including lunch) as well as package deals including accommodation.

Terraventuras (p173) Shuttles from Puerto Viejo (US$65).

Willie's Tours (p165) Shuttles from Cahuita (US$70).

Barra del Colorado

At 904 sq km, including the frontier zone with Nicaragua, Refugio Nacional de Vida Silvestre Barra del Colorado, or 'Barra' for short, is the biggest national wildlife refuge in Costa Rica. It is also one of the most remote – more so since Costa Rica's commercial airlines suspended service to the area in 2009.

The area has long been a favorite of sportfishers, who arrive to hook gar, tarpon and snook. Those who aren't into fishing will be rewarded with incredible landscape. The Ríos San Juan, Colorado and Chirripó all wind through the refuge and out to the Caribbean Sea – through a soggy wetland habitat made up of marshes, mangroves and lagoons. Here, you'll find West Indian manatees, caimans, monkeys, tapirs and three-toed sloths, plus a riotous bird population that includes everything from keel-billed toucans to white hawks. There are countless species of waterbird.

The village of Barra del Colorado lies near the mouth of the Río Colorado and is divided by the river into Barra del Norte and Barra del Sur. The airstrip is on the south side, but more people live along the north side. The area outside the village is swampy and there are no roads; travel is almost exclusively by boat.

🏃 Activities

Fishing is the bread and butter of area lodges, which can also organize custom wildlife-watching excursions along mangroves, lagoons and canals (from US$40).

Anglers go for tarpon from January to June and snook from September to December. Fishing is good year-round, however, and other catches include barracuda, mackerel and jack crevalle, all inshore; or bluegill, guapote (rainbow bass) and machaca in the rivers. There is also deep-sea fishing for marlin, sailfish and tuna, though this is probably better on the Pacific. Area lodges are experts at arranging fishing trips; dozens of fish can be hooked on a good day, so 'catch and release' is an important conservation policy of all the lodges.

🛏 Sleeping

Most of the area's lodging is west of the airstrip, on the south side of the river. Tarpon Land Lodge and Río Colorado Lodge are accessible on foot. Other lodges will have a boat waiting when you arrive with prior reservation. There are also a few basic family-run *cabinas* between the airstrip and the beach, charging US$25 to US$40 per night.

Tarpon Land Lodge CABINA $
(☑8818-9921; s/d US$24/32, incl sportfishing & full board US$250/350; ☒) Situated right next to the airstrip, this is Barra's budget option. At the time of research, new floors were being put in, and five new rooms were under construction (eight worn wood rooms remained in service). The attached restaurant-bar is a local gathering spot and a good place for fish *casados* (mains from US$6.50).

Silver King Lodge LODGE $$$
(☑8447-5988, in USA 877-335-0755; www.silver kinglodge.com; 3-day packages per person US$3850; ✻@✿☒) This excellent sport-fishing lodge caters to couples and families. Huge hardwood rooms have cane ceilings and lots of amenities. Outside, covered

walkways lead to a pool, Jacuzzi and sauna. Bounteous meals are served buffet-style and an open-air bar whips up cocktails. Rates include equipment, fishing license, air transport to and from San José and one cigar per day. No joke.

Río Colorado Lodge LODGE $$$
(☎2232-4063, in USA 800-243-9777; www.riocoloradolodge.com; r per person incl 3 meals US$195, incl 3 meals, 8hr fishing trip & happy hour US$585; ❄📶) Owned by a retired Mississippi lawyer, this 18-room lodge is housed in a rambling tropical-style building with breezy rooms connected by covered walkways, plus a pool table and an outdoor deck with satellite TV. Its bar, within walking distance of the landing strip, attracts a local crowd, and regular afternoon happy hours have reinforced its reputation as a 'party lodge.'

Getting There & Away

Public bus-boat transportation from Cariari is the cheapest transport option. Take the 4am or 2pm bus from Cariari to Puerto Lindo (US$5, 2½ hours), then transfer to the boat for Barra del Colorado (US$6, 20 minutes). Return boats from Barra del Colorado to Puerto Lindo leave at 5am and 3pm.

An alternative, more scenic way to reach Barra del Colorado is by chartering a boat from Tortuguero. The 90-minute trip costs upwards of US$100 (price varies depending on gas prices, season and number of passengers). A recommended guide is **Roberto Abram** (☎8818-8749), who can be contacted through Casa Marbella in Tortuguero village; he also leads local river trips originating in Barra del Colorado.

Otherwise, most folks get here on air charters from San José arranged by the individual lodges.

SOUTHERN CARIBBEAN

The southern coast is the heart and soul of Costa Rica's Afro-Caribbean community. Jamaican workers arrived in the middle of the 19th century to build the railroad and then stayed on to serve as labor for United Fruit. Also in this area, to the interior, are some of the country's most prominent indigenous groups – cultures that have managed to remain intact despite several centuries' worth of incursions, first from the Spanish, later from the fruit industry and currently from the globalizing effects of tourism. They principally inhabit the Cocles/Kèköldi, Talamanca Cabécar and Bribrí indigenous territories.

Naturally, this fascinating cultural bubble wouldn't remain isolated forever. Since the 1980s the southern coast has seen the arrival of surfers, backpackers and adventurous families on holiday – many of whom have stayed, adding Italian, German and North American inflections to the cultural stew. For the traveler, it is a rich and rewarding experience – with lovely beaches to boot.

Reserva Biológica Hitoy-Cerere

One of Costa Rica's most rugged and rarely visited reserves, **Hitoy-Cerere** (☎2206-5516; admission US$5; ⏲8am-4pm) is only about 60km south of Puerto Limón. The 99-sq-km reserve sits on the edge of the Cordillera de Talamanca, characterized by varying altitudes, evergreen forests and rushing rivers. This may be one of the wettest reserves in the parks system, inundated with 4000mm to 6000mm of rain annually.

The reserve is surrounded by some of the country's most remote indigenous reserves, which you can visit with a local guide.

Although there is a ranger station at the reserve entrance with bathrooms, there are no other facilities nearby. A 9km trail leads south to a waterfall, but it is steep, slippery and poorly maintained. When rivers are high, some crossings may be impassable. Jungle boots are recommended.

Getting There & Away

By car (4WD recommended) from Puerto Limón, head south to Penshurst. Just south of the Río Estrella bridge, head west on the signed road to Valle de la Estrella. Another sign at the bus stop sends you down a dirt road about 15km to the reserve.

Cahuita

Even as tourism has mushroomed on Costa Rica's southern coast, Cahuita has managed to hold onto its laid-back Caribbean vibe. The roads are made of dirt, many of the older houses rest on stilts and chatty neighbors still converse in Mekatelyu. A graceful black-sand beach and a chilled-out demeanor hint at a not-so-distant past, when the area was little more than a string of cacao farms.

Cahuita proudly claims the area's first permanent Afro-Caribbean settler: a turtle fisherman named William Smith, who moved his family to Punta Cahuita in 1828.

Now his descendants, along with those of so many other West Indian immigrants, run the backyard eateries and brightly painted bungalows that hug this idyllic stretch of coast.

Situated on a pleasant point, the town itself has a waterfront but no beach. For that, most folks make the five-minute jaunt up the coast to Playa Negra or southeast into neighboring Parque Nacional Cahuita.

◉ Sights

Playa Blanca BEACH
At the entrance to the national park. A good option for swimming.

★ Playa Negra BEACH
At the northwest end of Cahuita, Playa Negra is a long, black-sand beach flying the *bandera azul ecológica,* a flag that indicates the beach is kept to the highest ecological standards. This is undoubtedly Cahuita's top spot for swimming and is never crowded. When the swells are big, this place also has an excellent beach break for beginners.

Tree of Life GARDENS
(☑2755-0014, 8317-0325; www.treeoflifecostarica. com; adult/child US$15/7.50; ⊙11am tour Tue-Sun, closed May, Jun, Sep & Oct) This lovingly maintained wildlife center and botanical garden 3km northwest of town on the Playa Negra road rescues and rehabilitates animals while also promoting conservation through educational programs. The rotating cast of residents typically includes kinkajous, peccaries, sloths, monkeys and toucans. There's excellent English-language signage throughout. It's also possible to volunteer here; see the website for information.

Sloth Sanctuary of Costa Rica WILDLIFE RESERVE
(formerly Aviarios del Caribe; ☑2750-0775; www. slothsanctuary.com; 2hr group tours adult/child 5-12yr US$30/15, private half-day tours per person US$150; ⊙8am-2pm Tue-Sun) About 10km

Cahuita

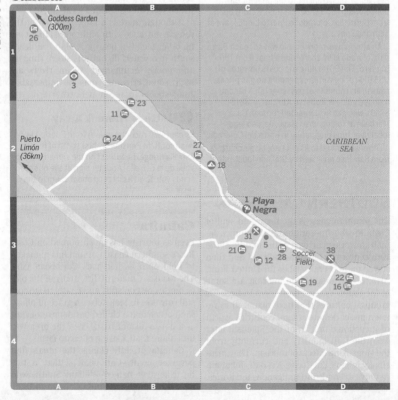

northwest of Cahuita, bordering the Río Estrella, the Arroyo family runs this private 88-hectare wildlife sanctuary dedicated to caring for injured and orphaned sloths. Visitors can observe these unique animals up close on group or private tours. (Irrefutable fact: there is nothing cuter than a baby sloth.) Though many of the reserve's rehabilitated sloths lack the skills to return to the wild, the Arroyos have successfully released more than 130 of them back into area forests.

☞ Tours

Snorkeling, horseback riding, chocolate tours and visits to nearby indigenous territories are standard offerings.

Centro Turístico Brigitte   HORSEBACK RIDING
(☑2755-0053; www.brigittecahuita.com; Playa Negra) Behind Reggae Bar in the heart of Playa Negra, this well-signed backstreet spot does it all, but specializes in horseback tours (three hours to full day, US$60 to US$110)

and surf lessons (US$35 including use of board). Brigitte also rents bicycles (US$8) and offers laundry (US$10 a load) and internet (US$2 per hour) services. Check the website or stop by in person for full details.

Also offers a couple of basic wood *cabinas* and two private single rooms, plus a good onsite restaurant.

Cahuita Tours   TOUR
(☑2755-0101, 2755-0000; www.cahuitatours.com) This is one of the most established agencies in town.

Snorkeling House   TOUR
(☑8361-1924; www.snorkelinghouse.com) Local tour guide and conservationist Fernando Brown launches his excellent snorkeling tours in Cahuita national park from Miss Edith's (p169), his family's restaurant. The tour includes a couple of stops where reef sharks, rays and numerous fish are often spotted, and concludes with a fresh fruit snack.

Roberto's Tours   FISHING
(☑2755-1148; aventurasrobertotour@gmail.com) Specializes in sportfishing tours *and* has a restaurant for cooking up your catch.

Willie's Tours   TOUR
(☑8917-6982, 2755-1024; www.williestourscosta rica.com; ◷8am-noon & 2-7pm Mon-Sat, 5-7pm Sun) A full-service tour agency that can also arrange further-flung tours and transport.

Mister Big J's   TOUR
(☑2755-0060, 8887-4695; ◷8am-7:30pm) Offers the usual range of tours.

🛏 Sleeping

There are two general areas to stay in Cahuita: the town center (which can be a little noisy) or north of town along Playa Negra. If walking between Playa Negra and the center at night, don't carry valuables; better yet, bike or take a taxi, especially if traveling alone.

🛏 In the Center

Cabinas Riverside   CABINA **$**
(☑8893-2252; d with/without kitchen US$30/25; ℗) Managed by friendly Cahuita local Peck Ferguson and family, this tidy budget place just around the corner from Kelly Creek ranger station offers nine simple rooms with mosquito nets and hot showers; five units that are a bit more expensive also come with

Cahuita

kitchens. The grassy yard abuts a swampy area perfect for spotting caimans, monkeys and sloths.

Cabinas Secret Garden　　　　　CABINA $
(☏2755-0581; koosiecosta@live.nl; dm/s/d/tr US$12/18/22/30; 🅿🛜) This tiny place with a lush garden has five tiled units with fans, mosquito nets, and hot-water showers in cubicle-style bathrooms, plus one five-bed dorm with cold showers. There's also a nice shared kitchen with free coffee.

Cahuita National Park Hotel　　　HOTEL $
(☏2755-0244; hotelnationalpark03@gmail.com; s & d US$50, tr & q US$65; 🅿❄🛜) The hotel-style rooms here are large and bare, with dowdy brown curtains and industrial tile floors, but you still might be tempted by the prime location right at the national-park entrance. Beach and ocean views from the upstairs terrace (and several rooms) are spectacular.

Cabinas Smith 1 & 2　　　　　　CABINA $
(☏2755-0068; s/d/tr with fan US$18/23/30, s/d/tr/q with air-con US$30/35/40/45; 🅿❄🛜) These clean rooms spanning two properties between the main drag and the waterfront are run by a friendly older couple with deep local roots. Eight units adjacent to the own-ers' home have TV, air-con and wi-fi; five

older fan-cooled units around the corner are primarily of interest to the seriously budget-minded. All share a guest kitchen.

Spencer Seaside Lodging　　　　CABINA $
(☏2755-0027; s US$16-20, d US$26-30; 🅿) Rooms at this long-standing, locally owned spot are rough around the edges but big – and nothing else at this price level can match the seaside setting within two blocks of the town center. Upstairs units have bet-ter views, as well as a shared terrace strung with hammocks.

⭐**Alby Lodge**　　　　　　　BUNGALOW $$
(☏2755-0031; www.albylodge.com; d/tr/q US$60/65/70; 🅿🛜) This fine lodge on the edge of the park has spacious landscaped grounds that attract howler monkeys and birds. Four raised bungalows (two sleeping three people, two sleeping four) are spread out, allowing for plenty of privacy. High ceilings, mosquito nets and driftwood details make for pleasant jungle decor. A common *rancho* (thatched gazebo) has excellent communal kitchen facilities.

Bungalows Aché　　　　　　BUNGALOW $$
(☏2755-0119; www.bungalowsache.com; bungalow s US$45, d US$50-55; 🅿🛜) In Nigeria, Aché means 'Amen,' and you'll likely say the same thing when you see these three spotless

polished-wood bungalows nestled into a grassy yard bordering the national park. Each octagonal unit comes with a lockbox, minifridge, kettle and small private deck with hammock. A three-bedroom vacation house (doubles US$70, up to seven people US$120) is available 1km inland.

Kelly Creek Hotel
CABINA $$

(☎ 2755-0007; www.hotelkellycreek.com; s/d/ste US$50/60/70, extra person US$10; [P][☎]) At this place just outside the national-park entrance, where sloths and caimans hang out, you may be serenaded by the dulcet squawks of the resident parrot. Draw closer and find five graceful natural wood *cabinas* with high ceilings, cream-colored linens and mosquito nets. Local artwork adorns the reception area, and the onsite restaurant serves breakfast (US$5).

Ciudad Perdida
BUNGALOW $$$

(☎ 2755-0303; www.ciudadperdidaecolodge.com; d standard/superior incl breakfast US$106/127, q US$212; [P][✻][☎]) 🌿 In a shady, peaceful spot bordering the national park, but only an eight-minute walk from Cahuita's town center, this eco-conscious lodge offers cute one- and two-room, candy-colored wood bungalows surrounded by landscaped gardens. All include hammocks, ceiling fans, refrigerators and safe boxes. One house has a Jacuzzi, three have kitchens and all have cable TV.

📖 Playa Negra

Cabinas Tito
BUNGALOW $

(☎ 8880-1904, 2755-0286; www.cahuita-cabinas-tito.com; d with/without hot water US$35/25, additional person US$10, 4-person houses US$70; [P][☎]) Only 200m northwest of Cahuita, yet surrounded by extensive tropical gardens and banana plants, this quiet family-run oasis offers seven brightly painted, clean and simple *casitas* (one with kitchen) plus a family-friendly Caribbean-style house. Tito, the kind and charming young host, is a recent university graduate who's actively seeking to create habitat for birds, frogs and other wildlife.

Cabinas Algebra
BUNGALOW $

(☎ 2755-0057; www.cabinasalgebra.com; bungalows US$20-35; [P][☎]) This long-standing place has three rustic hammock-equipped cabins tucked into a peaceful backyard garden at Playa Negra's northern end. The spacious, inviting front deck doubles as a

restaurant and common area, with wood floors, books, games and wi-fi. It's 2km northwest of Cahuita, but the owners offer free bus-station pickup with advance notice.

Camping María
CAMPGROUND $

(☎ 2755-0091; campsites per person US$8, incl tent rental US$10; [☎]) Seven sweet and well-spaced campsites share a gorgeous section of waterfront near the northern end of Playa Negra, shaded by coconut palms and a variety of fruit trees. Campers have access to rudimentary cooking facilities, two bathrooms with cold-water showers and an upstairs library and recreation room with guitar and pool table. María brews free morning coffee for everyone.

★ Playa Negra Guesthouse
BUNGALOW $$

(☎ 2755-0127; www.playanegra.cr; s/d US$64/79, cottages US$89-144; [P][☎][▦]) Owned by a delightful couple, this meticulously maintained place offers four charming rooms in a Caribbean-style plantation house, complemented by three kitchen-equipped storybook cottages. Tropical accents include colorful mosaics in the bathrooms and cozy wicker lounge furniture on the private verandas. A lovely pool, honor bar and BBQ area are tucked into the well-manicured garden dotted with fan palms. Every unit has thoughtful and homey touches, including a minifridge and coffeemaker, and the staff goes out of its way to help guests explore the area. A winner all around.

El Encanto B&B
B&B $$

(☎ 2755-0113; www.elencantocahuita.com; s/d US$80/90, d studio/ste US$105/210, extra person US$25, all incl breakfast; [P][☎][▦]) This pleasant B&B, only about 200m northwest of downtown Cahuita, is set in landscaped grounds dotted with easy chairs and hammocks. Demure bungalows have high ceilings, tile floors and firm beds draped in colorful textiles. The studio and upstairs apartment both have fully equipped kitchens, and the onsite spa and Jacuzzi are super *tranquilo*.

Casa Marcellino
CABINA $$

(☎ 2755-0390; www.casamarcellino.com; d US$85-96, q US$102-113; [☎]) In a peaceful garden setting, just inland down a side road between Cahuita and Playa Negra, you'll find this charming cluster of spotless wood cabins with fully equipped kitchens. More expensive units have large bathtubs, plus spacious porches with hammocks and retractable awnings. Monthly and weekly rates are available.

SELVA BANANITO

At the foot of Cerro Muchito, on the edge of Parque Internacional La Amistad, the family-run, 1200-hectare **Selva Bananito Lodge** (☏8375-4419, 2253-8118; www.selvabananito. com; 3-day packages US$588) has dedicated the last three decades to developing sustainable ecotourism and wise land-management practices.

While this lodge does not offer beach access, there is plenty to keep the adventurous traveler occupied: tree climbing, bird-watching, waterfall hiking and horseback riding. Rates, based on double occupancy, include three meals daily and transportation from San José, as well as the above-mentioned activities.

Conscious of their environmental impact, the owners employ solar energy, recycled hardwood and biodegradable products. They are deeply committed to preserving the Limón watershed (which provides Puerto Limón's drinking water) and have installed camera traps around their property to record the movements of wild cats and other fauna. They aim to become a wildlife corridor that will allow jaguars to move freely between Parque Internacional La Amistad and the Caribbean coast.

For those driving to the lodge, the turnoff is just south of the Río Vizcaya crossing (about 19km south of Limón). The lodge is about 8km inland. Detailed directions are posted on the website.

Cabinas Iguana
CABINA **$$**

(☏2755-0005; cabinas-iguana.com/en; d bungalow US$45-65, d without bathroom US$25; P🌊🛜❄) Set back from the beach on the road marked by the Reggae Bar, this family-run spot features rather faded but nicely shaded simple wood cabins of various sizes, all nestled into forested grounds with abundant wildlife.

La Piscina Natural
CABINA **$$**

(☏2755-0146; www.piscina-natural.com; d/tr US$50/65; P🛜🌊❄) Run by Cahuita native Walter and expatriate former schoolteacher Patty, this chilled-out gem of a spot near Playa Negra's northern end is a self-proclaimed 'Caribbean Paradise'. The small rooms, which share access to a huge kitchen and open-air lounge, are comfortable enough, but what really make this place special are the lush grounds, gorgeous waterfront and stunning, rock-fringed natural ocean-water pool.

Hotel La Diosa
BUNGALOW **$$$**

(☏2755-0055; www.hotelladiosa.net; bungalows incl breakfast US$100-170; P❄🛜❄) This relaxing spot on Playa Negra offers six well-constructed bungalows, some of which contain Jacuzzi tubs, air-conditioning and oceanfront terraces. The grounds include a tranquil pool, a *palapa*-topped restaurant and a meandering walkway to the beach. This is the spot for some serious R&R.

Coral Hill Bungalows
BUNGALOW **$$$**

(☏2755-0479, 8861-0063; www.coralhillbunga lows.com; d incl breakfast US$147; 🛜) Popular with honeymooners, these three immaculate private bungalows in a wildlife-friendly garden setting are done up with tropical decor: polished-wood floors, bamboo furniture, mosquito nets, hand-painted ceramic sinks and porches with hammocks and leather rocking chairs. Luxuries include pillow-top mattresses, high-thread-count sheets, fresh flowers and full breakfasts served by the gracious hosts. Follow signs from Reggae Bar.

Kenaki Lodge
BUNGALOW **$$$**

(☏2755-0485; www.kenakilodge.com; d incl breakfast US$113, d/q bungalow US$135/249; P🛜) Directly opposite Playa Grande (the next beach north of Playa Negra), this appealing place is the creation of expatriate Isabelle and Costa Rican tae kwon do master Roberto. Four bright, high-ceilinged modern rooms and two elegant bungalows with satellite TV and modern kitchen fixtures surround a spacious landscaped yard and a wooden breakfast deck.

Hotel Suizo Loco Lodge
BUNGALOW **$$$**

(☏2755-0349; www.suizolocolodge.com; s/d/ tr US$85/115/165, ste d/tr US$140/203, all incl breakfast; P🛜❄) Eleven immaculate, white-washed bungalows have king-size beds and folk-art decor at this serene family-friendly lodge (cribs available). All units have safe, minifridge, solar-heated showers and small, private terraces. The perfectly landscaped grounds contain an impressive mosaic-tile pool with a swim-up bar. It's along the road forking off the main Playa Negra road about 2km northwest of Cahuita.

Eating

This town offers some of the best Caribbean fare around, along with some surprisingly delicious Italian cuisine.

Cocoricó
ITALIAN $

(mains US$6-12; ⊘ 5-10pm Wed-Mon) The menu here revolves around pizza, pasta and other Italian-themed mains, but it's better known for its regular movie screenings. Free movies are shown every night, as are two-for-one cocktails from 5pm to 10pm.

Café y Delicias
INTERNATIONAL $

(breakfast US$3-4, dishes US$4-9; ⊘ 6:30am-5pm Mon-Sat, 7am-1pm Sun) Greet the morning with a cup o' joe and a warm cinnamon roll, or unwind in the afternoon with a refreshing *jugo*. Breakfast offerings include French toast and bacon, while the lunch menu revolves around salad, spaghetti and quiche. Hearty sandwiches on homemade wholegrain bread are perfect for beach picnics at the national park.

Smoothie Bar
& Crêpe Café
JUICE BAR, CREPERIE $

(juices US$2-4, crepes US$3-7; ⊘ 7am-5:30pm) At this friendly main-street spot, Sherilyn whips up fresh fruit crepes and juices mixed with water, milk, yogurt or ice cream. There's always an attractively priced juice of the day (US$2), but even better is the *agua de sapo*, a delicious, sinus-clearing Caribbean concoction made with lemon juice, water, brown sugar and loads of fresh ginger.

★ Sobre Las Olas
SEAFOOD $$

(☑ 2755-0109; pastas US$12-15, mains US$12-25; ⊘ noon-10pm Wed-Mon; ⌘) Garlic shrimp, seafood pasta, or fresh grilled fish of the day come accompanied by crashing waves and sparkling blue Caribbean vistas at this sweet spot owned by a lively couple. Cahuita's top option for romantic waterfront dining, it's only a 400m walk northwest of Cahuita, on the road to Playa Negra. Save room for the delicious tiramisu.

★ Miss Edith's
CARIBBEAN $$

(☑ 2755-0248; mains US$6-24; ⊘ 7am-8pm; ⌘) This long-time local restaurant serves a slew of Caribbean specialties and a number of vegetarian options. The service may be laid-back, and some dishes aren't spectacular, but the spicy jerk chicken and potatoes stewed in garlic are more than worth the wait.

Pizzeria CahuITA
PIZZA $$

(☑ 2755-0179; pizzas US$5-16; ⊘ 4-10pm Fri-Wed) As the red-white-and-green color scheme implies, the ITA here stands for Italy, motherland of the two expatriate families who opened this excellent, unpretentious pizzeria in 2013. Grab a seat at the aluminum tables on the cement back patio and enjoy a surf and insect serenade while you wait for your thin-crusted beauty to emerge from the wood-fired oven.

At the time of research, the owners were opening an adjacent hotel, the CahuITA Inn.

Restaurant La Fé Bumbata
SEAFOOD $$

(dishes US$7-16; ⊘ 7am-11pm) Chef and owner Walter, a Cahuita native, serves up tall tales and tasty meals at this reasonably priced spot. There's a laundry list of Tico and Caribbean items, but the main draw is anything doused in the restaurant's spicy-delicious coconut sauce.

Chao's Paradise
CARIBBEAN $$

(☑ 2755-0480; seafood mains US$11-18; ⊘ noon-10pm) Follow the wafting smell of garlic and simmering sauces to this highly recommended Playa Negra outpost that serves fresh catches cooked up in spicy 'Chao' sauce. The central Playa Negra open-air restaurant-bar has a pool table.

Palenque Luisa
Casa de Carnes
STEAK $$

(☑ 7039-9689; mains US$6-16; ⊘ 2-10pm Mon-Sat) In the corner veranda of an old house, this cozy spot specializes in filet mignon, tenderloin and T-bone steaks, but you'll also find plenty of other savory treats, including chicken in jalapeño or coconut sauce, pork chops, grilled seafood and *ceviche*.

Drinking & Nightlife

Coco's Bar
BAR

(www.facebook.com/cocosbar.cahuita; ⊘ noon-late) Low-key Cahuita is home to one insanely loud drinking hole: Coco's Bar. You can't miss it at the main intersection, painted Rasta red, gold and green and cranking the reggaetón up to 11. On some nights (usually on weekends) there's also live music.

Splash
BAR

(⊘ 10am-10pm) This outdoor bar has its own swimming pool and often hosts roots and reggae nights, private parties and other special events.

ℹ Information

The town's helpful website, www.cahuita.cr, has lodging and restaurant information, including pictures of many of the town's facilities and attractions. It also has a 'Cahuita Cam' showing live shots of Playa Blanca.

Banco de Costa Rica (☺9am-4pm Mon-Fri) At the bus terminal; has an ATM.

Internet Palmer (per hr US$2; ☺7am-7:30pm) Internet access in the heart of town.

ℹ Getting There & Around

The best way to get around Cahuita – especially if you're staying out along Playa Negra – is by bicycle. Several places around town rent bikes, including Mister Big J's (p165) in Cahuita and Centro Turístico Brigitte (p165) in Playa Negra. Most places charge between US$7 and US$10 per day.

Parque Nacional Cahuita

This small but beautiful **park** (admission US$5) – just 10 sq km – is one of the more frequently visited national parks in Costa Rica. The reasons are simple: the nearby town of Cahuita provides attractive accommodations and easy access; more importantly, the white-sand beaches, coral reef and coastal rainforest are bursting with wildlife.

Declared a national park in 1978, Cahuita is meteorologically typical of the entire coast (very humid), which results in dense tropical foliage, as well as coconut palms and sea grapes. The area includes the swampy **Punta Cahuita**, which juts into the sea between two stretches of sandy beach. Often flooded, the point is covered with cativo and mango trees and is a popular hangout for birds such as green ibis, yellow-crowned night heron, boat-billed heron and the rare green-and-rufous kingfisher.

Red land and fiddler crabs live along the beaches, attracting mammals such as crab-eating raccoon and white-nosed *pizotes* (coatis). White-faced capuchins, southern opossums and three-toed sloths also live in these parts. The mammal you are most likely to see (and hear) is the mantled howler monkey, which makes its bellowing presence known. The coral reef represents another rich ecosystem that abounds with life.

🏃 Activities

Hiking

An easily navigable 8km **coastal trail** leads through the jungle from Kelly Creek to Puerto Vargas. At times the trail follows the beach; at other times hikers are 100m or so away from the sand. At the end of the first beach, Playa Blanca, hikers must ford the dark Río Perezoso, or 'Sloth River,' which bisects Punta Cahuita. Inquire about conditions before you set out: under normal conditions, this river is easy enough to wade across, but during periods of heavy rain it can become impassable since it serves as the discharge for the swamp that covers the point.

The trail continues around Punta Cahuita to the long stretch of Playa Vargas. It ends at the southern tip of the reef, where it meets up with a road leading to the Puerto Vargas ranger station. Once you reach the ranger station, it's another 1.5km along a gravel road to the park entrance. From here, you can hike the 3.5km back to Cahuita along the coastal highway or catch a ride going in either direction.

Swimming

Almost immediately upon entering the park, you'll see the 2km-long **Playa Blanca** stretching along a gently curving bay to the

BUSES FROM CAHUITA

Autotransportes Mepe buses arrive and depart at the bus terminal 200 m southwest of Parque Central.

DESTINATION	COST (US$)	DURATION (HR)	FREQUENCY (DAILY)
Manzanillo	2.40	1	roughly two hourly, 7am-7pm
Puerto Limón	2.40	1½	about every 30mins, 6am-8pm
Puerto Viejo de Talamanca	1.50	½	roughly two hourly, 7am-7pm
San José	8.90	4	7am, 8am, 9:30am, 11:30am & 4:30pm
Sixaola	3.95	2	hourly, 6am-7pm; passes through Bribrí

east. The first 500m of beach may be unsafe for swimming, but beyond that, waves are generally gentle. (Look for green flags marking safe swimming spots.) The rocky Punta Cahuita headland separates this beach from the next one, Playa Vargas. It is unwise to leave clothing or other belongings unattended when you swim.

Snorkeling

Parque Nacional Cahuita contains one of the last living coral reefs in Costa Rica. While the reef represents some of the area's best snorkeling, it has incurred damage over the years from earthquakes and tourism-related activities. In an attempt to protect the reef from further damage, snorkeling is only permitted with a licensed guide. The going rate for one person is about US$25.

You'll find that conditions vary greatly, depending on the weather and other factors. In general, the drier months in the highlands (from February to April) are best for snorkeling on the coast, as less runoff results in less silt in the sea. Conditions are often cloudy at other times.

Volunteering

Though not renowned as a sea-turtle destination, Cahuita's beaches are nonetheless an important habitat for several breeds. Asociación Widecast (☑in San José 8818-2543; www.latinamericanseaturtles.com) has volunteering opportunities for those interested in assisting on in-water research projects and various conservation-related activities. Reserve in advance.

It's also possible to volunteer at Tree of Life (p164) wildlife-rescue center, on the road to Playa Negra.

✕ Eating

Boca Chica   ITALIAN, COSTA RICAN $
(☑2755-0415; meals US$8-10; ⊘8am-6pm) After a long, hot jungle hike, you may think you're hallucinating when you see this small, whitewashed place at the end of the road. It's not a mirage, just a well-placed bar-restaurant, run by charming expatriate Rodolfo and his wife, Karen. The menu features cold *jugos,* Caribbean specialties, homemade pastas and delicious *platos del día* from noon onward.

❶ Information

The Kelly Creek ranger station (☑2755-0461; admission by donation; ⊘6am-5pm) is at the southern end of town in Cahuita, while 3.5km

Parque Nacional Cahuita

down Hwy 36 takes you to the well-signed Puerto Vargas ranger station (☑2755-0302; admission US$5; ⊘8am-4pm Mon-Fri, 7am-5pm Sat & Sun).

Puerto Viejo de Talamanca

There was a time when the only travelers to the little seaside settlement once known as Old Harbor were intrepid surfers who padded around the quiet, dusty streets, board under arm, on their way to surf Salsa Brava. That, certainly, is no longer the case. This burgeoning party town is bustling with tourist activity: street vendors ply Rasta trinkets and Bob Marley T-shirts, stylish eateries serve global fusion everything and intentionally rustic bamboo bars pump dancehall and reggaetón. The scene can get downright hedonistic, attracting dedicated revelers who arrive to marinate in ganja and *guaro.*

Despite that reputation, Puerto Viejo nonetheless manages to hold on to an easy charm. Stray a couple of blocks off the main commercial strip and you might find yourself on a sleepy dirt road, savoring a spicy Caribbean stew in the company of local families. Nearby, you'll find rainforest fruit and cacao farms set to a soundtrack of cackling

Puerto Viejo de Talamanca

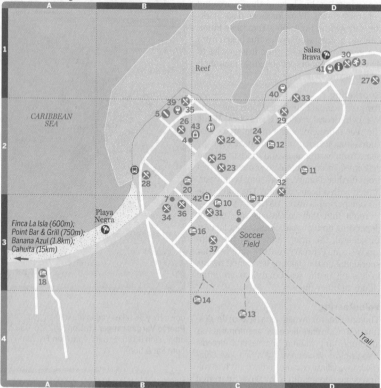

birds and croaking frogs, and wide-open beaches where the daily itinerary revolves around surfing and snoozing. So, chill a little. Party a little. Eat a little. You've come to just the right place.

◉ Sights

Finca La Isla   GARDENS
(☑ 2750-0046, 8886-8530; self-guided/guided tours US$6/12; ⊘ 10am-4pm Fri-Mon; P) ✿ West of town, this farm and botanical garden has long produced organic pepper and cacao, along with more than 150 tropical fruits and ornamental plants. Birds and wildlife abound, including sloths, poison-dart frogs and toucans. Informative guided tours (minimum three people) include admission, fruit tasting and a glass of fresh juice; alternatively, buy a booklet (US$1) and take a self-guided tour. Recently, the farm began making its own chocolate.

Aiko-logi   WILDLIFE RESERVE
(☑ 8997-6869, 2750-2084; aiko-logi-tours.com; day tours incl transport & lunch US$60, overnight stays per person incl meals US$99; P) ✿ Nestled into the Cordillera de Talamanca, 15km outside Puerto Viejo, this private 135-hectare reserve is centered on a former *finca,* on land fringed with dense primary rainforest. It's ideal for bird-watching, hiking and splashing around in swimming holes. Day tours from Puerto Viejo (or Cahuita) can be arranged, as can overnight tent platform stays and yoga classes. Reserve ahead.

🏃 Activities

Costa Rica Way (p181) is an excellent source of general information on local activities.

Hiking

There are superb coastal hiking opportunities located within 15km of Puerto Viejo in Parque Nacional Cahuita (p170) and the Ref-

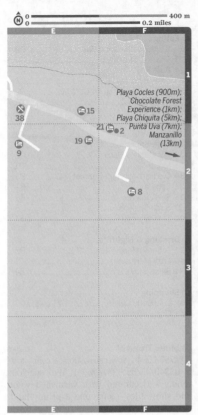

Playa Cocles (900m);
Chocolate Forest
Experience (1km);
Playa Chiquita (5km);
Punta Uva (7km);
Manzanillo
(13km)

ugio Nacional de Vida Silvestre Gandoca-Manzanillo (p186).

Surfing

Breaking on the reef that hugs the village is the famed Salsa Brava, a shallow break that is also one of the country's most infamous waves. It's a tricky ride – if you lose it, the waves will plow you straight into the reef – and definitely not for beginners. Salsa Brava offers both rights and lefts, although the right is usually faster. Conditions are best with an easterly swell.

For a softer landing, try the beach break at Playa Cocles – where the waves are almost as impressive and the landing far less damaging. Cocles is about 2km east of town. Conditions are usually best early in the day, before the wind picks up.

Waves in the area generally peak from November to March, and there is a surfing miniseason from June to July. From late March to May, and in September and October, the sea is at its calmest.

Several surf schools around town charge US$40 to US$50 for two hours of lessons. Stands around town rent boards from about US$20 per day.

Caribbean Surf School　SURFING
(📞8357-7703) Lessons by super-smiley surf instructor Hershel Lewis, widely considered the best teacher in the town. Recently he also started teaching paddle boarding.

One Love Surf School　SURFING
(📞8719-4654; jewell420@hotmail.com) Julie Hickey and her surfing sons Cedric and Solomon specialize in surf lessons, massage school and yoga classes for women and children.

🎓 Courses

Spanish School Pura Vida　LANGUAGE COURSE
(📞2750-0029; www.spanishschool-puravida.com) Located at the Hotel Pura Vida, this school offers everything from private hourly tutoring to intensive five-hours-a-day, multiweek classes.

👉 Tours

Tour operators generally require a minimum of two people on any excursion. Rates may be discounted for larger groups.

Gecko Trail Costa Rica　TOUR
(📞2756-8159, in USA & Canada 415-230-0298; www.geckotrail.com) This full-service agency arranges local tours as well as transportation, accommodations and tours throughout Costa Rica.

Terraventuras　TOUR
(📞2750-0750; www.terraventuras.com; ⏰7am-7pm) Offers overnights in Tortuguero, a shaman tour, and a Caribbean cooking class, along with the usual local tours. Also has its very own 23-platform, 2.1km-long canopy tour (US$58), complete with Tarzan swing.

Caribe Shuttle　TOUR
(📞2750-0626; caribeshuttle.com/puerto-viejo-tours) Based at Rocking J's hostel, this company offers a wide variety of tours in the Puerto Viejo area, and excursions to Bocas del Toro, Panama. It also provides transport to San José, northwestern Costa Rica and San Juan del Sur, Nicaragua.

Exploradores Outdoors　RAFTING
(📞2750-2020; www.exploradoresoutdoors.com; 1-day trips incl 2 meals & transportation from

Puerto Viejo de Talamanca

US$99) This outfit offers one- and two-day trips on the Ríos Pacuare and Reventazón. Staff can pick you up and drop you off in Cahuita, Puerto Viejo, San José or Arenal, and you're free to mix and match your pick-up and drop-off points. It has an office in the center of town.

Reef Runner Divers   DIVING
(☑ 2750-0480; www.reefrunnerdivers.net; 1-/2-tank dives US$65/100; ☉8am-6pm) If you are not certified, you can do a discover dive course for US$155 (includes two tanks) or spring for the full PADI certification for US$375.

🛏 Sleeping

Hostel Pagalú   HOSTEL $
(☑ 2750-1930; www.pagalu.com; dm/s/d US$12/30/33, s/d without bathroom US$25/28; P🤚) This peaceful, contemporary hostel offers a break from Puerto Viejo's party scene. Clean, airy dorms and doubles abound in niceties, including large lockers, charging stations for MP3 players and bunk-side reading lamps. There's a shared, open-air kitchen and a quiet lounge with tables and hammocks, plus a supply of spring water for refilling your own reusable bottle.

Cabinas Tropical   CABINA $
(☑ 2750-2064; www.cabinastropical.com; s/d/tr US$40/45/55; P🤚❄🤚) Ten spacious rooms – decorated with varnished wood and shiny tiles – surround a primly landscaped garden on the eastern end of town. The comfortable quarters are just part of the appeal: biologist owner Rolf Blancke leads excellent hikes, bird-watching excursions, and tours of a nearby fruit and spice farm (per person US$20 to US$65, minimum two people).

Lionfish Hostel   HOSTEL $
(☑ 2750-2143; www.facebook.com/thelionfish hostel; dm US$7-10, r US$25) Started by local surfers, this new hostel appeals to on-the-go types looking for like-minded adventurers. The dorms are basic and sometimes a bit stuffy, but it's a small price to pay for the bonfires and cookouts that take place out back on weekends. At the time of research, a Jacuzzi was under construction.

The hostel rents bikes (US$5 per day) and surfboards (US$20 for six hours), and also hooks guests up with affordable surf lessons and tours. An Italian restaurant upstairs and a fried chicken joint on the first level keep patrons well fed.

Jacaranda Hotel & Jungle Garden
CABINA $

(☎ 2750-0069; www.cabinasjacaranda.net; s/d/tr/q from US$30/45/50/55; P 🛜) In a blooming garden intersected by mosaic walkways, this place near the soccer field has 15 simple wood *cabinas* with spotless ceramic-tile floors and murals of flowers, along with a small, shared kitchen and patio. Yoga classes are available, and the onsite spa offers massage and bodywork.

La Ruka Hostel
HOSTEL $

(☎ 2750-0617; www.facebook.com/laruka.hostel; dm US$10, r with/without bathroom US$45/30; 🛜) If the cute painting of the surfing dog doesn't lure you in, the friendly welcome from owners Dannie and Dave will. Just east of town, this hostel has spacious common areas up front, a shared kitchen out back, plus dorm space and a couple of private rooms with shared bath upstairs.

Hotel Pura Vida
HOTEL $

(☎ 2750-0002; www.hotel-puravida.com; s/d/tr US$55/55/65, s/d/tr without bathroom US$40/45/55; P 🛜) This inn opposite the soccer field doubles as a Spanish school and offers solidly midrange amenities. Ten breezy, immaculate rooms come clad in polished wood, bright linens and ceramic-tile floors; many have charming views of the surrounding village. Showers are heated with solar power and there's a lounge with easy chairs and hammocks. Breakfasts, snacks and chilled beers are available.

Cabinas Guaraná
CABINA $

(☎ 2750-0244; www.hotelguarana.com; s/d/tr/q US$35/43/53/62; P @ 🛜) Amid a riotous tropical garden in town, 12 brightly painted concrete *cabinas* are decorated with wooden furniture and colorful folk tapestries. Each one comes with a small private terrace with hammock. There is a spacious shared kitchen and a vertigo-inducing tree house that offers spectacular sea views.

Rocking J's
HOSTEL $

(☎ 2750-0657; www.rockingjs.com; camping per person US$12, hammock US$10, dm/d/ste US$15/33/50/70; P 🛜) Puerto Viejo's biggest party hostel and 'hammock hotel' organizes full-moon parties and drinking games, sometimes to the chagrin of quieter neighbors. The accommodations are basic: tight rows of tents and hammocks, snug dorms and private doubles share rickety showers

in an environment brightened by a veritable explosion of psychedelic mosaics.

Escape Caribeño
BUNGALOW $$

(☎ 2750-0103; www.escapecaribeno.com; s/d/tr garden view US$70/75/85, ocean view US$90/95/105; P ✳ @ 🛜) Charming owners keep these 14 spick-and-span bungalows with spotless bathrooms, some on the beach side and others in the garden across the road, 500m east of town toward Playa Cocles. More expensive units are in lovely Caribbean-style structures with stained-glass shower stalls; all units have stocked minifridges, cable TV, fans and hammocks. Breakfast (US$5 to US$9 extra) is also available.

Kaya's Place
GUESTHOUSE $$

(☎ 2750-0690; www.kayasplace.com; s/d without bathroom US$40/43, d/ste US$55/87; P ✳ 🛜) Across the road from the beach at Puerto Viejo's western edge, this funky guesthouse has 17 snug, basic rooms, ranging from dim units with shared cool-water showers to more spacious garden rooms with air-con and private bathroom. The property also includes a bungalow, a private cabin and three apartments.

A 2nd-floor lounge is filled with hammocks and offers prime ocean views. The restaurant serves craft beer from a local brewery and bikes are available for rent.

Casa Verde
CABINA $$

(☎ 2750-0015; www.cabinascasaverde.com; s/d/tr/q US$78/84/110/120, s/d/tr/q without bathroom from US$52/60/68/92; P ✳ 🛜 ⚥) Under new ownership, this 17-room wonder features tiled walkways winding through gardens with tidy accommodations, each with high ceilings, stained-wood furniture, folk-art touches and private terraces with hammocks. Cheaper rooms are more basic, but the shared bathrooms and newly air-conditioned units shine. The pool is straight out of *Fantasy Island*. Credit cards accepted.

Coco Loco Lodge
BUNGALOW $$

(☎ 2750-0281; www.cocolocolodge.com; d US$55-69, d bungalow US$75-87; P @ 🛜) You'll find various accommodations at this quiet hotel. The most charming are the palm-thatched bungalows, featuring shining wood floors, minifridges and coffeemakers. All of these have private terraces with hammocks, offering views of the expansive garden. One large accommodation in the main house is ideal for a family and is equipped with a kitchen. Credit cards accepted.

OLIVER J DAVIS PHOTOGRAPHY / GETTY IMAGES ©

1. Cricket, Parque Nacional Tortuguero (p152)
Most visitors come to see the sea turtles, but Tortuguero teems with all kinds of wildlife.

2. Manzanillo (p186)
End your hike beachside in this relaxed, off-the-beaten-track village.

3. Parque Nacional Cahuita (p170)
Picture-perfect sunrises and coastal hiking await in this small national park.

4. Puerto Viejo de Talamanca (p171)
There are plenty of beautiful beaches on this stretch of coast.

WORTH A TRIP

CACAO TRAILS

Halfway between Cahuita and Puerto Viejo de Talamanca in Hone Creek, this **botanical garden and chocolate museum** (☑ 2756-8186; www.cacaotrails.com; Hone Creek; guided tours US$25; ⊙ 7am-4pm; ♿) has a couple of small exhibits devoted to indigenous and Afro-Caribbean culture, a lush garden bursting with bromeliads and heliconias, and an onsite chocolate factory where cacao is processed in traditional ways.

Two-hour tours include a visit to all of these spots, plus a hike to a nearby organic farm. Any bus between Cahuita and Puerto Viejo can drop you at the entrance. This is a great outing for kids.

Bungalows Calalú   BUNGALOW $$
(☑ 2750-0042; www.bungalowscalalu.com; s/d/tr US$40/55/65, d/tr/q with kitchen & air-con US$70/90/100; P ❄ ⚲ ☎) A lovely tropical-garden setting, a swimming pool and convenient parking are among the appealing features at this small cluster of bungalows within easy walking distance of town. Cheaper fan-cooled units have private front porches where you can listen to the chorus of chirping birds every morning. Family-friendly larger units come with air-con and kitchen.

Blue Conga Hotel   B&B $$
(☑ 2750-0681; www.hotelblueconga.com; r US$65-125; P ⚲ ☎) This backstreet B&B 1km east of town has 14 simple rooms in a two-story, tropical-style building. Best value are the six airy upstairs units, with high ceilings, clerestory windows, canopy beds with mosquito nets, handcrafted lamps, private terraces, coffeemakers and microwaves. Rooms downstairs are less inspiring. Breakfast is served on a lovely open-air garden deck, beside the pool.

Banana Azul   LODGE $$$
(☑ 2750-2035; www.bananaazul.com; d US$104-200, ste US$150-200, all incl breakfast; P ⚲ ☎) Removed from town, this romantic hotel sits astride a blissfully tranquil black-sand beach. Jungle-chic decor (white linens, mosquito nets, bromeliads in the showers) is complemented by fine ocean vistas from upstairs terraces. Best is the Howler Suite, a corner room with multidirectional views. There's also an onsite restaurant-bar, plus bike and boogie-board rentals. No children under 16. At the time of research, the construction of 18 new villas was underway on the property. The first villa should be completed by 2016; 17 more will follow by the end of 2017. The hotel will remain open throughout.

Cashew Hill Jungle Cottages   BUNGALOW $$$
(☑ 2750-0256, 2750-0001; www.cashewhilllodge.co.cr; cottages US$90-150; P ⚲ ☎) Perched on a lush hillside five minutes above town are seven bright, colorful and comfortable three- to eight-person cottages with full kitchens, loft-style sleeping areas and charming rustic touches. All have private decks or patios stocked with comfy chairs and hammocks, while the two-bedroom Playa Negra cabin offers exquisite ocean views. A yoga platform hosts classes daily.

✕ Eating

With the most diverse restaurant scene on the Caribbean coast, Puerto Viejo has the cure for *casado* overkill.

Find groceries at the local **Old Harbour Supermarket** (⊙ 6:30am-10pm) or the incongruous chain-store **MegaSuper** (⊙ 8am-9pm). Don't miss the Saturday organic market (p180), when area vendors and growers sell snacks typical of the region.

★ **Como en mi Casa Art Café**   CAFE $
(☑ 6069-6337, 6069-6319; www.comoenmicasacostarica.wordpress.com; cakes US$4, mains US$5-10; ⊙ 7am-4pm Thu-Tue; ☎) Owned by a friendly bohemian expat couple, this charming vegetarian cafe makes everything from scratch, from the jams to the hot sauces to the gluten-free pancakes. The walls are covered in local art and 10% of the coffee profit helps buy supplies for local schools. Oddly enough, you'll find this place above the butcher shop in the center of town.

Popular items include raw cakes, homemade lentil-bean burgers and gluten-free avocado wraps.

★ **Bread & Chocolate**   BREAKFAST $
(☑ 2750-0723; cakes US$4, meals US$6-9; ⊙ 6:30am-6:30pm Wed-Sat, to 2:30pm Sun; ☎) Ever had a completely homemade PB&J (bread, peanut butter and jelly all made from scratch)? That and more can be yours at this dream of a gluten-lover's cafe. Coffees are served in individual French presses; mochas come unconstructed so you have

the pleasure of mixing your own homemade chocolate, steamed milk and coffee; and everything else – from the gazpacho to the granola to the biscuits – is lovingly and skillfully made in-house.

Café Rico
CAFE **$**

(☎ 2750-0510; caferico.puertoviejo@yahoo.com; breakfast US$3-8; ☺ 5:30am-1pm; ☎) Home to some of Puerto Viejo's best home-roasted coffee, this cozy garden cafe serves breakfast accompanied by a plethora of other services: free wi-fi, a book exchange, a laundry, and rentals of bikes and snorkeling gear. Guests who stay in the attached *cabinas* get laundry and rentals free. A room is US$30 to US$50 with a discount for three or more nights.

Soda Shekiná
CARIBBEAN **$**

(☎ 2750-0549; mains US$7-12; ☺ 11:30am-9pm Wed-Mon) Delicious traditional Caribbean home cooking can be found at this backstreet eatery with wooden slab tables on an open-air terrace, just northwest of the soccer field. Everything is served with coconut rice and beans, salad and caramelized fried bananas.

Dee-Lite
ICE CREAM **$**

(☎ 8935-6547; gelati US$3-5; ☺ noon-8pm) Directly across from the bus stop, this authentic *gelateria* is the perfect place to cool off after a long, hot bus ride.

Sel & Sucre
FRENCH **$**

(☎ 2750-0636; meals US$4-10; ☺ noon-9:30pm; ☑) Dark coffee and fresh-fruit smoothies offer a nice complement to the menu of crepes, both savory and sweet. These delights are all prepared by the one and only chef Sebastien Flageul, meaning service can be slow. But it's worth the wait. At research time, a new hostel was underway upstairs.

De Gustibus
BAKERY **$**

(☎ 2756-8397; www.facebook.com/degustibusbakery; baked goods from US$1; ☺ 6:45am-6pm) This bakery on Puerto Viejo's main drag draws a devoted following with its fabulous focaccia (US$1 a slice), along with slices of pizza, apple strudels, profiteroles and all sorts of other sweet and savory goodies. Eat in, or grab a snack for the beach.

Pan Pay
BAKERY **$**

(☎ 2750-0081; dishes US$3-6; ☺ 7am-5pm) This popular corner spot on the beachside road in town is excellent for strong coffee, fresh baked goods and hearty wedges of fluffy Spanish omelet served with crisp tomato-

bread. There are sandwiches and other light meals, but it's the flaky chocolate croissants that make us want to jump out of bed in the morning.

★ Laszlo's
SEAFOOD **$$**

(mains US$16; ☺ 6-9:30pm) Whaddya get when you take a champion sport fisherman, born and raised in Transylvania, and transplant him to Puerto Viejo by way of New Jersey? Answer: an amazing, eclectic eatery with no sign and no menu that only opens when owner Laszlo catches enough fish. The day's catch comes with garlic and parsley, homemade French fries and grilled veggies. Yum.

Stashu's con Fusion
FUSION **$$**

(☎ 2750-0530; mains US$10-18; ☺ 5-10pm Thu-Tue; ☑) Stroll 250m out of town toward Playa Cocles to this romantic low-lit patio cafe serving up creative fusion cuisine that combines elements of Caribbean, Indian, Mexican and Thai cooking. Steamed spicy mussels in red-curry sauce and tandoori chicken in coconut are just a couple of standouts. Excellent vegetarian and vegan items round out the menu. Owner and chef Stash Golas is an artist inside the kitchen and out.

Miss Lidia's Place
CARIBBEAN **$$**

(☎ 2750-0598; dishes US$7-20; ☺ 11am-9:30pm Tue-Sun) A long-standing favorite for classic Caribbean flavors, Miss Lidia's has been around for years, pleasing the palates and satisfying the stomachs of locals and tourists alike. Fruit-and-veggie lovers will appreciate the ice-cold *batidos* (fresh fruit drinks) and the delicious assortment of broccoli, green beans, cauliflower, corn-on-the-cob, carrots and mushrooms accompanying most dishes.

Mopri
SEAFOOD **$$**

(☎ 2756-8411; www.pescaderiaymariqueriamopri. com; mains US$6-14; ☺ 10am-10pm; ☑) You'd never know it from Mopri's dingy facade or cheap plastic tables, but this place serves the best seafood in Puerto Viejo and possibly all of Costa Rica. The whole snapper and sizable lobster, which are also sold fresh at the adjacent fish market, are served up with a lip-smacking salsa *caribeño*.

Bikini Restaurant & Bar
FUSION **$$**

(☎ 2750-3061; mojitos US$3, mains US$5-15; ☺ noon-10:30pm) If frozen mojitos are your thing, get thee to Bikini. This hip new restaurant and bar opened in 2015, quickly attracting a crowd of revelers with its affordable cocktails and varied menu. Caribbean dishes, pasta, salads and sushi all pair well with strong drinks and a convivial atmosphere.

Koki Beach
LATIN AMERICAN $$$

(☑2750-0902; www.kokibeach.com; mains US$11-24; ⊙5-11pm Tue-Sun; 🛜) A high-end favorite for drinks and dinner, this sleek eatery cranks lounge music and sports colorful Adirondack chairs that face the ocean from an elevated wooden platform on the east end of town. There's a decent selection of Peruvian-inflected *ceviches*, plus meat and other seafood dishes, but slim pickings for vegetarians.

Café Viejo
ITALIAN $$$

(☑2750-0817; www.cafeviejo.com; mains US$10-28; ⊙6-11:30pm Wed-Mon) This pricey, sceney Mediterranean lounge and restaurant stands out for its fresh pastas, tasty pizzas, fancy cocktails and upscale, romantic ambiance. Its main-street location makes for excellent people-watching.

 Drinking & Nightlife

Restaurants often metamorphose into rollicking bar scenes after the tables are cleared. For excellent people-watching over beer, try Bikini Restaurant & Bar. If you want to see and be seen, hit Koki Beach or Café Viejo.

Lazy Mon
CLUB

(⊙12:30pm-2:30am) Puerto Viejo's most dependable spot for live music, Lazy Mon draws big crowds with reggae at happy hour (4pm to 7pm), then keeps things hopping with more of the same throughout the evening. The ping-pong and pool tables are popular gathering spots, and fire shows take place every Thursday night.

Salsa Brava
BAR

(☑2750-0241; ⊙11am-3am) Specializing in fresh seafood and open-grill cooking, this popular spot is the perfect end-of-day cocktail stop – hit happy hour from 4pm to 6pm and you'll also catch two-for-one mojitos for sunset overlooking the Salsa Brava surf break. On Friday and Sunday it brings in DJs for the popular reggae nights.

Point Bar & Grill
SPORTS BAR

(☑2756-8491; Playa Negra; ⊙11am-11pm; 🛜) If you happen to be traveling during football season (or any other sport season, for that matter), you don't have to miss the big game. Just head to this convivial spot on the beach northwest of town. Decent food, big screens and craft beer. Nuff said.

Johnny's Place
CLUB

(⊙11am-8pm, to 2am Wed, Fri & Sat) Once a beachside clubbing institution, Johnny's slowed after the party started getting out of control in 2015. The place shut down briefly and reopened under new ownership as a classy restaurant and bar with fancy cocktails. There are still DJs, dancing and occasional revelry on weekends, though.

 Shopping

Lulu Berlu Gallery
CRAFTS

(☑2750-0394; ⊙9am-9pm) On a backstreet parallel to the main road, this gallery carries folk art, clothing, jewelry, ceramics, embroidered purses and mosaic mirrors, among many other one-of-a-kind, locally made items. Out back, the popular restaurant Congo Reeff opened recently.

Organic Market
MARKET

(⊙6:30-11am Sat) Don't miss the weekly organic market, when area vendors and growers sell snacks typical of the region, particularly tropical produce and chocolate. Arrive before 9am or the best stuff will be long gone.

BUSES FROM PUERTO VIEJO DE TALAMANCA

All public buses arrive and depart from the bus stop along the beach road in central Puerto Viejo. The ticket office is diagonally across the street.

DESTINATION	COST (US$)	DURATION	FREQUENCY
Bribrí/Sixaola	1.50/3.35	30/90mins	roughly hourly, 6:30am-7:30pm
Cahuita/Puerto Limón	1.50/3.60	30/90mins	roughly hourly, 5:30am-6:30pm
Manzanillo	1.30	30mins	every 2hr, 6:45am-7:45pm (less frequently on weekends)
San José	10.90	5hr	7:30am, 9am, 11am & 4pm daily, plus 1pm Sun

ℹ️ Information

DANGERS & ANNOYANCES

Be aware that though the use of marijuana (and harder stuff) is common in Puerto Viejo, it is nonetheless illegal.

As in other popular tourist centers, theft can be an issue. Stay aware, use your hotel safe, and if staying outside of town avoid walking alone late at night.

INTERNET ACCESS

Costa Rica Way (☑2750-3031; www.costaricaway.info; ☺8am-6pm) Costa Rica Way operates a tourist-information center near the waterfront east of town, and lists hotel and restaurant info on its website.

Pipens Internet (☑2750-0486; per hr US$2; ☺9am-8pm) Desktops and wireless access. Right next to the bus station.

MONEY

Banco de Costa Rica (☺9am-4pm Mon-Fri) Two ATMs work on Plus and Visa systems, dispensing both colones and dollars. Sometimes they run out of cash on weekends, and they can be finicky; if one machine won't let you withdraw cash, try the other.

Banco Nacional (☺9am-4pm Mon-Fri, ATM 6am-10pm daily) Just off main street near the bridge into town. Dispenses colones only.

TOURIST INFORMATION

Puerto Viejo Satellite (www.puertoviejosatellite.com) has information on local lodgings, eating and activities.

ℹ️ Getting There & Around

BICYCLE

A bicycle is a fine way to get around town, and pedaling out to beaches east of Puerto Viejo is one of the highlights of this corner of Costa Rica. You'll find rentals all over town for about US$5 per day.

SHUTTLE

An ever-growing number of companies offer convenient van shuttles from Puerto Viejo to other tourist hotspots around Costa Rica and down the coast to Bocas del Toro, Panama. For an exhaustive list, see Gecko Trail's very helpful website. The following companies operate out of Puerto Viejo.

Caribe Shuttle (p173) Serves Bocas del Toro (Panama), San José and Tortuguero.

Gecko Trail Costa Rica (p173) Standard shuttle service to San José and Tortuguero; also offers good-value Adventure Connection packages that provide transport to San José or Arenal, with a half-day, 30km Río Pacuare rafting trip included in the price.

Interbus (☑4100-0888; www.interbusonline.com) Serves Arenal-La Fortuna, San José, Siquirres and Puerto Viejo de Sarapiquí.

Pleasure Ride (p162) Operates tours and transportation in the Caribbean, as well as reliable private vans to the rest of the country. It also runs an Airport Express to and from San José.

Playa Cocles, Playa Chiquita & Punta Uva

A 13km road winds east from Puerto Viejo, through rows of coconut palms, alongside coastal lodges and through lush lowland rainforest before coming to a dead end at the sleepy town of Manzanillo. The road was paved for the first time in 2003, dramatically shortening the amount of time it takes to travel this route. The roadway is narrow, however, so if you're driving, take your time and be alert for cyclists and one-lane bridges.

👁️ Sights

⭐Playa Cocles
BEACH

Playa Cocles has impressive waves for surfers who aren't so keen to break skin and bones on nearby Salsa Brava (Costa Rica's biggest break). It has lefts and rights, which both break close to the steep beach. Conditions are usually best from December to March, and early in the day before the wind picks up.

Jaguar Centro de Rescate
WILDLIFE RESERVE

(☑2750-0710; www.jaguarrescue.com; Playa Chiquita; adult/child under 10yr US$20/free; ☺tours 9:30am & 11:30am Mon-Sat; 🐾) Named in honor of its original resident, this well-run wildlife-rescue center in Playa Chiquita now focuses mostly on other animals, including raptors, sloths and monkeys. Founded by zoologist Encar and her partner, Sandro, a herpetologist, the center rehabilitates orphaned, injured and rescued animals for reintroduction into the wild whenever possible. Volunteer opportunities are available with a three-week minimum commitment.

The rescue center recently started additional tours at La Ceiba, 50 hectares of primary forest in the Gandoca-Manzanillo national wildlife refuge. Rehabilitated animals are released there, and tours are available in the morning and evening, with breakfast or dinner included. Prices range from US$55 to US$60.

⚡ Activities

The region's biggest draws involve surf, sand, wildlife-watching and attempts to get a decent tan between downpours. Playa Cocles is known for its great surfing and organized lifeguard system, which helps offset the dangers of the frequent riptides, while **Punta Uva** features the best and safest beaches for swimming.

Indulgence Spa SPA

(☑2750-0536; www.indulgencespa-salon.com; Playa Cocles; ☺11am-6pm Mon-Sat) The southern Caribbean's best day spa. It's onsite at La Costa de Papito.

Totem Surf School SURFING

(☑2750-0758; totemsurfschool.blogspot.com; Playa Cocles) This surf school offers group deals and packages.

Punta Uva Dive Center DIVING

(☑2759-9191; www.puntauvadivecenter.com; Punta Uva; 1-/2-tank dives from US$70/95) The center is clearly signposted off the main road in Punta Uva. Offers diving, PADI courses and snorkeling.

☞ Tours

Chocolate Forest Experience TOUR

(☑8341-2034, 8836-8930; www.caribeanscr.com/chocolate-tour; Playa Cocles; guided tours US$26; ☺tours 10am Mon, 10am & 2pm Tue & Thu, 2pm Fri & Sat) 🥾 Playa Cocles–based chocolate producer Caribeans leads tours of its sustainably managed cacao forest and chocolate-creation lab, accompanied by gourmet chocolate tastings.

Crazy Monkey Canopy Tour ADVENTURE TOUR

(www.almondsandcorals.com/activities/crazy-monkey-canopy-ride; per person US$45; ☺10am-2pm) The region's only canopy tour, operated by Almonds & Corals Lodge (p184) between Punta Uva and Manzanillo.

🛌 Sleeping

This stretch of beaches features some of the most charming and romantic accommodations in the country.

🛌 Playa Cocles

A broad stretch of white-sand beach lies just 1.5km east of Puerto Viejo, offering proximity to the village and its many restaurants, but plenty of peace and quiet, too.

Mi Casa Hostel CABINA $

(☑2750-0128; www.micasahostel.com; Playa Cocles; dm US$15, d/tr/q with fan US$35/45/55, with air-con US$65/75/85; P❄@🛜) Directly opposite the Playa Cocles beach break are these 12 clean, simple *cabinas* with tile floors and queen beds, some with air-con and cable TV. Four dorm rooms offer 16 beds total. Bikes can be rented onsite, and surfboard rental and lessons are available across the road. The bar next door has loud music and wild parties on Tuesday.

El Tucán Jungle Lodge CABINA $$

(☑2750-0026; www.eltucanjunglelodge.com; Playa Cocles; s/d/tr/q US$45/55/65/75; P🛜) Only 1km off the road, this jungle retreat feels miles from anywhere, making it ideal for bird-watchers. Four clean wooden *cabinas* on the banks of the Caño Negro share a broad patio with hammocks from which you can observe sloths, toucans and more. Upon request, the welcoming owners serve breakfast (per person US$7) and organize walks in the area.

Finca Chica BUNGALOW $$

(☑2750-1919; www.fincachica.com; Playa Cocles; bungalows US$65-130, per week US$520-1049; 🛜) Surrounded by lush tropical greenery, these four stand-alone wooden houses range from a two-person bungalow to an amazing three-story structure known as 'La Casita del Río' that sleeps up to six people. All have fully equipped kitchens, and three have spacious living and dining areas. It's tucked down a dead-end dirt driveway, a few hundred meters off the main road.

Paradise Island Lodge CABINA $$

(☑2750-0109; www.facebook.com/paradiseislandlodge; Playa Cocles; s/d US$90/120; P❄🛜🏊) Opposite the lifeguard tower at the main hub of the beach lies this efficient wooden lodge with 12 expansive rooms, all of which are equipped with safe, cable TV and handmade wood furnishings crafted from the slightly curved outer boards that are discarded during lumber processing.

La Costa de Papito BUNGALOW $$$

(☑2750-0080; www.lacostadepapito.com; Playa Cocles; d incl breakfast US$107, additional adult/child US$17/7; P🛜) Relax in rustic comfort in the sculpture-studded grounds at this popular Cocles outpost, which has wood and bamboo bungalows decked out with hand-carved furniture, stone bathrooms straight out of *The Flintstones* and roomy porches draped with hammocks. The onsite restaurant serves Caribbean specialties, while the rustic, palm-thatched Indulgence Spa offers massage and spa treatments.

Azánia Bungalows   BUNGALOW $$$
(☑2750-0540; www.azania-costarica.com; Playa Cocles; d incl breakfast US$113, additional person US$25; P@❄) Ten spacious but dark thatch-roofed bungalows are brightened up by colorful linens at this charming inn set on landscaped jungle grounds. Nice details include woven bedspreads, well-designed bathrooms and wide-plank hardwood floors. A free-form pool and a Jacuzzi nestle into the greenery, and there's an Argentine restaurant and bar.

Physis   B&B $$$
(☑8866-4405, 2750-0941; www.physiscaribbean.net; Playa Cocles; d US$100-110, tr US$135-150, all incl breakfast; ❄) Creature comforts abound at this four-bedroom B&B, tucked down a Playa Cocles side road and managed by expatriates Jeremy and Emily. There are free Netflix movies in the smaller downstairs units, satellite TV in the honeymoon suite, and super-strong wi-fi, sound systems, dehumidifiers, air-con and mini-fridges throughout. An upstairs deck with a well-stocked bar doubles as the breakfast area.

🛏 Playa Chiquita

It isn't exactly clear where Playa Cocles ends and Playa Chiquita begins, but conventional wisdom applies the name to a series of beaches 4km to 6km east of Puerto Viejo.

Villas del Caribe   HOTEL $$
(☑2233-2200, 2750-0202; www.facebook.com/villascaribe; Punta Uva; d US$80-85, villas US$115-165, all incl breakfast; P❄) With a prime location near the beach, this resort offers lovely, brightly painted rooms, comfortable beds, sitting areas and roomy bathrooms with Spanish tile. Junior villas also come with kitchenettes, while the two-story villas have ocean views, king-size beds, kitchens and BBQs. All have private decks with hammocks. Select villas have air conditioning.

La Kukula   BUNGALOW $$$
(☑2750-0653; www.lakukulalodge.com; Playa Chiquita; d/tr US$110/130, bungalows US$200,

houses US$250-400, all incl breakfast; ❄) 🌿 Three tastefully spaced 'tropical contemporary' bungalows bring guests close to nature with natural ventilation (super-high ceilings and screen walls) and open jungle views from the rainfall showers. The wood-decked pool is great for bird- and frog-watching. For larger groups, a three-bedroom house sleeps up to nine, with private kitchen and pool. Delicious included breakfasts feature homemade bread and marmalade.

Shawandha Lodge   BUNGALOW $$$
(☑2750-0018; www.shawandha.com; Playa Chiquita; d incl breakfast US$147, additional person US$30; P❄@❄) Immersed in greenery, with frogs, agoutis and other tropical critters close at hand, this upscale lodge has 13 private, spacious nature-themed bungalows painted in earth tones and equipped with large mosaic-tiled bathrooms. A meticulously maintained thatched *rancho* serves as an open-air lounge, and there's a French-Caribbean restaurant. A private path across the road leads to the beach.

Tierra de Sueños   BUNGALOW $$$
(☑2750-0378; www.tierradesuenoslodge.com; Playa Chiquita; bungalows incl breakfast US$95-165; P❄) 🌿 True to its name ('land of dreams'), this blissful garden retreat comprises seven adorable wood bungalows with mosquito nets and private decks. The quiet, tropical atmosphere is complemented by regular yoga and tai chi classes on an open-air platform. Laundry (US$15 per load) is available, as is wi-fi (in common areas only).

🛏 Punta Uva

Punta Uva is known for the region's most swimmable beaches, each lovelier than the next. To find the turnoff to the point (about 7km east of Puerto Viejo), look for the Punta Uva Dive Center sign.

Walaba Hostel   HOSTEL $
(☑2750-0147; www.walabahostel.com; Punta Uva; dm/s/d/tr/q without bathroom US$16/24/38/52/66, s/d cabinas with bathroom US$40/54) Funky, colorful and relatively cheap for Punta Uva, this ramshackle collection of open-air dorms, private rooms (including an 'attic' double reached by a ladder) and small cabins is surrounded by a garden and managed by a friendly couple. Guests share ample kitchen facilities, hot and cold showers, and a creaky-floored communal area with

games, books and DVDs. Bikes are available for rent (US$5 half-day, US$10 all day).

⭐ **Cabinas Punta Uva**   CABINA $$

(☑2759-9180; www.cabinaspuntauva.com; Punta Uva; cabinas with/without private kitchen US$90/65) Only steps from idyllic Playa Punta Uva, this cluster of three *cabinas* with tiled bathrooms, polished-wood verandas, hammocks and a shared open-air kitchen is dreamily hidden down a dead-end street in a verdant garden setting. Fall asleep to the sound of crashing waves and chirping insects and wake up to the roar of the resident howler monkeys.

⭐ **Tree House Lodge**   BUNGALOW $$$

(☑2750-0706; www.costaricatreehouse.com; Playa Chiquita; d US$200-390, extra person US$50; P) 🐾 Adventurers who like their lodgings whimsical will appreciate these five open-air *casitas*, including a literal 'tree house' – a two-story cabin build around a living sangrillo tree. All have kitchens, BBQs, spacious decks with easy chairs and hammocks, and private paths leading to a small white-sand beach. The newest house has a minigolf course around a tree in the living room.

Almonds & Corals Lodge   BUNGALOW $$$

(☑2271-3000, in USA 1-888-373-9042; www.almondsandcorals.com; r/master ste US$195/295, additional person from US$20, all incl breakfast; P@❄) 🐾 Buried in the jungle, this beachfront spot is popular with honeymooners. Its 24 palm-roofed suites are connected by wooden boardwalks, and feature four-poster beds, Jacuzzi tubs and patios with hammocks. Rooms are screened in for comfort, but you'll still enjoy the nightly serenade of insects and frogs. A breakfast buffet is included; other meals can be purchased at the restaurant.

Casa Viva   BUNGALOW $$$

(☑2750-0089; www.puntauva.net; Punta Uva; 1-bedroom houses US$100, 2-bedroom houses d/tr/q US$130/160/190; P❄🛜) Beautifully handcrafted by a master carpenter, these enormous, fully furnished hardwood houses, each with tiled shower, kitchen and wrap-around veranda, are set on a property that fronts the beach – an ideal spot in which to chill out in a hammock and observe the local wildlife. Weekly and monthly rates are also available.

Korrigan Lodge   BUNGALOW $$$

(☑2759-9103; www.korriganlodge.com; Punta Uva; d incl breakfast US$120; P) Nestled into a patch of jungle near the main road, these four thatch-roofed and concrete bungalows come with minibar, safe, modern bathroom and private terrace with hammock. All guests have access to free bikes. Breakfast is served in an open-air *rancho* surrounded by gardens.

🍴 Eating

If you want to stay close to Puerto Viejo while having access to a nice beach, Playa Cocles has a good mix of isolation and amenities, offering a wide variety of places to eat. After that, the pickings get thin until you get closer to Punta Uva, where you'll find a cluster of fantastic restaurants.

Pita Bonita   MEDITERRANEAN $

(☑2756-8173; Punta Uva; US$7-15; ⏲1-9pm Mon-Sat) For Turkish coffee, hummus and the best pita bread in the Caribbean, this is the place. The open-air eatery is ensconced in a tropical garden across from the Tree House Lodge in Punta Uva, making it a great stop before or after the beach. For adventurous eaters there's also *shakshuka*, an African dish with poached eggs and spicy tomato sauce.

Chocorart   CAFE $

(☑8866-7493; Playa Chiquita; snacks from US$2; ⏲10am-5pm Mon-Fri) This roadside cafe makes a perfect place to break your bike ride and get a quick chocolate fix. *Batidos*, coffee and ice cream are all available, but the real stars here are the brownies, hot chocolate and other delectables made from cocoa grown on the adjacent farm; excellent chocolate tours are also available here.

⭐ **Selvin's Restaurant**   CARIBBEAN $$

(☑2750-0664; Punta Uva; mains US$10-18; ⏲noon-8pm Thu-Sun) Selvin is a member of the extensive Brown family, noted for their charm, and his place is considered one of the region's best, specializing in shrimp, lobster, a terrific *rondón* and a succulent chicken *caribeño* (chicken stewed in a spicy Caribbean sauce).

Pura Gula   INTERNATIONAL $$

(☑8634-6404; mains US$12-20; ⏲2-4pm & 6-10pm) The short but solid menu at this casually elegant eatery includes beef tenderloin with blue goat cheese, pad thai, fillet of fish with shiitake mushrooms, and gnocchi. Everything's served on a pleasant open-air deck, just off the main road between Playa Chiquita and Punta Uva.

★ **La Pecora Nera** ITALIAN $$$
(📞 2750-0490; Playa Cocles; mains US$10-30; ⏰ 5:30-10pm Tue-Sun; 🖋️) If you splurge for a single fancy meal during your trip, do it at this romantic eatery run by Ilario Giannoni. On a lovely, candlelit patio, deftly prepared Italian seafood and pasta dishes are served alongside unusual offerings such as the delicate *carpaccio di carambola*: transparent slices of starfruit topped with shrimp, tomatoes and balsamic vinaigrette. There is an extensive wine list (from US$32 a bottle), but you can't go wrong with the well-chosen and relatively inexpensive house wines.

El Refugio ARGENTINE, INTERNATIONAL $$$
(📞 2759-9007; Punta Uva; mains US$15-25; ⏰ 5-9pm Thu-Tue) This tony Argentine-owned restaurant with only five tables is renowned for its rotating menu of three appetizers, five main dishes and three desserts. New offerings get chalked up on the board daily, anchored by perennial favorites such as red tuna in garlic, *bife de entraña* with chimichurri (beef in a marinade of parsley, garlic and spices) and *dulce de leche* crepes. Reserve ahead.

SOUTHERN CARIBBEAN INDIGENOUS COMMUNITIES

The area is home to a number of thriving indigenous communities, many of which can be visited by travelers. Brush up on a little local knowledge first.

Bribrí & Cabécar

At least two indigenous groups occupied the territory on the Caribbean side of the country from pre-Columbian times. The Bribrí tended to inhabit lowland areas, while the Cabécar made their home high in the Cordillera de Talamanca. Over the last century, members of both ethnic groups have migrated to the Pacific side. But many have stayed on the coast, intermarrying with Jamaican immigrants and even working in the banana industry. Today the Bribrí tend to be more acculturated, while the Cabécar are more isolated.

The groups have distinct languages (which are preserved to some degree), though they share similar architecture, weapons and canoe style. They also share the spiritual belief that the planet – and the flora and fauna contained within it – are gifts from Sibö (God). *Taking Care of Sibö's Gifts*, by Juanita Sánchez, Gloria Mayorga and Paula Palmer, is a remarkable record of Bribrí oral history.

Visiting Indigenous Communities

There are several reserves on the Caribbean slopes of the Cordillera de Talamanca, including the Talamanca Cabécar territory (which is more difficult to visit) and the Bribrí territory, where locals are more equipped to handle visitors.

The most interesting destination is Yorkín, in the Reserva Indígena Yorkín. While you are there, you can meet with a local women's artisan group, Mujeres Artesanas Stibrawpa, which offers demonstrations in roof thatching, cooking and basket-weaving. It's a rewarding trip, well worth the time and effort to get there (day trips US$70, overnights US$90).

Alternatively, you can visit the larger, modern village of Shiroles, about 20km west of Bribrí, where you can observe and participate in local chocolate production (half-day trip US$35). Half-day trips (US$25) also visit an iguana farm on the Kèköldi territory (this is a tiny ethnicity related to the Bribrí).

Note: it is not recommended to visit these territories independently. Not only are many spots difficult to reach, but in most cases villages do not have the infrastructure to accommodate streams of tourists. And of course, remember to be respectful – these are people's private homes and work spaces, not tourist attractions.

Terraventuras (p173) runs tours to Shiroles that can include a meeting with a shaman. Willie's Tours (p165) in Cahuita does a day trip to the Kèköldi territory and an overnight trip to Yorkin.

Manzanillo

The chill village of Manzanillo has long been off the beaten track, even since the paved road arrived in 2003. This little town remains a vibrant outpost of Afro-Caribbean culture and has also remained pristine, thanks to the 1985 establishment of the Refugio Nacional de Vida Silvestre Gandoca-Manzanillo, which includes the village and imposes strict regulations on regional development.

Activities are of a simple nature, *in* nature: hiking, snorkeling and kayaking are king. (As elsewhere, ask about riptides before heading out.)

Activities

Bad Barts SNORKELING
(🖉2750-3091; www.badbartsmanzanillo.com) Near the bus stop in Manzanillo, this outfit rents snorkel gear and kayaks, boogie boards, bicycles and scuba gear. Hours vary. Call ahead.

Sleeping

Cabinas Something Different HOTEL $$
(🖉2759-9014; r US$17-85; ❄) With 17 tidy rooms named for local wildlife, this long-standing hotel can accommodate families and groups of various shapes and sizes. Higher-end rooms come with air-con, minifridges, coffeemakers and even full kitchens.

Cabinas Manzanillo CABINA $$
(🖉2759-9033, 8327-3291; s/d US$40/60; P🛜) Run by the ever-helpful Sandra Castillo and Pablo Bustamante, these eight *cabinas* on Manzanillo's western edge are so clean you could eat off the tile floors. Cheery rooms have big beds, industrial-strength ceiling fans and spacious bathrooms. There's also a shared kitchen and bikes for rent ($10).

From Maxi's Restaurant, travel 300m west toward Punta Uva, then make a left onto the signposted dirt road.

Congo Bongo BUNGALOW $$$
(🖉2759-9016; www.congo-bongo.com; bungalows US$165-195, extra person US$15, per week US$990-1170; P🛜) About 1km outside Manzanillo towards Punta Uva, these seven charming cottages surrounded by dense forest (formerly a cacao plantation) offer fully equipped kitchens and plenty of living space, including open-air terraces and stra-

tegically placed hammocks that are perfect for wildlife-watching. A network of trails leads through the 6 hectares of grounds to the beautiful beach.

Eating

Cool & Calm Cafe CARIBBEAN $$
(🖉8843-7460; mains US$10-24; ⏱4-9pm Mon, 11am-9pm Wed-Sun) Directly across from Manzanillo's western beachfront, this front-porch eatery regales visitors with fine Caribbean cooking, from snapper to shrimp, and chicken to lobster, with a few extras like guacamole, tacos and veggie curry thrown in for good measure. Owner Andy offers Caribbean cooking classes and a 'reef-to-plate' tour where you dive for your own lobster or fish.

Maxi's Restaurant CARIBBEAN $$
(mains US$9-23, lobster US$24-80; ⏱noon-10pm; 🖉) Manzanillo's most famous restaurant draws a tourist crowd with large platters of grilled seafood, whole red snappers (*pargo rojo*), steaks and Caribbean-style lobsters (expensive and not necessarily worth it). Despite the somewhat lackadaisical service, the open-air upstairs dining area is a wonderful seaside setting for a meal and a beer with views of the beach and the street below.

ℹ Getting There & Away

Puerto Viejo & Puerto Limón Buses from Puerto Viejo to Manzanillo (US$1.20, 30 minutes) depart at 6:45am, 7:45am, 9:45am, 11:45am, 1:45pm, 4:45pm and 6:45pm, returning to Puerto Viejo at 7am, 8am, 10am, noon, 2pm, 4pm and 6pm. These buses all continue to Puerto Limón (US$4.90, two hours) for onward transfers.

San José Autotransportes Mepe also runs one direct bus daily between Manzanillo and San José (US$12, five hours), leaving Manzanillo at 7am and returning from San José at noon.

Refugio Nacional de Vida Silvestre Gandoca-Manzanillo

This little-explored refuge – called Regama for short – protects nearly 70% of the southern Caribbean coast, extending from Manzanillo all the way to the Panamanian border. It encompasses 50 sq km of land plus 44 sq km of marine environment. The peaceful, pristine stretch of sandy white beach is one of the area's main attractions. It's the center of village life in Manzanillo, and stretches for miles in either direction – from Punta Uva in the west to Punta Mona in the east. Offshore, a 5-sq-km coral reef is a teeming habitat for lobsters, sea fans and long-spined urchins.

 Activities

Hiking
A coastal trail heads 5.5km east out of Manzanillo to **Punta Mona**. The first part of this path, which leads from Manzanillo to Tom Bay (about a 40-minute walk), is well trammeled, clearly marked and doesn't require a guide. Once you pass Tom Bay, however, the path gets murky and it's easy to get lost, so ask about conditions before you set out, or hire a guide. It's a rewarding walk with amazing scenery, as well as excellent (and safe) swimming and snorkeling at the end.

Another, more difficult, 9km trail leaves from just west of Manzanillo and skirts the southern edges of the Pantano Punta Mona, continuing to the small community of **Gandoca**. This trail is not commonly walked, as most people access Punta Mona and Gandoca from the park entrance at the northern edge of the refuge, which is located on the road to Sixaola. If you want to try to hike this, be sure to hire a guide.

A third trail in the reserve takes visitors through the forest. Parts of this trail were previously dangerous or difficult to access, but it has recently been improved with a covered boardwalk made of wood and plastic.

Snorkeling & Diving
The undersea portion of the park cradles one of the two accessible living coral reefs in the country. Comprising five types of coral, the reefs begin in about 1m of water and extend 5km offshore to a barrier reef that local fishers have long relied on and researchers have only recently discovered. This colorful undersea world is home to some 400 species of fish and crustaceans. **Punta Mona** is a popular destination for snorkeling, though it's a trek so you may wish to hire a boat. Otherwise, you can snorkel offshore at **Manzanillo** at the eastern end of the beach (the riptide can be dangerous here; inquire about conditions before setting out). Also check out the Coral Reef Information Center at Bad Barts in Manzanillo.

Conditions vary widely, and clarity can be adversely affected by weather changes.

Kayaking
You can explore some of the area's waterways by kayak, available from Bad Barts; per hour US$6. Paddle out to the reef, or head up the **Quebrada Home Wark**, in the west of the village, or up the tiny **Simeon Creek**, at the east end of the village. These are short paddles, which is ideal if you've got kids.

Dolphin-Watching
In 1997 a group of local guides in Manzanillo identified tucuxi dolphins, a little-known species previously not found in Costa Rica, and began to observe their interactions with bottlenose dolphins. A third species – the Atlantic spotted dolphin – is also common in this area. This unprecedented activity has attracted the attention of marine biologists and conservationists, who are following these animals with great interest.

For dolphin-watching trips in the reserve (from US$53), contact Bad Barts. Keep in mind: in Costa Rica it is illegal to swim with dolphins. Be sure to keep a distance from the animals and refrain from touching or bothering them.

Turtle-Watching
Marine turtles – especially leatherback but also green, hawksbill and loggerhead – all nest on the beaches between Punta Mona and the Río Sixaola. Leatherbacks nest from March to July, with a peak in April and May. Local conservation efforts are under way to protect these nesting grounds since the growth of the area's human population has led to increased theft of turtle eggs.

During turtle season, no flashlights, beach fires or camping are allowed on the beach. All tourists must be accompanied by a local guide to minimize disturbance of the nesting turtles.

 Tours

★ **Florentino Grenald** TOUR
(☎8841-2732, 2759-9043; 4-hr tours per person from US$35) Local guide and former park ranger Florintino Grenald (Tino) is one of the most knowledgeable naturalists on the Caribbean. Since 1992 he's been handing out rubber boots and escorting guests through

his yard, a veritable tropical Eden, before taking them into the Gandoca-Manzanillo reserve, where he quickly spots caimans, frogs, snakes and whatever else happens to be nearby.

Abel Bustamante TOUR
(☑ 2759-9043) A recommended local guide.

Omar TOUR
(☑ 2759-9143) A recommended local guide.

🛏 Sleeping & Eating

Pack some snacks for a day hike, or call ahead to Punta Mona to make reservations for lunch there. The exotic garden contains plants from all over the world, making for some truly delicious salads. After the hike, grab a fruit smoothie and some delicious Caribbean food at Cool & Calm Café (p186), just a short walk north of the entrance to the refuge.

★ **Punta Mona** CABINA $$
(www.puntamona.org; cabinas incl 3 organic meals per person US$75; @) 🍃 Accessible only by foot or boat, this 35-hectare organic farm and retreat 5km southeast of Manzanillo is a thriving experiment in permaculture design and sustainable living. It grows over 200 varieties of fruit and nut trees and hundreds of edible greens, roots, veggies and medicinal plants, which comprise 90% of the huge vegetarian meals included in the daily rate.

Check the website for myriad educational and volunteer opportunities here, including yoga retreats and an adult jungle camp. To arrange accommodations and transportation, email contact@puntamona.org ahead of your visit.

Nature Observatorio CAMPGROUND $$$
(☑ 8628-2663; www.natureobservatorio.com; adult/child US$160/100) 🍃 Up 80ft in a tree within the Gandoca-Manzanillo wildlife refuge, this observation deck and tree house allows guests to experience life in the canopy of an old growth forest. The open-air, two-story accommodations feature hammocks and comfy beds from which monkeys, kinkajous and toucans are regularly spotted. To reach the platform, guests must climb the tree (harnesses provided).

The owner, an ardent conservationist, collects his customers in Manzanillo at 1pm each day and leads them on a 45-minute

hike to the tree, which he assists them in scaling on a rope ladder. Dinner and breakfast are delivered up the tree in a basket. The entire deck is just 60 sq m, and includes just two units that sleep two people each.

ℹ Information

An excellent photo book on the area, with commentary in Spanish and English, is *Refugio Nacional de Vida Silvestre Gandoca-Manzanillo* by Juan José Puccí, available locally.

Minae (☑ 2759-9100; ⊙ 8am-noon & 1-4pm) is located in the green wooden house as you enter Manzanillo, and generally has trail maps of the refuge.

ℹ Getting There & Away

Buses to Manzanillo drop off in front of Maxi's Restaurant (p186). From there, it's about 1km to the refuge's entrance. A newly constructed bridge allows guests to enter the park without having to wade through the water at high tide. Another good option for accessing different areas of the park is to hire a boat.

Bribrí

This bustling, no-stoplight town in the foothills of the Cordillera de Talamanca lies at a bend in the paved road that connects Cahuita to Sixaola and the Panama border. The village is primarily an agricultural center and a spot for nearby indigenous communities to take care of errands; most travelers just pass through on their way to the border or on local tours.

From Bribrí, a 34km paved road takes the traveler to the border at Sixaola.

◉ Sights

For information about tours to local indigenous villages, drive 2km west of town to Rancho Grande and ask for Catato (his house is just opposite Rancho Grande's football field).

Studio of Fran Vázquez GALLERY
(☑ 2751-0205) On the road to Bribrí, 350m north of the Sixaola turnoff, find the studio of this self-taught folk painter whose colorful acrylic landscapes are well known in Puerto Viejo and San José. Look for the brightly painted sign outside a small, one-story house. Call ahead to visit, as hours vary.

GETTING TO PANAMA

Welcome to Costa Rica's most entertaining border crossing! An old railroad bridge spans the churning waters of the Río Sixaola, connecting Costa Rica with Panama amid a sea of agricultural plantations. Until recently, oversize buses and trucks also plied this route – making for a surreal scene whenever one of these vehicles came clattering along the wood planks, forcing pedestrians to scatter to the edges. Today there's a parallel bridge for motor-vehicle traffic, inaugurated in mid-2012, but pedestrians still get the fun of walking across the old bridge.

From here, most travelers make for Bocas del Toro in Panama, a picturesque archipelago of jungle islands that is home to lovely beaches and endangered red frogs, and is easily accessible by regular water taxis from the docks at Almirante.

The border is open 7am to 5pm (8am to 6pm in Guabito, Panama, which is an hour ahead of Costa Rica), though one or both sides may close for lunch at around 1pm. At the entrance to the bridge, on the right-hand side, pay the US$7 Costa Rica departure tax and get your exit stamp at the Costa Rica immigration office (✆2754-2044). Once over the bridge, stop at Panama immigration to get your passport stamped and pay the US$4 entry tax. Note that Panama no longer requires tourist cards for foreigners entering from Costa Rica, but you will be required to show proof of onward travel out of Panama, such as a copy of your plane ticket home. Personal cars (not rentals) can cross here.

Guabito has no hotels or banks, but in a pinch you can exchange colones at the market across the street. From the border, half-hourly buses (US$1.25, one hour) run to Terminal Piquera in Changuinola, where you can transfer to one of the frequent buses to Almirante (US$1.75, 45 minutes) for the water taxi. Alternatively, from Guabito you can take a collective taxi (per person US$10, one hour) straight to Almirante. From this point, hourly water taxis (per person US$6, 25 minutes) make the trip to Bocas del Toro between 6:30am and 6pm.

For a more streamlined, if slightly more expensive, trip to Bocas del Toro, take one of the daily shuttles from Cahuita (p163) or Puerto Viejo de Talamanca (p181).

🛏 Sleeping & Eating

There are a few basic lodging options. Accommodations tend to fill up on market days (Monday and Tuesday).

Cabinas El Piculino   CABINA **$**
(✆2751-0130; d with fan/air-con US$34/50; P✳🛜) Connected to the great **soda** (casados US$7) run by the same family, this spotless place has 17 clean, simple, brightly painted rooms, some with hot showers; all have TV and most have air-con.

Restaurante Bribrí   COSTA RICAN **$**
(✆2751-0044; breakfast/casados US$3/6.50; ⏱5am-6pm Mon-Sat) Run by the helpful Carlos and Miriam, this busy restaurant adjacent to the bus stop serves breakfast, *casados,* chicken with rice, fried plantains and tamales.

ℹ Information

Banco Nacional (⏱8:45am-3:45pm) Has an ATM and changes US dollars. It's 100m north of the bus stop.

ℹ Getting There & Away

Buses arrive and depart hourly from in front of Restaurante Bribrí.
Puerto Limón, via Cahuita US$4.40; three hours; departs hourly from 6am to 7:45pm.
San José US$11.80; 5½ hours; departs 6:30am, 8:30am, 10:30am and 3:30pm.
Sixaola US$2.90; 30 minutes; departs hourly from 6am to 8pm.

Sixaola

This is the end of the road – literally. Bumpy tarmac leads to an old railroad bridge over the Río Sixaola that serves as the border crossing into Panama. Like most border towns, Sixaola is hardly scenic: it's an extravaganza of dingy bars and roadside stalls selling rubber boots.

🛏 Sleeping & Eating

Cabinas Sanchez   CABINA **$**
(✆2754-2105; d/tr US$20/30; 🛜) Cabinas Sanchez offers five spotless cabins and a trampoline, but no hot water.

From the border, head north along the lower road and walk about 100m to the tunnel on the left. After exiting the underpass, walk west another 100m to find the cabinas.

Scorpion Restaurant
CARIBBEAN $

(📞 6925-7890; casados US$5-9; ⊘ hours vary) If you must eat at the border, this Caribbean place is your best bet. Pork, beef, chicken, snapper and *patacones* (fried plantains) are all on the menu.

From the border, head north along the lower road for about 200m.

❶ Getting There & Away

The bus station is just north of the border crossing, one block east of the main drag.

Buses to either San José (US$13.15; six hours; 6am, 8am, 10am and 3pm) or Puerto Limón (US$6.30, three hours, hourly from 5am to 7pm) all stop at Bribrí and Cahuita.

There are also regular buses to Puerto Viejo de Talamanca (US$3.25, one hour, hourly between 5:30am and 7:30pm Monday through Saturday, every two hours on Sunday).

Northwestern Costa Rica

Best Places to Eat

➡ Café Caburé (p206)

➡ Café Liberia (p226)

➡ Hummingbird Café (p218)

➡ Monteverde Cheese Factory (p200)

➡ Orchid Coffee (p205)

Best Places to Sleep

➡ Casitas Tenorio (p217)

➡ Capulín Cabins & Farm (p202)

➡ Celeste Mountain Lodge (p217)

➡ Hotel Belmar (p204)

Why Go?

What did you come to Costa Rica for? To lounge on pristine beaches and ride glorious waves? To hike up volcanoes and soak in geothermal springs? To spy on birds and monkeys and get lost among ancient trees? The northwestern corner of Costa Rica packs in all this and more. Unlike any other part of Costa Rica, Guanacaste – in the far northwest – is a wide, flat expanse of grasslands and dry tropical forest, where savanna vistas are broken only by windblown trees. Further east, the Cordillera de Guanacaste rises majestically out of the plains in a line of sputtering, steaming volcanic peaks that beg exploration. Further south, higher altitudes create a misty, mystical cloud forest, teeming with life. What did you come to Costa Rica for? Here it is...

When to Go

➡ Guanacaste is Costa Rica's driest province, getting very little rain from November to April, when the winds bless (and blast) Bahía Salinas.

➡ By contrast, the 'green' season is very, very green in the cloud forest.

➡ From May to November, there are much fewer tourists and prices for accommodation are reduced.

➡ Humpback whales migrate up the coast in September and October.

➡ Other seasonal events to watch out for are the blooming of the yellow cortezes in March and the *fiestas Guanacastecas* that occur throughout the year.

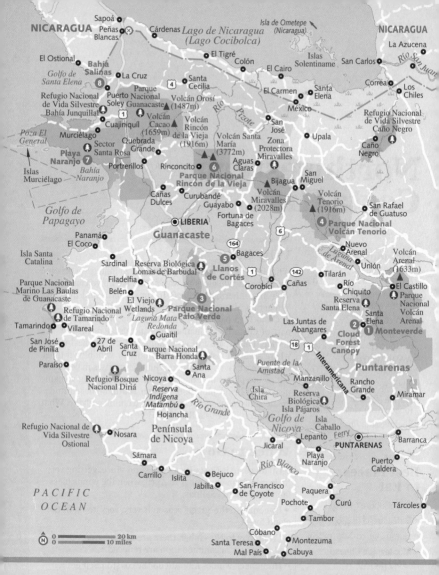

Northwestern Costa Rica Highlights

1 Spotting the resplendent quetzal through the mist at one of the reserves near **Monteverde** (p193).

2 Making like a monkey by zipping and swinging on the **Cloud forest canopy tour** (p198).

3 Checking off your bird list at **Parque Nacional Palo**

Verde (p221), Costa Rica's largest wetland sanctuary.

4 Hiking along the raging Río Celeste at the **Parque Nacional Volcán Tenorio** (p218), and marveling at her cerulean-blue waters.

5 Cooling off with a refreshing waterfall shower and bath at **Llanos de Cortés** (p223).

6 Trekking past waterfalls, thermal pools and volcanic vents at **Parque Nacional Rincón de la Vieja** (p228).

7 Surfing the legendary Witch's Rock at **Playa Naranjo** (p235).

8 Satisfying your need for speed with a kitesurfing course at **Bahía Salinas** (p238).

Parks & Reserves

Northwestern Costa Rica has a wealth of parks and reserves, ranging from little-visited national parks to the highlight on many visitors' itineraries, Monteverde Cloud Forest.

Parque Nacional Palo Verde (p221) Stay at the research station and take a guided tour to see some of the 300-plus bird species recorded in this rich wetland.

Parque Nacional Rincón de la Vieja (p228) Peaceful, muddy isolation can be found just outside of Liberia, where bubbling thermal activity abounds.

Refugio Nacional de Vida Silvestre Bahía Junquillal (p236) Another small, peaceful protected site, this refuge has a beach backed by mangrove swamp and tropical dry forest.

Reserva Biológica Bosque Nuboso Monteverde (p209) Costa Rica's most famous cloud forest, Monteverde receives a steady stream of visitors but still hasn't lost its magic.

Reserva Biológica Lomas de Barbudal (p221) If you're here in March, you might be lucky enough to catch the yellow blooms of the *corteza amarilla* tree in this tropical dry forest reserve.

Reserva Santa Elena (p198) With fewer crowds and higher elevation, this is a mistier and more mysterious place to experience the cloud forest.

Sector Santa Rosa (p233) Access legendary surf, hike through the largest stand of tropical dry forest in Central America and visit a historical battle site.

Sector Murcielago (p236) Brave the notorious roads to explore deserted beaches, or catch a boat to surf the country's most celebrated break.

ⓘ Getting There & Away

More and more visitors are flying directly into Liberia, a convenient international airport that makes for quick escapes to both northwestern Costa Rica and the beaches of the Península de Nicoya. Liberia is also a major transportation center for buses traveling the Interamericana, from the border with Nicaragua to San José. Regular buses also connect the Península de Nicoya to hubs such as Santa Cruz and Nicoya and coastal points beyond.

This is a heavily touristed region, so entrepreneurs have picked up on the need for more transportation options. If you're looking for a ride that's cheaper than a rented car and more comfortable (and faster) than a public bus, you'll probably be able to find a shuttle bus. Several companies ply the most popular routes.

MONTEVERDE & AROUND

Spread out on the slopes of the Cordillera de Tílaran, this area is a sprawling chain of villages, farms and nature reserves. The biggest population center – the village of Santa Elena – runs almost seamlessly into its next-door neighbor Cerro Plano and its next next-door neighbor, tiny Monteverde (which borders the namesake reserve).

The Reserva Biológica Bosque Nuboso Monteverde (Monteverde Cloud Forest Reserve) is the most famous one, but there are public and private properties of all shapes and sizes – from tiny family *fincas* (farms) to the vast Children's Eternal Rainforest – that blanket this whole area in luscious green. As a result, there are trails to hike, birds to spot, waterfalls to swim and adventures to be had everywhere you turn.

Monteverde & Santa Elena

Strung between two lovingly preserved cloud forests, this slim corridor of civilization consists of the Tico village of Santa Elena and the Quaker settlement of Monteverde, each with an eponymous cloud-forest reserve. The cloud forests around Monteverde and Santa Elena are premier destinations for everyone from budget backpackers to well-heeled retirees. On a good day, Monteverde is a place where you can be inspired about the possibility of a world in which organic farming and alternative energy sources are the norm. On a bad day, Monteverde can feel like Disneyland in Birkenstocks. Take heart in the fact that the local community continues to fight the good fight to maintain the fragile balance of nature and commerce.

◉ Sights

The sights in Monteverde and Santa Elena are mostly geared to bringing the wildlife a little closer, whether it's bats, butterflies, frog, snakes or flowers. These stops can be entertaining and educational – especially for children – but it's even more rewarding when you see these creatures in the wild. And you're in the wild, so go out there and see it.

Monteverde & Santa Elena

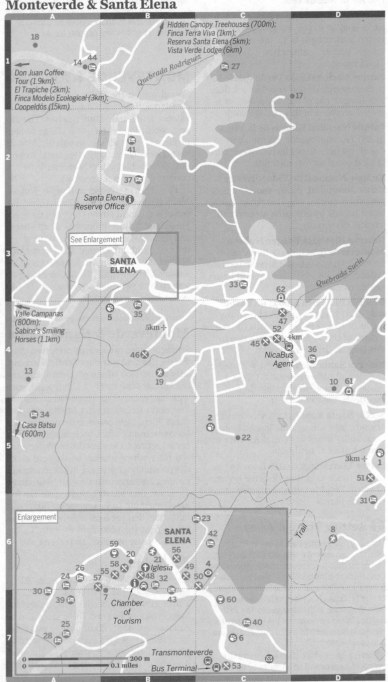

Hidden Canopy Treehouses (700m);
Finca Terra Viva (1km);
Reserva Santa Elena (5km);
Vista Verde Lodge (6km)

Quebrada Rodríguez

Don Juan Coffee
Tour (1.9km);
El Trapiche (2km);
Finca Modelo Ecológical (3km);
Coopeldós (15km)

Santa Elena
Reserve Office

See Enlargement

SANTA
ELENA

Quebrada Sucia

Valle Campanas
(800m);
Sabine's Smiling
Horses (1.1km)

5km

NicaBus
Agent

4km

Casa Batsu
(600m)

3km

Enlargement

SANTA
ELENA

Iglesia

Chamber
of
Tourism

Trail

Transmonteverde
Bus Terminal

0   200 m
0   0.1 miles

Jardín de Orquídeas
GARDENS

(Orchid Garden; ☑2645-5308; www.monteverde orchidgarden.net; Santa Elena; adult/child US$10/ free; ☺8am-5pm) This sweet-smelling garden in Santa Elena has shady trails winding past more than 400 types of orchid organized into taxonomic groups. On your guided tour, you'll see such rarities as *Platystele junger-mannioides,* the world's smallest orchid. If you have orchids at home, here's your chance to get tips from the experts on how to keep them beautiful and blooming.

Serpentarium
ZOO

(Herpentario; ☑2645-6002; www.skyadventures. travel; Santa Elena; adult/student/child US$13/ 11/8; ☺9am-8pm) A guide will show you around and introduce you to some 40 species of slithery snakes, plus a fair number of frogs, lizards, turtles and other cold-blooded critters. Your ticket entitles you to a return visit after dark, when all the nocturnal species come out. Guided tours leave every hour.

Monteverde Theme Park
ZOO

(Monteverde Frog Pond; ☑2645-6320; www.mon teverdethemepark.com; Santa Elena; per attraction $13-17, canopy tour adult/child $35/20; ☺9am-4:30pm, ranario to 8pm) Formerly known as the Ranario, or Frog Pond, this place has added an insect house, a butterfly garden and canopy tour – hence, it's now a theme park. The frogs are still the highlight: about 25 species reside in transparent enclosures lining the winding indoor jungle paths. Sharp-eyed guides point out frogs, eggs and tadpoles with flashlights. Your ticket entitles you to two visits, so come back in the evening to see the nocturnal species.

The canopy tour is a scaled-back version of this activity, with eight cables and a Tarzan swing. It's perfect for children and chickens who might be freaked out by the longer, higher, faster zip lines on offer.

Butterfly Garden
ZOO

(Jardín de Mariposas; ☑2645-5512; www.monte verdebutterflygarden.com; Cerro Plano; adult/ student/child US$15/10/5; ☺8:30am-4pm; ⓐ) Head here for everything you ever wanted to know about butterflies, with four gardens representing different habitats and home to more than 40 species. Up-close observation cases allow you to witness the butterflies as they emerge from the chrysalis (if your timing is right). Other exhibits feature the industrious leafcutter ant and the ruthless tarantula hawk (actually a wasp that eats

Monteverde & Santa Elena

tarantulas) and lots of scorpions. Kids love this place, and knowledgeable naturalist guides truly enhance the experience.

Bat Jungle ZOO
(☏2645-7701; www.batjungle.com; Monteverde; adult/child US$13/11; ☺9am-7pm; ⛶) The so-called Bat Jungle in Monteverde is a small but informative exhibit, with good bilingual educational displays and a free-flying bat habitat housing almost 100 bats. Make a reservation for your 45-minute tour to learn about echolocation, bat-wing aerodynamics and other amazing flying-mammal facts.

Day is night; night is day! The bats are on a reversed day/night schedule so they are most active from 9am to 5pm.

Friends Meeting House CHURCH
(www.monteverdequakers.org; Monteverde; ☺meetings 10:30am Sun, 9am Wed) This simple meeting house in Monteverde is the 'church' of the American Society of Friends, or the Quakers, who first settled this area and committed to protect a portion of the cloud forest.

In 1949 four Quakers in Alabama were jailed for their refusal to be drafted to fight in the Korean War. In response, a group of 44 Quakers from 11 families left the US and headed for (much) greener pastures, literally. The Quakers settled in Monteverde (Green Mountain) for two reasons – the absence of a military and the cool, mountain climate. Ensconced in their isolated refuge, they adopted a simple, trouble-free life of dairy farming and cheese production. Years later, in an effort to protect the watershed above its 15-sq-km plot in Monteverde, the Quaker community agreed to preserve the mountaintop cloud forest, eventually leading to the establishment of the reserve.

Monteverde Friends School CULTURAL CENTRE (www.mfschool.org; Monteverde; per person US$15; ☺ tours 8am Tue & Fri; ♿) Here's a great way for children to learn about and interact with the local culture: spend some time at the schoolhouse. With advance reservation, visitors can sit in on morning assembly and tour the grounds. Kids are even invited to attend a class (and recess!) with an English-speaking buddy.

Volunteers who can make a long-term commitment are invited to work with local students, providing tutoring, art projects, music lessons, technology assistance or other individualized attention.

🏃 Activities

In addition to the two biggies anchoring this area at the north and south, Monteverde and Santa Elena are home to dozens of smaller private reserves (not to mention the giant Children's Eternal Rainforest). The Monteverde and Santa Elena reserves are special – very special – because they are essentially the only cloud-forest reserves in the area. But if you want to immerse yourself in nature, get some exercise, spot some monkeys, admire a scenic vista, cool off in a waterfall, there are countless places to do so (most of which will be significantly less crowded than the Monteverde reserve).

Finca Modelo Ecologica OUTDOORS (☎ 2645-5581; www.familiabrenestours.com; treetops/canyoning/combo US$40/70/100; ☺ treetops 8am-4pm, canyoning 8am, 11am & 2pm) The Brenes family *finca* offers a number of unique and thrilling diversions. Their masterpiece is the two-hour canyoning tour, which descends six glorious waterfalls, the largest of which is 40m. No experience necessary, just an adventurous spirit. Treehuggers can climb a 132ft ficus tree, using ropes and rappels to go up and down.

The *finca* is located 2km north of Santa Elena in the village of La Cruz, but transportation from your hotel is included in the price.

Revive Healing Arts MASSAGE (☎ 8372-2002; www.revivehealingarts.com; Monteverde; treatments from US$50) Karen Gordon's signature offering, the Mountain Massage, is custom designed to soothe your aching muscles, no matter what adventures you have been up to. She also offers Reiki, craniosacral therapy and personalized retreat programs.

Curi-Cancha Reserve HIKING, BIRD-WATCHING (☎ 8356-1431, 2645-6915; www.curi-cancha.com; admission US$14, guided hike US$15, natural history tour US$45, bird tour US$60; ☺ 7am-3:30pm, guided hike 7:30am & 1:30pm) Bordering Monteverde but without the crowds, this lovely private reserve on the banks of the Río Cuecha is popular among birders. There are about 10km of well-marked trails, a hummingbird garden and a view of the continental divide. Make reservations for the guided hikes, including the early-morning bird walks and specialized three-hour natural history walks.

Santuario Ecológico HIKING (Ecological Sanctuary; ☎ 2645-5869; www.santuarioecologico.com; Cerro Plano; adult/student/child US$17/14/11, morning tour US$35/31/29, night tour US$30/25/23; ☺ 7am-5:30pm, morning tour 7am, night tour 5:30pm) This smallish sanctuary is set on private property comprising premontane and secondary forest, and coffee and banana plantations. Descend to an impressive 30m waterfall and cool off with a refreshing dip. These trails are not well trodden, so you're more likely to meet a coati or a sloth than another human being. Bird walks and night tours also available.

Bosque Eterno de los Niños HIKING (Children's Eternal Rainforest, BEN; ☎ 2645-5305; www.acmcr.org; adult/child admission US$12/free, guided hike US$22/14, transportation per person US$4; ☺ 7:30am-5:30pm, night hike 5:30pm; ♿) 🌿 What became of the efforts of a group of schoolchildren to save the rainforest? Only this enormous 220-sq-km reserve – the largest private reserve in the country. It is mostly inaccessible to tourists, with the exception of the well-marked 3.5km **Sendero Bajo del Tigre** (Jaguar Canyon Trail; ☎ 2645-5200; www.acmcr.org; admission adult/child US$12/free, night hike adult/student/child/transportation US$22/19/14/4; ☺ 8am-4pm, night

DON'T MISS

RESERVA SANTA ELENA

The exquisitely misty 310-hectare **Reserva Santa Elena** (☑ 2645-7107, 2645-5390; www.reservasantaelena.org; adult/student US$14/7, guided hike US$15; ☺ 7am-4pm) offers a completely different cloud forest experience to Monteverde. Cutting through the veiled forest, the 10km of dewy trails see much less traffic, retaining a magic that is sometimes missing at Monteverde. Open since 1992, this reserve was one of the first community-managed conservation projects in the country.

There's a **reserve office** (☑ 2645-5390; www.reservasantaelena.org; Colegio Técnico Profesional; ☺ 8am-4pm Wed-Fri) at the Colegio Técnico Profesional in town. The reserve itself is about 6km northeast of the village of Santa Elena. There's a simple restaurant, coffee shop and gift store. Note that all proceeds go toward managing the reserve as well as to environmental-education programs in local schools.

hike 5:30pm; ⛓), which is actually a series of shorter trails. At the entrance there's an education center for children and a fabulous vista over the reserve.

Make reservations in advance for the popular two-hour night hikes. The Estación Biológica San Gerardo, reachable from a rather gnarly 2½-hour trail from Reserva Santa Elena, is managed by BEN and has dorm beds for researchers and students, but you may be able to stay overnight with prior arrangements.

Cerro Amigos   HIKING

Take a hike up to the highest peak in the area (1842m) for good views of the surrounding rainforest and, on a clear day, Volcán Arenal, 20km away to the northeast. Behind Hotel Belmar in Cerro Plano, take the dirt road going downhill, then the next left. The trail ascends roughly 300m in 3km. Note that this trail does not connect to the trails in the Monteverde reserve.

SkyTram   SCENIC RIDE

(☑ 2479-4100; www.skyadventures.travel; Santa Elena; adult/student/child US$44/37/31) Owned by SkyTrek, SkyTram is a wheelchair-accessible cable car that floats gently over the cloud forest. On a clear day you can see from the volcanoes in the east to the Pacific in the west. Packages are available if you're also interested in the SkyTrek (canopy tour) and SkyWalk (hanging bridges).

🐦 Courses

Monteverde Institute   LANGUAGE COURSE

(☑ 2645-5053; www.monteverde-institute.org; Monteverde; weeklong courses US$375, homestay incl meals per day US$23) This nonprofit educational institute in Monteverde offers interdisciplinary courses in Spanish, as well as

more specialized programs in tropical ecology, conservation and ecotourism, among other topics. Courses are occasionally open to the public, as are volunteer opportunities in education and reforestation.

Centro Panamericano de Idiomas   LANGUAGE COURSE

(CPI; ☑ 2265-6306; www.cpi-edu.com; Cerro Plano; weeklong classes US$390; ☺ 8am-5pm) Specializes in Spanish-language education, with courses geared toward families, teenagers, medical professionals and retirees. For fun: optional dance and cooking classes are included with your tuition.

🐦 Tours

There's not a lot of diversity when it comes to tours in Monteverde. Most reserves offer guided hikes, morning bird walks and spooky night hikes. Other than that, you'll find canopy tours and coffee tours – both provide a good energy boost! Keep in mind that Monteverde works on a commission-based system, so take all unsolicited advice with a degree of skepticism.

Horse Riding

Sabine's Smiling Horses   HORSE RIDING

(☑ 2645-6894; www.smilinghorses.com; Monteverde; 2hr/3hr/all-day ride per person US$45/65/105; ☺ tours 9am, 1pm & 3pm) Conversant in four languages (in addition to equine), Sabine will make sure you are comfortable on your horse, whether you're a novice rider or an experienced cowboy. Her longstanding operation in Monteverde offers a variety of treks including a popular waterfall tour (three hours) and a magical full-moon tour (monthly). And yes, the horses really do smile.

Finca El Rodeo
HORSE RIDING

(✆ 2645-6306; www.caballerizaelrodeo.com; Santa Elena; per person $40-60) Based at a local *finca*, this outfit offers tours on private trails through rainforest, coffee plantations and grasslands, with plenty of pauses to spot wildlife and admire the fantastic landscapes. The specialty is a sunset tour to a spot overlooking the Golfo de Nicoya. *¡Que hermoso!*

Horse Trek Monteverde
HORSE RIDING

(✆ 8379-9827; www.horsetrekmonteverde.com; per person US$49-85) Owner and guide Marvin Anchia is a Santa Elena native, a professional horse trainer and an amateur naturalist who offers an excellent, intimate horseback-riding experience. Tours range from two-hour rides through the coffee plantations and scenic half-day rides in the cloud forest to all-day cowboy experiences. The horses are well cared for, well trained and a joy to ride.

Canopy Tours

Wonder where the whole canopy-tour craze was born? Santa Elena is the site of Costa Rica's first zip lines, today eclipsed in adrenaline by the nearly 100 imitators who have followed, some of which are right here in town. You won't be spotting any quetzals or coatis as you whoosh your way over the canopy, but if you came to Costa Rica to fly, this is the absolute best place to do it. If you want to explore the treetops without the adrenaline rush, several outfits also have systems of hanging bridges. Transportation from your lodging is included in the price.

Selvatura
CANOPY TOUR

(✆ 2645-5929; www.selvatura.com; canopy US$50, walkways US$30, each exhibit US$5-15; ⊙ 7:30am-4pm) One of the bigger games in town, Selvatura has 3km of cables, 18 platforms and one Tarzan swing over a stretch of incredibly beautiful primary cloud forest. In addition to the cables, it has 3km of 'Treetops Walkways,' as well as a hummingbird garden, a butterfly garden and an amphibian and reptile exhibition.

Selvatura is 6km north of Santa Elena, near the reserve, but there's a booking office in town.

Original Canopy Tour
CANOPY TOUR

(✆ 2645-5243; www.theoriginalcanopy.com; adult/student/child US$45/35/25; ⊙ 7:30am, 10:30am & 2:30pm) The storied zip-line tour that started the trend. With 15 cables, a Tarzan swing and a rappel through the center of an old fig tree, it's a lot more fun than most history museums. Your adrenaline rush may not be as big as at some of the other canopy tours, but you'll enjoy smaller groups and more emphasis on the natural surroundings.

After the tour, you are free to wander the 5km of hiking trails on the grounds of the Cloud Forest Lodge. It's 1km north of town, on the way to Reserva Santa Elena.

100% Aventura
CANOPY TOUR

(✆ 2645-6388; www.aventuracanopytour.com; Santa Elena; canopy adult/child US$50/40, bridges US$30/20; ⊙ tours 8am, 11am, 1pm & 3pm; ⊞) Aventura boasts the longest zip line in Latin America (which is nearly 1600m in case you were wondering). The 19 platforms are spiced up with a Tarzan swing, a 15m rappel and a Superman zip line that makes you feel as if you really are flying. It also has a network of suspension bridges, laced through secondary forest. Reservations required.

It's about 3km north of Santa Elena on the road to the reserve, but there's a booking office in town.

SkyTrek
CANOPY TOUR

(✆ 2645-5238; www.skyadventures.travel; Santa Elena; adult/student/child SkyWalk US$25/21/17, SkyTrek US$77/64/53; ⊙ 7:30am-5pm; ⊞) This seriously fast canopy tour consists of 11 platforms attached to steel towers that are spread out along a road and zoom over swatches of primary forest. We're talking serious speeds of up to 64km/h, which is probably why SkyTrek was the first canopy tour with a real brake system. The SkyWalk is a 2km guided tour over five suspended bridges; a night tour is also available.

Extremo Canopy
CANOPY TOUR

(✆ 2645-6058; www.monteverdeextremo.com; Santa Elena; canopy tour US$50, bungee US$70, Tarzan swing $40; ⊙ 8am-4pm; ⊞) Located in secondary forest, there's a canopy ride, allowing you to fly Superman-style through the air, the highest and most adrenaline-addled Tarzan swing in the area, and a bungee jump. One way or another, you will scream. The views are marvelous but they herd some pretty big groups through here, so it's not exactly a nature experience.

Guided Hikes

Ficus Trails
HIKING

(✆ 2645-6474; www.ficustrails.com; adult/student/child night hike US$25/20/15, natural history walk US$30/25/20, birding US$38) From the observation deck at this private reserve, you can

MONTEVERDE CHEESE FACTORY

Until the upswing in ecotourism, Monteverde's number-one employer was the **Monteverde Cheese Factory** (La Lechería; ☑ 2645-7090; www.monteverdecheesefactory.com; Monteverde; tours adult/child US$12/10; ☉ store 7:30am-5pm Mon-Sat, to 4pm Sun, tours 9am & 2pm Mon-Sat), which was started in 1953 by Monteverde's original Quaker settlers. Learn about the history of the Quakers in Costa Rica and their methods for producing and pasteurizing cheese on a two-hour tour of the factory (reservations required). You can also pop in any time to sample the creamy goodness. Bonus: now there's a Santa Elena outlet (p205), right next door to the Catholic church.

The Monteverde Cheese Factory is now the second-largest cheese producer in the country. It's no longer owned by the Quakers (it's now owned by the Mexican giant Sigma Alimentos), but the factory still uses their name and recipes, producing everything from a creamy Gouda to a very nice sharp, white cheddar, as well as other dairy products such as yogurt and, most importantly, ice cream. Don't miss the chance to sample Monte Rico, a Monteverde original.

see from the continental divide down to the San Luis falls, and out to the Golfo de Nicoya. The varied altitude means it's home to a huge diversity of flora and fauna, some of which you can spot on daily bird walks and night hikes. The tour guides are attentive and patient, guaranteeing a worthwhile experience.

Take the road to San Luis and follow the signs.

Valle Escondido   HIKING

(Hidden Valley; ☑ 2645-6601; www.valleescondido preserve.com; Cerro Plano; day use US$20, night tour adult/child US$25/15; ☉ 7am-4pm, night tour 5:30pm) Reserve in advance for the popular two-hour guided night tour, then come back the next day to explore the reserve on your own. Located behind Monteverde Inn in Cerro Plano, the well-marked trail winds through a deep canyon into an 11-hectare reserve, passing wonderful vistas and luscious waterfalls. During the day, Valle Escondido is quiet with few tourists, so it's recommended for birding and wildlife-watching.

Santa Maria Night Walk   TOUR

(☑ 2645-6548; www.nightwalksantamarias.com; Santa Elena; per person US$25; ☉ tour 5:30pm) Night walks have become so popular because 80% of the cloud-forest creatures are nocturnal. This one takes place on a private Santa Elena *finca*, with 10-hectare swathe of primary and secondary forest. Expert guides point out all kinds of wildlife that are active in the evening, ranging from snakes and spiders to sloths and kinkajous. Flashlights are provided.

Food & Drink

Café de Monteverde   COFFEE TOUR

(☑ 2645-7550; www.lifemonteverde.com; Monteverde; tour per person US$18; ☉ coffee tasting 7:30am-6pm, tours 8am & 1:30pm) 🍴 Stop by the shop in Monteverde to take a crash course in coffee and sample the delicious blends. Or, sign on for the three-hour tour on sustainable agriculture, which visits organic *fincas* implementing techniques like composting and solar energy. Learn how coffee growing has helped to shape this community and how it can improve the local environment.

Kind of makes you want to pour yourself another cup!

El Trapiche   COFFEE TOUR

(☑ 2645-7650; www.eltrapichetour.com; Santa Elena; adult/child US$32/12; ☉ tours 10am & 3pm Mon-Sat, 3pm Sun; 🏠) Visit this picturesque family *finca* in Santa Elena, where they grow not only coffee but also sugarcane, bananas and plantains. See the coffee process first-hand, take a ride in a traditional ox cart, and try your hand at making sugar. Bonus: lots of samples along the way, including sugarcane liquor, sugarcane toffee and – of course – delicious coffee. Kids love this one.

Don Juan Coffee Tour   COFFEE TOUR

(☑ 2645-7100; www.donjuancoffeetour.com; Santa Elena; adult/child US$35/15, night tour US$20; ☉ 7am-4:30pm, tours 8am, 1pm & 6pm) Don Juan does three in one, where you can learn about all your favorite vices (OK, maybe not *all* your favorites, but three of the good ones). It's a pretty cursory overview of how sugarcane is harvested and processed; how cacao beans are transformed into dark, decadent chocolate; and how coffee happens, from plant to bean to cup.

Caburé Chocolate Tour CHOCOLATE TOUR

(☑2645-5020; www.cabure.net; per person US$15; ☺tours 1pm & 4pm Mon-Sat) Bob, the owner of the Caburé chocolate shop in Monteverde, shares his secrets about the magical cacao pod and how to transform it into the food of the gods. There are plenty of opportunities for taste testing along the way, and you'll try your hand at making truffles.

🛏 Sleeping

Santa Elena and Monterverde are lined with lodgings, from fun and affordable hostels and friendly farmstays, to luscious and luxurious mountain lodges. They are packed into the village streets and spread out on the forested hills around town. Budget travelers will probably want to stay in Santa Elena, where they have more options and easier transportation. Midrange and high-end travelers might want to consider staying in nearby Cerro Plano or Monteverde, or even further afield. These places promise closer interaction with nature, though many require a vehicle (preferably, a 4WD).

Reservations are practically required during holiday weeks, and recommended throughout the high season. Prices drop 30% to 40% during the low season.

🛏 Santa Elena

★Casa Tranquilo HOSTEL $

(☑2645-6782; www.casatranquilohostel.com; dm US$10, d with/without bathroom US$30/22, all incl breakfast; P@🛜) At Casa Tranquilo, the wonderful Tico hospitality starts first thing in the morning with homemade banana bread. In addition to the excellent breakfast, staff lead free guided hikes, sharing their in-depth local expertise. The rooms are simple and spotless, some featuring skylights and gulf views. Colorful murals adorn the outside, so you'll know you are in the right place.

Pensión Santa Elena HOSTEL $

(☑2645-5051; www.pensionsantaelena.com; d without bathroom US$28, d with bathroom US$32-38, ste US$45-60, all incl breakfast; P@🛜) This full-service hostel right in central Santa Elena is a perennial favorite, offering budget travelers top-notch service and *pura vida*

hospitality. Each room is different, with something to suit every budget. The 'grand' rooms in the annex feature perks like superior beds, stone showers and iPod docks.

Cabinas Eddy CABINA $

(☑2645-6635; www.cabinas-eddy.com; d US$40-60, without bathroom US$35; P@🛜) This budget spot continues to get rave reviews for its amazing breakfasts, attentive service and delightful manager Freddy (son of Eddy, by the way). The rooms are spotless, as is the fully equipped communal kitchen. The balcony is a great place to relax with a cup of free coffee and take in the view.

Monteverde Backpackers HOSTEL $

(☑2645-5844; www.monteverdebackpackers.com; dm US$10-12, d/tr/q US$30/45/55, all incl breakfast; P@🛜) Small and friendly, Monteverde Backpackers is part of the Costa Rica Hostel Network. The wood-paneled rooms are clean and comfy enough, the showers are hot, the location in Santa Elena is quiet, and management is helpful. Freebies include coffee, hammocks and a sunset hike. Breakfast is DIY, so you can make 'em how you like 'em (eggs, that is).

Monteverde Luxury Hostel HOSTEL $

(☑2645-5157; www.monteverdeluxuryhostel.com; dm US$16, d US$58; P🛜) Think of a classy mountain lodge with lots of amenities, where you meet cool people and share adventures. That's the concept behind this hostel-lodge. Rooms range from stylish, six-bed dorms to private, semi-luxurious tree-top cabins. All guests are invited to the huge common area to listen to some tunes, access free wi-fi and sip happy-hour cocktails.

Prices include a guided hike on the woodsy grounds, home to friendly white-faced capuchin monkeys. Movie nights, barbecue dinners and other events make sure you have something to do after sunset.

Cabinas El Pueblo CABINA $

(☑2645-6192; www.cabinaselpueblo.com; d incl breakfast with/without bathroom from US$32/25; P@🛜) On a quiet road just steps from Santa Elena town, this pleasant hostel is run by an attentive Tico couple, Marlenny and Freddy. Well-furnished rooms are bright and clean, if cramped. You'll also find a communal kitchen, hammocks and – most importantly – an exceedingly warm welcome. All guests are gifted a treat from the family coffee plantation.

Cabinas & Hotel Vista al Golfo CABINA $

(☑ 2645-6321; www.cabinasvistaalgolfo.com; dm US$10, r with/without bathroom from US$30/20, ste US$50, all incl breakfast; P �)) Rooms in this bright, kitschy lodge are well kept, the showers are hot and the owners will make you feel right at home. The upstairs balcony rooms have great views of the rainforest and, on a clear day, the Golfo de Nicoya. There's nothing really special going on here, with the exception of an excellent common space, furnished with beanbags, hammock chairs and more awesome views.

Sleepers HOSTEL $

(☑ 8305-0113; www.sleeperssleepcheaperhostels. com; dm US$10, s/d US$25/30, all incl breakfast) You can't miss this lime-green and aqua-blue building in central Santa Elena. Downstairs it looks like a friendly restaurant, but it's actually a crowded communal kitchen, where happy travelers prepare and share meals. Upstairs it looks like a modern motel, but it's actually a hostel, where happy travelers surf the web and catch a breeze on the balcony. Rooms are spotless, with en suite bathrooms.

Hotel El Sueño HOTEL $

(☑ 2645-5021; www.hotelelsuenocr.com; s/d/tr/q incl breakfast US$30/40/55/75; P ☜) Smack dab in the middle of Santa Elena, this family-run hotel has friendly service, huge wooden rooms and a generous breakfast. The floors are squeaky and the water is lukewarm at best, but it's not a bad option for the price. There's a great shared balcony with sweeping views of the area.

★ Capulín Cabins & Farm CABINA $$

(☑ 2645-6719; www.cabinascapulin.com; cabina US$60-90; P ☜) Observe traditional farm life, hike the trails to spot birds and monkeys, or just swing in a hammock and watch the show in the sky. There are eight comfortable cabins of varying sizes – some with kitchens and some with fantastic views to the gulf. Your Tico farm family hosts could not be more generous in sharing their knowledge of the area.

Valle Campanas FARMSTAY $$

(☑ 2645-5631; www.vallecampanas.com; d US$75, family cabin US$120-175, all incl breakfast; P ☜) 🍃 A collection of four humble cabins are scattered around a family coffee and sugar plantation in Santa Elena. The functional cabins have new kitchens, wide porches with hammocks and plenty of polished wood. Trails wind around the *finca* grounds, allowing guests to visit the animals and observe a working farm. It produces eggs, milk, honey and produce, all of which you'll sample in the scrumptious breakfasts.

Arco Iris Ecolodge LODGE $$

(☑ 2645-5067; www.arcoirislodge.com; s/d/tr budget from US$33/44/54, standard US$70/90/100, superior US$105/120/135; P ☜) This clutch of pretty cabins is on a little hill overlooking Santa Elena and the surrounding forests. Rooms vary in size and style, but all are quite lovely, with lots of stained wood, rainforest showers and private terraces. A system of private trails winds through the property, including one that leads to a lookout with views to the Pacific.

Monteverde Rustic Lodge HOTEL $$

(☑ 2645-6256; www.monteverderusticlodge.com; d/tr/q incl breakfast US$75/90/125; P) Funny thing about the Rustic Lodge: it's not that rustic. The tree-trunk posts and furnishings play along with the theme, but the remodeled rooms are spotless, comfortable and even upscale. Decorated in subtle earth tones, the rooms have lots of stained wood, tile floors and floral curtains. The shared balcony or terrace overlooks a blooming garden. Your host, José, is a charmer.

Finca Terra Viva FARMSTAY $$

(☑ 2645-5454; www.terravivacr.com; d/casita incl breakfast US$60/90; P @ ☜) 🍃 A 300-acre working dairy *finca* surrounded by lush forest, this is a unique sleep that offers guests an authentic rural experience, with an element of environmental consciousness raising. Try your hand at feeding baby cows and making cheese at the organic dairy; hike on trails through farm and forest; and learn all about the measures the farm is taking to minimize its environmental footprint.

Terra Viva is about 3.5km north of town on the road toward Reserva Santa Elena.

Casa Batsu B&B $$

(☑ 2645-7004; www.casabatsu.org; d incl breakfast US$100; P ☜) A few years back, Carlos and Paula remodeled their family farmhouse, then they filled it with art and jazz and delicious food, and then they opened their doors to share the love with visitors. Three rooms are furnished with pillow-strewn beds, well-placed hammocks and striking stone showers. You'll enjoy the decadent breakfasts, for sure, but do stay for dinner one night, as Carlos is an amazing chef.

Hotel Claro de Luna
B&B **$$**

(☎ 2645-5269; www.clarodelunahotel.com; d incl breakfast US$75-97; P ﹫) This graceful old mahogany gingerbread-style house in Santa Elena is surrounded by gorgeous gardens bursting with heliconia, orchids and other tropical blooms. The rooms are simple but cheerful, with brightly painted interiors and floral quilts. Unfortunately, sound travels easily in this old house: get a deluxe room in the annex if you can.

Santa Elena Hostel Resort
LODGE **$$**

(☎ 2645-7879; www.costaricahostels.net; dm US$14, d with/without balcony US$58/52; P ❀ ﹫) With fish in the koi pond and monkeys on the rooftops, this newish hostel may seem like paradise. The shady grounds are strung with hammocks for sunny days, while there's a big stone fireplace for cool nights. The rooms have stained-wood walls and high sloped ceilings. It's worth paying for private balconies with sweet views.

Vista Verde Lodge
LODGE **$$**

(☎ 8380-1517, 2200-5225; www.vistaverdehotel. com; d/tr/q incl breakfast from US$77/88/99; P) 🏊 Wanna get away? Drive your 4WD 7km north of town to this remote, weather-beaten lodge, where you'll fall asleep to the sounds of the rainforest. Wood-paneled rooms with large windows take in views of Volcán Arenal and beyond. If it feels a little damp (as it does), head to the cozy common area to warm your feet beside the fire.

Some 4km of trails run through 64 hectares of primary and secondary forest. Hike to the waterfall, which provides the hydroelectric energy that this place runs on. The lodge is located about 4km past the Reserva Santa Elena.

Hotel Las Orquideas
B&B **$$**

(☎ 2645-5509; www.orquideasmonteverde.com; d/tr/q US$67/78/95; P ﹫) Surrounded by forest yet only 500m from Santa Elena town, this lovely little hotel is a pleasant base for your explorations. There's not a lot going on in the shiny wood guest rooms, but the place is set on gorgeous grounds with lots of wildlife. And your host Nidia is a gem.

Mar Inn B&B
B&B **$$**

(☎ 2645-5279; www.monteverdemarinn.com; d/q incl breakfast US$65/80; P ﹫ ﹫) This humble, homey B&B in Santa Elena is a family-run place that makes all guests feel warm and welcome. Rooms are rustic but comfortable, with stained wood walls, tile floors and big bathrooms. There's a communal kitchen and a shared balcony where rocking chairs are oriented toward those lovely sunset views of the Golfo de Nicoya.

Swiss Hotel Miramontes
HOTEL **$$**

(☎ 2645-5152; www.swisshotelmiramontes.com; r incl breakfast US$62-90; P ﹫) About 500m north of the soccer field in Santa Elena, this charming Euro-inspired retreat is well situated in a grove of pine trees and tropical flowers. Expansive grounds are landscaped with trails winding through the gorgeous orchid gardens. The eight wood-paneled rooms are a little stuffy but satisfactory, while the airy restaurant is light-filled and pleasant for breakfast.

Hidden Canopy Treehouses
BOUTIQUE HOTEL **$$$**

(☎ 2645-5447; www.hiddencanopy.com; d US$275, tree house from US$335, all incl breakfast; P ﹩ ﹫) Hidden within 13 acres of private rainforest are five stunning stilted tree houses, built of wood and windows. Guests relish the private tree-top balconies, luxurious bedding, waterfall showers, custom-made furniture and local artwork. There are two less expensive, less spacious, but equally attractive rooms in the main house. Prices include sunset drinks, featuring an amazing light show in the sky.

Hidden Canopy is 3km north of Santa Elena on the road to the reserve. No kids; two-night minimum.

Cloud Forest Lodge
LODGE **$$$**

(☎ 2645-5058; www.monteverdecloudforestlodge. com; s/d/tr/q incl breakfast US$102/113/124/135; P ﹫ ﹫) Sleep in the clouds: this hilltop lodge is up there, surrounded by 70 acres of primary and secondary forest. There are trails to walk, species to check off your bird list, and gulf views to marvel at. The wooden cabins are spacious and comfortable but hardly luxurious, though you'll enjoy the view from your private porch.

The Original Canopy Tour (p199) is right here at the lodge, which is about 1km from Santa Elena. It's a pleasant walk into town, but you'll get your exercise on the way back.

Hotel Poco a Poco
HOTEL **$$$**

(☎ 2645-6000; www.hotelpocoapoco.com; d incl breakfast US$150-175; P ﹩ ﹫ ﹫ ﹫) There's a lot to love about Poco a Poco. The spa, of course. The restaurant is also excellent, and the contemporary architecture is striking. The whole place is family-friendly, with a

OFF THE BEATEN TRACK

SAN LUIS ECOLODGE & RESEARCH STATION

Formerly a tropical biology research station, the drop-dead-gorgeous facility of **San Luis Ecolodge & Research Station** (www.uga.edu/costarica) is Monteverde's best-kept secret. Administered by the University of Georgia, it integrates academia with high-quality ecotourism and education. The 62-hectare campus is set on a cinematic jade plateau with cloud-forested mountains jack-knifing on three sides and keyhole sea views to the west. Travelers can soak up this stunning natural beauty when they stay at the **Ecolodge San Luis** (University of Georgia Costa Rica; ☑ 2643-7363; www.ecolodge sanluis.com; dm/s/d incl meals US\$54/84/154; P @ �).

Adjoining the southern reach of the Monteverde reserve, much of the campus overlooks the boiling waters of the Río San Luis. Its average elevation of 1100m makes it a tad lower and warmer than Monteverde, and bird-watchers have recorded some 230 species attracted by the slightly nicer weather. There's a working farm with tropical-fruit orchards and a coffee harvest from November to March, and a number of trails into primary and secondary forest.

From the main road between Santa Elena and Monteverde, turn south at the Hotel Fonda Vela and head down the mountain for three steep kilometers. Don't miss the distant view of the San Luis waterfalls as you descend. Look for a signed turnoff to the left. With advance warning, the lodge can also help with transportation.

small playground, kiddie pool, and ceramic critters peeking out in unexpected places. Rooms show off a sophisticated style, but you'll pay more for the upper-floor views.

🛏 Monteverde & Cerro Plano

Los Pinos Cabañas y Jardines LODGE **$$**
(☑ 2645-5252; www.lospinos.net; Cerro Plano; d standard/superior US\$85/140, ste d/tr US\$100/125, q US\$160-180; P ☎ ☀) 🌿 Fourteen free-standing *cabañas* are scattered around the peaceful, forested gardens of this 9-hectare property in Cerro Plano, which once formed part of the family *finca*. Each *cabaña* affords plenty of privacy, plus a fully equipped kitchen and small terrace, although they lack some basic niceties like storage and hammocks. The grounds have tons of birdlife, a playground, walking trails and an organic garden. An awesome option for families.

Hotel El Bosque HOTEL **$$**
(☑ 2645-5158; www.bosquelodgecr.com; Monteverde; d/tr/q incl breakfast US\$95/110/125; P ✻ ☀) On the edge of the Bosque Eterno de los Niños in Monteverde, this place is a pleasant surprise. Stand-alone wood cabins are surrounded by tropical gardens and primary forest, with many kilometers of trails to get lost on. Wildlife abounds – keep your eyes open for agoutis, coatis, cappuchin monkeys and amazing birds. Walking distance to pastries and pizza.

Reduced rates are sometimes offered online, especially for smaller rooms.

Mariposa B&B B&B **$$**
(☑ 2645-5013; www.mariposabb.com; Monteverde; s/d/tr/q US\$40/65/80/90, apt d/q US\$90/120, all incl breakfast; P ☀) Just 2km from the Monteverde reserve, this friendly family-run place has quite nice rooms with stained-wood walls, terracotta floors and beamed ceilings, not to mention a sweet local family looking after guests. It's nestled in the forest, with a sunny terrace for observing wildlife or just savoring a cup of local joe. The traditional Tico breakfast is a highlight.

Hotel El Viandante HOTEL **$$**
(☑ 2645-6475; www.hotelelviandante.com; Cerro Plano; s/d/tr/q incl breakfast US\$65/75/95/120; P @ ☀) Perched on a small but steep hill in Cerro Plano, this stone lodge is a solid choice. The rooms are pretty standard, with good mattresses, pinewood interiors and high ceilings, but the service is outstanding. Renzo and Grace extend a true and warm welcome. The pinnacle of this place is the top-floor lounge, with a 180-degree view of the surrounding landscape.

★ Hotel Belmar HOTEL **$$$**
(☑ 2645-5201; www.hotelbelmar.net; Cerro Plano; peninsula r US\$215-235, deluxe chalets US\$225-315; P @ ☀ ▤) 🌿 Every room at the Belmar boasts a spectacular view of forest or gulf (or both!). The gorgeous light-filled rooms are decked out with hand-crafted furniture,

high-thread-count linens and spectacular sunsets from the private balconies – and the higher you go, the more spectacular they are. Other perks include yoga classes, spa services and a fabulous restaurant with those same jaw-dropping views.

Incidentally, this place is a *real* ecoresort, boasting five leaves from the Certificate of Sustainable Tourism program. Solar-heated water, biodigested energy and rainwater harvesting are just a few of the sustainable practices at the Belmar.

Trapp Family Lodge   HOTEL $$$
(☑2645-5858; www.trapphotelmonteverde.com; d US$120-135; P✆) Here's some contemporary lux in the midst of the cloud forest. The 20 spacious rooms have high wooden ceilings, big bathrooms and fabulous views from picture windows (which overlook gardens or cloud forest). There's an elegant (but overpriced) restaurant on-site. And the Trapp family extends their renowned hospitality, promising warmth no matter what the weather.

You can't get much closer to the Monteverde reserve than here (less than 1km from the entrance). The trade-off, of course, is that it's far away from everything else.

✖ Eating

Santa Elena and Monteverde offer high quality but poor value in the kitchen. You'll be delighted by the organic ingredients, local flavors and international zest, but not by the high price tags. Even the local *sodas* and bakeries are more expensive than they ought to be. Santa Elena has most of the budget kitchens in the area, but there's good eating throughout the Monteverde swirl.

✖ Santa Elena

★**Orchid Coffee**   CAFE $
(☑2645-6850; mains US$4-12; ☉7am-7pm; ✆☑) ✐ If you're feeling peckish, go straight to this lovely cafe in Santa Elena, filled with art and light. Take a seat on the front porch and take a bite of heaven. It calls itself a coffee shop, but there's a full menu of traditional and nontraditional breakfast items, sweet and savory crepes, interesting and unusual salads, and thoroughly satisfying sandwiches. And coffee, too, but so much more.

Monteverde Cheese Factory Outlet   ICE CREAM $
(ice cream $US2-4; ☉10am-8pm) Now you don't have to trek all the way down to the Monteverde Cheese Factory to get the most delicious ice cream in Costa Rica. Just pop into this ice cream parlor in central Santa Elena and order yourself a scoop of coffee. Mmmmmm is for Monteverde.

Taco Taco   MEXICAN $
(☑5108-0525; www.facebook.com/tacotacomonte verde; mains US$5-8; ☉noon-8pm; ✆) Quick and convenient, this *taquería* offers tasty Tex-Mex tacos, burritos and quesadillas filled with shredded chicken, slow-roasted short rib, roasted veggies and battered mahimahi. The only difficulty is deciding (but you really can't go wrong). The deck in front of Pensión Santa Elena is perfect for people-watching, but the seating supply is limited, especially if you want a shady spot.

Sabor Tico   SODA $
(☑2645-5827; www.restaurantesabortico.com; mains US$5-8; ☉9am-9pm) ✐ Ticos and travelers alike rave about this local Santa Elena joint. Look for some tasty twists on the standard fare, such as *sopa da olla* (beef soup), *chorreada Tica* (fried corn cakes) and tamales (holiday fare, typically). The *gallos* (soft tortilla with delicious filling of your choice) are a perfect alternative to the more filling *casado* for lunch.

The original location is opposite the soccer field; there's a newer branch in the Centro Comercial.

Paz y Flora   VEGETARIAN $
(☑2645-6782; www.pazyflorarestaurante.com; mains US$7-10; ☑⌂) Good for the body, good for the soul and good for the earth. That's what Paz y Flora in Santa Elena strives for in its menu of vegetarian and vegan delights. It's a pretty comprehensive offering, with sandwiches, salads, pasta, rice and *rollitos*. It's all super fresh and deliciously satisfying. Look for the Buddha mosaic and you'll know you're in the right place.

SuperCompro   SUPERMARKET $
(☑2758-7351; ☉7am-9pm) A big and busy supermarket, at the main intersection in Santa Elena.

Toro Tinto   STEAK $$
(☑2645-6252; www.facebook.com/torotinto.cr; ☉noon-10pm) A Santa Elena newcomer, this Argentinean steakhouse lures in customers

with soft lighting and a cozy brick and wood interior. And it keeps them sated with steaks that are perfectly cut and grilled to order, not to mention unexpected specials and delicious desserts. The wine selection is good – mostly Chilean and Argentine – but pricey. This place will warm your cloud-soaked soul.

Tree House Restaurant & Café   CAFE $$

(☑ 2645-5751; www.treehouse.cr; mains US$7-18; ⊙ 11am-10pm; 🕱) It's a fine line between hokey and happy. But this restaurant – built around a half-century-old *higuerón* (fig) tree – definitely makes us happy. There's a menu of well-prepared if overpriced standards, from *ceviche* to *sopa Azteca* to burgers. The service is spot-on, and the atmosphere is quite delightful. It's a lively space to have a bite, linger over wine and occasionally catch live music.

El Jardín   INTERNATIONAL $$$

(☑ 2645-5057; www.monteverdelodge.com; Monteverde Lodge; lunch US$8-14, dinner US$16-22; ⊙ 7am-10pm; 🕱) 🍃 Arguably the 'finest' dining in the area. The menu is wide ranging, always highlighting the local flavors. But these are not your typical *tipica:* beef tenderloin served on a sugarcane kebab, pan-fried trout topped with orange sauce. The setting – with windows to the trees – is lovely and the service is superb. Romantics can opt for a private table in the garden.

Morpho's Restaurant   INTERNATIONAL $$$

(☑ 2645-7373; www.morphosrestaurant.com; mains US$8-20; ⊙ 11am-9pm; P🍴) Dine among gushing waterfalls and fluttering butterflies at this downtown restaurant in Santa Elena. Some call it 'romantic,' others call it 'kitschy' – but nobody can dispute the excellent, sophisticated menu, which combines local ingredients with gourmet flair. The results are sure to please any palate.

✖ Monteverde & Cerro Plano

Stella's Bakery   BAKERY $

(☑ 2645-5560; Monteverde; mains US$4-8; ⊙ 6am-10pm; 🕱📶) A bakery for birders. Come in the morning for strong coffee and sweet pastries, or come later for sandwiches on homemade bread and rich, warming soup. Whenever you come, keep on eye on the bird feeder, which attracts tanagers, mot-mots and an emerald-green toucanet.

Whole Foods Market   SUPERMARKET $

(Monteverde; ⊙ 7:30am-5:30pm) This is not the Whole Foods you might think it is, but you'll notice some similarities. This is a good but expensive place to pick up fresh produce, as well as spices and other imported ingredients you might not find in the big supermarket.

Café Caburé   CAFE $$

(☑ 2645-5020; www.cabure.net; Monteverde; lunch US$6-12, dinner US$14-20; ⊙ 9am-8pm Mon-Sat; P🕱) This Argentine cafe above the Bat Jungle in Monteverde specializes in creative and delicious everything, from sandwiches on homemade bread and fresh salads, to more elaborate fare like sea bass in almond sauce or filet mignon with chimichurri. Save room for dessert because the chocolate treats are high art.

Pizzería Tramonti   ITALIAN $$

(☑ 2645-6120; www.tramonticr.com; Monteverde; mains US$10-16; ⊙ 11:30am-9:30pm Mon-Sat; P🍴📶) Tramonti offers authentic Italian, specializing in fresh seafood, hearty pastas and wood-fired pizzas. There's a decent selection of wines from Italy and Argentina. With a greenery-filled dining room twinkling with lights, the ambience is relaxed yet romantic.

Quimera's   TAPAS $$

(☑ 2645-7037; Cerro Plano; tapas US$7-10) Come to this casual cafe in Cerro Plano for unexpected creations, like sea bass in ginger and rum, shrimp skewers in mango sauce, and roasted eggplant with smoked cheese and sun-dried tomatoes. The place promises 'Latin-infused tapas,' but the menu is actually infused with flavors and ingredients from all over the world, which is even better. Start yourself off with one of the house cocktails.

Johnny's Pizzería   PIZZA $$

(☑ 2645-5066; www.pizzeriadejohnny.com; Cerro Plano; mains US$11-24; ⊙ 11:30am-10pm; 🕱📶) Johnny's has been serving up wood-fired, thin-crust pizzas in Cerro Plano since 1993. Keep it simple with a margherita or let Johnny impress you with one of his creative combos (like the Monteverde, with prosciutto, green olives and home-grown organic leeks).

d'Sofia   FUSION $$$

(☑ 2645-7017; Cerro Plano; mains US$12-16; ⊙ 11:30am-9:30pm; 🕱) Sofia has established itself as one of the best places in town with its Nuevo Latino cuisine – a modern fusion of traditional Latin American cooking styles. Think plaintain crusted sea bass, seafood chimichanga or beef tenderloin with roasted red pepper and cashew sauce. The ambience is enhanced by groovy music, picture windows, romantic candle lighting and potent cocktails.

 Drinking & Nightlife

Nightlife in these parts generally involves a guided hike and nocturnal critters, but since this misty green mountain draws artists and dreamers, there's a smattering of regular cultural offerings. When there's anything going on you'll see it heavily advertised around town. Especially during the dry season, you'll see some action at the bars in Santa Elena.

Monteverde Beer House   BEER GARDEN
(☑8659-2054; www.facebook.com/monteverde beerhouse; Santa Elena; 🐦) It's not a brewery – contrary to the sign – but it does offer a selection of local craft beers. There's a shady deck out back and smiling servers on hand, so it's a perfect atmosphere for kicking back after a day of adventures. The Middle Eastern food (mains US$6 to US$10) is hit or miss, but if you're hungry, go for the shakshuka.

Bar Amigos   BAR
(☑2645-5071; www.baramigos.com; Santa Elena; ☺noon-3am) With picture windows overlooking the mountainside, this Santa Elena mainstay evokes the atmosphere of a ski lodge. But, no, there are DJs, karaoke, billiards and sports on the screens. This is the one consistent place in the area to let loose, so there's usually a good, rowdy mix of Ticos and tourists. The food is also surprisingly good.

 Shopping

⭐**Luna Azul**   JEWELRY
(☑2645-6638; www.facebook.com/lunaazulmon teverde; Cerro Plano; ☺9am-6pm) This supercute gallery and gift shop in Cerro Plano is packed to the gills with jewelry, clothing, soaps, sculpture and macramé, among other things. The jewelry in particular is stylish and stunning, crafted from silver, shell, crystals and turquoise.

Monteverde Art House   HANDICRAFTS
(Casa de Arte; ☑2645-5275; www.monteverde arthouse.com; Cerro Plano; ☺9am-6:30pm) You'll find several rooms stuffed with colorful Costa Rican artistry here. The goods run the gamut, including jewelry, ceramic work,

Boruca textiles and traditional handicrafts. There's a big variety, including some paintings and more contemporary work, but it's mostly at the crafts end of the artsy-craftsy spectrum. Great for souvenirs. Find it in Cerro Plano.

Casem   HANDICRAFTS
(Cooperativa de Artesanía Santa Elena Monteverde; ☑2645-5190; www.casemcoop.blogspot.com; ☺8am-5pm) Begun in 1982 as a women's cooperative representing eight female artists, today Casem has expanded to reportedly include almost 150 local artisans (eight of whom are men). It's a nice story, but a rather underwhelming selection of stuff, featuring embroidered clothing, painted handbags, polished wooden tableware, and some bookmarks and greeting cards.

 Information

EMERGENCY
Police (☑2645-6248) In Santa Elena.

INTERNET ACCESS
Nearly all hotels and hostels are wired with wi-fi, while some accommodations also offer computers with internet access. In any case, you can always check your email while you wait for your clean clothes at **L@undry Internet** (☑2645-7717; Santa Elena; ☺8am-8pm).

MEDICAL SERVICES
Consultorio Médico (☑2645-7778; Cerro Plano; ☺24hr) Across the intersection from Hotel Heliconia.
Red Cross (☑2645-6128; www.cruzroja.or.cr; ☺24hr) A hospital located just north of Santa Elena.

MONEY
The banks and ATMs are clustered in the southern part of Santa Elena.
Banco de Costa Rica (Cerro Plano; ☺9am-4pm Mon-Fri)
Banco Nacional (Santa Elena; ☺8:30am-3:45pm Mon-Fri, 9am-1pm Sat)
Banco Popular (☑2542-3390; Centro Comercial Plaza Monteverde, Santa Elena; ☺8:45am-4:30pm Mon-Fri)

POST
Correos de Costa Rica (Santa Elena; ☺8am-4:30pm Mon-Fri, to noon Sat) Across from the shopping mall.

TOURIST INFORMATION
Most hotels, hostels and guesthouses are eager to assist their guests, whether by booking tours or making transportation arrangements.

Chamber of Tourism (☎2645-6565; Santa Elena; ◷9am-noon & 1-7pm) Operated by the local chamber of commerce, this office promotes its member hotels and tour companies – so it's not necessarily an unbiased source.

Monteverde Info (www.monteverdeinfo.com) This great comprehensive website is chock full of information, with listings for hotels, tours, restaurants, transportation and more.

Monteverde Tours (Desafío Adventure Company; ☎2645-5874; www.monteverdetours. com) In partnership with Desafío Adventure Company, this tour agency and vacation planner can help you find the activity you are looking for. It can make arrangements for guided hikes, horseback riding, canopy tours, coffee tours and more, not to mention transportation like the taxi-boat-taxi to Arenal. It's a good resource if you're unsure how you want to spend your time.

❶ Getting There & Away

After resident protesters took to the streets in 2013, the transportation ministry announced that it would invest the necessary US$16 million to pave the 18km road from Guacimal to Santa Elena, which is the main access route to Monteverde. There was no sign of asphalt at the time of research, but this plan is moving forward and may be completed by the time you read this. Enjoy the smooth ride. Travel times will obviously be greatly reduced, but that's not the only change that road will bring.

CAR

While most Costa Rican communities regularly request paved roads in their region, preservationists in Monteverde have done the opposite. All roads around here are shockingly rough. Even if you arrive on a newly paved road via Guacimal, you'll still want a 4WD to get around to the more remote lodges and reserves.

There are three roads from the Interamericana: coming from the south, the first well-signed turnoff is at Rancho Grande (18km north of the Puntarenas exit). The first stretch of this route (from Sardinal to Guacimal) was paved in 2011. The remaining 17km (from Guacimal to Santa Elena) is scheduled to be paved in 2016. At the time of research, it took about three hours to drive to San José, but that time will be reduced with the road improvements.

A second, shorter road goes via Juntas, but it's not paved except for the first few kilometers. Finally, if coming from the north, drivers can take the paved road from Cañas via Tilarán and then take the rough road from Tilarán to Santa Elena.

If you're coming from Arenal, consider taking the lakeside route through Tronadora and Río Chiquito, instead of going through Tilarán. The roads are rougher, but the panoramas of the lake, volcano and surrounding countryside are magnificent.

There are two gas stations open for business in the area.

BUSES FROM SANTA ELENA

All buses stop at the bus terminal in downtown Santa Elena, where most of the budget digs are, and do not continue into Monteverde. You'll have to walk or take a taxi if that's where you plan to stay. On the trip in, keep an eye on your luggage, particularly on the San José–Puntarenas leg, as well as on the Monteverde–Tilarán run. Keep all bags at your feet and not in the overhead bin. Stories of theft and loss are legion.

DESTINATION	COMPANY	COST (US$)	DURATION (HR)	FREQUENCY
Las Juntas*	TransMonteverde	2	1½	4:30am
Puntarenas	TransMonteverde	3	3	4:30am, 6am, 3pm
Reserva Monteverde		1.20	30min	Departs 6:15am, 7:30am, 1:20pm, 3pm; returns 6:45am, 11:30am, 2pm, 4pm
San José	Tilarán Transportes	5	5	6:30am, 2:30pm
Tilarán, with connection to La Fortuna		3	2½ hours, seven hours in total	7am, 4pm

* Buses to Puntarenas can also drop you off in Las Juntas.

If you're traveling to Managua or Grenada in Nicaragua, you can make arrangements to meet the international bus en route on the Interamericana in Lagartos:

Monteverde Experts (☎2645-7263; www.monteverdeexperts.com) Agent for TicaBus.

NicaBus Agent (☎2645-7063)

The fastest route between Monteverde–Santa Elena and La Fortuna is a taxi-boat-taxi combo (US$25 to US$30, four hours, departs 8am and 2pm), which can be arranged through almost any hotel or tour operator in either town, including Monteverde Tours. A 4WD minivan takes you to Río Chiquito, meeting a boat that crosses Laguna de Arenal, where a van on the other side continues to La Fortuna. This is increasingly becoming the primary transportation between La Fortuna and Monteverde as it's incredibly scenic, reasonably priced and saves half a day of rough travel.

Bosque Nuboso Monteverde

Here is a virginal forest dripping with mist, dangling with mossy vines, sprouting with ferns and bromeliads, gushing with creeks, blooming with life and nurturing rivulets of evolution. It is so moving that when Quaker settlers first arrived in the area, they agreed to preserve about a third of their property in order to protect this watershed. The community later joined forces with environmental organizations to purchase 328 hectares adjacent to the already preserved area. This was called the **Reserva Biológica Bosque Nuboso Monteverde** (Monteverde Cloud Forest Wildlife Biological Reserve; ☎ 2645-5122; www.reservamonteverde.com; adult/concession/child under 6yr US$20/10/free; ⏰ 7am-4pm), which the Centro Científico Tropical (Tropical Science Center) began administering in 1975. Nowadays the reserve totals 105 sq km.

Monteverde Cloud Forest Reserve is the result of private citizens working for change, rather than waiting around for a national park administered by the government. As the underfunded Minae struggles to protect the national-park system, enterprises like this are more important than ever for maintaining cohesive wildlife corridors.

Because of the fragile environment, the Monteverde reserve allows a maximum of 160 people inside at any time. During the dry season this limit is usually reached by 10am. You can assure your admission by making advance reservations for a spot on a tour. Otherwise, be an early bird and arrive before the gates open.

🏃 Activities

Hiking
Visitors should note that the walking trails can be muddy, even during the dry season. You're essentially walking around in a cloud, so don't bother complaining, just bring rain gear, suitable boots and a smile. Many of the trails have been stabilized with concrete blocks or wooden boards, but unpaved trails deeper in the preserve turn sloppy during the rainy season.

There are 13km of marked and maintained trails – a free map is provided with your entrance fee. The most popular of the nine trails, suitable for day hikes, make a rough triangle (El Triángulo) to the east of the reserve entrance. The triangle's sides are made up of the popular **Sendero Bosque Nuboso** (1.9km), an interpretive walk through the cloud forest that begins at the ranger station, paralleled by the more open, 2km **El Camino**, a favorite of bird-watchers. The **Sendero Pantanoso** (1.6km) forms the far side of El Triángulo, traversing swamps, pine forests and the continental divide. Returning to the entrance, **Sendero Río** (2km) follows the Quebrada Cuecha past a few photogenic waterfalls.

Bisecting the triangle, the gorgeous **Chomogo Trail** (1.8km) lifts hikers to 1680m, the highest point in the triangle. Other little trails crisscross the region, including the worthwhile **Sendero Brillante** (300m), with bird's-eye views of a miniature forest. However, keep in mind that despite valiant efforts to contain crowd sizes, these shorter trails are among the most trafficked in the country.

The trail to the **Mirador La Ventana** (elevation 1550m) is moderately steep and leads further afield to a wooden deck overlooking the continental divide. To the west, on clear days you can see the Golfo de Nicoya and the Pacific. To the east you can see the Peñas Blancas valley and the San Carlos plain. Even on wet, cloudy days it's magical, especially when the winds are howling and fine swirling mist washes over you in waves. All over these woods, in hidden pockets and secluded gullies, that mist collects into rivulets that gather into threads that stream into a foaming *cascada*, visible from **Sendero Cascada**. From here the water pools, then forms into a gushing river, best glimpsed from **Sendero Río** or **Sendero Chuecha**. There's a 100m suspension bridge about 1km from the ranger station on **Sendero Wilford Guindon**. A mini Golden Gate suspended in the canopy, you can feel it rock and sway with each step.

There are also trails to three backcountry shelters that begin at the far corners of the triangle. Even longer trails, many of them

Life in the Cloud Forest

To explore the Monteverde cloud forest is to arrive at the pinnacle of Costa Rica's continental divide. A blast of swirling, misty euphoria surrounds you, where lichen-draped trees soar, exotic birds gossip, and orchids and bromeliads bloom. Life is abundant, throbbing and palpable.

Two Forests, Two Ecosystems

Warm, humid trade winds from the Caribbean sweep up forested slopes to the Reserva Biológica Bosque Nuboso Monteverde, where they cool and condense into clouds that congregate over the nearby Reserva Santa Elena. The two forests are each rich in diversity and oxygen, but the slight temperature and topographical differences mean that each has its own unique ecosystem.

Cloud Flora

The most abundant life form in the cloud forest, epiphytes seem to take over the trees they are growing on, yet they are not parasites and they do not harm their hosts. These clever plants get their nutrients from the floating mist, which explains their exposed roots. Look closely, and you'll see that one tree might be covered in dozens of epiphytes. This is one of the major reasons that cloud forests can claim such biodiversity: in Monteverde it's estimated that epiphytes represent almost 30% of the flora species.

The biggest family of epiphytes is the orchids, with nearly 500 species (the greatest diversity of orchids on the planet). Most amazingly, this figure includes some 34 endemic species – those that do not exist anywhere else.

1. Hiker on canopy walkway **2.** Green-crowned brilliant hummingbird **3.** Orchid

Cloud Birds

Playing an important role in the pollination of orchids and other blooming plants, hummingbirds are among the most visible of the cloud-forest creatures. Their unique ability to fly in place, backwards and upside down allows them to drink on the fly, as it were. There are some 30 species buzzing around; check them out at Cafe Colibri (p212), just outside the Monteverde reserve.

You'll hear the three-wattled bellbird long before you see him, as his distinctive song is supposedly one of the loudest bird calls on earth. As you might guess, he has three long wattles hanging from his beak.

The most famous cloud-forest resident is the resplendent quetzal. With long plumes of jade green and electric blue, this exotic beauty lives up to his name. Quetzals move seasonally between elevations, but if you're in the right place at the right time, a good bird guide should be able to find one.

Quaker Connection

The Quakers were the original conservationists here. In the early 1950s, about a dozen pacifist farming families decided to leave the US so that they would not be drafted to fight in the Korean War. They settled in this remote perch and called it Monteverde (literally 'Green Mountain'). The Quakers have been actively involved in protecting this unique environment ever since.

less developed, stretch out east across the reserve and down the Peñas Blancas river valley to the lowlands north of the Cordillera de Tilarán and into the Bosque Eterno de los Niños. If you have the time to spare, these hikes are highly recommended, as few tourists venture beyond the triangle. It's important to first talk to the park service, as you will be dealing with rugged terrain; a guide is highly recommended. Backcountry camping and sleeping in these shelters is normally no longer allowed.

Wildlife-Watching

Monteverde is a bird-watching paradise, with the list of recorded species topping out at more than 400. The resplendent quetzal is most often spotted during the March and April nesting season, though you may get lucky any time of year. Keep your ears open for the three-wattled bellbird, a kind of cotinga that is famous for its distinctive call. If you're keen on birds, a specialized bird tour is highly recommended.

For those interested in spotting mammals, the cloud forest's limited visibility and abundance of higher primates (namely human beings) can make wildlife-watching quite difficult, though commonly sighted species (especially in the backcountry) include coatis, howler monkeys, capuchins, sloths, agoutis and squirrels (as in 'real' squirrel, not the squirrel monkey). Most animals avoid the main trails, so get off the beaten track.

Tours

Although you can (and should) hike around the reserve on your own, a guide will provide an informative overview and enhance your experience. Make reservations at least a day in advance for park-run tours. The English-speaking guides are trained naturalists; proceeds benefit environmental-education programs in local schools. The reserve can also recommend excellent guides for private tours.

Bird-Watching Tours TOUR
(2645-5112; per person incl entry fee US$64; tours depart 6am) These early-morning guided bird walks usually last four to five hours, checking off as many as 40 species of birds (out of a possible 500). There's a three-person minimum, six-person maximum. Book in advance through the reserve office.

Night Tours TOUR
(with/without transportation US$25/20; tours depart 5:45pm) Two-hour night tours offer the opportunity to observe the 70% of regional wildlife that has nocturnal habits. Frogs, bats and other night critters are increasingly active as the sun sets. Tours are by flashlight (bring your own for the best visibility).

Natural History Tours TOUR
(2645-5122, reservations 2645-5112; adult/student excluding entry fee US$37/27; tours depart 7:30am, 11am & 1:30pm) Guided natural-history tours start with an informative 10-minute orientation, followed by a 2½- to three-hour walk in the woods. You'll learn all about the characteristics of a cloud forest and identify some of its most unique flora. Your ticket is valid for the entire day, so you can continue to explore on your own when the tour is over. Reservations required.

Sleeping & Eating

La Casona LODGE $$
(2645-5122; www.reservamonteverde.org; incl 3 meals & reserve admission per adult/child US$81/44) At the entrance to the Reserva Biológica Bosque Nuboso Monteverde, this mountain lodge is usually used by researchers and student groups, but it's open to tourists when there's room. The six plain private rooms feel rather institutional, but they're clean and comfortable – and you can't get any closer to the park. Plus your hard-earned cash directly contributes to protecting the cloud forest.

Restaurant RESTAURANT $
(plates US$5-10; 7am-4pm) There's a small restaurant at the entrance to the reserve, which has a decent variety of sandwiches, salads and typical dishes.

Cafe Colibri CAFE $
(2645-7768; coffee drinks US$2; 8am-5pm) Just outside the reserve gates, the 'hummingbird cafe' is a top-notch spot to refuel after a hike in the woods. The drinks will warm your body, but the humming of dozens of hummingbirds in the garden will delight your heart. An identification board shows the nine species that you're likely to see. Great photo ops.

Information

The visitors center, adjacent to the reserve gift shop, is where you can get information and buy trail guides, bird and mammal lists and maps,

LA ENSENADA LODGE

La Ensenada Lodge & Wildlife Refuge (☑ 2289-6655; www.laensenada.net; s/d/tr/q US$48/60/75/100, meals US$8-18; P 🛜 🌊), a wonderfully remote 800-acre *finca* and working cattle ranch, salt farm and papaya orchard, is an incredible setting for birding, horseback riding and good old-fashioned R&R. Rustic but comfortable wooden bungalows face out onto the Golfo de Nicoya, and have private solar-heated bathrooms and patios with hammocks – perfect for watching sunsets (or birds). There's also a restaurant, tennis courts, a romantically rickety jetty and a terrific trail network.

Containing primary and secondary forest (a rarity in this part of the country), as well as mangrove swamps at the mouth of the Río Abangares, this property has been declared a national wildlife refuge. Boat tours to the mangroves (per person US$82) offer the chance to glimpse dozens of bird species, caimans and crocs; horseback tours (US$27) take you through the tropical dry forest.

as well as souvenirs and postcards. Leave your passport to rent a pair of binoculars (US$10).

The annual rainfall here is about 3000mm, though parts of the reserve reportedly get twice as much. It's usually cool, with high temperatures around 18°C, so wear appropriate clothing. It's important to remember that the cloud forest is often cloudy (!). The reserve is managed by the Centro Científico Tropical and supported by donations through the **Friends of Monteverde Cloud Forest** (www.friendsof monteverde.org).

🛈 Getting There & Away

Public buses (US$1.20, 30 minutes) depart the Banco Nacional in Santa Elena at 6:15am, 7:30am, 1:20pm and 3pm. Buses return from the reserve at 6:45am, 11:30am, 2pm and 4pm. You can flag down the buses from anywhere on the road between Santa Elena and the reserve – inquire at your hotel about what time they will pass by. Taxis are also available for around US$10.

The 6km walk from Santa Elena is uphill but offers lovely views – look for paths that run parallel to the road. The bird-watching is magnificent, especially in the last 2km.

INTERAMERICANA NORTE

Despite Tico speed demons and lumbering big rigs, the Interamericana offers a wide-angle view of the region. The main artery connecting San José with Managua runs through kilometers of tropical dry forest and neat roadside villages to the open Guanacaste grasslands, where savanna vistas are broken only by windblown trees. Along the way, thin, (mostly) earthen roads branch off and wander up the slopes of hulking volcanoes shrouded in cloud forest, skirt hidden waterfalls and meander into vast estuaries that kiss pristine bays.

Montes de Oro

Northeast of Puntarenas, the region of Montes de Oro is a gold mining district that's tucked into the slopes and valleys of the Cordillera de Tilarán. A good number of day-trippers come up from Puntarenas and other coastal towns to fly through the trees on one of the country's biggest canopy tours. But otherwise, this area is largely off the beaten track, with few facilities catering to independent travelers. You'll need your own vehicle (a 4WD, of course) and a sense of adventure, but in Miramar, you'll discover a real Tico town that's largely untouched by tourism. And if you make it all the way up to Zapotal, at 1500m above sea level, you'll have unparalleled views all the way down to the Golfo de Nicoya and a cloud forest of your very own.

🏃 Activities

Colinas Verdes

Zapotal   HIKING, MOUNTAIN BIKING
(☑ 8829-0619, 2639-8516; www.colinasverdescr. com; admission to trails only US$10) You'll find a little bit of magic amid the clouds at Colinas Verdes, set on 35 hectares of emerald green hills and misty skies. Much of the property has been set aside for conservation and reforestation, but you'll find 4km of trails winding their way through the forest, with five hanging bridges, four short zip-line cables and countless stunning vistas.

❶ LUNCH BREAK

If you're driving on the Interamericana, Abangares makes an excellent lunch stop, with several appealing eateries right on the highway.

Mi Finca (☏ 2662-8686; mains US$8-12; ⏱ 6am-9pm; 🅿 🛜 👪) Nobody is saying that you should make a special trip to eat here. All we're saying is that it's a convenient pit stop with clean bathrooms, coffee to-go and an enticing pastry counter. And often a dozen or so scarlet and green macaws hanging out in the trees in the back. Located about 20km south of Cañas, across from the turnoff to Puente de Amistad.

Bar-B-Q Tres Hermanas (☏ 2232-6850; www.bbqtreshermanas.com; cnr Interamericana & Rte 18; mains US$7-18; ⏱ 7am-9pm; 🅿 🛜 👪) Long before you get here, you'll notice signs on the Interamericana advertising the best steakhouse in Guanacaste – Bar-B-Q Tres Hermanas. Believe the hype. This local landmark's specialty is barbecue beef and pork ribs, marinated and slow cooked for eight hours. It's located about 20km south of Cañas, at the turnoff for the Puente de Amistad. Look for the giant bull. It's a perfect pit stop if you're making the long drive to or from the Península de Nicoya. Kids will love the playground and everyone else will appreciate the spotless, almost swanky restrooms.

If you want to sleep in the clouds, there are four comfortable, hot-water cabins (double US$60) on the grounds. The lodge also organizes outings and tours on mountain bike – a thrilling way to explore this amazing area. At the northern end of Miramar, take the right-hand fork and drive about 14km on the very rough road to Zapotal.

Finca Daniel Adventure Park　　　ADVENTURE TOUR
(☏ 2639-8303, 8382-3312; www.adventuretours costarica.com; rope obstacle course US$60, canopy tour US$99-114) Just when you thought you had gone to a place where no tourist had gone before...there's a flag-waving, adrenaline-rushing, scream-inducing adventure park, catering to busloads of day-trippers coming up from the coast. It's purportedly among the biggest canopy tours in the country, with 25 cables and 11 waterfalls (some of them dip-worthy). There's also a unique rope obstacle course through the trees.

The place is definitely fun, but the big groups may be a detractor. If you don't have your own wheels, the adventure park can bus you in from Puntarenas, Jacó, the northern Península de Nicoya, or even San José.

🛏 Sleeping

There are a few lovely places to stay around Miramar and Zapotal, but they are all small and this place is remote, so make sure you reserve in advance so you're not stranded.

Finca El Mirador　　　B&B $$
(☏ 2639 8774; www.finca-mirador.com; d incl breakfast US$85; 🅿 ❄) Above Miramar, this sweet collection of bungalows is perched on the mountain slope, with majestic views across the plains and down to the coast. The bungalows are equipped with sloping wood ceilings and tile floors, full kitchens and hammock-strung terraces. Hiking trails wind their way around the property. Look for the turnoff about 4.5km north of Miramar.

Hotel Vista Golfo　　　HOTEL $$
(☏ 8382-3312, 2639-8303; www.adventurepark costarica.com; d/tr/q US$87/100/110, ste US$120-150, all incl breakfast; 🅿 ❄ 🛜 ❄) At the Finca Daniel Adventure Park, the on-site hotel is a pleasant place with a tranquil, mountain setting that's perfect for getting a little fresh air. Comfortable rooms have traditional decor and private terraces, some with sweeping views of the Golfo de Nicoya. Located 5km due north of Miramar.

❶ Getting There & Away

The town of Miramar is the capital of this district and the main population center. It's 6km north of the Interamericana on a good paved road. The small village of Zapotal is a further 16km northeast and it's a rough road into the clouds.

There are four buses a day connecting Miramar to San José (2½ hours). Nonetheless, this is a difficult area to navigate without your own car. Also, be advised that the roads here are frequently washed out during the rainy season, so a 4WD is highly recommended.

Cañas

If you're cruising north on the Interamericana, Cañas is the first town of any size in Costa Rica's driest province, Guanacaste. *Sabanero* (cowboy) culture is evident on the sweltering streets, where full-custom pickup trucks share the road with swaggering cowboys on horseback. It's a dusty, typically Latin American town, where almost everyone struts slowly and businesses shut down for lunch. It's all centered on the Parque Central and the decidedly atypical Catholic church.

Although you're better off basing yourself in livelier Liberia, Cañas is a good place to organize rafting trips on the nearby Río Corobicí or for exploring Parque Nacional Palo Verde.

⊙ Sights

Iglesia de Cañas   CHURCH
(cnr Calle Central & Av Central) You might not expect an architectural landmark in this otherwise innocuous town, so don't miss the local Catholic church, designed by famed local painter Otto Apuy. From top to bottom (including a 30m belfry) it's covered in psychedelic mosaics, taking the form of sinewy vines and colorful starbursts. The theme of the artwork ranges from religious stories to jungle scenes. The church is striking from afar, but up close the intricacy and artistry are amazing.

Las Pumas   ZOO
(☑2669-6044; www.centrorescatelaspumas.org; adult/child US$12/8; ⊙8am-4:30pm) This wild-animal shelter was started in the 1960s by the late Lilly Hagnauer, a Swiss environmentalist. It's the largest shelter of its kind in Latin America, housing big cats including pumas, jaguars, ocelots, jaguarundis and margays, plus a few deer, foxes, monkeys, peccaries, toucans, parakeets and other birds that were either orphaned or injured. It's located about 5km north of Cañas on the Interamericana.

The shelter is still operated by the Swiss Family Hagnauer, a local Cañas institution. This is a labor of love. The shelter does not receive any government funding and relies on visitor admission and donations to survive. Volunteers are always welcomed, but you'll need to make arrangements beforehand.

🏃 Activities

Ríos Tropicales   RAFTING
(☑2233-6455; www.riostropicales.com; adult/child US$65/50, white-water rafting US$105; ⊙departures 7am-3pm; ⊕) The popular Ríos Tropicales offers Class I–II family 'float tours' for flora and fauna viewing. For the more adventurous, there are Class III–V white-water rafting trips on Río Tenorio that feature a death-defying 3.6m drop. Ríos Tropicales operates out of the Rincón Corobicí restaurant, 4km north of Cañas.

Safaris Corobicí   RAFTING
(☑2669-6191; www.nicoya.com; Interamericana Km 193; 2hr tour US$52, 3hr bird-watching tour US$60, white-water rafting trip US$95; ⊙departures 7am-3pm; ⊕) These gentle rafting trips down the Río Corobicí emphasize wildlife observation rather than exciting white-water rafting. The river is Class I–II (in other words, pretty flat), but families and birders will love it. Swimming holes are found along the river. The company also offers one Class III–IV white-water trip each day. It's about 5km north of Cañas. Discounts for kids under 14.

🛏 Sleeping & Eating

Hotel Cañas   HOTEL $
(☑2669-0039; www.hotelcanascr.com; cnr Calle 2 & Av 3; s/d US$28/40; P ❋ 🛜) Here is a professionally run collection of decent tiled rooms with wooden beds, air-con and hot water, off the main drag. It's quiet and super clean. Portions in the popular restaurant are quite generous.

Hotel La Pacífica   HOTEL $$
(☑2669-6050; www.pacificacr.com; d/apt incl breakfast US$90/125; P ❋ @ 🛜 ≋) This former hacienda is now an attractive lodge with a delightful restaurant, located 4.5km north of Cañas on the Interamericana. Set on 9 hectares of dry tropical forest, the grounds are superb for birds and wildlife. Wooden furniture and hand-painted tilework adorn the spacious suites, which are decked with hammock-strung terraces.

The restaurant is highly recommended, with many of the ingredients grown on the family's nearby organic farm. The result is *tipica* meals (mains US$8 to US$24), prepared and presented with taste and grace.

Caña Brava Inn   HOTEL $$
(☑2669-1294; www.hotelcanabrava.com; cnr Interamericana & Av 5; s/d US$55/70; P ❋ 🛜 ≋) 🐾
The most upscale hotel in town has all the

BUSES FROM CAÑAS

All buses arrive and depart from Terminal Cañas at the northern end of town. There are a few *sodas* and snack bars, and you can store your bags at the desk.

DESTINATION	COMPANY	COST (US$)	DURATION (HR)	FREQUENCY
Liberia	Reina del Campo	3	1	8 daily, 6am-5:40pm
San José	Empresa La Cañera	5	3½	8 daily, 5:30am-5pm
Tilarán	Transporte Villana	1	30min	7 daily, 5am-3:30pm
Upala	Transportes Upala	3	2	3 daily (en route from San José)

modern amenities, including well-insulated rooms with flat-screen TV, comfy bedding and contemporary, dark-wood furnishings.

Rincón Corobicí   COSTA RICAN $$
(☑2669-1234; www.rinconcorobici.com; mains US$6-12; ☺8am-6pm; P☏) A great lunch stop, this attractive Swiss-run restaurant is 4km north of Cañas on the banks of the Río Corobicí. A terrace provides river and garden views, and a short trail follows the riverbank, where you can take a cool dip.

ⓘ Information

Banco Popular (☑2668-3900; cnr Av 3 & calle 5; ☺8:45am-4:30pm Mon-Fri, 8:15-11:30am Sat) Just a few blocks from Parque Central.
Hospital de Cañas (CAIS; ☑2668-4300; Rte 142; ☺24hr) The hospital is located 1.2km north of town on Rte 142.

Volcán Tenorio & Around

Part of the Área de Conservación Arenal (ACA), Parque Nacional Volcán Tenorio is a cool, misty, magical place highlighted by cloud forests and the icy-blue Río Celeste, the region's namesake. The park entrance is located just north of Bijagua (pronounced 'bee-hag-gwa'), which is the main base for visiting this natural wonder.

There are some fabulous mountain lodges in the Volcán Tenorio area, both near the park entrance and in the village of Bijagua, so spend a night or two if you have the time.

Bijagua

The only sizable town in the Tenorio sphere is Bijagua, a small farming community that's strung out along Hwy 6, halfway between the Interamericana and the bigger town of Upala.

Bijagua has been a sort of leader in the area of rural community tourism. It all started with the Heliconias Lodge, which is managed by a cooperative of local families, who recognized the importance of protecting the forest around them while pursuing their economic opportunities. With one project, the co-op found a way to achieve many goals: giving visitors the chance to get up close with the forest; earning a livelihood for themselves; preserving their natural resources; and spreading the love throughout the community, by offering training programs in English and environmental protection.

Heliconias Lodge has helped shape this town, as many former guides and staff have gone on to open their own companies and lodges, to further share the benefits of the tourist dollar.

⊙ Sights & Activities

Finca Verde Lodge   FARM
(☑2466-8069, 8918-4805; www.fincaverdelodge.com/activities; day/night tour US$12/14; P🐾) Sloths, frogs, snakes, butterflies and prolific birdlife inhabit the gorgeous grounds of this *finca*, worth a visit just to see firsthand the methods of a working organic farm. You'll meet plenty of resident animals, witness the life cycle of a butterfly and search for colorful tree frogs. The *finca* is located on a rather rough road a few kilometers southeast of the main highway. There are four comfortable cabins (including breakfast US$70 to US$100) on the grounds, as well as the recommended Hummingbird Cafe (p218).

Heliconias Lodge
Hanging Bridges   HIKING, BIRD-WATCHING
(☑2466-8483; www.heliconiaslodge.net; per person US$17) Get a different perspective on the forest when you see it from this trail of hanging bridges. It's any easy hike – about 2.5km, with three loooooong swinging bridges traversing the canopy. It's a beautiful spot – rife with butterflies and birdlife – and you're likely to have the trail to yourself. Located about 4km from the main road.

🛏 Sleeping

There is a shortage of budget options, but the little town of Bijagua has a pretty good range of places to stay. You'll find them on the main road, Hwy 6, or nestled into the hills east or west of town.

Río Celeste Backpackers
HOSTEL $

(☎8314-9784; www.facebook.com/riocelesteback packers; campsite/dm/d US$5/15/35; P🐾) The best budget option is this little house that has been turned into a hostel. There are two private rooms and one eight-bed dormitory; guests share two bathrooms, a kitchen and a small living area. There's a camping in the yard. Your host, Jorge, is an experienced naturalist who leads tours and runs a shuttle bus to Río Celeste (US$15 per person).

★ Casitas Tenorio
BUNGALOW $$

(☎8312-1248; www.casitastenorio.com; d incl breakfast US$80-120; P🐾) 🍃 This sweet family-run farm has a half-dozen simple, spacious *casitas* surrounded by wildlife. Owners Donald and Pip are committed to community rural tourism, and the charm of this place is experiencing life on the farm, visiting the animals and exploring the fruit tree–laden grounds. Your breakfast comes straight from the chickens! Drive about 2km southeast from Bijagua, on the road to Heliconia Lodge.

Cataratas Bijagua Lodge
BUNGALOW $$

(☎8937-4687; www.cataratasbijagua.com; d/tr/q incl breakfast US$70/85/100; P🐾) 🍃 Owners Warner and Carla turned their family's dairy farm into a beautiful ecolodge, with five rustic cabins set on gorgeous jungle grounds, with views of both Tenorio and Miravalles. The wildlife-filled grounds are ripe for exploring, with a river trail leading to a private waterfall. The place operates on power from a hydroelectric generator. Located 2km west of Bijagua: look for the turnoff near the Casita del Maiz. Warner and Carla don't speak much English, so brush up on your Spanish.

Sueño Celeste
B&B $$

(☎2466-8221; www.sueno-celeste.com; Hwy 6; d/tr/q US$95/120/145; P🐾) This cute, funky B&B at the southern end of Bijagua has a collection of stylish bungalows with polished-concrete floors, frilly bed linens, molded-concrete rain showers and beamed ceilings, scattered around a garden plot with Volcán Tenorio views. The fastidious French owners will make sure you are oriented and informed during your stay.

Hotel Cacao
HOTEL $$

(☎2466-6142; www.hotelcacaocr.com; s/d/tr/q incl breakfast US$60/75/95/115; P🌸🐾) Set in a yellow concrete building, this motel-style place has spacious rooms with new tiles and wooden beds, but little stylistic flourish. However, there is plenty of deck seating with lovely views of Volcán Miravalles. Follow the trail along the river to cool off in the local swimming hole. Located 300m northwest of the main highway.

Celeste Mountain Lodge
LODGE $$$

(☎2278-6628; www.celestemountainlodge.com; s/d/tr/q incl all meals US$165/210/250/290; P🐾) 🍃 Innovative and sustainable, this contemporary open-air hilltop lodge in the shadow of Volcán Tenorio is absolutely stunning. The 18 rooms are small but stylish, with wooden shutters that open onto immobilizing vistas. Winding through labyrinthine gardens, a trail is laid with geotextile (no more muddy shoes!), which makes for soundless hiking and prime bird-watching. The price includes meals at the excellent gourmet restaurant.

Hot water comes from solar power, and cooking gas is partially produced by kitchen waste. There's even an ingenious 'tropical hot bath,' heated by burning salvaged wood. The lodge is located at the end of a 3.5km-long, rough (4WD required) access road that begins at the northern end of Bijagua.

Finca Mei Tai
B&B $$$

(☎8411-7801; www.finca-meitai.com; d/tr/q incl breakfast US$100/120/140; P🐾🍽) Set on 100 acres of forest and pastures 2.5km west of Bijagua, nestled between two volcanoes, this family *finca* is crisscrossed by walking trails and dotted with farm animals. There are only two guest rooms, each with an abundance of natural light, local hardwoods and graceful details. Eric and Cecil built their place with the intention of living well, and helping others to do the same.

To get here, take the turnoff across from Pizzeria Barrigon.

Tenorio Lodge
LODGE $$$

(☎2466-8282; www.tenoriolodge.com; s/d/tr/q incl breakfast US$145/155/185/205; P@🐾) Located on a lush hilltop 1km south of Bijagua, with amazing views of Volcán Tenorio, this lodge has 12 romantic and roomy bungalows, featuring orthopedic beds, stone or wood floors and floor-to-ceiling windows with volcano views. On the 17-acre property you'll find a restaurant, two ponds, a heliconia garden, and two hot tubs to enjoy after a long day of hiking.

Eating

Sprinkled along Hwy 6, Bijagua has the requisite *soda,* pizzeria and a few other places to eat, in addition to the hotel restaurants. It's all pretty standard stuff, although you can experience the very beginnings of a farm-to-table movement at the Hummingbird Cafe.

Hummingbird Cafe INTERNATIONAL **$$**
(☑2466-8069; www.fincaverdelodge.com/hummingbird-cafe; mains US$8-12; ☺noon-9:30pm; ☑⚑) ❡ On the grounds of the Finca Verde Lodge (p216), this family restaurant is a surprising change of pace from the Tico fare in town. The emphasis is on fresh ingredients, many of which are grown right here on the farm. Specialties include red-chili enchiladas, fresh salads and, of course, tasty pizza pies. Come early (or stay late) and take a tour of the family's organic farm to see where your food is coming from.

❶ Getting There & Away

About 6km northwest of Cañas, a paved road branches off the Interamericana and heads north to Upala, passing between Volcán Miravalles to the west and Volcán Tenorio (1916m) to the east. Smack dab in the middle of these two mighty volcanoes sits the little town of Bijagua. It's about 40km north of Cañas and 27km south of Upala. Unfortunately, there is no gas here: fill your tank before you arrive. Buses between San José and Upala stop in Bijagua (US$8, four daily).

Parque Nacional Volcán Tenorio

They say that when God finished painting the sky blue, he washed his paintbrushes in the Río Celeste. The heavenly blue river, waterfalls and lagoons of **Parque Nacional Volcán Tenorio** (☑2200-0135; www.acarenaltempisque.org; adult/child US$12/2; ☺8am-4pm, last entry 2:30pm) are among the most spectacular natural phenomena in Costa Rica, which is probably why the park is known to locals simply as Río Celeste.

Established in 1976, this magical 184-sq-km national park remains a blissfully pristine rainforest abundant with wildlife. Soaring 1916m above the cloud rainforest is the park's namesake, Volcán Tenorio, which actually consists of three peaked craters: Montezuma, Tenorio I (the tallest) and Tenorio II.

Your first stop will be the Puesto El Pilón ranger station, which houses a small exhibit of photographs and dead animals. Pick up a free English or Spanish hiking map.

⚑ Activities

A well-signed trail begins at the ranger-station parking lot and winds 1.5km through the rainforest until you reach an intersection. Turn left and climb down a very steep but sturdy staircase to the **Catarata de Río Celeste**, a milky-blue waterfall that cascades 30m down the rocks into a fantastically aquamarine pool.

It's 400m further to the **Mirador**, where you'll have gorgeous views of Tenorio from the double-decker wooden platform. Further on is the technicolor **Pozo Azul** (Blue Lagoon). The trail loops around the lagoon 400m until you arrive at the confluence of rivers known as **Los Teñidores** (The Stainers). Here two small rivers – one whitish blue and one brownish yellow – mix together to create the blueberry milk of Río Celeste.

Note that swimming is strictly prohibited everywhere along this trail. The nearby hot springs were closed after some tourists were burned in 2011. Hiking to the volcano crater is also strictly prohibited.

Allow three to four hours to complete the entire hike. It's about a 7km round-trip, but parts of the trail are steep and rocky. The trail is wet and muddy year-round. Good hiking shoes or boots are a must. After your hike, you'll find an area to wash your footwear near the trailhead.

⛏ Sleeping

There are some sweet places to stay along the road to the national park, ranging from friendly budget *cabinas* to swanky mountains lodges. If you really want to get away from it all, there are a few lodges north of the park, in the vicinity of the village of San Miguel.

La Carolina Lodge LODGE **$$**
(☑2466-6393, from outside Costa Rica 843-343-4201; www.lacarolinalodge.com; per person incl meals US$80-100; ☑☎) Flanked by a roaring river and tucked into the trees on the volcano slope, this isolated lodge is also a working cattle ranch. Amazing organic meals – featuring poultry and meat from the farm – are cooked over an outdoor wood-burning stove. Cabins are rustic and romantic. The river is delicious for swimming, and a wood-fired hot tub is luxurious for soaking.

Room rates include guided hikes and horseback rides in the surrounding countryside. The lodge is about 1.3km west of the charming ranching hamlet of San Miguel; turn off the highway 5km north of Bijagua and follow the signs.

Posada Cielo Roto
CABIN $$

(☑ 2466-6049; www.cielorotocostarica.com; per person incl 3 meals US$80) These six wood cabins are perched on the northern slope of Volcán Tenorio. This is traditional Tico living, where dinner is cooked over a wood stove and guests gather around the fireplace after eating. And this is real Tico hospitality: Mario goes out of his way to extend the warmest of welcomes. Rates include a guided hike to Río Celeste and a horseback riding outing on the property. Cash only.

To get here, take the turn to San Miguel that is signposted 5km north of Bijagua. The *posada* is about 10km east on a brutal road.

Catarata Río Celeste Hotel
HOTEL $$

(☑ 8938-9927, 8876-4382; www.cataratarioceleste.com; d/bungalow/ste US$65/75/120; ℗ 🤶) Located about 1km from the park entrance, this family-run resort is spread out over nice landscaped grounds. There are six simple tiled rooms that share a hammock-strung terrace, as well as five more luxurious bungalows with Jacuzzis, outdoor showers and volcano views. Many different tours are on offer, as well as a pleasant open-air restaurant that attracts the tour groups passing through.

Cabinas Piuri
HOTEL $$

(☑ 8706-0617; www.facebook.com/cabinaspiuri; s/d incl breakfast US$35/50, planetarium r US$55, ste US$80; ℗ 🤶) About 1km past the park entrance, this unusual property is perched on a gorgeous slice of the milky-blue Río Celeste. The accommodations are varied, ranging from colorful *cabinas* with king-size beds to an egg-shaped, animal-sculpted 'planetarium.' Soak in an inviting stone dipping pool on the river banks or take this unique opportunity to swim in the magnificent river itself.

There's also a spacious restaurant with river and forest views.

Posada Río Celeste
CABINA $$

(☑ 8356-0285, for English 8978-2676; www.posadarioceleste.com; d incl breakfast US$70; ℗) This homey property offers clean, rustic rooms and hearty, home-cooked meals, all on a family farm in a rural ranching community 1km northeast of the park entrance. Two talkative parrots inhabit the blooming gardens. Staff can organize hiking and swimming in and out of the park.

Even if you're not staying here, this is a perfect pit stop for lunch, after hiking in the park. There's no menu: Wuilbert and his wife will serve up whatever they have cooking on their stove. Portions are huge, prices are reasonable.

Rio Celeste Hideaway
HOTEL $$$

(☑ 2206-4000; www.riocelestehideaway.com; d/ste incl breakfast US$280/340; ℗ 🤶) This elegant address is just 550m from the park gate. Sprinkled among lush landscaped grounds, the spectacular property has huge, 90-sq-m thatched *casitas* with wooden floors, pastel paint jobs and antique furnishings. Beds are covered with canopies and draped in 300-thread-count sheets. Even the bathrooms are luxurious here, with soaking tubs, outdoor showers, and 'his' and 'hers' basin sinks.

BACK ROADS BETWEEN TENORIO & MIRAVALLES

An epic back road, 4WD track links Tenorio to Miravalles. This is useful for road-trippers who wish to base themselves in Tenorio and visit Miravalles for the day (an itinerary that we recommend highly). About 12km south of Bijagua make a right where you see a sign toward the *pueblo* of Rio Chiquito. It's a rather small sign, and once you make the turn you'll be in the even smaller *pueblo*. The road narrows immediately and severely. Don't worry, there is no dead end. After fording a stream it goes crazy vertical. Shift into 4-low and grind up the 200m hill. At the top are marvelous vistas of the two mountains, acres of rangeland and the vast valley below. Then you'll go down again, ford another stream, navigate a steeper incline and be rewarded with massive views once more. By now you'll be in old Tico cattle country. Enjoy it. Within an hour you'll be dipping into hot springs.

❶ Getting There & Away

There's no bus to the national park. The closest you can get is Bijagua, from where you can book a tour at almost any hotel.

A 30km road connects Bijagua (Hwy 6) and Guatuso (Hwy 4), passing the national park (and many lodgings) along the way. The entrance to the national park is about 9km from Bijagua and 21km from Guatuso. This road is very rough in places (4WD required), so it's easier to approach from the west. But if you're coming from the La Fortuna area, and you have the appropriate vehicle, it's faster to brave the road from Guatuso.

Five kilometers north of Bijagua is the gravel road to San Miguel. Turning left at the San Miguel intersection will bring you to La Carolina Lodge (1.3km). The rough dirt road (4WD required) continues another 13km until it meets up with Hwy 4, the main Upala–Fortuna thoroughfare. Turning right will take you 4km down an even rougher road to the national-park gate.

Volcán Miravalles & Around

Volcán Miravalles (2028m) is the highest volcano in the Cordillera de Guanacaste, and although the main crater is dormant, the geothermal activity beneath the ground has led to its development as a hot-springs destination. Miravalles isn't a national park or refuge, but the volcano itself is afforded a modicum of protection by being within the Zona Protectora Miravalles.

North of Fortuna, the government-run Proyecto Geotérmico Miravalles is an ambitious project that uses geothermal energy to produce electricity, primarily for export to Nicaragua and Panama. It also produces about 18% of Costa Rica's electricity. A few bright steel tubes from the plant snake along the flanks of the volcano, adding an eerie, alien feel to the remote landscape.

Most of the hot springs facilities also have accommodations, but they are mostly pretty mediocre. If your budget does not accommodate top-end lodging, consider basing yourself in Tenorio.

🏃 Activities

Volcán Miravalles and other volcanoes are a critical source of renewable energy for Costa Rica. But the geothermal energy most people crave comes in liquid form. Most of the hot springs are north of the tiny village of Fortuna de Bagaces (not to be confused with La Fortuna de Arenal or Bagaces).

Río Perdido
HOT SPRING

(☑ 2673-3600; www.rioperdido.com; day pass adult/child US$40/30, spa treatment US$50) This fabulous facility – set amid an otherworldly volcanic landscape – is a wonderful way to soak in the soothing waters of Miravalles. The day pass allows access to miles of hiking trails, complete with waterfalls and panoramic views, as well as the thermal river and hot springs, where temperatures range from 32°C to 46°C. There's a swim-up bar, hanging bridges, and glorious views all around.

If you care to spend the night (or several) at Rio Perdido, eco-chic bungalows (single/double US$230/275) are contemporary and cool, with polished-concrete floors, bold patterns, lots of windows and raised terraces facing the forest.

Las Hornillas
HIKING, HOT SPRING

(☑ 8839-9769, 2100-1233; www.hornillas.com; tours incl lunch US$35-55; ⏰ 9am-5pm; 🖐) On the southern slopes of Miravalles, Las Hornillas has a unique lunar landscape, with bubbling pools and fumaroles on the property. Hike to see the volcanic action up close, then soak in three thermal pools and fly down a 250m slide. An additional tour involves a tractor ride and hanging bridges through the forest, to reach a series of spectacular waterfalls.

Spend the night in one of the rustic cabins (per person US$55) on the property, and you can soak in the pools by the light of the silvery moon.

Canyon Adventure
CANOPY TOUR

(☑ 2673-3600; www.rioperdido.com; adult/child US$60/50) You've done the canopy tours, but have you done a *canyon* tour? This new take on a tried-and-true adventure will have you zipping from platform to platform, most of which are mounted on rocks or canyon walls. The route is challenging and fun, with five zip lines, plus a series of bridges, swings and *ferratas* (steel cables).

Canyon Adventure also gives full access to the thermal river, hot springs and hiking trails.

Miravalles Volcano Adventure Center
CANOPY TOUR

(☑ 2673-0469; www.facebook.com/miravallesadventurecenter; canopy tour adult/child US$40/30, tours US$35-90, cabins US$30) There's something for everybody at this adventure center near the base of the volcano. The centerpiece of the complex is the canopy tour, which has 12 cables and hanging bridges

RESERVA BIOLÓGICA LOMAS DE BARBUDAL

Forming a cohesive unit with Palo Verde, the 26-sq-km **Reserva Biológica Lomas de Barbudal** (☑ 2659-9194; adult/child US$12/2; ☉ 7am-4pm) is a tropical dry forest reserve that's famous for its huge diversity of resident bees. If that doesn't make you want to come here, maybe the troops of white-faced capuchin monkeys will be more appealing.

In any case, Lomas de Barbudal is an accessible option for off-the-beaten-track, independent hiking. A small visitors center has maps and other information. You can explore the reserve on four different hiking trails; Sendero La Catarata rewards with an amazing waterfall that merits a dip.

Lomas de Barbudal is tropical dry forest, with a prolonged dry season that sometimes feels like a drought. Nearly 70% of the trees in the reserve are deciduous, and during the dry season they shed their leaves just like fall in a temperate forest. This allows the trees to conserve water and enables sunlight to filter through to facilitate the growth of thick underbrush.

The reserve protects several species of endangered trees, such as mahogany and rosewood, as well as the common and quite spectacular corteza amarilla. This tree is what biologists call a 'big-bang reproducer' – all the yellow cortezes in the forest burst into bloom on the same day, and for about four days the forest is an incredible mass of yellow-flowered trees. This usually occurs in March, about four days after an unseasonal rain shower.

Lomas de Barbudal is also known for its insects. There are about 250 species of bee in this fairly small reserve – representing about a quarter of the world's bee species. There are also more than 200 bird species, including endangered species such as the great curassow, king vulture, scarlet macaw and jabirú stork.

The turnoff to Lomas de Barbudal from the Interamericana is 14km southeast of Liberia and 12km northwest of Bagaces. From here it's 7km to the entrance of the reserve on a rough unpaved road. Some steep sections may require 4WD in the rainy season.

---

through fields and forest. The place also has an on-site spa, horseback-riding and other adventures, including an all-day expedition to the Miravalles crater.

El Guayacán HOT SPRING
(☑ 2673-0349; www.termaleselguayacan.com; adult/child US$10/8; ☉ 8am-10pm; ▣) Just behind Thermo Manía, this is a family *finca* that's hissing and smoking with vents and mud pots. There are eight thermal pools and one cold pool with a waterslide. You can also take a guided tour of the fumaroles (stay on the trail!). If you wish to spend the night, bed down in one of the clean, cold-water *cabinas* (single/double from US$30/60) brushed in bright colors or in a spacious villa with kitchenette.

Yökö Termales HOT SPRING
(☑ 2673-0410; www.yokotermales.com; adult/child US$10/8; ☉ 7am-10pm; ▣) Yökö has four hot springs and a larger pool with a small waterslide and waterfall, set in an attractive meadow at the foot of Miravalles. The views are magnificent, but there's little shade around the pools. The 12 canary-

tinted rooms (including breakfast US$40 to US$125) are comfy enough, with beamed and plywood ceilings. It's a decent, but not magical, sleeping option.

❶ Getting There & Away

Volcán Miravalles is 27km northeast of Bagaces. Head north on a paved road through the communities of Salitral and Torno, where the road splits. Take the left-hand fork to reach Guayabo, with a few *sodas* and basic *cabinas;* to the right, you'll find Fortuna de Bagaces, with easier access to the hot springs. The road reconnects north of the two towns and continues toward Upala.

There are hourly buses from Bagaces to and from Guayabo and Fortuna (US$1, 45 minutes).

Parque Nacional Palo Verde

The 184-sq-km **Parque Nacional Palo Verde** (☑ 2206-5965, 2680-5965; adult/child US$12/2, guided tours US$48; ☉ 8am-4pm) is a wetland sanctuary in Costa Rica's driest province. It lies on the northeastern bank of the mouth of the Río Tempisque and at the head of the Golfo de Nicoya. All the major rivers in the region drain into this ancient intersection of two basins, which creates a mosaic of habitats, including mangrove swamps, marshes, grassy savannas and evergreen forests. A number of low limestone hills provide lookouts over the park, and the park's shallow, permanent lagoons are focal points for wildlife. The park derives its name from the abundant *palo verde* (green tree), a small shrub that's green year-round. The park is contiguous in the north with the 73-sq-km Refugio de Vida Silvestre Dr Rafael Lucas Rodríguez Caballero and the Reserva Biológica Lomas de Barbudal.

Word to the wise: the mosquitoes are legendary in this place. By all means, bring insect repellent!

Activities

Wildlife-Watching

Palo Verde has the greatest concentrations of waterfowl and shorebirds in Central America, and over 300 bird species have been recorded here. Bird-watchers come to see the large flocks of heron (including the rare black-crowned night heron), stork (including the endangered jabirú), spoonbill, egret, ibis, grebe and duck. Forest birds, including scarlet macaws, great curassows, keel-billed toucans and parrots, are also common. Frequently sighted mammals include deer, coati, armadillo, monkey and peccary, as well as the largest population of jaguarundi in Costa Rica. There are also numerous reptiles in the wetlands, including crocodiles that are reportedly up to 5m in length.

The dry season (December to March) is the best time to visit, as flocks of birds tend to congregate in the remaining lakes and marshes. Plus, the trees lose their leaves, allowing for clearer viewing. Mammals are occasionally seen around the watering holes. That said, the entire basin swelters during the dry season, so bring adequate sun protection. During the wet months, large portions of the area are flooded, and access may be limited.

If you'd like some help spotting and identifying your furred and feathered, OTS offers guided bird walks and night tours.

Hiking

You can explore the park's well-maintained trails on your own or accompany the OTS guide on his or her regular one-hour guided walk (adult/child US$30/20). Pick up a map at the park entrance.

From the entrance, the first trailhead you'll reach is for the **Sendero Roco**, which is a short steep climb up to a scenic viewpoint over the lagoon. On a clear day you can see the Río Tempisque to the Golfo de Nicoya. Next along, the **Sendero Mapache** traverses three distinct habitats in a short 700m. See if you can tell the difference between the deciduous lowland, limestone and evergreen forests.

Along the shore of the lagoon, the 900m **Sendero El Pizote** is prime for spotting water birds. And at the far end of the park, beyond the ranger station, you can hike 1400m along the **Sendero La Cantera** to reach a splendid lookout over the whole area.

No matter which trail you choose, remember that it gets fiercely hot in the dry season, so carry ample water and a sun hat and avoid hiking during midday.

Tours

To fully appreciate the size and topography of the park, it's worth organizing a boat trip (per person US$57) down the Río Tempisque, a wide, brown, brackish river contained on either side by mangroves. Arrangements can be made through the OTS Hacienda Palo Verde Research Station.

Tour operators on the Península de Nicoya and in La Fortuna bring tour groups to Palo Verde, but if you can get here, you'll save plenty of money by arranging everything yourself.

Boat tours depart from the dock in Puerto Chamorro, which is on the main park road, 2km beyond the ranger station. If you arrive early enough, you may be able to show up and find a free spot on an outgoing boat.

El Viejo Wetlands   NATURE TOUR
(✆2296-0966; www.elviejowetlands.com; cultural tour US$25, mountain biking US$33, boat tour US$63; ⊙7am-3pm) Bordering Parque Nacional Palo Verde, this impressive facility is owned and operated by a successful sugarcane family that has devoted some 5000 acres to a wetlands refuge. In addition to hiking, biking and boat tours (some of which enter the national park), they also do a sugarcane demonstration. Meals are served in the historic and atmospheric Casona.

The main entrance to El Viejo is about 15km south of Filadelfia. Head southeast out of town on Calle 5 and follow the signs. El Viejo can also provide transportation from anywhere in the northern Península de Nicoya.

LLANOS DE CORTÉS

If you have time to visit only one waterfall in Costa Rica, make it **Llanos de Cortés** (admission by donation, parking US$4; ⊙8am-5pm). Scramble down a short, steep trail to reach this spectacular 12m-high, 15m-wide waterfall, which you'll be able to hear as soon as you get out of your car. The falls drop into a tranquil pond with a white sandy beach that's perfect for swimming and sunbathing. Go 'backstage' and relax on the rocks behind the waterfall curtain, or shower beneath the lukewarm waters. Apart from a portable toilet, there are no services here except for the occasional vendor selling coconuts or *ceviche*.

This beautiful hidden waterfall is located about 3km north of Bagaces; head north on the Interamericana, turn left on the dirt road after the Río Piedras bridge, then follow the bumpy road (4WD required) for about 1km. Turn right at the guarded gate where you'll make a donation (US$2 will do the job) in exchange for your admission. Continue down the dirt road about 300m to the parking area. Although the lot is guarded, it's not wise to leave valuables exposed in your car.

If you don't have a car, any bus traveling this part of the Interamericana can drop you at the turnoff, but you'll have to hike the 1.5km to the falls. On weekends this is a popular Tico picnic spot, but on weekdays you'll often have the waterfall to yourself.

🛏 Sleeping & Eating

**OTS Hacienda Palo
Verde Research Station** LODGE $$$
(☑ 2524-0607; www.ots.ac.cr; r incl meals per adult/child US$90/38; 🅿 🛜) Run by the OTS, Hacienda Palo Verde Research Station conducts tropical research and teaches university graduate-level classes. But it also has rustic cabins with bunk beds and fans, which are rented out to 'natural history visitors.' The research station is on a well-signed road 8km from the park entrance. Camping is also permitted here.

❶ Getting There & Away

The main road to the entrance, usually passable to ordinary cars year-round, begins from a signed turnoff from the Interamericana, opposite Bagaces. The 28km gravel road has tiny brown signs that direct you when the road forks. Once inside the park, another 8km brings you to the limestone hill, Cerro Guayacán (and the OTS Hacienda Palo Verde Research Station), from where there are great views; 2km further are the Palo Verde park headquarters and ranger station. You can drive through a swampy maze of roads to the Reserva Biológica Lomas de Barbudal without returning to the Interamericana, but be sure to inquire with rangers about road conditions.

Buses connecting Cañas and Liberia can drop you in Bagaces, opposite the turnoff to the park. If you're staying at the Palo Verde Research Station, the staff may be able to pick you up, but be sure to make advance arrangements.

Liberia

The sunny rural capital of Guanacaste has long served as a transportation hub connecting Costa Rica with Nicaragua, as well as being the standard-bearer of Costa Rica's *sabanero* culture. Even today, a large part of the greater Liberia area is involved in ranching operations, but tourism is fast becoming a significant contributor to the economy. With an expanding international airport, Liberia is a safer and more chilled-out alternative Costa Rican gateway to San José, which means more travelers are spending a night or two in this sweet town, knitted together by corrugated-tin fencing, mango trees and magnolias.

Most of the historic buildings in the town center are in need of a paint job. That said, the 'White City' is a pleasant one, with a good range of accommodations and services for travelers on all budgets. The streets in downtown Liberia are surprisingly well signed, a rarity in Costa Rica. Still, it's largely a launch pad for exploring Rincón de la Vieja National Park and the beaches of the Península de Nicoya, rather than a destination in itself.

◉ Sights

The blocks around the intersection of Av Central and Calle Real contain several of Liberia's oldest houses, many dating back about 150 years. There's a long-term plan to pedestrianize Calle Real (south of the park), which was the historic thoroughfare into and out of the city.

Liberia

Museo de Guanacaste MUSEUM

(☑ 2665-7114; cnr Av 1 & Calle 2; ⊗ 8am-4pm)
FREE At long last, the regional museum is
undergoing a major renovation, due to be
completed toward the end of 2016. The intention is that this historic building will no
longer be just the former city jail, but an actual museum with exhibits about the history
and culture of Guanacaste. Opening hours
may change.

La Agonía CHURCH

(La Iglesia de la Ermita de Nuestro Señor de la
Agonía; Av Central & Calle 9; ⊗ variable) With
whitewashed walls and twin pillars flank-
ing the front door, La Agonía typifies the
Spanish colonial architecture that earned
Liberia its nickname, the White City. This is
the city's oldest church, built in 1825. There
is supposedly an exhibit of art and culture
inside, but it's difficult to say for sure, as the
doors are usually locked tight.

Africa Safari
Adventure Park WILDLIFE RESERVE

(☑ 2288-1000; www.africasafaricostarica.com; tour
adult/child $50/35, 3-tour package adult/child
$115/105; ⊗ tours 9:30am, 11am, 1pm & 2pm)
Elephants, zebra, giraffes and other African
wildlife are right at home in the dry Guanacaste heat, as you can see at this private
wildlife reserve, located about 10km south
of Liberia. The safari tour allows you to get
up close and personal with the (sort of) wild
animals. Also on offer: kayaking, zip-lining,
horseback riding and ATVs.

🛏 Sleeping

Liberia is at its busiest during the dry season – reservations are strongly recommended
over Christmas, Easter and Día de Guanacaste and on weekends. During the wet
season, however, most of the midrange and
top-end hotels give discounts.

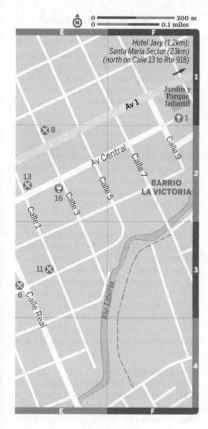

Hotel Javy (1.2km);
Santa María Sector (23km)
(north on Calle 13 to Rte 918)

Liberia

🔘 Sights

NORTHWESTERN COSTA RICA LIBERIA

and close to the bus station. Small, private rooms, mostly with bathrooms. There's a communal outdoor kitchen, overlooking a small yard, filled with flowers and hung with hammock. It's nothing fancy, but it's very friendly.

La Posada del Tope GUESTHOUSE $

(📲 2666-3876; www.facebook.com/hotellaposada deltope; Calle Real btwn Avs 2 & 4; d US$25; 🅿️ ⊖ @ 🛜) Rooms are in the *'casa real'* across the street from the wooden lobby. Set around an awesome garden and furnished with eclectic art and antiques, this place has a lot of personality. Rooms are decidedly basic and not that clean and bathrooms are shared (mostly), but the price is right. The bilingual Tico owner, Denis, is a wealth of information.

Hotel Javy HOTEL $$

(📲 2666-9253; www.hoteljavy.com; cnr Av 19 & Calle 19; d incl breakfast US$50; 🅿️ ❄️ 🛜) Isabella is your hostess with the *mostest*. This charming lady goes out of her way to make sure her guests are happy, not least preparing an enormous, delicious breakfast to send you off feeling satisfied. The rooms are light-filled and comfortable, with firm beds, incongruously formal furnishings and spotless new bathrooms.

The location, about 2km northeast of Parque Central, is not so convenient.

In town, most of the lodgings are budget and midrange options, but you'll find some high-end international chain hotels near the airport.

Hotel Liberia HOTEL $

(📲 2666-0161; www.hotelliberiacr.com; Calle Real btwn Avs Central & 2; dm US$13, s/d torre US$32/45, casona US$38/50; 🅿️ 🛜) It's hard to resist the glorious shady courtyard at this historic guesthouse, which is one of Liberia's best budget options. The most appealing *'casona'* rooms are set in the old building, where the high ceilings, tile floors and wooden furniture contribute to an old-fashioned ambience. Less atmospheric *'torre'* rooms and dorms are in the newer concrete building at the back of the courtyard.

Hospedaje Dodero HOSTEL $

(📲 8729-7524; www.hospedajedodero.yolasite.com; Av 11 btwn Calles 12 & 14; d US$25-30; ❄️ 🛜) Three things: super clean, super service

✖ Eating

Liberia has a good selection of restaurants, both in town and on the road going out to the airport. If you're taking the bus, pick up some snacks for the road at the traditional covered **market** (Ave 7 btwn Calles 10 & 12; ⊙ 6am-7pm Mon-Sat, to noon Sun), conveniently located next to Terminal Liberia.

Restaurante El Pilon   COSTA RICAN $
(📞 2666-0616; Calle Central btwn Avs 5 & 7; casados US$5-8; ⊙ 6:30am-4pm Mon-Sat) A great little find for fans of *casados*. This local diner serves at least 10 daily, featuring fresh *pescado* (fish), *pollo* (chicken), steak, lamb and more. Relax around wooden tables in the cool, dark-tiled dining room.

Café Liberia   ORGANIC $$
(📞 2665-1660; Calle Real btwn Avs 2 & 4; mains US$8-10; ⊙ 11am-9pm Tue-Sun, 3-9pm Mon; ✱ 🗟 🍴) This beautifully restored colonial-era building has heavy wooden furniture and frescoed ceilings, creating a romantic ambience for rich coffee and gourmet fare. Simple food is taken to new levels: *ceviche* (seafood marinated in lemon or lime juice, garlic and seasonings) is served with irresistible, warm, fresh-baked tortilla chips. It's also an atmospheric setting for live music and other occasional performances.

El Meson Liberiano   INTERNATIONAL $$
(📞 2666-1819; Calle 3; mains US$8-15; ⊙ noon-9pm; 🗟 🍴) A lovely historic hacienda, this 'Liberia house' is now one of the nicer restaurants in town, offering thoroughly modern presentations of pretty traditional food. The service is quite charming. But what makes this place is the delightful back patio, where the wooden tables are shaded by a big old mango tree.

Green House   VEGETARIAN $$
(Casa Verde; 📞 2665-5037; www.thegreenhouse costarica.com; Hwy 21; mains US$6-12; ⊙ 11am-9pm; 🗟 🍴 🍴) When they say 'green house' they mean it, as in a glass building filled with plants. Plus, there are green panels on the windows and – yes – many veggie options on the menu. Come into the light-filled dining room for a delightful fusion of flavors, such as grilled chicken with mango salsa and excellent fish tacos. Located on the road to the airport, about 8km west of town.

Pizza Pronto   PIZZA $$
(📞 2666-2098; cnr Av 4 & Calle 1; mains US$8-17; ⊙ 11am-11pm) This very cute, old-world pizzeria, where the wood is stacked next to the smoking courtyard oven, keeps it romantic and simple – just pizza, pasta and salads. The pizzas are delish, ranging from the recommended vegetarian option to the not-so-recommended taco pizza. Don't worry, you can choose from a long list of toppings and create your own.

Copa de Oro   RESTAURANT $$
(📞 2666-0532; cnr Calle Real & Av 2; mains US$5-16; ⊙ 11am-10pm Mon-Sat; 🗟 🍴) This congenial family restaurant is popular with locals and gringos alike. Try the rice and seafood house specialty, *arroz copa de oro*. The *casados* are excellent and there's a nice *ceviche* menu too.

Jauja   INTERNATIONAL $$$
(📞 2665-2061; www.facebook.com/jaujarestau rante; cnr Av 25 de Julio & Calle 10; mains US$8-15; ⊙ 11am-11pm; 🅿 🗟 🍴 🐾) This stylish, indoor-outdoor bar and cafe on the main drag is unique in Liberia for its upscale ambience and classy cuisine. Service is also excellent. Look for wood-fired pizza, tender grass-fed steaks and burgers on home-baked buns. The place is popular among LIberia's local professional set, as well as tourists and expats.

Toro Negro Steakhouse   STEAK $$$
(📞 2666-2456; cnr Ave Central & Calle 1; mains US$12-18; ⊙ noon-9:30pm; 🅿 🗟 🍴) Located in a beautiful colonial-era building, this family-friendly restaurant has an extensive international menu specializing in meat including New York strip, filet mignon and burgers. The rustic interior is inviting, but you can't beat the outdoor balcony for people-watching and enjoying the evening breeze.

🍷 Drinking & Nightlife

There is no shortage of watering holes in this young, lively town. It's up to you to decide if you want to drink at the sports bar, the cocktails bar, the cowboy bar or the art cafe. What kind of mood are you in?

★ Mariajuana   CAFE
(📞 2665-7217; www.facebook.com/mariajuanares taurante; ⊙ 3-10:30pm Tue-Sun; 🗟 🍴) There's a great mellow vibe at this alfresco bar, tucked into a big tree-shaded yard at the end of a dead-end street. It's part cafe and part gallery, with wind chimes in the air, African masks on the walls and a menu of coffee drinks, cocktails and bar food (mains US$6 to US$8). No better place in Liberia to spend a hot afternoon.

Palermo Lounge
COCKTAIL BAR

(☎2240-3325; cnr Av Central & Calle 3; ☺4pm-2am) One of the city's most pleasant places for a drink is this tropical garden, lush with greenery and waterfalls. There are also sports and music videos on the big screen, but the volume is usually turned down so patrons can enjoy the tranquil atmosphere. The menu offers very tasty pub grub and Tico fare.

Morales House
BAR

(☎2665-2490; cnr Av 1 & Calle 14; ☺3pm-2am) A real Guanacaste *sabanero* hangout, this barnlike bar has bull heads on the walls, blaring *ranchera* music and American sports on TV. Bonus: thick, juicy steaks for hungry buckaroos.

Information

MEDICAL SERVICES
Hospital Dr Enrique Baltodano Briceño (☎2666-0011, emergencies 2666-0318; Rte 918) Behind the stadium on the northeastern outskirts of town.

MONEY
Liberia probably has more banks per square meter than any other town in Costa Rica.

BAC San José (☎2295-9797; Centro Comercial Santa Rosa, Rte 21; ☺9am-6pm Mon-Fri, to 1pm Sat)

Banco de Costa Rica (☎2666-2582; cnr Calle Real & Av 1; ☺9am-4pm Mon-Fri)

Banco Nacional (☎2666-0191; Av 25 de Julio btwn Calles 6 & 8; ☺8:30am-7pm Mon-Fri, 9am-3pm Sat)

Citibank (cnr Interamericana & Av 25 de Julio; ☺9am-6pm Mon-Fri, to 12:30pm Sat)

ⓘ Getting There & Away

AIR
Located 12km west of Liberia, **Aeropuerto Internacional Daniel Oduber Quirós** (LIR; www.liberiacostaricaairport.net) serves as the country's second international airport, providing easy access to all those beautiful beaches without the hassle of San José. In January 2012 it unveiled its sleek, mod new US$35-million terminal.

The majority of international flights still go to the USA and Canada, in addition to some regional flights on Copa Air (to Panama) and

BUSES FROM LIBERIA

Buses arrive and depart from **Terminal Liberia** (Av 7 btwn Calles 12 & 14) and **Terminal Pulmitan** (Av 5 btwn Calles 10 & 12).

DESTINATION (COMPANY)	COST (US$)	DURATION (HR)	TERMINAL	FREQUENCY
Cañas (Reina del Campo)*	2	1½	Terminal Liberia	Half-hourly, 5:30am-5:30pm
Curubandé	2	40min	Terminal Liberia	6:40am, noon, 5pm
La Cruz/Peñas Blancas (Arrieta)	2.50	1½-2	Terminal Liberia	5:30am, 8:30am, 9am, 11am
Nicoya, via Filadelfia and Santa Cruz (La Pampa)	2.50	1½	Terminal Liberia	Half-hourly, 4:30am-8:20pm
Playa Flamingo (La Pampa)	3	1½	Terminal Liberia	6am, 8am, 10am, 11am, 12:30pm, 5pm, 6pm
Playa del Coco (Pulmitan)	1.50	1	Pulmitan	Hourly, 5am-11am, plus 12:30pm, 2:30pm, 6:30pm
Playa Hermosa (La Pampa)	2	1½	Terminal Liberia	5 daily, 7:30am-5:30pm
Playa Tamarindo (La Pampa)	3	2	Mercado Municipal	7 daily, 3:50am-12:30pm; hourly, 2pm-6pm
Puntarenas* (Reina del Campo)	3	3	Terminal Liberia	9 daily, 5am-3:30pm
San José (Pulmitan)	6	4	Pulmitan	14 daily, 3am-10pm

* It's quicker to jump off the San José–bound bus in your destination.

Taca (to Guatemala). Domestic flights mainly go to San José.

There are no car-rental desks at the airport; make reservations in advance, and your company will meet you at the airport with a car. Taxis from Liberia to the airport are about US$20. Or you can catch a bus in front of the Mercado Municipal (30 minutes, hourly) which runs from 5:30am to 6:30pm, Monday through Friday only.

NatureAir (☑ Aeropuerto Internacional Daniel Oduber Quirós 2668-1106, reservations 2299-6000; www.natureair.com; ⊗ 6am-5pm) To/from San José.

Sansa (☑ Aeropuerto Internacional Daniel Oduber Quirós 2668-1017, reservations 2290-4100; www.flysansa.com) To/from San José.

CAR

Liberia lies on the Interamericana, 234km north of San José and 77km south of the Nicaraguan border post of Peñas Blancas. Hwy 21, the main artery of the Península de Nicoya, begins in Liberia and heads southwest. A dirt road leads 25km from Barrio La Victoria to the Santa María entrance of Parque Nacional Rincón de la Vieja; the partially paved road to the Las Pailas entrance begins from the Interamericana, 5km north of Liberia.

There are more than a dozen rental-car agencies in Liberia (none of which have desks at the airport itself). Most companies will drop off your car at your hotel upon request.

Adobe (☑ 2667-0608, in USA 866-767-8651; www.adobecar.com; ⊗ 8am-5pm) One of the cheapest companies in Costa Rica.

Avis (☑ 2668-1196; www.avis.co.cr; ⊗ 6am-10pm)

Budget (☑ 2436-2062, 2668-1024; www.budget.com; ⊗ 6am-11:30pm)

Europcar (☑ 2668-6125; www.europcar.co.cr; ⊗ 8am-7pm Mon-Fri, to 4pm Sat, to 3pm Sun)

Mapache (☑ 2586-6300; www.mapache.com; ⊗ 6am-9pm Mon-Fri, to 7pm Sat & Sun) Green car rental. Mapache is 100% carbon neutral and has been awarded four green leaves by OTS.

Toyota Rent a Car (☑ 855-866-3486, 2668-1212, 2258-1213; www.toyotarent.com; ⊗ 7am-7pm)

VIP Car Rental (☑ 8941-1697, 2666-0052; www.vipcarrentaltours.com) Expect discount prices on well-maintained vehicles.

Parque Nacional Rincón de la Vieja

Given its proximity to Liberia – really just a hop, a skip and a few bumps away – this 141-sq-km national park feels refreshingly uncrowded and remote. The name means 'old lady's nook,' and it's named after the active Volcán Rincón de la Vieja (1895m), the steamy main attraction. The park also covers several other peaks in the same volcanic range, including the highest, Volcán Santa María (1916m). The park exhales geothermal energy. It bubbles with multihued fumaroles, tepid springs and steaming flatulent mud pots, as well as a young and feisty *volcancito* (small volcano). All of these can be visited on foot on well-maintained steep trails. Note the Las Pailas sector is closed on Monday.

🏃 Activities

Hiking

From the Santa María ranger station, there are some 12km worth of hiking trails which take in the hot springs. Since the 2012 eruptions, the trek to the summit of Rincón de la Vieja is no longer open to the public.

Sendero Las Pailas   HIKING

A circular trail known as Sendero Las Pailas – about 3km in total – takes you east of Las Pailas ranger station, past boiling mud pools *(las pailas)*, sulfurous fumaroles and a *volcancito*. This is the most popular (and most crowded) section of the park, as it's an easy but worthwhile trail with a lot to see.

As of 2016, part of this trail will be paved, allowing folks in wheelchairs (and strollers) the chance to see the *volcancito* and fumaroles.

Catarata La Cangreja   HIKING

About 350m west of the Las Pailas ranger station are two waterfall trails. Catarata La Cangreja is the classic, dropping 50m straight from a cliff into a small lagoon where you can swim. Dissolved copper salts give the falls a deep blue color. This trail winds through forest, past truly massive strangler figs, then on to open savannah spiked with yucca on the volcano's flanks, where views stretch as far as the Palo Verde wetlands and the Pacific beyond.

The hike to Catarata La Cangreja is 5.1km in each direction. The hiking itself takes about four hours, plus time to linger at the falls.

Branching off from the Cangreja trail, there is a trail to **Caratas Escondidas** (Hidden Waterfalls), which is 4.3km in each direction. This trail is less trafficked, but there is no swimming at the waterfall.

HOTTEST SPOTS FOR THERMAL POOLS & MUD POTS

Costa Rica's volcano-powered thermal pools and mud pots provide plenty of good, clean fun for beauty queens and would-be mud wrestlers alike.

Hot Springs Río Negro On the slopes of Volcán Rincón de la Vieja, with several pools in a jungle setting.

Eco Termales Hot Springs (p245) While some hot spots around Arenal charge outrageous fees to soak in sparkly surrounds, this place maintains its sense of elegance by limiting guest numbers.

Río Perdido (p220) Thermal pools, hanging bridges and low-key luxury characterize this thermal canyon experience near Volcán Miravalles.

Borinquen Mountain Resort & Spa (p233) The pinnacle of indulgent dirt exists in the remote heights of Rincón de la Vieja. If mineral mud is not your thing, you can opt instead for a skin treatment of coconut, cappuccino or chocolate.

Thermal Springs

There's no better way to recover from a grueling hike than by soaking in thermal springs. Many of the springs are reported to have therapeutic properties, which is always a good thing if you've been hitting the *guaro cacique* a little too hard.

In the Sector Santa María, a trail leads 2.8km west through the 'enchanted forest,' past the lovely Catarata Bosque Encantado (Enchanted Forest Falls), to sulfurous hot springs. Don't soak in them for more than about half an hour (some people suggest much less) without taking a dip in the nearby cold springs, 2km away, to cool off. If you want real-deal, volcano-created thermal pools, here they are: it doesn't get more 'natural' than this.

On the fringes of the park, there are several private facilities that have thermal pools with varying temperatures. No hiking required. Many companies and hotels offer tours to these sites from Liberia.

Hot Springs Río Negro   HOT SPRING
(☑ 2690-2900; www.guachipelin.com; per person US$10; ☺ 9am-5pm) Set in the dry forest along the Río Negro, this magical place is managed by the Hacienda Guachipelín. Ten natural, stone-crafted hot pools are accessible by a lovely wooded trail, with hanging bridges leading to pools on either side of the raging river. Pools range in temperature from 28°C to 53°C.

About 1km from the Las Pailas ranger station, turn toward Rincon de la Vieja Lodge and the Santa María sector. The hot springs will be on your right.

Canyon de la Vieja
Adventure Lodge   SPA, ADVENTURE TOUR
(☑ 2665-5912; www.thecanyonlodge.com; spa US$15, tours US$40-50; ☺ 8am-4pm) ✍ On the bank of the crystal-blue Río Colorado, this sprawling lodge operates a full-service spa, complete with cool and warm pools, mud baths and massage, and other treatments. The river current is strong, but the swimming hole is glorious for cooling off on a hot, sunny day (unfortunately, there's not much shade here). In addition to the spa, the adventure lodge offers horseback riding, tubing, rafting and canopy tours.

Accommodation (single/double including breakfast US$80/100) is also available.

Simbiosis Spa   SPA
(☑ 2666-8075; www.guachipelin.com; pools US$15, 50min treatment US$60-75; ☺ 9am-5pm) A short jaunt from the entrance to Rincón de la Vieja National Park, this spa takes advantage of the volcanic activity happening right on the property. Guests can see the boiling mud pools that are the source of their mud bath, and an on-site geyser occasionally puts on a show. There are only four pools (two warm, two cool), but there's a range of massage options.

☞ Tours

The lodges in the area can arrange tours such as horseback riding, mountain biking, guided waterfall and hot-spring hikes, rappelling, rafting and tubing on the lesser-known Río Colorado and, everyone's favorite cashburner, canopy tours. Tours are offered by Borinquen Mountain Resort (p233), Buena Vista Lodge (p233), Canyon de la Vieja

JERRY DRIENDL / GETTY IMAGES ©

1. Zip-lining in Santa Elena (p199)
Swing high through stunning cloud forest on one of Costa Rica's famed canopy tours.

2. Llanos de Cortés (p223)
This beautiful waterfall spills into a tranquil pond, perfect for swimming in.

3. Parque Nacional Rincón de la Vieja (p228)
A hotbed of geothermal activity, this park boasts vividly hued natural springs and a number of volcanoes.

4. Playa Naranjo (p235)
Magnificent coastal panoramas and legendary 3m curls at Witch's Rock – a pilgrimage point for surfers.

Adventure Lodge and Hacienda Guachi-pelín. Transportation from Liberia may also be provided, if needed.

🛏 Sleeping & Eating

There is a rustic cafe near the park entrance to Las Pailas, which will serve you a sandwich or sell you a bottle of water. But it's not much, so you're better off coming prepared with a picnic (and plenty of water). Otherwise, your eating options are mostly restricted to the hotels. There are a few *sodas* in Curubandé, if you want to change it up.

🛏 Sector Las Pailas

Cropping up on the road to Las Pailas is an eclectic collection of truly lovely lodges that are worth considering if you've got your own wheels.

El Sol Verde   CAMPGROUND $

(✆ 2665-5357; www.elsolverde.com; campsite US$9, tent houses US$27.50, d/q US$50/70; P 🛜) ❧ The lovely couple here in Curubandé village offer three Spanish-tiled, wood-walled rooms. Alternatively, bed down in the camping area, where there are a few furnished tent houses, a shared outdoor kitchen, solar-heated showers and plenty of space to pitch your own tent. The mural-painted terrace is a lovely place to relax, and you'll find hiking, swimming and wildlife in the immediate vicinity.

Casa Rural Aroma de Campo   HOTEL $$

(✆ 2665-0008, reservations 7010-5776; www.aromadecampo.com; s/d/tr/q US$55/76/104/123, bungalow $130, all incl breakfast; P 🛜🏊) Near the village of Curubandé, this serene, epiphyte-hung, hammock-strung oasis has six rooms with polished hardwood floors, open bathrooms, colorful wall art, mosquito nets and classy rural sensibility. Scattered around the property, an additional six pre-fab bungalows have bold colors and glass walls for better immersion in the forested setting. Delicious meals are served family-style in the courtyard. Warning: the pet parrot is an early riser.

Rincón de la Vieja Lodge   LODGE $$

(✆ 2200-0238; www.hotelrincondelaviejacr.com; s/d incl breakfast from US$60/70; P @ 🏊) ❧ Closest to the Las Pailas entrance, this rustic hacienda is on 400 hectares of protected land in breezy horse country. In addition to the 49 rustic rooms, there is a small pond,

a family-style restaurant and a canopy tour. The staff are utterly charming.

Rancho Curubandé Lodge   LODGE $$

(✆ 2665-0375; www.rancho-curubande.com; s/d/tr incl breakfast US$62/74/85, villa US$124; P ❄🛜) Set on a working *finca*, this is a pleasant, family-run place with horses for hire. There are 16 spotless and simple rooms with beamed ceilings and a wide common front porch lit by tasteful wrought-iron chandeliers. The two-bedroom villas are particularly good value. Located on the road to Las Pailas, about 600m from the Interamericana.

Hacienda Guachipelín   HOTEL $$$

(✆ 2666-8075; www.guachipelin.com; s/d/tr/q incl breakfast US$84/102/132/152; P ❄ @ 🛜🏊) This appealing 19th-century working cattle ranch is set on 12 sq km of primary and secondary forest. The 54 rooms are spacious and comfortable with traditional wood furniture and wide, welcoming verandas. All rooms enjoy lovely views of the volcano and surrounding grounds. You'll appreciate the welcome drink that awaits you when you check in. It's 10km from the park entrance.

Be warned that the on-site 'adventure center' makes this place feel a little like a vacation factory, catering largely to package tourists who descend for organized horse tours, in-house canopy tours and guided hikes in the national park.

🛏 Sector Santa María

There is one solitary sleeping option near the Sector Santa María, but it's not a bad choice.

Rinconcito Lodge   LODGE $$

(✆ 2666-2764, 2200-0074; www.rinconcitolodge.com; lodge s/d US$34/47, standard s/d $52/74, superior d $78; P 🛜) Just 3km from the Santa María sector of the park, this affordable option has attractive, rustic cabins that are surrounded by some of the prettiest pastoral scenery imaginable. The cheaper rooms are tiny, but they are also just as clean and fresh as you can imagine. The lodge also offers horseback riding and zip-lining tours.

🛏 Cañas Dulces Area

North of the road to Las Pailas is another, nearly roadless flank of the park, accessible from the charming *pueblo* Cañas Dulces. This is where dramatic shark-fin mountains draped in forest jut from pasture lands, and spectacular waterfalls thunder into valleys and bowls steaming with hot springs and scalding volcanic mud. Note that there is no access to the park from this side.

Buena Vista Lodge
LODGE **$$**

(☏ 2690-1414; www.buenavistalodgecr.com; d incl breakfast US$70-100; P 🛜 🏊) Part cattle ranch and part adventure lodge, this expansive place is set on 2000 acres in the western sector of the park. On the grounds are three waterfalls, thermal pools, a canopy tour, hanging bridges and a thrilling 400m mountain waterslide. Choose between rustic stained-wood rooms and more private log cabins with glorious views. This lodge caters to package tourists big time.

Accessible via the village of Cañas Dulces.

Borinquen Mountain Resort & Spa
RESORT **$$$**

(☏ 2690-1900; www.borinquenresort.com; d incl breakfast US$220-365; ✴ 🛜) The most luxurious resort in the area is located on the western flank of the park. It features nicely appointed bungalows with private decks and jaw-dropping mountain views, and all the expected adventure tours are on offer. The hot springs, mud baths and natural saunas are gorgeous and surrounded by greenery. A treatment at the elegant Anáhuac Spa (9am to 6pm) – suspended over the steaming jungle – is the icing on this decadent mud pie.

The resort is accessible via the village of Cañas Dulces.

ⓘ Information

The two main entrances to the park each have their own ranger station, where you sign in, pay admission and get free maps. Most visitors enter through **Las Pailas ranger station** (☏ 2666-5051; www.acguanacaste.ac.cr; adult/child 6-12yr/child 5yr & under US$15/5/ free; ⊗ 8am-4pm Tue-Sun, no entry after 3pm) on the western flank, where most of the trails begin. The **Santa María ranger station** (☏ 2666-5051; www.acguanacaste.ac.cr; adult/child US$15/5; ⊗ 7am-4pm, no entry after 3pm), to the east, is in the Hacienda Santa María, a 19th-century *rancho* that was reputedly once owned by US President Lyndon Johnson. This is your access point to the sulphorous springs.

ⓘ Getting There & Away

The Las Pailas sector is accessible via a good 20km road that begins at a signed turnoff from the Interamericana, 5km north of Liberia. It's paved for the first part of the drive past Curubandé. If you're not staying at the Hacienda

Guachipelín, you'll have to pay to drive on its private road, which costs US$1.50 per person and takes you to the park entrance.

The Santa María ranger station, in the east, is accessible via a rougher gravel road beginning at Barrio La Victoria in Liberia. Head east on Av 11, go around the stadium and continue north on Rte 918 for about 20km to the park entrance.

Both roads are passable to regular cars throughout the dry season, but a 4WD is required during the rainy season and is highly recommended at all other times. To travel between the two sectors you needn't double back to Liberia. One kilometer from the Las Pailas park entrance is the turn toward Rincón de la Vieja lodge, Río Negro hot springs and the Sector Santa María.

There's no public transportation to the park entrances, but a bus travels from Liberia to Curubandé three times daily in each direction (40 minutes). Any hotel in Liberia can arrange transport to the park for around US$20 per person. Alternately, you can hire a 4WD taxi from Liberia for about US$40 to Las Pailas, or US$65 to Santa María, each way.

The road to Cañas Dulces and beyond, toward Buena Vista Lodge and Borinquen Mountain Resort & Spa, is well signed about 11.5km north of Liberia, where it intersects with the Interamericana. Note that there is no access to the park from this side, so you'll have to go all the way back to the Interamerican and enter through Las Pailas.

Sector Santa Rosa

Established in 1971 as a national park, the Sector Santa Rosa (☏ 2666-5051; www. acguanacaste.ac.cr; adult/child US$15/5, surfing or snorkeling surcharge US$12; ⊗ 8am-4pm) is now a part of the much larger Area de Conservacion Guanacaste (ACG). This sprawling area was established to protect the largest remaining stand of tropical dry forest in Central America. With its primordial acacia thorn trees and tall jaragua grass, this rare landscape resembles the African savanna, though closer inspection reveals more American species of plants, including cacti and bromeliads.

Aside from the startling dry landscape, Santa Rosa contains some legendary surf breaks, important nesting beaches for several species of sea turtle, and deep historical gravitas. Difficult access means that most of the Santa Rosa sector is fairly empty, though it can get reasonably busy on weekends in the dry season, when Ticos flock to the park in search of their often-hard-to-find history.

Sights

Santa Rosa is the site of two game-changing battles from two different eras, ranking it among the country's most significant historical landmarks. This history is commemorated here with a museum and a monument. Although the park was established mainly due to historical and patriotic reasons, Santa Rosa also contains an important nesting site for olive ridley turtles and one legendary surf break.

La Casona   MUSEUM, HISTORIC BUILDING
(2666-5051; www.acguanacaste.ac.cr; with park admission free; 8-11:30am & 1-4pm) La Casona is the main edifice of the old Hacienda Santa Rosa. The battle of 1856 was fought around this building, and the military action is described with wonderful displays detailing (in English and Spanish) the old gold-rush route, William Walker's evil imperial plans, and the 20-day-battle breakdown. There are also exhibits on the region's natural history. Two hiking trails leave from behind the museum. La Casona is located near the park headquarters in the Santa Rosa sector.

Monument de los Heroes   VIEWPOINT, MONUMENT
(with park admission free) Climb up the steep staircase behind La Casona to reach a lookout point with a stunning view of three vol-

canoes. The monument itself was built to honor the heroes of the two important battles that took place in this vicinity.

Activities

Hiking

Several hiking trails originate near the park headquarters, including the gentle hike to the Mirador Valle Naranjo, with spectacular views of Playa Naranjo.

From the southern end of Playa Naranjo there are two hiking trails: Sendero Carbonal is a 5km trail that swings inland along the mangroves and past Laguna El Limbo, where the crocs hang out; Sendero Aceituno parallels Playa Naranjo for 13km and terminates near the estuary across from Witch's Rock.

The main road is lined with short trails to small waterfalls and other photogenic natural wonders.

Sendero Indio Desnudo   HIKING
Near the park headquarters, El Sendero Indio Desnudo is an 800m trail with signs interpreting the ecological relationships among the animals, plants and weather patterns of Santa Rosa. The trail is named after a common tree, also called gumbo limbo, whose peeling orange-red bark can photosynthesize during the dry season, when

---

SANTA ROSA IN HISTORY

This stretch of coast is famous among Ticos as a national stronghold. Costa Rica has been invaded three times, and the enemy has always surrendered in Santa Rosa.

The best known of these incidents is the Battle of Santa Rosa, which took place on March 20, 1856, when Costa Rica was invaded by the soon-to-be-self-declared president of Nicaragua, an uppity American named William Walker. Walker was the head of a group of foreign pirates and adventurers known as the 'Filibusters' that had already seized Baja and southwest Nicaragua and were attempting to gain control over all of Central America. In a brilliant display of military prowess, Costa Rican president Juan Rafael Mora Porras managed to assemble a ragtag group of fighters and surround Walker's army in the main building of the old Hacienda Santa Rosa, known as La Casona. The battle was over in just 14 minutes, and Walker was forever driven from Costa Rican soil.

Santa Rosa was also the site of battles between Costa Rican troops and invading forces from Nicaragua in the 20th century. The first – in 1919 – was a somewhat honorable attempt to overthrow the Costa Rican dictator General Federico Tinoco. Then, in 1955, Nicaraguan dictator Anastasio Somoza led a failed coup d'état. Today you can still see Somoza's abandoned tank, which lies in a ditch beside the road just beyond the entrance to the park.

The area's military history didn't end with Somoza. In the 1980s, US Marine lieutenant-colonel Oliver North illegally sold weapons to Iran and used the profits to fund the Nicaraguan Contras during the Sandinistas-Contra war. The troops' staging area was just north of Santa Rosa at Playa Potrero Grande (near the famous surf break now known as Ollie's Point).

the trees' leaves are lost (resembling a sun-burned tourist, or 'naked Indian,' as the the trail name translates).

Also seen along the trail is the national tree of Costa Rica, the guanacaste. The province is named after this huge tree species, which is found along the Pacific coastal lowlands. You may also see birds, monkeys, snakes and iguanas, as well as petroglyphs (most likely pre-Columbian) etched into rocks along the trail.

Mirador Valle Naranjo   HIKING
On the road to Playa Naranjo, and about 8km from shore, you'll pass a trailhead for the Mirador Valle Naranjo. It's a short 600m hump to a viewpoint with magical Naranjo vistas.

Surfing

Playa Naranjo   SURFING
(surfing surcharge US$12) A spectacular beach in the southernmost part of the Santa Rosa sector, Playa Naranjo is a pilgrimage point for wave riders who come to surf the legendary beach break at **Witch's Rock** (Roca Bruja), famous for its 3m curls (not recommended for beginners). Be careful of rocks near the river mouth, and crocodiles near the estuary as it's a rich feeding ground during the tide changes. There's a campground with pit toilets but no potable water, so be sure to bring your own. Call ahead regarding road conditions.

By the way, the beach is stunning, with a sweet, rounded boulder-strewn point to the north and shark-fin headlands to the south. Even further south, Nicoya and Papagayo peninsular silhouettes reach out in a dramatic attempt to out do each other.

Playa Naranjo is 18km from the park entrance and 11km from the Santa Rosa ranger station. The road from the station to the beach is notoriously bad. In fact, it's impassable except in the driest months, and even then requires a 4WD.

★ Ollie's Point   SURFING
Surfers make pilgrimages to this sector, near Playa Portrero Grande, to find the best right in all of Costa Rica. The famous surf break Ollie's Point offers a nice, long ride, especially with a southern swell. The bottom here is a mix of sand and rocks, and the year-round offshore is perfect for tight turns and slow closes. Shortboarding is preferred. Ollie's Point is only accessible by boat from Playa del Coco or Tamarindo.

Or you can do as Patrick and Wingnut did in Endless Summer II and crash-land your chartered plane on the beach (ahem, not actually recommended).

Wildlife-Watching
The wildlife in Santa Rosa is both varied and prolific, especially during the dry season, when animals congregate around the remaining water sources and the trees lose their leaves. More than 250 bird species have been recorded, including the raucous white-throated magpie jay, unmistakable with its long crest of manically curled feathers. The forests contain parrot and parakeet, trogon and tanager, and as you head down to the coast you'll be rewarded by sightings of a variety of coastal birds.

Dozens of species of bats have been identified in Santa Rosa. Other mammals you have a reasonable chance of seeing include deer, coati, peccary, armadillo, coyote, raccoon, three kinds of monkey, and a variety of other species – about 115 in all. There are also many thousands of insect species, including about 4000 moths and butterflies (just bring insect repellent).

Reptile species include lizards, iguanas, snakes, crocodiles and four species of sea turtle. The olive ridley sea turtle is the most numerous, and during the July to December nesting season tens of thousands of turtles make their nests on Santa Rosa's beaches, especially **Playa Nancite**. From August to December, *arribada* (mass arrival) takes place about once a month and lasts for four days. During September and October especially, it's sometimes possible to see as many as 8000 of these 40kg turtles on the beach at the same time. Playa Nancite is strictly protected and entry is restricted, but permission may be obtained from ranger station to observe *arribada*.

🛏 Sleeping
The accommodations at the Santa Rosa research station are usually occupied by visiting researchers. There's a shady developed campground (per person US$4) nearby, with picnic benches, grills, flushing toilets and cold-water showers. Playa Naranjo also has pit toilets and showers but no potable water – bring your own, and don't expect complete solitude. Everyone shares one sandy flat basin, only moderately sheltered from gusty wind by thin trees. There's a 25-person, two-night maximum. Bring tons of water.

SECTOR MURCIÉLAGO

Encompassing the wild northern coastline of the Península Santa Elena, the Sector Murciélago (Bat Sector) is where you'll find the isolated white-sand beach of Playa Blanca and the trailhead for the Poza el General watering hole, which attracts birds and animals year-round. Sector Murciélago is not accessible from the Santa Rosa sector.

To get to the northern Sector Murciélago, turn off the Interamericana near the police checkpoint that is 10km north of Santa Rosa. After 8km, bear left at the village of Cuajiniquíl. Continue on the gravel road for another 9km, passing such historic sights as the former hacienda of the Somoza family (it's currently a training ground for the Costa Rican police) and the airstrip that was used by Oliver North to 'secretly' smuggle goods to the Nicaraguan Contras in the 1980s. Continue straight until you cross a river, then hang a right and keep going straight over two more rivers until you reach the village of Murciélago and the park entrance.

Continue another 12km on a dirt road to the remote bays and beaches of Bahía Santa Elena and Bahía Playa Blanca. A 4WD is a must, and even then the road may be impassable in the wet season. Also, signage is nonexistent. Have fun!

Research Station   HOSTEL **$**
(☑ 2666-5051; www.acguanacaste.ac.cr; dm US$12) Make reservations in advance to stay in basic to grim eight-bed dorms with cold showers and electricity. Researchers get priority, but there's usually some room for travelers. Travelers can get their meals (US$6 to US$10) in the cafeteria on-site with reservations.

❶ Getting There & Away

Access to the Santa Rosa sector park entrance is on the western side of the Interamericana, 35km north of Liberia and 45km south of the Nicaraguan border. The well-signed main park entrance can be reached by public transportation: take any bus between Liberia and the Nicaraguan border and ask the driver to let you off at the park entrance; rangers can help you catch a return bus. You can also arrange private transportation from the hotels in Liberia for about US$20 to US$30 per person round trip.

From the entrance it's another 7km to park headquarters, where you'll also find the museum and the campgrounds. This office administers the Area de Conservación Guanacaste (ACG).

From this complex, a very rough track leads down to Playa Naranjo, 12km away. Even during the dry season this road is only passable to a high-clearance 4WD, and you must sign an eerie waiver at the park entrance stating that you willingly assume all liability for driving this road. The park also requires that you be completely self-sufficient should you choose to undertake the trip, which means bringing all your own water and knowing how to do your own car repair. During the rainy months (May to November) the road is open to hikers and

horses but closed to all vehicles; if you want to surf here, it's infinitely easier to gain access to the beach by hiring a boat from Playa del Coco or Tamarindo, further south.

Refugio Nacional de Vida Silvestre Bahía Junquillal

Overlooking the Bahía Junquillal, just north of the Sector Murciélago, this 505-hectare wildlife refuge (☑ 2666-5051; www.acguanacaste.ac.cr; adult/child 6-12yr/child 5yr & under US$15/5/free; ⊙ 7am-5pm) is another part of the vast Area Conservación de Guanacaste (ACG). The quiet bay and beautiful protected beach provide gentle swimming and snorkeling opportunities, making this a popular destination for Tico families on weekends and holidays. On a clear day, you'll see Volcán Orosí in the distance.

Two short trails (totaling 1.7km) hug the coast, traversing dry tropical forest, leading to a marine bird lookout in one direction and to the mangroves in the other. Keep your eye out for pelicans and frigate birds, as well as capuchin monkeys, coatis and other scavengers.

There is a campground (per person US$19) near the ranger station. Very popular among domestic tourists, it is outfitted with brick grills and picnic tables at every site. During the dry season especially, water is at a premium and is turned on for only one hour a day. There are pit latrines. If you don't care to camp, the nearest accommodations are 7km north, in Bahía Salinas.

ⓘ Getting There & Away

From the Interamericana, turnoff at the police checkpoint, following the signs about 8km to Cuajiniquíl. Just before you reach the village, turn right on the paved road and continue 4km to the park entrance. You'll know you're getting close when that glorious cobalt bay appears from out of nowhere on your left.

If you're coming from Bahía Salinas, take the paved road that heads south from El Soley. It hugs the coast, depositing you at Junquillal in a mere 7km.

La Cruz

La Cruz is the closest town to the Peñas Blancas border crossing with Nicaragua, and it's the principal gateway to Bahía Salinas, Costa Rica's premier kitesurfing destination. La Cruz itself is a fairly sleepy provincial town set on a mountaintop plateau, with lots of Tico charm and magical views of an epic windswept bay. El Mirador is a required stop, to stretch your legs and widen your worldview.

⊙ Sights & Activities

El Mirador Centro Turistico   VIEWPOINT

FREE Don't cruise through La Cruz without stopping at the oddly shaped 'tourist and cultural center' on the western edge of town. You might stumble onto an exhibit or a concert, but the main attraction is the jaw-dropping 180-degree view of Bahía Salinas. You can also peek into Nicaragua from here. The cafe at the back is a fine lunch stop.

Hacienda El Cenizaro   ADVENTURE TOUR

(☑ 8630-5050; www.haciendaelcenizaro.com; tours $99) On the road to Bahía Salinas, this attractive hacienda sits back from the road, overlooking its farmland spotted with bulls. It's an atmospheric location to hop on a horse – or an ATV if you prefer. Horseback riding tours traverse the tropical dry forest, but ATVs carry you to new heights for splendid views of the bay.

Spider Monkey Canopy Tour   CANOPY TOUR

(☑ 8893-4396; spidermonkeytours@hotmail.com; tour $45; ⊙ 8am-4pm) On the road to Bahía Salinas you'll find the requisite canopy tour, with 11 cables and a Tarzan swing. Get a new perspective on the tropical dry forest!

🛏 Sleeping

Amalia's Inn   INN $

(☑ 2679-9618; s/d US$25/35; ℗ 🏊) This yellow stucco house on a cliff isn't a bad place to spend the night. For starters, the shared terracotta terraces have stupendous bay views. Inside, homey rooms are furnished rather randomly, but the brick floors and wooden ceilings are attractive. Walls in the meandering house are hung with modernist paintings by Amalia's late husband, Lester Bounds.

Amalia's niece is now the lady of the house, and short of offering meals she'll make you feel right at home.

Hotel La Mirada   HOTEL $

(☑ 2679-9702; www.hotellamirada.com; d US$45-65; ℗ ❄ 🛜) Just off the Interamericana you'll find the town's spiffiest spot. Family owned and lovingly cared for, rooms are spacious and clean, with high, beamed ceilings and loft sleeping spaces. The biggest rooms have kitchenettes and air-con. Despite the name, there's no view to speak of.

Cañas Castillas   FARMSTAY $$

(☑ 8381-4030; www.canas-castilla.com; s/d/tr/q US$45/56/68/80; ℗ ❄ 🛜) On the banks of the peaceful Río Sapoa, about 5km north of La Cruz in Sonzpote, a half-dozen quaint cabins are surrounded by 68 hectares of tropical forest and farmland. The family *finca* includes cattle and horses, as well as oranges, passion fruit and loads of other tempting fruit trees, making for amazing bird-sighting opportunities. Hearty, home-cooked meals are available.

It's a perfect place to recover from a border crossing. You may end up staying for a while!

ⓘ Information

Change money in town to avoid the high rates at the border.

Banco Nacional (☑ 2212-2000; ⊙ 8:30am-3:45pm Mon-Fri) At the junction of the short road into the town center.

Banco Popular (☑ 2681-4600; ⊙ 8:45am-4:30pm Mon-Fri, 8:15-11:30am Sat) In the town center, just south of the Catholic church.

Cruz Roja (☑ 2679-9004, emergency 2679-9146) A small clinic just north of the town center on the road toward the border.

ⓘ Getting There & Away

The bus station is located on the western edge of town, just north of the road to Bahía Salinas. A **Transportes Deldú counter** (☑ 2221-2596; www.facebook.com/transportedeldu; ⊙ 7:30am-12:30pm & 1:30-6pm) sells tickets and stores luggage. To catch a TransNica bus to Peñas Blancas at the border and on to Managua

NORTHWESTERN COSTA RICA LA CRUZ

in Nicaragua, you'll need to flag down a bus on the Interamericana.

Peñas Blancas US$1, 45 minutes, 10 departures almost hourly from 5am to 5:30pm.

Playa Jobó US$1.50, 30 minutes, departs four times daily from 8:30am to 5:30pm from the bus terminal near Hotel Bella Vista.

San José via Liberia US$7, five hours, departs hourly from 5am to 7pm.

Bahía Salinas

Welcome to the kitesurfing capital of Costa Rica, where giddy riders shred beneath magnificent rainbows that arch over a wide bay, extending all the way to Nicaragua. The destination has a deconstructed nature – communities congregate on empty beaches, clumped with tropical forests that are home to howler tribes and linked by dirt roads. The result is a pleasingly *tranquilo,* rural vibe.

Bahía Salinas is a stunning, under-the-radar destination even if you don't ride wind. But not for long. The glorious sands of Playa Jabó are no longer deserted after the opening of a gigantic, 400-room, five-star resort. The road heading south is already partially paved and more development will certainly follow. For better and for worse.

 Activities

If wind isn't your thing, head around the point to Playa Jobó, a perfect, 300m-wide horseshoe of a bay with calm water and headlands sprouting with flowering trees, or Playa Rajada, set on the southernmost arm of Salinas. Rajada is ruggedly gorgeous and sheltered enough to be almost placid. In September and October, humpback whales often congregate here.

Boats can be rented in the village of El Jobó or at one of the local resorts to visit Isla Bolaños, a seabird refuge home to the en-

---

ⓘ **GETTING TO NICARAGUA**

Crossing the border into Nicaragua at Peñas Blancas is a highly variable experience, sometimes taking a half-hour or less, and sometimes taking multiple hours. Here's what you need to know:

➡ Peñas Blancas is a busy border crossing (open 6am to midnight), which can be a major hassle at peak times. Avoid crossing the border shortly before closing time and in the days leading up to major holidays.

➡ Make sure you have at least six months validity on your passport. If your passport is about to expire, you will be denied entry into Nicaragua.

➡ Most car-rental companies in Costa Rica won't allow you to take the vehicle out of the country. Leave your car in one of the nearby guarded parking areas (assuming you're coming back, of course).

➡ Costa Rica charges a $7 land exit fee, payable by credit or debit card.

➡ The border posts are about 1km apart. If you're on an international bus (TicaBus), you'll get a lift between posts. Otherwise, you'll have to hoof it. Hordes of generally useless touts will offer to 'guide' you through the simple crossing – let them carry your luggage if you like, but agree on a fee beforehand.

➡ Entering and leaving Nicaragua costs US$12, which must be paid in US dollars. You'll also be charged US$2 to enter the state of Rivas.

➡ You may be asked to show a proof of exit, such as a return bus ticket or a flight reservation out of Nicaragua.

➡ There are no banks at the border, but there are plenty of money-changers hanging around. Rates will be not be to your advantage, obviously.

There's a fairly fabulous duty-free shop waiting for you in Sapoá, the Nicaraguan equivalent of Peñas Blancas. Relax with your purchases on the 45-minute bus ride to Rivas (departing every 45 minutes or so). Rivas is a quiet transport hub, though its well-preserved 17th-century center is worth exploring. If you're good at bargaining (and you will have to bargain hard), there are a number of taxis waiting on the Nicaraguan side of the border to whisk you to Rivas (US$30).

dangered brown pelican (visits are restricted to April through November to avoid disturbing nesting seabirds). Ask around about fishing and diving trips to Isla Despense, Isla Caballo and Isla Murcielago, with its resident bull sharks.

Kitesurfing

Bahía Salinas is an internationally known mecca for kitesurfers between November and March, when the wind howls fairly consistently. The shape of the hills surrounding the bay funnels the winds into a predictable pattern (though it can be gusty, ranging between 20 and 40 knots), and the sandy, protected beaches make this a great place for beginners and experienced riders alike.

It's important to remember that there are inherent dangers to kiting (namely the risk of losing a limb – yikes!), so seek professional instruction if you're not experienced. The Professional Air Sports Association (PASA) and the International Kiteboarding Organization (IKO) have set standards for beginner instruction. You'll need to take a nine-hour certification course to rent gear and safely go out on your own.

The road follows the curve of the bay to the consistently windy beaches of **Playa Papaturro** and **Playa Copal**, the kiting vortex. It's an incredibly wide beige beach backed by scrubby manzanillo trees with views across the sea all the way to Nicaragua. It does get crazy windy here, so, though picturesque, it's not about beach-combing.

The turnoff to Papaturro is clearly marked. Playa Copal has two access roads. The first one is through the farmland behind Plaza Copal. (It's a public road, but you must close the gate behind you so the animals don't get out.) The second one is more clearly marked – follow the signs to KiteHouse.

Kiteboarding Costa Rica KITESURFING
(☑ 8370-4894; www.kiteboardincostarica.com; lessons per hr US$45-65) Operated out of the KiteHouse at the western end of Playa Copal, this is a highly regarding kitesurfing school. Instructors speak French and English. If you've already got your certification and you feel confident, you can also just rent equipment here.

Kitesurf School 2000 KITESURFING
(☑ 2676-1042, 8826-5221; www.bluedreamhotel. com; lessons per hr US$35-45; ⊙ 8am-8pm) Make reservations in advance to take lessons or rent gear at the area's original kite shop

(IKO certified). Formerly known as Kitesurf 2000, it's located at Blue Dream Hotel, 250m from Papaturro. Lessons are available in Spanish, English and Italian. Cash only.

Cometa Copal Kitesurfing KITESURFING
(☑ 8553-6764; www.kitesurfingincostarica.com; lessons per hr US$40; ⊙ Nov-May) Bob is an American instructor, lifeguard and emergency medical technician who runs this reputable kitesurfing school on Playa Copal. He can also set you up with simple accommodations (from US$50) with easy access to the beach.

🛏 Sleeping & Eating

Bike House B&B $
(www.thebikehousecostarica.com; cabina US$35; ☎) This friendly B&B caters to travelers who prefer their adventure with two wheels on the ground. Accommodations are simple and sweet, with a shady common porch with hammocks, and Carole also prepares delicious *tipica* (typical Costa Rican food). She can also help make arrangements for kitesurfing if you want to give it a try.

In addition to renting bikes (per day US$10), Carole leads a variety half-day and full-day cycling trips in the area.

Blue Dream Hotel HOTEL $
(☑ 2676-1042, 8826-5221; www.bluedreamhotel. com; dm US$17, standard s/d US$35/45, bungalow s/d US$52/58, ste s/d/tr $65/67/77; ⊙ Sep-Jul; P ✳ @ ☎) This friendly, groovy hotel offers marvelous views over Playa Papaturro from every single guest room on its terraced hillside. Rooms range from simple and comfortable with Spanish tiles to more spacious chalet-style with private balconies. All have access to a hammock-strung garden with the same amazing view. There's an Italian chef in the kitchen serving hearty breakfasts and good pizzas.

★ KiteHouse GUESTHOUSE $$
(☑ 2676-1045, 8370-4894; www.kiteboardingcos tarica.com; dm US$20-25, cabina US$55-70, villa from US$90; ⊙ Nov-May; ✳ ☎ ☀) This excellent operation has taken over the western end of Playa Copal, with kiteboarding lessons, rentals, a wide range of accommodations and a hilltop restaurant (6pm to 9pm Tuesday to Sunday). Every sleeping option – from dorm room to villa – has a terrific view of the beach. The rooms also have kitchenettes, as there are few other places to eat.

Plaza Copal SODA $

(☑ 8994-5292; www.facebook.com/plazacopal;
meals US$6-10; ⊙ 8am-10pm; 🅿 🛜) ● There's
a fantastic vibe at this outdoor *soda*, located
on the road down to Copal. Hungry kitesurfers congregate here to get their fill before
and after riding the wind. They can vouch
for the home-cooked meals, which are filling
and downright delectable. Place all orders
in advance for amazing coconut curry, grass-
fed beef steaks and fresh fish.

If you want easy access to the goods from
the kitchen, you can stay here in one of the
basic wooden rooms with shared bathrooms
(double US$25). The owner, Ulf, is also good
for travel information, including tips for getting to Nicaragua.

❶ Getting There & Away

From La Cruz, the road is paved at first, but
gravel for the last 9km. It leads down from the
lookout point in La Cruz past the small coastal
fishing community of Puerto Soley, at the eastern end of Playa Papaturro.

If you're driving from the south, there's a
paved route to El Soley. Don't count on your
map or GPS to know about this new road – but
figure it out as it will save you some time on
the bumps. Instead of driving all the way to
La Cruz, turn off the Interamericana near the
police check point, following signs to Cuajini-
quil. After about 8km, just before the village,
you'll bear right toward Junquillal. The paved
road follows the coast about 12km north to El
Soley, from where you'll pick up the gravel road
from La Cruz.

Buses (US$2) make the 30-minute run be-
tween the La Cruz bus terminal and the village of
Jobó three times a day in either direction. A taxi
to the beaches costs about US$20.

Arenal & Northern Lowlands

Best Places to Eat

➡ Restaurant Don Rufino (p254)

➡ Benedictus Steakhouse (p254)

➡ La Ventanita (p259)

➡ Gingerbread Hotel & Restaurant (p265)

Best Wildlife-Watching

➡ Arenal Natura (p245)

➡ Refugio Nacional de Vida Silvestre Caño Negro (p268)

➡ Chilamate Rainforest Eco Retreat (p280)

➡ Estación Biológica La Selva (p282)

Why Go?

You know about the region's main attraction: that now-dormant volcano, surrounded by old lava fields, bubbling hot springs and a stunning lake. Venture further onto the wild rivers and into the tropical jungle of the northern lowlands and you will discover real-life Costa Rica, where agricultural commerce and ecological conservation converge as a work in green progress. Stretching from the borderlands of Nicaragua south to the Cordillera de Tilarán, *fincas* (farms) of banana, sugarcane and pineapple roll across humid plains. Community tourism lives and breathes here, creating added revenue for a historically farm-based economy. You can spot a macaw in the wild, paddle into roaring rapids and cruise inky lagoons, all with lifelong resident guides, then nest in lodges that double as private rainforest reserves. When the tourist hordes get you down, make your way here for a refreshing blast of rural realism and an invigorating dose of wild beauty.

When to Go

➡ There's no dry season in the northern lowlands: the lush jungles surrounding the rivers in the region, such as the Río Frío and the Río Sarapiquí, receive rainfall at almost any time of year.

➡ There is a less-wet season, though, from January to April, when there's lower rainfall.

➡ Because there's so much rain, you can run the rivers any time of year, but they flow faster from July to December.

➡ Wildlife also abounds year-round, but skies will be clearer and trails less muddy from January to April.

➡ Fun *sabanero* street festivals take place in La Fortuna in February and in Ciudad Quesada (San Carlos) in April.

Arenal & Northern Lowlands Highlights

① Hiking up the Cerro Chato at **Parque Nacional Volcán Arenal** (p256) and gazing across the turquoise-blue crater lake at its summit.

② Soothing your weary muscles with a soak in volcano-heated pools at **Eco Termales Hot Springs** (p245).

③ Marvelling at sweeping lake or volcano views from your perch in charming **El Castillo** (p257).

④ Getting up close and personal with orphaned or injured wild animals at **Proyecto Asis** (p276).

⑤ Getting down and dirty while exploring the underworld in the **Venado Caves** (p275).

⑥ Exploring the lagoons, counting caimans and spying on spoonbills at the **Refugio Nacional de Vida Silvestre Caño Negro** (p268).

⑦ Listening to the racket made by great green macaws hanging at the almendros trees at **Boca Tapada** (p275).

⑧ Getting thrills and chills while riding the rapids of the **Río Sarapiquí** (p278).

⑨ **Wildlife-spotting** (p279) for howlers, sloths, peccaries and birdlife while exploring the grounds of your ecolodge.

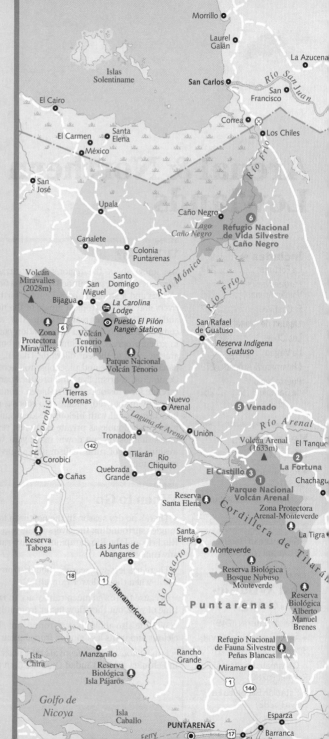

243

Parks & Reserves

0 ────── 20 km
0 ────── 10 miles

La Esperanza

Boca de
Sábalo

Castillo de la
Concepción

El Castillo

NICARAGUA

Alajuela

Llanura de
Guatusos

Río San Juan

Refugio Nacional de
Vida Silvestre
Mixto Maquenque

Trinidad

Refugio Nacional
de Vida Silvestre
Barra del Colorado

Boca
Tapada 7

Heredia

Boca de
Arenal

Cinco
Ceibas

Laguna
Astillero

Río Sarapiquí

Muelle de
San Carlos

(142)

(141)

Tres Amigos

Pital

(250)

Pital

(162)

Centro
Neotrópico
Sarapiquís

Chilamate

9

Puerto Viejo
de Sarapiquí

Estación Biológica
La Selva

Río Chirripó

Limón

Platanar

Jabillos

Aguas
Zarcas

(140)

8 La Virgen

(126)

Tirimbina
Rainforest
Centre

Horquetas

Florencia

Venecia

Río
Cuarto

Río Frío

4 Ciudad Quesada
(San Carlos)

Laguna Hule

San Miguel

Reserva
Cordillera
Volcánica
Central

(4)

Río Balsa

Cariblanco

Albergue
El Socorro

Parque Nacional
Volcán Poás

Santa
Clara

(32)

Guápiles

Bajos

Volcán Poás
(2704m)

Parque
Nacional
Braulio
Carrillo

Poasito

Vara
Blanca

Reserva
Forestal
Grecia

Reserva Forestal
Cordillera
Volcánica
Central

Parque
Nacional
Braulio
Carrillo

San Ramón

Sarchí

Sacramento

Monte de la
Cruz

(32)

Grecia

San Pedro
de Poás

(1)

ALAJUELA

San Isidro
de Heredia

HEREDIA

(3)

Alto
Palma

Parque Nacional
Volcán Irazú

Parks & Reserves

In addition to the famous must-see volcano, there are several notable refuges and parks in the northern lowlands, offering opportunities for low-key, crowd-free boat tours and wildlife-watching.

Parque Nacional Volcán Arenal (p256) Centered on the perfect cone of the eponymous volcano, the clouds will sometimes disperse, revealing the hulking giant.

Parque Nacional Braulio Carrillo (p279) Newly opened, the northern sector of Costa Rica's largest park has hardly any infrastructure, but it will likely be developed in coming years.

Refugio Nacional de Vida Silvestre Caño Negro (p268) The lagoons of Caño Negro attract a wide variety of birds year-round, though prime time for birdwatchers is between January and July.

Refugio Nacional de Vida Silvestre Mixto Maquenque (p275) Though there isn't much in the way of infrastructure at this refuge, local lodges can take you into this remote rainforest.

❶ Getting There & Away

It's easy to reach this region, which is crisscrossed by a couple of fast, new highways (with one more in the works). Coming up from San José or driving down from the Nicaraguan border near Los Chiles, you can be anywhere in the region within a few hours, if you have your own vehicle.

Traveling by bus may take a bit longer, but you can still reach most destinations without too much hassle. Ciudad Quesada (San Carlos) is a major transportation hub for the region where you may have to change buses, especially if you're journeying between the Arenal region and the Lowlands.

By contrast with Arenal, the Lowlands are still largely undiscovered by tourists (though this is changing). Having your own vehicle will allow you greater ease in getting to its appealingly far-flung reaches.

ARENAL & AROUND

Whether you approach from the west or from the east, the drive into the Arenal area is spectacular. Coming from Tilarán in the west, the paved road hugs the northern bank of Laguna de Arenal. The lake and forest vistas are riveting, but pay attention

to your driving and watch for potholes and coati jams. On either side of the road – up the green slope and down on the lakeside – lovely inns, hip coffeehouses and eccentric galleries appear like pictures in a pop-up book. Approaching from Ciudad Quesada (San Carlos), you'll have Volcán Platanar as the backdrop, as the road winds through this green, river-rich agrarian region, passing through prosperous towns bright with bougainvillea. If the weather cooperates, the resolute peak of Arenal looms in front of you.

The volcano may be dormant, but plenty of adventure still awaits you here. There are trails to hike, waterfalls to rappel down, and innumerable sloths to spot. No matter what your preferred method of exploring – hiking, biking, horseback riding, zip lining – you can do it here. And when your body says it's had enough, you can ease into a volcano-heated pool to soak your aches and pains away.

La Fortuna

First impressions of La Fortuna may be somewhat lacking, what with all the tourists and uninspired cinder-block architecture. But, with time, this town's charms are revealed. Here, horses graze in unimproved lots, spiny iguanas scramble through brush, sloth eyes peer from the riverside canopy, and eternal spring mornings carry just a kiss of humidity on their breath. And always, there's that massive volcano lurking behind the clouds or sparkling in the sun.

For most of its history, La Fortuna has been a sleepy agricultural town, 6km from the base of Cerro Arenal (Arenal Hill). In 1968, Arenal erupted violently after nearly 400 years of dormancy, and buried the small villages of Pueblo Nuevo, San Luís and Tabacón. Suddenly, tourists from around the world started descending on La Fortuna in search of fiery night skies and that inevitable blurry photo of creeping lava. La Fortuna is still one of the top destinations for travelers in Costa Rica, even though the great mountain stopped spewing its molten discharge in 2010.

◉ Sights

Catarata Río Fortuna   WATERFALL
(Map p248; www.cataratariofortuna.com; admission US$12; ⊙ 8am-5pm) You can glimpse the sparkling 70m ribbon of clear water that pours through a sheer canyon of dark volcanic rock

arrayed in bromeliads and ferns with minimal sweat equity. But it's worth the climb down and out to see it from the jungle floor. Though it's dangerous to dive beneath the thundering falls, a series of perfect swimming holes with spectacular views tile the canyon in aquamarine. This is also the trailhead for the difficult hike to Cerro Chato (p256).

From the turnoff on the road to San Ramón, it's about 4km uphill to the falls. On the way up, you'll enjoy spectacular views of Cerro Chato as you hike through pastures and past the small hotels lining the road.

Arenal Natura   PARK

(Map p248; 📞 2479-1616; www.arenalnatura. com; day/night/bird tour US$29/39/49; ⏱ 8am-5:30pm; 🚗) Located 6km west of La Fortuna, this is a well-manicured nature experience that includes frogs, turtles, snakes and crocs, all in their appointed places. The birdlife is also prodigious here. Excellent naturalist guides ensure that you don't miss anything hiding in the trees. Discounted rates for children and students.

Mirador El Silencio   NATURE RESERVE

(Map p248; 📞 2479-9900; www.miradorelsilencio.com) 🌿 Set on 555 acres, this private reserve is a mix of primary and secondary forest, located about 7 miles west of La Fortuna. This place is filled with life, from vibrant blue morpho butterflies to three species of monkeys, plus a wide variety of plant life. Four trails are marked with informative signs about the ecology of the place, not to mention a couple of fabulous lookouts.

Ecocentro Danaus   NATURE RESERVE

(Map p248; 📞 2479-7019; www.ecocentrodanaus. com; admission with/without guide US$18/12, guided night tour US$35; ⏱ 8am-4pm Mon-Sat, 9am-3:30pm Sun, night tour 5:30pm; 🚗) 🌿 This center, 2km east of town, has a well-developed trail system that's good for birding, as well as spotting mammals such as sloth, coati and howler monkey. The price of admission also includes a visit to a butterfly garden, a ranarium featuring poison-dart frogs, and a small lake containing caiman and turtles. Reserve in advance for the excellent night tour.

Activities

Bike Arenal   CYCLING

(Map p246; 📞 2479-7150; www.bikearenal.com; Av 319 A, Route 702; rental per day/week US$25/150, half-/full-day tour US$85/135; ⏱ 7am-6pm)

This outfit offers a variety of bike tours for all levels of rider, including a popular ride around the lake and a half-day ride to El Castillo. You can also do versions of these rides on your own. Make advance arrangements for rental and an English-speaking bike mechanic will bring the bicycle to you.

Hot Springs

Beneath La Fortuna the lava is still curdling and heating countless bubbling springs. There are free, natural hot springs in the area that any local can point you toward. If you're after a more comfortable experience, consider one of the area's resorts.

★ Eco Termales Hot Springs   HOT SPRING

(Map p248; 📞 2479-8787; www.ecotermalesfortuna.cr; admission US$36; ⏱ 10am, 1pm or 5pm; 🚗) 🌿 Everything from the natural circulation systems in the pools to the soft lighting is understated, luxurious and romantic at this gated, reservations-only complex about 4.5km northwest of town. Lush greenery surrounds the walking paths that cut through these gorgeous grounds. Only 100 visitors are admitted at a time, to maintain the ambience of serenity and seclusion.

Cocktails – served while you soak – come highly recommended.

Springs Resort & Spa   HOT SPRING

(Map p248; 📞 2401-3313, in USA 954-727-8333; www.thespringscostarica.com; 2-day admission US$60; ⏱ 8am-10pm; 🚗) If you're looking for a luxurious hot-spring experience, the Springs features 18 free-form pools with various temperatures, volcano views, landscaped gardens, waterfalls and swim-up bars, including a jungle bar with a waterslide. The whole scene is human-made, but it's lovely.

Paradise Hot Springs   HOT SPRING

(Map p248; www.paradisehotspringscr.com; adult/child US$23/15; ⏱ 11am-9pm) This low-key place has one lovely, large pool with a waterfall and several smaller, secluded pools, surrounded by lush vegetation and tropical blooms. The pools vary in temperature (up to 40°C), some with hydromassage. Paradise is much simpler than the other larger spring settings, but there are fewer people, and your experience is bound to be more relaxing and more romantic.

Lockers, towels and nonalcoholic drinks are included with admission. There's a restaurant if you want to eat or drink something more potent.

La Fortuna

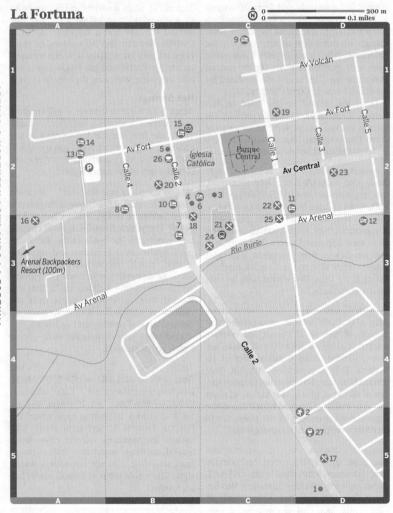

N 0 — 200 m
0 — 0.1 miles

Baldi Hot Springs HOT SPRING
(Map p248; ☎ 2479-9917; www.baldihotsprings.cr; with/without buffet US$56/34; ☺ 10am-10pm; ♨) Big enough so that there's something for everyone, Baldi, about 4.5km northwest of town, has 25 thermal pools ranging in temperature from 32°C to a scalding 67°C. There are waterfalls and soaking pools for chill-seekers and 'Xtreme' slides for thrill-seekers, plus a good-size children's play area. At night, the thumping music and swim-up bars attract a young party crowd, but drinks are pricey!

Tabacón Hot Springs HOT SPRING
(Map p248; ☎ 2519-1999; www.tabacon.com; day pass incl lunch or dinner adult/child US$85/30; ☺ 10am-10pm) ✍ Some say it's cheesy and some say it's fun. (We say it's both.) Broadleaf palms, rare orchids and other florid tropical blooms part to reveal a 40°C waterfall pouring over a fake cliff, concealing constructed caves complete with camouflaged cup holders. Lounged across each well-placed stonelike substance are overheated tourists of various shapes and sizes, relaxing.

La Fortuna

The spa, located 14km west of La Fortuna, is on the site of a 1975 volcanic eruption that killed one local. The former village of Tabacón was destroyed in the 1968 eruption, when 78 people were killed. Don't sweat it: the mountain is once again dormant. For now.

☞ Tours

Sometimes it seems like tour companies are taking over this town. Commissions are big business around here, so shop around before you book. And keep in mind that you can actually do many of these activities on your own – or by booking directly with the service provider. Be aware: what value is added by booking through a tour provider? Tour companies offer many packages that combine activities (canopy tour, guided hike, horseback riding etc) with a dip in the hot springs. Make sure you understand exactly what's included, especially admission fees to parks and springs.

Tour operators also offer a slew of pricey tours to distant destinations, such as Caño Negro, Río Celeste and Venado Caves. If you're short of time, this is a fine option, though you'll save yourself a ton of money (and probably have a much better experience) if you actually go to the place and organize a tour upon arrival.

★ Don Olivo Chocolate Tour   ECOTOUR
(☑ 6110-3556, 2469-1371; www.facebook.com/tour dechocolatedonolivo; tour US$25; ◷ 8am, 10am, 1pm & 3pm; ⊕) Let Don Olivo or his son show you around their family *finca*, showing off

their sugar cane, oranges and – of course – cocoa plants. The process of turning this funny fruit into the decadent dessert that we all know and love is truly fascinating. Bonus: lots of taste-testing along the way!

Alberto's Horse Tours   HORSEBACK RIDING
(Map p246; ☑ 2479-7711, 2479-9043; www.facebook.com/albertoshorses; per person US$85; ◷ 8:30am-1:30pm) Alberto and his son lead popular horseback-riding trips to the Catarata de la Fortuna. It's a three- or four-hour trip, but you'll spend about an hour off your horse, when you hike down to the falls for a swim or a photo op. Beautiful setting, beautiful horses. Cash only.

PureTrek Canyoning   CANYONING
(Map p248; ☑ 1-866-569-5723, 2479-1313; www.puretrekcanyoning.com; 4hr incl transportation & lunch US$100; ◷ 7am-10pm; ⊕) ✆ The reputable PureTrek leads guided rappels down three waterfalls, one of which is 50m high. Also included: rock climbing and 'monkey drop', which is actually a zip line with a rappel at the end of it. High marks for attention to safety and high-quality gear. It gets some big groups, but it does a good job keeping things moving.

Check-in at PureTrek headquarters, located in a tree house 6km west of town.

Nature Tours

Arenal Oasis   BIRD-WATCHING
(Map p248; ☑ 2479-9526; www.arenaloasis.com; night/bird walks US$40/55; ◷ 5:45pm) The Rojas Bonilla family has created this wild frog sanctuary, home to some 28 species of

Around La Fortuna

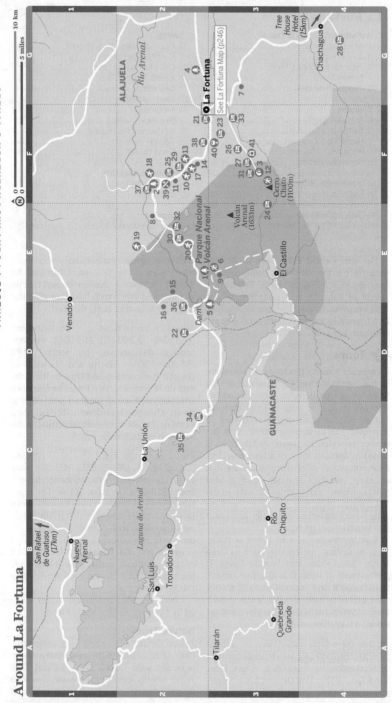

Around La Fortuna

croaking critters. The frogs are just the beginning of this night walk, which continues into the rainforest to see what other nocturnal animals await. If you're more of a morning person, it also does a bird-watching tour. Reservations recommended. Located 3km from La Fortuna's centre; hotel pickup costs US$10.

Jacamar
Naturalist Tours   HIKING
(Map p246; ☎ 2479-9767; www.arenaltours.com; Av Central; ⊘7am-9pm) Recommended for its variety of naturalist hikes, including Volcán Arenal, waterfall and hanging bridges. Customers rave about the guides' flexibility and attentiveness. Located on the ground level of Hotel Arenal Carmela.

Canoeing, Kayaking & Rafting

La Fortuna is not a river-running hub like you'll find in other parts of the country, but there are a few companies offering canoeing and kayaking in the area. If you wish to go white-water rafting, tour companies do take groups from La Fortuna to run the Sarapiquí and other distant rivers. Some offer the option to get dropped afterwards in San José or on the Caribbean coast – a good way to have some fun on a travel day.

Canoa Aventura   CANOEING
(☎ 2479-8200; www.canoa-aventura.com; canoe trip US$67; ⊘6:30am-9:30pm) 🏆 This long-standing family-run company specializes in canoe and float trips led by bilingual naturalist guides. Most are geared toward wildlife- and bird-watching.

Wave Expeditions   RAFTING, KAYAKING
(Map p246; ☎ 2479-7262; www.waveexpeditions. com; cnr Calle 2 & Av Fort; river trips US$70-100, kayaking US$54; ⊘7am-9pm) Wave Expeditions runs the wild Ríos Toro and Sarapiquí, as well as the mellower Balsa. You can kayak on Laguna de Arenal. There's also hiking, horseback riding, caving, canyoning and tortilla making.

Aguas Bravas   RAFTING, KAYAKING
(☎ 2479-7645; www.costaricaraftingvacation.com; rafting US$80-100, kayaking US$60; ⊘7am-7pm) The rafting trips take place on the Río Sarapiquí so it's not exactly in the area. But Aguas Bravas also offers hiking trips around the volcano, horseback riding to the falls and kayaking on Laguna de Arenal.

Canopy Tours

Arenal Paraíso Canopy Tours   CANOPY TOUR
(Map p248; ☑2479-1100; www.arenalparaiso.com;
tours US$45; ⏰8am-5pm; 🖈) A dozen cables
zip across the canyon of the Río Arenal, giving a unique perspective on two waterfalls,
as well as the rainforest canopy. Also includes admission to the resort's swimming
pool and 13 thermal pools, which are hidden among the rocks and greenery on the
hillside.

Athica Canopy   CANOPY TOUR
(☑2479-1405; www.athicacanopy.com; adult/child
US$48/38; ⏰8am, 10:30am, 1pm & 3pm) Operat-
ed by Jacamar Naturalist Tours, this canopy
tour is set up to give you a new perspective
on Volcán Arenal and the surrounding conservation area. There are 10 cables and 14
platforms, as well as the ever-popular Tarzan
swing. Athica offers the opportunity to add
on a two-hour horseback riding trip.

**Arenal Mundo
Aventura**   ADVENTURE TOUR
(Map p248; ☑2479-9762; www.arenalmundoaven
tura.com; adult/child adventure tours US$67/51,
hiking US$53/37; 🖈) An all-in-one adventure
park, this place offers various guided hikes,
rappelling and horseback riding, as well as
a canopy tour. It also hosts performances
of indigenous Maleku dance and song. It
is 2km south of La Fortuna, on the road to
Chachagua.

Canopy Los Cañones   CANOPY TOUR
(Map p248; ☑2479-1047; www.hotelloslagos.
com; adult/child US$50/35) 🌿 Located at the
Hotel Los Lagos, the Canopy Los Cañones
has 12 cables over the rainforest, ranging
from 50m to 500m long. The price includes
admission to a frog farm, crocodile farm,
butterfly farm, hot springs, natural pools
and waterslides, which are all on the hotel
grounds.

Ecoglide   CANOPY TOUR
(Map p248; ☑2479-7120; www.arenalecoglide.
com; adult/child US$55/45; ⏰7am-4pm; 🖈)
Ecoglide is the biggest canopy game in
town, featuring 13 cables, 15 platforms and a
'Tarzan' swing. The dual-cable safety system
provides extra security and peace of mind.

✨ Festivals & Events

Fiestas de la Fortuna   CULTURAL
(www.facebook.com/fiestasfortuna; ⏰mid-Feb)
The big annual bash features two weeks of
Tico-rules bullfights, colorful carnival rides,
greasy festival food, craft stands and unusual gambling devices. It's free, except for
the beer (which is cheap), and you'll have a
blast trying to decide between the reggaetón go-go dancers and the live *ranchero* and
salsa.

🛏 Sleeping

There are loads of places to stay in town.
In fact, the tourist infrastructure has over-
flowed out of town, so that now there are
lodges strung out along the roads heading
south and west. With Parque Nacional Volcán Arenal at their doorstep, many of these
places on the outskirts have hiking trails,
hot springs and volcano views right on the
property. The disadvantage is that restaurants and other facilities are limited outside
of town.

If you have your own transport, you
might even consider staying in the national
park at the Arenal Observatory Lodge (p257)
or in the small town of El Castillo, as you'll
be rewarded with fewer crowds and a more
rustic vibe.

Prices drop dramatically during the green
season (May to November). Look for discounts of 25% to 40%.

🛏 La Fortuna

Sleeping Indian Guesthouse   GUESTHOUSE $
(Map p246; ☑2479-8431, 8446-9149; sleeping
indianguesthouse@gmail.com; Av Fort; d US$45;
🛜) Ethnic insensitivities aside, this is a delightful 2nd-story guesthouse just north of
the church. Six sweet fan-cooled rooms have
lofty ceilings, tile floors, colorful paint jobs
and big windows. The spacious common
area includes a fully equipped kitchen, two
balconies with volcano views, and a homey
living room, well stocked with books, games
and funky artwork. The live-in owner is a
gracious host.

Arenal Hostel Resort   HOSTEL $
(Map p246; ☑2479-9222; www.arenalhostel
resort.com; Av Central; dm/s/d/tr/q US$17/50/
60/80/90; 🅿❄@🛜🏊) 🌿 Offering the best
of hostel and resort, this welcoming place
is arranged around a landscaped garden,
complete with hammocks, small pool,
party-place bar and volcano view. All rooms
are clean, spacious and air-conditioned,
with en suite bathrooms. A word of warning: a recurring complaint is that reservations were 'lost' or clients were 'bumped' to
Hostel Backpackers La Fortuna. This could

happen to *you*. By the way, Arenal Hostel Resort and Arenal Backpackers Resort do essentially the same thing, but they are not actually the same place.

Arenal Backpackers Resort HOSTEL $

(Map p248; ☑2479-7000; www.arenalbackpack ersresort.com; Av Central; dm US$14-18, tents s/d US$30/40, s/tw/d US$55/60/70; P❋@🅰🛋) The original hostel-resort in La Fortuna, this self-proclaimed 'five-star hostel' with volcano views is pretty cushy. Sleep on or-thopedic mattresses and take hot showers in your en suite bathroom (even in the dorms). Somewhere between dormitory and hotel is the covered tent city: raised tents have air mattress and electricity (but no proper walls, so you'll hear your neigh-bors loud and clear).

The main attraction is the landscaped pool with swim-up bar, where backpackers spend lazy days lounging with a cold beer. You'll be in a traveler's party bubble here. Not that there's anything wrong with that.

Hostel Backpackers La Fortuna HOSTEL $

(Map p246; ☑2479-9129; www.hostelbackpackers lafortuna.com; dm/s/d/tr/q US$15/45/50/70/85; P❋@🅰🛋) This is the most 'grown-up' hostel in town. The rooms are done in whites and beiges, and the courtyard is lush, lovely and strung with hammocks. Guests are invited to go down the street to the sis-ter property, Arenal Hostel Resort, to join the party (swimming pool, bar) and then to return here for quiet, comfort and a good night's sleep.

La Choza Inn INN $

(Map p246; ☑2479-9361; www.lachozainn hostel.com; Av Fort btwn Calles 2 & 4; dm US$10, s/d US$35/50, air-con US$10, all incl breakfast; P❋@🅰) With all the budget 'resorts' in town, it's refreshing to find a charming, old-fashioned, family-run inn, where kids and puppies interact with the guests and facilities are basic but the staff is always ac-commodating. Take your pick from the dark, palm-wood dorms or the attractive doubles boasting Arenal views from the balconies.

Fas B&B B&B $

(Map p246; ☑2479-9238; Calle 2; d incl breakfast US$60; P❋@🅰) Lovely blooming flowers deck the 2nd-floor terrace, inviting you into this cute motel-style lodging. Inside, you'll find good-value and personable service. Spotless rooms are painted in pastels, with beds dressed in tasteful quilts and walls

hung with tropical paintings. The place is small, however, and once you leave your room you're as good as on the street.

Hotel Monte Real HOTEL $$

(Map p246; ☑2479-9357; www.monterealhotel. com; Av Arenal btwn Calles 3 & 5; r US$85-95, ste US$110, all incl breakfast; P❋🅰🛋) A smart, modern motel property on the edge of town, next to the Río Burio. This excellent location combines the convenience of town with the nature and rusticity of the forest – meaning lovely gardens and wildlife at your doorstep. Spacious rooms have Spanish-tile floors, stained-wood ceilings and sliding glass doors, some with private balcony.

La Fortuna Suites GUESTHOUSE $$

(Map p246; ☑8577-1555; www.lafortunasuites. com; d/ste from US$55/95, all incl breakfast; P❋🅰) Here's a chance to luxuriate in some high-end amenities at midrange prices. We're talking high-thread-count sheets and memory-foam mattresses, custom-made fur-niture and flat-screen TVs, gourmet break-fast on the balcony and killer views. Despite all these perks, guests agree that the thing that makes this place special is the hospi-tality shown by the hosts. It's 300m west of Parque Central.

Hotel Central Loft HOTEL $$

(Map p246; ☑2479-9004; hotelcentralloft.com; cnr Calle 2 & Av Central; d/tr/q incl breakfast US$75/95/105; ❋🅰🛋) You can't get more central than the Hotel Central Loft, a sur-prisingly upscale place. Fresh, contemporary rooms have tile floors and wooden accents, with volcano views from the little balcony. Noise can be an issue, so you may want to bring your ear plugs.

Hotel Arenal Rabfer HOTEL $$

(Map p246; ☑2479-9187; www.arenalrabfer.com; Calle 1; s/d/tr/q incl breakfast US$75/85/100/115; P❋🅰🛋) Arguably the most architecturally appealing of the downtown options, with a striking shingled 2nd floor. Set up around a pebbled pool area and shady palm garden, the rooms are spacious with high slanted ceilings and fresh coats of paint. Functional but not fancy. Located on a quiet side street, two blocks from the action.

Hotel Las Colinas HOTEL $$

(Map p246; ☑2479-9305; www.lascolinasarenal. com; Calle 1 btwn Avs Central & Arenal; s/d/tr stand-ard US$70/80/100, with balcony US$80/100/110, all incl breakfast; P❋@🅰) 🌱 Stay here and you're likely to spend most of your time on the 2nd-story 'terrace garden,' with ample sun lounges and spectacular views of the volcano. The rooms are simple but stylish, with tile floors and cherry-stained furnishings. The rooms on the 1st floor are dark, so you'll pay more for the sunlit standard units with balconies.

West of La Fortuna

★Roca Negra del Arenal GUESTHOUSE $$
(Map p248; ☑2479-9237; www.hotelrocanegra delarenal.com; d/q US$80/110, breakfast US$7; P✳🛜☒) Plenty of feathered and furry friends roam the grounds at this gem of a guesthouse, located 2km west of town. Along with the ever-charming owner, they make for quite a welcome party. There are seven spacious rooms, each with stained-wood accents, huge tile bathrooms and semiprivate terraces facing the garden (complete with rockers).

But what makes this place so special? It's the paradisaical setting. The luscious tiled pool and Jacuzzi are surrounded with tropical gardens that are bursting with blooms and buzzing with bees and birds. If you came for R&R in exotic environs, look no further.

Arenal Oasis BUNGALOW $$
(Map p248; ☑2479-9526; www.arenaloasis.com; d US$78; P🛜) 🐾 Located only 3km from the center of La Fortuna but still surrounded by vegetation and wildlife, this place is truly an oasis. The accommodations are in dark but cozy log-cabin bungalows, with private porches facing the rainforest. It's a family-run operation that truly lends a personal touch.

Arenal Oasis is located just west of town, 1km south of the main road; turn off at the cemetery.

Hotel Campo Verde BUNGALOW $$
(Map p248; ☑2479-1080; www.hotelcampo verde.com; d/tr/q incl breakfast from $95/110/130; P🛜) An absolutely darling family-owned property, located 9km west of town. Canary-yellow wooden bungalows have vaulted beamed ceilings, two queen beds, lovely drapes and chandeliers, and a sweet tiled patio blessed with two waiting rockers. Book the wooden bungalows furthest from the road at the foot of the mountain, where the views are unbeatable.

Erupciones Inn B&B B&B $$
(Map p248; ☑2479-1400; www.erupcionesinn.com; d incl breakfast US$65-75; P✳🛜) You can ad-mire Arenal from every single colorful *cabina* at this riverside property 11km from La Fortuna. Take a seat on your private patio and take it in. The cheaper *cabinas* are a bit tired on the inside, while the more expensive ones are bigger and more polished. Overall, service is sweet. And did we mention the views?

El Silencio del Campo LODGE $$$
(Map p248; ☑2479-7055; www.hotelsilenciodel campo.com; d/tr/q incl breakfast US$215/255/280; P✳☒) This lovely lodge about 4km west of town has 24 stand-alone cabins that are luxurious without being showy. The property's pièce de résistance, though, is the hot spring – for guests only – with half a dozen decadent pools in a range of temperatures. Guests can also experience life on a working farm (try your hand at milking a cow) and feast on fresh eggs for breakfast.

Nayara Hotel, Spa & Gardens HOTEL $$$
(Map p248; ☑2479-1600; www.arenalnayara. com; r/ste incl breakfast US$320/440; P✳@🛜☒) This intimate and indulgent hotel, 6km west of town, has amassed a slew of awards for its Asian-inspired architecture, minimalist decor and richly romantic setting. The 24 rooms have exquisite furnishings and bedding, rich woods, high-tech gadgetry, outdoor showers and private outdoor Jacuzzis where you can soak up views of Volcán Arenal. Exquisite.

Arenal Volcano Inn INN $$$
(Map p248; ☑2479-1122; www.arenalvolcanoinn. com; s/d/tr from US$125/135/155; P✳🛜☒) Resembling an upper-middle-class suburb of Arenal, about 6km northwest of La Fortuna, this appealing lodging has sidewalks winding through perfectly manicured lawns, connecting the attractive bungalows and swimming pool. The bungalows are lined up on the hillside, opening to private terraces that face the mighty mountain. Inside, clean, white walls and linens are complemented by dark stained wood trimmings, with all the amenities to ensure your upper-middle-class comfort.

South of La Fortuna

Finca Luna Nueva LODGE $$
(☑2468-0864; www.fincalunanuevalodge.com; s/d/tr incl breakfast US$95/105/120; ☒) 🐾 Bordering the Children's Eternal Rainforest, this special place started as a spice farm then blossomed into an ecolodge. It's a pretty

impressive amalgam of sustainability and luxury, featuring lovely *casas* built from reclaimed wood, an ozonated swimming pool, solar-heated Jacuzzi, a huge medicinal plant garden and an amazing restaurant, supplied by the on-site organic farm. Located about 17km south of La Fortuna, in the village of San Isidro.

Hotel Cerro Azul
BUNGALOW $$

(Map p248; ☑2479-7360; www.ranchocerroazul. com; d/tr/q US$90/105/120; P✳☞) Five cute, shingled cabins face the parking lot but back up to the forest, with private porches overlooking the trees. A 200m trail leads to the rushing river, with the volcano beyond. The cabins have woody interiors and stylish details. Think: simple, natural, beautiful, comfortable.

Catarata Eco-Lodge
LODGE $$

(Map p248; ☑2479-9522; www.cataratalodge. com; s/d/tr/q incl breakfast US$80/85/100/115; P☞☒) ✐ Set at the base of Cerro Chato and surrounded by forest, this place is ideal if you want to get away from it all (but not too far away, as you're still just 4km from town). The digs are decent little Spanish-tile and wood rooms, with hammocks strung on the terrace. The restaurant is also recommended.

Chachagua Rainforest Hotel
HOTEL $$$

(Map p248; ☑2468-1020; www.chachaguarainfor esthotel.com; d/bungalow incl breakfast US$180/ 215; P⊜✳☞☒) Situated on a private reserve that abuts the Bosque Eterno de Los Niños, this hotel is a naturalist's dream. Part of the property is a working orchard, cattle ranch and fish farm, while the rest is humid rainforest. Explore it on hiking trails or on horseback. The rooms are nice but arguably overpriced, while the stylish, spacious bungalows are gorgeous as all get-out.

Drive 11km south of La Fortuna. On the southern side of Chachagua, fork right off the main road and follow the signs on a 2km dirt track that may require a 4WD in the rainy season.

Casa Luna Hotel & Spa
HOTEL $$$

(Map p248; ☑2479-7368; www.casalunahotel. com; s/d incl breakfast US$135/145; P✳@☞☒) The snazziest joint on this rustic road, this walled-off complex initially seems like a gated community. But, once inside, you'll see that the landscaped gardens and adobe-style lodgings are lovely. Wooden doors open into 36 elegant, split-level duplexes with tiny

private patios. There's a full menu of spa treatments, and guests rave about the attentive service.

Green Lagoon
HOTEL $$$

(Map p248; ☑2479-7700; www.greenlagoon.net; d US$110) Perched high up on the mountain above the Río Fortuna Catarata, this 'well-being resort' is great for birders and froggers, er, frog-lovers – especially with the resident naturalist on hand to point out specimens. The rooms are fairly plain, but comfortable. The 'wellness' comes in with spa services, garden and vegetarian restaurant. Rates include admission to hike to Cerro Chato.

✖ Eating

Unless you're eating exclusively at *sodas*, you'll find the restaurants in La Fortuna to be more expensive than in other parts of the country. But there are some excellent, innovative kitchens, including a few that are part of the farm-to-table movement. The restaurants are mostly clustered in town, but there are also places to eat on the road heading west.

Rainforest Café
CAFE $

(Map p246; ☑2479-7239; Calle 1 btwn Avs Central & Arenal; mains US$4-6; ⊙7am-8:30pm; ☞✐) We know it's bad form to start with dessert, but the irresistible sweets at this popular spot are beautiful to behold and delicious to devour. The savory menu features tasty burritos, *casados*, sandwiches etc. There's also a full menu of hot and cold coffee, including some tempting specialty drinks (Mono Loco = coffee, banana, milk, chocolate and cinnamon).

There's a dash of urban-coffeehouse atmosphere here. Must be the writing in the milk foam.

La Central
CAFE $

(Map p246; ☑2479-8080; cnr Calle 2 & Av Central; breakfast US$3, mains US$4-8; ⊙8am-6pm Wed-Mon; ☞✐) A breezy terrace, filled with greenery and art, this is a perfect stop for breakfast or lunch. The place touts natural healthy food, and you'll find lots of vegetarian options – fresh, hearty salads, a tasty veggie burger, and a Middle Eastern spread with hummus and baba ganoush. Come later in the day for fresh fruit-juice cocktails and occasional live music acts.

Soda Viquez
SODA $

(Map p246; ☑2479-7133; cnr Calle 1 & Av Arenal; mains US$6-10; ⊙7am-10pm; ✐) Travelers adore the 'local flavor' that's served up at

Soda Viquez (in all senses of the expression). It's a super-friendly spot, offering tasty *tipica,* especially *casados,* rice dishes and fresh fruit *batidos*. Prices are reasonable, portions ample.

Soda la Hormiga SODA $
(Map p246; Av Arenal; mains US$3-5; ☺6am-4pm) Locally beloved and set conveniently next door to the bus station, this open-air lunch counter is one of the quaintest, cheapest *sodas* in town. It does all the *casados,* as well as big breakfasts and burgers.

Mega Super SUPERMARKET $
(Map p246; Av Arenal; ☺7am-9pm Mon-Sat, to 8pm Sun) Next to the bus terminal, this spacious supermarket is a good place to visit before that long bus ride.

Chifa La Familia Feliz FUSION $$
(Map p246; ☏8469-6327; Calle 2; mains US$8-12; ☺11am-10pm; 🎀🖥🍴) If you're looking for a change of taste – a *real* change from *casados* and pizza – check this out. In case you didn't know, *Chifa* means 'Chinese food' in Peruvian-Spanish. So what we have here is Peruvian Chinese food, which is something special indeed. The chef goes out of his way to welcome and satisfy all comers.

Anch'io Ristorante & Pizzeria ITALIAN $$
(Map p246; ☏2479-7024; Av Central; mains US$10-18; ☺noon-10pm; 🅿🖥🍴) If you have a hankering for pizza, you can't do better than Anch'io, where the crust is crispy thin, the toppings are plentiful, and the pie is cooked in a wood-fired oven. Start yourself off with a traditional antipasto. Accompany with cold beer or a bottle of red. Add super service and pleasant patio seating. And you've got yourself a winner.

Café Mediterraneo ITALIAN $$
(Map p246; ☏2479-7497; Calle 2; mains US$8-12; ☺11am-10pm) It's worth the jaunt out of town to eat at this delightful osteria, which cooks up homemade pasta dishes and wood-fired pizza. Customers rave about the personable service and decadent desserts. Nutella pizza? *Sì, grazie!*

Kappa Sushi SUSHI $$
(Map p246; Calle 1 & Ave Fort; sushi & rolls US$7-10; ☺noon-10pm; 🍴) When you're surrounded by mountains and cattle farms, who's thinking of sushi? Well, think of it. The fish is fresh (you're not *that* far from the ocean) and the preparations are innovative. The dragon roll (shrimp tempura, avocado and eel sauce) is

a favorite. Sit at an outside table and enjoy the view of Arenal while you feast on raw fish – or go for the veg options.

Lava Lounge INTERNATIONAL $$
(Map p246; ☏2479-7365; www.lavaloungecostarica.com; Av Central btwn Calles 4 & 2; mains US$8-12; ☺7am-10:30pm; 🅿🎀🍴) This hip, open-air restaurant is a relief when you just can't abide another *casado.* There is pizza and pasta, wraps and salads, with loads of vegetarian options. Both food and service are variable, but the picnic tables and *palapa* roof create a cool, rustic vibe. Add colorful cocktails and occasional live reggae music, and the place is pretty irresistible.

★Benedictus Steakhouse STEAK $$$
(Map p248; ☏2479-1912; www.facebook.com/benedictussteakhouse; mains US$14-30; ☺noon-10pm) 🌿 Turn off the highway and drive about 1km up a steep, rough dirt road to arrive at this spectacularly situated steak house (tricky to find in the dark, so arrive before the sun goes down). You'll be rewarded with a gorgeous view, followed by an amazing meal. In addition to the meats, there is heavenly homemade bread, fantastic *ceviche* and tantalizing desserts.

The steaks come from free-range cattle that graze on grass in the pastures below the restaurant. They also raise lambs, chickens and pigs. Veggies come from the organic greenhouse. Farm to table direct. Speaking of tables, there are only a few of them, so make sure you reserve.

Restaurant Don Rufino INTERNATIONAL $$$
(Map p246; ☏2479-9997; www.donrufino.com; cnr Av Central & Calle 3; mains US$16-40; ☺11am-11pm) The vibe is trendy and the service is hopping at this indoor-outdoor grill. The highlight of the menu is the perfectly prepared grilled meats. If you're cutting back, go for Grandma's BBQ chicken (seasoned with chocolate, wrapped in a banana leaf) or the chef's special tuna (seasoned with ginger oil, served with rice noodles, tamarind sauce and cashew nuts).

🍺 Drinking & Nightlife

El Establo BAR
(Map p246; ☏2479-7675; Calle 2; ☺5pm-2am Wed-Sat) La Fortuna's raucous *sendero* bar with an attached disco fronts the bull ring and attracts an ever-enthusiastic local following. The age demographic here ranges from 18 to 88. That's almost always a good thing.

Vagabondo Reggae Bar
BAR

(Map p248; 2479-8087; Av Central; ⊙8pm-2am) Chill out with cheap beers and good vibes at this super-relaxed reggae bar, located about 2km west of town. Behind the lion's face, you'll find a dimly lit bar, populated by both Ticos and tourists, playing pool and (maybe) dancing.

Down to Earth
COFFEE

(Map p246; 2479-8568; www.godowntoearth. org; Calle 2; ⊙8am-8pm) This place is all about the coffee, which is brewed from single-origin beans from the owner's farm in the Dota Tarrazu Valley. There's no food here, just coffee – smooth, strong and revitalizing. Drink it, or buy some beans to take home. Sure, it's kind of pricey, but so is Starbucks.

Shopping

Hecho A Mano
HANDICRAFTS

(Handmade Art Shop; Map p246; 8611-0018; www.facebook.com/handmadeartshop; Calle 1; ⊙9am-10pm) There's no shortage of souvenirs for sale in La Fortuna. But this unique shop is something special, carrying an excellent selection of arts and crafts by local and national artists. You'll find representative pieces from Costa Rica's many subcultures, including Boruca masks, rasta handicrafts, lots of macrame and some lovely handmade jewelry.

Neptune's House of Hammocks
HOMEWARES

(Map p248; 2479-8269; ⊙8am-6pm) On the road to La Catarata de la Fortuna, it sells soft drinks and hammocks (US$50 to US$170). Take a breather and try one out.

ⓘ Information

MEDICAL SERVICES

Centro Medico Sanar (2479-9420; cnr Calle 5 & Av Fort; ⊙8am-8:30pm) Medical consultation, ambulance services and pharmacy.

Servicios Contables Mario Esquivel (2460-8989, 2479-7027; www.secmesa.com; Calle 1; ⊙24hr) Located in the Hotel Las Colinas building, this private clinic is open 24/7 and has English-speaking staff.

MONEY

Line up to get some colones (or dollars) at banks all around town.

BAC San José (cnr Av Fort & Calle 3; ⊙9am-6pm Mon-Fri, to 1pm Sat)

Banco de Costa Rica (Av Central; ⊙9am-4pm Mon-Fri)

Banco Nacional (cnr Calle 1 & Av Fort; ⊙8:30am-3:45pm Mon-Fri)

Banco Popular (2479-9422; cnr Av Central & Calle 5; ⊙8:45am-4:30pm Mon-Fri, 8:15-11:30am Sat)

POST

The **Correos de Costa Rica** (Map p246; Av Fort; ⊙8am-5:30pm Mon-Fri, 7:30am-noon Sat) is located northeast of the Parque Central.

ⓘ Getting There & Away

TAXI-BOAT-TAXI

The fastest route between Monteverde-Santa Elena and La Fortuna is the taxi-boat-taxi combo (formerly known as jeep-boat-jeep, which sounds sexy but it was the same thing). It is actually a minivan with the requisite yellow 'turismo' tattoo, which takes you to Laguna de Arenal, meeting a boat that crosses the lake, where a 4WD taxi on the other side continues to Monteverde. It's a terrific transportation option that can be arranged through almost any hotel or tour operator (US$25 to US$35, four hours).

This is increasingly becoming the primary transportation between La Fortuna and Monteverde as it's incredibly scenic and reasonably priced.

ⓘ Getting Around

BICYCLE

Biking is a reasonable option to get around town and reach some of the top tourist attractions. The challenging 7km ride from town to La Catarata is a classic. Make advance arrangement to rent a bike from Bike Arenal (p245) and they'll drop it off at your hotel.

CAR

La Fortuna is easy to access by public transportation, but nearby attractions such as the hot springs, Parque Nacional Volcán Arenal and Laguna de Arenal demand internal combustion (or a tour operator). If you're thinking of doing a day trip to Río Celeste, Caño Negro or Venada Caves, you might also consider renting a car for the day.

Adobe Rent a Car (2479-7202; www.adobe car.com; Av Arenal; ⊙8am-5pm)

Alamo (2479-9090; www.alamocostarica. com; cnr Av Central & Calle 2; ⊙7:30am-5:30pm)

BUSES FROM LA FORTUNA

The **bus terminal** (Map p246; Av Arenal) is on the river road. Keep an eye on your bags, particularly on the weekend San José run.

DESTINATION	COMPANY	COST (US$)	DURATION (HR)	FREQUENCY
Ciudad Quesada (San Carlos)	Auto-Transportes San José–San Carlos	2	1	12 daily, 4:30am to 7pm
San José*	Auto-Transportes San José–San Carlos	5	4	12:45pm, 2:45pm
San Ramon via Chachagua		2	2	6am, 9am, 12:30pm, 4pm
Tilarán, with connection to Monteverde**	Auto-Transportes Tilarán, departs from the Parque Central	3	3½	8am, 4:30pm

* Alternatively, take the bus to Ciudad Quesada, from where there are frequent departures to San José.

** To reach Monteverde (US$4, six to eight hours), take the early bus to Tilarán, where you'll have to wait a few hours for the onward bus to Santa Elena.

Parque Nacional Volcán Arenal

For most of modern history, Volcán Arenal was just another dormant volcano surrounded by fertile farmland. But for about 42 years – from its destructive explosion in 1968 until its sudden subsiding in 2010 – the volcano was an ever-active and awe-striking natural wonder, producing menacing ash columns, massive explosions and streams of glowing molten rock almost daily.

The fiery views are gone for now, but **Arenal** (Map p248; ☑2461-8499; adult/child US$15/5; ☺8am-4pm) is still a worthy destination, thanks to the dense forest covering her lower slopes and foothills, and her picture-perfect conical shape up top (often shrouded in clouds, but still). The Parque Nacional Volcán Arenal is part of the Area de Conservación Arenal, which protects most of the Cordillera de Tilarán. This area is rugged and varied, rich with wildlife and laced with trails.

🏃 Activities

Hiking

From the ranger station (which has trail maps available) you can hike the **Sendero Los Heliconias**, a 1km circular track that passes by the site of the 1968 lava flow. A 1.5km-long path branches off this trail and leads to an overlook. The **Sendero Las Co**ladas also branches off the Heliconias trail and wraps around the volcano for 2km past the 1993 lava flow before connecting with the **Sendero Los Tucanes**, which extends for another 3km through the tropical rainforest at the base of the volcano. To return to the parking area, you'll have to turn back – you'll get good views of the summit on the way.

From the park headquarters (not the ranger station) is the 1.3km **Sendero Los Miradores**, which leads down to the shores of the volcanic lake and provides a good angle for volcano viewing. Also from park headquarters, the **Old Lava Flow Trail** is an interesting and strenuous lower elevation trail following the flow of the massive 1992 eruption. The 4km round trip takes two hours to complete. If you want to keep hiking, combine it with the **Sendero El Ceibo**, a scenic 1.8km trail through secondary forest.

There are additional trails departing from Arenal Observatory Lodge and on a nearby private reserve.

Cerro Chato Trail   HIKING
(Map p248; www.arenalobservatorylodge.com; Arenal Observatory Lodge; day pass per person US$10) The ultimate hike in the national park, the Cerro Chato Trail meanders through pasture before climbing steeply into patches of virgin growth, reaching into misty sky. The trail crests Cerro Chato, Arenal's dormant partner, and ends in

a 1100m-high volcanic lake that is perfect for a dip. The hike is only 8km round trip, but it will take two to three hours each way.

The trail starts at the Arenal Observatory Lodge on the western side of the volcano, or there is an alternative, even more strenuous route that departs from La Catarata de la Fortuna (p244) and approaches from the east. If you're taking the western route, be sure to enter the Observatory Lodge to get on the correct trail; bypass the dodgy operation that has set up shop just outside the gates.

Waterfall Trail   HIKING
(Map p248; www.arenalobservatorylodge.com; Arenal Observatory Lodge; day pass per person US$10) This scenic hike departing from the Arenal Observatory Lodge is an easy, 2km round-trip hike to a 12m waterfall. The terrain starts out flat then descends into a grotto where you'll find a thundering gusher of a waterfall. You'll feel the mist long before you see its majesty.

Arenal 1968   HIKING
(Map p248; ☏2462-1212; www.arenal1968.com; admission US$12, mountain bike rental US$45; ☉7am-10pm) Right next to the park entrance, you'll find a private network of trails along the original 1968 lava flow. There's a *mirador* (lookout) which on a clear day offers a picture-perfect volcano view. Mountain bikes are available to ride on these trails. It's located 1.2km from the highway turnoff to the park, just before the ranger station.

☞ Tours

In addition to hiking, it's also possible to explore the park on horseback, mountain bike or ATV.

Arenal Wilberth Stables   HORSEBACK RIDING
(Map p248; ☏2479-7522; www.arenalwilberth stable.com; per person US$65; ☉7:30am, 11am & 2:30pm) Three-hour horseback-riding tours depart from these stables, at the foot of Arenal. The ride takes in forest and farmland, as well as lake and volcano views. The stables are opposite the entrance to the national park, but there's an office in town next to Arenal Resort Hostel.

⌂ Sleeping

Arenal Observatory Lodge   LODGE $$$
(Map p248; ☏2479-1070, reservations 2290-7011; www.arenalobservatorylodge.com; d/tr/q without bathroom US$100/$115/130, with bathroom from

US$140/155/185; ⓟ🖭@🛜🏊) Set high on the Arenal slopes, this sensational, sprawling lodge is the only accommodation in the national park. Rooms range from La Casona's rustic doubles with shared bathrooms and views from the porch, to plus junior suites, with king-size beds, local art and huge picture windows framing the volcano. Most of the rooms fall somewhere in the middle of this range.

There's a decent international restaurant on the grounds (as there's obviously nowhere else to eat in the area). There's also a small museum, with exhibits on the history, volcanology and hydrology of Arenal. Rates include access to the swimming pool and hiking trails, as well as a free guided walk each morning.

❶ Information

The **ranger station** (☏2461-8499; adult/child US$15/5; ☉8am-4pm) is on the western side of the volcano. The complex housing the station includes an information center and parking lot. From here, trails lead 3.4km toward the volcano.

❶ Getting There & Away

To get to the ranger station by car, head west from La Fortuna for 15km, then turn left at the 'Parque Nacional' sign and take the 2km good dirt road to the entrance on the left side of the road. You can also take an 8am bus toward Tilarán (tell the driver to drop you off at the park) and catch the 2pm bus back to La Fortuna.

If you are heading to Arenal Observatory Lodge, continue driving on the dirt road. About 3km past the ranger station you will come to a small one-lane bridge and parking area. After crossing the bridge you'll reach a fork in the road; left goes to Arenal Observatory Lodge and right goes to the village of El Castillo. Turn left and continue 2.6km to reach the lodge. This steep, hard-packed gravel and partially paved road is fine for most vehicles, but a 4WD is recommended.

A taxi from La Fortuna to either the lodge or El Castillo will cost about US$30.

El Castillo

The tiny mountain village of El Castillo is a beautiful, bucolic alternative to La Fortuna, if you don't mind the treacherous roads. This picturesque locale has easy access to Parque Nacional Volcán Arenal and amazing, up-close views of the looming mountain – with none of the traffic or tourist madness of its bigger neighbor.

There is a tight-knit expat community, some of whom have opened appealing lodges and top-notch restaurants. There are hiking trails and swimming holes. There are even a few worthy attractions – a butterfly house and an eco-zoo. The only thing El Castillo doesn't have is pavement. And maybe that's a good thing.

⊙ Sights

El Castillo-Arenal
Butterfly Conservatory
WILDLIFE RESERVE

(☑ 2479-1149; www.butterflyconservatory.org; adult/student US$16/11; ⊙ 8am-4pm) This is more than just a butterfly conservatory (although it has one of the largest butterfly exhibitions in Costa Rica). Altogether there are six domed habitats, a ranarium, an insect museum, a medicinal herb garden, and an hour's worth of trails through a botanic garden and along the river. The birding is also excellent at this peaceful place, which has wonderful volcano views.

Arenal EcoZoo
ZOO

(El Serpentario; ☑ 2479-1059; www.arenalecozoo. com; adult/child US$20/16; ⊙ 8am-7pm) This snake house offers a hands-on animal experience, as in, handling and milking a venomous snake. The EcoZoo is also home to a red-tailed boa (one of the largest snakes in the world), as well as frogs, amphibious lizards, iguanas, turtles, scorpions, tarantulas and butterflies. Come at feeding time if you want to see snakes devouring bugs, frogs and other snakes!

🏃 Activities

Rancho Adventure Tours
ADVENTURE TOUR

(☑ 8302-7318; www.ranchomargot.com; farm tour US$35, other tours US$55) Rancho Margot has a good selection of guided tours, including horseback riding on the southern side of Laguna de Arenal, kayaking on the lake, and touring the ranch to learn about the workings of a sustainable farm.

La Gavilana
TOUR

(☑ 2479-1747, 8433-7902; night hike US$45, waterfall tour US$90, Big Forest hike US$130) The adventurous folks at La Gavilana Herbs & Art offer a two-day 'extreme hike' of the Big Forest trail between El Castillo and San Gerardo (near Santa Elena). Traversing old-growth forests and raging rivers, hikers overnight at the rustic Rancho Maximo in San Gerardo. Dinner and breakfast are provided. La Gavilana offers a few additional adventures,

including an extended night hike and a one-day waterfall tour.

Sky Adventures
CANOPY TOUR

(☑ 2479-4100; www.skyadventures.travel; adult/ child SkyTrek US$77/53, Sky Tram US$44/37, Sky Walk US$37/26, Sky Limit US$77/53; ⊙ 7:30am-4pm) El Castillo's entry in the canopy-tour category has zip lines (Sky Trek), a floating gondola (Sky Tram) and a series of hanging bridges (Sky Walk). It's safe and well run, and visitors tend to leave smiling. A unique combo, Sky River Drift combines a zip line with tree-climbing (and jumping) and river tubing. There's also mountain biking on the property.

🛏 Sleeping

For a tiny place, El Castillo has an impressive range of accommodations, from funky budget lodgings to charming B&Bs to expansive eco-lodges. You'll find them clustered in the village and strung out along the lake shore. If you've got your tent, you can pitch it for free on the lakefront (take the dirt track just across from the church). Best views in town.

Essence Arenal
HOSTEL $

(☑ 2479-1131; www.essencearenal.com; d/tr/q from US$45/55/65, d without bathroom US$30, tents US$30; P @ 🛜 🌊) 🌿 Perched on a 22-hectare hilltop with incredible volcano and lake views, this 'boutique hostel' is the best cheap sleep in the Arenal region. Bed down in a basic but clean room or a fine hip-ified tent, done up with plush bedding and wood furnishings. It's an eclectic, positive-energy place, offering group hikes, yoga classes and good vibes. Guests participate in the loving preparation of vegetarian meals that will delight even the most hardcore carnivore; the restaurant is open 7am to 8pm. Turn left towards the Butterfly Conservatory and continue 1km uphill to the hostel.

Cabinas Los Tucanes
HOTEL $

(☑ 2479-1076; www.arenalcabinaslostucanes.com; d/tr/q US$55/65/80, breakfast US$5; 🛜) Here you'll find huge, bright, spotless and spacious rooms, with plain decor but fabulous vistas from the picture windows. The top-floor rooms catch a nice breeze off the terrace. Fanny and Licho take care of this place, and they'll take care of you too.

Majestic Lodge
GUESTHOUSE $$

(☑ 2479-1085, 8703-1561; www.majesticlodgecos tarica.com; r $95; P ❄ 🛜 🌊) With a prime perch overlooking Laguna de Arenal, this is a lovely boutique lodge. It's easy to hang out all day, enjoying the view from the covered deck or soaking in the gorgeous stone swimming pool (and Jacuzzi). The plush rooms in the lodge have beautiful handcrafted wooden furniture and exquisite tiled bathrooms, while 'Pie in the Sky' *cabinas* also have fully equipped kitchens.

Hummingbird Nest
B&B $$

(Nido del Colibri; ☑ 8835-8711, 2479-1174; www. hummingbirdnestbb.com; d/tr/q incl breakfast US$85/95/100; P ❋ ☎) At the entrance to town, a small path leads up the steep hill to this charming B&B, owned by a former flight attendant and all-round world traveler who found a small slice of paradise to call her own. Her quaint complex has two guest rooms and a garden full of hummingbirds. Soak the night away in a huge outdoor Jacuzzi in the garden. Two-night minimum.

★ Rancho Margot
RESORT, LODGE $$$

(☑ 8302-7318; www.ranchomargot.org; dm per person US$80, bungalow s/d US$250/415, all incl meals; P ☎ ☎ ☎) ✔ Part resort lodge, part organic farm, Rancho Margot is 152 acres of cinematic loveliness, set along the rushing Río Caño Negro and surrounded by rainforested mountains. There are comfortable dorm-style bunkhouse accommodations. If your budget allows, spring for a beautiful teak-furnished bungalow, its deck strung with a hammock and blessed with views of hulking mountains, weeping jungle and placid lake. Two-night minimum.

Prices include a two-hour guided tour of the farm and daily yoga classes. Hiking trails and (free) hot springs are at hand.

Nepenthe
B&B $$$

(☑ 8892-5501; www.nepenthe-costarica.com; d incl breakfast US$115; P ❋ ☎ ☎) The highlight of this sweet place is the spectacular, spring-fed infinity pool overlooking Laguna de Arenal. Lodge-like rooms are simple, tiled numbers with colorful artisanal accents, set in a gentle arc of a ranch-style building. Hammocks on the patio allow you to take it all in. Just down the hill, Agustino's Restaurante also comes highly recommended for dinner.

✖ Eating & Drinking

Your eating options are pretty limited in El Castillo, but there are some good ones – enough to keep you fed for several days at least. In addition to the few places in the vil-

lage, several lodgings on the outskirts have recommended restaurants. Of course, you have many more choices in La Fortuna, but you'll have to traverse 9km of bumpy gravel roads to get there.

★ La Ventanita
CAFE $

(☑ 2479-1735; mains US$3-5; ☒ 10:30am-9pm; ☒) *La Ventanita* refers to the 'little window' at Kelly's house where you place your order. Soon enough, you'll be devouring the best burrito or *chifrijo* (rice and pinto beans with fried pork and capped with fresh tomato salsa and corn chips) that you've ever had, along with a nutritious and delicious *batido* (smoothie). It's typical fare with a twist – pulled pork and bacon burritos, for example. Kelly is a wealth of information about the area, so ask away.

La Gavilana Herbs & Art
BAKERY $

(☑ 2479-1747; www.facebook.com/LaGavilana-HerbsandArt; items US$2-6; ☒ 8am-5pm Mon-Fri, 9am-2pm Sat) Meet Thomas and Hannah. He's Czech and makes the hot sauce and vinegar; she's American and bakes the cookies and breads. Their place is decked with paintings (by Hannah), while the grounds contain a food forest (by Thomas), filled with medicinal herbs and fruit trees. The whole place is filled with love, beauty and creativity. It's 100m uphill from Essence Arenal hostel.

Fusion Grill
FUSION $$

(☑ 2479-1949; www.fusiongrillrestaurant.com; mains US$8-15; ☒ 7am-10pm) Set in an open-air dining room with an incredible vista of the volcano, Fusion Grill shows off a little swank (at least, more than other restaurants in El Castillo). Chef Benedictus is rightly proud of his *ceviche*, but he has a full, solid menu, featuring steaks and seafood and phenomenal desserts.

Howlers Bar & Grill
BAR

(☑ 2479-1785; www.facebook.com/howlersbarand grill; ☒ noon-10pm Tue-Sun) This lakefront bar is a fun choice for a night out drinking in El Castillo. (Good thing, as it's your only choice.) The American-style pub grub is excellent, as is the cold draught beer. It's a popular place for the expat community to congregate, guaranteeing an upbeat, *pura vida* vibe.

❶ Getting There & Away

El Castillo is located 8km past the entrance to Parque Nacional Volcán Arenal. It's a rough gravel road, and it only gets worse once you get to the

CHLAUS LOTSCHER / GETTY IMAGES ©

1. Wildlife, Laguna de Arenal (p262)
Euphonias are among the many vividly hued birds to watch for in this scenic lake region.

2. Tabacón Hot Springs (p246)
Soak up the ambience amid lush flora and a 40°C waterfall cascading over an artificial cliff.

3. Catarata Río Fortuna (p244)
Best viewed from the jungle floor, this 70m waterfall pours through a canyon of fern-covered volcanic rock.

4. Volcán Arenal (p256)
Known for its massive eruptions from 1968 to 2010, Arenal is a rugged, awe-inspiring hiking destination.

village. A 4WD is required in the rainy season and recommended year-round.

There is no public transportation, but a private **shuttle bus** (☑ 8887-9141) runs from the MegaSuper in La Fortuna (one hour, US$10). The bus departs Rancho Margot at 6am, 10am and 4pm, returning from La Fortuna at 7am, 12:30pm and 5:15pm. The schedule is subject to change; reservations are required anyway so it's best to call ahead.

Laguna de Arenal

About 18km west of La Fortuna you'll arrive at a 750m-long causeway across the dam that created Laguna de Arenal, the largest lake in the country at 88 sq km. A number of small towns were submerged during its creation, but the lake now supplies valuable water to Guanacaste and produces hydroelectricity for the region. High winds also produce power with the aid of huge steel windmills, though windsurfers and kitesurfers frequently steal a breeze or two.

This is one of the premier road trips in Costa Rica. The road is lined with odd and elegant businesses; strong winds and high elevations give the lake a temperate feel and the scenic views of lakeside forests and Volcán Arenal are about as romantic as they come.

A drive around the lake reveals a string of sweet lodging options, from cozy B&Bs to yoga retreats to jungle spas, many of them foreign owned. The only population center of note is Nuevo Arenal, where you'll also find the only budget accommodations on the lake. Finances aside, these properties on the lake are enticing places to spend a night or two. Or 10. But be careful: there's a strong and growing community of expats around Laguna de Arenal – people who came for a visit and never left…

🏃 Activities

Laguna de Arenal offers scores of secluded bays and coves to explore as well as a forested island. You'll usually find a kayak concession set up on the western end of the dam, but take care because when the wind kicks in it can be a nightmare to make it back. This is also a popular route for cycling (inquire at Bike Arenal; p245), as well as a few other attractions in the area.

Mistico Hanging Bridges   CANOPY TOUR
(Puentes Cogantes de Arenal; Map p248; ☑ 2479-8282; www.misticopark.com; admission adult/child US$24/free, tours US$36-47; ⊙ 7:30am-4:30pm,

tours 6am, 9am & 2pm) Unlike the fly-by view you'll get on a zip-line canopy tour, a walk along these hanging bridges allows you to explore the rainforest and canopy from six suspended bridges and 10 traditional bridges at a more natural and peaceful pace. The longest swaying bridge is 97m long and the highest is 25m above the earth. All are accessible from a single 3km trail that winds through a tunnel and skirts a waterfall.

Reservations are required for guided bird-watching tours or informative naturalist tours. The Tilarán bus can drop you off at the entrance, but it's a 3km climb from the bus stop. There are also loads of tours from La Fortuna.

La Roca Canyoneering   ADVENTURE TOUR
(Map p248; ☑ 2479-9800; www.canyoneering laroca.com; tour US$95) Rappelling into river canyons, zip lines, hanging bridges, a Tarzan swing, swimming and snacks are packed into this adrenaline-pumping half-day tour. Make sure you bring a change of clothes, as you will get wet. La Roca is 4km from the dam; it also has an office at Sunset Tours (Map p246; ☑ 2479-9800; www.sunsettour.net; Calle 2; ⊙ 6:30am-9pm) in La Fortuna.

Arenal Kayaks   KAYAKING
(☑ 2694-4336; www.arenalkayaks.com; 2hr tour US$35) Two-hour guided paddle on Laguna de Arenal, including wildlife-watching and swim stops. Hotel pick-up included.

Represa Arenal

Forget for a moment that there are always ecological issues associated with dams and revel in the fact that this one created a rather magnificent lake. In the absence of wind, the glassy surface of Represa Arenal (Arenal Dam) reflects the volcano and the surrounding mountains teeming with cloud forest. Crowds congregate to admire the view and snap photos. (Unfortunately, there's no convenient place to stop, so you'll often encounter a minor traffic jam, especially at the dam's western end.)

At the eastern end of the dam, there's a hairpin turnoff and the road heads sharply up the hillside, leading to a small enclave of lodges and attractions.

🛏 Sleeping

Lost Iguana   RESORT $$$
(Map p248; ☑ 2479-1557; www.lostiguanacr.com; r/ ste incl breakfast US$275/310; 🅿 ❄ @ 🛜 🏊) This stylish and splashy tropical resort, just 1.5km

from the dam, is set among lush rainforest and rushing streams with glorious volcano views at every turn. Luxurious rooms have private balconies looking out on Arenal, beds made with Egyptian cotton sheets, a terra-cotta wet bar, and an invaluable sense of peace and privacy. Upgrade to a suite for a Jacuzzi tub or outdoor rain shower.

Also on the grounds: a romantic restaurant, a gorgeous bi-level pool with swim-up bar, and the well-equipped Golden Gecko Spa.

Arenal Lodge   LODGE $$$
(Map p248; ☑ 2479-1881; www.arenallodge.net; d standard/superior US$115/120, f US$150, junior ste US$165, all incl breakfast; P ※ ☎ ☒) Arenal Lodge is at the top of a steep 2.5km ascent, though the entire lodge is awash with views of Arenal and the surrounding cloud forest. Standard rooms are just that, but the spacious junior suites are tiled and have wicker furniture and a picture window or balcony with volcano views.

The grounds are crisscrossed by hiking trails, and the lodge also has a Jacuzzi, a billiards room, a restaurant and private stables.

❶ Getting There & Away

The Represa Arenal (Arenal Dam) is about 18km west of La Fortuna. It's an easy drive if you have your own vehicle. If not, there are plenty of tour operators (or taxis) who will bring you to this corner of the region. You can also wait for the bus to Tilarán, which runs twice a day.

Nuevo Arenal

Although steeped in aging *extranjero cultura* (expat culture), this two-horse town still feels very Tico. A rest stop for travelers heading to Tilarán and points beyond, it's certainly a pleasant (and cheap) place to spend the night. The tiny downtown also has a gas station, two banks, a supermarket and a bus stop near the park. It even has a rickety old *plaza del toros*.

In case you were wondering what happened to old Arenal, it's about 27m below the surface of Laguna de Arenal. In order to create a large enough reservoir for the dam, the Costa Rican government had to make certain, er, sacrifices, which ultimately resulted in the forced relocation of 3500 people. Today the humble residents of Nuevo Arenal don't seem to be fazed by history, especially since they now own premium lakeside property.

WINDSURFING

Consistent winds blow across northwestern Costa Rica, and this consistency attracts wind riders. Laguna de Arenal is rated one of the best windsurfing spots in the world, and kitesurfers sail here too. From late November to April, **Tico Wind** (☑ 2692-2002, 8383-2694; www.ticowind.com; SUP/kitesurf/windsurf rental per day US$20/90/96, windsurfing lessons per hr US$50; ☺ Nov-Apr) sets up camp on the lake shore and offers lessons in both. It has state-of-the-art boards and sails, with equipment to suit varied wind conditions. The launch is located 15km west of Nuevo Arenal. The entrance is by the big, white chain-link fence with 'ICE' painted on it. Follow the dirt road 1km to the shore. It gets a little chilly on Laguna de Arenal, and rentals usually include wetsuits, as well as harnesses and helmets.

🛏 Sleeping

There are a few budget options right in town, in addition to the expat-owned properties that line the lake.

Aurora Inn   HOTEL $
(☑ 2694-4245; r US$24; P @ ☎ ☒) You'd never know it from the street, but these rooms are rather sweet, spotless, spacious, wood cabin–like constructions with lovely lake views and vaulted beamed ceilings. Located on the eastern side of the square, it's one of the only budget options on Laguna de Arenal. The attached restaurant does decent pizza.

★ La Ceiba Tree Lodge   LODGE $$
(☑ 2692-8050, 8313-1475; www.ceibatree-lodge.com; s/d/tr/q from US$65/90/115/135; P ※ ☎) About 22km west of the dam, this lovely, laid-back lodge overlooks a magnificent 54m ceiba tree. Seven spacious, Spanish-tile rooms are hung with original paintings and fronted by Maya-inspired carved doors. Each room has rustic artifacts, polished-wood ceilings and vast views of Laguna de Arenal. The tropical gardens and spacious terrace make this mountaintop spot a tranquil retreat.

Agua Inn   B&B $$
(☑ 2694-4218; www.aguainnspa.com; d incl breakfast US$80; P ☎ ☒) The sound of the rushing river will lull you to sleep at this intimate

B&B on the banks of the rainforest-shaded Río Cote. This gorgeous property is designed for total relaxation and rejuvenation, with a jungle-shaded pool and a private lake trail. Four simple rooms feature soothing tones and plush linens, with a shared balcony providing a lovely view over the property.

Villa Decary
B&B **$$$**

(✆ 2694-4330, in US or Canada 1-800-556-0505; www.villadecary.com; r/casitas incl breakfast US$125/160; P❋🖢) This country inn 2km east of Nuevo Arenal is an all-round winner, offering epic views and unparalleled hospitality. Elegant, spacious rooms are decorated with bright serape bedspreads and original artwork, boasting balconies with excellent views of the woodland below and the lake beyond. There are larger *casitas* (sleeping four) with kitchenettes. The trails behind the house offer excellent opportunities for birding.

Decary also boasts one of the best collections of palm trees in Costa Rica, which explains why it's named for a French botanist who discovered a new species of palm. It's 24.5km west of the dam.

Lucky Bug B&B
B&B **$$$**

(✆ 2694-4515; www.luckybugcr.net; d/ste incl breakfast from US$100/120; P🖢🖫) Set on a rainforest lagoon, 3km west of Nuevo Arenal, the five blissfully isolated bungalows at the Lucky Bug feature works and decorative details by local artisans. Here are blond-wood floors, wrought-iron butterflies, hand-painted geckos, mosaic washbasins and end tables. Each room is unique and captivating. There's a rainforest trail in the grounds and kayaks for use on the lagoon.

There is also an on-site Caballo Negro Restaurant and the fabulously quirky Lucky Bug Gallery. Should you fall in love with a painting of a bug or something bigger, they can ship it for you.

La Mansion
INN **$$$**

(Map p248; ✆ 2692-8018; www.lamansionarenal.com; d/ste incl breakfast from US$205/225; 🖫) About 15.5km west of the dam, La Mansion enjoys amazing lake views from the cottages, pool and restaurant. The large split-level rooms feature king-size beds, private terraces and mural-painted walls. The fabulous infinity lap pool is surrounded by a relaxing patio and an ornamental garden featuring Chorotega pottery. Lovely all around.

With a bar shaped like the bow of a ship, on-site restaurant Le Bistro is a romantic spot for lunch or dinner, with panoramic views from the dining room and outdoor patio. It has a substantial menu of well-prepared European fare. There's quite a show at sunset.

Hotel Los Héroes
HOTEL **$$$**

(Map p248; ✆ 2692-8012, 2692-8013; www.pequenahelvecia.com; d US$95-125, ste US$125-150, all incl breakfast; P🖢🖫) Los Héroes looks like a Swiss village, centered on a charming chapel complete with chimes. The alpine chalet, midway between the dam and Nuevo Arenal, has large, immaculate but rather innocuous rooms. There's a working dairy on the grounds. A narrow-gauge train (Map p248; per person US$10; ⏱11:30am & 1pm) chugs up the hill, bringing guests to the revolving Rondorama Panoramic Restaurant (unique in Costa Rica!).

🍴 Eating & Drinking

Nuevo Arenal is a surprising little foodie Shangri-la, with enough eating options to keep you out of the kitchen for at least a week. In addition to the charming (and quite delicious) places in town, you'll also find one of the country's top-rated restaurants in a charming and disarming gingerbread house on the lake shore.

Moya's Place
CAFE, PIZZA **$$**

(✆ 2694-4001; mains US$6-12; ⏱11am-10pm) Murals, masks and other indigenous-inspired art adorn the walls at this friendly cafe. Take your pick from the delicious sandwiches, well-stuffed wraps and burritos, and tasty thin-crust pizza. This place is a sort of local gathering spot, where Ticos and expats alike gather to eat, drink and laugh. The food is good and the beer is cold.

Tinajas Arenal
CAFE **$$**

(✆ 2694-4667, 8926-3365; www.tinajasarenal.com; mains US$9-15; ⏱9am-9:30pm; 🖫🖩🖦) 🌊 With glorious sunsets and a dock for boat access, this new lakeside retreat is a hidden gem. The chef – who honed his skills nearby at La Mansion – has created a menu of traditional favorites and new surprises, using fresh seafood and organic ingredients grown right here. Sample the refreshing cocktail *a la casa*, Limon Hierba (lemonade with mint).

At the southern end of Nuevo Arenal, turn off the main road and follow the signs about 2km to Tinajas Arenal.

Los Platillos Voladores
ITALIAN **$$**

(☑2694-5005; www.facebook.com/losplatillosvol adores; mains US$6-14; ⊙11:30am-7:30pm) This Italian carry-out joint gets rave reviews for its homemade pastas, roast chickens and fresh salads. It's mostly Italian – the eggplant Parmesan is delectable – but the rotating menu features a variety of fish, chicken and meat dishes. If you have nowhere to go, you can enjoy your food on the patio with views to the lake.

It's located right in Nuevo Arenal, a half block from the lake road turnoff.

Las Delicias
SODA **$$**

(☑8320-7102; mains US$5-12; ⊙7am-9pm; 🛜) A cheap and cheerful *soda* near the top of the hill as you approach town, with ample wooden-table seating. It does Western-style breakfasts, pasta dishes, quesadillas and grilled steaks on the cheap, but it's known for its *casados*.

Tom's Pan
BAKERY **$$**

(☑2694-4547; mains US$9-16; ⊙8am-4:30pm Mon-Sat; P🛜) Better known as the 'German bakery,' thanks to the signs that litter the lake road, this landmark is a famous rest stop for road-trippers heading to/from Tilarán. Its breads, strudels and cakes are all homemade. It also has German sausages, sandwiches and beer. Surprisingly pricey for the setting.

★Gingerbread Hotel & Restaurant
INTERNATIONAL **$$$**

(☑8351-7815, 2694-0039; www.gingerbreadarenal. com; mains US$25-40; ⊙5-9pm Tue-Sat, lunch by reservation only; ☑) Don't miss the chance to eat at one of the best restaurants in northwestern Costa Rica. Chef Eyal is the larger-than-life, New York–trained Israeli chef who turns out transcendent meals from the freshest local fare. Favorites include mushrooms smothered in gravy, blackened tuna salad, and enormous, juicy, grass-fed burgers. It's big food that goes down well. Cash only.

If you want to sleep where you eat, book one of the sweet boutique rooms upstairs, each showcasing fabulous murals and other artwork by local creatives.

❶ Getting There & Away

Nuevo Arenal is 27km west of the dam, or an hour's drive from La Fortuna. There's not much public transportation in these parts, except the twice-daily bus that runs between La Fortuna and Tilarán.

West End of Laguna Arenal

The hamlet of Piedras anchors the western end of Laguna de Arenal. It's more of an intersection than a town, but it has attracted a group of expats who appreciate the spectacular lakefront scenery and the proximity to Tilarán. This is also where most of the windsurfing goes down.

🛏 Sleeping

There's plenty of good karma at this end of the lake, where you can stay in one of two uplifting yoga lodges.

★Living Forest
B&B **$$**

(☑8708-8822; www.lakearenalretreats.com; s/d US$60/65, dm/d/tr/q without bathroom US$30/ 50/70/80; P🛜🏊) Interior designer, massage therapist, yogi and free spirit: Johanna Harmala has combined these traits to create this inviting, inspiring retreat on the banks of the Río Sabalito, about 15km west of Nuevo Arenal. The jewel-toned rooms are furnished with attractive walnut beds, with shared or private access to beautiful open-air stone bathrooms.

There's a swimming hole, as well as yoga and spa services.

Mystica Lodge
LODGE **$$$**

(☑2692-1001; www.mysticacostarica.com; d incl breakfast US$120-150; ⊙noon-9pm; P@🛜) Here's an invitation to relax and reconnect – with nature, your body and your breath. Comfortable, colorful rooms have Spanish-tile floors, woven bedspreads, wooden accents and a wide, inviting front porch with volcano views. Yoga and meditation classes are held in a gorgeous sheltered hardwood yoga space overlooking a gurgling creek, and there's a tree house healing center for Reiki and massage.

🍴 Eating & Drinking

There are only a few restaurants strung out along the western end of Lagua de Arenal, but they are varied and delicious. You'll have no problem finding a lunch stop to please everyone in the car.

Rock River Rocks
INTERNATIONAL **$**

(☑8726-1200; www.facebook.com/rockriverrocks; mains US$6-9; ⊙8am-4pm Mon-Sat) High up on a hill, with views to the lake, is the new Rock River Rocks, featuring 'Gringo Grub and Books.' For breakfast, there's crazy good huevos rancheros or pumpkin maple French

LOCAL KNOWLEDGE

SCENIC ROUTE

If you're driving between Arenal and Monteverde, consider taking the scenic route through Tronadora and Río Chiquito instead of driving through Tilarán. The distance is a bit longer and the roads are a bit rougher, but the marvelous vistas are well worth it. Look for the turnoff to Río Chiquito about 1km east of Tronadora. Note: if you go this route, there are no gas stations between Nuevo Arenal and Santa Elena, and the gas gets guzzled on the rough mountain roads. Make sure you fill up when you can.

toast. For lunch, you might try a ground lamb burger, with goat cheese and roasted red peppers. For dessert, treat yourself to a new book.

Equus Bar-Restaurant　　　BBQ **$$**
(☏ 8389-2669; mains US$6-14; ⊗ 11am-midnight) Follow your nose to this authentic stone-built tavern, 14.5km west of Nuevo Arenal, where the meat is cooked in an open fire pit, producing decadent, delicious aromas. Take a seat at a wooden-slab picnic table and dig in. A local favorite, this place has been run by the same family for more than a quarter of a century.

Café y Macadamia　　　CAFE **$$**
(☏ 2692-2000; cafeymacadamia@yahoo.com; pastries & coffee US$2-4, mains US$6-13; ⊗ 8am-8pm; P ᛫) We should start by acknowledging that $4 is a lot for a muffin, BUT these banana macadamia nut muffins are irresistible, especially when accompanied by a cup of Costa Rica coffee and a spectacular view over Laguna de Arenal. About 20.5km west of Nuevo Arenal, this is a perfect pit stop during your drive around the lake.

Lake Arenal Hotel & Brewery　　　BREWERY
(☏ 2695-5050; www.lakearenalhotel.com; ⊗ 11am-9pm; ᛫) If you like beer, consider staying at the only hotel (that we're aware of) that has a microbrewery on-site, mixing up the hops and barley to bring you delicious and unusual beers, such as the LAB chili lager and piña blonde. Drink it while feeling the lake breezes and admiring the views at the top-floor restaurant (the food is also good here).

If you wish to spend the night, there are 21 rooms (single/double including breakfast from US$75/85) with rustic bohemian charm, featuring textured paint jobs and interesting art works. You'll pay more for lake views and private patios.

San Luis & Tronadora

San Luis and Tronadora are the tiny twin communities on the southern side of Laguna de Arenal. They are the last outposts of civilization before the landscape gets swallowed by eternal rainforest (the Children's Eternal Rainforest, to be exact) further south and east. A small contingent of travelers trickles through here – mostly windsurfers and wanderers – but this wild and windy corner of the lake feels blissfully undiscovered.

Brisas Del Lago　　　SODA **$$**
(☏ 2695-3363; mains US$6-11; ⊗ 11am-10pm Tue-Sat, 1-10pm Sun; P ᛫) If you don't mind a little detour, here is your lunch stop between Monteverde and Arenal. Simple Tico fare is done with panache at this dressed-up *soda*. They marinate chicken breasts in their own BBQ sauce, skewer Thai-style shrimp and sauce teriyaki chicken, and the garlic fish is sensational.

Where the lake road turns into the Tilarán road, turn toward the lake and head to the community of San Luis.

❶ Getting There & Around

On the southern side of Laguna de Arenal, the main lake road (Rte 142) takes a sharp turn south to head toward Tilarán. If you take the northbound road instead, it quickly turns to gravel and descends into the lakeside hamlets of San Luis and, 3km further, Tronadora. With dramatic lake and volcano views, these villages are surprisingly and delightfully untouristed.

Tilarán

Near the southwestern end of Laguna de Arenal, the small town of Tilarán has a laid-back, middle-class charm thanks to its long-running status as a regional ranching center. Nowadays, it's also the main commercial center for the growing community of expats that resides along the shores of Laguna de Arenal. Most visitors, however, are just passing through, traveling between La Fortuna and Monteverde. Because it's situated on the slopes of the Cordillera de Tilarán, this little hub is a much cooler alternative (in climate and atmosphere) than the towns along the Interamericana.

◉ Sights

★ Viento Fresco   WATERFALL

(☑ 2695-3434; www.vientofresco.net; adult/child entrance US$15/10, horseback tour US$55/45; ⊙ 7:30am-5pm; 🅟) Driving between Monteverde and Arenal, there is no good excuse for skipping this stop. Viento Fresco is a series of five cascades, including the spectacular Arco Iris (Rainbow Falls), which drops 75m into a refreshing shallow pool that's perfect for swimming. The 1.3km of trails are well maintained, but there are no crowds or commercialism to mar the natural beauty of this place. You'll probably have the falls to yourself, especially if you go early in the day.

Add on a horseback riding tour or grab lunch at the restaurant to support this family-run operation. It's located 11km south of Tilarán on the road to Santa Elena.

🎊 Festivals & Events

Vuelta al Lago Arenal   SPORTS

(www.vueltaallagoarenal.com; ⊙ Mar) They say that it's virtually impossible to circumnavigate the lake. But *they* have never participated in the Vuelta al Lago Arenal, an annual event in March, when some 4000 cyclists do just that. It takes two days – one off-road and one on – to complete the 148km route. Most participants camp along the route.

Transportation of camping equipment is provided but participants are responsible for their own provisions.

Fiestas de Toro   CULTURAL

(⊙ Apr) The *sabanero* tradition in Tilarán is honored on the last weekend in April with a rodeo that's popular with Tico visitors, and on June 13 with a *fiesta de toros* that's dedicated to patron San Antonio.

🛏 Sleeping & Eating

Right in the center of town, you'll find a few restaurants catering to the drive-through traffic between La Fortuna and Monteverde. Cheaper meals can be found in the *mercado* (market) beside the bus terminal, or pop into the supermarket that is across from the park.

Hotel Tilarán   HOTEL $

(☑ 2695-5043; s/d without bathroom US$14/22, with bathroom US$20/26; 🅟) As cheap as they come, rooms are tiny and cleanish. If you can get one of the rooms toward the back, this is a decent budget choice on the western side of Parque Central. There's an appealing retro bar on the street front.

Hotel Cielo Azul   HOTEL $$

(☑ 2695-4000; www.cieloazulresort.com; d incl breakfast US$75; 🅟🛜❄) Found 500m before town, coming from Nuevo Arenal, this hillside property has eight recently redone rooms with tiled floors, whitewashed walls and new bathrooms. There's a good-size pool with a waterslide and a pretty spectacular vista.

Hotel Guadalupe   HOTEL $$

(☑ 2695-5943; www.hotelguadalupe.co.cr; s/d incl breakfast US$40/60; 🅟❄🛜❄) This modern hotel attracts traveling business types, who make themselves at home in simple rooms, dressed up with jewel tones and tiled floors. Service is friendly and efficient. There is a decent restaurant on-site, as well as a swimming pool, kiddie pool and hot tub.

La Troja   COSTA RICAN $$

(☑ 2695-4935; www.facebook.com/latroja.restau rante; mains US$8-12; ⊙ 10am-9pm) This is a popular stop for both Ticos and tourists, and rightly so. The attractive wooden building

---

BUSES FROM TILARÁN

Buses arrive and depart from the terminal half a block west of Parque Central. Be aware that Sunday-afternoon buses to San José can sell out as much as a day in advance.

DESTINATION	COMPANY	COST (US$)	DURATION (HR)	FREQUENCY
Cañas	Transporte Villana	1	30min	7 daily, 5am-3:30pm
La Fortuna	Transporte Tilarán-San Carlos	5	3½	7am, 12:30pm
Puntarenas	Empresa Maravilla	4	2	6am, 1pm
San José		7	4	5am, 7am, 9:30am & 2pm daily; 5pm Saturday and Sunday only
Santa Elena/Monteverde	TransMonteverde	3	2½	7am, 4pm

has massive windows, offering a lovely vista over Laguna de Arenal. Reliably good Costa Rican fare includes grilled steaks, rotisserie chicken and delicious whole tilapia.

❶ Getting There & Away

Tilarán is 24km east of the Interamericana at Cañas, and 75km east of La Fortuna, via the paved but winding lake road. The route from Tilarán to Santa Elena and Monteverde is paved for the first stretch, but then it becomes steep, rocky and rough. A 4WD is recommended, though ordinary cars can get through with care in the dry season.

NORTHERN LOWLANDS

In the far reaches of the northern lowlands, the vast, steamy stretches of pineapple and banana plantations intermingle with rainforest, wetlands and undisturbed wildness. The region is crisscrossed by some swift highways, well-trafficked by trucks laden with fresh-picked fruit and hefty cattle on their way to market. Most travelers follow the trucks and cruise right by, heading to or from the Caribbean coast or Nicaragua. But those who venture off the highway and brave the bumpy roads will be rewarded. The rivers and lagoons along the Nicaraguan border provide habitats for an enormous diversity of bird life. Keep your eyes peeled, and you're likely to spot the rare green macaw, who is making a come-back in these parts.

Upala

Just 9km south of the Nicaraguan border in the northwestern corner of the northern lowlands, Upala is a small *ranchero* town with a bustling market and plenty of tasty *sodas*. It's a center for the area's ranching and rice industries; most visitors are Costa Rican business people who come to negotiate for a few dozen calves or a truckload of grain. It's a somewhat convenient publictransit stopover between the Volcán Tenorio area and the Caño Negro, but there's no reason to linger.

🛏 Sleeping & Eating

The busy market, just behind the bus terminal, opens early with several nice *sodas* dishing up good *gallos* (tortilla sandwiches), *empanadas* (turnovers stuffed with meat

or cheese) and just about everything else. Other restaurants are scattered about town.

Hotel Wilson   HOTEL $
(☑ 2470-3636;   www.facebook.com/hotelwilson upala; d incl breakfast US$45; P ❋ 🐾 ☎ ☒) One of the nicer Wilson properties, this is a motelstyle facility with a popular bar and restaurant and a big waterfall-fed swimming pool. The rooms are plain but clean, with mostly wood furniture and linoleum floors and other appreciated amenities.

Cabinas Maleku   CABINA $
(☑ 2470-0142; d with/without air-con US$36/32; P ❋ 🐾) Wrapping around a gravel parking lot, these cute and comfortable *cabinas* are blessed with mosaic-tile patios decorated with hand-painted Sarchí-style wooden chairs and plenty of potted plants. It's a cheerful cheapie, for sure. There's an attached *soda* too.

❶ Getting There & Away

From Upala, the well-maintained, paved Hwy 6 runs south via Bijagua, intersecting with the Interamericana just north of Cañas. Hwy 4, also paved, runs in a more southeasterly direction to Muelle de San Carlos (near La Fortuna). A rough, unpaved road, usually passable to all cars, skirts the Refugio Nacional de Vida Silvestre Caño Negro on the way to Los Chiles, the official border crossing with Nicaragua.

The bus terminal is right off the park. Taxis congregate here too. **Transportes Upala** (☑ 2221-3318) has one daily bus to Ciudad Quesada (San Carlos; US$2, two hours, 9:10am), and three daily services to San José (US$4, five hours, 4:30am, 5:15am and 9:30am), via Bijagua and Cañas. Twice-daily buses go to Caño Negro (US$2, one hour, 11am and 3pm).

Refugio Nacional de Vida Silvestre Caño Negro

Part of the Área de Conservación Arenal–Huetar Norte, this remote, 102-sq-km **refuge** (☑ 2471-1309; www.ligambiente.com; adult/child US$5/1; ⊙ 8am-4pm) has long lured anglers seeking that elusive 18kg snook, and birders hoping to glimpse rare waterfowl. During the dry season water levels drop, concentrating the birds (and fish) in photogenically (or tasty) close quarters. From January to March, when migratory birds land in large numbers, avian density is world class.

The Río Frío defines the landscape. South of the main Caño Negro dock it's a table-flat, swampy expanse of marsh and lagoon that

THE WEEPING FOREST

Extensive deforestation of the Caño Negro area began in the 1970s in response to increased population density and the subsequent need for more farmland. Although logging was allowed to proceed in the area for almost 20 years, the government took action in 1991 with the creation of the Refugio Nacional de Vida Silvestre Caño Negro. Since its creation, Caño Negro has served as a safe habitat for the region's aquatic and terrestrial birds, and has acted as a refuge for numerous migratory birds.

However, illegal logging and poaching have continued around the perimeter of the park, and wildlife has suffered. In the last two decades, one-time residents of the park including ocelots, manatees, sharks and macaws have vanished. Tarpon and caiman populations are decreasing, and fewer migratory birds are returning to the park each year. Additionally, anglers are reporting record lows in both the size and number of their catches.

Satellite images show that the lake is shrinking each year, and that water levels in the Río Frío are dropping rapidly. It's difficult to say with certainty what is causing these changes, though the farms surrounding Caño Negro require extensive irrigation, and sugarcane is nearly 10 times as water-intensive as wheat.

Locals are extremely worried about the stability of the park, as entire communities are dependent on fishing and tourism for their survival. In response to the growing need to regulate development in the region, residents have formed a number of organizations aimed at controlling development in the northern lowlands. If you want to support the Caño Negro community, book your tour in town and spend your tourist dollar locally.

is similar in appearance, if not size, to other famous wetlands such as the Florida Everglades or the Mekong Delta. North of town, it's a slender river that carves looming forest. During the wet season, the river breaks its banks to form one immense 800-hectare lake, then contracts during the dry months from January through April, when water levels drop so far that the river is barely navigable. By April it has almost completely disappeared – until the May rains begin. This cycle has proceeded without fail for millennia, and the small fishing communities that live around the edges of the reserve adapt to each seasonal nuance.

 Activities

Caño Negro is regarded among bird-watchers as one of the premier destinations in Central America. During the dry season, the sheer density of birds in the park is astounding, but the variety of species is also impressive. At last count, more than 300 species of bird live here at least part of the year. In the winter months, there are huge congregations of migratory ducks, as well as six species of kingfisher, herons, cormorants, three types of egret, ibises, rails, anhingas, roseate spoonbills, toucans and storks. The refuge is also the only reliable site in Costa Rica for olivaceous cormorants, Nicaraguan grackles and lesser yellow-headed vultures.

Conspicuous reptiles include the spectacled caiman, green iguana and striped basilisk. Howler monkeys, white-faced capuchins and two-toed sloths are common. Despite incursions from poachers, pumas, jaguars and tapirs have been recorded here in surprising numbers.

Caño Negro is also home to an abundance of river turtles, which were historically an important part of the Maleku diet. Prior to a hunt, the Maleku would appease the turtle god, Javara, by fasting and abstaining from sex. If the hunt was successful, the Maleku would later celebrate by feasting on smoked turtle meat and consuming large quantities of *chicha,* a spirit derived from maize. And, well, they probably had some sex too.

Mosquitoes in Caño Negro are damn near prehistoric. Bring bug spray or suffer the consequences.

 Tours

Hiring a local guide is quick, easy and full of advantages – you'll pay less, you'll be supporting the local economy, and you'll have more privacy when you're out on the water. If you're spending the night in the area, your lodge can make arrangements for a tour. Otherwise, there are a few local outfits with an office (or at least a sign) in the village center.

Sportfishing trips can also be arranged through the lodges. Be sure to inquire about obtaining a seasonal fishing licence, which is normally required. (Bring your passport.)

Pantanal Tour BOAT TOUR
(www.facebook.com/pantanal.toursa; tours US$30-50) Marlon Castro and Juan Ríos can take you in their boat for sportfishing or ecological tours of the lagoon. They also lead horseback riding trips and kayaking outings.

Paraíso Tropical BOAT TOUR
(📱8823-4026, 2471-1621; tours kayak US$20, horse US$25, boat US$50; ⊙8am-4pm) Visit Joel Sandoval Bardos at his office in town. He does a variety of nature tours around the refuge, including a two-hour boat tour of the lagoon (up to four people).

🛏 Sleeping & Eating

Caño Negro is a small village, so all the lodges have easy access to the lagoon.

If you tire of eating at your lodging, you'll find a small grocery store and a few *sodas* in the village.

Kingfisher Lodge CABINA **$**
(📱2471-1116; www.kingfisherlodgecr.com; r US$50-60; P🐕❄) Located about 400m from the village center, these rustic *cabinas* surround a well-kept lawn. They all have heavy wood furniture and hammock-strung porches. Your hosts, the Sequera brothers, are recommended refuge guides and boat captains. Note that the reception is located 400m east of here, in a house at the opposite end of the street.

★**Hotel de Campo Caño Negro** LODGE **$$**
(📱2471-1012; www.hoteldecampo.com; s/d incl breakfast US$80/95; P❄🛜🏊) Set in an orchard of mango and citrus trees next to the 'Chapel' lagoon, this friendly hotel is a fisher's and bird-watcher's paradise. After angling for tarpons or spying on spoonbills, relax in the ceramic-tiled *casitas,* decked with vaulted beamed ceilings and tasteful bedding. The stylish restaurant (7:30am to 9:30pm) – adorned with gushing fountains and twirling fans – serves top-notch Italian and seafood. Boats, guides, kayaks, and fishing equipment are all available for hire.

Caño Negro Natural Lodge LODGE **$$$**
(📱2471-1426; www.canonegrolodge.com; d incl breakfast US$145; P❄🛜🏊) 🖋 Perched on land that becomes a virtual island in the Río Frío during the rainy season, this lodge is surprisingly upscale. Well-appointed rooms have glass sliding doors, wooden and wrought-iron furnishings and tiny terraces facing the garden. Relax in the pool or Jacuzzi or stroll the leafy grounds, while the staff makes arrangements for boat tours of the lagoon.

❶ Information

There are no banks or gas stations in town. Visitors to the park should stop at the ranger station to pay their admission fee. It's located on the western edge of the village, near the Kingfisher Lodge.

❶ Getting There & Away

Thanks to improved roads, tour operators are now able to offer relatively inexpensive trips to Caño Negro from all over the country. However, you don't need them to explore the river. It's much more intriguing and rewarding to rent some wheels (or hop on a bus), navigate the rutted road into the rural flat lands and hire a local guide from Caño Negro village. It's also a lot cheaper, and it puts money directly into the hands of locals, thus encouraging communities in the area to protect wildlife.

The village of Caño Negro and the entrance to the park lie on the rough road connecting Upala and Los Chiles, which is passable to all cars during the dry season. However, this road is frequently washed out during the rainy season, when a 4WD is required.

During the rainy season and much of the dry season, you can also catch a boat (US$20 to US$30) to and from Los Chiles.

Plus, the following bus routes serve Caño Negro village:
Los Chiles (US$2, one hour) Departing Los Chiles at 5am and 2pm; departing Caño Negro at 6:30am, 1pm and 6pm.
Upala (US$2.50, one hour) Departing Upala at 11am and 3pm; departing Caño Negro at 6:30am, 1pm and 3pm.

Los Chiles

Seventy kilometers north of Muelle on a smooth, paved road through the sugarcane, and just 6km south of the Nicaraguan border at Las Tablillas, lies the sweltering farming town of Los Chiles. Arranged with dilapidated grace around a ragged soccer field and along the unmanicured banks of the leisurely Río Frío, the humid lowland village is charming by border-town standards (sex workers and foreboding 'import-export' types notwithstanding). It was originally settled by merchants and fisherfolk who worked on the nearby Río San Juan, much of which forms the Nicaragua–Costa Rica border.

With the opening of the new border crossing at Las Tablillas, international travelers are no longer obligated to pass through Los Chiles, though the scenic boat ride across the border is a pleasant way to go. This is also a good base for enjoying the water route to Caño Negro.

Tours

Los Chiles is a convenient base to organize boat trips to Caño Negro. Inquire at Restaurante Heliconia (p272) about these trips. Otherwise just head to the dock, where you can hire boat captains to take you up the lovely, chocolaty Río Frío during the dry season and all the way into Lago Caño Negro during the rainy season.

Three- to four-hour trips cost anywhere from US$50 to US$100 for a small group, depending on the size and type of boat. If possible, make arrangements a day in advance and get an early start in the morning: the earlier out, the more you'll see.

Sleeping & Eating

With the new border crossing at Las Tablillas, it's usually possible to cruise right by Los Chiles without spending the night. If that doesn't work for you, you'll find a limited selection of hotels in town.

Hotel y Cabinas Carolina   CABINA $
(2471-1151; r from US$30; P ✻ 🤙) Not your typical border-town accommodations. This friendly, family-run option gets rave reviews for attentive staff, spotless rooms and excellent local food. It's near the main highway, just a few blocks south of the bus station.

Hotel Wilson Tulipán   HOTEL $
(2471-1414; www.hoteleswilson.com; cnr Av 0 & Calle 4; s/d/tr incl breakfast US$30/45/60; P 🤙 ✻ 🤙) Brand-new rooms are set in a somewhat strange, ghost-town motel that's right down the road from the boat dock. There are older but still comfortable rooms in the main building too, but those get night noise from the lively bar and restaurant, which flaunts tasty seafood *tipica* and bad behavior.

ℹ️ GETTING TO NICARAGUA

If you're heading north to Nicaragua, your life just got easier, thanks to the construction of the Puente Santa Fe, a bridge that crosses the Río San Juan just north of the Nicaraguan border. As a result, there is a brand new border crossing at **Las Tablillas**, 6km north of Los Chiles:

➡ The border crossing at Las Tablillas (open 8am to 4pm) will eventually handle about 40% of the Costa Rica–Nicaragua traffic, so travelers can expect it will become increasingly busy over the next few years.

➡ Hourly buses connect Los Chiles and Las Tablillas (US$1, 15 minutes). Or, get the bus directly from San José or Ciudad Quesada (San Carlos).

➡ You will have to pay a Costa Rica land exit fee of US$7 at immigration, payable by credit or debit card only (no cash).

➡ After walking across the border, you'll go through Nicaraguan immigration. The entrance fee is US$12, payable in US dollars or cordobas.

➡ After exiting immigration, you can catch a boat up the river or hop on a bus or a *collectivo* to San Carlos (US$2.20, 30 minutes).

If you are entering Cosa Rica from Nicaragua, you can take an hourly bus to Los Chiles or Ciudad Quesada or catch the direct bus to San José, which departs at 2:30pm.

If you want to get to/from Nicaragua the old-fashioned way, you can still go to Los Chiles to go to the **immigration office** (Migración; 2471-1233; Calle 4 & Av 0; ⊙8am-6pm) and catch the boat up the river, but now there is only one round trip per day (US$10 to US$12, departing Los Chiles 1pm or whenever enough passengers show up to make it worthwhile, departing from Nicaragua at 9:30am). You'll avoid the Costa Rica land exit fee, but you'll still have to pay US$12 to enter Nicaragua. It's actually a more enjoyable trip than the land crossing, but it takes some time.

Restaurante Heliconia COSTA RICAN $
(☑8307-8585, 2471-2096; mains US$6-10; ⊙6am-10pm Mon-Fri, 7am-10pm Sat & Sun) Across from the immigration office, this is a decent option for lunch or a smoothie. It also provides information on tours and transportation; inquire about boat trips to Caño Negro or taxi rides to the border.

ℹ Information

Banco Nacional (☑2212-2000; Av 1 btwn Calles 0 & 1; ⊙8:30am-3:45pm Mon-Fri) Close to the central park and soccer field, changes cash and traveler's checks and has a 24-hour ATM.

Cruz Roja (Red Cross; ☑2471-2025, 2471-1037; cnr Calle 2 & Av 1; ⊙24hr) Located at the northwestern corner of the plaza.

Post Office (⊙8am-noon & 1-5:30pm Mon-Fri) One block west of the bus station.

ℹ Getting There & Away

BUS

All buses arrive and leave from the terminal behind Soda Pamela, near the intersection of Hwy 35. **Chilsaca** (☑2460-1886; www.chilsaca. com) has 16 daily buses to Ciudad Quesada (US$2.25, two hours) from 4:30am to 6pm; you can transfer here for La Fortuna. Autotransportes San Carlos (p98) has two daily buses to San José (US$6, five hours), departing at 5am and 3pm. There are also three departures to Caño Negro (US$4, 2½ hours) at 5am, 2pm and 5pm. Timetables are subject to change, so always check ahead.

HISTORY OF THE MALEKU

The Maleku (colloquially referred to as the Guatuso) are one of the few remaining indigenous groups in Costa Rica. Historically, they were organized into 12 communities scattered around the Tilarán-Guanacaste range and the Llanura de San Carlos. Although their numbers dwindled following the arrival of Spanish colonists, the population survived relatively intact until the early 20th century.

With the invention of the automobile, the US rubber industry started searching for new reserves to meet the increasing demand for tires. With the aid of Nicaraguan mercenaries, industry representatives scoured Central America for stable rubber reserves, which were found on Maleku-inhabited land. The resulting rubber war virtually wiped out the population, and confined survivors to a handful of communities. Today the Maleku number around 400, and live in the three *palenques* (indigenous settlements) of Sol, Margarita and Tonjibe.

As is the situation with most indigenous groups in Costa Rica, the Maleku are among the poorest communities in the country, and they survive by adhering to a subsistence lifestyle. Their diet revolves around corn and the *tipuisqui* root, a traditional food source that grows wild in the region. Fortunately, since the Maleku have a rich artisan tradition, they are able to earn a small income by selling traditional crafts to tourists. Historically, the Maleku were renowned for their impressive jade work and arrow craftsmanship. Nowadays, their crafts primarily consist of pottery, jewelry, musical instruments and other small trinkets for the tourist market.

The Maleku are also famous for their unique style of clothing made from *tana:* tree bark that has been stripped of its outer layer, soaked in water and then pounded thin on wooden blocks. After it has been dried and bleached in the sun, it can be stitched together like leather, and has a soft texture similar to suede. Although it's rare to see modern Maleku wearing anything other than Western-style clothing, *tana* articles are often offered for sale to tourists.

Despite being small in number, the Maleku have held on to their cultural heritage, perhaps more than any other indigenous group in Costa Rica. This is especially evident in their language, which is one of the oldest in the Americas and linguistically distinct from the Amazonian and Maya dialects. Today the Maleku still speak their language among themselves, and a local radio station, Radio Sistema Cultural Maleku, airs daily programs in the Maleku language. The Maleku have also maintained their ceremonial traditions, such as the seasonal custom of crying out to Mother Nature for forgiveness through ritualistic song and dance.

As with all indigenous reservations in Costa Rica, the Maleku welcome tourists, as craft sales are vital to their survival. You can access the *palenques* via Rte 143, though it's best to inquire locally for directions as the roads are poorly maintained and unsigned.

CAR

You're likely to get here via Hwy 35 from Muelle. Skid marks and reptilian road kill do break up the beautiful monotony of orange groves, sage-blue pineapple fields and dense sugarcane plantations. More scenic, if a little harder on your chassis, is the decent dirt road running for 50km from Upala, through Caño Negro, passable for normal cars throughout the dry season.

San Rafael de Guatuso

The main population center of this agricultural area, San Rafael de Guatuso is a small town without too much to offer travelers – except its central location, which offers easy access to some key destinations. The humble town itself is a decent base for exploring the fantastic Venado Caves to the south and the blue waters of Río Celeste and the Parque Nacional Volcán Tenorio to the west. The area is also home to the few remaining indigenous Maleku, who reside in *palenques* (indigenous settlements) near here.

Cabinas Los Almendros   CABINA $

(☑ 8887-0495; cabinaslosalmendros@gmail.com; r US$24; [P][❄][🐾][🛜]) A cute family-run motel with well-maintained rooms, blessed with a fresh coat of paint and lovely bedding and window treatments. Each room is named after a different jungle beast or bird, complete with hand-carved wooden sculpture. Set on the edge of town behind the Banco Nacional, this is easily the best choice in the area.

The folks at Los Almendros offer transportation and tours to the Maleku reservation, Venado Caves and Río Celeste (Parque Nacional Volcán Tenorio).

ⓘ Getting There & Away

Guatuso lies on Hwy 4, midway between Upala and Muelle de San Carlos (about 40km from each). Buses leave frequently for Ciudad Quesada, where you can connect to La Fortuna. There is also one daily bus to Tilarán (three hours, 7:30pm) via Nuevo Arenal, and three daily buses to San José (five hours, 8am, 11:30am and 3pm).

From Guatuso, a rough gravel and dirt road covers the 21km to the entrance of Parque Nacional Volcán Tenorio, and onward to Bijagua. For this route, a 4WD is required in the rainy season and recommended year-round.

Muelle de San Carlos

This small crossroads village – locally called Muelle – was once an important dock (hence the name) as it's the most inland

spot from which the Río San Carlos is navigable. These days it is sugarcane country and it serves as a rest stop for truckers and travelers. It's also only 27km east of La Fortuna. If you have your own wheels, Muelle can be a quaint, quiet base for visiting Arenal and environs.

◎ Sights

Centro Turistico Las Iguanas   BRIDGE

(Iguana Bridge; ☑ 2462-1107) This is a popular spot for tourists en route from La Fortuna to Caño Negro, but not for lunch. Countless iguanas hang out in the bamboo and trees above the river, providing some great photo ops. Walk across the bridge to see how many you can count – but watch your step! The bridge is 1.8km north of the main intersection in Muelle, where Rte 35 takes a sharp turn to cross the river.

🛏 Sleeping & Eating

There are a number of *sodas* and a small supermarket on the road toward Los Chiles that will do if you're looking for your *casado* fix. If you want to sample the local specialty – that's beef – drive a few kilometers south to Platanar, where steakhouses line the road. Or, visit the restaurant at the *subasta ganadera* (livestock auction) right near the main intersection.

Tilajari Resort Hotel   RESORT $$$

(☑ 2462-1212; www.tilajari.com; d incl breakfast from US$110; [P][❄][✳][@][🛜][🏊]) This country club turned luxury resort has well-landscaped grounds overlooking the Río San Carlos and comfortable, well-appointed rooms. The extensive list of amenities includes racquetball and tennis courts, restaurant, pool, sauna, spa and butterfly garden, plus access to the neighboring 400-hectare private rainforest reserve with several trails. The facilities are a bit dated but the place offers excellent value for the price.

The resort is 800m west of the intersection at Muelle, on the road to Ciudad Quesada.

Subasta Ganadera   STEAK $$

(☑ 2462-1000; www.subastasganaderascr.com; mains US$4-12; ⊙ bar 11am-11pm) Overlooking a bullpen, this place is bustling with hungry *campesinos* (farmers). It has an expansive menu of local dishes, and it's a great spot for a cold beer. Come for lunch on Tuesday or Thursday to see the cattle auction.

❶ Getting There & Away

A 24-hour gas station lies at the main intersection of Hwy 4 (which connects Ciudad Quesada and Upala) and Hwy 35 (running from San José to Los Chiles). Buses pass through en route to all of those destinations.

Ciudad Quesada (San Carlos)

The official name of this small city is Ciudad Quesada (sometimes abbreviated to 'Quesada'), but all the locals know it as San Carlos, and local buses often list San Carlos as the destination. It's long been a bustling ranching and agricultural center, known for its *talabaterías* (saddle shops). Although San Carlos is surrounded by pastoral countryside, the city has developed into the commercial center of the region – it's gritty and quite congested. Fortunately, there's no real reason to enter the city, except to change buses.

🏃 Activities

Ciudad Quesada is not exactly a destination in itself. But if you're driving this way, why not stop for a soak? Popular with Tico families, the thermal pools here are an affordable and pleasant alternative to the overdone, overpopulated springs in La Fortuna. The hot springs and resorts are located about 8km east of town, heading toward Aguas Zarcas.

El Tucano Resort HOT SPRING
(☑ 2460-6000; www.hoteltucano.com; admission US$20) This posh but aging resort is set amid gorgeous primary forest. The thermal springs are tapped into three warm pools of varying temperatures – perfect for soaking away your ills. The most unique feature is the spring-fed river that streams through the property, creating warm rapids and hot holes to delight local swimmers. It's a worthwhile and relaxing place to spend half a day.

The spacious, colonial-style rooms (doubles US$120 to US$135, suites US$145 to US$200) enjoy forest views from the terrace.

Termales del Bosque HOT SPRING
(☑ 2460-4740; www.termalesdelbosque.com; adult/child US$12/6) Luxury here is low-key, with therapeutic soaking available in seven natural hot- and warm-water springs. The stone pools are surrounded by lush greenery and built into the riverbank, in a forested valley populated by morpho butterflies.

✳ Festivals & Events

Feria del Ganado CULTURAL
(🕙 Apr) Celebrate the *sabanero* culture in San Carlos during the Feria del Ganado, which is held every April. The cattle fair and auction are accompanied by carnival rides and a *tope* (horse parade).

🛏 Sleeping

You wouldn't want to stay in Ciudad Quesada itself, but there are some resorts on the outskirts – 8km to 20km away – that offer pleasant alternatives to the tourist madness in La Fortuna. If you are stuck in town for some reason, there is no shortage of budget hotels around.

Tree Houses Hotel HOTEL $$$
(☑ 2475-6507; treehouseshotelcostarica.com; incl breakfast d US$100-175, extra person US$15) Fulfill your childhood fantasy by spending a

---

BUSES FROM CIUDAD QUESADA

Terminal Quesada is about 2km from the town center. Taxis (US$1) and a twice-hourly bus (US$0.50) make regular runs between town and the terminal, or you can walk if you don't mind hauling your luggage uphill. Popular bus routes from Ciudad Quesada:

DESTINATION	COMPANY	COST (US$)	DURATION (HR)	FREQUENCY
La Fortuna	Transpisa	2	1½	12 daily, 5:40am-9:30pm
Los Chiles	Chilsaca	5	2	14 daily, 4:15am-7:30pm; direct bus 3pm
Puerto Viejo de Sarapiquí	Transportes Linaco	4	2	8 daily, 4:40am- 6:30pm
San José	Autotransportes San José-San Carlos	5	2½	Hourly 4am-6pm; direct buses 6:40am & 6:15pm
Upala	Transportes Upala	5	3	5:45pm

WORTH A TRIP

VENADO CAVES

Four kilometers south of Venado (Spanish for 'deer') along a good dirt road, the **Venado Caves** (Cavernas de Venado; ☑ 2478-8008; www.cavernasdelvenadocr.com; adult/child US$22/12, photographer US$20; ☺ 8am-3pm, last admission 2pm) are an adventurous excursion into an eight-chamber limestone labyrinth that extends for almost 3km. A bilingual guide leads small groups on two-hour tours through the darkness, squeezing through narrow passes, pointing out the most interesting rock formations and encountering bats and bugs. You'll be provided with rubber boots, headlamps and helmets, as well as a shower afterwards. You'll definitely want to bring a change of clothes.

Any tour operator in La Fortuna can arrange this trip for you. If you're driving yourself, the caves are well signed from Hwy 4. Otherwise, Cabinas Los Almendros (p273) offers transportation from San Rafael de Guatuso.

few nights in one of these awesome treetop hideouts. With solid wood construction and big windows facing the rainforest, the comfortable cabins have all the amenities you would expect on the ground, plus fabulous wrap-around porches that bring you even closer to the birds and monkeys. Rates include a guided hike in the surrounding 80-acre forest preserve.

Tree Houses is about 27km southeast of La Fortuna and 17km northwest of Ciudad Quesada (San Carlos). Assuming you have your own vehicle, it's within striking distance of the activities around Arenal, but removed from the hullabaloo.

Boca Tapada

Here's an off-the-beaten-track destination for adventurous souls. The rocky roads and lack of signage (even less than usual!) could mean a few unintended detours, but it's worth the effort for a glimpse into the ecological extravaganza of pristine rainforest. On the roads that pass pineapple fields and packing plants, your fellow travelers will be commuting *caballeros* (cowboys) and *campesinos* going about their day-to-day business. And at the end of the road, you'll be rewarded with a luxuriant bit of rainforest replete with the song of frogs and rare birds, and an inkling of the symbiosis that can happen when humans make the effort. Local lodges offer rainforest tours into the **Refugio Nacional de Vida Silvestre Mixto Maquenque**.

🛏 Sleeping

Mi Pedacito de Cielo LODGE $$
(☑ 2200-4782, 8308-9595; www.pedacitodecielo.com; s/d/tr incl breakfast US$65/75/85; [P][🛜]) 🌿
Perched above the Río San Carlos, 'my little

piece of heaven' is a rustic retreat, with 14 wooden bungalows offering river and rainforest views. Swing in the hammock-chair to watch the sunset and listen to the rainforest come alive. Superfriendly service and excellent home-cooked meals are perks, as is the attached rainforest reserve with hiking trails.

Laguna del Lagarto Lodge LODGE $$
(☑ 2289-8163; www.lagarto-lodge-costa-rica.com; s/d/tr US$60/75/90, meals US$8-15; [P][🛜])
🌿 Surrounded by 500 hectares of virgin rainforest, this outpost is legendary among birders. Basic screened rooms share large, hammock-strung verandas. It's not fancy, but it's wild and lovely, with feeders and fruit on the grounds attracting toucans, tanagers and more. There are 16km of trails, and canoes to explore the surrounding lagoons, where caimans dwell and Jesus Christ lizards make tracks across the water's surface.

★Maquenque Eco-Lodge LODGE $$$
(☑ 2479-7785; www.maquenqueecolodge.com; s/d/tr incl breakfast from US$105/130/155; [P][🛜][🏊])
🌿 Set on 80 glorious, bird-filled hectares, 14 unique bungalows overlook a lagoon and tropical garden, while additional tree houses are perched in the nearby rainforest. The place is a birders' paradise, with countless species flocking to feeders and fruit trees on the grounds, and both scarlet and green macaws frequently spotted in the surrounding almendros trees.

Prices include a guided rainforest hike in the morning, a student-led tour of a local school and use of canoes on the lagoon, as well as the opportunity to support sustainable tourism by planting a tree in the rainforest.

WORTH A TRIP

PROYECTO ASIS

It's an animal rescue center. It's a volunteer project. It's Spanish classes. The community-based organization Proyecto Asis (☑2475-9121; www.institutoasis.com; adult/child US$31/18, incl volunteering US$54/31; ☺tours 8:30am & 1pm) is doing a lot of good, and you can help. The introductory experience is a 1½-hour tour of the wildlife rescue center, but it's worth springing for the three-hour 'volunteering' experience, which includes hands-on interaction with the animals. It's pricey, but the cause is worthy.

Asis also offers homestays in the local community. It's located about 20km west of Quesada, past the village of Florencia. Reserve at least a day in advance.

ℹ Getting There & Away

Getting to Boca Tapada is an adventure in itself. The nearest town of note is Pital, north of Aguas Zarcas. About 2km north of Pital, take a right at the fork (after the bus stop) and follow the signs. It's a slow, rough 40km, but worth it.

Buses reach Boca Tapada on a two-hour trip from Pital, departing Pital at 9:30am and 4:30pm. Leaving Boca Tapada, the buses to Pital depart at 5:30am and 12:30pm. You can reach Pital on frequent buses from Ciudad Quesada (US$2, 1½ hours) or four daily buses from San José (US$4, four hours).

The lodges can also arrange transfers from La Fortuna or San José.

SARAPIQUÍ VALLEY

This flat, steaming stretch of *finca*-dotted lowlands was once part of the United Fruit Company's vast banana holdings. Harvests were carried from the plantations down to Puerto Viejo de Sarapiquí, where they were shipped downriver on boats destined for North America. In 1880 a railway connected rural Costa Rica with the port of Puerto Limón, and Puerto Viejo de Sarapiquí became a backwater. Although it's never managed to recover its former glory as a transport route, the river again shot to prominence as one of the premier destinations in Costa Rica for kayakers and rafters. With the Parque Nacional Braulio Carrillo as its backyard, this is one of the best regions for wildlife-watching, especially considering how easy it is to get here.

San Miguel

If you're driving up from San José or Alajuela, Hwy 126 curves up the slopes of the Cordillera Central, leaving behind the urban bustle and passing Volcán Poás before descending again into pastureland. This is *campesino* country, where the plodding hoofbeat of cattle is about the speed of life, as the hard-to-spot rural speed bumps will remind you, if you take those curves too quickly. You're off the beaten track now, and if you're self-driving, you may as well linger, because there are few Costa Rican corners quite this beautiful and unheralded.

☞ Tours

Mi Cafecito   COFFEE TOUR

(☑2476-0215; www.micafecitocoffeetour.com; tour US$22) About 5km south of San Miguel, in the foothills of Volcán Poas, Mi Cafecito is the perfect coffee break if you're heading to/from the Sarapiquí Valley. Including more than 200 small farmers, this co-op shows off the whole process of growing, harvesting and roasting coffee beans, especially using organic farming practices. The walk through the farm also yields expansive views of the gorgeous Sarapiquí Valley.

Even if you don't want to take a tour, there is a big shady cafe where you can get a cup o' joe (and food too).

🛏 Sleeping & Eating

The best lunch stop near San Miguel is 5km south of town at Mi Cafecito Coffee Tour. In town, there is at least one *soda* which promises breakfast, as well as bird-watching, tourist information, *cabanas* and clean bathrooms.

Albergue El Socorro   FARMSTAY $$

(☑8820-2160; www.alberguee socorrosarapiqui.com; per person incl meals US$75; ℗@) Albergue El Socorro is a small family *finca*, located 1000m above sea level, on a plateau surrounded by a magnificent knife's edge of green mountains, tucked between the looming Cerro Congo and Volcan Poas. There are three cozy A-framed cabins, from where guests can explore trails through primary and secondary rainforest, discover waterfalls, swim in rivers, or help out on the dairy farm.

The owner was born and raised as a rancher here, but in 2009 a massive earthquake struck the area, destroying the road to San Miguel along with his home and dairy. This wonderful family rebuilt the ranch from scratch and incorporated a tourism component, which provides a rare opportunity to slow down and experience authentic rural Tico living. This is the real *pura vida*.

🛈 Getting There & Away

From Ciudad Quesada (San Carlos), Hwy 140 heads east for about 40km before terminating sharply when it runs into Hwy 126. This intersection – in the hills of the Cordillera Central – is where San Miguel is. You can't miss the sharp turn as the two highways merge and continue north for 12km toward La Virgen.

La Virgen

Tucked into the densely jungled shores of the wild and scenic Río Sarapiquí, La Virgen was one of the small towns that prospered during the heyday of the banana trade. Although United Fruit has long since shipped out, the town remains dependent on its nearby pineapple fields. And it still lives by that river.

For over a decade, La Virgen was the premier kayaking and rafting destination in Costa Rica. Dedicated groups of hardcore paddlers spent happy weeks running the Río Sarapiquí. But a tremendous 2009 earthquake and landslide altered the course of the river and flattened La Virgen's tourist economy. Some businesses folded, others relocated to La Fortuna. And a few held on. Now, independent kayakers are starting to come back and there are three river outfitters offering exhilarating trips on the Class II–IV waters of the Río Sarapiquí.

◉ Sights

Nature Pavilion   WILDLIFE RESERVE
(☏2761-0801; www.costaricanp.com; admission US$20; ⏱7am-5pm) Father and son Dave and Dave greet all comers to this 10-acre reserve on the Río Sarapiquí. It's a lovely setting in which to spy on feathered friends. There are several viewing platforms, with feeders attracting toucans, trogans, tanagers and 10 species of hummingbird. From here you can follow along a trail system that winds through secondary forest all the way down to the river. Bonus: free coffee.

Snake Garden   ZOO
(☏2761-1059; www.snakegardencr.com; adult/child US$15/10, night tour US$30/24; ⏱9am-5pm) Get face to face with 50 species of reptiles and amphibians, including poison-dart frogs, rattlesnakes, crocs and turtles. The star attraction is a gigantic 80kg Burmese python. Make reservations for the night tour, which shows off many species of frogs you won't see during the day.

☞ Tours

**Hacienda Pozo
Azul Adventures**   ADVENTURE TOUR
(☏2438-2616, in USA & Canada 877-810-6903; www.pozoazul.com; tours US$55-85) Specializes in adventure activities, including horseback-riding tours, a canopy tour over the lush jungle and river, rappelling, mountain biking, and assorted river trips. It's the best-funded tour concession in the area, catering largely to groups and day-trippers from San José.

🛏 Sleeping

Cabinas El Bosque   CABINA $
(☏2761-0204; r US$12; ☎) Basic but new *cabinas* are set off the main highway, 1km south of town. Rooms are set in little square houses with cold-water bathrooms, fans, new tiles and colorful curtains.

**Tirimbina Rainforest
Center & Lodge**   LODGE $$
(☏2761-0333; www.tirimbina.org; d incl breakfast US$90-110, day pass US$17; 🅿❄@☎) Located 2km from La Virgen, this is a working environmental research and education center. The spacious, comfortable accommodations are located at the lodge or at a more remote field station. Tirimbina reserve has more than 9km of trails, and tours include bird-watching, frog and bat tours, night walks and a recommended chocolate tour.

The 345-hectare private reserve is connected to the nearby Sarapiquís Rainforest Lodge (p278) by two long suspension bridges. Halfway across, a spiral staircase drops to an island in the river. Explore!

Hacienda Pozo Azul   BUNGALOW $$
(☏2438-2616, 2761-1360; www.haciendapozo azul.com; d/tr/q incl breakfast US$100/125/150; 🅿@☎) 🍃 Near the southern end of La Virgen, Pozo Azul features stylish 'tent suites' scattered on the edge of the tree line, all on raised polished-wood platforms and dressed with plush bedding and mosquito nets. At night, the frogs and wildlife sing you to sleep as raindrops patter on the canvas roof.

RUNNING THE SARAPIQUÍ

The Río Sarapiquí isn't as wild as the white water on the Río Pacuare near Turrialba, but it will get your heart racing. Even better, the dense jungle that hugs the riverbank is lush and primitive, with chances to glimpse wildlife from your raft.

You can run the Sarapiquí year-round, but December offers the biggest water. The rest of the year, the river fluctuates with rainfall. The bottom line is: if it's been raining, the river will be at its best. Where once there were nearly a dozen outfitters in La Virgen, now there are four. Two of them are actually based in Chilamate and one is in Puerto Viejo – but all ride the same rapids, offering roughly the same Class II–IV options at similar prices.

Aguas Bravas (☑ 2766-6525; www.aguasbravascr.com; rafting trips US$75, safari float US$65; ☉ 9am-5:30pm) This excellent and well-established rafting outfit has set up shop along the Río Sarapiquí (complete with on-site hostel). Aguas Bravas has two tours on offer: take a gentle safari float to spot birds, iguanas, caimans and other wildlife, or sign up to splash through 14km of 'extreme rapids' on the San Miguel section of the river.

Aventuras del Sarapiquí (☑ 2766-6768; www.sarapiqui.com; river trips US$60-80) A highly recommended outfitter, offering land, air and water adventures. Beside white-water rafting (both Class II and III/IV trips), you can also fly through the air on a 14-cable canopy tour. Or, stay down to earth with horseback riding, mountain biking or good old-fashioned hiking.

Sarapiquí Outdoor Center (☑ 2761-1123; www.costaricaraft.com; 2/4hr rafting trip US$65/90, guided kayak trips from US$90) Here is the local paddling authority. In addition to its own rafting excursions, it offers kayak rental, lessons and clinics. Indie paddlers should check in for up-to-date river information. If you need somewhere to sleep before you hit the water, you can crash in the simple rooms or pitch a tent here.

Green Rivers (☑ 8341-0493, 2766-6265; www.facebook.com/greenriverscostarica; tours US$60-80) Operating out of the Posada Andrea Cristina B&B, this outfit is run by the ever-amiable Kevín Martínez and his wife. They offer a wide variety of rafting and kayaking tours, from family-friendly floats to adrenaline-pumping, rapid-surfing rides. They also know their nature, so they do natural-history and bird tours too.

Tropical Duckies (☑ 8760-3787, 2761-0095; www.tropicalduckies.com; adult/child US$65/50; ☉ departs 9am & 1pm) Highly recommended for beginners and families, this outfit does tours and instruction in inflatable kayaks, which allow for a fun paddle even when the river is low. Paddle on flat moving water or Class III rapids (or somewhere in between). Reserve ahead.

Pozo Azul also has a restaurant-bar near the highway with a lovely riverside veranda, though it caters mostly to big tour groups.

Sarapiquís Rainforest Lodge   LODGE **$$$**
(☑ 2761-1415; www.sarapiquis.com; d with/without breakfast US$130/105; P☉❄@☎) ✆ About 2km north of La Virgen, this ecolodge offers a place to stay and eat, as well as an education in environmental conservation and pre-Columbian culture. Modeled after a 15th-century pre-Columbian village, the *palenque*-style thatched-roof buildings each contain a clutch of sparse but spacious rooms, with huge solar-heated bathroom and private terrace. The restaurant incorporates ingredients used in indigenous cuisine, many grown on the premises.

What's really special about the lodge are the unique attractions scattered about the grounds. The **Alma Ata Archaeological Park** is a Maleku archaeological site, estimated to be around 600 years old. There is also an exhibit of indigenous artifacts. The **ethnobotanical garden** includes a huge collection of medicinal plants, most of which were also used by indigenous groups.

Eating & Drinking

El Chante   SODA **$**
(☑ 2761-0032; www.facebook.com/restauranteelchante; mains US$6-10) This La Virgen favorite has recently moved up the street to new digs (next to the old Rancho Leona). The service is welcoming and the food is

tasty and filling. The place is popular (and it has televisions) so it can get loud in the evenings.

Restaurante Mar y Tierra COSTA RICAN $
(☑ 8434-2832; mains US$8-10; ☺ 8am-10pm) You can't miss this roadside restaurant, set in an A-frame in the middle of town. The seafood and steak restaurant is popular with both locals and travelers. Try the *arroz Mar y Tierra*, a Tico take on surf and turf.

Bar & Cabinas El Río BAR
(☑ 2761-0138; ☺ noon-10pm) At the southern end of town, turn off the main road and make your way down to this atmospheric riverside hangout, set on rough-hewn stilts high above the river. Locals congregate on the upper deck to sip cold beers and nosh on filling Tico fare.

From here, you can stumble right into your bed if you stay in one of the A-frame bungalows (with fan/air-con US$15/20) near the road.

❶ Getting There & Away

La Virgen lies on Hwy 126, about 8km north of San Miguel and 17km west of Puerto Viejo de Sarapiquí. It's a paved but curvy route (especially heading south, where the road starts to climb into the mountains). Buses ply this route from San José via San Miguel to Puerto Viejo, stopping in La Virgen along the way. Local buses run hourly between La Virgen and Puerto Viejo de Sarapiquí (US$1, 30 minutes) from 6am to 8pm.

In the very near future, the new Vuelta Kooper Chilamate Hwy, aka Hwy 4, will head west from here, eventually connecting the Sarapiquí Valley to Muelle and beyond.

Chilamate & Around

The narrow, paved Hwy 4 runs for about 15km between La Virgen and Puerto Viejo, connecting a few farming villages such as the don't-blink-or-you'll-miss-it hamlet of Chilamate. On the northern side, the road is lined with small businesses, prosperous family *fincas* and acres upon acres of picturesque pineapple plantations. On the southern side is the wild Río Sarapiquí, providing a dramatic landscape for a handful of excellent ecolodges.

Beyond the river, these lodges are surrounded by their own private reserves of primary and secondary forest, crisscrossed by hiking trails, which are begging for exploration. And beyond that, the landscape

merges seamlessly into the unexplored northern reaches of **Parque Nacional Braulio Carrillo**. Technically, travelers cannot access the park from here, but nothing stops the wildlife – an enormous diversity of birdlife and even mammals like monkeys, kinkajous and peccaries – from sneaking out and spying on unsuspecting passers-by.

The whole region – from La Virgen to Puerto Viejo – is defined by the Río Sarapiquí. Several of the river-running companies have set up shop east of town.

☞ Tours

While agriculture remains the primary money-maker in the region, many folks recognize that tourism also has a role to play in the local economy. And it doesn't have to be an either/or. Entrepreneurial local farmers have started supplementing their agricultural activities with farm tours, allowing visitors a view into Tico rural lifestyles, sustainable farming practices, and the ins and outs of producing delicious food.

Best Chocolate Tour FOOD, FARM
(☑ 8815-0031, 8501-7951; per person US$30; ☺ tours 8am, 10am, 1pm & 3pm) Where does chocolate come from? This local Chilamate family can answer that question for you, starting with the cacao plants growing on their farm. The two-hour demonstration covers the whole chocolate-making process, with plenty of tasting along the way.

Organic Paradise FOOD, FARM
(☑ 2761-0706; www.organicparadisetour.com; adult/child US$$35/14; ☺ 8am, 10am, 1pm & 3pm) Take a bumpy ride on a tractor-drawn carriage and learn everything you ever wanted to know about pineapples. The two-hour tour focuses on the production process and what it means to be organic, but it also offers real insight into Costa Rican farm culture, as well as practical tips like how to choose your pineapple at the supermarket.

The tour is very educational and surprisingly entertaining. And of course, you get to sample the goods.

🛏 Sleeping & Eating

This scenic stretch of Hwy 126 and Hwy 4 is home to a few excellent ecolodges. Good news for budget travelers: you don't have to stay at them to take advantage of their private trails and other interesting attractions.

WORTH A TRIP

CINCO CEIBAS

On the grounds of the huge, 1100-hectare Finca Pangola, there is a swathe of dense, green primary rainforest, home to some of the oldest and largest trees in all of Costa Rica. This is **Cinco Ceibas** (📞2476-0606; www.cincoceibas.com; full-day tour incl lunch US$125). And yes, there are five glorious ceiba trees that you see, as you walk 1.2km along the raised wooden boardwalk through the jungle. The stroll is paired with horseback riding, kayaking or an ox-cart ride, plus lunch, for a carefully choreographed adventure.

Cinco Ceibas offers transportation for day-trippers from San José or La Fortuna. If you have your own wheels, it's a one-hour drive on mostly gravel roads from La Virgen. From the highway north of town, take the turn off to Pueblo Nuevo. There is supposed to be a new highway in the works, which will make this journey faster and easier, so ask around before you set out.

Isla del Río   HOSTEL $

(📞2766-6525; www.aguasbravascr.com; dm US$12, r with/without bathroom US$40/35; 🅿🛜) After riding the rapids, you can hunker down at this riverside hostel, operated by Aguas Bravas. It's a clean, basic set-up with solid wooden beds, clean bathrooms and hearty breakfasts (US$6). There are trails for exploring, as well as an outdoor hangout area where you can lounge in a hammock, listen to the rushing river and recall your rafting adventure.

★Chilamate
Rainforest Eco Retreat   LODGE $$

(📞2766-6949; www.chilamaterainforest.com; dm US$30-35, s/d/tr/q incl breakfast US$90/110/130/155; 🅿🛜) 🐾 Family-run and family-friendly, this is an inviting and truly innovative retreat, where owners Davis and Meghan are dedicated to protecting the environment and investing in community. Built on 20 hectares of secondary forest, the solar-powered cabins are basic but full of character, with hand-crafted furniture and natural air-cooling. The restaurant serves incredible, fresh breakfast and dinner buffets, using local, organic ingredients.

Covered, flat walkways allow you to move between buildings in the complex without ever getting wet (after all, this is the rainforest!). Behind the cabins, 6km of paths wind through the jungle, where you're likely to spot sloths, monkeys, toucans, frogs, snakes and more. And when you can't take the heat, head to the nearby river swimming hole, complete with Tarzan swing from the bridge.

Selva Verde Lodge   LODGE $$$

(📞2761-1800, in USA & Canada 800-451-7111; www.selvaverde.com; s/d US$120/140, bungalow s/d US$140/170, all incl breakfast; 🅿❄🛜🏊)

In Chilamate, about 7km west of Puerto Viejo, this former *finca* is now an elegant lodge protecting 200 hectares of rainforest. Choose to stay at the river lodge, elevated above the forest floor, or in a private bungalow, tucked away in the nearby trees. Rooms have shiny wooden floors, solar-heated showers and wide verandas with views to the forest.

There are three walking trails through the grounds and into the premontane tropical wet forest, as well as medicinal and butterfly gardens, various boat tours on the Río Sarapiquí, and an on-site Italian kitchen.

La Quinta de Sarapiquí Lodge   LODGE $$$

(📞2761-1052; www.laquintasarapiqui.com; d/tr/q incl breakfast US$110/125/140; 🅿❄🛜🏊) 🐾 At this family-run lodge on the banks of the Río Sardinal, covered paths crisscross the landscaped garden, connecting thatched-roof, hammock-strung rooms. You can swim in the pretty saltwater pool or in the nearby river swimming hole; observe the creatures in the frog house, caimen nursery and butterfly garden; or hike the trails through secondary forest.

Even if you're not staying here, you can get a day pass (US$12) to explore the animal exhibits and hiking trails.

Rancho Magallanes   COSTA RICAN $$

(📞2766-5606; chicken US$5-12; ⊗10am-10pm) Rancho Magallanes is a sweet roadside restaurant with a wood-burning brick oven where they roast whole chickens and serve them quite simply with tortillas and banana salsa. You can dine with the truckers by the roadside or in the more upscale riverside dining area, painted with colorful jungle scenes.

Getting There & Away

Any bus between La Virgen and Puerto Viejo de Sarapiquí can drop you off at the entrances to the ecolodges along Hwy 4, while a taxi from La Virgen will cost from US$8 to US$10.

Puerto Viejo de Sarapiquí

At the scenic confluence of the Ríos Puerto Viejo and Sarapiquí, this was once the most important port in Costa Rica. Boats laden with fruit, coffee and other commercial exports plied the Sarapiquí as far as the Nicaraguan border, then turned east on the Río San Juan to the sea.

Today it is simply a gritty but pleasant palm-shaded market town. The town is adjusting to the new economy, as the local polytechnic high school offers students advanced tourism, ecology and agriculture degrees. The school even has its own reserve, laced with trails. Visitors, meanwhile, can choose from any number of activities in the surrounding area, such as bird-watching, rafting, kayaking, boating and hiking.

Tours

The boat traffic at the dock in Puerto Viejo is no longer transporting commuters who have somewhere to go. Nowadays, it's used primarily for tourist boats, which cruise the Ríos Sarapiquí and Puerto Viejo, looking for birds and monkeys. On a good day, passengers might spot an incredible variety of water birds, not to mention crocodiles, sloths, two kinds of monkeys and countless iguanas sunning themselves on the muddy riverbanks or gathering in the trees.

Ruta Los Heroes BOAT TOUR
(☎2766-5858; 2hr tour per person US$20; ⏲7am-3pm) The pink building near the dock is a boat-captain cooperative, offering river tours with ecological and historical emphasis. Make arrangements to leave as early as possible to beat the heat and see more wildlife. If the office is closed (as it sometimes is in the low season), you can negotiate directly with the captains you find at the dock.

Oasis Nature Tours BOAT TOUR
(☎2766-6260, 2766-6108; www.oasisnaturetours.com; full-day tour incl transportation from San José US$65-80) This is just one of several guides that runs boat tours on the local rivers. Also offers zip lining, rafting and other guided adventures.

Sleeping

This stretch of jungle boasts quite a range of accommodations, from budget bunks in town designed for local long-term plantation workers to several excellent lodges on the outskirts.

Cabinas Laura CABINA $
(☎2766-6316; s/d US$25/30; P ❄) Located on the road to the pier, this place is quiet and cheap. Rooms are simple but spotless, with new tiles, wooden furnishings and cable TV.

★**Posada Andrea Cristina B&B** B&B $$
(☎2766-6265; www.andreacristina.com; d incl breakfast US$58-62; P 📶) On the edge of town and at the edge of the forest, this charming B&B is a gem. The grounds are swarming with birds, sloths and monkeys, not to mention the frogs that populate the pond. Quaint cabins all have high, beamed ceilings, colorful paint jobs and private terraces. Or opt to stay in a funky tree house, built around a thriving Inga tree.

Your delightful host, Alex Martínez, is also a birding guide. He's active in environmental protection and runs Tierra Hermosa, a nearby wildlife reserve and rescue center. You'll see some of the 'clients' around the *posada*.

Hotel El Bambú HOTEL $$
(☎2766-6005; www.elbambu.com; d standard/superior incl breakfast US$90/105; P ❄ 📶 🏊) This big hotel is smack dab in the middle of town, with a popular restaurant and an inviting pool. The rooms are spacious and attractive enough, though it's worth springing for the 'superior,' which has a Jacuzzi tub and a private balcony facing the trees.

Hotel Gavilán HOTEL $$
(☎2234-9507; www.gavilanlodge.com; d/tr/q from US$70/85/100; P ❄ 📶 🏊) Sitting on a 100-hectare reserve about 4km northeast of Puerto Viejo, this former cattle *hacienda* is a bird-watching haven, with 5km of private trails on the grounds. The tired but cozy rooms have pastel paint jobs and wide porches, some with river views. Management is quite charming, offering private boat tours and bird walks upon request.

Hotel Ara Ambigua HOTEL $$$
(☎2766-7101; www.hotelaraambigua.com; d/tr/q incl breakfast from US$115/140/160; P ❄ 📶 🏊) About 1km west of Puerto Viejo, this countryside retreat offers oddly formal but well-equipped rooms, set on gorgeous grounds.

There are birds buzzing in the luscious, blooming gardens, poison-dart frogs in the *ranario* (frog pond) and caimans in the small lake.

Even if you're not staying here, the on-site pizzeria, La Casona, is an excellent place to grab lunch and spy on your feathered friends.

 Eating

Most of the lodgings in and around Puerto Viejo have on-site restaurants or provide meals. Otherwise, there are several *sodas* in Puerto Viejo de Sarapiquí and a supermarket at the western end of town.

Chicharronera Caballo Loco STEAK $
(☑ 8630-2320; www.facebook.com/chicharronera caballoloco; mains US$4-8; ⊙ 6am-8pm Mon-Sat, 11am-10pm Sun) This is an open-air joint, serving up *chicharones* (fried pork or beef rinds) and other meats just outside the livestock auction mart. Take your lunch inside to watch the auction action. The livestock sales can attract quite a crowd of *sabaneros* and other local characters, so it's great people-watching (and animal-watching, for that matter).

Restaurante La Casona PIZZA $$
(☑ 2766-7101; www.hotelaraambigua.com; meals US$8-16; ⊙ 8am-10pm; 🛜📶) At Hotel Ara Ambigua, this place is particularly recommended for its oven-baked pizza and typical, homemade cuisine served in an open-air *rancho*. The deck offers a sweet view of the gardens, where birds flutter by as you enjoy your meal.

ℹ **Information**

Banco Popular (☑ 2766-5658; ⊙ 8:45am-4:30pm Mon-Fri, 8:15-11:30am) is located near the dock; **Banco de Costa Rica** (⊙ 9am-4pm Mon-Fri) is at the entrance of town.

Cruz Roja (☑ administration 2764-2424, emergency 2766-6212) provides medical care.

ℹ **Getting There & Away**

The **bus terminal** (⊙ 5am-7pm) is right across from the park, near the Hotel El Bambú. Local buses run hourly between La Virgen and Puerto Viejo de Sarapiquí (US$1, 30 minutes) from 6am to 8pm.

Ciudad Quesada (Transportes Linaco) US$3, two hours, departs eight times daily from 4:40am to 6:30pm.

Guápiles (Transportes Guapileños) US$2, one hour, departs 10 times daily from 5:30am to 5pm.

San José (Autotransportes Sarapiquí and Empresarios Guapileños) US$2.50, two hours, departs 5am, 5:30am, 7am, 8am, 11am, 1:30pm, 3pm and 5:30pm.

Estación Biológica La Selva

Not to be confused with Selva Verde Lodge in Chilamate, Estación Biológica La Selva is a working biological research station equipped with laboratories, experimental plots, a herbarium and an extensive library. The station is usually teeming with scientists and students researching the nearby private reserve.

The area protected by La Selva is 16 sq km of premontane wet tropical rainforest, much of which is undisturbed. It's bordered to the south by the 476-sq-km Parque Nacional Braulio Carrillo, creating a protected area large enough to support a great diversity of life. More than 886 bird species have been recorded here, as well as 120 mammal species (including 70 species of bat and five species of big cat), 1850 species of vascular plant (especially from the orchid, philodendron, coffee and legume families) and thousands of insect species – with 500 types of ant alone.

☞ **Tours**

Remember that – practically speaking – it's always the rainy season here. If hiking, bring rain gear and footwear that's suitable for muddy trails, as well as insect repellent and a water bottle.

TS La Selva Research station HIKING
(☑ 2766-6565; www.threepaths.co.cr; guided hike US$35, bird-watching hike US$50; ⊙ guided hike 8am & 1:30pm, bird-watching hike 5:45am) Reservations are required for three-hour guided hikes with a bilingual naturalist guide. You'll head across the hanging bridge and into 57km of well-developed jungle trails, some of which are wheelchair accessible. Unguided hiking is forbidden, although you'll be allowed to wander a bit after your guided tour. You should also make reservations for the popular guided bird-watching hikes.

🛏 **Sleeping & Eating**

La Selva welcomes drop-ins for the lodgings at the research station, though it's best to phone ahead and reserve your accommodations.

OTS La Selva Research Station   LODGE $$$
(☎2766-6565; www.threepaths.co.cr; r per person incl meals from US$90-95; ℙ) Rooms are equipped with twin beds, private bathrooms, fans and balconies overlooking the forest. There are also family-style houses, as well as dorm rooms with bunk beds and shared bathrooms. Prices include meals and guided hikes.

ℹ Getting There & Away

Public buses between Puerto Viejo and Río Frío/ Horquetas can drop you off along the highway, which is 1km from the entrance to La Selva. Alternatively, catch a taxi from Puerto Viejo, which is about 4km away.

Horquetas & Around

South of Puerto Viejo de Sarapiquí, plantations line Hwy 4 and sprawl all the way to the marshes and mangroves of the Caribbean coast. To the west, the rugged hills of the Cordillera Central mark the northeastern boundary of Parque Nacional Braulio Carrillo. Most travelers on this scenic stretch of highway are either heading to the Caribbean coast or to the Central Valley. However, some are pulling off the road to visit one of the area's unique off-the-beaten-track destinations, like the world-class botanical garden at Heliconia Island or the backyard frog habitats at Frog's Heaven.

◉ Sights

Heliconia Island   GARDENS
(☎2764-5220; www.heliconiaisland.com; self-guided/guided tours US$10/18, d/q from US$80/ 100; ⊙8am-5pm; ℙ🐾) 🐾 Drive down a rugged road, walk across the bridge and enter a masterpiece of landscape architecture that is home to more than 80 varieties of heliconias, tropical flowers, plants and trees. The 2.3-hectare island overlooking the Río Puerto Viejois is also a refuge for 228 species of bird, including a spectacled owl who returns every year to raise her family. There are resident howler monkeys, river otters, sloths, and a few friendly dogs that will greet you upon arrival.

Dutch owners Henk and Carolien offer guided tours to show off the most memorable plants, including rare hybrids of heliconia found only on the island. They also own swatches of secondary forest on either side of the garden, which offers a wild forest buffer and attracts wildlife. The admission fee is waived for overnight guests, who stay in immaculate raised cabins with stone floors and breezy balconies. Heliconia Island is about 5km north of Horquetas.

Frog's Heaven   GARDENS
(Cielo de Ranas; ☎2764-2724, 8891-8589; www. frogsheaven.com; adult/child US$25/12; ⊙8am-8pm; 🐾) 🐾 The frogs hop free in this lovely tropical garden, which provides a perfect habitat for more than 20 species. On guided tours you're likely to see old favorites like the red-eyed tree frog and poison-dart frogs, as well as some lesser-known exotic amphibians, such as the translucent glass frog and the wrinkly Mexican tree frog. Come for the night tour to see a whole different frog world.

This place is also excellent for birding and – occasionally – spotting other creatures too. Reserve at least a day ahead. Located in Horquetas, diagonal from the church.

🛏 Sleeping

The tricky thing about the lodges in Horquetas is that they're not exactly in Horquetas. They use this address because it is the nearest vestige of civilization – but these lodges are out there. Some of them are *way* out there. Make reservations and follow instructions on how to get there. And don't forget your sense of adventure, because you're going to need it.

Yatama Ecolodge   LODGE $$
(☎7015-1121; www.facebook.com/yatamacr; per person incl 3 meals US$80) Are you willing to forgo some creature comforts for the chance to commune with the rainforest? At Yatama, you'll sleep in primitive wooden cabins with no electricity. You'll slog through the mud to glimpse frogs, birds and bugs. You'll eat satisfying food. You'll skip showers in favor of river swims. And you'll revel in the vibrancy of the forest around you.

Staff picks you up in Horquetas to make the treacherous, one-hour drive up to this primitive lodge on the edge of the Parque Nacional Braulio Carrillo. Bring: insect repellent, rubber boots and an adventurous spirit.

Rara Avis   CABINA $$$
(☎2200-4238, 2764-1111; www.rara-avis.com; s/d casitas US$70/130, lodge US$85/160, all incl meals) When they say remote, they mean remote. This private reserve, 13 sq km of high-altitude tropical rainforest, is accessible only

to guests who make the three-hour tractor ride up a steep, muddy hill. Accommodations are rustic: there's no electricity, though the kerosene lamps and starry skies are unforgettable. Prices include all meals, transportation from Horquetas and two guided hikes per day.

The private reserve borders the eastern edge of Parque Nacional Braulio Carrillo and has no real dry season. Bird-watching here is excellent, with more than 350 documented species, while mammals including monkeys, coatis, anteaters and pacas are often seen. Since getting here is time-consuming and difficult, a two-night stay is recommended. You can also arrange to travel on horseback instead of by tractor, but you'll have to hike the last 3km yourself.

Sueño Azul Resort RESORT $$$

(☑ 2764-1000; www.suenoazulresort.com; d US$120-150, extra person US$20; P❋🐾🛜🏊) Sueño Azul has a stunning perch at the confluence of the Ríos Sarapiquí and San Rafael. The vast property has hiking trails, a suspension bridge, a canopy tour and a waterfall, as well as a stable of gorgeous horses. The facility itself is looking worse for wear, but rooms are comfortable enough, with log beds and river views.

The restaurant, unfortunately, is overpriced and uninspiring – which is a shame, as there are no other options in the vicinity. From Horquetas, follow the signs over the suspension bridge to the property entrance, from where it's another 1.4km (with another precarious bridge crossing) to the resort itself.

❶ Getting There & Away

About 12 smoothly paved kilometers from Puerto Viejo de Sarapiquí is the village of Horquetas, around which you'll find the turnoffs for Frog's Heaven, Heliconia Island and the other resorts. From Horquetas it's another 15km to Hwy 32, which connects San José to the Caribbean coast and bisects Parque Nacional Braulio Carrillo on the way to San José.

Península de Nicoya

Best Places
to Sleep

➜ Hotel Quinta Esencia (p295)

➜ Villa Mango B&B (p316)

➜ Costa Rica Yoga Spa (p317)

➜ Camp SuperTramp (p321)

Most Beautiful
Beaches

➜ Playa Conchal (p298)

➜ Playa Junquillal (p309)

➜ Playa Carrillo (p324)

➜ Playa San Miguel (p326)

Why Go?

Maybe you've come to the Península de Nicoya to sample the sapphire waters that peel left and right, curling into perfect barrels up and down the coast. Or perhaps you just want to hunker down on a pristine patch of sand and soak up some sun. By day, you might ramble down rugged roads, fording rivers and navigating ridges with massive coastal views. By night, you can spy on nesting sea turtles or take a midnight dip in the luxuriant Pacific. In between adventures, you'll find no shortage of boutique bunks, tasty kitchens and indulgent spas to shelter and nourish body and soul. Whether you come for the thrills or just to chill, the Nicoya Peninsula delivers. You'll find that the days (or weeks, or months) drift away on ocean breezes, disappearing all too quickly.

When to Go

➜ During September and October, peak rainfalls swell rivers, making some roads impassable.

➜ The peninsula is at its most lush in September and October: the air isn't nearly as dusty, the whales are migrating and prices are cheap.

➜ From May to November, accommodations rates are lower. Prices rise significantly during holiday weeks (Christmas, New Year's and Easter).

Península de Nicoya Highlights

1 Diving down deep to spy on sea turtles, manta rays and bull sharks at **Playa del Coco** (p288).

2 Catching morning swells and relishing afternoon asanas in **Nosara** (p312).

3 Marveling at Mother Nature's ways in **Refugio Nacional de Fauna Silvestre Ostional** (p319) during *arribada*, the mass arrival of nesting ridley turtles.

4 Sitting beneath the palms at **Playa Carrillo** (p324) and watching a spectacular sunset.

5 Devouring delectable *ceviche* and ice-cold *cerveza* at **LocosCocos** (p327) on a postcard-perfect beach.

6 Surfing luscious breaks and feasting on farm-fresh cooking in **Mal País** and **Santa Teresa** (p328).

7 Kayaking and swimming in the bioluminescent waters of **Refugio Nacional de Vida Silvestre Curú** (p343).

8 Hiking to a wilderness beach at the tip of the peninsula at **Reserva Natural Absoluta Cabo Blanco** (p335).

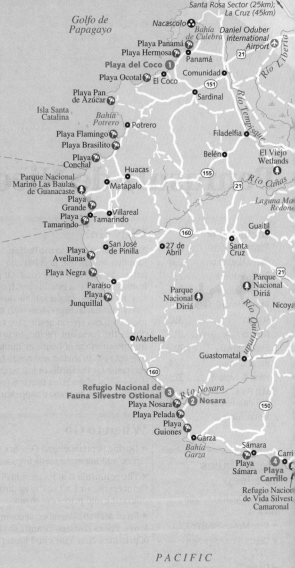

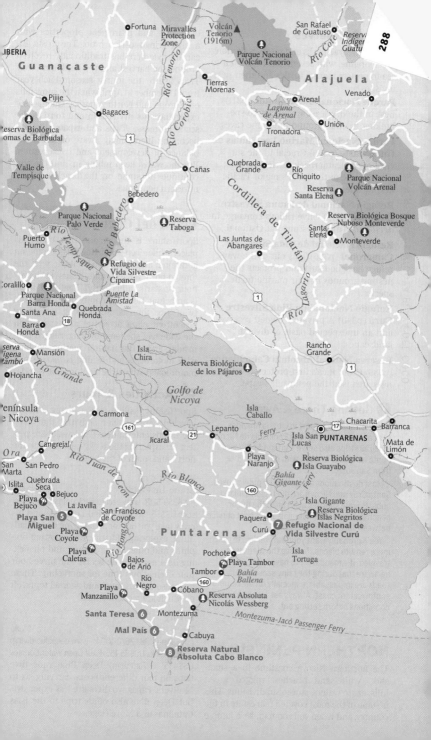

IBERIA

Fortuna

Miravalles
Protection
Zone

Volcán
Tenorio
(1916m)

San Rafael
de Guatuso

Reserva
Indígena
Guatu

Guanacaste

Parque Nacional
Volcán Tenorio

Alajuela

Río Cote

Pijije

Tierras
Morenas

Venado

Bagaces

Arenal

Reserva Biológica
omas de Barbudal

Laguna
de Arenal

Río Corobicí

Unión

Tronadora

Valle de
Tempisque

Tilarán

Cañas

Quebrada
Grande

Río
Chiquito

Parque Nacional
Volcán Arenal

Bebedero

Cordillera de Tilarán

Reserva
Santa Elena

Río Tenorio

Reserva
Taboga

Santa
Elena

Reserva Biológica Bosque
Nuboso Monteverde

Parque Nacional
Palo Verde

Las Juntas de
Abangares

Monteverde

Puerto
Humo

Río Tempisque

Río Bebedero

Refugio de
Vida Silvestre
Cipanci

Coralillo

Parque Nacional
Barra Honda

Puente La
Amistad

Santa Ana

Quebrada
Honda

Isla
Chira

Barra
Honda

erva
ígena
ambú

Mansión

Río Lagarto

Río Grande

Reserva Biológica
de los Pájaros

Rancho
Grande

Hojancha

Golfo de
Nicoya

Península
e Nicoya

Carmona

Isla
Caballo

Isla
Cabuya

Chacarita

Barranca

Cangrejal

Jicaral

Lepanto

Ferry

Isla San
Lucas

PUNTARENAS

Mata de
Limón

Ora

Río Juan de León

Playa
Naranjo

Reserva Biológica
Isla Guayabo

San
Marta

San Pedro

Río Blanco

Bahía
Gigante

Islita

Quebrada
Seca

Bejuco

Isla Gigante

Reserva Biológica
Islas Negritos

Playa
Bejuco

La Javilla

San Francisco
de Coyote

Puntarenas

Paquera

Curú

Refugio Nacional de
Vida Silvestre Curú

**Playa San
Miguel**

Playa
Coyote

Río Bongo

Pochote

Isla
Tortuga

Playa
Caletas

Bajos
de Arió

Playa Tambor

Río
Negro

Tambor

Bahía
Ballena

Playa
Manzanillo

Cóbano

Reserva Absoluta
Nicolás Wessberg

Santa Teresa

Montezuma

Montezuma-Jacó Passenger Ferry

Mal País

Cabuya

**Reserva Natural
Absoluta Cabo Blanco**

Parks & Reserves

Most of Nicoya's parks and reserves lie along the shoreline, with several stretching out to sea to protect marine turtles and their nesting sites.

Parque Nacional Barra Honda (p311) Best in the dry season; you can go spelunking in underground limestone caves.

Parque Nacional Marino Las Baulas de Guanacaste (p298) Crucial to the survival of the leatherback turtle, this park protects one of the turtle's major Pacific nesting sites.

Refugio Nacional de Fauna Silvestre Ostional (p319) Olive ridleys converge in *arribadas* (mass nestings) at Ostional.

Refugio Nacional de Vida Silvestre Camaronal (p326) This out-of-the-way refuge has good surf and protects the nesting grounds of four marine turtle species.

Refugio Nacional de Vida Silvestre Curú (p343) A privately owned reserve and an unexpected oasis of diverse landscapes.

Reserva Natural Absoluta Cabo Blanco (p335) Costa Rica's first protected wilderness area is at the peninsula's cape.

❶ Getting There & Away

The international airport in Liberia provides easy access to much of the Península de Nicoya. Small airstrips also serve Tamarindo, Nosara, Punta Islita and Tambor, with regular flights from San José.

Most destinations are served by public buses; Santa Cruz and Nicoya are the region's inland hubs. Private shuttles also run to the major beach destinations (including a fast boat service between Jacó and Montezuma).

You'll probably want your own vehicle to reach more remote places. To drive the roads less traveled, it's mandatory to have a 4WD, but be aware that during the rainy season many roads are impassable, especially on the remote southwestern coast. Always ask locally about conditions before setting out.

NORTHERN PENINSULA

The northern Nicoya coastline in a snapshot: white-sand beaches, rugged green hills, azure waters, stucco subdivisions. This is some of the most coveted real estate in the country, and when you zoom in, it's a jumble of resorts and retirement properties with a high gringo-to-Tico ratio. The Costa Rican lifestyle here has traditionally revolved around the harvest and the herd, but today Ticos live by the tourist season. Each year from December to April, when the snow falls on Europe and North America, Guanacaste experiences its dry season and tourists descend en masse. Ticos and expats alike are becoming increasingly aware of the tricky balance of development and conservation. But the waves keep rolling in, and the sun continues to smile on the beaches of the northern peninsula.

Playa del Coco

Sportfishing is the engine that built this place, while deep-sea diving has become an additional attraction. You'll mingle with the foreign-born anglers and divers at happy hour (it starts rather early). That said, there is an actual Tico community here, and plenty of Tico tourists. Stroll along the grassy beachfront plaza at sunset and gaze upon the wide bay, sheltered by long, rugged peninsular arms, the natural marina bobbing with motorboats and fishing *pangas* (small motorboats). All will be right in your world.

🏃 Activities & Tours

Sportfishing, sailing, scuba diving and sea kayaking are popular activities that keep the troops entertained. Sea kayaks are perfect for exploring the rocky headlands to the north and south of the beach.

Pacific Coast Stand-Up Paddle WATER SPORTS
(☑8359-5118; www.pacificcoastsuptours.com; lessons US$35, tours US$65-85) Let Jorge and his crew take you out for an amazing day of paddling, exploring hidden coves, spotting dolphins and other sea creatures, and picnicking on a near-private beach. The three-hour tour even allows time for snorkeling. These guys also do surf tours and snorkel tours, all of which are recommended.

Diving

Deep Blue Diving DIVING
(☑8349-0498, 2670-1004; www.deepblue-diving.com; 2 tanks US$85-155, PADI Open Water Courses US$435; ◉7am-6pm) Deep Blue runs dive trips on four different boats, carrying six to 14 divers. Papagayo dives are less expensive, but Deep Blue also offers trips to the Islas Catalinas and Murciélagos.

DIVERS DO IT DEEPER

The northern peninsula is one of the best and most easily accessible dive destinations in the country, though visibility varies greatly (9m to 15m, and sometimes up to 20m). Typical dive sites include:

➡ Volcanic rock pinnacles near the coast

➡ Isla Santa Catalina (about 20km to the southwest)

➡ Isla Murciélago (40km to the northwest, near the tip of Península Santa Elena)

There is no colorful hard coral such as you would see at a reef, but the sites make up for it with abundant marine life. Plenty of turtles and pelagics meander through, including mantas, sharks and whales. You'll be lost in huge schools of smaller tropical fish. These waters are sometimes home to humpback whales, who can be heard underwater during calving season (January to March) and seen during migration season (June and July).

Isla Santa Catalina and Isla Murciélago both host migrant manta rays from December to late April, and Murciélago is also known for its regular sightings of resident bull sharks. Divers also head to Narizones, which is a good deep dive (about 27m), while Punta Gorda is an easy descent for inexperienced divers.

Rich Coast Diving
DIVING

(☑ 2670-0176; www.richcoastdiving.com; 2 tanks from US$85, Open Water Courses US$450; ☺ 7:30am-6pm) This Dutch outfit is one of the largest dive operations in Coco. They offer the regular range of local dives (good for sharks, rays and schools of fish) as well as more expensive trips to the Islas Catalinas and Murciélagos.

Summer Salt
DIVING

(☑ 2670-0308; www.summer-salt.com; 2 tanks from US$85) This friendly Swiss-run dive shop has professional, bilingual staff. Snorkelers are also welcome on the dive boats

Fishing

Blue Marlin
FISHING

(☑ 2670-2222; www.sportfishingbluemarlin.com; half-day from US$500) Takes sports fishers out on eight different cruises, ranging from the 28ft *Sea Fox* to the luxury 55ft *Jackpot*. Fishers routinely hook sailfish, marlin, *dorado* (mahimahi) and roosterfish. This company practices catch and release with all species.

Dream On Sportfishing
FISHING

(☑ 8735-3121; dreamonsportfishing.com; half-/full-day trips from US$500/800) This team of fishing enthusiasts will take you out on one of three excellent boats, ranging from 25ft to 35ft, all fitted for your comfort. They do anything they can to make your day – even clean your catch!

 Festivals & Events

Fiesta Cívica
CULTURAL

(www.facebook.com/fiestasplayasdelcoco2015; ☺ Jan) During the last week in January the town hosts a multiday Fiesta Cívica, with bullfights, rodeos, dancing and plenty of drinking.

🛌 Sleeping

Garden House at M&M
HOSTEL $

(☑ 2670-0273; gardenhouse@hotelmym.com; La Chorrera; dm $20-25, d $60; ❄ 🋀 🉑) There are plenty of budget *cabinas* in Coco but this is the only proper hostel. After many changes in name and management, the property is now known as the Garden House, and is operated by the good folks behind Hotel M&M (p290). There are three dorm rooms, a handful of privates and a sweet swimming pool, all within striking distance of the beach.

Villa del Sol
HOTEL $$

(☑ 2670-0085, in Canada 866-793-9523, in USA 866-815-8902; www.villadelsol.com; La Chorrera; r incl breakfast US$85, apt US$100; 🅿 ❄ @ 🋀 🉑) About 1km north of the town center, this leafy, tranquil property attracts monkeys, iguanas and a good variety of birdlife, in addition to the happy travelers lounging on hammocks. The main building has stylish rooms with sunset-view balconies. In the back building, studio apartments (sleeping four) offer excellent value. Walk to the beach in five minutes or less.

Pato Loco Inn GUESTHOUSE $$

(☎2670-0145; www.patolocoinn.com; d/tr/q incl breakfast US$58/68/78; P❄@📶🏊🐾) Richard and Mary Cox offer a warm welcome to Coco Beach, with a wide range of rooms, a friendly bar and the best American breakfast in town (think biscuits and gravy). Most of the rooms feature stenciling or thematic murals, hand-painted by Mary herself. Stop by for Monday or Friday happy hour to shoot the breeze with the expats.

Hotel M&M HOTEL $$

(☎2670-1212; www.hotelmym.com; s/d/tr incl breakfast US$34/54/70; P📶) A romantic beachfront hacienda with an all-wood balcony overlooking the boardwalk. Fan-cooled rooms have ceramic tiled floors, beamed ceilings and cold-water showers. This simple place is one of the only beachfront properties in Coco. And if the beach is not your thing, you're invited to take a dip in the pool at sister property Garden House (p289).

Toro Blanco HOTEL $$

(☎8950-6126, 2670-1707; www.toroblancoresort.com; s/d US$50/90; P❄📶🏊) This mustard-yellow, two-story colonial-style building surrounds a courtyard with a lovely swimming pool and swim-up bar. Apartments are outfitted with engraved headboards, wooden wardrobes, kitchenettes and flat-screen TVs. The private terraces are decked with pink flamingos and white bulls, so there's that, too.

Hotel La Puerta del Sol HOTEL $$$

(☎2670-0195; www.lapuertadelsolcostarica.com; d/ste incl breakfast US$113/158; P❄📶🏊) This unpretentiously luxurious Mediterranean-inspired hotel is a short walk from the town and the beach, but a world away from the traffic and the noise. There are two large suites and eight huge pastel-colored rooms, with polished brick and concrete floors, king-sized beds and private terraces. The grounds are lush with blooming tropical flowers surrounding a glorious pool.

Hotel Chantel BOUTIQUE HOTEL $$$

(☎2670-0389; www.hotelchantel.com; d incl breakfast US$99-110, ste US$120-125; P❄📶🏊🐾) Perched on a cliff overlooking the coast, this intimate hotel is a step up from other local lodgings. Eleven rooms have tasteful wood and wicker furniture, contemporary artwork on the walls, and private terraces with stunning vistas of Playa del Coco. The breezy rooftop restaurant (the Lookout) and the elegant infinity pool share the same panoramic view.

It's a short drive from town: just south of Flor de Itabo, head west off the main road and follow the signs.

Rancho Armadillo HOTEL $$$

(☎8336-9645, 2670-0108; www.ranchoarmadillo.com; d incl breakfast standard US$204, deluxe US$244-278; P❄📶🏊) Near the entrance to town, this private estate is on a hillside about 600m off the main road (mostly paved), with ocean views to remind you where you are. It's set on 25 acres with plenty of wildlife, and the seven rooms are decorated with individually crafted furniture, hand-woven tapestries and local artwork. Self-catering gourmands will appreciate the fully equipped professional kitchen.

Eating

Coco's main drag is lined with places to eat, though it's hard to distinguish one from another on this noisy, crowded street. Our favorite places are on the beach (of course) or tucked away in the quieter corners of town. Not surprisingly, this town excels at seafood.

Soda La Teresita SODA $

(☎2670-0665; mains US$5-10; ⏰6:30am-9pm Mon-Sat, to 5pm Sun) Located at the crossroads of the main drag and the beach, this place can't be beaten for people-watching in Coco. It's also your best bet for lunch, whether you're hankering for a *torta* (sandwich) or a traditional *casado* (set meal). Teresita also cooks up a hearty breakfast.

Congo CAFE $

(☎2670-1265; www.costaricacongo.com; mains US$6-10; ⏰8am-7pm; P📶🖉) Part cafe, part funky retail boutique, Congo's interior is groovy with arched booths, rattan sofas and a deconstructed wood-and-granite coffee bar. They serve all the espresso drinks and an array of healthy sandwiches, salads and breakfasts.

★**Lookout** SEAFOOD $$

(☎8755-7246; www.thelookoutcoco.com; oysters US$2-3, small plates US$6-15; ⏰3-10pm Tue-Sun; 📶🖉) So many things to love about the Lookout: sustainably harvested Pacific oysters, locally brewed craft beers, and a small but intriguing menu of snacks, *ceviches* and sandwiches. And then there's the view. It's a stunner, taking in the Golfo de Papagayo and the Cordillera de Guanacaste in the distance. Located on the top floor of the Hotel Chantel.

La Dolce Vita ITALIAN $$
(☑ 2670-1384; www.ladolcevitacostarica.com; La Chorrera; mains US$10-18; ☺ 8am-10pm; 🖉) Set in the Pueblito Sur development about 500m north of the main drag, this is the local expat choice for wood-fired pizza in Playa del Coco. The restaurant is lovingly set in a brick courtyard sprinkled with candlelit tables around a gurgling fountain. They also do a range of pastas, unique preparations of seafood and traditional grills.

Citron FUSION $$$
(☑ 2670-0942; www.citroncoco.com; mains US$15-20; ☺ 5:30-10pm Mon-Sat) The contemporary menu features fresh ingredients and innovative preparations, including a few enticing specials from the wok (think sea bass poached with scallions, soy sauce and sesame oil). Save room for a decadent Mediterranean dessert. Despite the shopping-mall setting, you can dine in the sophisticated, minimalist dining room or on an open-air deck, surrounded by pochote trees.

🍷 Drinking & Nightlife

La Vida Loca BAR
(☑ 2670-0181; www.lavidalocabeachbar.com; ☺ 11am-11pm) Across a creaky wooden footbridge on the south end of the beach is where you'll find this hangout, popular among gringos and Ticos alike. It's a classic beach bar, with pool tables, live music and good vibes. If you're hungry, order up some comfort food such as burgers, nachos, meat loaf, chili dogs, clam chowder and more.

Tiki Coco Place BAR
(☑ 2670-0711; www.tikicoco.bar; ☺ 10am-11pm; 🛜) Get a front row seat for the ongoing beach volleyball match or, even better, a killer sunset. This open-air beach bar offers beach-accented gastropub fare, ice-cold beers and hand-crafted cocktails, not to mention service with a smile. Happy hour specials nightly from 3pm to 9pm.

ⓘ Information

Police are located southeast of the plaza by the beach.

The few people arriving at Playa del Coco by boat will find the **Immigration Office** (☑ 2670-1133; www.migracion.go.cr; ☺ 8am-4pm Mon-Fri) near the police station.

ⓘ Getting There & Away

It's easy to get to Playa del Coco, which is located less than 40km from Liberia and only 25km from that airport. The nearest gas station is in Sardinal, about 7.5km inland from Playa del Coco.

All buses arrive and depart from the main terminal, south of town.

Liberia US$2; one hour; departs hourly from 5am to 11pm.

San José Pulmitan (p98) US$10; five hours; departs 4am, 8am and 2pm.

Playa Hermosa

Playa Hermosa ('beautiful beach') is a lovely, wide and languid sheltered bay, framed by headlands and sprinkled with coconut palms and olive trees. Although it's only 5.5km (by road) north of Playa del Coco, and development is springing up rapidly along this entire coastline, Hermosa feels more remote.

🏃 Activities & Tours

BA Divers DIVING
(☑ 2672-0032; www.badivers.cr; 2-tank dives from US$120; ☺ 7am-5pm) BA's very experienced and efficient crew will take you out on the *Legend* to hit the local dive sites around Playa Hermosa. Longer trips to the Bat Islands are also on offer. Located on the main road at the southern end of town.

North Pacific Tours FISHING
(☑ 8398-8129; www.northpacifictours.com; fishing from US$400, surfing from US$275) This fish and surf operation knows where to find the biggest fish and the biggest breaks. Captain Mauricio and first mate Daniel will take you on their 26ft fishing boat, *Don Manual,* for coastal fishing, snorkeling and/or surfing. Split-charters available.

🛏 Sleeping

Congo's Hostel & Camping HOSTEL $
(☑ 2672-1168; www.congoshostel.com; dm incl breakfast US$12-15; 🅿 ❄ 🛜) This decent, friendly budget option is on the second beach access road, just one block from the beach. It's a ramshackle but relaxed place, offering hammocks, secure parking and an

open-air communal kitchen. The four-bed dorm rooms have metal beds with worn mattresses, and a bathroom in each. Breakfast is coffee and bread.

La Gaviota Tropical HOTEL $$$
(☎2672-0011; www.lagaviotatropical.com; r/ste US$140/160; ₽❋☎❄) It's ingenious: a vertical hotel. All five huge suites – fully equipped and impeccably decorated – face the glorious sea. Climb to the top floor to cool off in the small but spectacular infinity pool. Downstairs, you can enjoy an excellent meal at Roberto's restaurant (☎2672-0011; www. lagaviotatropical.com; mains US$9-18; ⊙11am-10pm; ☎) or walk a few steps to the sand.

Hotel El Velero HOTEL $$$
(☎2672-1017, 2672-0036; www.costaricahotel. net; d US$113; ₽❋☎❄) Just steps from the beach, this resort hotel has 22 spacious rooms decorated with woodwork, bamboo beds with colorful bedspreads, wicker ceiling fans, and granite washbasins. Ask for a seafront room on the 2nd floor for maximum views. The staff might be the friendliest folks on the beach, going out of their way to get to know their guests and provide superior service.

Hotel La Finisterra BOUTIQUE HOTEL $$$
(☎2672-0227; www.lafinisterrahotel.com; d/ste from US$175/232; ₽❋@☎❄) Notched into the southern headland, this stylish boutique hotel has only 10 rooms and suites, all with stunning ocean views. Rooms are clean and comfortable with big picture windows. Common areas also enjoy a fabulous panorama of surf, sand and sky. It's a steep hike down to the water, if you actually want to get your toes wet.

✖ Eating

Aqua Sport COSTA RICAN $$
(☎2672-0151; www.facebook.com/aquasportcr; mains US$10-20; ⊙10am-10pm; ☎) This colorful, fun beach bar is an excellent place to pass an evening feasting on burgers or fish tacos and swilling beers. Or sample the Peruvian specialties, such as *lomo saltado* (salted pork), *diabla* octopus (spicy with tomato sauce) and of course *ceviche*. Hammocks hang from the rafters and Adirondack chairs sit right on the sand. *¡Que rico!*

Ginger MEDITERRANEAN $$
(☎2672-0041; www.gingercostarica.com; tapas US$6-13; ⊙5-10pm Tue-Sun; ✐) On the east side of the main road, you'll see this stun-

ner cantilevered into the trees. This is not the restaurant you would expect to find in an unassuming beach village. The chic ambience complements a gourmet list of Asian- and Mediterranean-inspired tapas, fresh-fruit cocktails and a decent wine list. Reservations recommended for dinner during busy seasons.

ⓘ Getting There & Away

BUS
Buses to Liberia and San José depart from the main road on the northern end of the beach and make a stop in Sardinal.
Liberia La Pampa (☎2665-7530, 2686-7245) US$2; 1¼ hours; departs eight times from 6am to 7pm.
San José Tralapa (p98) US$11; six hours; departs 5am.

CAR
Coming from Liberia, you'll drive west for 14km, crossing the steel bridge and entering the village of Comunidad. Right before the Do-It Center, turn right and drive another 1.6km. Turn left at the sign for Playa Panama. Continue 11km and turn left onto the road that will take you into Hermosa. The entire route is paved, albeit windy.

If you have some time, it's worth exploring the beaches along the Golfo de Papagayo. Playa Panamá is right in the middle of the gulf with mangroves on one side, and a placid bay that feels almost like a lake. In between are the rustic Playa Bonita and Playa Buena.

Playa Ocotal

There is not much of a town here – just a few vacation rentals and an attractive resort. That's one reason it feels like a rustic outpost amid the condo-mania of the northern peninsula. The beach is gray and wooded, and the northernmost corner is quite picturesque. The water is warm and placid, and you can snorkel around the rocks at the southern end.

It's about 4km southwest of Playa del Coco by paved road; it's worth a trip simply to eat at Father Rooster's.

🏃 Activities

Rocket Frog Divers DIVING
(☎2670-1589; www.scuba-dive-costa-rica.com; 2 tanks US$85-165; ⊙8am-6pm) An awesome upstart dive shop on the Los Almendros property de Ocotal that hits 22 local dive sites and motors out to the Islas Catalinas to dive with

mantas. The 36ft, purpose-designed *Pacific Express* promises to make it to distant dive sites in half the time of other vessels.

Monkey Farm VOLUNTEERING
(☑8853-0165; www.themonkeyfarm.org; horseback riding US$45-60; ⊗8am-4pm) 🏖 A small team of enthusiastic international volunteers has started this experiment in sustainability. It's an animal rescue center; and, it's an organic farm. It's entirely volunteer run, so stop in (for a day or for a month) to take a tour and lend a helping hand. Call before visiting to make sure staff are on hand.

The Monkey Farm also offers horseback riding tours (on the beach or in the forest) to raise money for their efforts.

🛏 Sleeping & Eating

Los Almendros de Ocotal APARTMENT $$
(☑2670-1560; www.losalmendrosrentals.com; studio/apt/villa US$82/180/237; 🅿️❄️@🛜🏊) Perched on the hillside just above the beach, these studios and apartments are a great option for divers, beach bums and self-caterers. Studios sleep two, apartments sleep four and villas sleep six. The fancier units have a private pool and terrace.

Father Rooster Bar & Grill PUB FOOD $$
(☑2670-1246; www.fatherrooster.com; mains US$10-16; ⊗11:30am-9:30pm; 🛜) This colorful gastropub by the sea serves up tasty sandwiches and American pub fare, as well as top-notch (though expensive) cocktails. You cannot beat the location, whether you sit in the rockers on the shaded wooden terrace or at tables under the palms sunk into the sand. *¡Pura vida!*

❶ Getting There & Away

There are hourly buses between Liberia and Playa del Coco, some of which continue on to Ocotal. Otherwise, a taxi should cost under US$10.

Bahía Potrero

Although they're lined up in a row, Playas Danta, Pan de Azúcar, Potrero, Flamingo, Brasilito and Conchal have little in common. The beaches range from gray sand to white sand to crushed seashells, with a wide variety of development along the way. It's gratifying to know that even here – along this busy strip of coastline – it's still possible to find a pretty *playa* without another soul on it.

WORTH A TRIP

DIAMANTE ECO ADVENTURE PARK

Here's an attempt to fit all of Costa Rica into one adventure park. The oceanfront **Diamante Eco Adventure Park** (☑8682-2369; www.diamanteecoadventurepark.com; Playa Matapalo; packages from US$58; ⊗8:30am-5:30pm) offers almost every activity in the book, including ATV tours, fishing, hiking, biking, horseback riding, kayaking, snorkeling, scuba diving, stand-up paddling, surfing and zip lining. There's also an animal sanctuary and a botanical garden. And, in case you need a rest after all that adventure, a beach strung with hammocks.

Coming from the north, it's tempting to take the road from Sardinal to Potrero. Keep in mind there's a reason why locals call this route the 'Monkey Trail.' The first 8km of gravel road leading to the small town of Nuevo Colón is fine, but the second half is pretty brutal, and should only be tackled in dry season with a 4WD. The Monkey Trail begins 5km west of El Coco; turn right at the Castrol Oil sign and follow the signs for **Congo Trail Canopy Tour** (☑2666-4422; congotrail@racsa.co.cr; US$35; ⊗8am-5pm). At the 'T' intersection in Nuevo Colón, turn left, bear left at the fork and continue for 5km until you reach Congo Trail Canopy. From there, it's a hair-raising 6km drive to Bahía Potrero.

To avoid the rough roads, return to the main peninsular highway from El Coco, then head south through Filadelfia and on to Belén (a distance of 18km), from where a paved road heads 25km west to Huacas. Take the road leading north until you hit the ocean in Brasilito. If you turn right and head north, you'll pass Playa Flamingo and Bahía Potrero before reaching Playa Pan de Azúcar. If you make a left instead and head south, you will end up at Playa Conchal.

Potrero

Several beaches – largely undeveloped – are strung along this low-key bay. Playa Prieta is a gorgeous black-sand beach, with crystal-blue waters and lush green vegetation, making for a colorful landscape indeed. The small cove is ideal for swimming,

DON'T MISS

PLAYA PAN DE AZÚCAR

Although buses stop at Potrero, travelers with their own ride can continue 3km north on a paved road to 'Sugar-Bread Beach,' named for the strip of sugary white sand that's protected at both ends by rocky headlands. This is one of the most scenic stretches of road in all of northern Costa Rica, as dry rugged cliffs sheer down into aquamarine coves sheltered by offshore islets. The ocean here is calm, clear and perfect for snorkeling. The remote location – and the lack of cheap accommodations – create an atmosphere of total seclusion.

Luxury at the **Hotel Sugar Beach** (☑ 2654-4242; www.sugar-beach.com; d/ste with breakfast from US$158/280; P🌬@🛜🏊) is simple and understated, but undeniably classy. Floor-to-ceiling windows, private balconies and stunning views are just a few of the features you might enjoy in your room. A walking path winds through lovely landscaped grounds, down to the sweets sands of Pan de Azúcar. Overheard in the lobby: 'Now this is vacation.'

sunbathing and strolling. To the south, the gorgeous white-sand beach at Playa Penca curves around another little cove, where stand-up paddle boarders ply the sheltered turquoise bay toward gleaming offshore islets. Further south is the more developed 'town' beach, Playa Potrero.

There's a small fishing *pueblo* (village) at Potrero, just beyond the northern end of the eponymous beach. This is where the bus line ends, so these beaches won't see the weekend rush found at Brasilito.

Cacao Lodge   HOTEL **$$**
(☑ 2654-4145; www.facebook.com/cacaolodgecr; d with breakfast US$52; P🌬🛜🏊) Oddly situated on the main drag north of Potrero, this little place is set up like a roadside motel – a strip of rooms facing the pool, facing the road. That said, the place has a boutique feel, with batik fabrics adorning earth-toned walls. It's a 15-minute walk to Playa Penca.

Hotel Isolina   HOTEL **$$$**
(☑ 2654-4333; www.isolinabeach.com; d/tr/q incl breakfast from US$102/113/104; P🌬@🛜🏊) These attractive yellow concrete buildings are a comfortable and affordable option, with kitchenettes and multiroom options to accommodate families. The rooms are plain, with wood furniture and whitewashed walls; but the landscaped grounds are lovely, with two swimming pools, shady palms and blooming heliconias. At the north end of Playa Potrero, it's a short walk to Playa Penca, so that's a two-fer.

Shack   AMERICAN **$**
(☑ 2654-6038; www.facebook.com/TheShackCR; mains US$5-17; ⊙8am-10pm; P🛜) Set beneath a stilted tin roof twirling with ceiling fans,

this fabulous diner is Potrero's favorite spot to grab a bite. Come for breakfast when homemade bagels and sausages are served. Lunch and dinner feature Tex-Mex flavor, and they also do pizza, lobster rolls and more. Bonus: live music!

La Perla   BAR
(☑ 2654-4500; www.facebook.com/perlasbar; ⊙4pm-late; 🛜) You need to know La Perla, as it serves as the landmark by which all directions are given (next to La Perla, 300m south of La Perla etc). You might also want to know about its highly lauded Saturday night rib dinners. Live music, bar games and good-old-fashioned comfort food keep the expat community happy.

ℹ Getting There & Away

Departing Potrero, buses begin their route on the southeast corner of the soccer field. All buses go via Flamingo.

San José Tralapa US$13; six hours; departs 2:45am, 9am and 2pm.

Santa Cruz Folklórica, US$3; two hours; departs eight times per day from 6am to 9:40pm.

Playa Flamingo

Any time a once-pristine slice of paradise sprouts McMansions and condos and gets stitched up with a network of roads, there is a tendency to point fingers and raise hell about what was and what now is. And, yes, at Flamingo it does feel like the developers won. But that does not change the fact that this sugary, postcard-worthy white-sand and shell beach is glorious. Kissed by a serene blue sea with the rugged keys of the Catalinas floating off in the distance, it attracts a local Tico scene along with package tourists. Nose the air if you must, but why not enjoy the place?

Mariner Inn INN $

(☏2654-4081; www.marinerinn.com; d/q from US$39/45, ste US$68; P✳︎🐾🛜❄️) Overlooking the harbor, this old-school inn is an excellent deal in an expensive town. Rooms are from another era but they're not too shabby, featuring dark wood beds, ceramic tile floors and a fresh coat of paint. The biggest draw is the bar – an old sailor's hang.

La Cuchara Verde VEGETARIAN $$

(☏8811-0222; mains $8-12; ⊙9am-5pm Mon-Sat; 🛜🐾) ✿ 'Positive food' is what is promised at this good-vibe vegetarian cafe. Burgers, sandwiches, pastries and egg dishes will sate your animal-free appetite. Wash it down with an organic iced tea or a fresh-fruit smoothie. Good for your body, good for the earth.

Angelina's SEAFOOD $$$

(☏2654-4839; www.angelinasplayaflamingo.com; pizza US$13-19, mains US$16-29; ⊙11:30am-10pm) Relatively formal for Costa Rica, Angelina's offers fine dining in a breezy, open-air setting, upstairs at the Plaza. Innovative seafood preparations feature tropical fruits and local flavors. Frugal travelers can feast on thin-crust pizzas with unique toppings or delectable pasta dishes.

Beach House BAR

(☏2654-6203; www.beachhouseplayaflamingo. com; ⊙11am-9pm; 🛜👶) It's hard to resist this colorful shack on the beach offering cold fruity cocktails and glorious sunset views. Seafood and pub fare are on the menu. For entertainment purposes, there's live music and a playroom for kids. (Parents take note: kids eat for free on Friday nights.)

❶ Getting There & Away

Buses depart from the traffic circle near the town entrance and travel via Brasilito. Schedules change often, so ask locally about departure times as well as the best place on the road to wait for the bus.

Liberia La Pampa US$3; two hours; departs 5am, 10:30am, 12:30pm and 3:40pm.

San José Tralapa US$13; six hours; departs 9am and 2pm.

Santa Cruz Transportes Folklórica (☏2680-3161; transportesfolklorica.com) US$2; one hour; departs 12 times per day from 6am to 10pm.

Brasilito

Unlike the other touristy towns along this stretch, Brasilito feels like an authentic *pueblo,* complete with town square, beachfront soccer pitch, pink-washed *iglesia* (church) and friendly Tico community. All of which makes up for the beach, which has its (much) betters on either side. Fortunately, it's just a short stroll along the sea to sugary Conchal.

🛏 Sleeping

Diversion Tropical CABINA $

(☏2654-5519; www.diversiontropical.com; s/d/tr US$39/45/51; P✳︎🐾🛜❄️) Here's an outstanding deal in a busy, roadside location. Tiled rooms are clean but cramped, with upstairs rooms giving a glimpse of the ocean (which is 300m away). Guests have free use of snorkel gear, while kayaks and mountain bikes are available for rental. Communal facilities (aka the 'Fun Zone') include an outdoor kitchen and grill, a book exchange, board games and darts.

★Hotel Quinta Esencia B&B $$

(☏2654-5455; hotel-quintaesencia.net; d with breakfast US$75; P✳︎🐾🛜❄️) An awesome, artistic vibe pervades this chilled-out lodging, built around the trees on the northern edge of Brasilito. The comfortable guest rooms feature driftwood, bamboo and neutral tones, accented by ribbons of color. Co-owner Stephanie is an artist, and you'll see her work scattered about the premises. There's a lot of love here.

Hotel Brasilito HOTEL $$

(☏2654-4237; www.brasilito.com; r US$64-90; P✳︎🛜) On the beach side of the plaza, this basic hotel offers simple, clean rooms with wood floors and ceiling fans, lined up along a wide balcony. Sea-view rooms are a little more, but worth the splurge. Otherwise, the patio's hammocks are ideal for soaking up the sunset. Budget rooms (no air-con) are also available.

Conchal Hotel HOTEL $$$

(☏2654-9125; www.conchalcr.com; d incl breakfast US$99-120; P✳︎@🛜❄️) This bougainvillea- and palm-dappled lodge is a sweet retreat. Spacious rooms are fitted with unique design touches, such as beamed ceilings and wrought-iron furniture. Enjoy the lovely gardens while lounging poolside or from the privacy of your patio. A simple but

Golfo de
Papagayo

○ Liberia

Playa Pan de
Azúcar ○

Playa
Junquillal ○

Golfo de
Nicoya

PACIFIC
OCEAN

Playa
Carrillo ○

Playa
San Miguel ○

Reserva Natural
Absoluta Cabo Blanco ○

 Undiscovered Nicoya

When it comes to beautiful beaches, Península de Nicoya is blessed richly indeed. Development here is uneven, which means there are plenty of hidden nooks, secluded coves and pristine paradises that remain unexploited.

Of course, you can't just take a direct flight to paradise; you have to work for it. In Costa Rica, that usually means switching to 4WD, driving over some brutally bumpy roads, and perhaps fording a river or two. (NB: This itinerary is not recommended during the rainy season.) Hang on tight and embrace the adventure: it's worth the effort to discover your own secret spot.

Your first destination is **Playa Pan de Azúcar** (p294), accessible via the infamous Monkey Trail. It's a rough ride but you won't care once you reach this jigsaw of rugged cliffs and clandestine coves. The only place to sleep is the Hotel Sugar Beach (p294) – a sweet choice. Heading south, you'll pass through resort towns like **Playa Flamingo** (p292) and fishing villages like **Brasilito** (p295). The main road detours inland, so you can buzz right by Tamarindo. It's not until you reach **Playa Junquillal** (p309) that you'll start to feel you're really out there. And you are. Unless the surf's up, this stunning wilderness beach is often deserted.

Keep moving south, skipping Nosara and Sámara, but stopping at **Playa Carrillo** (p324), a white-sand beauty, framed by granite and backed by towering palms. Locals descend from the village to watch the sunset. You should join them.

The area between Carrillo and Santa Teresa remains one of the peninsula's most isolated and wonderful stretches of coastline. Tackle the rugged roads and you'll be rewarded with miles of abandoned beaches backed by forest-covered hills. Our favorite is **Playa San Miguel** (p326), at once desolate and divine. Don't miss sundowners at LocosCocos (p327).

Your final stop is the **Reserva Natural Absoluta Cabo Blanco** (p335), a nature reserve that covers the entire tip of Península de Nicoya. Here, the evergreen forests and wilderness beaches are mostly empty of visitors. Hike the Sendero Sueco to the tippety tip, a pebble beach with a gorgeous confluence of turquoise waters and green vegetation. This is as far south as you can go on the peninsula.

Top: Playa Carrillo (p324)
Bottom: Playa Flamingo (p294)

scrumptious continental breakfast is served at the Papaya Restaurant (which is also recommended for other meals).

Eating & Drinking

Papaya Restaurant SEAFOOD $
(☑2654-9125; www.conchalcr.com; mains US$8-15; ⊙7am-10pm Thu-Tue; 🔊🅿) Vegetarians and seafood lovers, rejoice! For the former, there are all-day breakfasts, power salads and falafel wraps. For the latter, there are seafood salads, fresh grilled fish and jumbo shrimp. Come during the day for big burritos and flatbread sandwiches, or come at night for fancier fare. The restaurant is at the Conchal Hotel (p295).

Spot INTERNATIONAL $$
(☑2654-5463; www.facebook.com/thespotbrasilito; tapas US$6-8, mains US$10-12; ⊙7am-10pm; 🔊🅿) Downstairs from the Hotel Brasilito, this is a fresh, open-air patio serving a wide range of international fare, from French *petit déjeuner* (breakfast) to Mediterranean tapas to American burgers. Tropical decor and ocean views promise a pleasant experience.

Getting There & Away

All buses to/from Playa Flamingo travel through Brasilito (originating in Liberia, Santa Cruz or San José). There are three daily buses to San José. Buy tickets in advance at the **Tralapa Agencia** (☑2221-7202; ⊙8am-6pm Mon & Wed-Sat, 8am-3pm Sun, closed noon-1pm) at the north end of Brasilito.

Playa Conchal

Just 1km south of Brasilito is Playa Conchal, a gorgeous stretch of sea and sand backed by palms. Conchal rates among the most beautiful beaches in Costa Rica. The name comes from the billions of *conchas* (shells) that wash up on the beach, and are gradually crushed into coarse sand. The shallows drift from an intense turquoise to sea-foam green deeper out, a rarity on the Pacific coast. If you have snorkeling gear, this is the place to use it.

The beach is often packed with locals, tourists and countless vendors, but on weekdays during low season, Playa Conchal is pure paradise. The further south you stroll, the wider, sweeter and more spectacular the beach becomes.

The easiest way to reach Conchal is to simply walk 15 minutes down the beach from Playa Brasilito. You can also drive along the sandy beach road, though you'll be charged US$2 to park.

Playa Grande

Playa Grande is a wide, gorgeous beach, famous among conservationists and surfers alike. By day, the offshore winds create steep and powerful waves, especially at high tide. By night, an ancient cycle continues, as leatherback sea turtles bearing clutches of eggs follow the ocean currents back to their birthplace. The beach stretches for about 5km from the Tamarindo estuary, around a dome rock – with tide pools and superb surf fishing – and on to equally grand Playa Ventanas. The water is exquisite, warm, clear and charged with dynamic energy. Even confident swimmers should obey those riptide signs, as people have drowned here.

Since 1991 Playa Grande has been part of the Parque Nacional Marino Las Baulas de Guanacaste, which protects one of the most important leatherback nesting areas in the world. During the day, the beach is free and open to all, which is a good thing as the breaks off Playa Grande are fast, steep and consistent. At night, however, it is only possible to visit the beach on a guided tour, to ensure that nesting cycles continue unhindered.

Sights

Parque Nacional Marino Las Baulas de Guanacaste PARK
(☑2653-0470; adult/child US$12/2, turtle tours incl admission US$30; ⊙8am-noon & 1-5pm, tours 6pm-2am) Las Baulas national marine park encompasses the entire beach at Playa Grande, as well as the adjacent land and 220 sq km of ocean. Playa Grande is one of the world's most important nesting areas for the *baula* (leatherback turtle). In the evenings from October to March, rangers lead tours for visitors to witness this amazing cycle of life. Canoe tours explore the mangroves, which are home to caimans and crocodiles, as well as numerous bird species such as the roseate spoonbill.

But the main attraction is the nesting of the world's largest species of turtle, the leatherback, which can weigh in excess of 400kg. Nesting season is from October to March. It's fairly common to see green turtles lay their eggs here on any given night, but leatherbacks are much less common.

The leatherback is critically endangered and, despite increased conservation efforts, fewer leatherbacks are nesting on Playa Grande each year. In an effort to protect the dwindling population, park rangers collect eggs and incubate them to increase their chances of survival. Even so, sea turtles must hatch on the beach and enter the water by themselves, otherwise memory imprinting does not occur, and the hatchlings will never return to their birthplace to nest. It's estimated that only 10% of hatchlings survive to adulthood.

The park office is by the northern entrance to Playa Grande. Many hotels and tourist agencies in Tamarindo book tours that include transportation, as well as park admission and a guided tour.

The show kicks off anytime after 9pm. Tourists are not allowed on the beach until the turtles have made it to dry sand. (Be prepared to wait. It could be a very long night – but well worth it.) Guards with two-way radios will alert your guide, who will accompany you to a designated viewing area. Photography, filming and lights of any kind are prohibited to protect the turtles. Over the span of one to two hours, you can watch as the turtle digs its nest, lays about 80 to 90 silver shiny eggs and then buries them in the sand.

Activities

Surfing

Surfing is the main motivation for coming to Playa Grande, and it is indeed spectacular. There are two main beach breaks – one at either end of the beach – especially at high tide in the early morn. Unfortunately, when the surf's up the breaks get crowded, so chat up some locals to learn their secrets.

Frijoles Locos Surf & Spa   SURFING
(☑ 2652-9235; www.frijoleslocos.com; boards per hour US$10-20, 90min lessons US$30; ☺ 9am-5pm) An all-purpose surf shop where you can rent surfboards and sign up for lessons. Afterward, you can recover with a deep tissue massage or other spa treatments. This place also rents just about everything you need to guarantee a great day at the beach, including bikes, snorkel gear, boogie boards and shade tents. Enjoy!

Playa Grande Surf Camp   SURFING
(☑ 2653-1074; www.playagrandesurfcamp.com; board rental per day US$20, 2hr lessons US$40) In addition to board rentals and surf lessons, this outfit also offers surf packages which include accommodations and transportation to the best breaks on the peninsula. Located in the southern part of Playa Grande.

Wildlife-Watching

Playa Grande is a wilderness beach, nearly surrounded by mangrove swamps. Protected by the Tamarindo Wildlife Sanctuary (in addition to the Las Baulas national park), this place is teeming with wildlife – and not only turtles. Local guides lead canoe expeditions in the Tamarindo estuary, where you can spot crocs, monkeys, anteaters and *pizotes* (coatis), not to mention a stunning variety of birds.

Black Turtle Tours   WILDLIFE WATCHING
(☑ 8534-8664; per person US$20-30) Paddle a canoe through the saltwater jungle that dominates the Tamarindo Wildlife Sanctuary, at the southern end of Playa Grande. This maze of mangroves – including five different species – is home to a spectacular array of flora and fauna. Your guide, Jhonathan, will help you spot it.

These tours are especially rewarding during the dry season, when the surrounding arid forest forces more species into the 'saltwater forest,' resulting in an incredible density of wildlife.

Sleeping

Lodgings are located at the two ends of Playa Grande. At the northern end, you'll find the heart of the village, with Hotel Las Tortugas, the main beach entrance, the ranger station and the bulk of facilities. At the southern end, a handful of guesthouses have opened up in the Palm Beach Estates development, where there's another beach access point. Further south is Hotel Bula Bula and the boats to Tamarindo.

Playa Grande Surf Camp   CABINA $
(☑ 2653-1074; www.playagrandesurfcamp.com; dm US$15-20, d US$45; ℗❄☂☷) Aside from boards, lessons and trips, the surf camp is also a great budget accommodations option. Three cute, thatched, A-frame *cabinas* have private porches and hammocks, just steps from the beach. There are also two breezy elevated *cabinas* that sleep four. Surf packages available.

★ **La Marejada Hotel** BOUTIQUE HOTEL **$$**
(☑2653-0594, in USA & Canada 800-559-3415; www.hotelswell.com; r incl breakfast US$90; ❄🛜❄) Hidden behind a bamboo fence, this stylish nest is a gem. The eight elegantly understated rooms have stone tile floors, rattan and wooden furnishings, and queen beds. There's not a lot of space here, but it's lovingly cared for and generously shared. Surf lessons and spa services offered onsite, not to mention an excellent restaurant.

Indra Inn GUESTHOUSE **$$**
(www.indrainn.com; r US$79; P❄🛜) It's not too fancy at Indra Inn, but it doesn't have to be. Grounds are blooming with fruit trees and hung with hammocks. Rooms are newly renovated and simply decorated. And owners Matt and Natalia are charming hosts. Other perks include irresistible breakfasts, daily yoga classes, impromptu jam sessions and good vibes.

El Manglar & Mi Casa Hostel HOTEL **$$**
(☑2653-0952; www.micasahostel.com; d/q/ste from US$50/70/80; P❄🛜❄) Near the southern end of the beach this funky, friendly faux-dobe villa property offers a room to suit every budget. All categories of room are quite smart, with fresh paint and sturdy wood furnishing. The villas offer particularly good value, complete with king-size beds, kitchen, living area and private patio. Steps from the waves.

Sugar's Monkey HOTEL **$$**
(☑2653-0719; www.sugarsmonkey.com; d/q US$60/90; P❄🛜❄) Sugar's Monkey has new management, a new name and a new vibe – both rooms and restaurant got a revamp. The wood-paneled rooms are dark, but you can get your vitamin D lounging on your semiprivate terrace. Or at the beach, which is a few steps away.

Hotel Cantarana INN **$$$**
(☑2653-0486; www.hotel-cantarana.com; Palm Beach Estates; s/d US$105/130; P❄🛜❄) This is a lovely, intimate inn nestled into the semigated Palm Beach Estates. The spacious and luxurious rooms each have a private terrace overlooking the glittering pool and gorgeous gardens. A highlight is the restaurant, set on the 2nd-floor terrace amid the treetops. Open for breakfast and dinner, the kitchen creates some tasty concoctions from local ingredients.

Rip Jack Inn INN **$$$**
(☑2653-0480, in USA 800-808-4605; www.ripjackinn.com; d from US$102; P❄🛜❄) Named for two canine amigos, this comfy, convivial inn has a handful of rooms that are clean, modern, and artfully painted, each featuring a small patio with a hammock. In addition to a place to lay your head, Rip Jack has a yoga studio with daily classes, surf gear for rent and an amazing 'treetop' restaurant.

Hotel Bula Bula HOTEL **$$$**
(☑2653-0975; www.hotelbulabula.com; r with breakfast US$125; P❄🛜❄) At the southern end of town, Hotel Bula Bula has decked out its rooms with king-size beds, tropical paint jobs and whimsical local art. The grounds are gorgeous and the front porch is well equipped with rattan rockers. Most importantly: cocktails. The Great Waltini's hardwood bar puts out some seriously potent drinks, including rum yummies, margaritas and the mysterious Siberian.

✖ **Eating & Drinking**

Cafe Del Pueblo ITALIAN **$$**
(☑2653-2315; mains US$10-18; ⊙5-9pm) Just east of town, this open-air Italian restaurant is a gem. Thin-crust pizzas get good reviews, and regulars rave about the innovative seafood preparations, tender steaks and homemade pasta dishes. Dine under the stars on the patio. Reservations recommended on weekends.

Shakas Beach Bar BAR
(☑4702-4742; www.facebook.com/shakasbeachbar) Here's a charming spot with a cool surf vibe. Painted surfboards decorate this breezy place, where you can find a seat at the bar or lounge on big beanbag pillows on the deck. The menu is limited, but folks rave about the big burgers, craft beers and fish tacos.

ℹ **Information**

Playa Grande Clinic (☑2653-2767, 24hr emergency 8827-7774; www.facebook.com/pgclinic) If you get rolled too hard in the surf and need a doctor, find this clinic next to Kike's Place.

ℹ **Getting There & Away**

There are no buses to Playa Grande, but the road is paved so it's an easy drive. Alternatively, catch a boat across the estuary from Tamarindo to the southern end of Grande (around US$2 per person, from 7am to 4pm). From Playa Grande arrange your boat to Tamarindo at Hotel Bula Bula.

Playa Tamarindo

Well, they don't call it Tamagringo for nothing. Tamarindo's perennial status as Costa Rica's top surf and party destination has made it the first and last stop for legions of tourists. It stands to reason, then, that this is the most developed beach on the peninsula with no shortage of hotels, bars and restaurants.

Despite its party-town reputation, Tamarindo is more than just drinking and surfing. It forms part of Parque Nacional Marino Las Baulas de Guanacaste, and the beach retains an allure for kids and adults alike. Foodies will find some of the best restaurants in the country. Families and students will appreciate the fierce competition that has kept lodging prices reasonably low. And Tamarindo's central location makes it a great base for exploring the northern peninsula.

Activities

Costa Rica Stand-Up
Paddle Adventures   ADVENTURE SPORTS
(📋8780-1774; costaricasupadventures.com; rental from US$25, lessons/tours US$75/115) Yoga classes on the ocean: here's your chance to do sun salutations on a stand-up paddle board. If you prefer more traditional SUP activities – say, paddling – they do that too. Lessons take place right on the beach at **Nogui's** (📋2653-0029; mains US$10-22; ⊙6am-10pm Thu-Tue), while tours go out to ride the surf or explore the flat waters of the estuaries.

Ser Om Shanti Yoga Studio   YOGA
(📋8591-6236; www.seryogastudio.com; Plaza Tamarindo, 2nd floor; classes from US$15) There's a full schedule of daily Hatha and Vinyasa yoga classes, as well as Pilates and restorative yoga. It all takes place in a bright, airy studio on the top floor of Tamarindo plaza.

Surfing

Like a gift from the surf gods, Tamarindo is often at its best when neighboring Playa Grande is flat. The most popular wave is a medium-sized right that breaks directly in front of the Tamarindo Diria hotel. The waters here are full of virgin surfers learning to pop up. There is a good left that's fed by the river mouth, though be advised that crocodiles are occasionally sighted here, particularly when the tide is rising (which is, coincidentally, the best time to surf). There can be head-high waves in front of the rocks near Le Beach Club.

More advanced surfers will appreciate the bigger, faster and less crowded waves at neighboring beaches: Playa Langosta, on the other side of the point; Playas Avellanas, Negra and Junquillal to the south; and Playa Grande to the north.

There are countless surf schools offering lessons and board rental in Tamarindo. Surf lessons hover at around US$45 for 1½ to two hours, and most operators will let you keep the board for a few hours beyond that to practice.

Iguana Surf   SURFING
(📋2653-0091; www.iguanasurf.net; board rental US$20, group/semiprivate/private lessons US$45/65/80; ⊙8am-6pm) Iguana Surf has been giving lessons for some 25 years, so they probably know what they are doing. Excellent for couples, families or anyone. The two-hour lesson includes a rash guard and locker, in addition to the surfboard. After your lesson, all gear is half-price.

Learn Improve Surf Company   SURFING
(📋8316-0509; www.learnimprovesurfcompany.com; lessons per person US$30-70) Edgar Sanchez wants to teach you how to surf. This upstart company excels at offering instruction for all ages and abilities. It also takes more advanced wave riders on surf tours to Playa Avellanas and Playa Grande.

Kelly's Surf Shop   SURFING
(📋2653-1355; www.kellysurfshop.com; board rental per day/week US$20/120, group/semiprivate/private lessons US$50/65/90; ⊙9am-6pm) One of the best surf shops in the area, Kelly's has a terrific selection of newish boards that it rents by the day or week. Premium boards cost a bit more. Staff are super informative, with lessons, advice and other recommendations to get you out on the waves.

Matos Surf Shop   SURFING
(📋2653-0845; www.matossurfshop.com; Sunrise Commercial Center; board rental per day US$10; ⊙8am-7pm) In addition to giving lessons and renting boards, this place also does surf photography and video (in case you wanted to star in your own version of *Endless Summer*). Tamarindo's cheapest rates for board rental and sales. There is another outlet in Playa Grande.

Playa Tamarindo

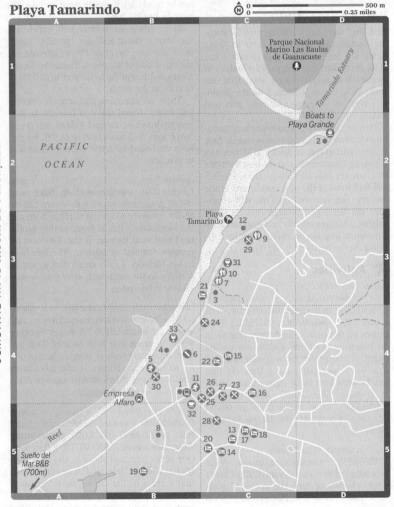

Diving

Tamarindo is a surf town. But that doesn't mean there is nothing to see below the waves. Enticing dive sites in the vicinity include the nearby Cabo Velas and out to the Islas Catalinas.

Freedive Costa Rica DIVING
(☑ 8353-1290; www.freedivecostarica.com; Plaza Conchal; free diving US$35-55, snorkeling US$55, spearfishing US$145; ⊗ 9:30am-5:30pm) Owner Gauthier Ghilain claims free diving is 'the most natural, intimate and pure form of communion with the underwater world.' It

requires no bulky gear and minimal training. He promises a safe and super-fun environment in which to learn how to explore the deep blue sea in new ways.

Tamarindo Diving DIVING
(☑ 8583-5873; tamarindodiving.net; 2-tank dives US$110) It's called Tamarindo Diving, but Davide Gabbi actually takes clients on a boat that departs from Playa Flamingo and heads out to the Islas Catalinas. (It's a trade-off: you'll spend more time on the road but less time on the boat motoring to your destination.) Turtles, dolphins and whales are

Playa Tamarindo

often spotted from the boat, while eagle rays, sharks and manta rays are lurking below the surface.

Agua Rica Diving Center DIVING
(☑ 2653-0094, 2653-2032; www.aguarica.net; 2 tanks from US$80, certification US$550) Tamarindo's longest-standing dive shop takes clients to the nearby Cabo Velas and out to the Islas Catalinas. Snorkel tours also go out a few times a day. Agua Rica is a professional outfit but if they don't have enough divers on board they may cancel the trip.

Courses

Instituto de Wayra LANGUAGE COURSE
(☑ 2653-0359; www.spanish-wayra.co.cr; per week from US$320; ☉ 7:30am-5:30pm Mon-Fri, 10am-4pm Sun) A Spanish program that offers small class sizes and an immersive experience. The school recommends (and arranges) homestays so students have more opportunities to practice.

Coastal Spanish Institute LANGUAGE COURSE
(☑ 2653-2673; www.coastalspanish.com; per week from US$310) This Spanish school is located right on the beach in downtown Tamarindo (which may make it more difficult to concentrate on your grammar and vocabulary). The place specializes in weekly surf and Spanish packages, which include 20 hours of Spanish classes and six hours of surf instruction, as well as board rental.

Tours

There are tour agencies all around town, offering surf lessons of course, but also boat tours, canopy tours, snorkeling trips, ATV rentals, sea kayaking and stand-up paddling. Bike and board rental is also easy to find.

Asociación de Guías Locales ECOTOUR
(☑ 2653-1687; www.sinac.go.cr/AC/ACT/PNMarino Baulas; boats to Playa Grande US$3, turtle tours US$25-35; ☉ 7am-4pm) Stop by this local guide office to book a turtle tour to Las Baulas national park or a kayak tour of the mangroves in the nearby Tamarindo Wildlife Sanctuary. Giant leatherback turtles nest at Las Baulas (Playa Grande) from October to March. Unfortunately, numbers have been way down in recent years, so turtle sighting is not guaranteed.

Sleeping

Tamarindo is packed with lodging options in all price ranges, including all manner of hostels, guesthouses and high-end resorts. Although the city can feel a bit oppressive, with crowded streets and nonstop heat, it's not that hard to escape the hullabaloo by staying on the south side of town. Things quiet down pretty quickly when you leave the main drag.

We list high-season rates; rates drop significantly during other times of the year.

Tamarindo Backpackers
HOSTEL $

(☑2653-1720; www.tamabackpackers.com; dm US$15, d from US$50; P❋@🛜≋) This attractive yellow hacienda has a great vibe that welcomes all comers. Private rooms (mostly with shared bathroom) are excellent value, with Spanish-tiled floors, mural-painted walls, beamed ceilings and flat-screen TVs. The dorms are quite clean but otherwise unspectacular. Outside, hammocks are strung in the tropical gardens and around a small pool. Five-minute walk to the beach.

La Botella de Leche
HOSTEL $

(☑2653-0189; www.labotelladeleche.com; dm US$13-15, d US$40; P❋@🛜≋) With a relaxed vibe, this congenial spot – aka 'the bottle of milk' – is recommended for its warm and attentive management and fully air-conditioned rooms and dormitories. Stenciled walls pretty up the otherwise plain rooms. Facilities include a shared kitchen, surfboard racks, hammocks and a TV lounge.

Pura Vida Hostel
HOSTEL $

(☑8747-8780; www.puravidahostel.com; dm US$15-18, d with/without bathroom US$60/50; ❋@🛜) Inside this leafy compound are dorms and private rooms accented by trippy murals and mirrored mosaics. The vibe is friendly and super chill, especially in the common *rancho,* furnished with hammocks and rocking chairs. They sometimes organize open-mike nights and other live music. Also: free bikes and boards.

Blue Trailz Hostel
HOSTEL $

(☑2653-1705; dm/r US$15/69; ❋@🛜) Across the street from the beach, this immaculate and intimate hostel is popular among the surfer set. Budget travelers appreciate the clean, cool dorms (with air-con) as well as the attentive service from the staff. Guests get reduced rates on boards, bikes, lessons and tours. Sweet.

Beach Bungalows
B&B $$

(☑8800-0011; www.tamarindobeachbungalows. com; d incl breakfast US$90; P🛜≋) 🌱 Shaded by palms, these two-story teak bungalows feel like a luxurious retreat. In each bungalow, the upstairs is a rich yet rustic sleeping area, while the downstairs is an open-air poolside chill-out lounge. Guests enjoy a decadent breakfast, as well as free use of bikes, a gas grill and a common kitchen.

Hotel Mahayana
HOTEL $$

(☑2653-1154; www.hotelmahayana.com; d US$62; P❋🛜≋) The Mahayana is a sweet retreat, away from the hustle and bustle of the main drag. Spotless, citrus-painted rooms are fitted with high ceilings, big windows and private terraces (with hammocks). The courtyard contains a small, cool pool and an outdoor kitchen, which is at your disposal.

Villas Macondo
HOTEL $$

(☑2653-0812; www.villasmacondo.com; s/d/tr US$50/60/70, with air-con US$75/85/95, apt US$125-170; P❋@🛜≋) Although it's only 200m from the beach, this establishment is an oasis of serenity in an otherwise frenzied town – it's also one of the best deals around. Beautiful modern villas with private hammocks and patios surround a solar-heated pool and tropical garden. Larger apartments are equipped with full kitchens, making them ideal for families.

Hotel Luamey
BOUTIQUE HOTEL $$$

(☑2653-1510; www.hotelluamey.com; d from US$150; P❋🛜≋) Simply exquisite, this boutique hotel is an oasis of serenity and beauty in the midst of Tamarindo chaos. Spacious cabana suites are decorated in soothing earth tones, with dark wood furnishings, stone showers and private patios (where breakfast is served). Service is super accommodating. Free use of surfboards.

Tamarindo Bay Boutique Hotel
BOUTIQUE HOTEL $$$

(☑2653-2692; www.tamarindobayhotel.com; d incl breakfast from US$124; P❋🛜≋) 🌱 Here's a romantic getaway for grownups only, where contemporary design goes hand-in-hand with environmental consciousness. Slick, modern rooms have king-size beds and rainforest showers. Bikes, snorkel gear and surfboards are at your disposal. But our favorite feature is the swimming pool, complete with multicolored LED lighting and recycled plastic decking.

Sueño del Mar B&B
B&B $$$

(☑2653-0284; www.sueno-del-mar.com; d US$205, casitas US$265-325; P❋@🛜≋) This exquisite B&B on Playa Langosta is set in a stunning faux-dobe Spanish-style *posada* (guesthouse). The six rooms have four-poster beds, artfully placed crafts and open-air garden showers, while the romantic honeymoon suite has a wraparound window with sea views.

There's private beach access beyond the pool and tropical garden, and a priceless, pervasive atmosphere of seclusion and beauty. No children allowed.

Arco Iris
BOUTIQUE HOTEL **$$$**

(www.hotelarcoiris.com; d incl breakfast US$130-160; P❄🛜🏊) This is a lovely, low-key collection of bungalows, set on the quiet eastern edge of town. Outstanding and personable service is the hallmark of this operation. Pristine, modern rooms and lush gardens make for an idyllic setting. The onsite restaurant, Seasons, is a highlight.

Villa Amarilla
B&B **$$$**

(✎2653-0038; www.hotelvillaamarilla.com; d incl breakfast US$120-140; P❄🛜🏊) It's hard to resist this fun and funky yellow house backing up to the beach. Upon arrival, you'll be greeted with a shot of tequila and a warm smile. The rooms are not that fancy but they do feature tile floors, handmade furniture and whimsical paint jobs. The whole place is laid-back and lovely. NB: must love dogs.

🍴 Eating

★ La Bodega
BREAKFAST, SANDWICHES **$**

(✎8395-6184; www.labodegatamarindo.com; Nahua Hotel; mains US$6-8; ⊙7am-3pm Mon-Sat; 🛜🍴♿) This delightful shop and cafe specializes in unique combinations of ingredients, focusing on fresh, local and organic. For breakfast, they do amazing things with eggs, while lunch is a daily changing menu of unique sandwiches and salads. Any time of day, you can't go wrong with banana bread or lemon scones and a cup of fresh brewed java.

★ Green Papaya
MEXICAN **$**

(✎2652-0863; www.facebook.com/Gr33nPapaya; mains US$5-10; ⊙9am-10pm Tue-Sun; ❄🛜🍴♿) Swing on up to the bar for a breakfast burrito or pull up a tree-stump stool to sample the terrific tacos at this fantastic new addition. The mahimahi tacos are perfection in a tortilla, while non-meat-eaters will appreciate the multiple veggie options. You'll go loco for the Coco Loco dessert. Everything is funky, fresh and friendly – don't miss it.

Surf Shack
BURGERS **$**

(✎2653-2346; www.facebook.com/surfshacktamarindo; mains US$5-10; ⊙11am-9pm; 🛜♿) If you are craving a big bad burger, Surf Shack has you covered, with a good selection of patties, thick-cut onion rings and irresistible milkshakes. Tin-can walls and surfboard decor create a super laid-back vibe, enhanced by the drinks coming from the bar. It's steps from the beach; the sea breeze is the perfect accompaniment to anything you order.

El Casado del Carro
COSTA RICAN **$**

(casados US$4; ⊙noon-3pm) Doña Rosa has been delivering top-notch *casados* from her late-model Toyota hatchback for more than a decade. Her devoted Tico following lines up daily at noon, and she generally sells out by 2pm. You'll get your meal in a Styrofoam platter (nobody's *perfecto*), usually with yucca or plantains, rice, chicken or beef, and some tasty black beans.

Falafel Bar
LEBANESE **$**

(✎2653-1268; www.facebook.com/tamarindofalafelbar; mains US$5-8; ⊙10am-10pm Wed-Mon; 🍴) When you get tired of *casados* (as you do), head to this Middle Eastern cafe for all the faves: shawarma, falafel, tabbouleh, hummus and kebabs. The pita bread is made fresh daily. And now the place has improved on the 'bar' part with the recent acquisition of an alcohol license.

Sprout
INTERNATIONAL **$$**

(✎2653-2374; mains US$10-12; ⊙11am-10pm Mon-Sat; 🛜🍴♿) Sprout specializes in – wait for it – healthy food. Here, 'healthy' is a code word for fresh, nutritious and delicious, with a menu featuring giant salad bowls, veggie wraps and straight-out-of-the-surf seafood (including amazing fish tacos). Wash it down with a glass of organic wine and you'll be feeling fine.

La Baula
PIZZA **$$**

(✎2653-1450; www.facebook.com/PizzeriaLaBaula; mains US$10-15; ⊙5:30-10:30pm; 🍴♿) The best pizza in Tamarindo, by some accounts. This casual open-air restaurant has real wood-fired pizzas with a wide variety of toppings, as well as pastas and other Italian fare. It's also one of the most family-friendly restaurants in town, with a playground to keep the kids entertained. The open-air, woodsy setting requires insect repellent.

Seasons by Shlomy
MEDITERRANEAN **$$$**

(✎8368-6983; www.seasonstamarindo.com; Hotel Arco Iris; small plates US$8-12, mains US$18-20; ⊙6-10pm Mon-Sat; 🍴) Don't leave town without eating here. Israeli chef Shlomy offers a short list of carefully selected and perfectly prepared dishes. Depending on the availability of ingredients, you might start with grilled octopus or a lobster-leek terrine. Follow up with seared tuna in a honey chili marinade or filet mignon in red wine sauce. Perfection on a plate.

The understated yet elegant open-air restaurant has indoor seating and romantic poolside tables. Reservations are recommended here.

Dragonfly Bar & Grill ASIAN $$$

(☑ 2653-1506; www.dragonflybarandgrill.com; mains US$18-22; ☺ 5:30-10pm Mon-Sat; P 🛜 🌙) Dragonfly is beloved for its refined menu and its upscale tiki-bar atmosphere. The open-air dining room has twinkling lights and lanterns, with a subtle dragonfly motif throughout. The eclectic menu leans Asian, but fuses elements from around the world. Go for the Buddha Bowl filled with goodness or the fiery Thai beef served on glass noodles. Desserts are also divine.

 ## Drinking & Nightlife

During the high season (and on weekends year-round), the main drag in Tamarindo has the festive feel of spring break, with happy patrons spilling out onto the beach, drink in hand. The 'scene' unfolds all around you. If you're not sure where to start, go for sundowners at any bar or restaurant on the beachfront strip.

Cafe Tico CAFE

(☑ 8861-7732; www.facebook.com/cafeticotamarindo; ☺ 7am-5pm Mon-Fri, to 3pm Sat; 🛜 🍴) Walk in. Take a deep breath. Smell the coffee brewing? That's why you are here. Sip it on the shady patio while snacking on a homemade pastry. *Pura vida.*

El Be! BAR

(☑ 2653-0178; ☺ 11am-close) Formerly Le Beach Club, this place has changed languages (and added an exclamation point!) but the cool vibe remains the same. Lounge on beach beds or hammocks and listen to the DJ do his stuff. Happy hour (4pm to 7pm) features drink specials, live jazz music and fabulous sunsets. It's not a bad option for food if you're feeling peckish.

Sharky's SPORTS BAR

(☑ 2653-4705; www.sharkysbars.com; ☺ 11:30am-2:30am Thu-Tue, 5pm-2:30am Wed) If you're looking for a place to watch the big game, look no further than Sharky's. Besides nine screens showing sports, there are burgers and wings and lots of beer. There's a nightly lineup of fun and games, including karaoke night on Tuesday and ladies' night on Saturday. Get ready to get your drink on.

Aqua Disco CLUB

(☑ 8934-2488; www.facebook.com/Discoteque Aqua; ☺ 4pm-2am) Aqua Disco is a proper nightclub with a thumping dance floor, and a breezy deck that's critical for the cooldown. Come early for free drinks (with a small cover charge). Come really early for two-for-one cocktails and sunset views. Or, come really really early (or stay really late) for a mean breakfast burrito.

 ## Information

BAC San José (Plaza Conchal; ☺ 8:30am-3:30pm)

Backwash Laundry (☺ 8am-8pm Mon-Sat) Get your filthy unmentionables washed, dried and folded.

BUSES FROM PLAYA TAMARINDO

The **Empresa Alfaro** (☑ 2653-0268; ☺ 7:30am-5:30pm Mon-Sat, 9am-3:30pm Sun) office is near the beach, while other buses depart from the bus stop in front of Pacific Park.

DESTINATION	COMPANY	PRICE (US$)	DURATION (HR)	DEPARTURES
Liberia		3	2½	12 times per day 3:30am-6pm
San José	Alfaro	11	5½	3am & 5:30am
San José	Tralapa	11	5½	7am
Santa Cruz		2	1½	6am, 8:30am & noon

Private shuttle buses offer a faster (albeit more expensive) option. **Tamarindo Shuttle** (☑ 2653-0505; www.tamarindoshuttle.com) provides comfortable and convenient transfers from Tamarindo to destinations around the country, including both airports. **Tropical Tours** (☑ 2640-1900, 2640-0811; www.tropicaltourshuttles.com) has daily shuttles that connect Tamarindo to San José, as well as several destinations in the southern part of the Nicoya peninsula.

Banco de Costa Rica (Plaza Conchal) Twenty-four hour ATM.

Coastal Emergency Medical Service (☑ 2653-1974, emergency 8835-8074; ⊙ 24hr)

ⓘ Getting There & Away

Surfers and other beach party people flock to Tamarindo by air, bus and car. If you choose your lodging wisely, there's no need for a car in this town, as you can walk to the beach and book tours of other outings in the area.

AIR

The airstrip is 3km north of town; a hotel bus is usually on hand to pick up arriving passengers. During high season, **Sansa** (☑ 2290-4100; www. flysansa.com; Tamarindo Airport) has three daily flights to and from San José (one way US$140), as does NatureAir (one way US$124). If you go for the promotional fares, you can get pretty good discounts on these prices.

CAR

By car from Liberia, take Hwy 21 to Belén, then Hwy 155 via Huacas to Tamarindo. A taxi costs about US$50 to or from Liberia.

Amazingly, there's no gas station here. For that, you'll have to drive 15 paved kilometers to Huacas, hang a right and go up the hill. The gas station is 4km ahead, on the right.

ⓘ Getting Around

Here's a great service. **Avellanas Express** (US$6; ⊙ 8am-5pm) runs a surf shuttle to area beaches. There are three different 'lines' from Tamarindo: back and forth to Playa Grande; south to Avellanas and Negra; and north to Conchal and Flamingo. Based at Neptuno Surf Shop.

Stop by the Asociación de Guías Locales (p303) at the northern end of the beach to hire a boat to cross the estuary to Playa Grande (US$3).

Playas Avellanas & Negra

These popular surfing beaches have some of the best, most consistent waves in the area, made famous in the surf classic *Endless Summer II.*

Playa Avellanas is an absolutely stunning pristine sweep of pale golden sand. Backed by mangroves in the center and two gentle hillsides on either end, there's plenty of room for surfers and sunbathers to have an intimate experience even when there are lots of heads in town.

Playa Negra is also undeniably romantic. Though the sand is a bit darker and

the beach is broken up by rocky outcrops, gorgeous dusty back roads link tide pools of expat shredders who picked this place to exist (and surf) peacefully. Though there isn't much local soul here, the beach itself is a beaut.

🏃 Activities

The waves at Playa Avellanas are decent for beginners and intermediate surfers. Little Hawaii is the powerful and open-faced right featured in *Endless Summer II,* while the beach break barrels at low tide. Still, advanced surfers get bored here, so they go to Playa Negra, which is blessed by a world-class right that barrels. Further south is (hush hush) Playa Tortuga, an epic break for advanced surfers only. The waves are best between April and November, but start getting good in March.

Avellanas Surf School   SURFING (☑ 2653-1531; avellanas-surf-school.com; lessons adult/child US$45/50, board rental per day US$20; ⊙ 8am-5pm) Mauricio Ortega is a local guy who loves to surf and wants to share his expertise and lifestyle with anyone who cares to partake. He and his wife Dialan run this highly rated surf school, and rent out a handful of cabins and villas close to the waves.

Playa Negra SUP Wave Riders   SURFING (☑ 8702-7894; www.playanegrasupwaveriders.com; lessons US$65-85, tours US$50-70) In less than two hours, you'll learn how to stand up and paddle, either in the flats of the local estuary or out on the open ocean waves. If you already know what you are doing, rental boards are also available.

🛏 Sleeping

There's not really a village here – just a series of surf-oriented lodgings strung out along the road that connects the two beaches. That said, there's a nice range of sleeping options, from hippy surf camps to more sophisticated guesthouses and villas. If you prefer to sleep out under the stars, you'll find a few places to string a hammock or pitch a tent at the southern end of Playa Avellanas.

Casa Surf   GUESTHOUSE **$** (☑ 2652-9075; www.casa-surf.com; Playa Avellanas; dm per person US$15; 🅿) 🏄 Casa Surf looks tropically terrific, with its bamboo exterior and palm thatch roof. Inside, you'll find simple, clean rooms – brightly painted

PENÍNSULA DE NICOYA PLAYAS AVELLANAS & NEGRA

and fastidiously kept – with shared access to a bathroom and kitchen. The upstairs hammock deck is an enticing place to spend an afternoon (or a night). Also available: bike rental, book exchange, community guitar.

The casa offers an excellent-value surf, sleep and eat option (US$30), which includes two meals daily and surfboard rental.

Kon Tiki   HOSTEL $

([📱]2652-9117; www.kontikiplayanegra.com; Playa Negra; r per person US$20; [P][🛜]) Along the road from Avellanas, this low-key and inviting place has a rambling collection of fruit-colored cabins on stilts. In the middle of it all is a rickety pavilion where guests swing in hammocks and devour pizza and other affordable fare. Bathroom facilities are shared. The place is popular with surfers and howler monkeys.

Peace Retreat   B&B $$

(www.peaceretreat.ca; Playa Negra; s/d without bathroom US$60/75, with bathroom US$80/100; [P][🛜][❄]) Sweet screened teak cabins are sprinkled around the jungly grounds, while additional rooms are perched above the central Casa Yoga. This is a place for relaxing and detoxing, rejuvenating and rejoicing. Morning yoga classes are open to the community. 'Retreat' packages are also available.

Café Playa Negra   GUESTHOUSE $$

([📱]2652-9351; www.cafeplayanegra.com; Playa Negra; s/d/tr/q US$55/75/90/100; [P][❄][🛜][❄]) These stylish, minimalist digs upstairs from the cafe have polished concrete floors and elevated beds, dressed with colorful bedspreads and other artistic touches. There's a groovy shared deck with comfy hammock chairs and an inviting swimming pool.

The downstairs cafe is worth a stop no matter where you are sleeping. Look for delectable sandwiches and super-fresh seafood.

Las Avellanas Villas   APARTMENT $$

([📱]2652-9212; www.lasavellanasvillas.com; Playa Avellanas; d/tr/q US$90/100/110, air-con US$10; [P][❄][🛜]) Thoughtfully designed, these five stunning *casitas* are oases of tranquillity and balance, with private teak terraces, polished concrete floors, indoor greenery, open-air showers, and large windows streaming with natural light. For practical matters, there are surfboard racks and hammocks (of course). Full kitchens make this option perfect for families or groups. The grounds are about 800m from the beach.

Rocky Point Surf Lodge   CABINA $$

([📱]2652-9270; www.playanegrasurflodge.com; Playa Negra; s/d without bathroom US$30/40, s/d/tr/q with bathroom US$55/65/75/85, all incl breakfast; [❄][🛜][❄]) The quaint *cabinas* at Rocky Point are set around a gorgeous tropical garden, teeming with hummingbirds, butterflies and parakeets. The simple rooms have freshly painted walls and a few artistic details. Guests also have access to a shared terrace and plenty of hammocks. Don't skip out on lunch at the onsite Jalapeño Eatery & Market.

Mauna Loa Surf Resort   BUNGALOW $$

([📱]2652-9012; www.hotelmaunaloa.com; Playa Avellanas; d/tr/q from US$90/113/136; [P][❄][🛜][❄]) This hip spot offers a straight shot to the beach. Paths lead from the gorgeous pool area through a lush garden to attractive podlike bungalows. Look for open-air showers and swaying hammocks outdoors, and pastel-brushed walls and comfy orthopedic beds indoors. Prepare meals in the communal kitchen or grab a bite at the onsite Italian restaurant.

🍴 Eating

A legendary beach cafe that's named after a pig: that's the main thing that's going on when it comes to eating in these surfer outposts. Otherwise, travelers should explore the hotel restaurants, as some of them offer truly special experiences.

★ Jalapeño Eatery & Market   MEXICAN $

([📱]2652-9270; www.playanegrasurflodge.com; Playa Negra; mains US$7-10; [🕙]8am-4pm Mon-Sat) There's something special about this glorified taco bar. Ingredients are organically produced or locally sourced – or they are not going into this food. Tortillas are hand-rolled; hot sauce and other condiments are made onsite; chickens and eggs come from the neighbor's farm. Even the fish is usually speared by the chef/owner. (So don't complain if it takes longer than you expected.)

Lola's on the Beach   CAFE $$

([📱]2652-9097; mains US$6-12; [🕙]10am-5pm Tue-Sun; [P][🛜]) Hang out at this stylish beach cafe while waiting for the waves. Slanted wood chairs are planted in the sand beneath thatched umbrellas. A tree-stump bar overlooks an open kitchen, where the beachy cuisine is tops.

In case you're wondering, Lola was an enormous and lovable pig, aka the queen of Avellanas. She has since passed, but her legacy lives on in 'little' Lolita!

Villa Deevena FUSION $$$
(☑ 2653-2328; www.villadeevena.com; mains US$18-28; ☺ 7am-9pm; P ❋ ☎) Foodies drive from all over Guanacaste to sample the fare at this hidden gem. It's worth the search for this otherworldly restaurant, which is the brainchild of *chef de cuisine* Patrick Jamon. Start off with a fresh-fruit-juice cocktail while you peruse the menu of masterpieces. Look for perfect preparations of seafood, slow roasted meats and one-of-a-kind desserts.

The property also offers simple but sensual luxury at its minimalist bungalows (double US$124). Swish accommodations – decorated with hardwood and soothing tones – surround the glittering saltwater pool.

ℹ Getting There & Away

BUS

There is no public transportation between Tamarindo and these beaches, though surf camps often organize trips. You can also catch a ride on the Avellanas Express (p307), which departs Tamarindo at 9am, 11am, 2pm and 3:50pm, with two of these shuttles going all the way to Playa Negra. To return to Tamarindo, the shuttle departs from Playa Negra at 10am and 3pm, and from Avellanas at 10:15am, 11:40am, 3:15pm and 6pm.

CAR

From Tamarindo, drive 5km inland to the village of Villareal, and turn right on to the dirt road. This road becomes progressively worse as you get further from Tamarindo and it usually requires a 4WD. If you're not coming from Tamarindo, drive west from Santa Cruz on the paved highway, through 27 de Abril to Paraíso, then follow the signs to the beach of your choice. As always, do not leave valuables in your car, especially at the beaches.

Playa Junquillal

Hard to pronounce and almost as difficult to find, Junquillal (say 'hoon-kee-yal') is a 2km-wide gray-sand wilderness beach that's absolutely stunning and mostly deserted. To the south, a dome boulder crumbles into a jutting rock reef and beyond that is a vast, 200-hectare estuary carved by the Río Nanda Mojo. To the north is a narrow rise of bluffs sprouting clumps of palm trees. Sunsets are downright surreal with blinding golds, molten oranges and shocking pinks. The sea does swirl with fierce rip currents, however, and when it gets big, surfers descend from Negra. Even when the surf isn't high, it's dangerous out there. Don't let kids or even intermediate swimmers venture out alone.

With far more Ticos than tourists, Junquillal has an inviting authenticity unique in the northern peninsula. The nearest town is 4km inland at Paraíso.

🛌 Sleeping

El Castillo Divertido HOTEL $
(☑ 8351-5162, 2658-8428; www.castillodivertido.com; s US$20-30, d US$30-50; P ☎) This colorful castle, decked out with crenellated walls and carved masks, is just 100m from the beach, offering panoramic views from the rooftop bar. Take advantage of the one-of-a-kind kayaking tours through the Río Nanda Moja and surrounding mangroves. On Friday nights, all guests are invited to partake of cold drinks and delicious grilled carnage at a weekly sunset BBQ.

★ **Mundo Milo Ecolodge** BUNGALOW $$
(☑ 2658-7010; www.mundomilo.com; d incl breakfast US$67-77; P ☎ ☀) ✎ The most creative nest in the area is this unique eco-lodge, where attention to detail is paramount. Choose between three fan-cooled, sky-lit bungalows, each surrounded by lush vegetation and styled after a different world region (Africa, Mexico, Persia). The pool is an artful arc overlooking dry tropical woodland, with monkeys howling, birds chanting and waves crashing in the distance.

ℹ Getting There & Away

You can reach this tiny beach town by public transportation, as long as you're in no rush.

BUS

Buses depart from Junquillal to Santa Cruz (US$3, 1½ hours) at 6am, 9am, 12:30pm and 4:30pm; you can catch the bus anywhere along the main road. Buses from Santa Cruz to Junquillal depart from the Mercado Municipal at 5am, 10am, 2:30pm and 5:30pm.

CAR

If you're driving, it's about 16km by paved road from Santa Cruz to 27 de Abril, and another smooth 17km into town.

LOCAL KNOWLEDGE

GUAITIL

An interesting excursion from Santa Cruz, Guaitil is a small artisanal potter community, where attractive ceramics are made from local clays, using earthy reds, creams and blacks in pre-Columbian Chorotega style. Ceramics are sold outside the potters' houses and also in San Vicente, 2km beyond Guaitil. If you ask, you can watch part of the potting process, and local residents will be happy to give you a few lessons for a small price.

From Junquillal, it's possible to drive 35km south to Nosara via the legendary surf spot of Marbella. However, this is a very rough dirt road for 4WD only and it may be impassable in the rainy season. There are no gas stations on the coastal road and little traffic, so ask locally before setting out. It's easier to reach beaches south of Junquillal from Nicoya.

Santa Cruz

A stop in Santa Cruz, a *sabanero* (cowboy) town typical of inland Nicoya, provides some of the local flavor missing from foreign-dominated beach towns. Unfortunately, there aren't any attention-worthy sights, so most travelers' experience of Santa Cruz consists of changing buses and buying a mango. However, the town is an important administrative center in the region, which gives it a healthy middle-class appeal, and it serves as a good base for visiting Guaitil.

About three city blocks in the center of Santa Cruz burned to the ground in a devastating fire in 1993. An important landmark is the vacant-lot-looking field known as Plaza de Los Mangos, which was once a large grassy square with three mango trees. Soon after the fire the attractive and shady Parque Bernabela Ramos opened 400m south of Plaza de Los Mangos.

🛏 Sleeping

Hotel La Pampa HOTEL $
(☑ 2680-0586; s/d from US$36/40; P ❄ 🛜) A good budget option, this peach-tinted hotel is 50m west of the Plaza de Los Mangos. It isn't all that inspiring from the outside, but the rooms are clean and modern, providing a decent place to lay your head.

La Calle de Alcalá HOTEL $$
(☑ 2680-0000; www.hotellacalledealcala.com; s/d incl breakfast US$63/84; P ❄ 🛜 ⛱) With its stucco arches and landscaped garden around a pool, this hotel gets points for design. Carved wooden doors open into small tiled rooms with rattan furnishings. It's one block due east of the bus terminal; a convenient stopover option.

❶ Getting There & Away

Santa Cruz is 57km from Liberia and 25km south of Filadelfia on the main peninsular highway. A paved road leads 16km west to 27 de Abril, from where dirt roads continue to Playa Tamarindo, Playa Junquillal and other beaches. There's a gas station off the main intersection with the highway.

CENTRAL PENINSULA

Long the political and cultural heart of Guanacaste, the inland region of the central peninsula looks and feels palpably more 'Costa Rican' than the beach resorts of the northern coast. Over generations, the dry tropical forest has been cut down to make way for the *sabaneros'* cattle, but stands of forest remain, interspersed between *fincas* (farms) and coastal villages, sometimes backing stretches of wild, empty beaches. Though the areas around Sámara and Nosara are developing steadily, many foreigners who are drawn to the rugged coastline are active in its conservation. The central peninsula remains rife with secluded beaches, small villages and endless possibilities for getting 'off the map.'

Nicoya

A hub between the beaches and ranches, the big cities and *pueblitos*, Nicoya offers a blast of Tico time. Truckers, road trippers and locals converge around a grid, packed with commerce and crowned with a gorgeous *iglesia* that makes the leafy Parque Central worth a loiter.

That said, there's no reason to linger longer than you need to. Nicoya is not fabulous. Just real.

Situated 23km south of Santa Cruz, Nicoya was named after an indigenous Chorotega chief who welcomed Spanish conquistador Gil González de Ávila in 1523 (a gesture he regretted). In the following centuries, the Chorotega were wiped out by the colonists, though the distinctive facial features of the local residents are a testament to their heritage.

🛏 Sleeping & Eating

Mundiplaza Hotel
HOTEL $

(☑ 2685-3535; Calle 3; d US$40; ❄ 🛜) Located right in the center of Nicoya, this is a perfectly pleasant place to spend the night. With colorful paint jobs and new tile bathrooms, it's spotlessly clean and well maintained. The shared balcony has striking views to the Nicoya hills, though the road noise can be excessive.

Bobo's Burger House
FAST FOOD $

(☑ 8757-7777; www.facebook.com/BobosBurger House; Calle Central & Av 2; mains US$4-8; ⊙ 11am-10pm Mon-Sat; 🛜☑🍴) Bobo knows his burgers. He makes them from premium beef, chicken or fish, and lets you pick the toppings from the organic veggie bar. Even if you're not a meat-eater you have options here. Thick, crispy steak fries round out the meal. And for dessert? Save room for Bobo's *helado burguesa* – vanilla ice cream sandwiched between two chocolate chip cookies.

Cafe Daniela
SODA $

(☑ 2686-6148; www.facebook.com/cafedaniela; Calle 3; mains US$4-10; ⊙ 7am-9pm; 🍴) A popular *soda* serving appetizing *típica* bites. Think: *gallo pinto* (stir-fry of rice and beans) in the morning, and fish, beef, chicken and veggie *casados* (set meals) later on. All served in bright tiled environs.

ℹ Information

Banco de Costa Rica (Calle Central; ⊙ 8:30am-3pm Mon-Fri)

Banco Popular (Calle 3; ⊙ 9am-4:30pm Mon-Fri, 8:15-11:30am Sat) Also has a 24-hour ATM at Hospital La Anexión.

Hospital La Anexión (☑ 2685-8400; ⊙ 24hr) The peninsula's main hospital is on the north side of Nicoya.

Parque Nacional Barra Honda

Parque Nacional Barra Honda is situated about halfway between Nicoya and the mouth of the Río Tempisque. The main attraction of this inland park is a massive underground system of caverns composed of soft limestone, carved by rainfall and erosion over a period of about 70 million years. Speleologists have discovered more than 40 caverns, some reaching as far as 200m deep, though to date only 19 have been fully explored. There have also been discoveries of pre-Columbian remains dating to 300 BC.

Stop in Nicoya to grab some goods for a picnic (and plenty of water), as there is nowhere to eat in the vicinity of Barra Honda.

◉ Sights

Parque Nacional Barra Honda Caverns
CAVE

(☑ 2659-1551; adult/child US$12/2; ⊙ trails 8am-4pm, caverns 8am-1pm) This 23-sq-km national park protects a system of some 40 caverns. The only cave with regular public access is the 41m-deep La Terciopelo, which has incredible speleothems – calcite figures that rise and fall in the cave's interior. It's quite the underground art museum. Stalagmites, stalactites and a host of beautiful formations have evocative names such as fried eggs, organ, soda straws, flowers and shark's teeth. Call the ranger station one

BUSES FROM NICOYA

Most buses arrive at and depart from the bus terminal southeast of Parque Central.

DESTINATION	COMPANY	COST (US$)	DURATION (HR)	DEPARTURES
Liberia	Transportes La Pampa	2.60	2	Every 30-60min, 7am-8:30pm
Playa Nosara	Empresa Traroc	3.60	2	4:45am, 10am, 12:30pm, 3:30pm & 5:30pm Mon-Sat. No early bus Sun
Sámara & Playa Carrillo	Empresa Traroc	3.60	1½	10 daily, 6am-8pm
San José	Empresa Alfaro	9	5	5 daily

day in advance to make arrangements for the four-hour guided tour (US$29, including park admission).

Unlike some caverns in other places, Barra Honda is not developed for wide-scale tourism, which means that it feels less like a carnival attraction and more like a scene from *Indiana Jones*. So, don your yellow miner's hat and sturdy boots, and be prepared to get down and dirty. The descent involves ladders and ropes, so you should be reasonably fit; children must be at least 12 years old.

The dry season is the only time that tourists are allowed to enter the caves, though the hiking is fine at any time of year. As always, carry several liters of water and let the rangers know where you are going. Sneakers or, preferably, boots are necessary if you will be caving. You will also need a 4WD vehicle to drive from the ranger station to the parking area near the caves.

🏃 Activities

The Barra Honda hills have a few well-marked hiking trails through deciduous, dry tropical forest. Before or after visiting the cave, you can hike 3.5km to the top of Cerro Barra Honda, which has a *mirador* (lookout point) with a view of Río Tempisque and Golfo de Nicoya. You won't need a guide to hike the trails.

🛈 Getting There & Away

To reach Barra Honda by public transportation, take a bus from Nicoya to Santa Ana (US$3.50, twice daily except Sunday), which will get you within striking distance (about 1km away). Alternatively, take a taxi from Nicoya for about US$20 round-trip. You can arrange for your driver to pick you up at a specified time.

If you have your own vehicle, take the peninsular highway south out of Nicoya toward Mansión and make a left on the access road leading to Puente La Amistad. From here, continue another 1.5km and make a left on the signed road to Barra Honda. The dirt road will take you to the village of Barra Honda then wind to the left for another 6km, passing Santa Ana, before ending at the national park gate. The road is clearly marked, and there are several signs along the way indicating the direction of the park. After the village of Barra Honda, the road is unpaved, but in good condition.

If you are coming to the park from Puente La Amistad, you will see the access road to Barra Honda signed about 16km after leaving the bridge.

Nosara & Around

Nosara is a cocktail of international surf culture, stunning back-road topography, jungled microclimates, moneyed expat mayhem and yoga bliss. It recalls Malibu, Oahu's North Shore and Byron Bay, Australia, while remaining completely its own – only in Costa Rica – incarnation.

Here, three stunning beaches are stitched together by a network of swerving, rutted earth roads that meander over coastal hills and kiss the coast just west of the small Tico village of Nosara. Inland are remnant pockets of luxuriant vegetation that attract birds and other wildlife. The area has seen little logging, partly because of the nearby wildlife refuge.

The area is spread out along the coast and inland, making wheels a necessity. Five miles inland, Nosara village is where you'll find supplies and gas, as well as the airport. Most accommodations, restaurants and beaches are in Playa Pelada to the north and Playa Guiones to the south. There are many unidentified little roads, which makes it hard to navigate if you don't know the place. For a handy map visit the website of Nosara Travel (www.nosaratravel.com).

⊙ Sights

Playa Garza   BEACH

From the south, the first beach you'll come to is Playa Garza, still a sleepy Tico fishing village with an arc of pale brown sand, and headlands on either side of the rippling bay. Fishing boats bob 100m from shore and there's a point break to the north side. There are a few *cabinas* and *sodas* here, and lots of sand space with precious few tourists.

Playa Guiones   BEACH

Playa Guiones is quite simply a sip of raw nectar: a wide, generous, undeveloped arc of marbled sand, with a few pebbles and shells mixed in, excellent beach breaks and plenty of space. It's an easygoing place for surfers, surf dogs and surf babies – you might just see unattended strollers lodged in the wet sand at low tide.

Check out Playa Guiones for the best beach break in the Central Peninsula, especially when there is an offshore wind. Although the beach is usually full of surfers, fortunately there are plenty of take-off points.

Playa Pelada
BEACH

North of Guiones, Playa Pelada is rough and rugged, and less endowed with surfers and luxury (which could be viewed as a luxury in itself). Things feel both spookier and more profound in Pelada. This beach lacks surf, so it's wonderful for children. It also has sheared-away boulders tumbling into a foaming sea, two alluring beachside restaurants and a fishing village intimacy that Guiones lacks.

Refuge for Wildlife
ZOO

(⌂ 8708-2601, 2682-5049; www.refugeforwildlife. com; Nosara; per person US$50; ⊘ by appointment) Make an appointment for an educational visit to this animal rescue center. Brenda Bombard is an incurable animal lover who has devoted the last 16 years to caring for injured and abandoned howler monkeys. Two-hour tours are highly informative, sharing information about the habits of howler monkeys and the center's efforts to rescue and release them (with an impressive 85% success rate). Volunteer opportunities also available.

Sibu Sanctuary
ZOO

(⌂ 8413-8889; sibusanctuary.org; admission US$65; ⊘ tours 10:30am) Reservations are absolutely required to visit this wildlife sanctuary, set on 50 glorious acres of jungle and garden. The sanctuary is dedicated to rescuing, rehabilitating and eventually releasing howler monkeys who have been injured or abandoned. The educational visits include some time with the primates, as well as a guided tour of the beautiful grounds. The price is high, but it all goes to support the good work of this private center.

Sibu Sanctuary is located in the village of Santa María, due west of Nosara village.

⚐ Activities & Tours

Playa Ponies
HORSEBACK RIDING

(⌂ 2682-5096; playaponies.org; 1hr/2hr/half-day tours US$40/55/90; ▣) Carrie and Neno want to take you riding on jungly trails and windswept beaches, with special routes designed for families with children.

Miss Sky
TOUR

(⌂ 2682-0969; www.missskycanopytour.com; Nosara; adult/child 5-12yr US$75/50; ⊘ tours 8am & 1:30pm) Miss Sky's zip lines run from mountainside to mountainside above a pristine private reserve. If you can keep your eyes open, you'll be rewarded with glorious views

of forest, sea and sky. The two daily tour times follow different routes. The morning route is 6.5km with 13 cables, yielding views of Playa Ostional and Río Montaña (complete with waterfall). The afternoon route has only eight cables covering 4.5km, overlooking Playas Pelada and Guiones and Nosara village.

Reserva Biológica Nosara
HIKING

(⌂ 2682-0035; www.lagarta.com; admission US$6; ⊘ 8am-4pm) The private 35-hectare reserve behind the Lagarta Lodge has trails leading through a mangrove wetland down to the river and beach. Stop in the Lagarta lobby to pick up a map of a two-hour self-guided tour. This is a great spot for birding, reptile-spotting and other wildlife-watching. Boat tours of the mangroves are also available.

Tica Massage
SPA

(⌂ 2682-0096; www.ticamassage.com; Playa Guiones; massages US$35-75; ⊘ 9am-6pm) After a hard day of surfing, treat yourself to a (totally legit) spa treatment at Tica Massage, in the Heart of Guiones Wellness Center. Services cater especially to surfers; or opt for a foot massage, a face massage or an invigorating 'Sea Glow' massage.

Surfing

Safari Surf
SURFING

(⌂ 2682-0113, from US or Canada 866-433-3355; www.safarisurfschool.com; Playa Guiones; 1-week packages from US$1580; ⊘ 7am-7pm) This all-inclusive surf school offers one-week packages, complete with lodging, meals, surf lessons and gear, as well as some extra activities (depending on the package). Different packages cater to budget travelers and women, in addition to the 'signature' Tortuga package. The quality of surf instruction is universally praised.

Coconut Harry's
SURFING

(⌂ 2682-0574; www.coconutharrys.com; Playa Guiones; board rental per day US$15-20, lessons adult/child US$45/35; ⊘ 7am-5pm) At the main intersection in Guiones, this popular surf shop offers top-notch private lessons, as well as board rental and stand-up paddle rental. Conveniently, there's a second location near the main break at Playa Guiones.

Juan Surfo's Surf Shop
SURFING

(⌂ 2682-1081; www.surfocostarica.com; Playa Guiones; board rental per day US$15-20, lessons per hour US$45; ⊘ 8am-6pm) Juan Surfo is a highly recommended surf teacher who gives

Surfing the Peninsula

For decades, surfers have descended to this rugged peninsula in search of the perfect wave. Now the spectacular coastline is dotted by enticing beach towns with good vibrations and epic surf. You can surf almost anywhere along this coastline, but here are a few of our favorite spots.

Playa Grande

Playa Grande (p298) is across the river and a world away from tourist-jammed Tamarindo. It doubles as a national park that protects leatherback turtle nesting grounds, which means the wide, rambling beach is damn near pristine. The wave shapes up beautifully with head-high sets year-round. The village has a little hub at either end of the beach, where you'll find a handful of tasty kitchens and comfy inns catering to the visiting surfers.

Playas Avellanas & Negra

South of Tamarindo, you'll find two of the most celebrated surf spots on the peninsula, though the nearby villages still retain that appealing atmosphere of rusticity and remoteness. Playa Avellanas (p307) is an understated yet elegant place to nest, within reach of white-sand beaches and a break that is kind to beginners. Nearby, the surf swells big and gnarly at Playa Negra (p307), breaking on beautiful dark sand. To dodge the crowds, seek out the still-hidden waves tucked between all the big names.

Nosara

Within striking distance of three different beach breaks, Nosara (p312) offers consistent surf and a welcome cloud of hippie-chic comfort. The town is a maze of rough dirt roads, backed by lush

1. Playa Avellanas (p307) 2. Playa Santa Teresa (p328) 3. Playa Grande (p298)

rainforest – although it is growing and changing rapidly. Here, yoga studios and spa treatments are the antidote for your surf-sore body.

Mal País & Santa Teresa

At the southern end of the peninsula, Mal País (p328) and Santa Teresa (p328) are favored by young, hip and sexy surfers from around the world. The beach is long and the swell is consistent, which means you can generally find your own space – particularly if you drive to the far northern beaches. There's a wonderful farm-to-table movement happening here, so you'll be well fed throughout your stay. And when you need a break from the waves, escape to the nearby Reserva Natural Absoluta Cabo Blanco (p335), the country's oldest protected area.

SURF CAMPS

Want to surf and soak up the sun without dealing with the logistics of where to stay and what to eat? Consider one of the following all-inclusive surf camps:

➡ **Malpaís Surf Camp** (p330), Mal País

➡ **Al Chile** (p328), Santa Teresa

➡ **Peaks & Swells Surf Camp** (☎2642-0067; www.surfcamppeaksnswells.com) Montezuma

➡ **Safari Surf** (p313) Nosara

➡ **Casa Surf** (p307) Playa Avellanas

➡ **Witch's Rock Surf Camp** (Map p302; ☎2653-1262; www.witchsrocksurfcamp.com; one week from US$868) Tamarindo

➡ **Blue Trailz** (Map p302; ☎2653-1705; www.bluetrailz.com) Tamarindo

➡ **Playa Grande Surf Camp** (p299) Playa Grande

lessons at Playa Guiones. His shop offers the regular rentals, transportation and surf tours, as well as some rooms for rental at the nearby Surf Lodge. Located on the northern loop road, 200m from the beach.

Yoga

Nosara Yoga Institute
YOGA

(☑ 2682-0071; www.nosarayoga.com; Playa Guiones; classes US$15) This well-known yoga institute hosts a wide variety of 90-minute, drop-in classes (four to six daily during high season). Classes range from Vinyasa to restorative to core strengthening. If you want more, it also holds workshops, retreats and instructor training courses for beginner and advanced students in a beautiful jungle setting. Located in the hills near Playa Guiones; follow signs from the first access road.

Nosara Wellness
YOGA

(☑ 2682-0360; www.nosarawellness.com; Playa Pelada; classes US$14, private sessions from US$60) This wellness center offers everything from massage and acupuncture to pilates and yoga. If that's all too mainstream for you, sign up for a session of aerial yoga, which promises to 'realign you from the compression of gravity.'

🛏️ Sleeping

The main access roads to Playa Guiones are lined with hostels, hotels, guesthouses and more. Some of the Playa Pelada options are up in the hills, away from the beach. Prices outside of high season can be 20% lower or better.

⭐ 4 You Hostal
HOSTEL $

(☑ 2682-1316; www.4youhostal.com; Playa Guiones; dm/s/d/bungalow US$18/30/40/55; P ✴ 🛜) A fantastic hostel close to the Guiones action. The high-end minimalist design makes this evolutionary flophouse (read: dorm) feel luxurious. Within the dorm are three pods that have walls that don't quite reach the soaring ceiling, allowing for extra privacy. The place is decked out with Balinese furniture and plenty of hammocks, not to mention a spotless community kitchen and rooftop terrace.

Nosara Beach Hostel
HOSTEL $

(☑ 2682-0238; www.nosarahostel.com; Playa Guiones; dm/d US$20/65; 🛜) Lounge in a hammock on the breezy porch, overlooking iguana-filled gardens. You're steps from the surf. You have a stone shower to wash away the sand and a comfy wooden bunk to crash

on. There's a big communal kitchen, a spacious TV room and – bonus – foosball. The vibe is super chill. All is right in your world.

⭐ Villa Mango B&B
B&B $$

(☑ 2682-1168; www.villamangocr.com; Playa Pelada; s/d/tr/q incl breakfast US$84/96/113/130, air-con US$10; P ✴ 🌀 🛜 🛋) Set high on a hillside with views of both bays, at this B&B in the trees you can't help but relax. The spacious rooms have a Mediterranean flair, with gorgeous views and rustic stone and wood details. Lounge on the luxurious terrace, swim in the salt-water pool or take a short stroll down to the isolated stretch of beach.

Lagarta Lodge
LODGE $$

(☑ 2682-0035; www.lagarta.com; Playa Pelada; r s/d/tr/q US$85/90/96/102, ste s/d/tr/q US$136/142/147/152; P ✴ 🛜 🛋) At the northern end of Pelada, a road dead-ends at this 12-room lodge, set high on a steep hill above a 50-hectare reserve (great for birding and wildlife-spotting). At the time of research this hotel was closed for renovation and so information will be subject to change.

Large rooms have high ceilings, stucco walls and private patios, while suites take advantage of floor-to-ceiling windows and extra living space. The panoramas are priceless. The balcony restaurant is worth a visit just for the spectacular views of the river, mountains, sea and sunset, though the rotating menu of international and Tico specialties is also appealing.

Green Sanctuary
GUESTHOUSE $$

(☑ 8320-9822; hotelgreensanctuary.com; Playa Guiones; d/tr incl breakfast US$95/111; ✴ 🛜 🛋) It's a bit of a hike to the beach (700m), but that's the only complaint about this mod spot in the woods. A stone path winds through the trees, connecting a handful of stylish modular units. Each has a private terrace, complete with hammock. The layout affords surprising privacy. Take the southernmost access road and head all the way up the hill.

Giardino Tropicale
LODGE $$

(☑ 2682-4000; giardinotropicale.com; Playa Guiones; d/ste US$95/120, air-con US$15; P ✴ 🛜 🛋) 🌿 An appealing lodge set amid the namesake tropical garden. The standard rooms are small but sweet, with inviting, hammock-strung terraces. The suites are more spacious, with kitchenettes and nature-themed murals adorning the walls. Cool off (or get some exercise) in the luxuriously large lap pool. Hearty breakfasts are served at the poolside restaurant.

Refugio del Sol
GUESTHOUSE $$

(✆ 2682-0287, 8825-9365; www.refugiodelsol.net; Playa Pelada; s/d/tr US$35/55/65, d with kitchen US$65; P🐾🅿🤙) A short stroll from the sand, this rustic lodge is decked out with ceramic tiled floors, beamed ceilings, wood furnishings, candles and lanterns, and other soulful touches. Rooms open on to a wide L-shaped patio with hammocks. There's a communal kitchen, or you can partake of tasty Spanish cooking at the onsite restaurant.

Gilded Iguana
HOTEL $$

(✆ hotel 2682-0450, restaurant 2682-0259; www.thegildediguana.com; Playa Guiones; r with/without air-con from US$95/75; P✳🤙🏊) Down the second access road to Guiones, this long-standing hotel for anglers and surfers has well-furnished rooms with tile floors, big windows and shared terraces. The atmosphere is laid-back and the place is clean, comfortable and friendly. The cheaper rooms are close to the bar and tend to be noisy.

The tasty restaurant (mains US$9 to US$14) serves generous platters of fish tacos, fajitas and seafood specials; the attached bar is a popular gringo hangout, with live music on Tuesday and Friday nights.

★ Costa Rica Yoga Spa
LODGE $$$

(✆ 2682-5212, 2682-0192; costaricayogaspa.com; Nosara; per person incl 3 meals from US$112; P🤙) 🍃 This gorgeous mountaintop retreat takes care of all of the details, providing delightful accommodations, gourmet vegetarian meals, yoga classes and transportation to the beach. The most affordable lodging is in shared rooms – offering less privacy, but still featuring teak furniture, polished concrete floors and balconies with rewarding views.

Living Hotel & Spa
BOUTIQUE HOTEL $$$

(✆ 2682-5201; www.livinghotelnosara.com; Playa Guiones; d incl breakfast US$150; P✳@🤙🏊) Relax amid the simplicity and serenity of this tropical paradise. Pristine white rooms have tile floors, shiny wood ceilings and pretty stenciled walls. Tropical gardens surround the sparkling swimming pool, with plenty of communal sp ace in the thatch-roof *rancho*. Located on the north beach access road.

Refresh your palate with a fresh-squeezed juice or some other healthy treat from the Living Cafe; refresh your mind and muscles with something from the full menu of spa treatments.

Bodhi Tree
HOTEL $$$

(✆ 2682-0256; bodhitreeyogaresort.com; Playa Guiones; per person from US$135; P✳🤙🏊) Set on a lush hillside, this yoga resort is traversed by a gurgling river, complete with waterfall. The setting is gorgeous and serene – perfect for reconnecting with your breath, your body and the nature around you. The most affordable accommodations are simple, offering comfortable beds and ample storage space, as well as shared bathrooms with stone sinks and open-air showers.

Yoga classes are held in a magnificent open-air studio with 360 degrees of canopy views. All rates include one daily class.

Olas Verdes
HOTEL $$$

(✆ 2682-0608; olasverdeshotel.com; Playa Guiones; s/d/tr incl breakfast from US$210/260/310; P✳🤙🏊) With a prime location close to town and the beach, this new all-suite hotel has a lot to offer. Accommodations are spacious and stylish, featuring handcrafted furniture and designer fixtures, high ceilings and plenty of light. It may just be the unexpected perks that make it worth the price, including complimentary laundry service and refillable water bottles.

✗ Eating

Seekretspot
GELATERIA $

(✆ 2682-1325; Playa Pelada; gelati US$3-6; ⏱hours vary; 🤙) The secret is out: come to this sweet shack for an authentic gelato or sorbetto, made with love by Stefano and Frederica. For local flavor, go for coffee or coconut. If you need a pick-me-up, there are also fresh-brewed espresso drinks. Perfectly situated on your way from Playa Pelada.

Robin's Cafe & Ice Cream
CAFE $

(✆ 2682-0617; www.robinsicecream.com; Playa Guiones; mains US$6-8, ice cream US$3; ⏱8am-5pm Mon-Sat, 10am-4pm Sun; 🤙🍴) Perfectly suited to the health-conscious yogis and surfers who live in and visit Nosara. You'll see Robin working the kitchen, preparing a welcome menu of sweet and savory crepes, tempting wraps, and sandwiches on homemade, whole-wheat focaccias. If you must indulge your sweet tooth (trust us, you must), the ice cream is homemade and sublime.

Rosi's Soda Tica
SODA $

(☑2682-0728; Playa Guiones; mains US$3-6; ☺8am-3pm Mon-Sat) Now with two prominent locations, this is the favorite *soda* in Guiones and it's a damn good one. It's a perfect spot for breakfast, whether it's banana pancakes or huevos rancheros. At lunchtime, Rosi keeps it real with *casados* (set menus) and the like. She prepares everything as you watch (and wait). It takes time, but you can't rush perfection.

Taco! Taco!
MEXICAN $

(☑2682-0574; Playa Guiones; tacos US$4-8; ☺11am-4pm; ☑🏠) Every beach town needs an open-air *taquería* where surfers and beach bums can get a quick fix. In Nosara, it's Taco! Taco!, right on the main road into town. They do tacos and only tacos, stuffed with slow-cooked meat, fresh fish or grilled veggies, and topped with savory salsas and delectable guacamole. This place has earned its exclamation points.

Beach Dog Café
CAFE $$

(☑2682-1293; www.facebook.com/beachdogcafe; Playa Guiones; mains US$6-10, dinner mains US$12-15; ☺7am-3pm daily, to 10pm Wed & Sat; ℗🏠☑) Just steps from the beach, this groovy cafe is decadent and delicious. Try banana bread French toast for breakfast, or uberpopular fish tacos for lunch. Dinner is served only a couple of nights a week, but they occasionally host live music and show movies on the beach.

Burgers & Beers
BURGERS $$

(☑2682-5558; www.facebook.com/burgersandbeerscr; Playa Guiones; mains US$10-15; ☺noon-10pm; 🏠☑) Take your pick from half a dozen burgers and you'll get a plump, juicy patty of goodness, served on a fresh bun with big french fry wedges. It's not only about the beef: there's a veggie burger and a fish of the day. Also noteworthy are the dozen craft beers on tap. Can't beat it.

La Luna
INTERNATIONAL $$$

(☑2682-0122; Playa Pelada; dishes US$12-24; ☺11am-11pm Mon-Fri, 8am-11pm Sat & Sun) Located on the beach, this trendy restaurant-bar has cushy couches right on the sand, perfect for sunset drinks. The interior is equally appealing, with soaring ceilings, a gorgeous hardwood bar and walls adorned with work by local artists. Asian and Mediterranean flourishes round out the eclectic menu, and the views (and cocktails) are intoxicating. Call ahead for reservations.

Marlin Bill's
SEAFOOD, BURGERS $$$

(☑2682-0458; Playa Guiones; meals US$12-25; ☺11am-10pm Mon-Sat) Across the main road from the Guiones swirl, this old-timers' restaurant has views all the way to the ocean. The casual, open-air dining room is a perfect place to feast on grilled tuna, *ceviche* and other fresh seafood. Bill is famous for his burgers, so if you are hankering for the taste of home, he's your man.

🍷 Drinking & Nightlife

Hear live music and get your groove on at the bar at Kaya Sol (☑2682-1459; www.kayasol.com; Playa Guiones; dm US$23, d US$73-94; ✳🏠☑) or down the street at the Gilded Iguana (p317). The Beach Dog Café also has live music when open in the evenings. Head to Bar Olga (☑8404-6316; www.facebook.com/BarOlgas; Playa Pelada; mains US$8-16; ☺10am-10pm) after dark for drinking and dancing.

ℹ Information

Banco Popular (☑2682-0011, 2682-0267; Playa Guiones; ☺9am-4:30pm Mon-Fri, 8:15-11:30am Sat)

Nosara Travel (☑2682-0300; www.nosaratravel.com; Playa Guiones; ☺9am-3pm Mon-Fri) Download a decent Nosara map from the website.

NosaraNet & Frog Pad (☑2682-4039; www.thefrogpad.com; Playa Guiones; ☺9am-7pm Mon-Sat, 10am-6pm Sun; 🏠) An all-purpose stop for information, supplies and communication. Dave can answer any question – ever. You can also buy some reading material, rent a movie (or bike or surfboard) and surf the internet.

Police (☑2682-0317; Nosara) Next to the Red Cross and post office on the southeast corner of the soccer field in Nosara village center.

ℹ Getting There & Away

You can get here by airplane or bus, and there are many accommodations options close to the beach; so you don't really need your own vehicle in Nosara. That said, it's a sprawling area so you'll appreciate a car if you intend to explore the environs.

AIR

NatureAir (p97) has two daily flights to and from San José for about US$141 one way.

BUS

Local buses depart from the *pulpería* (corner grocery store) by the soccer field. Traroc buses depart for Nicoya (US$3.60, two hours) at 5am, 7am, noon and 3pm. To get to Sámara, take any bus out of Nosara and ask the driver to drop you off at *'la bomba de Sámara'* (Sámara gas station). From there, flag down one of the buses traveling from Nicoya to Sámara.

CAR

From Nicoya, a paved road leads toward Playa Sámara. About 5km before Sámara, turn onto a windy, bumpy (and, in the dry season, dusty) dirt road to Nosara village (4WD recommended). It's also possible (in the dry season) to drive north to Ostional, Junquillal and Paraíso, though you'll have to ford a few rivers. Ask around before trying this in the rainy season, when Río Nosara becomes impassable.

There are two gas stations in Nosara village, and a handful of rental car agencies in the Nosara area:

Economy Rent a Car (☑ 2299-2000; www.economyrentacar.com; Playa Guiones)

National (☑ 2242-7878; www.natcar.com; Playa Guiones; ☺ 8am-5pm)

Refugio Nacional de Fauna Silvestre Ostional

This 248-hectare coastal **refuge** (☑ 2683-0400; www.sinac.go.cr/AC/ACT/RVSOstional; adult/child US$12/2, turtle tours incl admission US$20) extends from Punta India in the north to Playa Guiones in the south, and includes the beaches of Playa Nosara and Playa Ostional. It was created in 1992 to protect the *arribadas* (mass nestings of the olive ridley sea turtles), which occur from from July to December (peaking in September and October). Ostional is one of two main nesting grounds for this turtle in Costa Rica, along with Playa Nancite in Parque Nacional Santa Rosa.

Outside of *arribada,* Ostional is usually deserted. But there is 5km of unbroken beach here, sprinkled with driftwood and swaying coconut palms. It's an ideal spot for surfing and sunbathing, birding and beachcombing.

Activities

Surfing

Surfers catch some good lefts and rights here just after low tide. Otherwise, this stretch of sea is notorious for strong currents and isn't suitable for swimming (unless you're green and have flippers).

Wildlife-Watching

Ostional is rife with sea creatures, even in addition to the turtles. Rocky Punta India at the northwestern end of the refuge has tide pools that abound with marine life, such as sea anemones, urchins and starfishes. Along the beach, thousands of almost transparent ghost crabs go about their business, as do the bright-red Sally Lightfoot crabs.

The sparse vegetation behind the beach consists mainly of deciduous trees and is home to iguanas, crabs, howler monkeys, *pizotes* (coatis) and many birds. Near the southeastern edge of the refuge is a small mangrove swamp where there is good bird-watching.

Tours

Mass arrivals of nesting turtles occur during the rainy season every three or four weeks (usually on dark nights preceding a new moon) and last about four nights. It's possible to see turtles in lesser numbers almost any night during nesting season. In the dry season, a fitting consolation prize is the small number of leatherback and green turtles that also nest here. Many tour operators in the region offer tours to Ostional during nesting season, or you can arrange with local guides to visit independently.

Associación de Guías Locales ECOTOUR
(☑ 2682-0428; www.facebook.com/Asociacion.Guias.Ostional; turtle tours per person US$8) You can't miss the local guides' office in Ostional, located on the main road just south of the plaza. During *arribada,* the guides lead 30-minute tours on the beach starting around 4pm and continuing until after dark. Early risers can also go for a tour shortly before sunrise. Check the website for details.

Sleeping & Eating

Most turtle tourists come on tours or drive themselves from Nosara or Sámara; but there are a few simple guesthouses in town for those who care to spend the night (and avoid driving on the treacherous road in the dark). North of the village, there are a few fancier accommodations options.

Ostional Turtle Lodge LODGE $
(☑ 2682-0131; www.ostionalturtlelodge.com; s/d/tr/q from US$26/40/56/70; P❋☎) A great guesthouse with only five simple rooms equipped with the basics (pay more for air-con), as well as a more spacious and stylish

chalet. Guests spend most of their time in the exquisite community *rancho* with hammocks, backed by mangroves, overlooking pastureland and within earshot of the sea.

Albergue Arribadas LODGE $$

(☑ 2682-0790; www.arribadas.com; cabins US$70; P ✳ ☎) This lodge is smack dab in the center of town, so it's noisy. Otherwise, it's good value, offering spacious four-person cabins with high ceilings and private baths. The place is frequented by groups of students and volunteers tracking turtles, but anyone can stay here. These folks are turtle experts, so they can help with tour arrangements.

Luna Azul HOTEL $$$

(☑ 2682-1400; hotellunaazul.com; d incl breakfast US$170; P ✳ ☎ ☑) This elegant hotel is a surprise, with its spacious bungalows and inviting infinity pool. From the outdoor showers to the private terraces, this is a place for relaxing – and perhaps eyeing a monkey or a bird or two. Luna Azul is about 4km north of Ostional village.

Treetops Inn INTERNATIONAL $$$

(☑ 2682-1335; costaricatreetopsinn.com; lunch/dinner per person US$32/62; ⊘ lunch 11am-2pm, dinner by reservation) Jack and Karen Hunter are renowned for their decadent five-course candlelit dinners, their potent piña coladas and their engaging storytelling. The prix-fixe meals feature the best of local ingredients, especially seafood and tropical fruit. It all takes place on a shaded deck with marvelous views of the forest canopy and the ocean beyond.

The couple also rents out two rooms – one that is actually in the treetops, and another bungalow on the beach. Located about 8km north of Ostional in the village of San Juanillo.

🛈 Getting There & Away

Ostional village is about 8km northwest of Nosara village. During the dry months there is one daily bus from Santa Cruz (two hours), departing Ostional at 5am and returning from Santa Cruz at 12:30pm. Times change, so be sure to confirm. In any case, at any time of the year the road can get washed out by rain. Hitchhiking from Nosara is reportedly easy.

If you're driving, you'll need a 4WD, as the journey requires at least one river crossing. Ask locally about conditions before setting out. From the main road joining Nosara beach and village, head north and cross the bridge over the Río Nosara. After 2km, you'll reach a T-junction. Take the left fork (which is signed) and continue about 6km north to Ostional.

Beyond Ostional, the dirt road continues on to San Juanillo and Marbella before arriving in Paraíso, northeast of Junquillal. Again, inquire locally before attempting this drive, and don't be afraid to use your 4WD.

Playa Sámara

Is Sámara the black hole of happiness? That's what more than one expat has said after stopping here on vacation and never leaving. On the surface it's just an easy-to-navigate beach town with barefoot, three-star appeal. The crescent-shaped strip of pale-gray sand spans two rocky headlands, where the sea is calm and beautiful. It's not spectacular, just safe, mellow, reasonably developed, easily navigable on foot and accessible by public transportation. Not surprisingly, it's popular with vacationing Ticos, foreign families and backpackers, who enjoy Sámara's palpable ease and tranquillity. But be careful, the longer you stay the less you'll want to leave.

If you've got some extra time and a 4WD, explore the hidden beaches north of Sámara, such as Playas Barrigona and Buenavista.

🕏 Activities & Tours

No matter what you like to do at the beach, you can probably do it at Playa Sámara. Expert surfers might get bored by Sámara's inconsistent waves, but beginners will have a blast. Otherwise, there's hiking, horseback riding and sea kayaking, as well as snorkeling out around Isla la Chora. Take a break from the beach to explore the forested hillsides on foot or on zip line.

Pato Surf School SURFING

(☑ 8761-4638; patossurfingsamara.com; board rental per day US$15, lessons US$30-40) Set right on the beach, Pato offers inexpensive and quality board rental, as well as beginner surf instruction. Pay for a lesson and get free board rental for five days! Also on offer: stand-up paddle rental and lessons; kayak rental and tours; and snorkel gear. Plus, massage on the beach and occasional beach yoga. What else do you want?

C&C Surf School SURFING

(☑ 8599-1874; www.cncsurfschool.com; board rentals per day US$15, lessons group/private US$40/60; ⊘ 8am-8pm) A great choice, offering lessons for individuals, pairs and small groups. Especially recommended for beginners. Owner Adolfo Gómez is a champion longboarder who has represented Costa Rica in the Central American Surfing Games.

Samara Trails HIKING
(☑ 2656-0920; samaratrails.com; adult/child US$40/30; ☺ 7am & 3pm, with reservation) This hike departs from the office across from Wingnuts, then follows a 6km route through a mango plantation and into the Werner Sauter Biological Reserve, a private reserve located in the hills above Sámara. In two hours, your naturalist guide covers the history of the area and the ecology of the dry tropical forest.

Birds, bugs and monkeys are usually sighted. You'll have great views along the way (including a sunset, if you take the afternoon tour).

Wingnuts CANOPY TOUR
(☑ 2656-0153; www.wingnutscanopy.com; adult/child US$60/45; ☺ tours 8am, 9am, noon & 1pm) One entrepreneurial family has found a way to preserve their beautiful, wild patch of dry tropical forest: by setting up a small-scale canopy tour. Family-owned and professionally run, this 10-platform operation is unique for its personal approach, as groups max out at 10 people. The price includes transportation from your hotel in Sámara.

Flying Crocodile SCENIC FLIGHTS
(☑ 2656-8048; www.flying-crocodile.com; per person US$110) About 6km north of Sámara in Playa Buenavista, the Flying Crocodile offers ultralight flights over the nearby beaches and mangroves. Onsite there is also a pretty cool hotel, set on jungly grounds and populated by wildlife.

Leo Tours ADVENTURE TOUR
(☑ 8995-6820; leotourssamara.com; kayak-snorkel per person US$40) Leo has kayaks, he has fishing rods, he has snorkel gear and he even has a boat. That means he'll take you out for any kind of water fun you crave, from sea kayaking to sport fishing. A favorite tour is kayaking out to Isla la Chora, where you can relax, hunt for iguanas (as in try to find them) and snorkel around the island. Look for Leo on the beach in front of Gusto (☑ 2656-0252; mains US$10-17; ☺ 9am-11pm; P �).

🍴 Courses

Centro de Idiomas Intercultura LANGUAGE COURSE
(☑ 2656-3000; www.samaralanguageschool.com; courses per week with/without homestay US$460/315) Centro de Idiomas Intercultura is right on the beach, which makes for a pleasant – if not always productive – place to study. Language courses can be arranged with or without a family homestay. Courses for kids are also available.

🛏 Sleeping

If you're staying in town, it's nearly impossible to be more than two blocks from the beach. Many hotels, hostels and charming guesthouses are clustered in the small rectangular grid that borders the sand. If you prefer to be further away from the action, there are some real gems west of town. Generally, budget options have cold-water showers only, while midrange and top-end facilities have hot water.

★ **Camp Supertramp** HOSTEL $
(☑ 2656-0373; campsupertramp.com; campsite US$8, dm US$14-16) There's something truly unique going down at Camp Supertramp, 1.5km west of Sámara and 600m from the beach. The list of things to love is long: Thomas (the owner), Jukebox (his dog), the jungle shower, the fire pit, the 1971 VW bus, the ping-pong table, and more. Sleep in the multilevel Monkey Room or the comfy-bed Delux Dorm. The vibe here is fun-filled and super chill.

El Cactus Hostel HOSTEL $
(☑ 2656-3224; www.samarabackpacker.com; dm US$14, d US$34-48; ☞☀) Brightly painted in citrus colors, El Cactus is a great option for Sámara's backpacker set, especially those who prefer serenity over revelry. Fresh rooms have wooden furniture, clean linens and hot-water showers. Hammocks hang around a small pool, and a fully fitted kitchen is also available. Located on a side street in the center of town, 100m from the beach.

Hotel Matilori HOSTEL $
(☑ 2656-0291; hostelmatilori.com; dm/s/d/tw US$16/30/36/32; P ☞) A terrific-value hostel with private rooms (and shared bathrooms) in the main house and cozy dorm rooms (sleeping four or six) in the newer annex. All the rooms have fresh coats of jewel-toned

paints, and guests have use of an updated kitchen and a shady patio. Endearing owners Fran and Jen welcome you with a *cerveza* on arrival!

Las Mariposas
HOSTEL $

(🖉 8703-3625, 2656-0314; www.hostelmariposas.com; hammock US$8, dm US$12-15, d without bathroom US$30-38; 🛜) On a rough dirt road near the language school, this fun, friendly hostel guarantees a good time, as long as you're in the right frame of mind. It's got wooden rooms and dorms, plenty of swaying hammocks, paper lantern lighting and a communal kitchen. It's just 60m from the sand.

La Mansion B&B
B&B $$

(🖉 2265-0165; www.samarabeach.com/lamansion; s US$40, d US$50-80, ste US$150; 🅿️❄🛜) This whitewashed concrete hacienda is on a quiet street, twirling with fans and bursting with colorful knickknacks. There's loads of charm: rooms are spacious and bright, and the breakfast is huge and delicious.

Sámara Palm Lodge
GUESTHOUSE $$

(🖉 2656-1169; www.samarapalmlodge.com; d US$70-80; 🅿️❄🛜🏊) An inviting little lodge on the edge of town. Eight spotless rooms feature tropical decor, with stained wood furniture, tile floors and bold colorful artwork. They face a lush garden and enticing swimming pool. It's a little west of town but just a five-minute walk to the beach.

Tico Adventure Lodge
LODGE $$

(🖉 2656-0628; www.ticoadventurelodge.com; tw/d/q/apt US$57/74/90/160; 🅿️❄🛜🏊) The US owners are proud of the fact that they built this lodge without cutting down a single tree, and they have every reason to be – it's pretty sharp. Nine double rooms and several larger apartments are surrounded by lush vegetation and old-growth trees. There's an outdoor kitchen and cookout area for communal use.

It's about 200m from the beach, on the main road between Sámara and Carrillo. Street noise can be a problem.

Entre Dos Aguas
GUESTHOUSE $$

(🖉 2656-0998; www.hoteldosaguas.com; d US$52-57, tr/q US$64/72, ste US$94-110; 🅿️🛜🏊) This fantastic little inn offers the charming personality and artistic atmosphere of a boutique hotel at the price of a roadside motel. Seven simple rooms have private stone showers, vibrant woven linens and many homey touches – all with access to an inviting common courtyard and lush gardens. It's just north of the main intersection on the road to Nicoya.

Casa del Mar
HOTEL $$

(🖉 2656-0264; www.casadelmarsamara.net; s/d/tr with bathroom US$80/80/90, without bathroom US$40/50/65; 🅿️❄🛜) 🌿 Surrounding a big mango tree and a tiny swimming pool are 17 rooms with whitewashed stucco walls and tile floors. The rooms that share a bathroom are a steal. The beach, where the hotel provides chairs and towels for its guests, is right across the street. Staff is friendly and attentive: if you need something, just ask!

⭐ LazDivaz
B&B $$$

(🖉 2656-0295; lazdivaz.com; d US$136-147; 🅿️🛜) They call it a B&C. No breakfast, just coffee. These three darling *casitas* are perched in the sand, about 400m east of the village center. The lodgings are simply decorated, but immaculately clean and exceedingly comfortable. Your main entertainment here will be swinging in a hammock and watching the sea and sky. *Pura vida.*

Las Ranas
LODGE $$$

(🖉 2656-0609; www.lodgelasranas.com; d/tr US$118/135; 🅿️❄🛜🏊) A sharp stucco lodge with a king's location. We're talking nearly 180-degrees of ocean vistas from the restaurant, pool and upper rooms. And those rooms are gorgeous, with canopy beds, granite tile floors, balconies, soaring beamed ceilings and (coming soon) kitchenettes. It's a few kilometers west of town, so you'll need wheels.

But it's worth the trip, as the leafy grounds are alive with birdlife and other animals. Spotted here: a stunning pair of western tanagers.

El Pequeño Gecko Verde
BUNGALOW $$$

(🖉 2656-1176; www.gecko-verde.com; d US$124-160, q US$210; 🅿️❄🛜🏊) A hidden slice of heaven. Contemporary and classy, these bungalows have beds dressed in plush linens, artisanal carvings on the walls, private terraces with hammocks and outdoor dining areas, and outdoor stone showers. On-site amenities include a saltwater swimming pool with waterfall, lush gardens and a fabulous open-air restaurant and bar. Located several kilometers west of town.

Sámara Tree House Inn
BUNGALOW $$$

(🖉 2656-0733; www.samaratreehouse.com; incl breakfast d poolside US$113-153, beachfront

US$170; [P][✳][🛜][🏊]) These six stilted tree houses for grown-ups are so appealing that you might not want to leave. Fully equipped kitchens have pots and pans hanging from driftwood racks, huge windows welcome light and breezes, and hammocks hang underneath. The pricier units face the beach. You can't get much closer than this.

Sámara Paraíso
HOTEL $$$

(📞 2656-2341; samaraparaiso.com; studio/ste incl breakfast US$136/226; [P][✳][🛜][🏊]) Welcome to paradise. A handful of brand-new thatch-roof bungalows are scattered about the tree-filled grounds, promising plenty of privacy. From your terrace, you can spy on monkeys, birds and more. Polished wood and crisp linens deck the interiors, each of which can accommodate up to four people. It's about 500m to a 'secret' beach. Shhh.

✕ Eating

★ Lo Que Hay
MEXICAN $

(📞 2656-0811; www.loquehaybeachbar.com; tacos US$2, mains US$5-10; ☺ 7am-late) This rocking beachside *taquería* and pub offers six delectable taco fillings: fish, chorizo, chicken, beef, pork, veggie. The grilled avocados stuffed with *pico de gallo* are choice. Even *sin* tacos, a good time will be had as the bar crowd sips into the wee small hours.

Roots Bakery
BAKERY $

(📞 8924-2770; www.facebook.com/rootsbakery cafeEnSamara; items US$3-5; ☺ 7am-4pm; 🛜) The carrot cake is really good; and the spinach quiche is better. But the cinnamon buns are otherworldly – so rich and gooey and sweet and chewy that you might have to do penance after you eat one. Required eating.

Roots is on the main drag, opposite the turnoff to Carrillo.

Ahora Sí
VEGETARIAN $

(📞 2656-0741; www.ahorasi.isamara.co; mains US$5-11; ☺ 8am-10pm; [P][🛜][🍴]) A Venetian-owned vegetarian restaurant and all-natural cocktail bar. They do smoothies with coconut milk; gnocchi with nutmeg, sage and smoked cheese; soy burgers and yucca fries; wok stir-fries; and thin-crust pizzas. All served on a lovingly decorated tiled patio.

Luv Burger
VEGETARIAN, BURGERS $$

(📞 2656-3348; www.luvburger.com; mains US$5-8; ☺ 8am-5pm; 🍴) 'Luv' is the operative word here. Feel it, veggies. There are burgers, but they are not made of meat. Neither are the sandwiches, salads or *casados*. It's all veggie,

all the time, from vegan pancakes for breakfast to guilt-free ice cream for dessert. Even the coffee drinks are made only with soy or almond milk. See how delicious animal-free can be.

Sámara Organics – Mercado Organico
MARKET $$

(📞 2656-3046; samaraorganics.com; drinks US$2-5; ☺ 7am-8pm) It's not cheap, but self-caterers (and anybody with a dietary restriction) will appreciate this cafe and market, well-stocked with organic produce and delicious prepared foods. Come get your healthy food fix.

El Lagarto
BARBECUE $$

(📞 2656-0750; www.ellagartobbq.com; mains US$11-20; ☺ 3-11pm; 🛜) Grilled meats are the big draw at this beachfront alfresco restaurant, studded with old trees. Watching the chefs work their magic on the giant wood-fired oven is part of the fun. The Surf & Turf is highly recommended, as are the cocktails.

Casa Esmeralda
SODA $$

(📞 2656-0489; www.facebook.com/casaesmeral da.samara; mains US$9-18; ☺ noon-9:30pm Mon-Sat) A favorite with locals, this is a dressed-up *soda* with tablecloths, faux-dobe walls and excellent food. The menu ranges from the expected *(arroz con pollo)* to the exotic (Italian octopus appetizer), all of which is fantastic. When the place gets busy, as it does, be prepared to wait.

La Dolce Vita
ITALIAN $$

(📞 2656-3371; www.facebook.com/ladolcevita. samara; US$8-15) Life is sweet when you're sitting under a giant *palapa* on the sand, drinking a smoothie and watching the surfers. This is a popular spot for pizza and sundowners, thanks to affable Italian owners and a prime beachfront locale.

Life is even sweeter when your bed is just a few meters away. The brand-new interior-facing guest rooms have bamboo furniture and jewel-painted walls.

🍷 Drinking & Nightlife

Flying Taco
BAR

(📞 8409-5376; ☺ noon-2am; 🛜) This joint is a laid-back, Tex-Mex beach bar. It's open for lunch – and the grub is recommended – but it's more fun to come at night, when you can also listen to live music, sing karaoke, play poker and drink margaritas. But don't skip the tacos.

La Vela Latina — BAR

(☑ 2656-2286; ⊙ 11am-midnight; 🛜) Here's your sunset happy hour spot. Settle into a comfy chair on the sand and order a bucket of icy beers or a perfectly blended cocktail at this beach bar. There's also a menu of sophisticated *bocas* (appetizers) and American-style pub grub.

Bar Arriba — SPORTS BAR

(☑ 2656-1052; www.facebook.com/SamarArriba; ⊙ 5:30pm-2am) The requisite sports bar in this surf town is Bar Arriba, located upstairs on the main drag. The place shows international sporting matches on its flat screens, so they're bound to be showing your game. The food is surprisingly satisfying: try the yucca fries (pub grub with a Central American twist).

ℹ Information

Banco Costa Rica (⊙ 9am-4pm Mon-Fri, ATM 24hr) Just off the main road, across from the soccer field.

Banco Nacional (☑ 2656-0086; ⊙ 9am-5pm Mon-Fri) Located next to the church.

La Vida Verde (Green Life; ☑ 2656-1051; greenlife@samarabeach.com; per kg US$3; ⊙ 8am-6pm Mon-Sat) Drop your dirty duds off at this laundry, 75m west of Banco Nacional. Or call ahead for pick-up and delivery.

Post Office (⊙ 8am-noon & 1:15-5:30pm Mon-Fri) Located in the same building as the police station, on the main road where it meets the beach.

Samara Info Center (☑ 2656-2424; www.samarainfocenter.com; ⊙ 9am-9pm) Located in front of Lo Que Hay, the Info Center is run by the amiable Brenda and Christopher. It's basically a tour consolidator, but they can help with accommodations, restaurant recommendations, transportation and simply answering questions about Sámara and Carrillo. And they book tours.

Samarabeach.com Surf this excellent website to get the skinny on Sámara, including a decent tourist map of the village and beach.

ℹ Getting There & Away

Playa Sámara lies about 35km southwest of Nicoya on a paved road. No flights were operating out of the Sámara airport (PLD) at research time.

Traroc buses go to Nicoya (US$3.60, one hour) 10 times a day from 5:30am to 7pm. Heading in the opposite direction, the same buses go to Playa Carrillo.

Playa Carrillo

About 4km southeast of Sámara, Carrillo is a wide, crescent-shaped beach with clean white sand, cracked granite headlands and a jungle backdrop. On weekends and holidays, the palm-fringed boulevard is lined with cars and the beach crowded with Tico families. At other times, it's practically deserted. The little town is on a hillside above the beach and attracts a trickle of sunbathers and surfers working their way down the coast.

◉ Sights & Activities

La Selva — WILDLIFE RESERVE

(☑ 2656-2236; adult/child US$15/10; ⊙ 8am-8pm) Up the hill and about 200m east of the beach, La Selva is a small but well-maintained wildlife refuge, with monkeys, iguanas, alligators, *pizotes* (coatis) and other critters. You can use your ticket twice: come in the morning before the heat of the day, then return around sunset when the nocturnal creatures wake up. This is a private venture, and the price of admission pays to protect and rehabilitate these animals. Warning: wear open-toed shoes at your own risk (fire ants).

Kingfisher Sportfishing — FISHING

(☑ 8358-9561, 2656-0091; www.costaricabillfishing.com; half-day excursions from US$900) A well-known local outfit offering deep-sea fishing on board the *Kingfisher*. Captain Rick and his crew provide top-notch service. Packages include accommodations at the luxurious Villa Oasis.

Carrillo Tours — TOUR

(☑ 2656-0543; www.carrillotours.com; ⊙ 8am-7pm) On the road up the hill, Carrillo Tours organizes turtle tours, snorkeling, kayaking, horseback riding and trips to Palo Verde.

🛏 Sleeping

There are a handful of guesthouses in the village of Puerto Carrillo. At the eastern end of the beach, take the turnoff that leads steeply uphill. It's a 15-minute walk (quicker on the way back down).

La Posada — B&B $

(☑ 2656-3131; laposada.co.cr; d incl breakfast US$40-50; 🅿 ❄ 🛜) High on the hill with sweeping panoramas of the trees and the sea, this B&B is a sweet retreat. Simple rooms have wood and wicker furniture and tropical flourishes. It's worth the extra US$10 for an ocean-view room, which also includes a breezy terrace and rocking chairs from which to take in that view. Yoga classes are held on the communal terrace.

La Tropicale   BUNGALOW $$
(☑ 2656-0159, 8884-9471; playacarrillocostarica. com; d/q incl breakfast US$60/140; P ✳ 🛜 🐾)
Across from La Selva wildlife reserve is a fun, funky, fabulous inn that has ramshackle charm and plenty of hip touches. Two colorful macaws stand guard at the porch, from where a stony path winds around the sparkling swimming pool and through mango, papaya and coconut trees. Standalone bungalows are draped with bold linens, lit with funky light fixtures and hung with original art.

The laid-back management style may be off-putting for some, but the place has a great vibe.

Cabinas El Colibrí   CABINA $$
(☑ 2656-0656; www.cabinaselcolibri.com; s/d/tr/q from US$60/70/80/90; P ✳ 🛜 🐾) Here's a collection of pleasant, spacious *cabinas* with hammocks on the porch. The brightly painted interiors have high vaulted ceilings and sturdy wood furnishings. There are kitchenettes in the apartments, but don't miss the chance to dine at the attached steakhouse, which serves traditional Argentine *parrilladas* (grilled meats), *empanadas* and fresh grilled tuna.

Hideaway Hotel   BOUTIQUE HOTEL $$$
(☑ 2656-1145; www.thehideawayplayasamara.com; d/tr/q incl breakfast US$157/190/225; P ✳ 🛜 🐾)
Midway between Carrillo and Sámara, this attractive whitewashed place is noteworthy for its super service and intimate atmosphere. A dozen spacious tiled suites all overlook the pleasant pool and blooming gardens. The airy restaurant is excellent. There is a small beach at the end of the road; alternatively, Playa Carrillo is a 15-minute walk.

❶ Getting There & Away

There is an airstrip just northwest of the beach, but it has not been in use for several years. Buses operated by **Traroc** (☑ 2685-5352; traroc.com) originate in Estrada, just east of here. From Carrillo, the buses go to Sámara, then continue on to Nicoya (US$3.60, 90 minutes, 10 daily).

Islita & Around

The coast southeast of Playa Carrillo remains one of the peninsula's most isolated and wonderful stretches of coastline, mainly because much of it is inaccessible and lacking in accommodations. But if you're willing to tackle rugged roads or venture down the coastline in a sea kayak (or possibly on foot), you'll be rewarded with abandoned beaches backed by pristine wilderness and rugged hills.

Islita is a pretty little town centered on a church and a soccer field, spruced up by artwork. The place looks unexpectedly prosperous, thanks to the efforts of the Hotel Punta Islita, which channels funding into the local community.

There are a few small breaks in front of the hotel, where you'll find a gorgeous cove punctuated with that evocative wave-thrashed boulder that is Punta Islita. At high tide the beach narrows, but at low tide it is wide, and as romantic as those vistas from above.

◉ Sights

Museo Islita   MUSEUM
(◷ 8am-4pm Mon-Sat) **FREE** Facing the soccer field, this little museum is an imaginative contemporary art house, crusted with mosaic murals. It's basically a studio and gallery, featuring artwork and handicrafts by local artists. Pick up a map for the **Arte Contemporáneo al Aire Libre** (open-air contemporary art museum), which includes mosaics, carvings and paintings that adorn everything from houses to tree trunks around the village.

Ara Project   ZOO
(☑ 8351-7849; www.thearaproject.org; admission by donation US$20; ◷ 4-5pm) A local NGO that is dedicated to the conservation of Costa Rica's two species of macaw: the great green macaw and the scarlet macaw. The group rehabilitates injured or rescued birds and eventually reintroduces them into the wild.

This breeding center and reintroduction site has an informative visitor center with lots of info about the organization, as well as a lookout point, where guests can watch the scarlet macaws as they return to their roost. It's quite a sight.

**Refugio Nacional de
Vida Silvestre Camaronal** WILDLIFE RESERVE
(Playa Camaronal; ☑ 2656-2080; www.sinac.go.cr/
AC/ACT/RVSCamaronal; admission US$6; ⊗8am-
6pm) A good beach and point break lies
north of Punta Islita at Playa Camaronal, a
charcoal gray stretch of sand strewn with
driftwood and sheltered by two headlands.
This beach also happens to be a protected
nesting site for leatherback, olive ridley,
hawksbill and black turtles, which explains
its wildlife refuge status. Hotel Punta Islita
offers turtle tours to Camaronal, as do tour
operators in Sámara and Carrillo.

🍽 Sleeping & Eating

Aside from the venerable Hotel Punta Islita,
there are no lodgings in the immediate area.
You can camp on the beaches (without facilities) if you are self-sufficient.

Hotel Punta Islita RESORT $$$
(☑ 2231-6122; www.hotelpuntaislita.com; d incl
breakfast from US$280; 🅿❄@🛜🏊) 🐾 This
hilltop hotel has 57 fully equipped rooms
with staggering ocean views. (If you spring
for a suite, you'll enjoy this view from a
private outdoor Jacuzzi.) The infinity pool
and surrounding grounds are stunning.
The amenities onsite do not stop, includ-
ing a full-service spa, a beach club with a
sunken pool bar and lounges on a rolling
lawn.

This luxury resort serves as an exam-
ple of how to ethically operate a hotel. In
addition to implementing sustainability
measures and organizing community arts
projects, it has sponsored the construction
of various public buildings, including the
village church (which hosts many destina-
tion weddings, so that was a win-win).

❶ Getting There & Away

There's no public transportation to Punta Islita,
aside from the daily flight from San José. In any
case, you'll probably want your own vehicle to
explore the coastline, preferably a 4WD.

There's a brand new permanent bridge over
the Río Ora, so the 10km journey between Puer-
to Carrillo and Punta Islita just got a lot easier.
South of the bridge, the road condition is less
reliable; proceed with caution during the rainy
season.

From December to April, five days a week,
NatureAir flies between San José and Punta
Islita (one way US$141).

Playas San Miguel & Coyote

Two of the most gorgeous – yet least visited –
beaches in Costa Rica are on this southern
stretch of the peninsula, just south of Beju-
ca. Playa San Miguel is a stunning, desolate
beach buffeted by a hulking granite head-
land and backed by elegant coconut palms.
There are a few excellent restaurants spread
out on the beach, but not much more. Playa
Coyote, to the south, is likewise a wilderness
beach, but at high tide much of the fine,
silver-gray sand gets swallowed up. Both
beaches serve as nesting grounds for olive
ridley turtles.

A number of in-the-know foreigners have
settled in the area and opened accommoda-
tions and restaurants near the shoreline. If
you're looking for a proper village, La Javil-
la is located 2km inland from Playa San
Miguel; further south, San Francisco de Coy-
ote is 4km inland from Playa Coyote.

◎ Sights & Activities

You can surf crowd-free beach breaks off San
Miguel, particularly when the tide is rising.
At Coyote there is an offshore reef that can
be surfed at high tide. When swimming, you
are advised to take precautions as the surf
can pick up, and there are not many people
in the area to help you in an emergency. If
you have your own sea kayak, these beach-
es (as well as nearby Islita) are perfect for
coastal exploration.

Mike's Jungle Butterfly Farm GARDENS
(☑ 2655-8070, 8719-1703; www.facebook.com/
junglebutterflyfarm; tours adult/child US$20/10;
⊗9am-3pm Mon-Sat) Mike's beautiful 47-acre
mountainside property includes walking
trails and a butterfly *rancho*. In addition to
the butterflies, you might spot howler mon-
keys, agoutis and iguanas. He also has colo-
nies of wild bees; you can buy their honey in
the gift shop. Book ahead for a tour.

If you need a place to lay your weary
head, Jungle Mike has two cute cottages
(US$65) on a hill overlooking a sublime
stretch of coast. You can also pitch a tent
on his farm.

Turtle Trax VOLUNTEERING
(turtle-trax.com) Located in San Francisco de
Coyote, Turtle Trax collaborates with the
venerable Programa Restauracion de Ti-
burones y Tortugas Marinas (PRETOMA;

pretoma.org) to offer opportunities to visiting volunteers who want to help monitor the turtle beaches in the area. Tasks include patrolling the beach, recording data, collecting eggs, maintaining the hatcheries and releasing the newly hatched *tortuguitas.*

Turtle Trax will organize affordable (rustic) housing and transportation for volunteers. Other opportunities include working in the local schools and collecting trash on the beach.

Sleeping

There's a smattering of unique and lovely lodgings spread out along this coast, though they are few and far between. Alternatively, both villages have *cabinas* that are acceptable options in which to pass a night. You can camp on either beach if you're self-sufficient, but there are no services.

Laguna Mar BOUTIQUE HOTEL **$$**
(☑ 2655-8181, in USA 704-851-8181; www.lagunamarhotel.com; Javilla; d incl breakfast US$74-93; P ❄ 🛜 ☲) In the center of the unassuming village of La Javilla (2km from the beach), this semiswanky hotel is incongruous with the setting, but still lovely. The rooms are simple but sophisticated, with high-thread-count linens, flat-screen TVs and contemporary flair. They are set around the sublime three-in-one swimming pool. Extra props for the excellent European restaurant.

Rhodeside B&B B&B **$$**
(☑ 2655-8006; www.rhodesidebedandbreakfast.com; d incl breakfast US$70; P ❄ 🛜) Edmund's signs offering iced coffee and espresso drinks will surely lure you in. This breezy green casa is set on the hillside north of San Miguel. Chickens poke around the grounds, while guests sip coffee and relax in rockers on the porch. If you care to stay longer, there are a handful of tiled rooms and an open-air *rancho* with great views.

Cristal Azul B&B **$$$**
(☑ 2655-8135; cristalazulhotel.com; d from US$254; P 🛜 ☲) Spectacular panoramas surround you at this hilltop retreat, where the four *cabinas* feature floor-to-ceiling windows, open-air showers and super-comfortable beds. It's worth the treacherous journey to spend a few days swinging in a hammock or lounging around the infinity pool (which really does seem to go on forever). Eager to share their little piece of paradise, your hosts are delightful.

 ## Eating

★ LocosCocos SEAFOOD **$$**
(www.locoscocos.com; Playa San Miguel; mains US$5-12; ⏱ 11am-sunset Tue-Sun; 🚗) Best. Beach. Bar. And that's saying something in Costa Rica. On an amazing, nearly deserted stretch of beach, Henner serves up his secret-family-recipe *ceviche* out of an old shipping container. Ice cold beers cap off this near-perfect experience. Also, if you time it right, you might get to see an amazing show in the sky (aka sunset).

El Barco INTERNATIONAL **$$**
(☑ 8566-9717; el-barco-costarica.com; mains US$9-12; ⏱ 11:30am-10pm; 🛜 🌱) It looks like a boat, but it's actually a building, facing a sweet slice of sand on Playa Coyote. Hokey, perhaps, but there's nothing gimmicky about the delicious and nutritious creations coming out of the kitchen. Fresh salads, hearty sandwiches and more substantial pasta and rice dishes will keep you sated.

Pizza Tree PIZZA **$$**
(☑ 2655-8063; pizzas US$9-12; ⏱ noon-10pm; P 🌱) If there is anything more fun than eating pizza in a tree house, we're not sure what it is. Take a seat at the top of this ramshackle, Seuss-like structure and feast on thin-crust pizzas and focaccias from the wood-fired brick oven. The owner is Italian but the concept is purely Tico.

❶ Getting There & Away

You can reach these beach towns by bus, but they are rather remote with minimal facilities, so you may feel stranded if you don't have your own vehicle. If your plans are limited to lounging on a deserted beach, you should be OK.

Empresa Arsa (☑ 2650-0179; transportesarsa.com) has two daily buses from San José that take about four hours to reach the beach (optimistically). The buses depart San José at 6am and 3:30pm. Return buses leave Bejuco at 4:45am and 2:30pm, passing through San Miguel and Coyote a half-hour or an hour later. This service is sketchy in the rainy season and the trip may take longer if road conditions are bad.

SOUTHERN PENINSULA

Word has spread about the hippie-chic outposts of Montezuma and dusty yet glamorous Santa Teresa. During the dry season, packs of international surfers and wanderers arrive, hungry for the wild beauty and soul-stirring waters on either side of the peninsula. In between – at the very southern tip of the Península de Nicoya – lies the first natural reserve in Costa Rica.

It used to require hours of sweaty bus rides and sluggish ferries from the mainland to access this tropical land's end, but these days there are more roads and regular boat shuttles, making the southern peninsula altogether more accessible. But if you have the time and money (and a thirst for adventure), embrace the gritty, arduous drive down the rugged western coast, which requires river crossings and low-tide beach traverses, muddy jungle slogs and steep narrow passes. It's hard work, but your arrival in paradise is all the sweeter for it.

Mal País & Santa Teresa

Get ready for tasty waves, creative kitchens and babes in board shorts and bikinis, because the southwestern corner of Península de Nicoya has all that and more. Which is why it's become one of Costa Rica's most life-affirming destinations. Here, the sea is alive with wildlife and is almost perfect when it comes to shape, color and temperature.

The hills are dotted with stylish boutique sleeps and sneaky kitchens run by the occasional runaway, top-shelf chef. Sure, there is a growing ribbon of mostly expat development on the coastline, but the hills are lush and that road is still rutted earth (even if it is intermittently sealed with aromatic vats of molasses). The entire area unfurls along one coastal road that rambles from Santa Teresa in the north through Playa El Carmen, the area's commercial heartbeat, then terminates in the fishing hamlet of Mal País.

◉ Sights

Playa El Carmen   BEACH
Playa El Carmen, downhill from the main intersection, is a good beach break that can be surfed anytime. The beach is wide and sandy and curls into successive coves, so it makes good beachcombing and swimming terrain too.

Playa Santa Teresa   BEACH
Playa Santa Teresa is a long, stunning beach that's famous for its fast and powerful beach break. The surf is pretty consistent and can be surfed at virtually any time of day. At the north end of the beach, Roca Mar – aka Suck

Rock – is an awesome point break and a local favorite. The break La Lora is named for the nightclub that marks the turnoff from the main road, so that's how you find it.

Playa Hermosa   BEACH
Somewhere north of town, Playa Santa Teresa ends and Playa Hermosa starts. This gorgeous beach deserves it's *hermosa* moniker and then some. It's wide and flat and spectacular at low tide. Apparently, the beach nearly disappears at high tide. Somewhere between low and high is surf tide, when you can ride the wide beach break left or right from center. You can surf the point break (at the north end of the beach) at any time.

Playa Manzanillo   BEACH
About 8km north of the Playa El Carmen intersection, Playa Manzanillo is a combination of sand and rock that's best surfed when the tide is rising and there's an offshore wind.

🏃 Activities

Surfing is the *raison d'être* for most visits to Santa Teresa and Mal País, and perhaps for the town itself. Most travelers want to do little else, except maybe stretch their muscles with a little yoga. That said, it's a gorgeous, pristine coastline: horseback riding or fishing trips can be easily arranged.

Surfing
The long, flat beach stretches for many kilometers along this southwestern coast of the peninsula. The entire area is saturated with surf shops. This is a good place to pick up an inexpensive board, which you can probably sell later. Most of the local shops also do rentals and repairs; chat them up to find out about their secret surf spots.

Kina Surf Shop   SURFING
(☏ 2640-0627; www.kinasurfcostarica.com; Santa Teresa; lessons per person US$50, board rentals per day US$12-20; ⊙9am-5pm) A terrific, efficient surf shop near the break in Santa Teresa. Kina claims to have the best selection of rental boards in the area, with 60-something quality boards available. The 90-minute lessons for beginner, intermediate and advanced surfers also come highly recommended.

Al Chile Surf Shop   SURFING
(☏ 2640-0959; www.alchilesurfshop.com; Santa Teresa; group/private lessons US$45/50) 'Al Chile' is a slang phrase that means something like

'For real!' As in 'In one lesson you'll be riding the white water – *al chile*!' The charming husband-wife team here guarantee it. If you don't want a lesson, they will still rent you a top-notch board.

Nalu Surf School SURFING
(☑ 2649-0391, 8358-4436; nalusurfschool.com; Santa Teresa; board rental per day US$10-20, group/private lessons US$50/65) Located 300m north of the Playa El Carmen intersection, this surf school is recommended for its fun and professional approach to instruction. Lessons usually take place at Playa El Carmen, but these guys will also transport you to other breaks in the area. The shop has a good selection of boards for rental and purchase.

Freedom Ride SUP WATER SPORTS
(☑ 8737-8781, 2640-0939; www.sup-costarica. com; Mal País; rental half-/full day US$25/40, lessons per person US$50; ☺ 9am-6pm) A stand-up paddle place with sharp management and excellent safety and instruction techniques. Andy offers lessons for first-timers and rentals for old-timers, as well as tours that are entertaining for anyone.

Yoga

Many surfers know that yoga is the perfect antidote to their sore flippers. Several studios in the area offer drop-in classes.

Yoga Studio at Nautilus YOGA
(☑ 2640-0991; www.hotelnautiluscostarica.com; Santa Teresa; group/private classes US$12/60; ☺ 9am & 6pm) What's not to love about rooftop yoga? Twice-daily classes are held on the deck at the Nautilus Boutique Hotel (p331), offering lovely views over the village. They offer Vinyasa flow and kundalini, power and restorative yoga. Located up the road from Hostal Brunela.

Casa Zen YOGA
(☑ 2640-0523; www.zencostarica.com; Santa Teresa; classes per person US$9) Three or four daily classes take place in a lovely 2nd-story, open-air studio, surrounded by trees. Most of the classes are a Hatha-inspired Vinyasa flow, but there's also cardio fit and other styles. Yoga by candlelight is a sublime way to transition from day to night. Multiclass packages are available.

Horizon Yoga Hotel YOGA
(☑ 2640-0524; www.horizon-yogahotel.com; Santa Teresa; classes per person US$12) Offers two classes daily, in a serene environment overlooking the ocean. About 100m north of Supermarket Ronny, turn off the main road and drive 50m up the hill.

🛏 Sleeping

Frank's Place is the landmark that occupies the main corner at Playa El Carmen. Stretching to the north, Santa Teresa is a dusty, mellow hamlet that's crammed with guesthouses, cafes and surf shops. Stretching to the south, Mal País is more sparsely developed and more densely forested, offering a quieter atmosphere.

Don Jon's BUNGALOW $
(☑ 2640-0700; www.donjonsonline.com; Santa Teresa; dm US$15-20, bungalow US$45-70, apt US$80-120; P❄️🛜) Just past the soccer field, Don Jon's place is the perfect base for surfers and anybody looking to 'relax to the max.' Rustic teak bungalows are creatively decorated and quite appealing, while attractive Spanish-tiled dorms have high-beamed ceilings and plenty of hammocks in the garden.

The restaurant knows its audience, serving filling breakfasts, giant burritos, delicious fish tacos and strong drinks. Located 100m from the surf.

Cuesta Arriba HOSTEL $
(☑ 2640-0607; www.cuestaarriba.com; Santa Teresa; dm US$15, d US$50-60, all incl breakfast; ☺ 9am-7pm; P❄️🛜🛏) This is a thinking person's hostel, attracting a cultivated crowd of travelers who appreciate the orderly atmosphere. En suite bathrooms, polished concrete floors, colorful tapestries and mosaic tile embellishments look lovely in both shared and private rooms. Communal areas include a big well-stocked kitchen area, a breezy terrace upstairs and a garden with hammocks.

Casa Zen GUESTHOUSE $
(☑ 2640-0523; www.zencostarica.com; Santa Teresa; dm/d/tr/q incl breakfast US$15/35/42/50; P🛜) This lovely Asian-inspired guesthouse is decked out in celestial murals and happy Buddha sculptures. The colorful but basic rooms share super-clean bathrooms and two fully equipped kitchens. Some guests have complained that the thin walls and passing traffic detract from the Zen atmosphere; but we would argue that the noise is just an opportunity to practice more Zen. Just down the alley from Casa Zen is our favorite swimming beach in the

area. With white and powdery sand, it's protected by rock reefs on both sides. Lovely hangout spot.

Wavetrotter
HOSTEL $

(☑2640-0805; wavetrottersurfhostel.com; Santa Teresa; dm US$15, r without bathroom US$35; P🛜) An excellent option for hostel hoppers, not just surfers, Wavetrotter is a simple place, with all-wood six-bed dorms overlooking a vast common area. There are private rooms in the garden, which is also home to howlers and iguanas. There is a huge communal kitchen and – major bonus – the whole place is spotless.

It's one block east of the main road: turn right before Pizza El Pulpo.

★Casa Pampa
GUESTHOUSE $$

(☑2640-0684; casapampa.com; Santa Teresa; r US$35, ste US$75-85; P🌬🛜) 🦋 Possibly the best deal in all of Santa Teresa. The location is super convenient – surrounded by an overflowing garden, on a quiet road, yet still close to town and the beach. The modest surf chalet has six spic-n-span rooms with kitchenettes and an outdoor lounge area. Rinse off on your return from the waves.

All rooms have air-con but you'll pay more to use it. Located next to Casa Zen.

Casa Azul
GUESTHOUSE $$

(☑2640-0379; www.hotelcasaazul.com; Santa Teresa; r with/without ocean view US$100/70, casitas/ste US$150/400; P🛜🏊) You can't get much closer to the waves than this fabulous electric-blue house, looming over the garden, pool and beach. Sharing a communal kitchenette and an outdoor BBQ, the three downstairs rooms are attractive with ceramic-tile floors, wrought-iron beds and plenty of light. The secluded garden *casita* has a private patio with sea views.

Pachamama
HOTEL $$

(☑2640-0195; www.pacha-malpais.com; Mal País; bungalows US$65-75, houses US$160; P🛜) This sweet earth-loving property offers tremendous value, especially in its quaint faux-dobe bungalows, each with a kitchenette and lovely shady front porch. There's also a wicked two-story, two-bedroom house with a romantic wooden loft. Wildlife abounds in the tropical garden. It's 1km from the Playa El Carmen intersection, 1km from Cabo Blanco and 50m from the beach.

Hotel Meli Melo
HOTEL $$

(☑2640-0575; hotelmelimelo.com; Santa Teresa; d/tr/q US$60/70/80; P🌬🛜) Here's a cheerful B&B, smack dab in the center of town and close to the main surf break. Clean, colorful rooms have all the standard amenities, plus a private terrace, a common kitchen, tropical gardens and an outdoor shower (the latter should be required in a surf town like this). Meli takes great pride in her namesake hotel and it shows.

Malpaís Surf Camp & Resort
LODGE $$

(☑2640-0031; www.malpaissurfcamp.com; Mal País; dm US$17, d with/without bathroom US$73/40, villa from US$108; P🌬@🛜🏊) There are comfortable, private cabanas and more luxurious digs, but the best deal at this surfers' lodge is the open-air *rancho,* with a tin roof and pebble floors, which you can share with three other surfers. Explore the landscaped tropical grounds, swim in the luscious pool, grab a cold beer in the open-air lounge and soak up the good vibes.

Funky Monkey Lodge
BUNGALOW $$

(☑2640-0272; www.funky-monkey-lodge.com; Santa Teresa; d US$96-102, apt US$136-192; P🌬@🏊) Located 200m north of the soccer field, this funky lodge has sweet, rustic bungalows built out of bamboo. Each has an open-air shower, balcony with hammock and access to a communal kitchen. Also: ping-pong, pool and board games...good times!

Funky Monkey's restaurant turns out some amazing things (eg banana pancakes for breakfast). No matter where you are staying, be sure to stop by on a Wednesday or Saturday night for super sushi.

Star Mountain
LODGE $$

(☑2640-0101; starmountaineco.com; Mal País; s/d/tr US$69/85/95, casitas US$159-169; P🛜🏊) 🦋 Set on a 90-hectare private reserve, replete with birds, butterflies and monkeys, Star Mountain is a true escape back to nature. The lodge has four spacious guest rooms, a wide porch with hammocks and rockers, a yoga studio and a glorious pool. It's 2km from the beach in Mal País. Turn off the main road at Mary's Restaurant.

Three kilometers of trails traverse the grounds, which you can explore on foot or on horseback.

Cabinas Playa
CABINA $$

(☑2640-0137; santateresasurfhostels.com; Santa Teresa; dm US$10-12, d US$50, q US$72-100; P🌬🛜🏊) Vying for the title of 'closest to the break,' this is also one of the friendliest places in town, thanks to super-attentive owners Amir and Idan. The rooms are plain but clean. The heart of the hostel is the cool common hangout area, complete with pool table and movie projector (surf clips are very popular here).

★**Canaima Chill House** BOUTIQUE HOTEL $$$
(☑ 2640-0410; www.hotel-canaima-chill-house.com; Santa Teresa; d/q US$100/130; P ⊛ 🕿) A 'chill house' is an apt descriptor for this eight-room boutique eco-chic hotel, set in the jungle. Super-stylish suites have breezy indoor-outdoor living areas, well-equipped kitchens, awesome hanging bamboo beds and loads of natural materials (such as stone grotto showers).

The Chill House is set in the hills, so you'll want wheels. Turn off the main road at Hostal Brunella and drive 500m east.

Guests share the Jacuzzi and plunge pool, and commune in the sunken pillow lounge.

Moana Lodge BOUTIQUE HOTEL $$$
(☑ 2640-0230, toll-free in USA 888-865-8032; moanacostarica.com; Mal País; r standard/deluxe US$105/145, ste US$245-280; P ⊛ ⊛ 🕿) A simply stunning boutique property etched into the wooded hillside above Mal País. Standard rooms are all-wood garden cottages, decked out with African art. Make the climb to the junior suites for 180-degree views of the coast. There are wood floors throughout, rain showers inside and outside, and sliding glass doors. The top-shelf Papaya Lounge (p334) shares that stunning perch.

**Atrapasueños
Dreamcatcher Hotel** BOUTIQUE HOTEL $$$
(☑ 2640-0080; www.atrapasuenos.net; Santa Teresa; d incl breakfast US$140-160, apt US$200; P ⊛ ⊛ 🕿) Steps from the beach, this family-owned place offers the intimacy of a B&B and the luxury of a boutique hotel. With a balcony or terrace overlooking lush gardens, the rooms have hardwood floors, exotic art and tapestries, and big glass sliding doors. A lovely mosaic pool is surrounded by a sun terrace with an outdoor shower.

Nautilus Boutique Hotel BOUTIQUE HOTEL $$$
(☑ 2640-0991; www.hotelnautiluscostarica.com; Santa Teresa; villa d/q US$165/270; P ⊛ 🕿) ✎
If you're looking for a healthy, relaxing retreat with a bit of luxury, Nautilus is for you. Each villa has a living area, fully equipped kitchen and private deck. Even better, the

design incorporates plenty of wood, natural elements, local artwork and fine linens.

Besides being a boutique hotel, Nautilus is also a 'wellness center,' offering twice daily yoga classes (p329) and amazing, healthy food at the onsite restaurant Olam.

Horizon Yoga Hotel HOTEL $$$
(☑ 2640-0524; www.horizon-yogahotel.com; Santa Teresa; d US$140-150, q US$250; P ⊛ @ 🕿) Replete with fountains and profound beauty, this stunning terraced property on the Santa Teresa hillside offers barefoot elegance at its best. There is a range of rooms, including family-friendly villas with private pools. A better choice is the stilted bamboo bungalows, which have decks with hammocks and massive 180-degree ocean views.

The same views are available at the onsite vegetarian restaurant, which serves strong coffee and herbal tea, fruit smoothies and satisfying breakfasts.

🍴 **Eating**

Zwart Cafe CAFE $
(☑ 2640-0011; Santa Teresa; mains US$4-8; ⏱ 7am-5pm; 🕿) Zwart means 'black' in Dutch, but this shabby-chic, artist-owned gallery and cafe is all white (or mostly, damn dust!). You'll love the surf-inspired Technicolor canvases, the lively outdoor patio and the popular breakfasts, including chocolate chip pancakes and breakfast burritos. At lunch it's all about the burritos. There's a dynamite used bookstore here too.

Caracolas SODA $
(☑ 2640-0525; Mal País; mains US$4-13; ⏱ 7am-9pm; P ⊛ 🖐) The lone *soda* on this end of the coast. It serves *típica* on timber tables in a garden that rolls on to the rocky beach. The place does all the usual chicken, beef and seafood dishes, as well as sandwiches and salads. But the reason to come here is to feel the ocean breeze and stare at the setting sun.

Burger Rancho BURGERS $$
(☑ 2640-0583; www.facebook.com/BurgerRancho; Santa Teresa; mains US$10-12; ⏱ 10am-10pm; ✎) Get your burger on at this open-air *rancho*. Check the blackboard for daily changing specials, including veggie options like a portobello mushroom burger; fish options like the Hawaiian tuna burger; and other unique options like a chorizo burger. There's other food too, but why would you want to do that?

ROB FRANCIS / ROBERT HARDING / GETTY IMAGES ©

1. Playa Carrillo (p324)

This wide, crescent-shaped beach is popular with Tico families on weekends.

2. Turtles, Refugio Nacional de Fauna Silvestre Ostional (p319)

Arribadas (mass nestings of olive ridley sea turtles) take place from July to December.

3. Nosara (p312)

Take in stunning sunset views as you horseback ride along the beach.

4. Playa Guiones (p312)

A popular spot for surfers, boasting the Central Peninsula's best beach break.

Pizzeria Playa Carmen
PIZZA **$$**

(☑ 2640-0110; restaurantepizzeriaplayacarmen.
com; Playa El Carmen; mains US$8-23; ☺ 9am-
10pm) This is a pizza place right on the
playa – hard to beat. It's a popular spot for
sundowners, thanks to the happy hour spe-
cials (two-for-one drinks) and the amazing
show that takes place in the sky. Come hob-
nob with the locals and enjoy.

★ Koji's
JAPANESE **$$$**

(☑ 2640-0815; www.santa-teresa.com/kojis; Playa
Hermosa; sushi US$5-10; ☺ 5:30-9:30pm Wed-
Sun) Koji Hyodo's sushi shack is a twinkling
beacon of fresh, raw excellence. The atmosphere and service are superior, of course,
but his food is a higher truth. The grilled
octopus is barely fried and sprinkled with
sea salt; there's a sweet crunch to his lobster
sashimi, sliced tracing-paper thin and sprinkled with fresh ginger.

It's 2km north of Florblanca. If you cross
the bridge, you've gone too far. Reservations
recommended.

Mary's Restaurant
ORGANIC **$$$**

(☑ 2640-0153; www.maryscostarica.com; Mal
País; pizza US$10-16, mains US$14-22; ☺ 5:30-
10pm Thu-Tue) Located at the far end of Mal
País village, this unassuming, open-air res-
taurant has a polished concrete floor, wood
oven, pool table and blackboard menu. It
offers delicious wood-fired pizzas, home-
made bacon and sausage, grilled seafood
and fresh produce straight from the farm.
It's all fabulous. Its secret? Using only fresh,
organic ingredients from local farms and
fishers.

Papaya Lounge
INTERNATIONAL **$$$**

(☑ 2640-0230; moanacostarica.com; Mal País;
tapas US$6-12; ☺ 7:30-10am daily & 5-10pm Wed-
Mon) The top-shelf Moana Lodge (p331) is
on a stunning perch and has jaw-dropping
views and Latin-inspired tapas. The emphasis on local ingredients results in delights such as beef braised in chili and
coffee, and seafood skewers in habanero
and passion fruit glaze. If you're wondering
how much to order, two tapa per person
should do the trick.

🍷 Drinking & Nightlife

It's no mystery where the party is going on:
Thursdays at Kika, Sundays at Roca Mar
and any night of the week – around sunset –
at Pizzeria Playa Carmen.

Roca Mar
BAR

(☑ 2640-0250; Santa Teresa; ☺ noon-9pm; 🛜)
Tucked away at Blue Surf Sanctuary at the
northern end of town, this is a pretty perfect beach lounge that attracts a local expat crowd. Beanbags are stuck in the sand,
and hammocks are slung in the trees – all
perfectly positioned for sunset. On Sunday
evenings, they host an official Sunset Party –
a family-friendly event with live music and
fire dancers and such.

Kika
LIVE MUSIC

(☑ 2640-0408; www.facebook.com/kika.santate
resa; Santa Teresa; ☺ 5pm-2am) This Argentine-
owned restaurant is a popular spot for dinner
and drinks by candlelight (Grandma's pork
gets rave reviews). But things really pick up
after dark on Thursday, when a local punk-
rock-ska cover band takes the stage, attracting a lively crowd for drinking and dancing.
Good band, bad band? Don't think too hard,
rockers, there's music in the air!

ℹ Information

Next door to Frank's Place, **Banco de Costa
Rica** (☑ 2211-1111; Playa El Carmen; ☺ 9am-4pm
Mon-Fri) has a 24-hour ATM. Directly across the
street at the Centro Comercial Playa El Carmen
you'll find a branch of **Banco Nacional** (☑ 2640-
0598; Playa El Carmen; ☺ 1-7pm Mon-Fri) with
an ATM.

malpais.net is a useful website with lots of
local information, including a handy map of the
area.

ℹ Getting There & Away

BUS

All buses begin and end at Ginger Café, 100m
south of Cuesta Arriba hostel, but you can flag
the bus down anywhere along the road in Santa
Teresa. At Frank's Place, the buses turn left and
head inland toward Cóbano.

A direct bus to San José via the Paquera ferry
departs at 7:30am and 3:30pm (US$13, six
hours). Local buses to Cóbano (US$2, 45 min-
utes) depart at 7am and noon.

Montezuma Expeditions (☑ 2642-0898;
www.montezumaexpeditions.com; Santa Te-
resa) organizes shuttle-van transfers to San
José, Tamarindo and Sámara; Jacó, La Fortuna,
Liberia and Monteverde; Manuel Antonio; and
Dominical.

CAR

Consider renting a car if you want to check out
some of the more distant breaks.

Alamo (🖉2242-7733; www.alamocostarica.com; Playa El Carmen; ⊙7:30am-5:30pm) Located at Frank's Place.

Budget (🖉2640-0500; www.budget.co.cr; Centro Comercial Playa El Carmen; ⊙8am-6pm Mon-Sat, to 4pm Sun) Next to Banco Nacional.

ℹ️ Getting Around

Santa Teresa and Mal País are dirt-road types of towns: during the dry season, life gets extremely dusty. Consider using a bicycle to get around town, so you're not contributing to the problem. If you must drive, please go slowly. The closest gas station is 2km up the Cóbano road from Playa El Carmen. Taxis between Mal País, Playa El Carmen and Santa Teresa range from US$4 to US$8.

Reserva Natural Absoluta Cabo Blanco

Just 11km south of Montezuma is Costa Rica's oldest protected wilderness area. Cabo Blanco (🖉2642-0093; adult/child US$12/2; ⊙8am-4pm Wed-Sun) comprises 12 sq km of land and 17 sq km of surrounding ocean, and includes the entire southern tip of the Península de Nicoya. The moist microclimate on the tip of the peninsula fosters the growth of evergreen forests, which are unique when compared with the dry tropical forests typical of Nicoya. The park also encompasses a number of pristine white-sand beaches and offshore islands that are favored nesting areas for various bird species.

Cabo Blanco is called an 'absolute' nature reserve because visitors were originally not permitted (prior to the late 1980s). Even though the name hasn't changed, a limited number of trails have been opened to visitors, but the reserve remains closed on Monday and Tuesday to minimize environmental impact.

🏃 Activities

There are no facilities in Cabo Blanco, so be sure to bring plenty of food and water. The closest place to stock up is about 2km away in Cabuya.

Hiking

From the ranger station, the **Sendero Sueco** (Swedish Trail) leads 4.5km down to a wilderness beach at the tip of the peninsula, while the **Sendero Danes** (Danish Trail) is a spur that branches from Sendero Sueco and reconnects 1km later. So, you can make this small 2km loop and stay in the woods, or take on the considerably more difficult but much more rewarding hike to the cape, heading down one way and taking the other path back up. Be advised that the trails can get very muddy (especially in the rainy season) and are fairly steep in certain parts – plan for about two hours in each direction.

The wide, sandy pebble **beach** at the end of the trail is magnificent. It's backed by jungle, sheltered by two rugged headlands including one that stretches out into a rock reef with island views just offshore. The water is striped turquoise at low tide, but the cool currents still make for a refreshing dip. Visibility isn't always great for snorkeling but you may want to bring a mask anyway. Driftwood is smooth, weathered and piled haphazardly here and there. There are even picnic tables and a grill, if you care to get ambitious. Simply put, it is a postcard,

PENÍNSULA DE NICOYA RESERVA NATURAL ABSOLUTA CABO BLANCO

THE WESSBERG LEGACY

The reserve at Cabo Blanco was originally established by a Danish–Swedish couple, the late Karen Mogensen and Olof Nicolas Wessberg, who settled in Montezuma in the 1950s and were among the first conservationists in Costa Rica. In 1960 the couple was distraught when they discovered that sections of Cabo Blanco had been clear-cut. At the time, the Costa Rican government was primarily focused on the agricultural development of the country, and had not yet formulated its modern-day conservation policy. Karen and Nicolas, as he was known, were instrumental in convincing the government to establish a national park system, which eventually led to the creation of the Cabo Blanco reserve in 1963.

The couple continued to fight for increased conservation of ecologically rich areas. Tragically, Olof was murdered in 1975 during a campaign in the Península de Osa. Karen continued their work until her death in 1994, and today they are buried in the Reserva Absoluta Nicolás Wessberg, the site of their original homestead.

and should be required for visitors to the southern peninsula. Leave the beach by 2pm to get out before the park closes.

Wildlife-Watching

Monkeys, squirrels, sloths, deer, agoutis and raccoon abound at Cabo Blanco. Armadillos, *pizotes* (coatis), peccaries and anteaters are also occasionally sighted.

The coastal area is known as an important nesting site for the brown booby, mostly found 1.6km south of the mainland on Isla Cabo Blanco (White Cape Island). In fact, the name 'Cabo Blanco' was coined by Spanish conquistadors when they noticed that the entire island consisted of guano-encrusted rocks. Seabirds in the area include the brown pelican and the magnificent frigate bird.

ℹ Getting There & Away

Buses (US$1.50, 45 minutes) depart from the park entrance for Montezuma at 7am, 9am, 11am and 3pm, passing through Cabuya about 15 minutes later. A taxi from Montezuma to the park costs about US$20.

Cabuya

This tiny, bucolic village unfurls along a rugged dirt road about 7km south of Montezuma. Populated by a tight-knit community of Ticos and expats, it is a hidden gem with easy access to the Cabo Blanco reserve, ideal for those looking to chill. Don't miss the amazing Cabuya ficus tree, which claims to be the largest strangler fig in Costa Rica, measuring 40m high and 22m in diameter!

The beach here is rocky and not great for swimming or surfing. But you're a short walk from Playa los Cedros, a great surf spot that is halfway between Montezuma and Cabuya. Alternatively, at low tide you can walk across the natural bridge to Isla Cabuya, which has a small sandy beach and good snorkeling spots, as well as an evocative island cemetery. Keep an eye on the tides or you'll have to swim back!

🛏 Sleeping

El Ancla De Oro   CABINA $

(🖉 2642-0369; www.hotelelancladeoro.com; s/d US$15/25, cabinas US$35-45; ℗🖥) This rustic outpost gets mixed reviews from readers. But it seems to be a decent option for budget travelers who want to experience life in the treetops. The best accommodations

are secluded stand-alone 'jungalows,' where you're likely to spot howler and white-faced monkeys from bed. Located on the road to Montezuma.

Hotel Celaje   CABINA $$

(🖉 2642-0374; www.celaje.com; s/d/tr/q incl breakfast US$75/90/105/120; ℗❄🖥🌊) This sweet spot is a collection of spacious, stained-wood A-frame bungalows set on a sublime palm-dappled slice of shore. The grounds are decorated with artistic touches, like coconut lamps and seashell mobiles. The place is right on a beautiful beach, which is not great for swimming due to rocks; but the pool is glorious!

Howler Monkey Hotel   HOTEL $$

(🖉 2642-0303; www.howlermonkeyhotel.com; s/d/tr/q US$80/100/110/120; ℗🖥🌊) Follow the signs down the side road to find these large rustic A-frame bungalows with kitchenettes (useful, as eating options are limited in Cabuya). The place is right on a slice of very quiet, rocky beach. The friendly owners are a wealth of information, and also offer bikes and kayaks. And yes, it's called Howler Monkey Hotel for a reason: expect a wake-up call.

🍴 Eating

Panadería Cabuya   CAFE $

(🖉 2642-1184; cabuyabeach.com; mains US$3-17; ⊙6:30am-8pm Mon-Sat, to 6pm Sun; 🖥) A local landmark. Set on a tropical patio, this inviting cafe serves up a stellar menu including fresh bread, pastries and strong coffee for breakfast, as well as soups and sandwiches for later in the day. If you have a thing for tall, dark and handsome, you should meet the chocolate cake.

Café Coyote   PIZZA $

(🖉 2642-0354; www.cabuyabeach.com; mains US$5-11; ⊙8am-10pm; 🖥) Jenny can help you with just about anything you need, from calling a taxi to organizing an adventure outing, pouring you a cold *cerveza* or making you a tasty pizza (her specialty). She also offers delicious breakfast options and other meals to sate your appetite at any time of day.

Soda Marvin   SODA $

(mains US$4-10; ⊙7am-9pm; 🖥🖉) Here's your local family-run *soda,* offering all your Tico favorites. Non-meat-eaters will be surprised and delighted by the excellent vegetarian *casado,* but there's also seafood pasta, fish fajitas, filling breakfasts and the ever-important, strong, dark coffee.

ℹ️ Getting There & Away

Driving from Montezuma, it's a straight shot 7km down the coast to the village of Cabuya. Buses make this run – en route to Cabo Blanco – four times a day in either direction.

If you find Café Coyote you have found the road to Mal País, which is about 7km due west on the stunningly scenic Star Mountain Rd (passable only during the dry season). Make sure you have a 4WD, especially during the rainy season, as these roads are rugged and there is at least one river crossing.

Montezuma

Montezuma is an immediately endearing beach town that demands you abandon the car to stroll, swim and (if you can stroll a little further) surf. The warm and wild ocean and that remnant, ever-audible jungle has helped this rocky nook cultivate an inviting, boho vibe. Typical tourist offerings such as canopy tours do a brisk trade here, but you'll also bump up against Montezuma's internationally inflected, artsy-rootsy beach culture in yoga classes, volunteer corps, veggie-friendly dining rooms and neo-Rastas hawking uplifting herbs. No wonder locals lovingly call this town 'Montefuma.'

It's not perfect. The accommodations are particularly poor value, and the eateries can be that way too (though there are some absolute gems). But in this barefoot *pueblo*, which unfurls along several kilometers of rugged coastline, you're never far from the rhythm and sound of the sea, and that is a beautiful thing.

◎ Sights

Picture-perfect white-sand beaches are strung along the coast, separated by small rocky headlands, offering great beachcombing and ideal tide-pool contemplation. Unfortunately, there are strong riptides, so inquire locally before going for a swim.

Playa Montezuma   BEACH

The best beach close to town is just north of Cocolores restaurant, where the sand is powdery and sheltered from big swells. This is your glorious sun-soaked crash pad. The water's shade of teal is immediately nourishing, the temperature is perfect and fish are abundant. At the north end of the beach, look for the trail that leads to a cove known as Piedra Colorada. A small waterfall forms a freshwater pool, which is a perfect swimming spot.

PLAYA COCOLITO

Here's your chance to see a waterfall crashing down a cliff, straight onto the rocks and into the ocean. And yes, it is as spectacular as it sounds. El Chorro Waterfall is the *pièce de résistance* of Playa Cocolito, which is itself pretty irresistible.

It's a hot, two-hour, 12km hike from Montezuma: leave at sunrise to spot plenty of wildlife along the way. Alternatively, this is a popular destination for horseback riding. In any case, be sure to bring water and snacks as there are no facilities here.

The waters here are a dreamy, iridescent azure, with pink rocky cliffs creating two inviting swimming areas. It's far enough from the action that you are likely to have the place to yourself.

Playa Grande   BEACH

About 7km north of town, Playa Grande is the best surf beach in the area. It's a 3km-plus stretch of waves and sand, which never gets too crowded as it requires a 30-minute hike to get here. But what a hike it is, wandering along between the turquoise waters of the Pacific and the lush greenery of the Montezuma Biological Reserve.

Playa Grande is sometimes a destination for topless or nude sunbathers. This is not the cultural norm in Costa Rica, so please be discreet if you're trying to get rid of your tan lines.

Montezuma Gardens   GARDENS

(📞2642-1317; www.montezumagardens.com; admission US$4; ⏰8am-4pm) About 1km south of town, alongside the waterfall trail, you can take a tour through this lush *mariposario* (butterfly garden) and nursery where the mysterious metamorphoses occur. You'll learn about the life cycles and benefits of a dozen local species, of which you'll see many colorful varieties. There's also a B&B located here (rooms US$57 to US$80).

★ Montezuma Waterfalls   WATERFALL

(parking US$2) A 40-minute river hike leads to a waterfall with a delicious swimming hole. Further along the trail, a second set of falls offers a good clean 10m leap into deep water. Reach the 'diving platform' from the trail: do not try to scale the slippery rocks! Daring

Montezuma

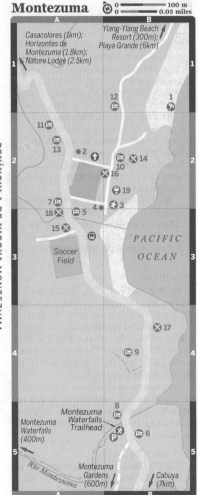

Casacolores (1km);
Horizontes de
Montezuma (1.8km);
Nature Lodge (2.5km)

Ylang-Ylang Beach
Resort (300m);
Playa Grande (6km)

PACIFIC
OCEAN

Soccer
Field

Montezuma
Waterfalls
(400m)

Montezuma
Waterfalls
Trailhead

Río Montezuma

Montezuma
Gardens
(600m)

Cabuya
(7km)

Montezuma

tience with new surfers of all ages. Daily lessons take place on Playa Grande, with no more than three people in the class. Surfboard, rash guard and fresh fruit are included. They also offer week-long camps for families, surfer chicks and yogis.

Montezuma Yoga   YOGA
(☑ 2642-1311, 8704-1632; www.montezumayoga. com; per person US$14; ⊙ classes 8:30am & 6pm daily) Anusara-inspired instruction, which pairs Iyengar alignment principles with a Vinyasa flow, is available in a gorgeous studio kissed by ocean breezes, sheltered by a peaked tin roof and serenaded by the sounds of nature. The Sunday night candlelight class is a close-to-heaven experience. On the grounds of Hotel Los Mangos.

Proyecto Montezuma   VOLUNTEERING
(☑ 2642-0271; www.proyectomontezuma.com) ✐ Proyecto Montezuma is an innovative volunteer program that not only gives to the community but also fosters cultural exchange, pays fair wages to its employees and gives back for donating your time and

souls can test their Tarzan skills on the rope that swings over a third set. A lot of travelers enjoy these thrills but a few of them have died, so do it at your own risk.

As you head south past Hotel La Cascada, there's a parking area, then take the trail to the right just after the bridge. You'll want proper hiking footwear.

🏃 Activities

Young Vision Surf School   SURFING
(☑ 8669-6835; youngvisionsurf.com; 2hr lessons US$45) Manny and Alvaro get rave reviews for their knowledge, enthusiasm and pa-

energy. Choose from projects such as teaching, environmental clean-up or sea turtle protection.

Courses

La Escuela del Sol COURSE
(☑8884-8444; www.laescueladelsol.com) Based at the Hotel El Tajalin, this eclectic educational vortex offers Spanish, surf, yoga, fire dance and scuba instruction. In other words, there is no excuse to leave Montezuma without a bilingual, underwater, surf warrior, dreadlocked hippie soul.

☞ Tours

Tour operators around town rent everything from bodyboards to bikes. They can also arrange speed-boat transfers to Jacó and private shuttle transfers to other places.

The most popular tour is a boat trip to Isla Tortuga (p345), which costs around US$50 including lunch, fruit, drinks and snorkeling gear. Although the island is certainly beautiful (the *most* beautiful in Costa Rica, by many accounts), travelers complain that the outing feels like a tourist circus, especially during high season when the entire island is full of boat tours.

Also popular are guided hikes in Cabo Blanco and horseback riding to Playa Cocolito.

Sun Trails TOUR
(Montezuma Waterfall Canopy Tour; ☑2642-0808; www.montezumatraveladventures.com; tours US$45; ◷9am-3pm) This 2½-hour canopy tour is operated by the tour company Sun Trails. After you've flown down nine zip lines, you'll hike down – rather than up – to the waterfalls. Bring your swimsuit, so you can jump off the rocks and cool off. Book at the Sun Trails office in town.

Cabo Blanco Travelers TOUR
(☑2642-1125, 8835-0270; www.caboblancotravelers.tk) Local guide Gerardo Canti leads nature hikes in Cabo Blanco, sharing the knowledge of local flora and fauna garnered from his Chorotega ancestors. Other tours include horseback-riding, sportfishing and snorkeling trips to Isla Tortuga. He also rents a few sweet bungalows in town.

🛏 Sleeping

Montezuma is a town distinguished by poor-value lodging, so it makes sense to book in advance. Note that some hotels have a three-night minimum during holiday weeks. There's a sprinkling of guesthouses and boutique hotels above Montezuma, off the road to Cóbano, some of which are highly recommended, but all of which are only suitable if you have wheels.

★ Luz en el Cielo HOSTEL, B&B $
(☑8811-3700, 2642-0030; www.luzenelcielo.com; dm US$18-28, d/q US$90/136; ℙ🛜) In the heart of the jungle but two minutes from town, this homey hostel and B&B is an inviting retreat. Crowded dorm rooms are super clean with sturdy wood furniture and lockers, while the new 'luxury' dorms are more spacious, with TVs, private balconies and en suite bathrooms. The treetop *cabinas* are also wonderful. Amazing breakfasts (included in rates), enticing hammocks and super-friendly staff.

Luna Llena HOSTEL $
(☑2642-0390; www.lunallenahotel.com; dm/s/d without bathroom US$15/28/38, d with bathroom US$55-65; ℙ🛜) On the northern edge of town on a hilltop overlooking the bay is a budget option which is absolutely delightful and truly unique. The rooms are all simple but stylish, colorful and clean; most have balconies. There are two kitchens, a BBQ grill and a breezy communal lounge with rattan chair-swings and stunning ocean views. Wildlife abounds in the surrounding trees.

Hotel Los Mangos HOTEL $
(☑2642-0076; www.hotellosmangos.com; r without/with bathroom US$35/75, bungalows US$90; ℙ❄🛜🏊) Scattered across mango-dotted gardens, this whimsical hotel has plain, painted-wood rooms in the main building and attractive (though dark) octagonal bungalows that offer more privacy. Monkeys populate the mango trees and yoga classes are held in the gorgeous, ocean-view yoga pavilion.

Hotel Pargo Feliz CABINA $
(☑2642-0064; d US$35-50; 🛜) You can't beat the location of these beachfront *cabinas* in the heart of Montezuma. Rooms are simple, clean and fan-cooled. The communal balcony and garden terrace have relaxing hammocks with sea views, and at night the surf will lull you to sleep.

Downtown Montezuma Hostel HOSTEL $
(☑8516-6921; www.facebook.com/dtmontezuma; dm US$14, d with/without bathroom US$45/35; 🛜) This funky little two-story hostel has art

on all the walls, a clean communal kitchen and plenty of hammocks for your swinging pleasure. Rates all include all-you-can drink coffee and make-your-own pancakes for breakfast. The rooms – four-bed dorms and private doubles – are nothing special, but guests love the fun, friendly vibe. Quiet time after 11pm is strictly enforced.

Luz de Mono LODGE **$$**
(☏2642-0090; www.luzdemono.com; r/ste incl breakfast US$75/95; ⓟ🔊🌊) A sweet stone lodge built into a lush inlet of remnant jungle, just a few steps from the beach. The upstairs 'suites' have high palm-beamed ceilings, wood furnishings, and new tile throughout. The cheaper downstairs rooms are not all that, but they all have access to a lovely pool area (with kiddie pool), an open-air *rancho* and shady grounds with abundant wildlife. Discounts available for cash payment.

Casacolores BUNGALOW **$$**
(☏2642-0283; www.casacolores.com; 1-/2-bedroom casas US$84/135; ⓟ🔊🌊) Seven bright houses (each painted and named for a color of the rainbow) are fully equipped with kitchens and big porches with hammocks. They're set amid blooming tropical gardens, with a stone-rimmed swimming pool onsite. The location is sort of a no-man's land (a 20-minute uphill hike from town) but there's plenty of wildlife wandering around these jungly grounds.

Horizontes de Montezuma GUESTHOUSE **$$**
(☏8403-6838; www.facebook.com/hotelhorizon tesdemontezuma; d US$85; ⓟ🔊🌊) This gem is situated about 2km north (and uphill) from Montezuma, in a colonial-style building surrounded by spectacular blooming gardens. Rooms are crisp, clean and impeccable, with a few fine stylistic touches. Private verandas yield glorious views of the forest canopy. The hosts go above and beyond to make sure their guests are supremely satisfied.

Hotel El Jardín CABINA **$$**
(☏2642-0074; www.hoteleljardin.com; d US$75-95, casas US$130; ⓟ✳@🔊🌊) This hillside hotel has 15 stained-wood *cabinas,* some with stone bathrooms, wide balconies and ocean views. The grounds are landscaped with tropical flowers and lush palms. The centerpiece is surely the bilevel swimming pool, complete with whirlpool and waterfall, making this place quite a nice little three-star resort.

Hotel La Cascada HOTEL **$$**
(☏2642-0057; www.lacascadamontezuma.com; s/d incl breakfast US$30/60, air-con US$10; ⓟ✳🔊) At the mouth of the river, en route to the waterfalls, this classic Montezuma hotel has 15 simple, sharp wooden rooms with flowy curtains and crisp white sheets. A huge 2nd-floor terrace faces the ocean and has hammocks perfect for swinging, snoozing or spying on the local troop of howlers.

The onsite restaurant is the perfect place to recover from your waterfall hike by sucking down a smoothie.

Nature Lodge LODGE **$$**
(☏2642-0124; www.naturelodge.net; d incl breakfast U$97-165; ⓟ✳🔊🌊) About 3km north of Montezuma on the road to Cóbano, this 16-hectare ranch is adjacent to the Reserva Absoluta Nicolás Wessberg. The lodge has 12 simple but elegant rooms in a lovely hacienda, beautifully landscaped, with a pool deck blessed with ocean and woodland views.

Anamaya Resort RESORT **$$$**
(☏2642-1289; anamaya.com; per week incl 3 meals from US$1125; ⓟ🔊🌊) Self-billed as a 'mind, body, and soul retreat,' Anamaya's perch is pretty damn special. Set on a hilltop with ocean panoramas and weeping jungle on all sides, this environment is certainly dramatic enough to spark enlightenment, if only for a heartbeat. The ample yoga space floats off the main house and has that insane aforementioned view, as does the adjacent infinity pool. It's a magical place to spend a week.

Prices include seven nights of lodging and three meals per day. Yoga classes, surf lessons and lots of other activities are available as 'retreat add-ons.'

Ylang-Ylang Beach Resort RESORT **$$$**
(☏2642-0636, in USA 888-795-8494; www.ylang ylangresort.com; tents/r/bungalows incl breakfast & dinner US$200/250/333; ✳🔊🌊) Walk 15 minutes north along the beach to this lush four-star property, complete with beautifully appointed rooms and bungalows, and a palm-fringed swimming pool, yoga center, gourmet organic restaurant and spa. The decor is lovely and tropical, with tile floors, stenciled walls and colorful tapestries. All accommodations have outdoor terraces facing the glorious sea.

Does that say US$200 for a tent? Yes, it does. It's actually a tent *cabin*, with a wooden floor, private bathroom and king-size bed, but still, it's a tent.

Hotel Amor de Mar
B&B $$$

(☑2642-0262; www.amordemar.com; d without/ with ocean view from US$102/135, villas from US$312; P🐾) A lovely B&B with 11 unique rooms, replete with exquisite touches like timber-framed mirrors, organic lanterns, and rocking chairs on a terrace. Then there's the palm-dappled lawn that rolls out to the tide pools and the Pacific beyond. It's gorgeous to look at but surprisingly noisy, despite being on the edge of town. Also, we can't get behind the US$18 breakfast.

🍴 Eating & Drinking

Montezuma is experiencing the same food revolution that is taking place on other parts of the peninsula. Local ingredients are meeting international chefs, with magnificent results. Montezuma is also good for traditional Tico fare, often with ocean-side service. Most of the restaurants are clustered around the central park and along the beach.

Kalibó
CAFE $

(☑2642-4545; mains US$3-8; ⊙6am-9pm; 🅟) A tiny place with an open kitchen and half a dozen tables, across from the bus stop. This perfect breakfast stop does homemade pastries, fresh fruit smoothies and strong local coffee. It also serves salads, sandwiches and proper meals. It's a charmer.

Soda Monte Sol
SODA $

(☑8849-4962; mains US$5-14; ⊙7am-9pm) A cute, colorful *soda* that does all the *típica* dishes, tasty and affordable *casados*, pastas, burgers and a variety of juices and smoothies. All is served at a leisurely pace in a humble dining room touched with grace. Great people-watching spot.

★Cocina Clandestina
LATIN AMERICAN $$

(☑8315-8003; www.facebook.com/clandestina montezuma; mains US$8-12; ⊙noon-9pm Tue-Sat; 🐾) The secret is out. The hottest new restaurant in Montezuma is this awesome, artistic place in the trees at the butterfly gardens (p337). Look for innovative takes on Central American standards, such as daily changing taco specials and delectable chicken mole enchiladas. Vegetarians are joyfully accommodated with yam and lentil cakes or *chilles rellenos*. The beverage of choice is Butterfly Beer, brewed onsite.

Tierra y Fuega
ITALIAN $$

(☑2642-1593; mains US$8-15; ⊙5-10pm; P🐾) Take a taxi (or drive in the dark!) up to this Italian gem in the hills above Montezuma. This Italian outpost looks as though it's straight out of the Tuscan countryside, complete with brick ovens warming the kitchen and chickens roasting over the fire. The menu is mostly pizza and pasta, but the flavors are divine – not surprising given the ingredients are all imported from Italy or grown onsite.

Cocolores
INTERNATIONAL $$

(☑2642-0348; mains US$9-22; ⊙5-10pm Tue-Sun) Set on a beachside terrace lit with lanterns, Cocolores is one of Montezuma's top spots for an upscale dinner. The wide-ranging menu includes curries, pasta, fajitas and steaks, all prepared and served with careful attention to delicious details. Prices aren't cheap but it's worth it.

Puggo's
MIDDLE EASTERN $$

(☑2642-0325; mains US$10-20; ⊙noon-11pm) A locally beloved restaurant decorated like a bedouin tent, Puggo's specializes in Middle Eastern cuisine, including falafel, hummus, kebabs and aromatic fish, which they dress in imported spices and herbs and roast whole. Cap it off with a strong cup of Turkish coffee.

Orgánico
VEGETARIAN $$

(☑2642-1322; mains US$8-12; ⊙8am-9pm; 🐾) When they say 'pure food made with love,' they mean it – this healthy cafe turns out vegetarian and vegan dishes such as spicy Thai burgers, a *sopa azteca* with tofu, smoothies and more (as well as meaty options too). Avocado ice cream is something everyone should try. There's live music almost nightly, including a wildly popular open mike on Monday nights.

Playa de los Artistas
INTERNATIONAL $$$

(☑2642-0920; www.playamontezuma.net/playa delosartistas.htm; mains US$9-18; ⊙5-9pm Mon-Fri, noon-9pm Sat) Most romantic dinner ever. If you're lucky, you'll snag one of the tree-trunk tables under the palms. The international menu with Mediterranean influences changes daily, though you can always count on fresh seafood roasted in the wood oven. The service is flawless, the cooking is innovative, and the setting is downright dreamy. Cash only (back to reality).

Chico's Bar BAR

(⊙11am-2am) When it comes to nightlife, Chico's is the main (only?) game in town, which means that everybody ends up here eventually – old, young, Ticos, tourists, rowdy, dowdy – especially on Thursday nights, which is reggae night. Snag a table on the back patio for a lovely view of the beach and beyond.

ⓘ Information

The only ATM in town is a BCR *cajero automático* located across from Chico's Bar. The nearest full-service bank is in Cóbano. For money exchange, tour operators in town will take US dollars, euros or traveler's checks.

Right next to the bus stop, **El Parque** (✆2642-0164; ⊙7am-8pm) is a central place to get your laundry done.

ⓘ Getting There & Away

BOAT

Zuma Tours (✆2642-0024; www.zumatours.net) operates a fast water shuttle connecting Montezuma to Jacó in an hour. At US$40 or so, it's not cheap, but it'll save you a day's worth of travel. From Montezuma, boats depart at 9:30am daily, and the price includes van transfer from the beach to the Jacó bus terminal. From Jacó, the departure to Montezuma is at 11am. During the high season, they may run an additional shuttle, departing Montezuma at 1:30pm and departing Jacó at 3pm. Book in advance from any tour operator. Also, dress appropriately; you will get wet.

CAR

Although the road from Paquera to Cóbano is paved, the stretch between Cóbano and Montezuma is not, and it can be brutal. During the rainy season you will need a 4WD. In the village itself, parking can be a problem, though it's easy enough to walk everywhere.

Playas Pochote & Tambor

These two mangrove-backed, gray-sand beaches are protected by Bahía Ballena, the largest bay on the southeastern peninsula, and are surrounded by small fishing communities. In the past 15 years, the area has slowly developed as a resort destination, but for the most part, Pochote and Tambor are mellow, authentic Tico beaches, providing plenty of opportunities for hiking, swimming, kayaking and even whale-watching.

The beaches begin 14km south of Paquera, at the mangrove shrouded, fishing *pueblo* of Pochote, and stretch for about 8km southwest to Tambor. The two villages are divided by the narrow estuary of the Río Pánica.

It should also be said that there is one rather conspicuous all-inclusive mega-resort in the Tambor area – Hotel Barceló Playa Tambor. The huge place has a convention center and golf course, but once you're in the *pueblo*, you won't even know it's there.

Both beaches are safe for swimming and kayaking, and there are occasional whale sightings in the bay. Pochote and Tambor also have easy access to the Refugio Nacional de Vida Silvestre Curú and all that it has to offer.

🛏 Sleeping

★ **Mar y Sol Ecotel** GUESTHOUSE $

(✆2683-1065, 8980-0040; d/q US$30/50; P🅿❄🛜) The location seems odd – stuck on a side road with no beach in sight – but the attentive owners and art-filled premises make it an excellent budget option. Eight rooms have been thoughtfully designed and decked out with custom furniture and

---

BUSES FROM MONTEZUMA

Buses depart Montezuma from the sandy lot on the beach, across from the soccer field. Buy tickets directly from the driver. To get to Mal País and Santa Teresa, go to Cóbano and change buses.

DESTINATION	PRICE (US$)	DURATION	DEPARTURES
Cabo Blanco via Cabuya	1.50	45min	8 buses 5:30am-8pm
Cóbano	2	1hr	8:15am, 10:15am, 12:15pm & 4:15pm
Paquera, via Cóbano	3	2hr	3:45am, 6am, 10am, noon, 2pm & 4pm
San José	14	5hr	7:30am & 3:30pm

Montezuma Expeditions (✆2642-0919; www.montezumaexpeditions.com; US$40-70) operates daily private shuttles to San José, La Fortuna, Monteverde, Jacó, Manuel Antonio, Dominical, Tamarindo, Sámara and Liberia.

mural-painted walls. Air-con and hot water are available on request. And actually, the beach is only 400m away, you just can't see it from here.

Out front, the gorgeous, hand-hewn wood bar is lit by wine-bottle lamps, invented and designed by the owner. It's an excellent place to grab a *cerveza*, or a pizza from the wood-fired oven.

Cabinas Cristina   CABINA $
(☎2683-0028; r US$36-56; P🖥) Located just 50m from the beach, and across from Tambor's rather romantically ramshackle Victorian church, this old standby has simple and spotless rooms, and a small but tasty home-style restaurant. The owners are warm and welcoming and offer valuable travel tips. Room prices vary with size and amenities.

Tambor Tropical   BOUTIQUE HOTEL $$$
(☎2365-2872; www.tambortropical.com; ste incl breakfast US$170-230; P✱🖥🌊) Romantically set on the beach amid a palm-fringed garden, Tambor Tropical is a lovely boutique hotel with stunning architecture. The 12 roomy, hexagonal suites all have dark wood interiors, full kitchens and private verandas, most with sunrise views. The place is a boon for birders: nearly 300 species have been spotted on or around the property.

Hotel Costa Coral   BOUTIQUE HOTEL $$$
(☎2683-0207; hotelcostacoral.com; r US$199-225; P✱🖥🌊) New management has breathed new life into this charming hotel in the center of Tambor. Ten classy rooms surround a gorgeous garden that is bursting with blooms. Recommended restaurant and spa onsite. The glorious beach is a mere five-minute walk away.

🛈 Getting There & Away

The airport is just north of the entrance to Hotel Barceló Playa Tambor. Hotels will arrange pickup at the airport for an extra fee. Between them, Sansa (p97) and NatureAir (p97) (one way US$115 to US$134) have up to a dozen daily flights to and from San José.

There's a **Budget** (☎2436-2085; www.budget.co.cr; ⊘8am-6pm Mon-Sat, to 4pm Sun) car-rental place 4km from the Tambor airport. It has a free shuttle to and from the 'terminal.' If you're not renting wheels, you can hop on one of the Paquera–Montezuma buses passing through here.

Refugio Nacional de Vida Silvestre Curú

Situated at the eastern end of the peninsula and only 6km south of Paquera, the tiny, 84-hectare Refugio Nacional de Vida Silvestre Curú (☎2641-0100; www.curuwildliferefuge.com; admission US$12; ⊘7am-3pm) holds a great variety of landscapes, including dry tropical forest, semideciduous forest and five types of mangrove swamp. The rugged coastline is also home to a series of secluded coves and white-sand beaches that are perfect for snorkeling and swimming, while hiking trails traverse varied but beautiful landscapes.

🏃 Activities & Tours

Visitors have access to 17 well-marked, easy to moderate trails, through the various landscapes. Or, join a variety of tours – horseback riding on the beach, kayaking through the estuary, snorkeling around the coves, or hiking with a naturalist guide. Local fauna includes iguanas, deer, three types of monkey, agoutis and pacas, plus three species of cat. Crabs, lobsters, chitons, shellfish, sea turtles and other marine creatures can be found on the beaches and in the tide pools. Bird-watchers have recorded more than 232 bird species.

Turismo Curú   TOUR
(☎2641-0004; www.curutourism.com; snorkeling per person US$40; ⊘8am-9pm) Anything that you might want to do at Curú wildlife refuge, Luis can make it happen. A boat trip to Isla Tortuga includes snorkeling at Islas Mortreros and a BBQ on the beach. The most unique offering is the evening Bioluminescence Tour, which involves kayaking to beautiful Quesera beach and swimming and snorkeling in the luminescent waters.

🛏 Sleeping

Refugio Nacional de Vida Silvestre Curú Cabinas   CABINA $
(☎2641-0100; curuwildliferefuge.com; r per person US$30, meals US$10) There are six rustic *cabinas* on the grounds of the wildlife reserve. The accommodations are bare and the showers are cold, but they are beautifully situated about 50m from the waves. Also, you'll be in good company (white-faced capuchin monkeys, primarily). Your reserve fee

is included in the cost of the room. Advance arrangements required.

❶ Getting There & Away

The entrance to the refuge is clearly signed on the paved road between Paquera and Tambor (about 6km from Paquera). Alternatively, the Paquera–Montezuma bus passes this way.

Paquera

The tiny village of Paquera is about 12km by road from Playa Naranjo and 4km from the Paquera ferry terminal. Paquera is not much of a destination in its own right, but it's a useful base for a few days of exploring in Refugio Nacional de Vida Silvestre Curú and the offshore islands. Short of that, you might want to spend a night here if you arrive on a late ferry from Puntarenas – instead of tackling those challenging roads in the dark.

⏝ Sleeping

While there are some budget *cabinas* right in town, there's nothing to be gained by staying there. You're better off staying on the outskirts (or in the hills, if you can afford it), for a more peaceful setting.

Mapi's Cabins   CABINA **$**
(☑ 2641-1133; costarica4vacation.com; r US$36; ❄) If you're looking to spend the night in Paquera, Mapi's is a comfortable stop. Your room price includes a comfortable bed, cool air-con and warm showers. Bonus: fill up

---

MUST LOVE CATS

Since 1992, **Profelis** (Feline Conservation Program; ☑ 2641-0644, 2641-0646; www.grafischer.com/profelis) has taken care of confiscated felines that were injured, abandoned or otherwise unable to survive in the wild. The center welcomes volunteers, especially veterinary students, biologists and experienced animal keepers.

Profelis is headquartered at Hacienda Matambú, a private wildlife reserve in San Rafael de Paquera, about 5km west of Paquera.

The project concentrates on smaller felines, including the margay, ocelot and jaguarundi, with the goal of rehabilitating the animals and reintroducing them into the wild.

---

on mangoes and other tropical fruits grown onsite. This is a very popular stop for hummingbirds, so bring your camera! The place is located just north of town, along the road to the Paquera ferry.

Hotel Vista Las Islas   HOTEL **$$$**
(☑ 2641-0817; hotelvistalasislas.com; d US$192; P ❄ 🛜 🏊) As implied by the name, the amazing panoramic view of the islands is the selling point here. It really is spectacular, and you can enjoy it from your private balcony, from the restaurant or from the magnificent infinity pool. It's a short walk to Playa Órganos, where you can swim, surf or stand-up paddle.

❶ Getting There & Away

All transportation is geared to the arrival and departure of the Puntarenas ferry. If either the bus or the ferry is running late, the other will wait.

BOAT

Ferry Naviera Tambor (☑ 2661-2084; www.navieratambor.com; adult/child/bicycle/motorcycle/car US$1.65/1/4.50/7/23) leaves daily at 5:30am, 9am, 11am, 2pm, 5pm and 8pm. The trip to Puntarenas takes about an hour. Buy a ticket at the window, reboard your car and then drive on to the ferry; you can't buy a ticket on board. Show up at least an hour early on holidays and busy weekends. The terminal contains a *soda* where you can grab a bite while waiting for the boat.

BUS

Buses meet arriving passengers at the ferry terminal and take them to Paquera, Tambor and Montezuma. They can be crowded, so try to get off the ferry fast to secure a seat. Most travelers take the bus from the terminal directly to Montezuma (US$3, two hours). Many taxi drivers will tell you the bus won't come, but this isn't true. There are no northbound buses.

Islands Near Bahía Gigante

The waters in and around the isolated Bahía Gigante, 9km southeast of Playa Naranjo, are studded with rocky islets and deserted islands. Isla San Lucas is tucked into the Golfo de Nicoya, while lovely Islas Gigante and Tortuga hang off the southeastern corner of the peninsula. These idyllic outposts are popular destinations for sportfishers and sea kayakers, scuba divers and snorkelers, who relish the fantasy of exploring some uncharted desert isle.

☞ Tours

In addition to party cruises (p351) departing from Jacó, tour operators in Jacó and Montezuma offer smaller-scale excursions to these islands, especially Isla Tortuga. Hotels in Tambor can also make the arrangements.

Turismo Curú (p343) offers a half-day boat trip to Isla Tortuga, which is only 3km from the wildlife refuge. This unique tour makes an effort to avoid the crowds by visiting in the morning (when other boats are still en route) and hitting lesser-known spots.

Hotel Vista Las Islas in Paquera has the advantage of proximity to Tortuga. Its all-day tour includes snorkeling and lunch, as well as kayaking or horseback riding. The hotel also offers day trips to Isla San Lucas.

☞ Isla Tortuga

Isla Tortuga is actually two uninhabited islands, just offshore from Refugio Nacional de Vida Silvestre Curú. This stunner – a quintessential tropical paradise – is widely regarded as the most beautiful island in Costa Rica. The pure white sand feels like baby powder; gargantuan coconut palms tower overhead; and clear turquoise waters lap up on the shores. Snorkelers usually enjoy good visibility and a wide variety of sea life, although there is no reef here. Jet skis and kayaks are sometimes on offer, depending on your tour.

Unfortunately, Tortuga receives heavy boat traffic from tour operators from Montezuma and Jacó, and the crowds quickly detract from the magic of this place. If possible, avoid weekends and holidays. Even better, avoid high season.

☞ Isla San Lucas

The largest island in Bahía Gigante (just over 600 hectares) is about 5km off the coast from Playa Naranjo. From a distance, it seems like a beautiful desert island, but the 'Island of Unspeakable Horrors' has a 400-year history as one of the most notorious prisons in Latin America. In 2001 the island was declared a national park. Visitors can expect to learn about the island's checkered history and explore the 100-year-old remains of the prison. Most tours also allow time to hike the trails and relax on the island's sandy shores.

Isla San Lucas was first used by Spanish conquistadors as a detention center for local tribes in the 16th century. Later, the Costa Rican government used the island to detain political prisoners until 1992. Writer José León Sánchez wrote about his experiences as a prisoner in his book *La Isla de Hombres Solos* (Island of the Lonely Men). Sánchez spent 30 years in this jail for a crime he didn't commit; he was later absolved of the crime.

Nowadays, visitors can explore the remains of the prison and church and bear witness to the island's history of suffering and redemption.

Playa Naranjo

This tiny village next to the ferry terminal is nothing more than a few *sodas* and small hotels that cater to travelers either waiting for the ferry or arriving from Puntarenas. There isn't any reason to hang around.

Playa Naranjo Inn HOTEL **$**
(☎2641-8290; hotelplayanaranjo@gmail.com; d incl breakfast US$40; ［P꙰❋꙰］) If you do get stuck at the port for a night, you can bed down at Playa Naranjo Inn, a motel-style accommodations facing a swimming pool. The rooms are comfortable enough, with heavy wood and wicker furniture, though the showers are cold. There is a restaurant here, too.

❶ Getting There & Away

All transportation is geared to the arrival and departure of the Puntarenas ferry, so don't worry – if one is running late, the other will wait.

BOAT

The **Coonatramar ferry** (☎2661-1069; www.coonatramar.com; adult/child/bicycle/motorcycle/car US$2/1/4/6/18) to Puntarenas departs daily at 8am, 12:30pm, 4:30pm and 8:30pm, and can accommodate both cars and passengers. The trip takes 1½ hours. If traveling by car, get out and buy a ticket at the window, get back in your car and then drive on to the ferry. You cannot buy a ticket on board. Show up at least an hour early on holidays and busy weekends, as you'll be competing with a whole lot of other drivers to make it on.

BUS

Buses meet the arriving ferry and take passengers on to Jicaral, for travel on to the more northerly parts of the peninsula. If you're headed to Montezuma or Mal País, take the other ferry from Puntarenas to Paquera.

CAR

If you are driving yourself, it's unlikely that you'll need to pass this way. Heading north, you'll be better off driving over the Puente de la Amistad to the peninsula instead of taking the ferry. And heading to Mal País or Montezuma, you should take the Puntarenas-Paquera ferry. That said, Rte 21 is a mostly paved road that connects Playa Naranjo to Nicoya (via Jicaral). It is also possible to get to Paquera (and further to Mal País or Montezuma) via a scenic, rugged and steep but passable road over three inland ridges with magical vistas of Bahía Gigante. A 4WD is recommended, especially in the rainy season when there might be rivers to cross.

Central Pacific Coast

Why Go?

Stretching from the rough-and-ready port of Puntarenas to the tiny town of Uvita, the central Pacific coast is home to both wet and dry tropical rainforests, sun-drenched sandy beaches and a healthy dose of wildlife. On shore, national parks protect endangered squirrel monkeys and scarlet macaws, while offshore waters are home to migrating whales and pods of dolphins.

With so much biodiversity packed into a small geographic area, it's no wonder the coastal region is often thought of as Costa Rica in miniature. Given its close proximity to San José and the Central Valley and highlands, and its well-developed system of paved roads, this part of the country is a favorite weekend getaway for domestic and international travelers.

While threats of unregulated growth and environmental damage are real, it's also important to see the bigger picture, namely the stunning nature that first put the central Pacific coast on the map.

Best Places to Eat

➡ Citrus (p402)

➡ Gabriella's (p374)

➡ Graffiti (p363)

➡ Sabor Español (p398)

When to Go

➡ Rains fall heavily between April and November – the best time to hit the waves in Playa Hermosa and Jacó.

➡ Whale-watching in Uvita is at its best between December and March and July till November.

➡ Festival fans will want to visit from around mid-January to late February, when music and art gatherings light up Jacó and Uvita.

Best Undiscovered Beaches

➡ Matapalo (p387)

➡ Playa Esterillos (p366)

➡ Playa Hermosa (p365)

➡ Playa Palo Seco (p367)

Central Pacific Coast Highlights

① Watching troops of monkeys, slow-moving sloths and gliding brown pelicans at **Parque Nacional Manuel Antonio** (p383).

② Surfing the beach breaks of **Jacó** (p358), **Playa Hermosa** (p365) and **Dominical** (p390) – or learning how.

③ Sampling some of the coast's most sophisticated cuisine in **Ojochal** (p400).

④ Scanning the horizon for pods of breaching humpback whales from the deserted

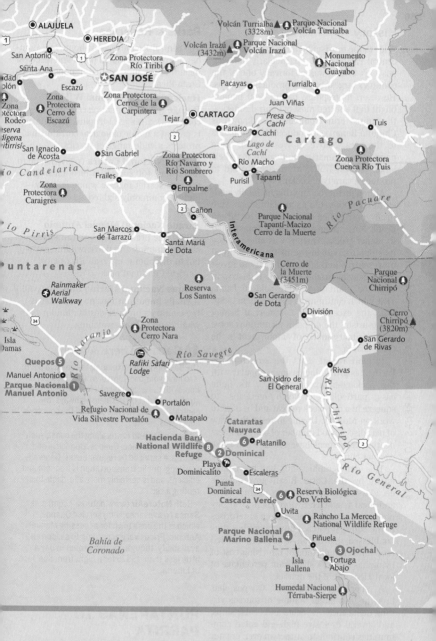

beaches of **Parque Nacional Marino Ballena** (p399).

⑤ Learning to paddleboard in the mangroves of **Quepos** (p370).

⑥ Swimming in the waterfalls of **Cataratas Nauyaca** (p391) and **Cascada Verde** (p396).

⑦ Looking for giant crocodiles and squawking pairs of scarlet macaws at **Parque Nacional Carara** (p354).

⑧ Getting a guided animal-spotting tour at **Hacienda Barú National Wildlife Refuge** (p387).

History

Prior to the tourism boom in Costa Rica, the central Pacific coast – particularly the Quepos port area – was historically one of the country's largest banana-producing regions. However, in response to the 1940 banana blight that affected most of Central America, the United Fruit Company (also known as Chiquita Banana) introduced African palms to the area. Native to West Africa, these palms are primarily cultivated for their large, reddish fruits, which are pressed to produce a variety of cooking oils.

Although the banana blight finally ended in the 1960s, the palm plantations were firmly entrenched and starting to turn a profit. Since palm oil is easily transported in tanker trucks, Quepos was able to close its shipping port in the 1970s, which freed up resources and allowed the city to invest more heavily in the palm-oil industry. In 1995 the plantations were sold to Palma Tica, which continues to operate them today. With the exception of commercial fishing and tourism, the oil palm plantations serve as the primary source of employment in the Quepos area.

In more recent years, this stretch of the Pacific has grown increasingly popular with the package-holiday crowd, as it's quite easy – particularly for North Americans – to squeeze in a one-week retreat and be back to work on Monday. Unable to resist the draw of paradise, a good number of baby boomers nearing retirement have relocated to these warmer climes.

This demographic shift has been facilitated by the Costa Rican government's decades-old policy of offering tax incentives and legal residence to foreigners who buy property or start businesses and enterprises in the country. Foreign investment has thus far blessed this region with vitally needed economic stimuli, though the rising cost of living has priced a significant percentage of local Ticos out of the market.

A sparkling marina at Quepos has brought in a larger volume of tourists visiting Costa Rica on yachts and cruise ships, and several exclusive high-end gated communities continue to attract an even greater number of wealthy immigrants. Things are indeed changing quickly along this stretch of coastline, though it's difficult to imagine that the authenticity of the coastal fishing villages, agricultural plantations and protected areas could ever be lost.

Parks & Reserves

The central Pacific coast is home to a number of excellent national parks and reserves, including the most visited national park in Costa Rica.

Hacienda Barú National Wildlife Refuge (p387) A small reserve that encompasses a range of tropical habitats and is part of a major biological corridor that protects a wide range of species.

Parque Nacional Carara (p354) Home to more than 400 species of bird, including the rare scarlet macaw, which is, amazingly, a commonly sighted species in the park.

Parque Nacional Manuel Antonio (p383) The pristine beaches, rainforest-clad mountains and dense wildlife never fail to disappoint in Costa Rica's most touristed national park.

Parque Nacional Marino Ballena (p399) A vitally important marine park; this is the country's premier destination for both whale- and dolphin-watching.

ⓘ Getting There & Away

The best option for exploring the coast in depth is to have your own form of private transportation. With the exception of a few odd unpaved stretches of dirt off the main highways, the central Pacific coast has some of the country's best roads.

Major cities and towns along the coast, such as Puntarenas, Jacó, Quepos, Dominical and Uvita, are serviced by regular buses. Generally speaking, public transportation is frequent and efficient, and is certainly more affordable than renting a car.

Both **NatureAir** (www.natureair.com) and **Sansa** (www.sansa.com) service Quepos, which is the base town for accessing Manuel Antonio. Prices vary according to season and availability, though you can expect to pay a little less than US$75 for a flight from San José or Liberia.

PUNTARENAS TO PARRITA

The northern reaches of the central Pacific coast extend from the maritime port of Puntarenas, a historic shipping hub that has fallen on harder times, to the booming town of Quepos, which is the main access point for Parque Nacional Manuel Antonio. In between are vast swaths of forested hillsides and wilderness beaches, which together protect large concentrations of remarkable wildlife, including some very impressive crocodiles. However, the local spotlight is fixed firmly on the surfing town of Jacó, which plays host to a colorful cast of characters, and its upmarket satellite – Playa Herradura, the yachtie haven. If the waves in Jacó are not challenging enough, nearby Playa Hermosa throws down the gauntlet with some of the most powerful waves on the Pacific coast.

Puntarenas

Port cities the world over have a reputation for polluted waters, seedy streets and slow decay, which might be a traveler's first impression of Puntarenas, Costa Rica's formerly prosperous, coffee-exporting gateway to the Pacific. As the closest coastal town to San José, Puntarenas has been a popular escape for landlocked Ticos, and some still come here on weekends. But during the week the activity along the oceanfront promenade slows to a languid pace – all the better to enjoy the beachfront *sodas* (inexpensive eateries) and busy market.

The city's ferry terminal is a convenient way to connect to pristine beaches on the central Pacific coast or to southern Nicoya, and Puntarenas is the jumping-off point for the almost-mystical Isla del Coco. Travelers mainly pass through here en route to somewhere else; but if you stay here overnight, you'll feel the vibe of a genuine working Tico town and find a couple of attractions.

Sights & Activities

Palacio Municipal   ARCHITECTURE
(Av 3 & Calle 9) Built in place of the previous Municipal Palace that burned down, this rather unusual 1970s structure with jutting upper floors, designed by architect Jorge Bertheau, is definitely the most unusual building in town. Beautiful or hideous? You decide!

Casa Fait   ARCHITECTURE
(Av 3 & Calle 3) Quite possibly the most beautiful building in Puntarenas, Casa Fait is a 1920s flight of fancy by the Italian immigrant Alberto Fait Rocchi. It's a curious mix of Victorian-style influences and a touch of art nouveau.

Parque Marino del Pacífico   AQUARIUM
(✐2661-5272; www.parquemarino.org; adult/under 12yr US$5.80/3.20; ☉9am-4:30pm Tue-Sun; P🚼) This marine park is popular with families and has an aquarium that showcases manta rays, nurse sharks, Nemo (we mean clown fish) and other creatures from the Pacific. The park sits on the site of the old train station and has a tiny splash pool for kids, snack bar, gift shop and information center.

Museo Histórico Marino   MUSEUM
(✐2661-5036, 2256-4139; Av Central btwn Calles 3 & 5; ☉9:45am-noon & 1-5:15pm Tue-Sun) FREE This dusty museum describes the once-proud history of Puntarenas through audiovisual presentations, old photos and artifacts. At the time of research it was closed for an indefinite period.

Casa de la Cultura   GALLERY
(✐2661-1394; Av Central btwn Calles 3 & 5; ☉10am-4pm Mon-Fri) FREE Casa de la Cultura has an art gallery with occasional exhibits as well as a performance space offering seasonal cultural events. Outside there's a pedestrial passageway with contemporary sculptures.

Paseo de los Turistas   PROMENADE
(Tourists' Promenade) Stroll beside the beach on the Paseo de los Turistas, a pedestrian boulevard stretching along the southern edge of town. Cruise ships make day visits to the eastern end of this road, and a variety of souvenir stalls and *sodas* are there to greet passengers. On weekend nights, this is the place to knock back beers and find the party.

☞ Tours

Calypso Cruises   BOAT TOUR
(✐2661-0585, 2256-2727; www.calypsocruises.com; Av 3, near Calle 5; day trips adult/student/child under 7yr US$145/135/80) This long-established, top-class, gringo-owned catamaran makes day trips to Tortuga's brilliant white beaches, mostly catering to Puntarenas cruise-ship crowds. Trips come with a picnic lunch, fresh fruit, snacks and booze.

Odyssey Tours   ADVENTURE TOUR
(✐8319-1315, 2635-2221, 8994-6245; www.odysseytourscr.com; day trip to Isla Tortuga per person US$150) Diego and Alvaro, a pair of friendly bilingual brothers, host a variety of customizable day tours and come with a slew of excellent recommendations. In Puntarenas they're mostly known for their luxury day trip to Isla

PUNTARENAS PAST & PRESENT

Prior to the mid-20th century, Puntarenas was the largest and most significant open-water port in Costa Rica. Some of the finest coffees to fill European cups were carried to the continent on Puntarenas-registered freighters, and the steady flow of capital transformed Puntarenas into the 'Pearl of the Pacific.' However, after the construction of the railway leading from the Central Valley to Puerto Limón in 1890, a more direct shipping route to Europe initiated the city's decline in importance, though Puntarenas did manage to remain a major port on the Pacific coast. While present visitors get a whiff of the city's glory in the lovely stone church at its center, modern history has left many unattractive sights: polluted waters, eroding structures and tacky souvenir stands that close up when the hulking cruise ships leave port.

Tortuga on their Manta Raya catamaran that comes complete with two Jacuzzis and an underwater viewing window.

Festivals & Events

Fiesta de La Virgen del Mar   RELIGIOUS
(Festival of the Virgin of the Sea) Puntarenas celebrates the Fiesta de La Virgen del Mar on the Saturday closest to July 16. Lavishly decorated fishing boats and yachts sail around the harbor, seeking protection from the Virgin for another year at sea. There are also boat races, a carnival, and plenty of food, drinking and dancing.

Sleeping

Hotel Cabezas   HOTEL **$**
(☑ 2661-1045; Av 1 btwn Calles 2 & 4; s/d without bathroom US$17/25, with bathroom US$25/35; P ❖ ☎) This no-nonsense budget option is an excellent choice. Get buzzed in and head up the stairs to the pastel-painted rooms with functional overhead fans and screened windows, which means you'll sleep deeply without needing air-con. Although you certainly shouldn't leave your valuables strewn about, this cheapie is safe, secure and surprisingly quiet.

Cabinas Joyce   CABINA **$**
(☑ 2661-4290, 5006-4290; cnr Calle 4 & Av 2; s/d from US$25/35; P ❖ ☎) This is the best option near the bus station – a spotless little joint of tiled rooms overseen with a hawkish eye by Joyce. Fairly charmless but convenient.

Hotel La Punta   HOTEL **$$**
(☑ 2661-0696; www.hotellapunta.net; cnr Av 1 & Calle 35; s/d US$70/84; P ❖ ☎ ⛱) For early morning ferry departures, Hotel La Punta is an appealing choice. Conveniently located one block from the dock, its 10 rooms are arranged around a landscaped courtyard and small pool. Comfortable accommodations feature terracotta floors, cable TV and fridge. The nicest option in Puntarenas proper.

✗ Eating

The freshest, cheapest food is available in the stands and *sodas* near the Central Market. This is also the stomping ground of a motley mix of sailors, drunks and prostitutes, but the scene is raffish rather than dangerous – during the day, at least. More restaurants are along the Paseo de los Turistas between Calles Central and 3, but some of the sit-down options are touristy and overpriced.

Marisquería Kaite Blanco   SEAFOOD **$**
(☑ 2661-5566; Av 1 btwn Calles 17 & 19; dishes US$7-12; ⊗ 10am-late) On the north side of town, this rambling restaurant is popular with locals, and serves good seafood and a variety of tasty *bocas* (appetizers). We're particularly partial to their spicy clams. If you really want to see the place swinging, the open-air courtyard comes to life on weekends with live music and all-night dancing.

La Casona   COSTA RICAN **$**
(☑ 2661-1626; cnr Av 1 & Calle 9; casados US$6-12; ⊗ 8am-6pm) This lemon-yellow house is an incredibly popular lunch spot, attracting countless locals who jam onto the shaded, greenery-laden deck across from Parque Mora y Cañas. Portions of grilled fish are heaped, and soups are served in bathtub-sized bowls – bring your appetite.

★ El Shrimp Shack   SEAFOOD **$$**
(☑ 2661-0585; Av 3 btwn Calles 3 & 7; meals US$8-18; ⊗ 11:30am-3:30pm Tue-Sun; ☎) Offering the most upscale dining in Puntarenas, El Shrimp Shack's silly name belies a gracious

interior – wood-paneled walls, marble-topped tables, antique light sconces and a stunning stained-glass ceiling, all within a century-old house with harbor views. Shrimp dishes feature prominently, though other options include burgers and excellent *ceviche*. Old-school service.

Drinking & Nightlife

Entertainment in the port tends to revolve around boozing and flirting. On the weekends, follow crowds of Ticos to the countless bars lining Paseo de los Turistas.

Capitán Moreno's   CLUB
(☑ 2661-6888; cnr Paseo de los Turistas & Calle 13; ☺ 11am-6pm Mon-Fri, 10am-8pm Sat & Sun) A time-honored spot for shaking some booty, with a huge dance floor right on the beach. Popular with a younger Tico crowd.

El Oasis del Pacífico   CLUB
(☑ 2661-6368; cnr Paseo de los Turistas & Calle 5; ☺ 9am-10pm Sun-Thu, to 1am Fri & Sat) A popular spot with a lengthy bar and a warehouse-sized dance floor. We hope you enjoy reggaetón.

❶ Orientation

Situated at the end of a sandy peninsula (8km long but only 100m to 600m wide), Puntarenas is just 110km west of San José by paved highway. The city has 60 calles (streets) running north to south, but only five avenidas (avenues) running west to east at its widest point. The southerly promenade, where you'll find the cruise-ship pier and some restaurants, is called the Paseo de los Turistas. As in all of Costa Rica, street names are largely irrelevant, and landmarks are used for orientation.

❶ Information

The major banks along Av 3, to the west of the market, exchange money and are equipped with 24-hour ATMs. There's also a Banco de Costa Rica (BCR) ATM opposite the pier on Paseo de los Turistas.

Puntarenas Tourism Office (Catup; Cámara de Turismo de Puntarenas; ☑ 2661-2980; Paseo de los Turistas; ☺ 8am-5:30pm Tue-Fri, 8am-12:30pm Sat; ☎) Opposite the pier on the 2nd floor of Plaza del Pacífico. It closes for lunch.

❶ Getting There & Away

Car and passenger ferries bound for Paquera and Playa Naranjo depart several times a day from the **northwestern dock** (Av 3 btwn Calles 31 & 33). If you are driving and will be taking the car ferry, arrive at the dock early to get in line. The vehicle section tends to fill up quickly and you may not make it on. In addition, make sure that you have purchased your ticket from the walk-up ticket window before driving onto the ferry. You will not be admitted onto the boat if you don't already have a ticket.

Schedules change seasonally and can be affected by inclement weather. Check with the ferry office by the dock for any changes. Many of the hotels in town also have up-to-date schedules posted.

Coonatramar (☑ 2661-1069; www.coonatramar.com; adult/child US$2/1.10, bike/car US$4/18) has daily departures to Playa Naranjo (for transfer to Nicoya and points west) at 6:30am, 10am, 2:30pm and 7:30pm.

Naviera Tambor (☑ 2661-2084; www.navieratambor.com; adult/child US$1.60/1, bike/car US$4.40/23) has daily departures to Paquera (for transfer to Montezuma and Mal País) at 5am, 9am, 11am, 2pm, 5pm and 8:30pm.

❶ Getting Around

Buses marked 'Ferry' run up Av Central and go to the ferry terminal, 1.5km from downtown. The taxi fare from the San José bus terminal in Puntarenas to the northwestern ferry terminal is about US$2.

Buses for the port of Caldera (also going past Playa Doña Ana and Mata de Limón) leave from the market about every hour and head out of town along Av Central.

BUSES FROM PUNTARENAS

Buses for San José depart from the large navy-blue building on the north corner of Calle 2 and Paseo de los Turistas. Book your ticket ahead of time on holidays and weekends. Buses for other destinations leave from across the street, on the beach side of the Paseo.

DESTINATION	COST (US$)	DURATION (HR)	FREQUENCY
Jacó	2.20	1½	8 daily 4:30am-5:30pm
Quepos	3.80	3½	5 daily 4:30am-3pm
San José	5.10	2½	hourly 4am-9pm
Santa Elena, Monteverde	3	3	8:15am & 2:15pm

Around Puntarenas

The road heading south from Puntarenas skirts the coastline, and a few kilometers out of town you'll start to see the forested peaks of the Cordillera de Tilarán in the distance. Just as the port city fades into the distance, the water gets cleaner, the air crisper and the vegetation more lush. At this point, you should take a deep breath and heave a sigh of relief – the Pacific coastline gets a whole lot more beautiful as you head further south, with beaches, surfing opportunities and mangroves aplenty. South of Puntarenas you'll find good waves (for experienced surfers only) and bird-watching opportunities in the coastal mangroves.

⊙ Sights & Activities

Playa San Isidro   BEACH
About 8km south of Puntarenas is Playa San Isidro, the first 'real' beach on the central Pacific coast. It's popular with beachcombers from Puntarenas.

Playa Doña Ana   BEACH
(entry US$3, parking US$2) The pair of beaches known as Playa Doña Ana is relatively undeveloped and has an isolated and unhurried feel. Surfers can find some decent breaks here, though, like Playa San Isidro, they are more popular for Tico beachcombers on day trips from Puntarenas, especially during weekends in high season. There are snack bars, picnic shelters and changing areas, and supervised swimming areas

Boca Barranca   SURFING
About 12km south of Puntarenas is, according to some, the third-longest left-hand surf break in the world. Conditions here are best at low tide, and it is possible to surf here year-round. However, be advised that there isn't much in the way of services out here, so be sure that you're confident in the water and seek local advice before hitting the break.

Mata de Limón   BIRD-WATCHING
Around 20km south of Puntarenas is Mata de Limón, a picturesque little hamlet situated on a mangrove lagoon, locally famous for its bird-watching. If you arrive during low tide, you'll see flocks of feathered creatures descending on the lagoon to scrounge for tasty morsels. Mata de Limón is divided by a river, with the lagoon and most facilities on the south side.

❶ Getting There & Away

Buses heading for the Caldera port depart hourly from the market in Puntarenas, and can easily drop you off at any of the spots along the highway. If you're driving, the break at Boca Barranca is located near the bridge on the Costanera Sur (South Coastal Hwy), while the entrance to Playa Doña Ana is a little further south (look for a sign that says 'Paradero Turístico Doña Ana'). The turnoff for Mata de Limón is located about 5.5km south of Playa Doña Ana.

Parque Nacional Carara

Situated at the mouth of the Río Tárcoles, the 52-sq-km **Parque Nacional Carara** (admission US$10; ⊙ 7am-3pm Dec-Mar, 8am-4pm Apr-Nov) is only 50km southeast of Puntarenas by road or about 90km west of San José via the Orotina highway. Straddling the transition between the dry forests of Costa Rica's northwest and the sodden rainforests of the southern Pacific lowlands, this national park is a biological melting pot of the two. Acacias intermingle with strangler figs, and cacti with deciduous kapok trees, creating heterogeneity of habitats with a blend of wildlife to match.

Carara is the famed home to one of Costa Rica's most charismatic bird species, the scarlet macaw. While catching a glimpse of this tropical wonder is a rare proposition in most of the country, macaw sightings are virtually guaranteed at Carara. And, of course, there are more than 400 other avian species flitting around the canopy, as well as Costa Rica's largest crocodiles in the waterways – it's best to leave your swimming trunks at home!

The park's three trails can easily be explored in half a day; come early to maximize wildlife sightings.

The dry season from December to April is the easiest time to go, though the animals are still here in the wet months. March and April are the driest months. Rainfall is almost 3000mm annually, which is less than in the rainforests further south. It's fairly hot, with average temperatures of 25°C (77°F) to 28°C (82°F), but it's cooler within the rainforest. An umbrella is important in the wet season and occasionally needed in the dry months. Make sure you have insect repellent.

Crocodile Bridge   WILDLIFE RESERVE
If you're driving from Puntarenas or San José, pull over by the Río Tárcoles bridge, also known as Crocodile Bridge. If you scan

the sandbanks below the bridge, you'll have a fairly good chance of seeing as many as 30 basking crocodiles. Although they're visible year-round, the best time for viewing them is low tide during the dry season.

Crocodiles this large are generally rare in Costa Rica as they've been hunted vigorously for their leather. However, the crocs are tolerated here as they feature prominently in a number of wildlife tours that depart from Tárcoles. And, of course, the crocs don't mind, as they're hand-fed virtually every day.

Indigenous Burial Sites   CEMETERY

With the help of a hired guide, it's possible to visit the archaeological remains of various indigenous burial sites located within Parque Nacional Carara, though they're tiny and for enthusiasts only. At the time of the Europeans' arrival in Costa Rica, these sites were located in an area inhabited by an indigenous group known as the Huetar (Carara means 'crocodile' in the Huetar language). Unfortunately, not much is known about this group, as little cultural evidence was left behind. Today the few remaining Huetar are confined to several small villages in the Central Valley.

 Activities

Wildlife-Watching

The most exciting bird for many visitors to see, especially in June or July, is the brilliantly patterned scarlet macaw, a rare bird that is commonly seen in the Parque Nacional Carara. Its distinctive call echoes loudly through the canopy, usually moments before a pair appears against the blue sky. If you're having problems spotting them, it may help

to inquire at the ranger station, which keeps tabs on where nesting pairs are located.

Dominated by open secondary forest punctuated by patches of dense, mature forest and wetlands, Carara offers some superb bird-watching. More than 400 species of bird inhabit the reserve, though your chances of spotting rarer species will be greatly enhanced with the help of an experienced guide. Some commonly sighted species include orange-billed sparrows, five kinds of trogon, crimson-fronted parakeets, blue-headed parrots, golden-naped woodpeckers, rose-throated becards, gray-headed tanagers, long-tailed manikins and rufous-tailed jacamars (just to name a few!).

Birds aside, the trails at Carara are home to several mammal species, including red brockets, white-tailed deer, collared peccaries, monkeys, sloths and agoutis. The national park is also home to one of Costa Rica's largest populations of tayras, weasel-like animals that scurry along the forest floor. And, although most travelers aren't too keen to stumble upon an American crocodile, some truly monstrous specimens can be viewed from a safe distance at the nearby Crocodile Bridge.

According to the park rangers, the best chance of spotting wildlife is at 7am, when the park opens.

Hiking

Some 600m south of the Crocodile Bridge on the left-hand side is a locked gate leading to the **Sendero Laguna Meándrica**. This trail penetrates deep into the reserve and passes through open secondary forest and patches of dense mature forest and wetlands. About 4km from the entrance is

SCARLET MACAWS

With a shocking bright-red body, blue-and-yellow wings, a long, red tail and a white face, the scarlet macaw (*Ara macao*) is one of the most visually arresting birds in the neotropical rainforest. It also mates for life and can live up to 75 years. Flying across the forest canopy in pairs, uttering their loud, grating squawks – there are few birds in Costa Rica with such character, presence and beauty.

Prior to the 1960s the scarlet macaw was distributed across much of Costa Rica, though trapping, poaching, habitat destruction and increased use of pesticides devastated the population. By the 1990s the distribution was reduced to two isolated pockets: the Península de Osa and Parque Nacional Carara.

Fortunately, these charismatic creatures are thriving in large colonies at both locales, and sightings are virtually guaranteed if you have the time and patience to spare. Furthermore, despite this fragmentation, the International Union for the Conservation of Nature continues to evaluate the species as 'Least Concern,' which bodes well for the future of this truly emblematic rainforest denizen.

GARABITO, INDIGENOUS HERO

The area encompassed by Parque Nacional Carara was once home to a legendary indigenous hero, a local *cacique* (chief) named Garabito. Commanding a vast area from the Golfo de Nicoya to the Central Valley, he led a fierce struggle against the Spanish in the mid-16th century.

At the time, a favorite tactic of the Spanish conquistadors throughout Latin America to weaken native resistance was to turn tribes against each other and decapitate the tribal leadership – literally. Although each story has grisly variations, the fate of captured *caciques* often involved public humiliation at a show trial, brutal torture and decapitation. Sometimes, the heads of *caciques* would be mounted and displayed.

Garabito was a different story. The popular chieftain constantly disrupted the Spanish establishment in the Pacific region and, in 1560, Guatemalan high command dispatched a military force to arrest him. Garabito, who claimed to have never spent two nights in the same bed, eluded capture, but the Spanish managed to seize his wife, Biriteka, as a hostage. Garabito countered by having one of his followers dress up as the chieftain and allow himself to be captured. While the camp celebrated catching who they thought was Garabito, the real Garabito escaped with his wife. The ruse is a celebrated victory of Costa Rica's indigenous underdogs, but eventually Garabito too had to accept defeat at the hands of the Spanish. Senior in years and lacking the support that had fueled his earlier series of rebellions, Gabarito surrendered in the 1570s, and was even baptized as a Christian.

Laguna Meándrica, which has large populations of heron, smoothbill and kingfisher. If you continue past the lagoon, you'll have a good chance of spotting mammals and the occasional crocodile, though you will have to turn back to exit.

Another 2km south of the trailhead is the **Carara ranger station** (⊙7am-3pm Dec-Mar, 8am-4pm Apr-Nov), where there are bathrooms. There are two short trail loops within the park that pass through the sultry, mulchy semi-gloom of the rainforest, characteristic of most of the park. They are accessed via the short, paved, wheelchair-accessible **interpretative trail** that begins at the ranger station. The first, **Sendero Las Aráceas**, is 1.2km long and links up with the second, **Sendero Quebrada Bonita** (another 1.5km). Sendero Quebrada Bonita is your best bet for seeing wildlife such as agoutis and ample birdlife, as it's furthest from the main road.

Guides can be hired at the ranger station for US$30 per person (two-person minimum) for a two-hour hike.

ⓘ Information

DANGERS & ANNOYANCES

Heavy tourist traffic along the Pacific coast has resulted in an unfortunate increase in petty theft. Vehicles parked at the Laguna Meándrica trailhead are occasionally broken into, and although there may be guards on duty, it is advised that drivers leave their cars in the lot at the Carara ranger station and walk along the Costanera Sur for 2km north or 1km south. Alternatively, park beside Restaurante Los Cocodrilos (tip the parking attendants on your return).

ⓘ Getting There & Away

Any bus traveling between Puntarenas and Jacó can leave you at the park entrance. You can also catch buses headed north or south in front of Restaurante Los Cocodrilos. This may be a bit problematic on weekends, when buses are full, so go midweek if you are relying on a bus ride. If you're driving, the entrance to Carara is right on the Costanera and is clearly marked.

Tárcoles & Around

The small, unassuming town of Tárcoles is little more than a few rows of houses strung along a series of dirt roads that parallel the ocean. As you'd imagine, this tiny, dusty Tico town isn't much of a tourist draw, though the surrounding area is perfect for fans of the superlative, especially if you're interested in seeing what's claimed to be the country's tallest waterfall and some of its biggest crocodiles.

◉ Sights

★ **Catarata Manantial de Agua Viva**　　　　　　　WATERFALL
(☑2645-1017; admission US$20; ⊙8am-3pm) This 200m-high waterfall is claimed to be the highest in the country. From the en-

trance, it's a steep 3km (45-minute) hike down into the valley; at the bottom, the river continues through a series of natural swimming holes. The falls are most dramatic at their fullest, during the rainy season, though the serene rainforest setting is beautiful any time of year. A 5km dirt road past Hotel Villa Lapas leads to the primary entrance to the falls. Keep an eye out for brightly colored poison-dart frogs as well as the occasional pair of scarlet macaws.

Pura Vida Gardens & Waterfalls   GARDENS
(✔2645-1001; www.puravidagarden.com; adult/under 10yr US$20/10; ☺8am-5pm) Just before the village of Bijagual, this private botanical garden offers great vistas of Manantial de Agua Viva cascading down the side of a cliff, and there are some pleasant hiking trails where you might see nesting toucans and other wildlife. The on-site restaurant caters to the Adventure Dining (www.adventure diningcostarica.com) crowds.

At the time of research this place was up for sale, so its future is uncertain.

🖙 Tours

This area is known for crocodile-watching tours, and travelers anywhere near this part of the coast will be bombarded with advertisements and flyers for them. Although it will be hard for adrenaline junkies to resist, some of these tours have a dubious impact on the natural habitat of the magnificent animals who lurk in the mudflats of the Río Tárcoles. Although they are definitely a spectacle to behold, it's frustrating to watch the crocodiles being hand-fed by some of the tour guides; it's illegal to feed wildlife in Costa Rica. If you do visit the crocodiles on a tour, ask a lot of questions and do your part to encourage responsible interaction with the animals. Tours usually cost US$35 per person for two hours.

Jungle Crocodile Safari (✔2637-0656; www.junglecrocodilesafari.com; per person US$35) is one of the better companies with an office in Tárcoles. The tours leave from town or you can arrange to be picked up at your hotel.

🛏 Sleeping

★**Hotel Manga Rosa**   BOUTIQUE HOTEL **$$$**
(✔4702-1166, in USA 800-259-5981; www.bou tiquehotelmangarosacostarica.com; r US$300; P🅿❄🛜🏊) Up in the hills and surrounded by jungle, and with remarkable views of the Pacific coast from its infinity pool, this intimate six-room boutique hotel is located just before Pura Vida Gardens and Waterfalls, 6km from Tárcoles. Light, bright spacious rooms with the coast spread out beneath, a gourmet restaurant, splashes of modern art and top-of-the-range furnishings seal the deal.

Hotel Villa Lapas   RESORT **$$$**
(✔2637-0232, 2439-1816; www.villalapas.com; all-inclusive r from US$199; P🅿❄🛜🏊) 🍃 Located on a private reserve comprising both secondary rainforest and tropical gardens, this resort offers rooms housed in an attractive Spanish colonial–style lodge. Guests can unwind in relative comfort in between guided hikes along the on-site trail network, bird-watching trips, canopy tours and soaks in the pool. Geared toward a birding crowd, the pace here is slow and low-key.

Alongside the Río Tarcolito, the hotel grounds include the kitschy 'Santa Lucia Town,' which has a couple of souvenir shops and a wedding chapel.

❶ Getting There & Away

Any bus between Puntarenas and Jacó can leave you at the entrance to Tárcoles. If you're driving, the entrance to the town is right on the Costanera Sur and is clearly marked. Local buses between Orotina and Bijagual can drop you off at the entrance to the Parque Nacional Carara.

Playa Herradura

Until the mid-1990s, Playa Herradura was a rural, palm-sheltered beach of grayish-black sand that was popular mainly with campers and local fishers. In the late 1990s, however, Herradura was thrown into the spotlight having been used as the stage for the Ridley Scott movie *1492: Conquest of Paradise*. Rapid development ensued, resulting in the construction of one of the most high-profile marinas in the country, the Los Sueños marina.

Playa Herradura represents one possible future for the central Pacific coast. Sprawling complexes of condos, fancy hotels and high-rise apartments are slowly encircling the bay and snaking up the mountainside, while the marina features rows of luxury yachts and sportfishing vessels. The southern half of the beach, at the end of the Playa Herradura Road, however, is a world apart from the landscaped grounds traversed by golf buggies: it remains stubbornly local, with picnicking Ticos and bars with pounding music.

🛌 Sleeping

You have to pay to play in Playa Herradura, so consider moving further down the coast to Jacó if you're not prepared to bunk down in the top-end price bracket.

★ **Hotel Villa Caletas** BOUTIQUE HOTEL **$$$**
(☎ 2630-3000; www.hotelvillacaletas.com; r US$283-505, ste US$555-815; ❖❄@🛜☃) ✿ Although the views of the Pacific are amazing, what makes this bluff-top hotel truly unique is its architectural fusion, incorporating elements as varied as tropical Victorian, Hellenistic and French colonial. The ultra-exclusive accommodations are located on the tiny headland of Punta Leona, perched high on a dramatic hillside at the end of a serpentine driveway just north of Playa Herradura.

Each room is arranged amid the tropical foliage of the terraced property, affording a singular sense of privacy and isolation. The room interiors are tastefully decorated with art and antiques, with windows looking onto spectacular views. There is also a French-influenced restaurant, several semi-private infinity pools, and a private 1km trail leading down the hillside to the beach.

★ **Zephyr Palace** BOUTIQUE HOTEL **$$$**
(☎ 2637-3000; www.zephyrpalace.com; ste US$515-1824; ❖❄@🛜☃) On the same property as the elegant Villa Caletas, its over-the-top sibling takes the decadence to another level of luxury. At this marble palace, seven individually decorated themed suites that wouldn't look out of place in Las Vegas evoke the splendor of ancient Rome, pharaonic Egypt and Asia. But no futuristic Space Suite? The turnoff is signposted just north of Playa Herradura.

🍴 Eating

La Puesta del Sol COSTA RICAN **$**
(☎ 2637-8003; mains from US$5; ❖ 11am-11pm; ❄) Right on the 'local' side of the beach, this lively eatery and bar shelters those to whom manicured golf courts are anathema. The menu is all about *casados* (set meals) and *ceviches* and the sunset goes well with your beer.

Dolce Vita CAFE **$**
(☎ 2630-4250; cakes from US$3; ❖ 7am-6pm; ❄🛜) Good coffee, quiches, proper bagels, chunky muffins and plenty of delectable desserts are found inside this little cafe right on the marina.

Bambú SUSHI **$$**
(☎ 2630-4333; Marina Village; mains from US$9; ❖ 11:30am-10pm; ❄🛜) On the waterfront overlooking the rows of gleaming yachts, this spot serves an appropriate selection of Poseidon's subjects. We're particularly partial to the rolls called Dragon, Spicy Lobster and Sunburn (way better than it sounds!), and the sampler sashimi platter hits the spot when paired with an Asahi beer.

Jimmy T's Provisions SUPERMARKET **$$**
(☎ 2637-8636; www.jimmytsprovisions.com; Los Sueños Marina; ❖ 6:30am-7pm Mon-Sat, 7:30am-5pm Sun) For those looking to self-cater in style, Jimmy T's is a dream come true. His small store on the docks of the Los Sueños marina caters mostly to the yachting set, but it's stacked floor to ceiling with organic, imported and rare-in-Costa Rica delicacies. Italian cheeses, grass-fed meat, Asian foods – it's a dream come true for self-caterers with *mucho* cash.

❶ Getting There & Away

The Herradura turnoff is on the Costanera Sur, about 6km after the Costanera Sur leaves the edge of the ocean and heads inland. From here, a paved road leads 3km west to Playa Herradura. There are frequent local buses (US$2, 20 minutes) connecting Playa Herradura to Jacó.

Jacó

Few places in Costa Rica generate such divergent opinions as Jacó. Partying surfers, North American retirees and international developers laud it for its devil-may-care atmosphere, bustling streets and booming real-estate opportunities. Observant ecotourists, marginalized Ticos and loyalists of the 'old Costa Rica' absolutely despise the place for the *exact* same reasons.

Jacó was the first town on the central Pacific coast to explode with tourist development and it remains a major draw for backpackers, surfers, snowbirds and city-weary *josefinos* (inhabitants of San José). Although working-class Tico neighborhoods are nearby, open-air trinket shops and tour operators line the tacky main drag which, at night, is given over to a safe but somewhat seedy mix of binge-drinking students, surfers and scantily clad ladies of negotiable affection.

While Jacó's lackadaisical charm is not for everyone, the surfing is excellent, the restaurants and bars are generally great and the nightlife can be a blast.

🏃 Activities & Tours

Tour companies offer a huge array of activities in and around Jacó, from surfing (there are numerous surfing schools) and sea kayaking to horseback riding, canopy tours, ATV tours and more extreme canyoning and waterfall-jumping adventures.

Virtually every shop, hotel and restaurant in town books tours, as Jacó operates on a lucrative commission-based system. As you'd imagine, it's hard to know who is greasing whose palms and who is running tours. Still, you shouldn't book anything from touts on the streets, and if an offer from a vendor seems too good to be true, then most likely it is. Talk to your lodgings and fellow travelers for recommendations, and it's usually better to go for companies that specialize in one (or a small handful) of activities rather than a catch-all operator that claims they can arrange everything under the sun.

Kayak Jacó   KAYAKING
(☑ 2643-1233; www.kayakjaco.com; tours from US$75) This reliable, responsible company facilitates kayaking and sea-canoeing trips that include snorkeling excursions to tropical islands, in a wide variety of customized day and multiday trips. Though it does have a presence at Playa Agujas, 250m east of the beach, it's best to phone or email in advance.

Mt Miros   HIKING
A worthwhile pastime that few tourists are aware of is following the trail up Mt Miros, which winds through primary and secondary rainforest and offers spectacular views of Jacó and Playa Hermosa. The viewpoint is several kilometers uphill. Note that the trailhead is unmarked, so ask a local to point it out to you.

Serenity Spa   SPA
(☑ 2643-1624; www.serenityspacr.com; Av Pastor Díaz; ⊙ 9:30am-7pm Mon-Sat, to 5pm Sun) Serenity Spa, east of Calle Bohío, offers the full range of spa services, from facial scrubs and body wraps to reflexology.

Surfing

Although the rainy season is considered best for Pacific coast surfing, Jacó is blessed with consistent year-round breaks. Even though more advanced surfers head further south to Playa Hermosa, the waves at Jacó are strong, steady and a lot of fun for intermediate surfers. Jacó is also a great place to learn to surf or start a surf trip as many places offer lessons and it's easy to buy and sell boards here.

If you're looking to rent a board for the day, shop around as the better places will rent you a board for US$15 to US$20 for 24 hours.

Tortuga Surf Camp   SURFING
(☑ 2463-3348; www.tortugasurfcamp.com; surfing lessons from US$60; ⊙ 9am-5pm) Regardless of your age or ability, this is one of the top places in Jacó to learn to surf or improve your technique. Michael and his crew are very patient and encouraging.

Vista Guapa Surf Camp   SURFING
(☑ 2643-2830, in USA 409-599-1828; www. vistaguapa.com) Six-time national surf champion Álvaro Solano runs the highly respected Vista Guapa Surf Camp, which comes highly recommended; great for beginners. SUP (stand-up paddleboarding) classes and rental also arranged. Weekly rates including full board start at around US$1150. Check the website for directions.

Carton Surf Shop   SURFING
(☑ 2643-3762; www.cartonsurfboards.com; Calle Madrigal; per day US$20; ⊙ 8am-5pm Mon-Sat, 10am-3pm Sun) A good place to rent boards, run by the friendly Villalobos brothers, near the beach at the southern end of the main drag on Calle Madrigal.

Swimming

Jacó is generally safe for swimming, though you should avoid the areas near the estuaries, which are polluted. Be advised that the waves can get crowded with beginner surfers who don't always know how to control their boards, so keep your wits about you and stay out of their way. Riptides occasionally occur, especially when the surf gets big, so inquire about local conditions and keep an eye out for red flags marking the paths of rips.

Horseback Riding

Be wary of winging it here; readers have reported incidents of horse abuse in Jacó and visitors will see malnourished and mistreated animals on offer near the beach.

Discovery Horseback Tours   HORSE RIDING
(☑ 8838-7550; www.horseridecostarica.com; rides from US$80) Nearby beach and rainforest rides are available through this highly recommended outfit, run by an English couple who offer an extremely high level of service and professionalism and who clearly take excellent care of their horses.

Jacó Center

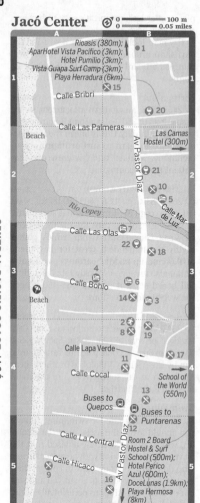

Jacó Center

Activities, Courses & Tours
1	Jacó Canyoning	B1
2	Serenity Spa	B4

Sleeping
3	Buddha House	B3
4	Hotel de Haan	A3
5	Hotel Mar de Luz	B2
6	Hotel Poseidon	B3
7	Posada Jacó	B3

Eating
8	Caliche's Wishbone	B4
9	El Hicaco	A5
10	Graffiti	B2
11	Green Room	B4
12	Lemon Zest	B5
13	Más x Menos	B4
14	Namaste	B3
15	Side Street Bistro	B1
16	Soda a Cachete	B5
17	TacoBar	B4
18	The Wok	B3
19	Tsunami Sushi	B4

Drinking & Nightlife
20	Bar Nirvana	B1
21	Monkey Bar	B2
22	Surf Dogs	B3

area belong to Vista Los Sueños, which offers 14 cables accessed by tractor cart through the lush hillside. They also arrange recommended horse-riding and waterfall tour combos and ATV adventures, though the latter is not hugely ecofriendly.

🎓 Courses

School of the World   LANGUAGE COURSE
(☑ 2643-2463; www.schooloftheworld.org; 1-/4-week package from US$355/1136) This popular school and cultural-studies center offers classes in Spanish, surfing, yoga, art, GoPro and photography (choose your ideal combo). The impressive building and activities center also houses a cafe and art gallery. On-site lodgings can be arranged, either in shared or private rooms.

🎉 Festivals & Events

Jungle Jam   MUSIC
(www.junglejam.com) This four-day mid-March music festival, held at DoceLunas Hotel, brings together rock, reggae, funk and soul artists. Past participants have included Steel Pulse, Perro Bravo, Thicker Than Thieves and Paul Damon.

Adventure Tours

Jacó Canyoning   ADVENTURE SPORTS
(☑ 2643-1834; www.jacocanyoning.com; Av Pastor Díaz; tours US$79-159; ⊙ 7am-9pm) This experienced, safety-conscious operator arranges some of the most adrenaline-charged excursions in town, from tamer waterfall rappelling to extreme canyoneering, cliff jumping and paddleboarding.

Vista Los Sueños Day Tours   ADVENTURE TOUR
(☑ 2637-6020, in USA 321-220-9631; www.canopy vistalossuenos.com; tours from US$90; ⊙ hourly tours 8am-3pm) The longest zip lines in the

🛌 Sleeping

Jacó has hosted a variety of tourists for years, and there's a wide spread of places to lay your head. From concrete-block dives to spendy upscale resorts, there's a lot to choose from in just a few blocks.

The center of town, with its many bars and discos, means that noise might be a factor in where you choose to stay. The far northern and southern ends of town have more relaxed and quieter accommodations.

Reservations are highly recommended on weekends in the dry season and become critical during Easter, the week between Christmas and New Year's Eve, and during the mid-March Jungle Jam music festival.

Low-season rates are as much as 30% to 40% lower than high-season rates. If you plan on a lengthy stay (more than five days), ask about long-term rates.

★ Room 2 Board
Hostel & Surf School   HOSTEL $
(📞2643-4949, in the USA 323-315-0012; www. room2board.com; dm from US$16, r with/without bathroom from US$59/62; 🅿✳@🖥✖) Now *this* is a hostel. Brand new, spacious and professionally run, it has a buzzy on-site cafe, dedicated staff who arrange tours and surfing lessons, and various configurations of rooms spread across three floors. The hammocks on the roof terrace catch the breeze, dorms come with excellent mattresses, rain showers and lockers, and there are yoga classes and movie screenings.

Rooms without bathroom are slightly pricier because they automatically come with air-con; en suite rooms come with fan only. Several rooms have family-friendly furniture configurations, and surf lessons for older kids.

Buddha House   GUESTHOUSE $
(📞2643-3615; www.hostelbuddhahouse.com; Av Pastor Díaz; dm US$18, s with/without bathroom US$70/35, d with/without bathroom US$80/40; 🅿✳🖥✖) Bold colors and modern art create an artistic atmosphere at this 'boutique hostel,' where the best private rooms are spacious suites. Communal areas include a breezy patio, a spotless kitchen and even a small pool, and the staff are lovely. What's less lovely is the noise: the hostel is next to a bar that parties late into the night.

Hotel de Haan   HOSTEL $
(📞2643-1795; www.hoteldehaan.com; Calle Bohío; dm US$12, r from US$30; 🅿@🖥✖) A hostel rather than a hotel, this Dutch-Tico outpost is popular with backpackers and surfers on a budget. Basic private rooms have hot-water bathrooms and are tidy but dark; dorms share bathrooms. The open-air kitchen overlooks the pool area, and is a great place to meet and hang out with fellow travelers, which some guests do late into the night.

Las Camas Hostel   HOTEL $
(📞8639-4241, 8533-7619; www.lascamashostel.com; Dorado Sol; dm with/without air-con US$13/11, r US$30; 🅿@🖥✖) This young backpacker start-up is a highly personable shoestring offering, kind of like a buddy's house. Las Camas puts you minutes away from the beach and the nightlife, yet guests seem content spending more of their time on the expansive rooftop deck. Rooms are a bit rough around the edges, but shabbiness is easy to forgive at this price range.

★ Hotel Perico Azul   HOTEL $$
(📞2643-1341; www.hotelpericoazuljaco.com; r/studio/ste US$60/75/160; 🅿✳🖥✖) Tucked away off a quiet side street, this small hotel is difficult to fault. The rooms and apartments are light and spotless, with bright splashes of color, there's a small pool to relax around, staff go out of their way to make you feel welcome, and owner Mike runs the recommended Tortuga Surf Camp (p359); surfing packages can be arranged.

AparHotel Vista Pacífico   HOTEL $$
(📞2643-3261; www.vistapacifico.com; r/ste incl breakfast from US$79/110; 🅿🖥✖) Located on the crest of a hill just north of Jacó (off Bulevar), this gem of a hotel is run by a warm young Canadian couple. Homey, comfortable rooms and suites with kitchen facilities come in a variety of configurations. Its favorable elevation offers not only panoramic views of the coastline and valley but also blessedly cool breezes. Kids under 12 stay free; child-friendly tours can be organized.

Hotel Mar de Luz   HOTEL $$
(📞2643-3259; www.mardeluz.com; Calle Mar de Luz; d/f/apt incl breakfast US$93/125/153; 🅿✳🖥✖) This adorable little hotel with Dutch-inspired murals of windmills and tulips has tidy and attractive air-conditioned rooms (outfitted with fridges, microwaves and coffeemakers) and stone-walled villas that are perfect for families. The friendly Dutch owners (who also speak Spanish, English, German and Italian) offer two swimming pools, several BBQ grills and plenty of useful information.

The owners are also extremely committed to fighting drugs and prostitution in Jacó, and are at the forefront of an admirable campaign to clean up the city.

Posada Jacó
HOTEL $$

(☑2643-1951; www.posadajaco.com; Calle Las Olas; ste US$90; P ❋ 🛜 ☲) Surprisingly quiet given it's only steps from Jacó's main drag, this tiny creekside hotel has a well-kept garden and pool area with a communal BBQ. Suites are the best deal here, complete with kitchenettes and terraces in low-key, friendly environs.

Hotel Poseidon
HOTEL $$

(☑2643-1642; www.hotel-poseidon.com; Calle Bohío; d incl breakfast from US$95; P ❋ @ 🛜 ☲) It's hard to miss the huge Grecian wooden carvings that adorn the exterior of this small American-run hotel. On the inside, tidy rooms are accented with stylish furniture and mosaic tiles (though the furniture looks weathered) and include amenities like fridges. There's a pool with swim-up bar, a small Jacuzzi, a decent open-air restaurant and the town's only sports bar.

★ Hotel Pumilio
BOUTIQUE HOTEL $$$

(☑2643-5678; www.hotelpumilio.com; r from US$250; P ❋ 🛜 ☲) In a wonderfully peaceful location along an unpaved road 2.5km north of Jacó, this intimate hotel caters to travelers who want to do their own thing yet repose in style. Luxurious rooms come with king-sized beds, rain showers and outdoor kitchenettes. The pool with waterfall is surrounded by lush greenery. There are rental bikes for pedaling down to Jacó.

DoceLunas
HOTEL $$$

(☑2643-2211; www.docelunas.com; Costanera Sur; r/ste incl breakfast US$178/201; P ⊜ ❋ 🛜 ☲) Situated in the foothills across the highway, 'Twelve Moons' is a heavenly mountain retreat consisting of only 20 rooms sheltered in a pristine landscape of tropical rainforest. Each teak-accented room is uniquely decorated with original artwork, and the luxurious bathrooms feature double sinks and bathtubs. Yoga classes, offered regularly, are free with room rates.

A full spa uses the hotel's own line of beauty products, and you can swim in a free-form, waterfall-fed pool. The open-air restaurant serves everything from marlin *ceviche* to vegan delicacies. To reach the hotel, make a left off the Costanera just after the third signed entrance for Playa Jacó.

Eating

The quality of fare in Jacó is high, and aside from the Quepos and Manuel Antonio area, the city proudly boasts the most diverse offering of international cuisine on the central Pacific coast. While the vast majority of eateries cater primarily to Western palates, there are still a few local spots that have weathered the storm of change.

★ Side Street Bistro
FUSION $

(☑2643-2724; Calle Bribri; sandwiches US$6-10; ⊙11am-4pm Mon, 11am-9pm Tue-Sat, 9am-5pm Sun) Ever since it opened, this little bistro has won over local and visiting fans with fresh, creative sandwiches such as the BBQ-pulled-pork sloppy joe, coffee-and-cacao-rubbed tenderloin and the reuben and the shrimp po'boys. There are local craft beers to wash them all down. And the breakfasts, oh, the breakfasts! Butter pecan waffles, maple bacon whiskey eggs Benedict... In a word: awesome.

★ Namaste
INDIAN $

(☑8482-6867; Calle Bohío; mains US$6-12; ⊙8am-7pm; 🛜🍴) You'll find this friendly little place by the delicious smells of Indian spices. Breakfast specials include *shakshuka* (Israeli-style eggs fried up with tomatoes and herbs), while the rest of the day you can feast on falafel, Bombay masala fish, chicken curry, baba ghanoush and other flavorful Middle Eastern and Asian dishes. Their smoothies are remarkable, too.

Soda a Cachete
COSTA RICAN $

(☑8633-1831; Av Pastor Díaz; meals US$5-9; ⊙8am-8pm) Although many of the local *sodas* have been pushed out by gringo palates, this little place survives through its loyal following, who drop by for huge, excellent breakfasts and set lunches. A few bucks will get you rice, beans, a fish or meat dish of the day and some juice. It's across from the Red Cross.

The Wok
ASIAN $

(☑2643-6168; Av Pastor Díaz; mains US$4-8; ⊙11am-9pm; 🍴) The Wok's pan-Asian menu is courtesy of the Dutch owner who lived in Asia for a while and it's reliably good – especially the stir-fries and the ribs (only available on Wednesdays). The scattered tables facing Jacó's main street also provide primo people-watching. It's next to the Budget car-rental place.

Más x Menos SUPERMARKET **$**

(Av Pastor Díaz; ⊘8am-10pm) This Western-style supermarket has an impressive selection of fresh produce, and local and international culinary items.

★**Graffiti** INTERNATIONAL **$$**

(☑2643-1708; www.grafficr.com; Av Pastor Díaz, Pacific Center, No 23; mains US$10-31; ⊘5-10pm Mon-Sat; 🕿🖉) Graffiti is tucked away at the Pacific Center; its decor is what you might expect from the name, and live music on weekends ups its game, but the spotlight here is fixed on the plate. The famous cacao-and-coffee-encrusted filet mignon is exceptional, complemented by the likes of macadamia-and-passion-fruit catch of the day, decadent cheesecake and creative cocktails. Reservations are highly recommended.

Tsunami Sushi JAPANESE **$$**

(☑2643-3678; www.tsunamisushicr.com; Av Pastor Díaz, Mall II Galeone, 2nd fl; meals US$11-30; ⊘5-10pm Sun-Thu, to 1am Fri; ✳🕿) Reservations are recommended at this sleek and popular sushi spot, one of the best on the central Pacific coast. We're particularly partial to their spicy tuna and ghost rolls, and cucumber martinis. Play your cards right and various specials throughout the week can save you some serious colones.

Caliche's Wishbone INTERNATIONAL **$$**

(☑2643-3406; Av Pastor Díaz; meals US$9-19; ⊘noon-10pm Thu-Tue; ✳🕿) Overseen by the charming Caliche, this has been a Jacó favorite for years and years. The eclectic menu includes pizzas, pitas, blackened tuna sashimi, pan-seared sea bass, and fish and shrimp tacos, though its justifiable fame comes from the fact that everything is quite simply fresh, delicious and good value. It's south of Calle Bohío.

Green Room FUSION **$$**

(☑2643-4425; Calle Cocal; mains US$9-20; ⊘9am-11pm; 🕿🖷) With an emphasis on creativity and fresh ingredients (these guys work with local organic farms), Green Room serves imaginative fare such as sweet-potato-crusted mahimahi, seared tuna with tamarind glaze and ribs with passion-fruit BBQ sauce, along with a supporting cast of salads, melts, wraps and burgers (plus a kids' menu). There's live music on Friday nights, courtesy of local or visiting musicians.

TacoBar INTERNATIONAL **$$**

(☑2643-0222; www.tacobar.info; Calle Lapa Verde; meals US$7-15; ⊘7am-10pm Tue-Sun, 11am-10pm Mon; 🕿🖉) A one-stop shop for grilled fish, salads and smoothies. Get your mint lemonade in the gargantuan 1L size or your greens at the salad bar featuring more than 20 kinds of exotic and leafy components. And, of course, there's the obligatory fish taco, which may be one of the planet's greatest food combinations. The *ceviche's* a letdown, though.

Rioasis PIZZA **$$**

(☑2643-3354; Plaza Jacó, Av Pastor Díaz; pizzas US$10-16; ⊘11:30am-10pm; ✳🕿🖉🖷) Admit it – sometimes pizza seems like *the best thing ever* in the moment. When it comes to Rioasis' wood-fired pie, topped with all kinds of gourmet goodness, it usually is. There's a kids' menu, too. The place is next to the river, right by the bridge.

★**Lemon Zest** FUSION **$$$**

(☑2643-2591; www.lemonzestjaco.com; Av Pastor Díaz; mains US$15-37; ⊘5-10pm; ✳🕿🖉) Chef Richard Lemon (a former instructor at Le Cordon Bleu Miami) wins many accolades for one of Jacó's swishest and imaginative menus. The roster of upscale standards – Caribbean-style jerk pork chop, red-quinoa-crusted shrimp with passion-fruit sauce, seared spicy ahi tuna with wilted spinach – is carried out with due sophistication, accompanied by a well-matched wine list. An excellent splurge.

El Hicaco SEAFOOD **$$$**

(☑2643-3226; www.elhicaco.net; Calle Hicaco; mains US$20-40; ⊘11am-midnight) This oceanside spot brims with casual elegance and is regarded as one of the finer dining experiences in Jacó. Although the menu is entirely dependent on seasonal offerings, both from the land and the sea, the specialty of the house is seafood, prepared with a variety of sauces highlighted by Costa Rica's tropical produce. Service can be glacially slow.

🍺 Drinking & Nightlife

Jacó isn't the cultural capital of Costa Rica; it's where people go to get hammered and party the night away. There are numerous raging bars and dance clubs that cater to good-times-seeking expats and travelers, but choose your venues carefully, as prostitution figures prominently.

Bar Nirvana
BAR

(☑8429-5255; Av Pastor Díaz; ⊙7pm-2am)
Great mojitos and a very chilled-out owner/
bartender who built the place from scratch
and is happy to chat to you. Good for after-
dinner drinks and gets raucous as the night
wears on.

Monkey Bar
CLUB

(☑2643-2357; Av Pastor Díaz; ⊙9pm-2:30am
Tue-Sun) Attracting a young crowd of locals
and visitors, Monkey Bar pumps with good
times, reggaetón and pheromones.

Surf Dogs
BAR

(☑2643-3342; www.surfdogsbar.com; Av Pastor Díaz; ⊙10am-late Tue-Sun) Chill out with
hamburger sliders, icy beers and decadent
daiquiris served at tables crafted from surfboards. It's definitely a surfer bar (think
foosball and dartboards). But it's also a dai-
quiri bar, with at least eight different kinds
on the menu. On Friday and Saturday nights
it helps if you're good at lip reading (it gets
loud).

❶ Orientation

Playa Jacó is about 2km off the Costanera,
3.5km past the turnoff for Herradura. The
beach itself is about 3km long, and hotels and
restaurants line the road running just inland.
The areas on the northern and southern fringes
are the most tranquil and attractive, and are the
cleanest.

Note that, in an effort to make foreign visitors
feel more at home, the town has placed street-
name signs on most streets, although the locals
continue to use the traditional landmark system.

❶ Information

There's no independent tourist information
office, though several tour offices will give information. Look for the free monthly Jaco's Guide
or the quarterly Info Jaco.

For cash, there are ATMs along the main Av
Pastor Díaz, though the best rates will be found
at the big branches like Banco Popular.

DANGERS & ANNOYANCES

Aside from occasional petty crime such as pickpocketing and breaking into locked cars, Jacó is
not a dangerous place by any stretch. However,
the high concentration of wealthy foreigners
and comparatively poor Ticos has resulted in a
thriving sex and drugs industry. To be fair, the
local council has done an admirable job cleaning
things up in recent years, and these vices are not
as public as they once were. But this is not to say
that Jacó is now squeaky clean.

Jacó is the epicenter of Costa Rica's prostitution scene. Assuming that the working girl or
guy is over 18 (not always a given), prostitution
is legal in Costa Rica, but travelers who wish to
explore this dark corner of Costa Rican nightlife
should carefully consider the health and safety
risks and negative social impacts.

Locals warn against walking alone on the beach
at night, as there have been several muggings.

❶ Getting There & Away

AIR

NatureAir and Alfa Romeo Aero Taxi (☑2735-
5353; www.alfaromeoair.com) offer charter
flights. Prices are dependent on the number
of passengers, so it's best to try to organize a
larger group if you're considering this option.

BOAT

The jet-boat transfer service that connects Jacó
to Montezuma is, far and away, the most efficient
way to get between the central Pacific coast and
the Península de Nicoya. The journey across the
Golfo de Nicoya only takes about an hour (compared to about seven hours overland), though at
US$40 it's definitely not cheap. (For US$10 you
can bring a bicycle or surfboard.) The bonus?
Sometimes travelers see dolphins along the ride.
Several boats leave daily from Playa Herradura,
2km north of town. Reservations are required
and the most consistent departures are with
Zuma Tours (☑2642-0050, 2642-0024; www.
zumatours.net) at 11am. It's a beach landing, so
wear the right shoes.

BUS

Gray Line (www.graylinecostarica.com), Easy
Ride (www.easyridecr.com) and Monkey Ride
(www.monkeyridecr.com) run shared shuttles
from Jacó to popular destinations such as San
José (from US$40), Manuel Antonio (from
US$35), Dominical/Uvita (from US$45), Sierpe
(from US$55), Puerto Jiménez (US$79) and Monteverde (from US$53). Easy Ride also offers direct
shuttles to Granada, Nicaragua (8:30am, US$99).

Buses for San José stop at the Plaza Jacó
mall, north of the center. The bus stops for other
destinations are opposite the Más x Menos
supermarket: stand at the bus stop (Av Pastor
Díaz) in front of the supermarket if you're headed north; stand at the bus stop (Av Pastor Díaz)
across the street if you're headed south. Buses
originate in Puntarenas or Quepos, so consult
your lodgings about the latest schedule and get
to the stop early.

Puntarenas US$2.20; 1½ hours; 12 daily
between 5am and 7:30pm.

Quepos US$2.70; 1½ hours; 12 daily between
6am and 7pm.

San José US$5.50; 2½ hours; eight daily
between 6am and 7pm.

ⓘ Getting Around

Getting around in Jacó is easy on foot; strolling the length of town in flip-flops takes about 20 minutes.

BICYCLE

Several places around town rent out bicycles, mopeds and scooters. Bikes can usually be rented for about US$5 an hour or US$10 to US$15 per day, though prices change depending on the season. Mopeds and small scooters cost from US$30 to US$50 per day (many places ask for a cash or credit-card deposit of about US$200).

CAR

There are several rental agencies in town, so shop around for the best rates.

Budget (☑2643-2665; Av Pastor Díaz, near Calle Bohío; ⊘8am-5pm Mon-Sat, to 4pm Sun) International car-hire company.

Economy (☑2643-1719; Av Pastor Díaz; ⊘8am-6pm) South of Calle Ancha.

Playa Hermosa

Regarded as one of the most consistent and powerful breaks in the whole country, Hermosa serves up serious surf that commands the utmost respect. You really need to know what you're doing in these parts – huge waves and strong riptides are unforgiving, and countless surfboards here have wound up broken and strewn about on the shoreline. Unless you're a hardcore surfer, it's best to stick to gentler breaks near Jacó, but there's nothing to stop you from coming up here and watching the action.

Several places on the Pacific coast are named 'beautiful beach' in Spanish, and this 10km-long strip of gray sand is hardly the loveliest of the lot. Billed as an upscale alternative to Jacó, minus the hookers and the traffic, Hermosa hasn't quite avoided development, with condos popping up along the beach like mushrooms. Still, for now, it is very much a slow-paced beach village.

🏃 Activities

★ **Surfing**   SURFING
Most of the wave action takes place at the northern reaches, where there are half a dozen clearly defined beach breaks. These break very near the shore, particularly in the rainy season between May and August.

Conditions are highly variable, but you can expect the maximum height to top out around high tide. Swell size is largely dependent on unseen factors such as current

and offshore weather patterns, but when it gets big, you'll know. At times like these, you really shouldn't be paddling out unless you have some serious experience under your belt. Playa Hermosa is not for beginners, and even intermediate surfers can get chewed up and spat out here. To watch and appreciate, park at the small road by the Backyard Hotel and wander out to the beach.

Vida Asana Retreat Center   YOGA
(☑8483-7603, in the USA 201-726-2677; www.vidaasana.com) This hillside retreat offers fully customizable packages combining yoga, surfing and healthy organic meals. Reservations for 'weekend recharge retreats' are highly recommended, and prices are dependent on the size of your party, the season and the extent of requested instruction. The accommodations are breezy, rustic and set amid lush jungle. Signposted along the dirt road from the south end of Hermosa.

🎊 Festivals & Events

National Surfing Championship   SPORTS
If you don't think you can hack it with the aspiring pros, you might want to give the surf on this beach a miss. However, consider stopping by in late July or late August, when local pro surfers descend for the annual national surf competition. Dates vary, though the event is heavily advertised around the country, especially in neighboring Jacó.

🛌 Sleeping

Most accommodations in Playa Hermosa are clustered along a few hundred meters of highway and the beach road paralleling it, which basically comprise the village. Rates vary wildly depending on season and demand, and they're often negotiable.

Hotel Brisa del Mar   CABINA $
(☑2643-7076, 8816-2294; cabinasbrisadelmar@hotmail.com; s/d/tr US$30/45/50; P❄🛜) A classic no-frills surfers' crash pad popular with Ticos, this Floridian-run spot has basic rooms with air-con, private hot shower and cable TV, as well as a communal kitchen where you can self-cater. If the surf is looking too small (or too big!), you can pass the time on the basketball court or with a few games of table tennis.

★ **Tortuga del Mar**   LODGE $$
(☑2643-7132; www.tortugadelmar.net; r US$89, studio from US$99; P❄@🛜🏊) This newish lodge is sheltered amid shady grounds,

and has just a handful of rooms housed in a two-story building, presided over by helpful Lilly and her husband. Tropical modern is the style, with lofty ceilings constructed from hardwoods, catching every gust of the Pacific breezes. The best bit? The wooden deck out front to watch the surfing action.

The larger studios are spacious and even feature mini-kitchenettes that make self-catering a real possibility within this price bracket.

Hotel Cabinas Las Olas
CABINA **$$**

(☏2643-7021; r US$50-75, skybox US$110; P❄🐾🏊) This distinctive three-story A-frame building is home to an awesome 'skybox room', a teak-accented, ocean-facing penthouse where you can fall asleep to the sounds of the surf and wake to a surf check. You can also rent one of several beachside rooms, from spartan budget digs to bigger rooms with kitchenettes. Multiday surfing, SUP and yoga packages are available here.

Costanera
B&B **$$**

(☏2643-7044; www.costaneraplayahermosa.com; r incl breakfast without/with air-con US$55/65; P❄🐾) Blink and you may miss Costanera, a tidy Italian-run B&B – so look carefully for the yellow buildings, as it's a great deal in this neighborhood. Five rooms of various sizes and shapes have vaulted wooden ceilings and beachfront terraces, with hammocks for post-surf relaxation. The owners' pitbulls are not overly friendly.

★ Sandpiper Inn
HOTEL **$$$**

(☏2672-0046; www.sandpipercostarica.com; r US$90-145; P❄🐾🏊) A central waterfront location with hammocks strung up so that guests can watch the surfing action in comfort, a little pool with a miniature waterfall, and comfortable rooms make this a top upmarket choice. It's hard not to make friends with Greg the owner and the grounds are full of iguanas and other local wildlife.

Marea Brava
RESORT **$$$**

(☏2643-7111; www.mareabravacostarica.com; r US$120, penthouse US$330; P❄🐾🏊) Tucked away into the northernmost corner of Hermosa's beachfront road, this creeper-clad hotel is one of the more characterful places in the village. The rooms are spacious and comfortable, but you can hang out by the two pools and bar even if you're not a guest (day pass US$14) and it's right on the waterfront. Very popular with weekending Ticos.

Eating

★ Bluegrass Cafe & Bakery
BAKERY **$**

(☏8945-9885; Costanera Sur; mains US$3-7; ⊙7am-3pm Wed-Sat, 7am-1pm Sun; 🐾) Hot cinnamon rolls, wholegrain and jalapeño-cheddar bread and banana-cream pies are all lovingly handmade by a superfriendly Texan – who also serves up pulled-pork and chicken curry with rice or in sandwich form. Worth a stop for quality baked goods and Shannon's impromptu bluegrass stylings. (There's also a bluegrass jam every Sunday afternoon; visiting musicians welcome.) Near the first beach entrance.

Jungle Surf Café
CAFE **$**

(meals US$5-9; ⊙8am-9pm Thu-Tue high season only) If you're looking for a quick bite between sets, this so-laid-back-it's-soporific cafe is a local institution that offers everything from kebabs and fish tacos to cold beer and fruit smoothies, but we're particularly keen on the seared tuna.

Backyard Bar
INTERNATIONAL **$**

(☏2643-7011; mains US$5-12; ⊙noon-late; 🐾) Backyard Bar's expansive menu serves the usual surfer fare (tacos, pizza, burritos), but none of it is likely to set your tastebuds alight. As the town's de facto nightspot, the Backyard Bar occasionally hosts live music, heavy pours at its nightly happy hour and a local surf contest every Saturday from 4pm until sunset (your chance to nab US$300!).

❶ Getting There & Away

Located only 5km south of Jacó, Playa Hermosa can be accessed by any bus heading south from Jacó. Frequent buses running up and down the Costanera Sur can easily pick you up, though determined surfers can always hail a taxi (with surf racks) or hitchhike.

Playa Esterillos

Only 15 minutes south of Jacó but a veritable world away, Playa Esterillos lures those who simply want to catch some surf, sun and scenery (sans scene), as there isn't much else to do along this miles-long expanse of beach. Playa Esterillos is signed off the highway in several sections: Esterillos Oeste (West), Centro (Central) and Este (East). Esterillos Oeste has a mini-supermarket, a couple of *sodas*, a tiny tour office and a Tico-village vibe absent in Jacó, while Esterillos Este has more of a resort feel, with upscale accommodations and a string of holiday homes along the beachfront.

🛏 Sleeping & Eating

Cheaper accommodations, popular with Ticos, are found in Esterillos Oeste, while Esterillos Este caters to a more upmarket clientele.

Hotel La Dolce Vita   HOTEL **$$**
(☑ 2778-7015; www.hotel-ladolcevita.biz; s/d from US$55/79; P ❄ 🛜 🐾) The intimate Hotel La Dolce Vita is just meters away from the beach. The pool may be small, but you can fall asleep, lulled by the sound of the waves, and in the morning have your breakfast served on your private terrace at a time of your choosing. The almond trees by the hotel attract scarlet macaws.

⭐**Alma del Pacífico**   RESORT **$$$**
(☑ 2778-7070, in the USA 410-727-6444; www.alma delpacifico.com; Esterillos Este; bungalow from US$305, villa from US$410; P ❄ 🛜 🐾) Each individually designed villa at this remarkable resort encompasses intriguing design elements, including wooden-lattice ceilings, sheer walls of glass framing private gardens, concrete-poured furniture done up with custom leatherwork, and impossibly intricate mosaic tile work. There is also an on-site restaurant specializing in gourmet and organic healthy fare, and an immaculate palm-fringed infinity pool that faces the crashing surf.

Hotel Pelicano   HOTEL **$$$**
(☑ 2778-8105; www.pelicanbeachcostarica.com; r/ste from US$94/170; P ♿ ❄ 🛜 🐾) The long-standing beachside Hotel Pelicano hits a sweet spot: it's affordable, safe, homey and on a dreamy stretch of the Pacific. The rooms are a bit rustic but open to balconies overlooking a small pool. Guests can take in sunsets, go surfing or splash around in the waves. The catch? It's fairly isolated; your only eating option is the on-site restaurant.

The hotel welcomes school groups and offers a variety of tours suitable for older children.

⭐**Los Almendros**   INTERNATIONAL **$$**
(☑ 2778-7322; Esterillos Oeste; mains from US$8; ⌚ 4-10pm Mon-Sat) Around 50m west of the soccer field in Esterillos Oeste, an expat has decided to take a global theme and run with it a few miles. The results? Delectable tuna steaks, Caribbean-style curry, red snapper with homemade salsa, pad thai, black-bean soup and more. The dishes are beautifully executed, the atmosphere convivial and the service sweet. It's worth traveling for.

ⓘ Getting There & Away

While buses connecting Jacó with Quepos can drop you off at the access roads into Playa Esterillos, getting there and around is easiest with your own set of wheels.

OFF THE BEATEN TRACK

PLAYA PALO SECO & AROUND

Playa Palo Seco (aka Isla Palo Seco) is a quiet, unhurried black-sand beach that's off the beaten track and located near mangrove swamps with good opportunities for bird-watching. Just south of the Río Parrita, a 6km dirt road connects the eastern edge of Parrita to the beach. Another popular excursion is to visit Isla Damas, which is actually the tip of a mangrove peninsula that becomes an island at high tide. Most people arrive here on package tours from Jacó or Quepos, though you can hire a boat to take you to and from the island.

It's worth making a detour to stay at **Beso del Viento** (☑ 2779-9674; www.besodel viento.com; incl breakfast r without/with air-con from US$84/108; P ❄ 🛜 🐾) if you relish privacy – this lovely, adult-only French-run B&B lives up to its name ('Kiss of the Breeze') and is located in a garden setting across the road from the isolated beach. Charming wooden-floored rooms are comfortably outfitted and decorated with an elegant eye for detail, with tiled bathrooms and immaculate linens. Your lovely hosts serve superb French meals, rent kayaks and bikes, and can arrange tours for guests.

Parrita is about 40km south of Jacó, and can be reached on any bus heading south from there. After Parrita, the coastal road dips inland through more palm-oil plantations on the way to Quepos.

SANDRA LEIDHOLDT / GETTY IMAGES ©

1. Jacó (p358)
Postcard-perfect sunsets in a bustling beach town.

2. Scarlet macaws, Parque Nacional Carara (p354)
Sightings of this beautiful species are virtually guaranteed at Carara.

3. Surfing at Jacó (p359)
Consistent year-round breaks make this a terrific place to learn how to surf.

4. White-faced capuchins, Parque Nacional Manuel Antonio (p383)
Spot these playful primates at Costa Rica's most popular national park.

PARQUE NACIONAL MANUEL ANTONIO & AROUND

As visitors arrive at this small outcrop of land jutting into the Pacific, the air becomes heavy with humidity, scented with thick vegetation and alive with the calls of birds and monkeys, making it suddenly apparent that *this* is the tropics. The reason to come here is the Parque Nacional Manuel Antonio, one of the most picturesque bits of tropical coast in Costa Rica.

If you get bored of cooing at the baby monkeys scurrying in the canopy and scanning for birds and sloths, the turquoise waves and perfect sand provide endless entertainment. However, as it's one of the country's most popular national parks, little Quepos, the once sleepy fishing and banana village on the park's perimeter, has ballooned with this tourism-based economy, and the road from Quepos to the park is overdeveloped. Despite this, the rainforested hills and the blissful beaches make the park a stunning destination worthy of the tourist hype.

Quepos

Located just 7km from the entrance to Manuel Antonio, the small, busy town of Quepos serves as the gateway to the national park, as well as a convenient port of call for travelers in need of goods and services. Although the Manuel Antonio area was rapidly and irreversibly transformed following the ecotourism boom, Quepos has largely retained an authentic Tico feel.

While many visitors to the Manuel Antonio area prefer to stay outside Quepos, accommodations in town are generally very good value, and there's a burgeoning restaurant scene that belies the town's small size. Quepos is also gridded with easy-to-walk streets, which provide the opportunity to interact with the friendly locals.

🏃 Activities

Diving

The dive sites are still being developed in the Quepos and Manuel Antonio area, and some of the diving outfits take customers as far as Isla del Caño. The dive sites are away from the contaminated beaches, so water pollution is not a problem when diving.

Oceans Unlimited DIVING
(☑ 2777-3171; www.scubadivingcostarica.com; 2-tank dive US$110) 🤿 This shop takes its diving very seriously, and runs most of its excursions out to Isla Larga and Isla del Caño, which is south in Bahía Drake (connected via a two-hour bus trip). It also has a range of specialized PADI certifications, and regular environmental-awareness projects that make it stand out from the pack.

It's located 400m up the road to Parque Nacional Manuel Antonio.

Sportfishing

Sportfishing is big here, and offshore ventures are said to be best from December to April, when sailfish are being hooked. By and large this is a high-dollar activity and you can expect to pay upwards of US$1000 to hire a boat for the day. If you want to shop around a bit, visit the office of **Marina Pez Vela** (☑ 2774-9000; www.marinapezvela.com), 500m south of the town center, which can connect you with captains of boats best suited to your needs.

Quepos Sailfishing Charters FISHING
(☑ 2777-2025, toll free in USA 800-603-0015; www.queposfishing.com) This Quepos-based outfitter gets good reviews from sportfishers and offers charters on a fleet of variously sized boats, whether you're after sailfish, marlin, dorado or wahoo. Rates vary significantly depending on season, number of people and size of boat. It also offers packages that include accommodations and transfers.

Tours

There are numerous reputable tour operators in the Quepos area, who specialize in everything from white-water rafting on nearby rivers and mangrove kayaking to newly introduced paddleboarding tours and waterfall tours of the Pacific coast.

★**Paddle 9** ADVENTURE TOUR
(☑ 2777-7436; www.paddle9sup.com; tours US$60-150) These new kids on the block are a young, passionate, safety-conscious team who've introduced SUP (stand-up paddleboarding) to Quepos (the tour leader's a pro) and who delight in showing visitors around the Pacific coast. Apart from their three-hour mangrove or ocean paddleboarding tours, their most popular outing is a seven-hour tour that involves swimming in various waterfalls, with a paddleboarding intro.

Unique Tours   ADVENTURE TOUR

(☏8396-0679, 2777-1119; www.costaricaunique tours.com) This established local operator organizes entertaining rafting tours of the Río Savegre, ocean and mangrove kayaking outings and more. But what makes them unique is that they're the only operator to do coastal hikes to Parque Nacional Manuel Antonio. Prices vary depending on group size.

H2O Adventures   ADVENTURE SPORTS

(Ríos Tropicales; ☏2777-4092; www.h2ocr.com) The venerable Costa Rican rafting company Ríos Tropicales has a hugely popular franchise in Quepos called H2O Adventures who organize rafting outings on the Naranjo, El Chorro and Savegre rivers, as well as kayaking and tubing outings. Rates for Class II to IV rapids are US$70.

Titi Canopy Tours   ADVENTURE TOUR

(☏2777-3130; www.titicanopytour.com; Costanera Sur; day/night tours US$70/80; ⊙tours 7:30am, 9:30am, 11:30am, 1:30pm, 3:30pm & 5:30pm) Offering zip-lining adventures during the day and night, this outfit has friendly, professional guides and a convenient location just outside of central Quepos (150m south of the hospital). Tour rates include drinks, snacks and local transportation; group discounts are available.

Iguana Tours   ADVENTURE TOUR

(☏2777-2052; www.iguanatours.com; ⊙6:30am-9pm) 🖉 With tours that leave for destinations all over the central Pacific coast, this adventure-travel shop offers reputable river rafting, sea kayaking, horseback riding, mangrove tours and dolphin-watching excursions. It's no fly-by-night operation – it's been around since '89 – and has a proven commitment to ecotourism principles, although it can be a bit disorganized sometimes.

🛏 Sleeping

Staying in Quepos offers a cheaper alternative to the sky-high prices at many lodges on the road to Manuel Antonio. It can also be more convenient, as all the banks, supermarkets and bus stops are in Quepos. Reservations are recommended during high-season weekends and are necessary during Easter and the week between Christmas and New Year's Eve.

⭐**Villas Jacquelina**   GUESTHOUSE $

(☏8345-1516; www.villasjacquelina.com; Calle 2; r US$35-70, apt US$130; P❄🛜❄) By far the best budget option in town, this large, ram-

RAINMAKER AERIAL WALKWAY

A privately owned rainforest, **Rainmaker Aerial Walkway** (☏2777-3565, in USA 540-349-9848; www.rainmakercosta rica.org; entry US$20, guided tours US$30-35) offered the first aerial walkway in Central America. From its tree-to-tree platforms, there are spectacular panoramic views of the surrounding primary and secondary rainforest and there are myriad opportunities here for great bird-watching as well as the occasional monkey sighting.

A large colorful sign marks the turnoff for Rainmaker on the Costanera Sur 15km west of Quepos.

bling building with various configurations of rooms (with/without bathrooms) is run by the indomitable Steve, an Arizonian transplant with energy to spare and tons of local knowledge, who can help arrange tours. There are large hangout spaces with hammocks and good breakfasts, and a vibe of friendly camaraderie prevails among guests.

Several rooms are geared toward families with kids, furniture-wise, and there's a child-friendly pool.

Pura Vida Hostel   HOSTEL $

(☏2777-2321; www.puravidahostelmanuelantonio. com; dm US$10-15, r per person US$15-20, all incl breakfast; ❄@🛜) From the rainbow-hued facade to the interior murals, this place is nothing if not colorful. The rooms have tropical-colored walls, bright linens, tile floors and lockers. Big, shared balconies overlook the jungle-covered hills, where you're likely to spot squirrel monkeys passing through. It's on the southern edge of town on the road to Manuel Antonio.

Hotel Papa's Papalotes   HOTEL $

(☏2777-3774; www.papaspapalotes.com; Av 2; s without/with air-con US$35/45, d without/with air-con US$45/55; ❄🛜) A decent budget choice in central Quepos, with private rooms a better bargain than at some nearby hostels. The decor won't make your social-media posts, but the place is clean and secure. If you opt for fan-only, you'll be woken up by the dawn chorus of traffic passing along the street; pack earplugs.

Quepos

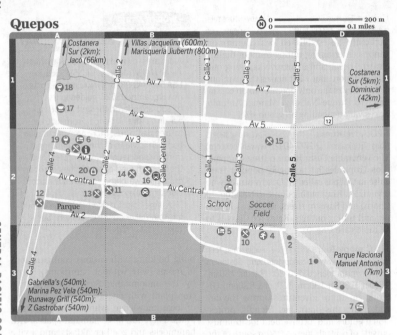

Quepos

⊙ Activities, Courses & Tours
1 H2O Adventures	D3
2 Iguana Tours	C3
3 Paddle 9	D3
4 Quepos Sailfishing Charters	C3

⊜ Sleeping
5 Hotel Papa's Papalotes	C3
6 Hotel Sirena	A2
7 Hotel Villa Romántica	D3
8 Wide Mouth Frog Backpackers	C2

⊗ Eating
9 Brooklyn Bakery	A2
10 Chicken On The Run	C3

11 Escalofrío	B2
12 Farmers' Market	A2
13 L'Italo	A2
14 Mercado Central	B2
15 Mini Price	C2
16 Soda Come Bien	B2

⊙ Drinking & Nightlife
17 Café Milagro	A1
18 Cuban Republik Disco Lounge	A1
Dos Locos	(see 11)
19 El Gran Escape	A2

⊙ Shopping
20 Jaime Peligro Books & Adventures	A2

Wide Mouth Frog Backpackers HOSTEL **$**
(☏ 2777-2798; www.widemouthfrog.org; Apartado 256; dm US$12, r with/without bathroom US$50/40; ⓟ❄@🛜🏊) Secure but resting on its laurels, this backpacker outpost has been overtaken by many local competitors. Pros? Spacious doubles, clean shared bathrooms, well-equipped kitchen and a large, open-air dining area that encourages socializing. Cons? Some staff members won't win congeniality prizes, the cheaper private rooms are cell-like, wi-fi is patchy and, dorms aside, the place is overpriced.

Breakfast is available for only US$3, there's a TV lounge with a free DVD library and wifi, a couple of lazy dogs padding around and a security guard watching the place and cars (street parking only) after hours. WMF is a perfect staging area for Manuel Antonio.

Hotel Sirena BOUTIQUE HOTEL **$$**
(☏ 2777-0572; www.lasirenahotel.com; Av 3; s/d incl breakfast from US$89/99; ⓟ❄🛜🏊) This intimate boutique hotel is a welcome part of the Quepos scene, and is easily the best midrange option in town. The Sirena's

whitewashed walls, blue trim and aromatherapy offer a slice of breezy Mediterranean serenity. In the rooms, guests enjoy crisp white linens, cable and a mini-fridge. Rooms upstairs get much better light but some windows face the corridor.

Hotel Villa Romántica HOTEL $$

(☑2777-0037; www.villaromantica.com; Av 4; s/d incl breakfast from US$68/98; P⊛@☎❋) A short walk southeast from the town center brings you to this peaceful garden oasis; rooms are dimly lit but comfortable enough, though the showers are threadbare and renovation is badly needed. If you're looking for a compromise between the convenience of staying in Quepos and the intimate proximity to nature found in Manuel Antonio, this is a passable choice.

✖ Eating

One benefit of staying in Quepos proper is the accessibility of a wide range of dining opportunities. The **Mercado Central** (Central Market; Av 1; meals from US$4; ☺hours vary) is packed with produce vendors and good *sodas* too numerous to list, so follow your nose and the locals. Self-caterers should also check out the **farmers' market** (Calle 4; ☺4pm Fri-noon Sat) near the waterfront, where you can buy directly from farmers, fisherfolk, bakers and other food producers.

★Marisquería Jiuberth SEAFOOD $

(☑2777-1292; mains from US$7; ☺11am-10pm) Run by a hardworking fisherman's family, this local institution with brightly tiled floors serves some of the best seafood in town, yet is practically unknown to visitors because it's tucked out of the way. Whether you have the catch of the day, or the moreish, satisfying fish soup, the portions are wonderfully generous and the service attentive. Follow unpaved Calle 2 out of town.

★Brooklyn Bakery BAKERY $

(Av 3; bagels US$1.50, mains US$5-8; ☺7:30am-6pm Mon-Sat; ☎☑) Real New York–style bagels and lox! (a real rarity in Costa Rica). Rye bread! Iced coffee! This adorable little bakery bakes its fresh wares every morning, as well as serving light bites throughout the day and delicious specials at lunchtime, such as Italian meatball sandwiches and oxtail ravioli.

L'Italo DELI $

(☑2777-4129; Calle 2; sandwiches US$5-7; ☺9am-6pm Mon-Sat) This deli makes excellent sandwiches with imported Italian meats and cheeses, served with a side of ill grace from the grumpy waiter, but perfect for toting on excursions to Manuel Antonio.

Chicken On The Run FAST FOOD $

(mains US$4-16; ☺8am-9pm Mon-Sat) If it's crispy fried chicken you're craving, this is the best little joint in town. Grab a wing or breast to go, or bring some friends for a sit-down meal of an entire roast chicken with all the trimmings. *Casados* are a bargain, too.

Soda Come Bien CAFETERIA $

(☑2777-2550; Av 1; mains US$3.50-8; ☺6am-5pm Mon-Sat, to 11am Sun) The daily rotation of delicious cafeteria options might include fish in tomato sauce, *olla de carne* (beef soup with rice) or chicken soup, but everything is fresh, the ladies behind the counter are friendly and the burly portions are a dream come true for hungry shoestringers. Or, pick up a fresh *empanada* before or after a long bus ride.

Mini Price SUPERMARKET $

(Av 5; ☺8am-9pm Mon-Sat, 10am-6pm Sun) Self-caterers rejoice! This large new supermarket stocks imported cheese, meats, chocolate and a vast array of wines, imported beers and liquor.

★Z Gastrobar FUSION $$

(☑2777-6948; Marina Pez Vela; mains US$15-25; ☺7:30am-10pm; P☎) Bright, open to the breeze from all sides and with colorful cushions strewn on its comfy couches, this is a terrific spot for lingering over a coffee and dessert, or over a lunch of dorado *ceviche* in coconut milk or an imaginative salad. The arty presentation matches the terrific flavors and the service is excellent.

Runaway Grill AMERICAN $$

(☑2519-9095; Marina Pez Vela; mains US$12-25; ☺noon-11pm; P⊛☎) An all-round crowd pleaser, Runaway Grill's menu spans steaks, wraps, salads, tacos, burgers, sandwiches and more. Portions are sizable and come with a sea view, the mint lemonades are refreshing and enormous, and the service is friendly (though they struggle sometimes when the place is packed).

Escalofrío ITALIAN $$

(☑2777-1902; Av Central; mains US$10-22; ☺2:30-10:30pm Tue-Sun; ⊛☎) Gelato lovers should make a point of stopping here, to choose from more than 20 flavors of the heavenly stuff. This spacious alfresco restaurant may also be the only game in town on Sunday night during slow season, a godsend especially if you enjoy thin-crust wood-fired pizza.

★ **Gabriella's** SEAFOOD **$$$**
(☑ 2519-9300; Marina Pez Vela; mains US$25-35; ⊙ 5-11pm; P ✳ 🔊) A serious contender for the region's best restaurant, Gabriella's does many things well. The veranda catches the sunset, the service is attentive, but the food is the real star, with a great emphasis on fresh fish and seafood. We're particularly big fans of the seared tuna with chipotle sauce and the spicy sausage and shrimp pasta. In a word: terrific.

 Drinking & Nightlife

The nightlife in Quepos has a good blend of locals and travelers, and it's cheaper than what you'll find in the Manuel Antonio area. If you are looking for something a bit more sophisticated, however, it's easy enough to jump in a taxi. Keep in mind that the action won't start warming up until around 10pm.

Café Milagro CAFE
(☑ 2777-1707; www.cafemilagro.com; Calle 4; ⊙ 7am-5pm Mon-Sat) Café Milagro sources its coffee beans from all over Costa Rica and produces a variety of estate, single-origin and blended roasts to suit any coffee fiend's palate, with 1% of its profits going to environmental causes via international nonprofit 1% for the Planet. Unlike its other, bigger branch en route to Manuel Antonio, this is takeout coffee only; no meals (drinks cost US$3.50 to US$7).

Cuban Republik Disco Lounge CLUB
(☑ 8345-9922; ⊙ 9pm-3am Thu-Sun) Cuban Republik hosts the most reliable party in central Quepos, and it has some kind of drink special nearly every night if you arrive early (before 10:30pm or 11pm). Later, the DJs get loud, the drinks get more pricey. Women get in for free before 11pm on Friday night and it's a nice, mixed Tico and gringo scene (cover charge is US$4).

El Gran Escape BAR
(☑ 2777-0395; Av 3; ⊙ 6am-11pm; 🔊) This long-standing pub has relocated back to central Quepos from Marina Pez Vela. Expect sports on the big screen, delicious (though pricey) burgers and prompt bar staff.

Dos Locos BAR
(☑ 2777-1526; Av Central; ⊙ 7am-11pm Mon-Sat, 11am-10pm Sun) This popular pseudo-Mexican restaurant is the regular watering hole for the local expat community, and serves as a venue for the occasional live band. Opening onto the central cross streets of town, its fun for people-watching (and cheap Imperials). There's an English-language trivia night every Thursday. Added bonus: breakfast is served all day.

ℹ️ **Orientation**

Downtown Quepos is a small checkerboard of dusty streets that are lined with a mix of local- and tourist-oriented shops, businesses, markets, restaurants and cafes. The town loses its well-ordered shape as it expands outward, but the sprawl is kept relatively in check by the mountains to the east and the water to the west.

BUSES FROM QUEPOS

Scheduled private shuttles, operated by Gray Line, Easy Ride and Monkey Ride, run between Quepos/Manuel Antonio and popular destinations such as Jacó (US$35), Monteverde (US$55), Puerto Jiménez (US$79), San José (US$49) and Uvita (US$35).

All buses arrive at and depart from the busy, chaotic main terminal in the center of town. If you're coming and going in the high season, buy tickets for San José in advance at the **Transportes Morales ticket office** (☑ 2777-0263; ⊙ 7-11am & 1-5pm Mon-Sat, 7am-1pm Sun) at the bus terminal; *colectivo* fares (not listed) to San José are slightly cheaper and take two hours longer.

DESTINATION	COST (US$)	TIME (HR)	FREQUENCY
Jacó	2.70	1½	10 daily 4:30am-5:30pm
Puntarenas	3.80	3	8 daily 4:30am-5:30pm
San Isidro de El General, via Dominical	3.80	3	5:30am, 11:30am, 3:30pm
San José	7	3½	6 daily 4:30am-4:45pm
Uvita, via Dominical	8	2	6:30am, 9:30am, 5:30pm

South of the town center is the Marina Pez Vela, whose marine slips opened to much fanfare in 2010, and which now features some of the best restaurants in town.

ⓘ Information

The best source of books for travelers within miles is **Jaime Peligro Books & Adventures** (🖉 2777-7106; www.queposbooks.com; Calle 2; ☉ 9:30am-5:30pm Mon-Sat), which has a complete selection of local guides, literature in a number of languages and tons of local information.

Look out for *Quepolandia*, a free English-language monthly magazine that can be found at many of the town's businesses.

Both **Banco de San José** (Av Central; ☉ 8am-5pm Mon-Fri) and **Coopealianza** (Av Central; ☉ 8am-5pm Mon-Fri) have 24-hour ATMs on the Cirrus and Plus systems. Other banks will all change US dollars and traveler's checks.

DANGERS & ANNOYANCES

Theft can be a problem, and the usual common-sense precautions apply: lock valuables in a hotel safe and never leave anything in a car.

When leaving bars late at night, walk in a group or take a taxi. Women should keep in mind that the town's bars attract rowdy crowds of plantation workers on weekends.

Note that the beaches in Quepos are polluted and not recommended for swimming. Go over the hill to Manuel Antonio instead, where some of the dreamiest waters in Costa Rica await.

ⓘ Getting There & Away

Both **NatureAir** (www.natureair.com) and **Sansa** (www.sansa.com) service Quepos. Prices vary according to season and availability, though you can pay a little less than US$75 for a flight from San José or Liberia. Flights are packed in the high season, so book (and pay) for your ticket well ahead of time and reconfirm often. The airport is 5km out of town, and taxis make the trip for a few thousand colones (do not pay more than US$8), depending on traffic.

ⓘ Getting Around

Buses between Quepos and Manuel Antonio (US$0.50) depart roughly every 30 minutes from the main terminal between 7am and 7pm, and less frequently after 7:30pm.

A number of international car-rental companies, such as **Budget** (🖉 2774-0140; www.budget.co.cr; Quepos Airport; ☉ 8am-5pm Mon-Sat, to 4pm Sun), operate in Quepos; reserve ahead and reconfirm to guarantee availability.

Colectivo taxis run between Quepos and Manuel Antonio (US$1 for a short hop). A private taxi will cost a few thousand colones. Catch one at the **taxi stand** (Av Central) south of the market. The trip between Quepos and the park should cost about US$15.

Quepos to Manuel Antonio

From the Quepos waterfront, the steep, narrow winding road swings uphill and inland for 7km before reaching the beaches of Manuel Antonio village and the entrance to the national park. This route passes over a number of hills awash with picturesque views of forested slopes leading down to the palm-fringed coastline.

This area is home to some of Costa Rica's finest hotels and restaurants and while shoe-stringers and budget travelers are catered for, this is one part of the country where those with deep pockets can bed down and dine out in the lap of luxury.

Watch out for local drivers careening around the bends at high velocities, and exercise caution and drive and walk with care, especially at night. Driving to Quepos from Manuel Antonio at around 6pm to 7pm means condemning yourself to sitting in practically immovable traffic.

◉ Sights & Activities

Manuel Antonio Nature Park & Wildlife Refuge   WILDLIFE RESERVE
(🖉 2777-0850; adult/child US$15/8; ☉ 8am-4pm; 🖈) This private rainforest preserve and butterfly garden breeds about three dozen species of butterfly – a delicate population compared to the menagerie of lizards, reptiles and frogs that inspire gleeful squeals from the little ones. A jungle night tour (5:30pm to 7:30pm, US$39/29 per adult/child) showcases the colorful local frogs and their songs, while day tours (US$15/8 per adult/child) introduce you either to the fluttering or the slithering denizens (or both; joint tickets US$25).

Amigos del Río   ADVENTURE TOUR
(🖉 2777-0082; www.adradventurepark.com; tours US$135) Pack all of your canopy-tour jungle fantasies into one day on Amigos del Río's '10-in-One Adventure,' featuring zip lining, a Tarzan swing, rappelling down a waterfall and more. The seven-hour adventure tour includes a free transfer from the Quepos and Manuel Antonio area as well as breakfast and lunch. Amigos del Río is also a reliable outfit for white-water-rafting trips.

X MARKS THE SPOT

Locals have long believed that a treasure worth billions and billions of dollars lies somewhere in the Quepos and Manuel Antonio area, waiting to be discovered. The legend was popularized by English pirate John Clipperton, who befriended the coastal Quepoa during his years of sailing to and from the South Pacific. Clipperton's belief stemmed from a rumor that in 1670 a number of Spanish ships laden with treasure escaped from Panama City moments before it was burned to the ground by Captain Henry Morgan. Since the ships were probably off-loaded quickly to avoid being raided at sea, a likely destination was the San Bernardino de Quepo Mission, which had strong loyalty to the Spanish crown.

John Clipperton died in 1722 without ever discovering the legendary treasure, and the mission closed permanently in 1746, as most of the Quepoa had succumbed to European diseases. Although the ruins of the mission were discovered in 1974, they were virtually destroyed and had long since been looted. However, if the treasure was indeed as large as it's described in lore, it is possible that a few gold doubloons could still be lying somewhere, waiting to be unearthed.

Manuel Antonio Surf School　SURFING
(MASS; ☑ 2777-4842, 2777-1955; www.manuelantoniosurfschool.com; group lesson US$65) MASS offers friendly, safe and fun small-group lessons daily, lasting for three hours and with a three-to-one student-instructor ratio. Find its stand about 500m up the Manuel Antonio road south of Quepos.

Cala Spa　SPA
(☑ 2777-0777, ext 220; www.sicomono.com; Hotel Sí Como No; treatments US$70-140; ⊙ 10am-7pm) If you're sunburned and sore from exploring Manuel Antonio – even better if you're not – the Cala Spa offers aloe body wraps, citrus salt scrubs and various types of massage to restore body and spirit. Open daily by appointment only.

🛏 Sleeping

The Quepos–Manuel Antonio road is skewed toward ultra-top-end hotels, but plenty of noteworthy midrange and budget options are hidden along the way. Low-season rates can be 40% lower than high-season rates. Reservations are a must for busy weekends and holidays. Although sleeping options along the Quepos–Manuel Antonio road are closer to the park than those in Quepos, many still require a taxi or a long walk along the busy road to reach the park.

★**Hostel Plinio**　HOSTEL $
(☑ 2777-6123; dm/d US$15/60; ❄ 🕏 🏊) Attuned to backpacker needs, Hostel Plinio ticks most boxes: a convenient location near Quepos, a large pool and ample common areas with hammocks and sofas for socializ-

ing, a gracious owner, an efficient tour desk and superior doubles with jungle views for couples wanting more privacy. The downside? The roadside location, meaning some rooms are noisy, and the wi-fi doesn't reach everywhere.

★**Vista Serena Hostel**　HOSTEL $
(☑ 2777-5162; www.vistaserena.com; incl breakfast dm US$11-18, bungalows without/with air-con US$50/60; P @ 🕏) Perched scenically on a quiet hillside, this memorable hostel allows gringo backpackers to enjoy spectacular ocean sunsets from a hammock-filled terrace and strum the communal guitar. Accommodations range from spartan econo-dorms to plusher dorms to bungalows for those who want a bit more privacy. Super-friendly owners Sonia and Conrad are commendable for their efforts in assisting countless travelers.

To top it off, a short trail hike through local farmland leads to a remote wilderness beach.

Backpackers Manuel Antonio　HOSTEL $
(☑ 2777-2507; www.backpackersmanuelantonio. com; dm/d incl breakfast US$12/35; P ❄ @ 🕏 🏊) This locally owned hostel has a very sociable vibe and a good location – relatively near the entrance of the park and walking distance from a good grocery store. The dorms are clean and secure (if small), and there's a grill and pool out back for socializing. Larger rooms, with a bunk and double bed, are good for groups of friends.

Didi's B&B　B&B $$
(☑ 2777-5185; www.didiscr.com; s/d US$58/67; ❄ 🕏 🏊) Run by a well-traveled Italian couple,

Didi's is the pick of the guesthouse lot, with four appealing rooms with TVs encroached on by the surrounding jungle. Opting for fan-only makes the room rate even more reasonable. Three-course Italian dinners (US$20) can be prepared on request using whatever owner Ezio has picked up at the market.

Hotel Mimos   HOTEL $$

(☎2777-0054; www.mimoshotel.com; d/ste from US$83/178; 🅿❄@🛜🏊) Run by kind and attentive staff, this whitewashed and wood-trimmed hotel has spacious, clean, terracotta-tiled rooms. The property is connected by lovely stone paths, bringing guests to two palm-fringed swimming pools, a glowing Jacuzzi and a restaurant serving Caribbean-influenced dishes. Investment in better mattresses and bed linen would go some way toward making this good place great.

Hotel Tres Banderas   HOTEL $$

(☎2777-1871; www.hoteltresbanderas.com; d/ste incl breakfast US$92/135; 🅿❄🛜🏊) This welcoming roadside inn is owned by a Polish-born US citizen – hence the very appropriate moniker, *tres banderas* (three flags). The 14 doubles and three suites are spacious affairs with imported tiles and local woods and, while some could use a bit of air, all come with jungle-facing terraces furnished with leather rocking chairs. Good for wildlife sightings.

Dinner is often prepared on an outdoor grill and guests congregate to dine together around the deep central pool, which lends a communal flourish to the property.

Hotel Mono Azul   HOTEL $$

(☎2777-2572; www.hotelmonoazul.com; r US$60-90, ste from US$125, child under 12yr free; 🅿❄@🛜🏊) The Mono Azul is decent value and a good family option – nestled in a tropical garden and decorated throughout in a rainforest theme, rooms are arranged around three pools. Skip the restaurant, though. Ten per cent of hotel receipts are donated to Kids Saving the Rainforest (KSTR), founded here by two local schoolchildren in 1999.

The girls were concerned about the endangered *mono tití* (Central American squirrel monkey). Many of these adorable critters were being run over on the narrow road to the national park or electrocuted on overhanging electrical cables, so KSTR purchased and erected monkey 'bridges' across the road (you can see them, often in use, as you head to the park). All proceeds from the hotel's on-site souvenir shop also go directly to KSTR.

★ Gaia Hotel & Reserve   BOUTIQUE HOTEL $$$

(☎2777-9797, in the USA 800-226-2515; www.gaiahr.com; r from US$435; 🅿❄🛜🏊) This luxurious pile comprises studios, terrace suites and three-story villas and offers nature tours within its expansive grounds – a former wildlife rehabilitation center. The restaurant – one of the best in the region – makes the most of fresh produce. Escapism and relaxation are greatly aided by the cascading pools and the spa treatments. Adults only.

★ Arenas del Mar   BOUTIQUE HOTEL $$$

(☎2777-2777; www.arenasdelmar.com; r incl breakfast US$374-860; 🅿❄🛜🏊) 🌿 This visually arresting hotel and resort complex is consistently shortlisted among Costa Rica's finest upscale hotels. The rooms are designed to incorporate the beauty of the natural landscape, to great effect, especially when you're staring down the coastline from the lofty heights of your private open-air Jacuzzi. Boons include wildlife roaming the property, expertly prepared seafood and the sustainability tour.

★ Hotel Sí Como No   HOTEL $$$

(☎2777-0777; www.sicomono.com; r US$260-328, ste US$401-424, child under 6yr free; 🅿❄🛜🏊) 🌿 This flawlessly designed hotel is an example of how to build an ecofriendly resort. The rooms are accented by rich woods and bold splashes of tropical colors, and come with sweeping balconies. The hotel has two pools (one for kids, one for adults only, both with swim-up bars), two Jacuzzis, a health spa and two excellent restaurants. Sustainable construction and practices include energy-efficient air-con units, recycling water for landscaping use and solar-powered

---

ℹ️ GOT KIDS?

The Quepos to Manuel Antonio stretch of road is home to the lion's share of accommodations and restaurants in these parts, but it's worth pointing out that many of the high-end boutique hotels and upscale eateries are not always very welcoming to babies and young children, so check your accommodations' policy.

If you find yourself walking along the narrow, winding road (there is no shoulder), keep a close eye on your children at all times.

Manuel Antonio Area

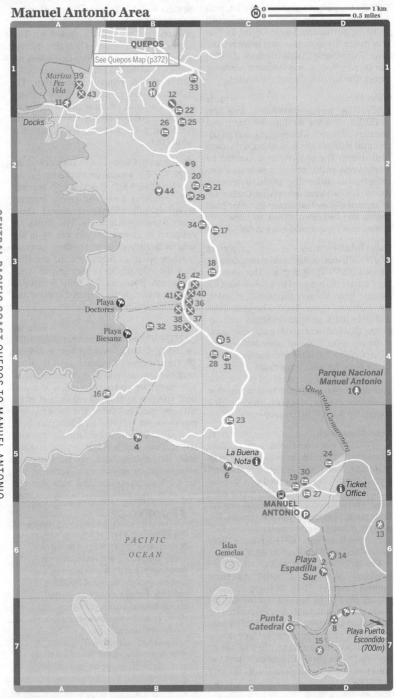

N
0 ————— 1 km
0 ————— 0.5 miles

QUEPOS
See Quepos Map (p372)

Marina Pez Vela
Docks

Playa Doctores

Playa Biesanz

Parque Nacional Manuel Antonio
Quebrada Camaronera

Ticket Office

La Buena Nota

MANUEL ANTONIO

PACIFIC OCEAN

Islas Gemelas

Playa Espadilla Sur

Punta Catedral

Playa Puerto Escondido (700m)

water heaters. No surprise, then, that Sí Como No is one of the 30-odd hotels in the country to have been awarded five out of five leaves by the government-run Certified Sustainable Tourism (CST) campaign.

Makanda by the Sea
VILLA $$$

(☎ 2777-0442; www.makanda.com; studio/villa incl breakfast from US$298/452; [P][✳][@][🖥][≈]) Comprising just six villas and five studios, in a stellar bluff-top location, Makanda has an unmatched air of intimacy and privacy. Villa 1 (the largest) will take your breath away – one entire wall is open to the rainforest and the ocean. The other villas and studios are air-conditioned and enclosed, though they draw upon the same minimalistic, Eastern-infused design schemes.

The grounds are also home to a beautiful infinity pool and Jacuzzi, both offering superb views out to sea, as well as a series of flawless Japanese gardens in which you can stroll and reflect on the beauty of your surroundings. And, if you're still not impressed, you can access a private beach by taking the 552 steps down the side of the mountain – bliss! Note that guests must be 16 or older.

Hotel Costa Verde
HOTEL $$$

(☎ 2777-0584; www.costaverde.com; efficiency units/studios from US$153/182, Boeing 727 home US$563; [P][✳][@][🖥][≈]) This collection of rooms and studios occupies a verdant setting frequented by troops of monkeys. Efficiency units incorporating teak trim and furnishings face the encroaching forest, while more expensive studios have full ocean views. Beware: the cheapest units are near the road! The most coveted accommodation is the airplane-tree-house hybrid made out of a decommissioned Boeing 727 fuselage.

The 727, which juts out of the jungle in the most surreal way, has two bedrooms with three queen-sized beds, two bathrooms, kitchenette and private terrace. The owners of Costa Verde are also the masterminds behind several eateries along the road to Manuel Antonio, including El Avión bar (also fashioned from a retired fuselage).

Manuel Antonio Area

CENTRAL PACIFIC COAST QUEPOS TO MANUEL ANTONIO

Babaloo Inn
HOTEL $$$

(✎2777-3461; www.babalooinn.com; r US$101-168; P✳🛜▣) Standard rooms at the Babaloo Inn come with private balcony overlooking a lush tropical garden. However, we're partial to the larger king rooms featuring dramatic ocean views, comfortable sitting area, over-sized beds and shower, small kitchenette and enough space for a family of four. All rooms come with fully stocked minibar and DVD player, perfect for a rainy day.

✗ Eating

Falafel Bar
MEDITERRANEAN $

(✎2777-4135; mains US$5-9; ⊘11am-7pm; 🛜✎) Adding to the diversity of cuisine to be found along the road, this falafel spot dishes up authentic Israeli favorites. You'll also find plenty of vegetarian options, including couscous, fresh salads, stuffed grape leaves, fab fruit smoothies and even french fries for the picky little ones.

Sancho's
MEXICAN $

(✎2777-0340; mains from US$5; ⊘8am-10pm; 🛜) A great view from the open-air terrace, potent house margaritas, excellent fish tacos and humongous chile verde burritos are just some of the draws at this friendly gringo-run joint. A place to knock back a few beers with friends in a convivial, chilled-out atmosphere, rather than woo your date.

Super Joseth
SUPERMARKET $

(✎2777-1095; ⊘7am-10pm) Although it's a godsend for self-caterers, Super Joseth is a grocery stop that's reflective of its location – a bit pricey, stocked with imported meats, cheeses, cookies and chocolate for foreign travelers, and very busy. It has an excellent wine and liquor selection and also sells sunblock and upscale picnic goods.

★ El Patio de Café Milagro
FUSION $$

(✎2777-2272; www.cafemilagro.com; mains from US$7; ⊘7am-10pm) This is a fine stop for fancy coffee drinks, and even better for decadent breakfasts (banana pancakes with macadamia nuts), sandwiches (mango mahimahi wrap) and sophisticated interpretations of Tico fare for dinner (Creole pork tenderloin). The patio itself is a lovely setting surrounded by tropical gardens; you can also order your sandwich packed for a picnic in the park.

★ Café Milagro
CAFE $$

(✎2777-0794; www.cafemilagro.com; mains US$8-23; ⊘7am-9:30pm; 🛜✎) With a menu full of vibrant, refreshing delectables – like gazpacho, salads tossed with mango and chaycote squash in passion-fruit dressing, fish tacos with chunky guacamole, or banana-macadamia pancakes – this appealing cafe is worth a stop morning, noon or night. Like its sister cafe in Quepos, it also serves a mean cuppa joe.

★ Lush Tapas & Lounge
FUSION $$

(✎2777-3939; Plaza Vista II; tapas US$10-12; ⊘3pm-late Mon-Sat; 🛜✎) On the 2nd floor of Plaza Vista II, the tables and chairs of this new tapas bar face the sunset and there are few better places to be at that time of day, cocktail in hand. There's a succinct tapas menu to complement your drink, with interesting flavor combinations and meticulous presentation. The mini-pulled-pork burgers and fish-and-mango *ceviche* stand out.

Agua Azul
INTERNATIONAL $$

(✎2777-5280; www.cafeaguaazul.com; meals US$10-25; ⊘11am-10pm Thu-Tue; 🛜) Perched on the 2nd floor with uninterrupted ocean views, Agua Azul is a killer lunch spot on this stretch of road – perfect for early morning park visitors who are heading back to their hotel. The breezy, unpretentious open-air restaurant, renowned for its 'big-ass burger,' also serves up the likes of fajitas, panko-crusted tuna and smoked-trout salad.

Claro Que Sí
SEAFOOD $$

(✎2777-0777; Hotel Sí Como No; meals US$9-22; ⊘11am-8pm; 🛜🍴) ✐ A casual, family-friendly restaurant that passes on pretension without sacrificing quality, Claro Que Sí proudly serves organic and locally sourced food items that are in line with the philosophy of its parent hotel, Sí Como No. Guilt-free meats and fish are expertly complemented with fresh produce, resulting in flavorful dishes typical of both the Pacific and Caribbean coasts.

Restaurante Barba Roja
SEAFOOD $$

(✎2777-0331; www.barbarojarestaurant.com; meals US$9-22; ⊘10am-10pm Tue-Sun) A Manuel Antonio area institution, the Barba Roja is both a lively bar and a seafood-and-steak spot with a respectable sushi menu and weekly specials (Friday is smoked-rib night). The terrace affords fantastic ocean views, best enjoyed with a local Libertas y La Segua craft brew (pints are US$6) or Mexican-style *michelada*.

La Luna
INTERNATIONAL $$

(✎2777-9797; www.gaiahr.com; Gaia Hotel; mains US$8-24; ⊘6am-11pm; 🛜✎) Unpretentious and friendly, La Luna makes a lovely spot for a special-occasion dinner, with a spectacular backdrop of jungle and ocean. An international menu offers everything from spicy tuna and mango tacos to mahimahi *ceviche* to lobster tails, with a Tico-style twist – such as grouper baked *en papillote*, with plantain purée and coconut milk. Separate vegetarian menu available.

⭐ **Kapi Kapi Restaurant**   FUSION $$$
(✆ 2777-5049; www.restaurantekapikapi.com; meals US$16-40; ⏰ 4-10pm; ❄ 🛜 🍴) While there is some stiff competition for the title of best restaurant in the area, this Californian creation certainly raises the bar. The menu at Kapi Kapi (a traditional greeting of the indigenous Maleku) spans the globe from America to Asia. Pan-Asian-style seafood features prominently; macadamia-nut-crusted-mahimahi, lobster ravioli and sugarcane-skewered prawns are all standouts.

🍹 Drinking & Nightlife

Ronny's Place   BAR
(✆ 2777-5120; www.ronnysplace.com; ⏰ noon-10pm) The insane views at Ronny's Place, of two pristine bays and jungle on all sides, make it worth a detour (just for a drink – don't bother eating here). While plenty of places along this stretch of road boast similar views, the off-the-beaten-path location makes it feel like a secret find. Look for the well-marked dirt road off the main drag.

El Avión   BAR
(✆ 2777-3378; ⏰ 11:30am-late; 🛜) Constructed around a 1954 Fairchild C-123 plane, allegedly purchased by the US government in the '80s for the Nicaraguan Contras but never used, this striking bar-restaurant is a great spot for a beer and stellar sunset-watching. Skip the food, though, and double-check the check, as complaints have been made about inaccuracies. In 2000 the enterprising owners of El Avión purchased the plane for the surprisingly reasonable sum of US$3000 (it never made it out of its hangar in San José because of the Iran-Contra scandal that embroiled Oliver North and his cohorts), and proceeded to cart it piece by piece to Manuel Antonio. It now sits on the side of the main road, where it looks as if it had crash-landed into the side of the hill.

Salsipuedes   BAR
(✆ 2777-5019; ⏰ 7am-10pm Wed-Mon) With fantastic views at sunset, Salsipuedes ('leave if you can') is a great place for tapas (US$7 to US$9) and beer – or for the more adventurous, cocktails made with *guaro* (a local fire-

water made with sugarcane). Leave if you can after a few of those! Quesadillas, *ceviche* and white bean and chicken stew are some of the tapas on offer.

☆ Entertainment

Sí Como No Cinema   CINEMA
(✆ 2777-0777; www.sicomono.com; Hotel Sí Como No; tickets US$7; ⏰ 8:30pm) This 45-seat theater shows a fun rotation of popular American movies. Admission is free if you spend US$10 at the hotel's restaurant or bar.

ℹ Information

La Buena Nota (✆ 2777-1002; buennota@racsa.co.cr; ⏰ 10am-6pm) A decent source of tourist information for this area.

ℹ Getting There & Away

Every 30 minutes or so local buses and shared taxis connect Quepos with Manuel Antonio (20 minutes). The public bus from Quepos will let you off anywhere along the road.

A word of caution: driver visibility is limited along parts of the narrow, steep and winding road, particularly during low-light and foul-weather conditions.

Manuel Antonio Village

As you travel the road between Quepos and Parque Nacional Manuel Antonio, the din from roaring buses, packs of tourists and locals hunting foreign dollars becomes increasingly loud, reaching its somewhat chaotic climax at Manuel Antonio village. Hordes descend on this tiny oceanside village at the entrance to the country's most visited national park. Don't show up all bright-eyed and bushy-tailed, expecting deserted beaches and untouched tropical paradise. Higher primates tend to be the most frequently sighted species, especially during the congested dry season, when tour groups arrive en masse.

But come here in low season or on a Monday, and you'll find a tranquil little village with waves sedately lapping at the white sand. And, when troops of monkeys climb down from the forest canopy to the tropical sands, you can get up close and personal with some marvelous wildlife.

🛏 Sleeping

The village of Manuel Antonio is the closest base for exploring the national park, though the selection of sleeping options is more

GAY GUIDE TO MANUEL ANTONIO

For jet-setting gay and lesbian travelers the world over, Manuel Antonio has long been regarded as a dream destination. Homosexuality has been decriminalized in Costa Rica since the 1970s – a rarity in all-too-often machismo-fueled, conservative Central America – and a well-established gay scene blossomed in Manuel Antonio soon after. Gay and lesbian travelers will find that it's unlike any other destination in the country.

It's not hard to understand why Manuel Antonio first started attracting gay travelers. Not only is the area stunningly beautiful but it has also long attracted liberal-minded individuals. There is a burgeoning artist community and a sophisticated restaurant scene; check out www.gaymanuelantonio.com for a full list of gay and gay-friendly accommodations, events, restaurants and bars.

Sights & Activities

During daylight hours, the epicenter of gay Manuel Antonio is the famous **La Playita**, a beach with a long history of nude sunbathing for gay men. Alas, the days when you could sun in the buff are gone, but La Playita is still widely regarded as a playful pick-up scene for gay men.

Sleeping

A significant number of hotels in the Manuel Antonio area advertise themselves as being gay-friendly and even the ones that don't are unlikely to discriminate. If you want to enjoy the freedom and peace of mind that comes with staying at exclusively gay accommodations, book a room at the gay-owned and operated Hotel Villa Roca, a collection of brightly whitewashed rooms and apartments situated around a central pool and sundeck. The expansive view from the pool takes in an uninterrupted view of the water and rocky offshore islands. This is also the place to catch incredible sunsets. Otherwise, Gaia Hotel & Reserve (p377) offers understated luxury amid its own private slice of protected wilderness.

Drinking & Nightlife

The Manuel Antonio area has always been proud to host one of the most sophisticated and cosmopolitan restaurant scenes on the central Pacific coast. A few venues have particularly good gay-oriented events. **Karma Lounge** (☏ 2777-7230; www.facebook.com/karmaloungema; ☷ 6pm-midnight Tue-Sun) is a friendly spot with an excellent happy hour and Lush (p380) serves imaginative tapas coupled with sunset views.

---

varied in Quepos or on the Quepos–Manuel Antonio stretch of road. It's also completely overrun with foreigners.

Backpackers Paradise Costa Linda　　　　　HOSTEL $
(☏ 2777-0304; www.costalindabackpackers.com; r per person from US$12; P❄@☎) Calling this backpacker pad a paradise is stretching the truth like a rubber band, but you can't beat the price when you can amble out to the beach or the national park in five minutes. While the staff is a bit harried, and the shared bathrooms could be cleaner, the cocktail and beer prices are easy on the wallet.

★ **Hotel Villa Roca**　　　BOUTIQUE HOTEL $$$
(☏ 2777-1349; www.villaroca.com; r/apt incl breakfast from $125/175; P❄☎☀) This gay-owned, intimate hotel caters to many of Manuel Antonio's gay travelers; it's particularly popular with men. The upstairs rooms are breezier. All guests and visitors must be 18 years or older. You can sun your buns around the beautiful, clothing-optional pool, where you may be joined by a couple of resident iguanas.

Hotel Vela Bar　　　　　HOTEL $$$
(☏ 2777-0413; www.velabar.com; r US$110-160, casita from US$130, ste from US$180; P❄@☎) This attractive little hotel offers light, bright, spacious and contemporary rooms and suites, set around an oval pool and overlooking lush gardens. Its rooms recently underwent a serious upgrade, and the price tag and the comfort are worth it, considering that you can stroll over to the park entrance in two minutes.

Hotel La Posada · BUNGALOW $$$
(☎ 2777-1446; www.laposadajungle.com; bungalows incl breakfast US$110-135, apt US$185-235; P ❃ 🛜 🏊) These secluded jungle bungalows and fully equipped apartments (sleeping four to six guests) all come with kitchenette, TV with DVD player, safe and terrace, and are clustered around a small pool. But the real beauty of staying here is the location right next to the park – from your lodgings you'll see squirrel monkeys and other wildlife crisscrossing the trees and rooftops.

Hotel Playa & Cabinas Espadilla · HOTEL $$$
(☎ 2777-2113, 2777-0903; www.espadilla.com; cabina/r from US$127/200; P ❃ 🛜 🏊) Two favorably located properties in one: the hotel is centered on a smallish swimming pool and tennis courts, and the more affordable *cabinas* across the road are slightly closer to the beach. While the accommodations are fairly bland for the price, and the hot water could be more consistent, you do have extremely convenient park and beach access from here.

ℹ Information
La Buena Nota (☎ 2777-1002; ⊙ 8am-6pm), at the northern end of Manuel Antonio village, serves as an informal tourist information center.

ℹ Getting There & Away

BUS
The bus stop in Manuel Antonio is at the end of the road into the village that runs along the beach. Buses depart Manuel Antonio beach for San José (US$9.10, three hours) 15 times daily between 4am and 5:30pm. Buy tickets well in advance at the Quepos bus terminal.

Buses for destinations other than San José leave from the main terminal in Quepos.

Local buses (US$0.50, 20 minutes, every 30 minutes) and shared taxis connect Manuel Antonio village with Quepos.

CAR
Driving the winding 7km road between Quepos and Manuel Antonio village on any day but Monday means spending time in traffic jams and potentially exorbitant parking fees.

Parque Nacional Manuel Antonio

A place of swaying palms and playful monkeys, sparkling blue water and a riot of tropical birds, **Parque Nacional Manuel Antonio** (☎ 2777-0644; park entrance US$16; ⊙ 7am-4pm Tue-Sun) is the country's smallest (just 19.83 sq km) and most popular national park. It became a protected area in 1972, preserving it from being razed to make room for a coastal development project. It's a truly lovely place; the clearly marked trail system winds through rainforest-backed white-sand beaches and rocky headlands, the wildlife (iguanas, sloths, monkeys) is plentiful, and the views across the bay to the pristine outer islands are gorgeous.

The downside? The crowds. Visitors are confined to around 6.8 sq km of the park (the rest is set aside for ranger patrols battling poaching) and the place gets packed when mid-morning tour buses roll in. Get here early (7am) and head for the furthest reaches of the park for a bit of tranquillity and the best chances to spot wildlife.

👁 Sights
There are four beautiful beaches – three within the park and one just outside the park entrance. The beaches are often numbered – most people call Playa Espadilla (outside the park) '1st beach,' Playa Espadilla Sur '2nd beach,' Playa Manuel Antonio '3rd beach,' Playa Puerto Escondido '4th beach' and Playa Playitas '5th beach.' Some people begin counting at Espadilla Sur, which is the first beach in the park, so it can be a bit confusing trying to figure out which beach people may be talking about. Regardless, they're all equally pristine, and provide sunbathing opportunities; check conditions with the rangers to see which ones are safe for swimming.

Playa Espadilla · BEACH
This wide stretch of white sand is found just outside the park entrance, in front of Manuel Antonio village.

★ Playa Espadilla Sur · BEACH
The exposed Playa Espadilla Sur is to the north of Punta Catedral and swimming here can be dangerous. The beach is a half-hour hike from the park entrance.

★ Punta Catedral · POINT
Geography fun fact: this isthmus that's the centerpiece of the park is called a *tombolo* and was formed by the accumulation of sand between the mainland and the peninsula beyond, which was once an island. At its end, the isthmus widens into a rocky peninsula, with thick forest in the middle, encircled by Sendero Punta Catedral. There

are good views of the Pacific Ocean and various rocky islets – nesting sites for brown boobies and pelicans.

Along this land bridge are the park's two amazing beaches, Playa Manuel Antonio, on the ocean side, and the slightly less visited (and occasionally rough) Playa Espadilla Sur, which faces Manuel Antonio village. With their turquoise waters, shaded hideouts and continual aerial show of brown pelicans, these beaches are dreamy.

Playa Manuel Antonio   BEACH
With its turquoise waters, this lovely beach fronts a deep bay, sheltered by the Punta Catedral on the west side and a promontory on the east. This is the best beach for swimming, but it also gets the most crowded with picnicking families, so get here early.

Turtle Trap   ARCHAEOLOGICAL SITE
At the western end of Playa Manuel Antonio you can see a semicircle of rocks at low tide. Archaeologists believe that these were arranged by pre-Columbian indigenous people to function as a turtle trap. (Turtles would swim in during high tide, but when they tried to swim out after the tide started receding, they'd be trapped by the wall.)

Playa Puerto Escondido   BEACH
This gorgeous horseshoe-shaped beach, accessed via the Sendero Puerto Escondido, is only reachable at low tide, so check with rangers first or risk getting stranded. Strong currents preclude swimming, but it's excellent for sunbathing.

🏃 Activities
The average daily temperature is 27°C (80°F) and average annual rainfall is 3875mm. The dry season is not entirely dry, merely less wet, so you should be prepared for rain (although it can also be dry for days on end). Make sure you carry plenty of drinking water, sun protection and insect repellent. Pack a picnic lunch if you're spending the day.

Hiking
Sendero El Perezoso   HIKING
The main trail (1.3km) that connects the park entrance with the other trails is paved and wheelchair-accessible. A new trail was added in 2015, its boardwalk parallel to the road; it provides a quieter alternative to the crowds along the main stretch. Here you'll find numerous tour groups trying to spot birds and sloths through their guides' telescopes.

A bit of eavesdropping on the numerous guides along this stretch will provide solo shoestring travelers an informal lesson on the many birds, sloths and monkeys along the way.

Sendero La Catarata   HIKING
This 900m trail branches off the main Sendero El Perezoso and leads to an appealing little waterfall.

Sendero Principal   HIKING
The longest trail in the park, the 2.2km Sendero Principal fringes Playa Espadilla Sur in the Manuel Antonio village.

★ Sendero Punta Catedral   HIKING
This 1.4km loop takes in the whole of Punta Catedral, passing through dense vegetation and with glorious views of the Pacific and the offshore islands. The blink-and-you'll-miss-it 200m Sendero La Tampa cuts across part of the loop.

Sendero El Mirador   HIKING
Heading inland and into the forest from the east side of Playa Manuel Antonio, this 1.3km trail climbs to a lookout on a bluff overlooking Puerto Escondido and Punta Serrucho beyond – a stunning vista. Rangers reportedly limit the number of hikers on this trail to 45.

Sendero Playas Gemelas
& Puerto Escondido   HIKING
This, the second-longest trail in the park (1.6km), is steep and slippery during the wet months and leads to the quiet Playa Puerto Escondido through dense forest and across a creek. For Playas Gemelas, take the turnoff halfway along.

Wildlife-Watching
Increased tourist traffic has taken its toll on the park's wildlife, as animals are frequently driven away or – worse still – taught to scavenge for tourist handouts. To its credit, the park service has reacted by closing the park on Monday and limiting the number of visitors to 600 per day during the week and 800 per day on weekends and holidays.

Even though visitors are funneled along the main access road, you should have no problem seeing animals here, even as you line up at the gate. White-faced capuchins are very used to people, and normally troops feed and interact within a short distance of visitors; they can be encountered anywhere along the main access road and around Playa Manuel Antonio. The capuchins are the worst culprits for snatching bags, so watch your stuff.

You'll probably also hear **mantled howler monkeys** soon after sunrise. Like capuchins, they can be seen virtually anywhere inside the park and even along the road to Quepos – watch for them crossing the monkey bridges that were erected by several local conservation groups.

Coatis can be seen darting across various paths and can get aggressive on the beach if you're eating. Three-toed and two-toed **sloths** are also common in the park. Guides are extremely helpful in spotting sloths, as they tend not to move around all that much.

However, the movements of the park's star animal and Central America's rarest primate, namely the **Central American squirrel monkey**, are far less predictable. These adorable monkeys are more retiring than capuchins, and though they are occasionally seen near the park entrance in the early morning, they usually melt into the forest well before opening time. With luck, however, a troop could be encountered during a morning's walk, and they often reappear in beachside trees and on the fringes of Manuel Antonio village in the early evening.

Offshore, keep your eyes peeled for pantropical spotted and bottlenose **dolphins**, as well as humpback **whales** passing by on their regular migration routes. Other possibilities include orcas (killer whales), false killers and rough-toothed dolphins.

Big **lizards** are also a featured sighting at Manuel Antonio – it's hard to miss the large ctenosaurs and green iguanas that bask along the beach at Playa Manuel Antonio and in the vegetation behind Playa Espadilla

Sur. To spot the well-camouflaged basilisk, listen for the rustle of leaves along the edges of the trails, especially near the lagoon.

Manuel Antonio is not usually on the serious bird-watchers' trail of Costa Rica, though the list of **birds** here is respectable. The usual suspects include the blue-gray and palm tanagers, great-tailed grackles, bananaquits, blue dacnises and at least 15 species of hummingbird. Among the regional endemics you should look out for are the fiery-billed aracaris, black-hooded antshrikes, Baird's trogons, black-bellied whistling ducks, yellow-crowned night herons, brown pelicans, magnificent frigate birds, brown boobies, spotted sandpipers, green herons and ringed kingfishers.

Tours

Hiring a wildlife guide costs US$20 per person (two-person minimum) for a two-hour tour. In the past, the only guides allowed in the park were members of Aguila (a local association governed by the park service), and recognized guides from tour agencies or hotels. However, these days the guys wearing Aguila shirts tend to be parking touts, and uncertified guides hang around by the park entrance, essentially charging tourists money for the privilege of looking through their telescope.

To make sure you find someone who is able to spot animals and birds and explain their role in the park ecosystem, opt for recommended guides such as **Lenny Montenegro** (☑ 8875-0437), or else ask to see the guide's ICT (Costa Rican Institute of Tourism) license to ascertain that they're the real deal.

ⓘ MONKEY BUSINESS

There are a number of stands on the beach that cater to hungry tourists, though everything is exuberantly overpriced and of dubious quality. Plus, all the food scraps have negatively impacted the monkey population. Before you offer a monkey your scraps, consider the following risks to their health:

➡ Monkeys are susceptible to bacteria transmitted from human hands.

➡ Irregular feeding will lead to aggressive behavior as well as create a dangerous dependency (picnickers in Manuel Antonio suffer downright intimidating mobs of them sometimes).

➡ Bananas are not their preferred food, and can cause serious digestive problems.

➡ Increased exposure to humans facilitates illegal poaching as well as attacks from dogs.

It goes without saying: don't feed the monkeys. And, if you do happen to come across someone doing so, take the initiative and ask them politely to stop.

We can testify to the fact that hiring a good guide dramatically improves your chances of wildlife sightings and lets you see animals and birds that you most likely would not have spotted by yourself.

ℹ Information

The **ticket office** (📞 2777-5185; park entrance US$16; ⏰7am-4pm Tue-Sun) is around 20m from the park entrance on your left. The ranger station is just before Playa Manuel Antonio.

DANGERS & ANNOYANCES

Watch out for the manzanillo tree (*Hippomane mancinella*) – it has poisonous fruits that look like little crab apples, and the sap exuded by the bark and leaves is toxic, causing the skin to itch and burn. Warning signs are prominently displayed beside examples of this tree near the park entrance.

ℹ Getting There & Away

The entrance and exit to Parque Nacional Manuel Antonio lies in Manuel Antonio village, connected to Quepos by frequent daily buses (20 minutes, every 30 minutes). Buses also depart for San José (US$9.10, three hours) 15 times daily between 4am and 5:30pm, some stopping in Quepos, some not.

Note that the road to Manuel Antonio is very narrow and congested, so it's suggested that you leave your car at your hotel and take an early morning bus to the park entrance instead, then simply walk in.

LA COSTA BALLENA

South of Quepos, the well-trodden central Pacific tourist trail begins to taper off, evoking the feel of the Costa Rica of yesteryear – surf shacks and empty beaches, roadside *ceviche* vendors and a little more space. Intrepid travelers can have their pick of any number of deserted beaches and great surf spots. The region is also home to the great bulk of Costa Rica's African palm–oil industry, which should be immediately obvious after the few dozen kilometers of endless plantations lining the sides of the Costanera.

QUALMS ABOUT PALMS

As you drive the Interamericana between Jacó and Quepos, or the roads leading to Puerto Jiménez and Sierpe, you can hardly fail to notice the vast expanses of African palms growing in regimental lines. Their fruit is harvested and processed into palm oil, a versatile product in cooking oils, biofuel, chocolate, cosmetics, chemical and farming industries – you name it!

Within three years of planting, the palms are ready for harvesting and a single hectare of palms can produce up to 30 metric tons of fruit bunches annually. Seed pods are cut from the tree, then steamed at processing plants to separate the seeds, which are then passed through a grinder to release oil.

The first palms were planted in Costa Rica in 1897 in order to diversify the holdings of the American-owned United Fruit Company, and later they replaced bananas as Costa Rica's biggest cash crop following the banana blight in the 1940s. Today, Costa Rica is the leading producer of palm oil in the Americas, and Palma Tica is the largest producer of palm oil in the country.

Much of the work in Costa Rican oil palm plantations is done by Nicaraguan migrant workers, as it's demanding and badly paid. Workers are required to keep the palms free of insects, so they must clear growth on the forest floor between the palms and apply poison to the trunks. There's a certain element of danger involved; the dry palm leaves and undergrowth between the rows of palms is the favorite habitat of the fer-de-lance, one of Costa Rica's deadliest snakes.

Those travelers who've seen the devastation caused by palm-oil cultivation in Indonesia, Malaysia and elsewhere – deforestation, the destruction of primary forests and habitats of endangered animals – will look at these kilometers of palm-oil plantations with some dismay. There are ways of producing palm oil in a sustainable manner and in accordance with global ethical standards, as certified by the Roundtable on Sustainable Palm Oil (www.rspo.org), but that is not happening with all Costa Rican palm-oil producers. Palma Tica, for example, has received a fair amount of bad press due to environmental degradation caused by its rendering plants, as well as for child and international migrant labor issues.

Known as the Costa Ballena, the beauteous length of coastline between Dominical and Ojochal focuses on three things: surfing (Dominical), whale-watching (Uvita) and gourmet cuisine (Ojochal). For the time being, the area retains an easygoing, unjaded allure despite the growing numbers discovering its appeal.

Matapalo

Off the Quepos–Dominical stretch of highway, Matapalo has been off most travelers' radar screens, though without good reason, as this vast, palm-fringed, gray-sand beach has some truly awesome surf. With two river-mouth breaks generating some wicked waves, Matapalo is recommended for intermediate to advanced surfers who are comfortable dealing with rapidly changing conditions, though there's usually a local lifeguard on duty. Matapalo is not the best beach for swimming as the transient rips here are about as notorious as they come, but it's perfect for sunbathing and observing the surfing action.

Sleeping & Eating

The accommodations are spread along the beach, with a couple of options along the access road that links the main village with the beach.

Albergue Suiza GUESTHOUSE $
(☑2787-5220; r from US$38; P❄🛜) Slightly set back from the beach road, this Swiss-run guesthouse is the best budget bet for Matapalo, with nine super-clean guest *cabinas* (air-con costs US$15 extra per night).

⭐**Charlie's Jungle House** GUESTHOUSE $$
(☑8544-3144, 2787-5005; www.charliesjunglehouse.com; r US$65-85; P❄🛜🐾) Run by the effusive Tricia, this guesthouse halfway along the beach road has five spacious, jungle-themed and colorful rooms, the largest with kitchenettes. The on-site Jungle Cafe serves wholesome meals. Tricia is hugely knowledgeable about the area, and arranges outings for guests – from trips to the local waterfalls to horseback riding and surfing lessons.

Dreamy Contentment BUNGALOW $$
(☑2787-5223; www.dreamycontentment.com; bungalow/villa from US$84/452; P❄🛜) By the beach, this Spanish-colonial property with impressive woodworking and towering trees throughout offers bungalows equipped with functional kitchenettes, the cheapest geared toward backpacking couples. The real star attraction is the villa, which has the kitchen of your dreams, a beachfront veranda and a princely bathroom complete with hot tub.

Rafiki Beach Camp CABINA $$$
(☑2787-5014; www.rafikibeach.com; tent incl breakfast US$119-128; ❄🛜🏊) Near the end of the beach road you'll find these friendly and laid-back luxury safari-style beachfront tents – all with electricity, tiled bathroom with hot shower and ocean views. There's a pool overlooking the ocean, adjacent to a *rancho* with a communal kitchen. Many guests stay here in conjunction with Rafiki Safari Lodge packages, kayaking down to Matapalo.

⭐**Langosta Feliz** SEAFOOD $$
(☑2777-5214; mains US$7-25; ⏱8am-10pm) Right across the Interamericana from the entrance to Matapalo village, this informal place serves some of the best seafood around. The lobster may or may not be happy, but diners certainly are, when presented with a seafood platter overflowing with razor clams, mussels, crab claws and lobster. A 'small' platter is plenty for two. Grilled fish and breakfasts also available.

Getting There & Away

Buses between Quepos and Dominical can drop you off at the turnoff to the village; from there it's a couple of kilometers to this off-the-beaten-track beach. There are also four buses daily from Quepos to Matapalo at 5:30am, 9:30am, 11:30am and 3:30pm (US$1.20, 30 minutes) that enter the village proper.

Hacienda Barú National Wildlife Refuge

Located on the Pacific coast 3km northeast of Dominical on the road to Quepos, this wildlife refuge (☑2787-0003; www.haciendabaru.com; admission US$10; ⏱7am-5pm) forms a key link in a major biological corridor called the Path of the Tapir. It comprises around 330 hectares of private and state-owned land that has been protected from hunting since 1976. The range of tropical habitats that may be observed here include pristine beaches, riverbanks, mangrove estuaries, wetlands, primary and secondary forests, tree plantations and pastures.

OGPHOTO / GETTY IMAGES ©

1. Parque Nacional Marino Ballena (p399) **2.** Humpback whale breaching, Parque Nacional Marino Ballena (p399) **3.** Tanager (p495) **4.** Catarata Manantial de Agua Viva (p356)

CLAUDE HUOT / SHUTTERSTOCK ©

Reserves of the Central Pacific Coast

Costa Rica's best road trip follows the Costanera Sur, along a string of fantastic natural parks. With wet and dry tropical forests and long beaches, these parks are alive with brightly colored birds, curious monkeys and a veritable army of iguanas – all of which show off the country's stunning biodiversity.

Rancho La Merced National Wildlife Refuge (p396) Surrounding Parque Nacional Marino Ballena on the southern part of the central Pacific coast, this former cattle ranch has excellent horse trails, primary and secondary forest, and miles of mangrove channels.

Parque Nacional Marino Ballena (p399) It's appropriate that this lovely, relatively quiet national park is shaped like a whale's tail; from the beaches it's possible to spot the migrating giants as they swim near shore.

Hacienda Barú National Wildlife Refuge (p387) Excellent trails and naturalist-led hikes make this the best birdwatching spot on the central Pacific coast. And just in case spotting rare tropical birds doesn't thrill you, there's also a zip line.

Catarata Manantial de Agua Viva (p356) With macaws overhead, this picture-perfect jungle waterfall drops 183m from one swimmable pool to the next. It's best during the rainy season, when the flows are full.

WORTH A TRIP

RAFIKI SAFARI LODGE

Nestled into the rainforest, with a prime spot right next to the Río Savegre, the **Rafiki Safari Lodge** (☎2777-2250, 2777-5327; www.rafikisafari.com; s/d incl all meals from US$167/289, child under 5yr free; ⓟ@🛜🏊) 🐾 combines all the comforts of a hotel with the splendor of a jungle safari – and getting here is half the fun. The owners, South African expats who have lived in the area for years, have constructed 10 luxury tents on stilts equipped with modern bathroom, private porch and hydroelectric power. All units are screened in, allowing you to see and hear the rainforest without actually having creepy-crawlies in your bed. There's a spring-fed pool with a serious waterslide and ample opportunities for horseback riding, bird-watching (more than 350 species have been identified), hiking, white-water rafting and unplugging. And of course, South Africans are masters on the *braai* (BBQ), so you know that you'll eat well alongside other guests in the *rancho*-style restaurant. This place makes for a great three-day stay; it's too remote to warrant the transport for only one night, but guests exhaust all the activities on offer after three days.

The entrance to the lodge is located about 15km south of Quepos in the small town of Savegre. From here, a 4WD dirt road parallels the Río Savegre and leads 7km inland, past the towns of Silencio and Santo Domingo, to the lodge. However, if you don't have private transportation, the lodge can arrange all of your transfers with advance reservations. Word to the wise: bring your own flashlight to supplement the standard-issue loaner that comes with your room keys.

This diversity of habitat plus its key position in the Path of the Tapir account for the multitude of species that have been identified in Hacienda Barú. These include 351 birds, 69 mammals, 94 reptiles and amphibians, 87 butterflies and 158 species of tree. Ecological tourism provides this wildlife refuge with its only source of funds, so guests are assured that money spent here will be used to further the conservation of tropical rainforest.

🏃 Activities & Tours

There is an impressive number of guided tours on offer. You can experience the rainforest canopy in three ways – a platform 36m above the forest floor, tree climbing, and a zip line called 'Flight of the Toucan.' In addition to the canopy activities, Hacienda Barú offers bird-watching tours, hiking tours, and two overnight camping tours in both tropical rainforest and lowland beach habitats. Hacienda Barú's naturalist guides come from local communities and have lived near the rainforest all of their lives. Even if you don't stop here for the sights, the on-site store carries an excellent selection of specialist titles for bird-watchers.

For people who prefer to explore the refuge by themselves, there are 7km of well-kept and marked, self-guided trails, a bird-watching tower, 3km of pristine beach, an orchid garden and a butterfly garden.

🛏 Sleeping & Eating

Hacienda Barú Lodge LODGE $$
(r incl breakfast $96-107; ⓟ🛜) Hacienda Barú Lodge consists of six clean, fan-cooled two-bedroom cabins located 350m from Barú beach. Guests staying here receive free admission to the refuge.

Hacienda Barú Restaurant COSTA RICAN $
(mains from US$7; ⊙8am-9pm) This red-tile-roofed, open-air restaurant by the ticket office serves a variety of tasty Costa Rican dishes.

ⓘ Getting There & Away

The Quepos–Dominical–San Isidro de El General bus stops outside the hacienda entrance. The San Isidro de El General–Dominical–Uvita bus will drop you off at the Río Barú bridge, 2km from the hacienda office.

A taxi from Dominical costs about US$7.

If you're driving, the El Ceibo gas station, 50m north of the Hacienda Barú Lodge, is the only one for a good distance in any direction.

Dominical

Dominical hits a real sweet spot with the travelers who wander up and down its rough dirt road with a surfboard under an arm, balancing the day's activities between surfing and hammock hang time. And although some may decry the large population of expats and gringos who have hunkered down here and the sheer volume of cars on its main street, proud residents are quick to point out that Dominical recalls the mythical 'old Costa Rica' – the days before the roads were all paved, and when the coast was dotted with lazy little towns that drew a motley crew of surfers, backpackers and affable do-nothings alike. Dominical has no significant cultural sights, no paved roads and no chain restaurants, but for those who come here to surf or to swing in a hammock, the place is just right.

◉ Sights

★Cataratas Nauyaca   WATERFALL

(☑ 2787-0541, 2787-0542; www.cataratasnauyaca. com; horseback tour US$70, hike admission US$5; ☺ tours depart 8am Mon-Sat) This center, owned and operated by a Costa Rican family, is home to the coast's most impressive waterfalls, which cascade through a protected reserve of both primary and secondary forest. The family runs horseback-riding tours to the falls (reservations required; Dominical pickup available), where visitors can swim in the inviting natural pools. Alternatively, you can hike to the falls in one hour or so if you're in decent shape.

The center is located 10km up the road from Dominical to San Isidro.

★Alturas

Animal Sanctuary   NATURE RESERVE

(☑ 2200-5440; www.alturaswildlifesanctuary.org; minimum donation adult/under 12yr US$25/15; ☺ 9-11am & 1-3pm Tue-Sun) Around 1.5km east and uphill from Dominical, this animal sanctuary takes in injured and orphaned animals as well as illegal pets, its mission being to rehabilitate those that can be and reintroduce them to the wild, and look after those that cannot. During the two-hour tour you're introduced to its residents: a macaw missing an eye, monkeys that were caged since infancy, Bubba the famous coatimundi, a caracara with a psychological problem and more. Entertaining, educational and a terrific cause.

Parque Reptilandia   ZOO

(☑ 8308-8855, 2787-0343; www.crreptiles.com; adult/child US$12/6; ☺ 9am-4:30pm; P ⊞) This reptile and amphibian haven, 7km up the Dominical–San Isidro road, is home to everything from alligators and crocodiles to turtles and poison-dart frogs. Our favorite is the viper section, where you can see Costa Rica's deadliest creatures, such as the fer-de-lance, pit viper and the black-headed bushmaster. Friday is feeding day, with live mice introduced into snake enclosures, which your kids may or may not love. Don't miss the ginormous anaconda!

☂ Activities & Tours

Pineapple Kayak Tours   KAYAKING

(☑ 8362-7655, 8873-3283; www.pineapplekayak tours.com; tours US$20-75) Run by a friendly young Tico-American couple, Pineapple Kayak Tours runs kayaking and stand-up paddleboarding (SUP) trips to local caves, rivers and mangrove forests. Find its office next to the police station in Dominical. The newest addition to the roster is Friday SUP yoga classes.

CENTRAL PACIFIC COAST DOMINICAL

SURF DOMINICAL

Dominical owes its fame to its seriously sick point and beach breaks, though surf conditions here are variable. There is a great opportunity to learn surfing in the white-water beach breaks, but beware of getting in too deep, as you can really get trashed out here if you don't know what you're doing. If you're just getting started, stay in the white water or make for the nearby Playa Dominicalito, which is a bit tamer.

Sunset Surf (☑ 8917-3143, 8827-3610; www.sunsetsurfdominical.com; Domilocos; all-inclusive packages per week from US$1415; ☺ 8am-4:30pm) Operated by Dylan Park, who grew up surfing the waves of Hawaii and Costa Rica, Sunset offers a variety of packages (including one for women only). It has a three-to-one student-instructor ratio and Park is an excellent teacher. Day lessons (from US$55) also available.

Costa Rica Surf Camp (☑ 8812-3625, 2787-0393; www.crsurfschool.com; Hotel DiuWak; all-inclusive packages per week from US$1190) This fantastic, locally owned surf school prides itself on a two-to-one student-teacher ratio, with teachers who have CPR and water-safety training and years of experience. The amiable owner, Cesar Valverde, runs a friendly, warm-hearted program. Rainy-season surf packages start from US$552.

Dominical Surf Adventures RAFTING, SURFING
(2787-0431; www.dominicalsurfadventures.com; 8am-5pm Mon-Sat, 9am-3pm Sun) A bit of an adventurer's one-stop shop, where visitors can book white-water-rafting trips, kayaking, snorkeling and dive trips and surf lessons (from US$50) from its humble little desk on the main drag. Rafting trips start at US$80 (for runs on the Class II and III Guabo) and include a more challenging run on the Río Coto Brus' Class IV rapids.

Bamboo Yoga Play YOGA
(2787-0229; www.danyasa.com; classes US$20) Complementary as yoga is to surfing, it's no wonder the practice is sweeping across Costa Rica. This lovely Dominical studio offers a variety of classes for all levels, including unique dance-yoga-flow hybrid styles and even burlesque dance. The studio also serves as a center for yoga and arts retreats.

Courses

Adventure
Education Center LANGUAGE COURSE
(2787-0023, in USA & Canada 800-237-2730; www.adventurespanishschool.com) This school runs one-week Spanish-language programs, starting at US$260 without accommodations. Private lessons are available, as are discounts for longer periods of study. Various lodging options are available, from homestays to hotels.

Festivals & Events

Envision Festival CULTURAL, MUSIC
(www.envisionfestival.com) Held in Dominical during the first week of March, this is a festival with a new-age bent, bringing together fire dancers, yoga and jam bands.

Sleeping

Dominical proper is home to the majority of the area's budget accommodations, while midrange and top-end places are popping up on the outskirts of town. There are additional options in the nearby mountaintop village of Escaleras. Although most of the year Dominical has an unflappably laid-back vibe, the place goes bananas over the holidays, when Ticos flock to the coast. Travelers on the thinnest of shoestrings can probably get away with camping on the beach.

Montañas de Agua HOTEL $
(2787-0200; www.montanasdeagua.com; d with/without air-con US$50/30, apt US$75; P❄☎) Dominical's best budget option is hidden among the lush foliage at the top of the southern spur road, south of the main drag. Even the cheapest rooms are well maintained, have tile floors, wide-plank ceilings, hot-water showers and small porches strung with hammocks. The grounds are beautiful, the staff are friendly and it's steps from the beach.

Piramys/Cool Vibes Hostel HOSTEL $
(dorm 8353-6428, private rooms 2787-0196; www.hosteldominical.com; dm/r US$12/32; P@☎) At this rambling beachfront hostel at the southern end of town, the corrugated-iron roof and tarpaulin protect the open-air dorm with beds draped in mosquito nets. Downstairs, the private rooms are fairly basic but comfortable. A huge, airy lounge has hammocks and TV, and there's a bar, communal kitchen and surfboards for rent. Dorms are first come, first served.

Posada del Sol HOTEL $
(2787-0085; d from US$37; P☎) There are only five rooms at this charming, secure, tidy little place on the main drag; no advance reservations are taken. There are basic comforts – hammocks outside each room, a sink to rinse out your salty beach gear and a clothesline for drying. Single travelers should check out the tiny single in the back. Located 30m south of the school.

Que Nivel CABINA $
(2787-0127; www.qndominical.com; dm US$10, r with/without air-con US$45/30) This may not be the best choice for restless sleepers or lovers of light, but it's affordable and near the beach. Concrete rooms downstairs are dark and humid, although they come with air-con and are decorated in cheery colors. Upstairs, fan-only rooms get better light. There's a shared kitchen and a lively restaurant-bar. The surfboards for rent are pretty worn.

Danyasa Yoga Retreat GUESTHOUSE $$
(2787-0229; www.danyasa.com; s/d/ste US$48/83/98; ❄☎) ✎ To visualize Danyasa, imagine eight refurbished cargo containers set amid tranquil greenery, each turned into a snug room or grander suite, with shared outdoor bamboo showers (suites are en suite) and a guest kitchen. Now imagine water features in the shape of Buddha's head, yoga and dance classes designed to unleash your Inner Goddess and align your chakra, and you're there.

Hotel y Restaurante Roca Verde   HOTEL $$

(☑ 2787-0036; www.rocaverde.net; r US$100; P✸@🖳🏊) Overlooking the beach about 1km south of town, this US-owned hotel has common spaces with tile mosaics, festive murals and rock inlays. The 10 tropical-themed rooms are comfortable and have terracotta-tile floors and pretty handpainted flora and fauna decorating the walls. The real action takes place in the festive open-air bar and pool, and decent restaurant.

Albergue Alma de Hatillo   B&B $$

(☑ 8850-9034; www.cabinasalma.com; r US$70-140; P✸@🏊) Consisting of immaculate cabins clustered beneath the fruit trees in the village of Hatillo, 6km west of Dominical, this friendly B&B is run by Sabina, a charming Polish woman. Boons? Fresh produce from the property for breakfast and the owner's innate helpfulness. Banes? The location near the highway detracts from the tranquillity of the yoga classes in the open-air studio.

Domilocos   HOTEL $$

(☑ 2787-0244; www.domilocos.com; r incl breakfast from US$90; P✸🖳🏊) On the road at the southern end of town, Domilocos is a solid, if rather overpriced, midrange option, with Mediterranean-inspired grounds, an attractive (but occasionally malfunctioning) plunge pool lined with potted plants and a decent restaurant, ConFusione. Tile-floored rooms with solid beds and bamboo furniture are basic and could use some sprucing up, but are spacious and clean.

★Costa Paraíso   BOUTIQUE HOTEL $$$

(☑ 2787-0025; www.costa-paraiso.com; d US$140-150; P✸🖳🏊) In a prime spot overlooking a rocky cove in Playa Dominicalito, this snug hideaway with Costa Rica's steepest driveway lives up to its name. Each of the five rooms is beautifully appointed in a modern tropical style, with tile floors, wood beams and windows oriented to catch ocean breezes and views. The in-house restaurant (p394) is a destination in itself.

All but one room (which does come with fridge and coffeemaker) has a kitchenette. Keep an eye out for the tiny sign on the ocean side, 2km south of Dominical – it's a sharp turn that goes steeply downhill.

★Mavi Surf Hotel   BOUTIQUE HOTEL $$$

(☑ 2787-0429; www.mavi-surf.com; r US$130; P♻✸🖳🏊) At the top end of the surfer market, this delightful lime-green hotel is run by friendly Italians Max and Barbara.

It's a two-minute walk to the beach, but far enough from the 'doof doof doof' of mainstreet bars, with surfing racks by each spacious, air-con room and bamboo partitions offering some privacy on the breezy terrace. Excellent breakfast included.

Cascadas Farallas   LODGE $$$

(☑ 2787-8378; www.waterfallvillas.com; ste/villa from US$190/300; P✸🏊) This spiritual retreat, 6km from Dominical along the San Isidro road, is located beside a series of cascading waterfalls. Balinese-style suites and villas are decked out from floor to ceiling with Asian art, and all have balconies facing the waterfalls. Regular yoga and meditation sessions are balanced with exclusively vegan cuisine. This eco-retreat has no TV and no wi-fi.

🍴 Eating

El Pescado Loco   SEAFOOD $

(mains US$8-9; ⊙noon-6pm) This little outdoor shack has only seven menu items, but when it comes to fish and shrimp tacos with chipotle sauce and chunky guacamole, it's totally nailed the flavors. Your quest to find the perfect fish taco may be over. Our only quibble: how about real cutlery instead of disposable?

Del Mar Taco Shop   TACOS $

(tacos US$4; ⊙10am-9pm) On the approach to the beach, an American expat cooks up some of the Pacific coast's best tacos in this casual surfer hangout. We prefer the fish tacos to the shrimp, which are overwhelmed a little by the batter. Chunky burritos are also available and the guacamole is superb.

Cafe Mono Congo   CAFE $

(☑ 8384-2915; mains US$4-9; ⊙6:30am-7pm; 🖳🍴) Perch on a swing at the bar or at a riverside table to enjoy the best espresso in town, hands down. This open-air cafe also dishes up tasty, simple breakfasts and (largely veggie) lunches, using organic local produce. Find it at the junction of the road into town and the main drag – couldn't be simpler.

Café de Ensueños   CAFE $

(meals US$5-9; ⊙6am-8pm) Run by a lovely Tico family, this local cafe is tucked away at the end of the southern spur road. Organic coffee drinks, fresh juices and hearty breakfasts are all served alfresco under a covered terrace – an excellent spot for a quiet, unhurried morning. Extra hungry? Go for the gut-busting Special Breakfast.

Soda Nanyoa
COSTA RICAN **$**

(☑ 8637-1176; mains US$5-8; ☺ 6am-10pm; 🛜) In a town that caters to gringo appetites with inflated price tags, Nanyoa is a gratifying find: an authentic, moderately priced, better-than-most Costa Rican *soda*. The big pinto breakfasts and fresh-squeezed juice are ideal after a morning session on the waves, and at night it lets patrons bring their own beer from the grocery across the street.

★ ¿Por Qué No?
FUSION **$$**

(☑ 2787-0025; www.cpporqueno.com; mains US$8-20; ☺ 7am-1:30pm & 5:30-9:30pm Tue-Sun, 7-11am Mon; 🛜 ☑ 🍴) Blackberry-and-cream-cheese-stuffed French toast, anyone? (Served with *real* maple syrup – this Canadian-run establishment doesn't mess around.) It's worth making a reservation for lunch or dinner – the creative, well-executed Tico-fusion dishes at this restaurant at the Costa Paraíso hotel (p393), such as blackened catch of the day with mango salsa and pulled pork, represent some of the best eats around here.

Organic, locally sourced ingredients are used whenever possible. Dishes like mango jerk chicken, vegetarian cassoulet and wood-fired pizza are quite reasonably priced, especially considering the quality and freshness, and the gorgeous oceanfront location can't be beaten.

Maracutú
VEGETARIAN, INTERNATIONAL **$$**

(☑ 2787-0091; www.maracatucostarica.com; meals US$10-18; ☺ 11am-1am; 🛜 ☑) This mellow, reggae-spouting 'natural restaurant' hits a lovely high note in Dominical. It serves mostly vegetarian and vegan dishes that span the globe, from falafel and burritos to Thai curries, with pescatarian-friendly fish tacos and wasabi tuna thrown in for good measure. The food is made from organic and locally sourced produce where possible. Maracutú also hosts lots of live music and DJs.

Dominical Sushi
SUSHI **$$**

(☑ 8826-7946; mains US$8-13; ☺ noon-10pm) In an open-air setting overlooking the River Barú, this beachfront sushi place takes advantage of the fresh tuna and other fish caught daily in Dominical. We're big fans of their tuna sashimi and unagi and rainbow rolls and the menu is complemented by a selection of Japanese beers and sake.

Patron's
AMERICAN **$$**

(mains from US$10; ☺ 8am-11pm) Dominating the main drag, Patron's is where you come for a game of billiards, Caesar salad and surf and turf, live jazz some evenings and a solid gringo crowd.

Drinking & Nightlife

The village loves to party, though the scene changes from night to night. Maracutú hosts lots of live music and DJs, and there's live music at Patron's also.

Tortilla Flats
BAR

(☑ 2787-0033; ☺ noon-late) The beachfront Tortilla Flats is the de facto place for surfers to enjoy sunset beers after a day in the water (skip the food, though). Its open-air atmosphere and easy vibes reflect the clientele, with surf videos on continuous loop, but continents may drift before you get served.

🛍 Shopping

Bookstore by the Seashore
BOOKS

(bookstorebytheseashore@gmail.com; ☺ 11am-4pm Mon-Sat) The central Pacific coast is a virtual desert when it comes to good English-

BUSES FROM DOMINICAL

Gray Line, Easy Ride and Monkey Ride offer private and shared shuttle services to popular destinations such as Jacó, San José, Monteverde, Tamarindo and Sierpe; Easy Ride has direct services to Granada, Nicaragua.

Buses pick up and drop off passengers along the main road in Dominical.

DESTINATION	COST (US$)	DURATION (HR)	FREQUENCY (DAILY)
Jacó	2.70	1½	10 daily 5am-6pm
Palmar	2	1½	4:45am, 10:30am, 3pm
Quepos	5.50	1	5:45am, 8:25am, 12:35pm, 12:45pm, 4:35pm, 4:45pm
San José	10.85	4½	5:45am, 2pm
Uvita	1	20 minutes	8 daily 4:45am-6:30pm

language bookstores, so readers who love actual paper books will want to stock up here. A shop on the road into town, Bookstore by the Seashore is packed with well-curated used fiction, nonfiction and genre titles, in excellent condition, and most for five bucks a pop.

ℹ️ Orientation

The Costanera Sur bypasses the town entirely; the entrance to the village is immediately past the Río Barú bridge. There's an unpaved main road through the village, where many of the services are found, and a beach road parallel to the ocean. About 100m south of the intersection is a southern spur road with some more accommodations and a cafe.

ℹ️ Information

There's a **Banco de Costa Rica** (BCR; ☎2787-0381; ☺9am-4pm Mon-Fri) on the highway just outside of town, and a postal service upstairs in the same small shopping center.

Dominical Information Center (☎2787-0454, 8651-9090; www.dominicalinformation. com; ☺6am-8pm) On the main strip, near the entrance to Dominical, this tourist info center has useful maps of town and bus timetables for the entire region. Bus ticket, shuttle and tour booking services available.

DANGERS & ANNOYANCES

Waves, currents and riptides in Dominical are very strong, and there have been drownings in the past. Watch for red flags (which mark riptides), follow the instructions of posted signs and swim at beaches that are patrolled by lifeguards. If you're smart, the beach is no problem, but people do die here every year.

Also, Dominical attracts a heavy-duty party crowd, which in turn has led to a burgeoning drug problem.

ℹ️ Getting There & Away

Taxis to Uvita cost US$10 to US$20, while the ride to Quepos costs US$60 and to Manuel Antonio it's US$70. Cars accommodate up to five people, and can be hailed easily in town from the main road.

Escaleras

Escaleras, a small community scattered around a steep and narrow dirt loop road that branches off the Costanera, is famed for its sweeping views of the coastline. If you want to make it up here, you're going to need a 4WD to navigate one of the coun-

try's most notoriously difficult roads. Needless to say, the locals weren't kidding when they named the place *escaleras* ('staircase'). Aside from the scenic views, travelers primarily brave the road to relax in a mountain retreat that's still close enough to the action in Dominical and Uvita.

🛏️ Sleeping & Eating

⭐ **La Tierra Divina**   B&B $$
(www.latierradivina.com; cabins US$80-99; Ⓟ❄️🛜) This brand new B&B consists of three unusual round cabins with fans, conical roofs and ocean views, surrounded by encroaching jungle; howler monkeys drop by for an occasional visit. Owners Becky and Troy are very helpful. The turnoff is 3km south of Dominical: first left through Dominicalito, then first right after the soccer field and 3km up the dirt road.

Bella Vista Lodge   LODGE $$
(☎8315-6026; www.costaricabellavistalodge.com; cabins $75-90; Ⓟ🛜) One of the first places you'll come to along the main Escaleras road is Bella Vista Lodge, a remote *finca* (farm) with several shiny-wood cabins on the property. Run by gregarious Bert, it's a chilled-out place where guests take their meals together, and the owner's friends throw impromptu concerts. 4WD required to reach the property.

Pacific Edge   CABINA $$
(☎2200-5428, 8935-7905; www.pacificedge.info; cabin/bungalow from US$70/100; Ⓟ❄️🛜🏊) Pacific Edge is located on a different access road that's 1.2km south of the first entrance to Escaleras. The owners are a worldly North American–British couple who delight in showing guests their slice of paradise. Four cabins are perched on a knife-edge ridge about 200m above sea level, while larger, family-friendly, fully equipped bungalows accommodate up to six. 4WD only.

Those interested in indigenous culture will find an excellent selection of Boruca masks here.

Villa Escaleras   VILLA $$$
(☎8823-0509, in USA & Canada 866-658-7796; www.villa-escaleras.com; villa for 4/6/8 people US$240/280/320, casa US$70; Ⓟ❄️🛜🏊) About 2km up the Escaleras road, Villa Escaleras has a spacious four-bedroom villa accented by cathedral ceilings, tiled floors, colonial furnishings and a palatial swimming pool. Twice-weekly maid service and a

wraparound balcony awash with panoramic views make the setting complete. There's also a smaller *casa*; both have a three-night minimum stay. 4WD essential.

Bar Jolly Roger AMERICAN $
([icon] 8706-8438; 10 wings US$10; [icon] 4-10pm; [icon]) If you have a hankering for chicken wings, Bar Jolly Roger offers 19 varieties, in addition to burgers, pizzas, cold beers and good margaritas. This friendly expat outpost is up the southern entrance to Escaleras. Look for the smiley-face Jolly Roger sign.

ⓘ Getting There & Away

The first entrance to Escaleras is 4km south of the San Isidro de El General turnoff before Dominical, and the second is 4.5km past the first one. Both are on the left-hand side of the road and poorly signed.

Uvita

Just 17km south of Dominical, this sweet little village consists of a few dirt roads, lined with farms, guesthouses and tiny shops, a cluster of strip malls by the main Costanera Sur entrance, and a scattering of hotels in the jungle-covered hills above. With its gentle pace of life, it should give you a good idea of what the central Pacific coast was like before the tourist boom.

Uvita's main attraction is Parque Nacional Marino Ballena, a pristine marine reserve famous for its migrating pods of humpback whales and its virtually abandoned wilderness beaches, but there are also good waterfalls nearby and once a year it holds the country's biggest hippie-fest, the Envision Festival.

Held a short distance from the main entrance to Uvita, the sweet little farmers' market is a good place to mingle with locals and longtime expats, and purchase locally grown fruit and vegetables, honey and home-cooked foods.

⊙ Sights

Uvita is a perfect base for exploring Costanera Sur, which is home to some truly spectacular, and largely empty beaches, as well as a waterslide in the shape of Cascada Verde.

★**Cascada Verde** WATERFALL
(admission US$2; [icon] 8am-4pm) Around 2.5km inland and uphill (toward the Cascada Verde hostel), this waterfall plunges into an invit-

ing deep pool, perfect for a refreshing dip. The best part? The waterfall also acts as an exhilarating natural waterslide with a 6ft drop at the end; take the path to the top, lie down, cross your arms and let gravity take care of the rest!

Rancho La Merced
National Wildlife Refuge NATURE RESERVE
([icon] 2743-8032, 8861-5147; www.rancholamerced.com; tours US$35-45; [icon] 7:30am-5:30pm) A few kilometers before Uvita, opposite the turnoff to Oro Verde, is this 506-hectare national wildlife refuge (and former cattle ranch), with primary and secondary forests and mangroves lining the Río Morete. Here you can take guided nature hikes, horseback-riding tours to Punta Uvita and bird-watching walks.

You can also stay at La Merced in a 1940s farmhouse, which can accommodate up to 10 people in double rooms of various sizes (doubles US$85).

Reserva Biológica
Oro Verde NATURE RESERVE
([icon] 8970-1315, 8843-8833) A few kilometers before Uvita you'll see a signed turnoff to the left on a rough dirt road (4WD only) that leads 3.5km up the hill to this private reserve on the farm of the Duarte family, who have lived in the area for more than three decades. Two-thirds of the 150-hectare property is rainforest, and there are guided hikes (US$35), night tours (US$30) and 6am bird-watching walks (US$30). Reserve in advance.

Farmers' Market MARKET
([icon] 8am-1pm Sat) Held a short distance from the main entrance to Uvita, along the unpaved road, this sweet little farmers' market on Saturdays is a good place to mingle with locals and longtime expats, and purchase psychedelic jewelry, locally grown fruit and vegetables, honey and home-cooked foods.

🏃 Activities & Tours

Whale-watching is a huge attraction here, with humpback whales visiting the waters surrounding Parque Nacional Marino Ballena twice a year (December to April and July to November).

★**Mad About Diving** DIVING
([icon] 2743-8019; www.madaboutdivingcr.com) Friendly, safe and professional diving operator, offering dives in the Parque Nacional Marino

Ballena and full-day scuba excursions to Isla del Caño in Bahía Drake (US$165). Two-tank dives from US$95.

Bahía Aventuras ADVENTURE TOUR
(📞 2743-8362, 8846-6576; www.bahiaaventuras. com) A well-regarded tour operator in Uvita, Bahía Aventuras has tours running the gamut, including surfing lessons (US$70), snorkeling (US$75) and whale-watching (US$90) in the Marino Ballena National Park, diving around Isla del Caño in Bahía Drake (US$189), and hiking, spanning the Costa Ballena to Corcovado.

Uvita
Adventure Tour KAYAKING, MOUNTAIN BIKING
(📞 2743-8008, 8918-5681; www.uvitadventure tours.com; mountain-biking/kayaking tour from US$35/65) Run by young, enthusiastic owner Victor, this small tour company offers highly recommended tours including exhilarating mountain-biking adventures, kayaking through the mangroves and snorkeling at the marine park.

🎪 Festivals & Events

⭐ **Envision Festival** ART, MUSIC
(www.envisionfestival.com) Four days of spoken word, music, yoga, performance art, permaculture, dreadlocks and DJs happen in Uvita in late February for the 'Costa Rican Burning Man' festival. Attendees set up camp in a jungle setting near the beach in Uvita where you might spot thousands of naked hippies.

There's even a tent where you can test your legally dubious substances for purity, to know exactly what you're taking. The festival's philosophy is: some revelers will invariably 'experiment' with mind-altering substances, so it's best to make the experience safer.

🛏 Sleeping

The main entrance to Uvita leads inland, east of the highway, where you'll find a number of eating and sleeping options. More guesthouses, *sodas* and local businesses are west of the highway, along the bumpy dirt roads that surround the edges of the park.

⭐ **Cascada Verde** HOSTEL $
(📞 2743-8191, 8593-9420; www.cascadaverde-cos tarica.com; dm/s/d from US$11/22/34; 🅿@📶) If you're looking for a quiet retreat in the jungle, this hostel, run by a young German couple, is for you. About 2km uphill from Uvita, it features jaw-dropping jungle views from the dining terrace, a large communal kitchen, plenty of indoor and outdoor spaces for relaxing, appealingly designed rooms with bamboo partitions, and a waterfall a short walk away.

Because of the open architecture style, be aware that there's very little noise privacy – but you'll also hear the jungle symphony surrounding you. Rooms can be configured to accommodate kids and child-friendly tours can be organized.

Flutterby House HOSTEL $
(📞 8341-1730, 2743-8221; www.flutterbyhouse.com; campsite US$7, dm US$14, d US$40-120; 🅿@📶) 🍃 Is it possible to fall in love with a hostel? If so, the ramshackle collection of colorful *Swiss Family Robinson*–style tree houses and dorms has beguiled us. The place is run by a pair of Californian sisters, and the clientele here tends to be of the barefoot, surfing variety. Socialize at the bar.

It rents out boards and bikes, sells beer for a pittance, has a tidy, open-air communal kitchen as well as a restaurant, and employs downright visionary sustainability practices. Great location a short stroll from Marino Ballena's beaches; it's near the south entrance gate of the park. Follow the signs from the Costanera Sur.

Tucan Hotel HOSTEL $
(📞 2743-8140; www.tucanhotel.com; campsite/ hammock/dm US$10/10/14, d from US$44; 🅿❄@📶) Located 100m inland from the main highway, this cheapie is popular with international travelers of all ages. The rooms are arranged around a semi-open communal area, and there are also simple tents and hammocks, as well as the lofty tree house. Bonuses include a shared kitchen, daily movies at 4pm, an Italian restaurant and a convivial atmosphere.

⭐ **Finca Bavaria** BOUTIQUE HOTEL $$
(📞 8355-4465; www.finca-bavaria.de; Interamericana Km 167; s/d from US$72/83; 🅿📶🏊) This German-run inn comprises a handful of appealing rooms with wooden accents, bamboo furniture, romantic mosquito-net-draped beds and the best breakfast along the coast (US$8). The grounds are lined with walkways and hemmed by jungle, though you can take in sweeping views of the ocean from the hilltop pool. Look for the signed dirt road at Km 167.

Cabinas Los Laureles   CABINA $$
(☑ 2743-8235, 2743-8008; www.cabinasloslaure
les.com; s/d from US$34/55; ⓟ@🖧) Set up on
a forested property with a short trail run-
ning through it, this 14-room spot slightly
uphill from the Costanera Sur offers authen-
tic Costa Rican hospitality. Of the friendly
Tico family that runs the place, son Victor
(who runs Uvita Adventure Tour, p397) is
bilingual and conscientious about refer-
ring guests to other locally run businesses.
The restaurant serves delicious homemade
casados.

★ **Hotel Cristal Ballena**   BOUTIQUE HOTEL $$$
(☑ 2786-5354; www.cristal-ballena.com; Costanera
Sur; r US$225-295; ⓟ❋🖧≋) 🖉 About 7km
south of Uvita, surrounded by 12 hectares of
private nature reserve and with killer views
of the coast from its hillside location, this
Austrian-run boutique hotel is one of the
top birding hotels in Costa Rica, with knowledgeable guides arranging bird-watching
excursions. An excellent restaurant, light,
bright rooms, vast, gorgeous suites and a
tranquil ambience complete the picture.

Two nature trails (800m and 2km) run
across the property, where you're very likely
to spot some wildlife during early morning
rambles, as well as some of the 250 bird
species resident in the surrounding tropical
lowland forest. The gift store sells colorful
Boruca masks of excellent quality.

Bungalows Ballena   BUNGALOW $$$
(☑ 2743-8543, 8667-2803; www.bungalowsbal
lena.com; apt/bungalow US$130/260; ⓟ🖧≋)
These fully outfitted apartments and stand-
alone bungalows are popular with Tico
families and large groups. All have kitchens,
wi-fi and satellite TV. The place is outfitted
for kids – there's a playground and a big,
welcoming pool in the shape of a whale's
tail. Find it 300m north of the park's main
entrance.

🍴 Eating

★ **Sibu Cafe**   CAFE $
(☑ 2743-8674; coffee US$1.60-4; ☉ 7:30am-7pm
Mon-Sat; ❋🖧🖉) Serving the best coffee for
miles around, this little cafe hides in the
strip-mall part of Uvita. Latte art, chunky
brownies and homemade lemon pie are all
on the menu. Want something more sub-
stantial? The hardworking couple here also
make excellent salads, thin-and-crispy pizza
pie, veggie juice and fruit smoothies.

Roadshack Deli   INTERNATIONAL $
(mains US$6-9; ☉ 11am-7pm Mon-Sat; 🖉)
Around 50m down the main Uvita road
from the highway turnoff, this open-air,
ramshackle spot is a gathering place for
offbeat customers craving veggie wraps,
braised pork and other sandwiches (we like
the Mother Clucker) and imaginative salads.
Wash it all down with homemade *kombu-
cha* (fermented tea drink). This is an infor-
mal community center, too.

★ **Sabor Español**   SPANISH $$
(☑ 2743-8312, 8768-9160; mains US$8-22; ☉ 6-
9:30pm Tue-Sun; 🖧) Having had a successful run in Monteverde, charming Spanish
couple Heri and Montse realized that they
wanted to live by the ocean – to Uvita's good
fortune. Thus, their sublime gazpacho, pael-
la, *tortilla española* and other Spanish specialties can now be savored with sangria in
a lovely *rancho* setting, at the end of a dirt
road in Playa Uvita.

The Baker Bean   PIZZA, CAFE $$
(☑ 2743-8700; mains US$7-18; ☉ 6am-8pm;
❋🖧🖉) Just north of the main entrance
to Uvita on the Costanera Sur, this odd-
ly named joint is half-pizzeria, half-cafe.
Locals and expats descend on the cafe for
good, strong morning coffee, filled bagels
and Argentinean-style empanadas (ideal
for picnicking), while in the restaurant half,
Armando the chef serves up ample pizzas,
some topped with imported ingredients.

ⓘ Orientation

The area off the main highway is referred to
locally as Uvita, while the area next to the beach
is called Playa Uvita and Playa Bahía Uvita (the
southern end of the beach). The beach area is
reached through two parallel roads that are
roughly 500m apart – they make a C-shape
connecting back to the road. The first entrance
is just south of the bridge over the Río Uvita and
the second entrance is in the center of town. At
low tide you can walk out along Punta Uvita, but
ask about conditions locally before heading out
so that the rising water doesn't cut you off.

ⓘ Information

You can find bus schedules, an area map and
other useful information at www.marinoballena.
org. Also keep an eye out for the free print mag-
azine *Ballena Tales*, a wonderful resource for
visitors, with bilingual articles, tide charts and
listings of local businesses from Dominical to
the Osa Peninsula.

DANGERS & ANNOYANCES

When enjoying the local beaches, be aware that personal possessions that are left unattended have been known to melt away into the jungles that fringe the shorelines.

In fact, it's best not to bring anything valuable to the beach with you. Until recently, petty theft was the worst problem around the national park and area beaches, and unfortunately, a few in-person (non-violent) robberies have taken place in the not-so-distant past. Get the latest word from the staff at your accommodations.

❶ Getting There & Away

Most buses depart from the two sheltered bus stops on the Costanera in the main village.

Dominical US$1; 30 minutes; 10 daily between 4:45am and 5:30pm.

Quepos US$8; two hours; departs 4:40am, 5am, 11am, 1pm and 4pm.

San José US$10.50; 3½ hours; departs 5:30am and 1pm.

Private shuttle companies – Gray Line, Easy Ride and Monkey Ride – offer pricier transfers from Uvita to Dominical, San José, Quepos, Jacó, Puerto Jiménez and other popular destinations.

Parque Nacional Marino Ballena

This stunner of a **marine park** (☑2743-8236; admission US$6; ⊙7am-6pm), created in 1989, protects coral and rock reefs surrounding several offshore islands. Its name comes not only from the humpback whales that breed here but also because of the Punta Uvita 'Whale Tail,' a distinctive sandbar extending into a rocky reef that, at low tide, forms the shape of a whale's tail.

Despite its small size, the importance of this area cannot be overstated, especially since it protects migrating humpback and pilot whales, three types of dolphin and nesting sea turtles, not to mention colonies of seabirds and several terrestrial reptiles.

Although Ballena is relatively off the radar of many coastal travelers, this can be an extremely rewarding destination for beach-lovers and wildlife-watchers. The lack of tourist crowds means that you can enjoy a quiet day at the beach in near solitude – a rarity in Costa Rica. You might even see dolphins in the surf or a humpback breaching.

Activities

The beaches at Parque Nacional Marino Ballena are a stunning combination of golden sand and polished rock. All of them are virtually deserted and perfect for peaceful swimming and sunbathing.

There is some decent surfing near the river mouth at the southern end of Playa Colonia.

Diving & Snorkeling

The coral reefs around the offshore islands are a good place to experience the park's underwater world, unlike the coral reefs near the shore that were heavily damaged by sediment run-off from the construction of the coastal highway. To delve into the underwater beauty of the park, go on a diving or snorkeling trip with the Argentinean-run Mad About Diving (p396).

Wildlife-Watching

Heading southeast from Punta Uvita, the park includes mangrove swamps, estuaries and rocky headlands. The lack of visitors means you'll have a number of quiet opportunities for good bird-watching.

The park is home to or frequently visited by a number of wildlife species, including common, bottlenose and pantropical spotted dolphins and a variety of lizards. The offshore islands are important nesting sites for frigate birds, brown boobies and brown pelicans, and from May to November, with a peak in September and October, olive ridley and hawksbill turtles bury their eggs in the sand nightly. However, the star attraction are the pods of humpback whales that pass through the national park from July to November and December to April, as well as occasional pilot whales.

Scientists are unsure as to why humpback whales migrate here, though it's possible that Costa Rican waters may be one of only a few places in the world where the whales mate. There are actually two different groups of humpbacks that pass through Parque Nacional Marino Ballena – whales seen in the fall migrate from Californian waters, while those seen in the spring originate from Antarctica and come here to breed and rear their babies.

Whale- and dolphin-watching trips are run by several tour companies in Uvita, including highly professional Bahía Aventuras (p397).

ℹ️ Information

There are four entrances to the park, the most commonly used being the **ranger station** (☎2743-8236; ⏰7am-6pm) in Playa Uvita (follow the main road through Uvita), followed by the one along a dirt road that runs past Flutterby House in Uvita; there is now a ranger station (read: wooden shack) there also. All park entrances are open from 7am to 6pm.

DANGERS & ANNOYANCES

The beaches of Parque Nacional Marina Balleno are notorious for bag-snatchings. Leave your bag on the sand near the bushes for a second and you're unlikely to ever see it again. Local residents are putting pressure on the park authorities to improve security in the park and also to provide working toilet facilities.

Another annoyance are the enterprising parking touts who charge visitors 2000 colones to park near the main entrance to the park. If you park on the street, you're not legally obliged to pay them anything. Better still, park nearby and walk to the entrance.

ℹ️ Getting There & Away

Parque Nacional Marino Ballena is best accessed from Uvita or Ojochal, by private vehicle, a quick taxi ride or by walking.

Ojochal

Of the trio of villages – Dominical, Uvita and Ojochal (the sporty one, the wildlife one and the gourmet one) – that make up the Costa Ballena, this laid-back, spread-out village is the culinary epicenter, with a multicultural expat population. Its friendly, well-integrated vibe has a distinctly different feel from that of surfer-dominated Dominical, although just north of Ojochal the largely undiscovered wilderness beach of Playa Tortuga is home to occasional bouts of decent surf.

Its excellent dining scene aside, Ojochal also serves as a convenient base for exploring nearby Parque Nacional Marino Ballena, and despite its small size there are plenty of accommodations in and around the village to choose from. Wildlife-lovers may wish to linger longer to learn more about the locally based turtle conservation project.

Reserva Playa Tortuga   NATURE RESERVE
(☎2786-5200; www.reservaplayatortuga.org; ⏰9am-3pm Mon-Fri) FREE Set up in 2009 by Costa Rican scientists, this excellent program runs several projects: studying and protecting from extinction the olive ridley turtle that nests on Playa Tortuga, monitoring the crocodilian population in the reserve and the human impact on their ecosystem, and community outreach: teaching local children the importance of protecting wildlife. Volunteers are very welcome. The reserve office is down a dirt road almost directly across from the entrance to Ojochal.

🛏️ Sleeping

There are a number of places to stay in Ojochal village, and more sleeping options spread out along the Costanera Sur.

REVIVING ROOTS

Ojochal's namesake, once on the verge of extinction in the area, is making a slow comeback. Though the tall, leafy *ojoche* tree (*Brosimum alicastrum*) takes about 30 years to mature, making this a long-term project, the local community has begun putting the *ojoche* back into Ojochal.

As Ojochal's population grew through the 1950s, most stands of *ojoche* were felled for cattle grazing and lumber. But in the same decade the tree's starchy fruit provided nourishment to many local families during severe drought. The pulp of the fruit can be eaten raw, boiled, or made into flour. The fruit (also known as the 'Maya nut,' though not a true nut) has a low glycemic index and high protein content, and is rich in fiber, fat, folate, iron and antioxidants.

Around 2009 the grassroots community group Comité de Ojoche began to replant *ojoche* trees in the area in an effort to re-establish Ojochal's connection with its roots (so to speak), and to save the tree from local extinction while reforesting the area with a nutritious and culturally valuable food source.

Hotel Villas Gaia offers walking tours of the 'Ojoche Route,' and you can buy *ojoche* flour from the local women's entrepreneurial association, which helps to fund the *ojoche*-revival project.

★ **Hotel El Mono Feliz** HOTEL $

(✆ 2786-5146; www.elmonofeliz.com; r US$35-50, bungalow US$75-100; ✳🏠🏊) Around 3km inland from Ojochal's entrance, this sweet little spot is run by a friendly Dutch couple – knowledgeable longtime residents of the Costa Ballena. The forested property is hemmed in by a trickling brook and this is the only wallet-friendly place in Ojochal, with tidy, fan-cooled rooms, and cabins and hammocks strung by a small pool. A couple of the rooms are geared toward families with kids, furniture-wise.

Diquis del Sur B&B $$

(✆ 2786-5012; www.diquiscostarica.com; r from US$62; 🅿✳🏠🏊) In Ojochal proper, around 1.5km in, this B&B is run by a delightful French-Canadian couple who make it feel like a home away from home. Accommodations are in a variety of fairly modest rooms, though all have kitchenettes conducive to self-catering. There's also a good restaurant on-site, and the well-maintained property is landscaped with flowers and fruit trees.

There are also villas for long-term rental. An interesting side fact: the property is named after the 'Diquis Spheres,' which are pre-Columbian stone balls, many of which were found in this area. Can organize kid-friendly tours.

★ **El Castillo** BOUTIQUE HOTEL $$$

(✆ 2786-5543; www.elcastillocr.com; r US$275-395, ste US$525; 🅿✳🏠🏊) Even the most jaded of guests will give an involuntary gasp of surprise when faced with the tremendous view from the infinity pool at this bluff-top hotel. Comprising just four rooms and two suites, decked out with four-poster beds and rain showers, this intimate place organizes outings to a private island. Planning to propose to your sweetie? Do it here.

There's also an excellent restaurant, Azul, open to non-guests.

★ **La Cusinga** LODGE $$$

(✆ 2770-2549; www.lacusingalodge.com; Interamericana Km 166, Finca Tres Hermanas; dm US$95, r US$136-204; 🅿) 🌿 This lovely ecolodge with breezy wood-and-stone rooms is a model of sustainable practices. It's also a relaxing place to unplug – in place of TVs there are yoga classes. Located on a private reserve, it has access to hiking, bird-watching, snorkeling and swimming in the Parque Nacional Marino Ballena. Whole-

some meals feature mostly organic produce. It's about 5km south of Uvita.

Hotel Villas Gaia CABINA $$$

(✆ 8382-8240, 2786-5044; www.villasgaia.com; villa incl breakfast from US$85-101, casa US$153; 🅿@🏠🏊) 🌿 Around 500m north of the Ojochal entrance is this beautifully kept collection of shiny wooden cabins with shaded porches, set in tranquil forested grounds. An excellent restaurant serves a variety of international standards, and the hilltop pool boasts a panoramic view of Playa Tortuga. The beach is a pleasant 20-minute hike along a dirt path that winds down the hillside.

Lookout at Playa Tortuga BOUTIQUE HOTEL $$$

(✆ 2786-5074; www.hotelcostarica.com; Interamericana Km 175; d US$107-168; 🅿✳@🏠🏊) This beautiful hilltop sanctuary is home to a dozen brightly painted bungalows awash in calming pastels. The grounds are traversed by a series of paths overlooking the beaches below, but the highlight is the large deck in a tower above the pool. Here you can pursue some early morning bird-watching, or perhaps some late-afternoon slothful lounging. Excellent Mexican restaurant (p402), too.

✖ Eating

Ojochal is *the* culinary enclave along the Costa Ballena, with influences ranging from Mediterranean to Indonesian, and it's home to a patisserie, pizzeria and farmers' market. You can find Ojochal's eateries listed at www.elsabordeojochal.com. All restaurants are well signposted throughout the village.

★ **Ballena Bistro** FUSION $

(✆ 2786-5407; www.ballenabistro.com; Costanera Sur, Km 169; mains US$4-12; ⏲11am-3pm Tue-Sun; 🏠🍴) The main attraction of multi-use, barn-like Goathouse 169, this bistro offers welcome, diverse fodder for your belly and your Instagram feed. Feast on the likes of garlic hummus, chèvre-orange salad, pulled-pork burgers and Brazilian coconut fish soup. Wraps, fresh juices and cold beers round out the menu. This is a smashing spot to break up a long drive.

★ **Azul** FUSION $$

(El Castillo; lunch mains from US$8-28, 2-/3-course dinner US$25/31; ⏲noon-10pm; 🏠🍴) At this chic little restaurant inside El Castillo, with killer views of the Pacific coast, your taste buds will be singing your praises when you treat them to superb spicy gazpacho, goat's cheese ravioli and expertly seared steak. There's terrific attention to presentation and taste, and the Mediterranean-style three-course dinners are worth a splurge.

★ **Citrus** INTERNATIONAL **$$**
(☑ 2786-5175; mains US$14-24; ⊙ 5:30-9pm Mon-Sat; ☎ ☑) With an outdoorsy ambience and merrily lit with twinkling fairy lights, this is one of Ojochal's most celebrated restaurants. Chef Marciano draws on her diverse background (French, Moroccan, Swedish…) to create her fresh and flavorful fusion dishes, presented with flair. Expect the likes of seafood red curry, gravadlax with horseradish, garlicky escargots, and a moreish Choco-Choco flourless chocolate cake.

★ **Exotica** INTERNATIONAL **$$**
(☑ 2786-5050; mains US$10-23; ⊙ 11am-9pm Mon-Sat) This phenomenal gourmet restaurant is worth planning your evening around. In a sultry, jungle ambience with orchids everywhere, the nouveau French dishes each emphasize a breadth of ingredients brought together in masterful combinations. Some of the highlights include Tahitian fish carpaccio, wild-duck breast with port-pineapple reduction and their signature dessert – the chili-tinged chocolate Devil's Fork. Reservations recommended.

Salsa MEXICAN **$$**
(☑ 2786-5074; Interamericana Km 175; mains from US$10; ⊙ 11am-10pm; ☎) By day you're treated to light bites such as fish tacos and fried calamari, but it's particularly worth coming here in the evenings for some authentic Mexican flavors, especially the dark, rich Oaxacan *moles*, Veracruz-style snapper and fresh salsas. It's inside Lookout at Playa Tortuga.

★ **Ylang-Ylang** INDONESIAN **$$$**
(☑ 2786-5054; www.facebook.com/YlangYlang Restaurant; mains US$25; ⊙ 5:30-10pm Wed-Sat early Dec-early Apr; ☎ ☑) The only Indonesian restaurant in Central America, this characterful Dutch-run place is immensely popular for the authentic, fiery flavors of their dishes (they grow their own Asian herbs). Dishes such as *daging rendang* (beef simmered with spices in coconut milk) and *ikan ketcap* (snapper with galangal and tamarind) are meant to be shared. With

only 12 guests per night, advance reservations are essential.

❶ Getting There & Away

Daily buses between Dominical and Palmar can drop you off near any of the places along the highway and also at the entrance of Ojochal village. However, to reach most places in Ojochal proper, it's best to have a car.

Gray Line, Easy Ride and Monkey Ride shuttles connect Ojochal with popular destinations along the Pacific coast and the Osa Peninsula.

PARQUE NACIONAL ISLA DEL COCO

A tiny speck of green amid the endless Pacific, Isla del Coco (☑ 2258-8750; www.cocos island.org; park entrance fee for 10-day trip US$490) looms large in the imagination of the adventurer: jagged mountains and tales of treasure, a pristine and isolated ecosystem filled with wildlife and some of the world's best diving. Remember the opening shot of *Jurassic Park*, where the helicopter sweeps over the sea to a jungle-covered island? That was here.

As beautiful as the island may be, its terrestrial environs pale in comparison to what lies beneath. Named by PADI as one of the world's top 10 dive spots, the surrounding waters of Isla del Coco harbor abundant pelagics, including one of the largest known schools of hammerhead sharks in the world.

Isla del Coco (aka Cocos Island) is around 500km southwest of the mainland in the middle of the eastern Pacific, making it Costa Rica's most remote destination.

History

In 1526 Spanish explorer Joan Cabezas stumbled onto Isla del Coco, though it wasn't noted on maps until its second discovery by French cartographer Nicolás Desliens in 1541; prior to being 'discovered' by Europeans, Isla del Coco received pre-Columbian seafaring visitors from Colombia and Ecuador. In the centuries that followed, heavy rainfall attracted the attention of sailors, pirates and whalers, who frequently stopped by for fresh water, seafood and coconuts.

Between the late 17th and early 19th centuries, Isla del Coco became a way station for pirates who are rumored to have hidden countless treasures here. The most famous was the storied Treasure of Lima, a trove of gold and silver ingots, gold laminae scavenged from church domes and a solid-gold, life-sized sculpture of the Virgin Mary. 'X marks the spot,' right? Not really. More than 500 treasure-hunting expeditions have found only failure. In fact, in 1869 the government of Costa Rica organized an official treasure hunt. They didn't find anything, but the expedition resulted in Costa Rica taking possession of the island, a treasure in itself, and it was declared a national park in 1978.

Settlers arrived on the island in the late 19th and early 20th centuries, though their stay on Isla del Coco was short-lived. However, they did leave behind domestic animals that have since converted into feral populations of pigs, goats, cats and rats – all of which threaten the natural wildlife.

Activities

Diving
The diving is excellent, and is regarded by most as the main attraction of the island. But strong oceanic currents can lead to treacherous underwater conditions, and Isla del Coco can only be recommended to intermediate and advanced divers with sufficient experience. Divers bring gloves to cling onto the rocks.

The island has two large bays with safe anchorages and sandy beaches: Chatham Bay is located on the northeast side and Wafer Bay is on the northwest.

The island's marine life is hugely varied, with 18 species of coral, 57 types of crustacean and abundant fish, sea turtles, schools of manta rays, dolphins and sharks. Just off Cocos are a series of smaller basaltic rocks and islets, which constitute some of the best dive sites.

Isla Manuelita is a prime spot, home to a wide array of fish, ray and eel, as well as schools of manta rays. Shark also inhabit these waters, including huge schools of scalloped hammerhead as well as whitetips, which are best spotted at night. Dirty Rock is another main attraction – a spectacular rock formation that harbors all kinds of sea creatures.

Diving is possible year-round, but the best time to see sharks is the May–November rainy season.

Aggressor
DIVING

(☎ in USA & Canada 800-348-2628; www.aggres sor.com) Operates a fleet of liveaboard diving boats to different destinations around the world. Offers eight- and 10-day land and sea expedition charters on *Okeanos Aggressor I* and *Okeanos Aggressor II* from Puntarenas to Isla del Coco from US$5500 per person.

Undersea Hunter
DIVING

(☎ 2228-6613, in USA 800-203-2120; www.under seahunter.com) Runs liveaboard 10- and 12-day land and sea expeditions to Isla del Coco from Puntarenas, with room for 14 to 18 people, from US$5645 per person.

Hiking
Even though this is the turf of hard-core divers, making landfall and exploring is worth the time and effort.

Rugged, heavily forested and punctuated by cascading waterfalls, Cocos is ringed and transected by an elaborate network of trails. The highest point is at Cerro Iglesias (634m), where you can soak up spectacular views of the lush, verdant island and the deep blue Pacific.

Note that visitors to the island must first register with the park rangers, though your tour company will most likely make all the necessary arrangements well in advance.

Because of its remote location, Isla del Coco is the most pristine national park in the country and one of Costa Rica's great wildlife destinations. Since the island was never linked to the Americas during its comparatively short geological history, Cocos is home to a very large number of rare endemic species.

Heading inland from the coastal forests up to the high-altitude cloud forests, it is possible to find around 235 unique species of flowering plants, 30% of which are found only on the island. This incredible diversity of flora supports more than 400 known species of insects – 65 endemics, as well as a striking range of butterflies and moths, are included in this count. Scientists believe that more remain to be discovered.

Of the 87 recorded species on the island and neighboring rocks, the most pronounced are the aquatic birds: brown and red-footed booby, great frigatebird, white tern and brown noddy. There are also three terrestrial endemics, namely the Cocos cuckoo, Cocos flycatcher and Cocos finch.

CENTRAL PACIFIC COAST PARQUE NACIONAL ISLA DEL COCO

ℹ Information

Área de Conservación Marina Isla del Coco
(Acmic; ☎ in San José 2258-8750, in San José
2250-7295; www.cocosisland.org; ⊙ 8am-3pm
Mon-Fri) In order to protect the conservation
status of the island, all visitors must apply for
a permit at this Área de Conservación Marina
Isla del Coco office in San José. However,
unless you're sailing to the island on a private
boat, tour operators will make all the necessary
arrangements for you.

ℹ Getting There & Away

The only way to get here is via a liveaboard
diving boat. With advance reservations, both
of the liveaboard diving tour companies in
Puntarenas will arrange transfers from either
San José or Liberia to Puntarenas, which is the
embarkation/disembarkation point for tours.
It takes 32 hours by boat from Puntarenas to
Isla del Coco.

Southern Costa Rica & Península de Osa

Best Ecolodges

➡ Danta Corcovado Lodge (p452)

➡ El Remanso Lodge (p445)

➡ Esquinas Rainforest Lodge (p455)

➡ Luna Lodge (p443)

Best Off-the-Beaten-Track

➡ Parque Internacional La Amistad (p425)

➡ Reserva Biológica Dúrika (p420)

➡ Reserva Indígena Boruca (p420)

➡ Playas San Josecito, Nicuesa & Cativo (p456)

Why Go?

From the chilly heights of Cerro Chirripó (3820m) to the steamy coastal jungles of the Península de Osa, this sector of Costa Rica encompasses some of the country's least-explored and least-developed land. Vast tracts of wilderness remain untouched in Parque Internacional La Amistad, and the country's most visible indigenous groups – the Bribrí, Cabécar, Boruc and Ngöbe – maintain traditional ways of living in their remote territories.

Quetzal sightings around San Gerardo de Dota are not unusual, and scarlet macaw appearances throughout the coastal region are the norm. Besides the easily spotted birds, and monkeys, sloths and coatis roaming the region's abundant parks and reserves, in Parque Nacional Corcovado there's also the rare chance to spy on slumbering tapir. Meanwhile, the rugged coasts of the Golfo Dulce and Península de Osa captivate travelers with abandoned wilderness beaches, world-class surf and opportunities for rugged exploration. This is the land for intrepid travelers yearning for something truly wild.

When to Go

➡ Trekking in Corcovado, and also up Cerro Chirripó is best during the dry season (late December through March).

➡ Surfing is at its best in Pavones during the April to October rainy season, though there are beginner waves year-round.

➡ The best time for quetzal sightings is during the nesting season between February and May, which also coincides with the fruiting of the wild avocado, their favorite food.

Southern Costa Rica & Península de Osa Highlights

1 Hiking the remote coast and rich rainforest of **Parque Nacional Corcovado** (p439), the country's premier wilderness experience.

2 Climbing atop Costa Rica's tallest peak to watch the sunrise from **Cerro Chirripó** (p416).

3 Catching a ride on one of the world's longest left breaks at the slow-paced surfing paradise of **Pavones** (p457).

4 Looking for resplendently feathered quetzals in the cool highlands of **San Gerardo de Dota** (p409).

5 Snorkeling, hiking and wildlife-spotting along the wild coast of **Bahía Drake** (p429).

6 Celebrating the vibrant **Fiesta de los Diablitos** (p421) at the Reserva Indígena Boruca.

7 Immersing yourself in rural tourism at the former gold-mining villages of **Dos Brazos** (p449) and **Rancho Quemado** (p435).

8 Contemplating the mysteries of the pre-Columbian stone spheres at **Sitio Arqueológico Finca 6** (p427).

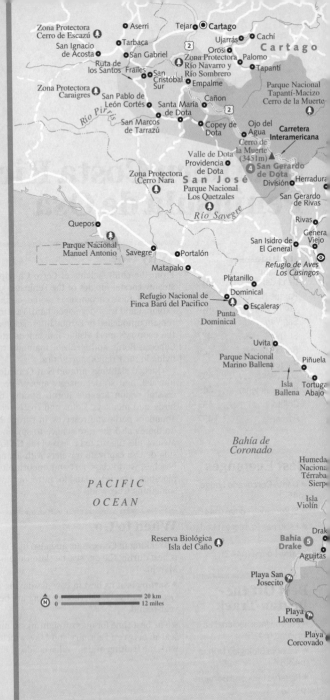

History

Costa Rica's indigenous population was almost entirely wiped out through both the direct and indirect effects of colonization. Spanish conquistadors eventually gave way to Catholic missionaries, though the end result was the same, namely the complete disruption of pre-Columbian life in the New World.

Even as late as the 20th century, indigenous groups were actively disenfranchised from the Spanish-dominated society. In fact, citizenship was not granted to the indigenous population until 1949, and reservations were not organized until 1977. In the intervening decades, indigenous groups have been allowed to engage in their traditional languages and customs.

On the Osa, the vast majority of the peninsula was never populated or developed by Ticos. In fact, because of the remoteness of the region, commercial logging was not a threat until the early 1960s. Although this tumultuous decade saw the destruction of much of Costa Rica's remaining primary forests, Osa was largely spared. By 1975, however, international companies were greedily eyeing the peninsula's timber and gold. Fortunately, these ambitions were halted when researchers petitioned President Daniel Oduber to establish a national park.

In recent years the peninsula has attracted the attention of wealthy foreigners, who have snatched up some prime real estate, but there's hope that development will be more sustainable in this part of the country, particularly since there is a vested interest in keeping the peninsula green.

Parks & Reserves

As the country's premier ecotourism destination, the Península de Osa has a plethora of parks, reserves and wildlife refuges. Beyond the Osa, the southern zone has its own wealth of less-visited protected lands. The following is only a list of absolute highlights.

Parque Internacional La Amistad (p425) This enormous bi-national park is shared with Panama and protects a biological corridor of incredible ecological significance.

Parque Nacional Chirripó (p416) Home to Costa Rica's highest and most famous peak, Cerro Chirripó, which on a clear day offers views of both the Pacific and the Caribbean.

Parque Nacional Corcovado (p439) Osa's shining crown jewel, and one of Costa Rica's last true wilderness areas.

Reserva Biológica Isla del Caño (p438) A tiny but spectacular marine and terrestrial park, popular with snorkelers, divers and biologists.

ⓘ Getting There & Away

The main towns in the region are well-connected by buses, with the exception of Puerto Jiménez, Bahía Drake, Zancudo and Pavones, which each have only a couple of bus connections daily. To explore southern Costa Rica in depth, it's best to have your own 4WD. That said, it's fairly easy to connect via bus to departure points for Amistad and Chirripó. Note that addresses in this part of the country are virtually nonexistent, and the numbered posts (counting the kilometers from San José) along the Carretera Interamericana are used to locate places.

Getting to Osa demands one of two things: lots of patience or flying in. Given the reasonable cost of flights, a good option for exploring the peninsula is to fly if your time is limited (you can then rent a vehicle in Puerto Jiménez). If you choose to drive, you'll need a 4WD and plenty of confidence: many roads in Osa are extremely poor and there are river crossings involved.

Easy Ride shuttles connect Puerto Jiménez to San José and popular destinations along the Pacific coast.

Sansa (⌨ 2290-4100; www.flysansa.com) serves Palmar, which is a jumping-off point for the southern zone. Prices vary according to season and availability, but usually you can expect to pay just under US$75 for a flight from San José or Liberia.

THE ROAD TO CHIRRIPÓ

Traveling south from San José, the road to Parque Nacional Chirripó passes through gorgeous countryside of redolent coffee plantations and cool, misty cloud forest. It bisects the Zona de los Santos, a collection of highland villages that bear sainted names: San Pablo de León Cortés, San Marcos de Tarrazú, San Cristóbal Sur, San Gerardo de Dota, Santa María de Dota – the last renowned for its superb, ecologically produced coffee. Further south in the Valle de El General, family-run *fincas* (farms) dot the fertile valley, though the action tends to center on San Isidro de El General, southern Costa Rica's largest town and major transportation hub.

Travelers aiming for this region tend to have one of two goals in mind: hiking up Cerro Chirripó, Costa Rica's tallest mountain and challenging high-altitude hike, and trying to spot the resplendent quetzal in the dense cloud forest that cloaks Cerro de La Muerte.

San Gerardo de Dota

San Gerardo de Dota is unlike any other place in Costa Rica – a bucolic mountain village run through by a clear, rushing river and surrounded by forested hills that more resemble the alps than the tropics. It's set deep within a mountain valley; the air is crisp and fresh, and chilly at night, and the orchard-lined Savegre basin hosts numerous high-altitude bird species that draw birdwatchers from around the world.

Activities

One of the best places to go bird-watching and hiking in the area is Parque Nacional Los Quetzales, though you're just as likely to spot the elusive quetzal along the private trails in the grounds of Savegre Hotel de Montaña and Paraíso Quetzal Lodge, the latter a little way from San Gerardo (both allow access to non-guests for a fee), or at a particular spot along the river (ask your lodgings where it is), which gets crowded with binocular-bearing twitchers at dawn. Your accommodations can arrange a birding guide for Parque Nacional Los Quetzales to maximize your chances of spotting the likes of collared trogons and emerald toucanets, as well as the quetzal. Travelers who wish to do extensive hiking in the area are advised to collect maps before they arrive.

A challenging 9km trail runs up from San Gerardo to Cerro de la Muerte; the trailhead is in the Savegre Hotel grounds. It's easier to hike down (five hours), but best done with a guide as the trailhead down is not as easy to find as the one going up. An easy 1km trail rambles along the Río Savegre to a pretty waterfall at the south end of the San Gerardo valley.

Quetzals are spotted particularly frequently every April and May (during breeding season) and are fairly common throughout the rest of the year.

Sleeping

Ranchos la Isla & Restaurante Los Lagos   CAMPGROUND $
(☑ 2740-1009; campsite per person US$10; P) This attractive property just across from Cabinas El Quetzal offers a handful of campsites

on metal-roofed platforms alongside a small river. The accommodating Chinchilla families arrange guided hikes to nearby waterfalls in the hope of spotting the elusive quetzal. If you're looking for a hot meal, the on-site restaurant is a modest affair serving up country-style *casados* (set meals; US$7 to US$10).

Cabinas El Quetzal   CABINA $$
(☑ 2740-1036; www.cabinaselquetzal.com; per person incl 2 meals US$65; P🛜) This simple cluster of four family-run, riverside *cabinas* (some with wood-burning stoves) has a homespun feel. The included meals are lovingly prepared – naturally, fresh trout is on offer. The rooms are without frills (tile floors, small sitting areas, no TVs), but they're clean, comfortable and stocked with a pile of blankets in the likely event of a chilly night.

★ **Trogon Lodge**   LODGE $$$
(☑ 2293-8181; www.trogonlodge.com; s/d from US$109/134) Hemmed in by cloud forest and with the Río Savegre crossing the property, Trogon Lodge is home to over 175 bird species, including that feathered prize – the quetzal – found along the marked hiking trails. Beautifully landscaped gardens, an excellent restaurant and delightful little touches, such as hot-water bottles delivered to your cabin, make this a superb choice.

TALAMANCA TROUT FISHING

While most sportfishers flock to the coast for a big catch, the crystal-clear waters and the cool air of the cloud forest make for a hypnotic, tranquil setting, and the fish – here, rainbow trout – are no less tasty.

The trout here are not native. Supposedly, they were first introduced to Central American rivers by the US military in Panama and the healthy fish made their way north into Costa Rican waters.

In order to maintain healthy populations, fishers are strongly encouraged to limit stream fishing to catch-and-release. If you want to take home your trout for dinner, fish in one of the local spring-fed ponds, which are well stocked with 30cm to 50cm trout. Success is guaranteed and you just pay for what you take home (about US$4.50 per kilogram). This is a great option for kids and folk with poor fishing karma.

Truchas Selva Madre (2571-1364, 2571-1817; www.truchasselvamadre.com; Interamericana Sur, 2km north of Km 64; 8am-5pm) A popular local fishing spot that is home to a well-stocked trout pond and hiking trails – good for a full day of fun. You can grill your catch right here.

Ranchos La Isla (2740-1009; San Gerardo de Dota; hours vary) Borrow equipment to fish in the river and ponds, then bring your catch back and have the staff fry it up for dinner.

Savegre Hotel (2740-1028; San Gerardo de Dota; 8am-4pm) This lodge provides equipment and guides for fly-fishing in the Río Savegre, or you can fish in the picturesque pond and pay for what you catch.

★ **Savegre Hotel**   LODGE $$$
(2740-1028, in USA & Canada 866-549-1178; www.savegre.com; s/d/ste incl 3 meals US$136/190/254;) Operated by the Chacón family since 1957, this lodge is hugely popular with bird-watchers, since the quetzal nests along the 30km of trails on the 400-hectare property. The gorgeous, wood-paneled rooms and suites have wrought-iron chandeliers and wooden furniture surrounding a stone fireplace. The on-site spa provides pampering and the professional guides organize birding, horseback riding and hiking outings. The trail network is open to nonguests (US$10 per person).

Dantica Cloud Forest Lodge   LODGE $$$
(2740-1067; www.dantica.com; r/ste incl breakfast from US$101/287;) The most elegant place in San Gerardo, this upscale lodge consists of lovely stucco bungalows with colorful Colombian architectural accents. The modern comforts – leather sofas, plasma TVs, Jacuzzis and track lighting – are nice, but the stunning vistas over the cloud forest steal the scene. The downside? The rooms get very cold at night in spite of the ethanol-burning stoves. A nature reserve complete with private trails is just steps away, as is a spa for post-hike pampering. If the price tag is too steep, instead you can stop by to browse the gallery's collection of art from all over Latin America, visit the gift store or book a romantic dinner at the Tico-continental **Restaurant Le Tapir** (mains from US$11 to US$23).

🍴 Eating

La Comida Típica Miriam   COSTA RICAN $
(2740-1049; meals US$6-10; 7am-7pm;) One of the first places you will pass in San Gerardo, about 6km from the Interamericana, is this cozy house advertising *comida típica* – regional specialties. Eating here is almost like receiving a personal invitation to dine in a Tico home: the food is delicious and abundant, and the hospitality even more so.

Miriam also rents a few cabins (US$40) in the woods behind the restaurant: a modest but comfortable place to spend a night or two.

Café Kahawa   CAFE $
(2740-1081; mains US$5-10; 7am-6pm;) With alfresco tables sitting above the river, funky skull art and sparkling fish tanks filled with fingerling trout, this atmospheric spot prepares trout in many excellent ways (and there are a few non-fishy dishes). Variations on the theme – such as trout in coconut sauce and trout *ceviche* – can't be found just anywhere. Located toward the southern end of the valley.

ℹ Getting There & Away

The turnoff to San Gerardo de Dota is near Km 80 on the Interamericana. From here, the steep road down into the valley alternates between paved and dirt; it's best to have a 4WD. Take it slowly, as two-way traffic necessitates a bit of negotiation. Buses between San José and San Isidro de El General can drop you at the turnoff, but bear in mind that the village spreads along 9km of road, so you may have a fair hike ahead of you.

Parque Nacional Los Quetzales

Spread along both banks of the Río Savegre, Parque Nacional Los Quetzales (☎ 2514-0403; admission US$10; ☺ 8am-4pm) officially became a national park in 2005. At an altitude of 2000m to 3000m, Los Quetzales covers 50 sq km of rainforest and cloud forest lying along the slopes of the Cordillera de Talamanca.

The park's lifeblood is the Río Savegre, which starts high up on the Cerro de la Muerte and feeds several glacial lakes before pouring into the Pacific. This region is remarkably diverse – the Savegre watershed contains approximately 20% of the country's registered bird species.

True to the park's name, the beautiful quetzal is here (best spotted during the March–June nesting season), along with the trogon, hummingbirds and sooty robin. Avians aside, the park is home to endangered species including jaguars, Baird's tapirs and squirrel monkeys. The park also has premontane forests, the second-most endangered life zone in Costa Rica.

ℹ Information

The park has no facilities for tourists aside from the small **ranger station** (☎ 2514-0403; ☺ 8am-4pm), which collects fees. From here, a modest network of ill-maintained bird-watching trails radiates into the forest. All the lodges around San Gerardo de Dota organize hiking and bird-watching tours, and it's best to come with a guide to get the most out of your visit.

ℹ Getting There & Away

The park is bordered by the Interamericana; the entrance is just past Km 76. Any bus along this route can drop you off at the ranger station, though most people arrive in a private vehicle.

Cerro de la Muerte

Between Empalme and San Isidro de El General, the Interamericana reaches its highest point along the famed Cerro de la Muerte (3451m). The 'Hill of Death' received its moniker during its pre-highway days, when crossing the mountains required travel on foot or horseback and many travelers succumbed to exposure.

It's still an exciting drive, snaking the fog-shrouded spine along a path riddled with blind corners, hair-raising cliffs and careless drivers who take huge risks to overtake slower road users. The upside? Exquisite panoramic views of the Cordillera de Talamanca.

Cerro de la Muerte marks the northernmost extent of the *páramo,* a highland shrub and tussock grass habitat typical of the southern zone. This Andean-style landscape is rich in wildlife and is home to many of the same species found in nearby Parque Nacional Chirripó. On the way to San Isidro the road descends through three other biospheres: cloud forests, montane and premontane forest.

🛏 Sleeping & Eating

There are several lodges spread out along this stretch of highway. Note that addresses in this part of Costa Rica are nonexistent, so accommodations tend to be listed by their 'Km' distance marker.

Bosque del Tolomuco   B&B **$$**
(☎ 8847-7207; www.bosquedeltolomuco.com; Interamericana Km 118; cabin from US$65; 🅿 🛜 ✸) Named for the sly tayra (tree otter) spotted on the grounds, this cutesy B&B is run by a lovely, chatty Canadian couple. There are five spacious, light-filled cabins, the most charming of which is the secluded 'Hummingbird

DON'T MISS

THE MAKER MET HIS MAKER

Although the treacherous drive across the Cerro de la Muerte might offer ample opportunities to meet your maker, look to the heavens about 6km north of San Isidro. There you'll see a giant lump of melted plastic, perched precariously on the edge of a cliff above. It used to be a towering statue of Christ, but was struck by lightning in 2015.

Cabin.' The grounds offer 5km of hiking trails, ample opportunities to indulge in bird-watching and some magnificent views of Los Cruces and Chirripó.

A made-to-order gourmet dinner is available with advance notice. Day hikers who want to stretch their legs and get off the road can hike the network of trails for US$3.

Mirador de Quetzales CABINA $$
(☑ 8381-8456, 2200-4185; www.quetzalesdecostarica.com; Interamericana Km 70; cabins per person incl 2 meals US$65; P) About 1km west of the Interamericana, this excellent option consists of a cluster of wooden cabins, warmed by electric heaters. Prices also include an early morning 'quetzal quest' along the 4km trail shaded by immense cypress trees – the feathered beauties reside in these forested hills year-round. Non-guests can wander the system of trails for a small fee (US$7).

Mirador Valle del General LODGE $$
(☑ 8384-4685, 2200-5465; www.valledelgeneral.com; Interamericana Km 119; d/tr incl breakfast US$55/70; P🛜) The main feature of the restaurant at this aptly named lodge is the panoramic view that complements local specialties such as fried trout. Below the restaurant, eight spotless rooms built entirely from cultivated wood are brightened by colorful indigenous tapestries and the spectacular valley views. Guests can ramble the nature trails in search of tanagers and other local feathered life.

★Paraíso Quetzal Lodge LODGE $$$
(☑ 2200-0241; www.paraisoquetzal.com; Interamericana Km 70; r per person incl breakfast from US$60, half-board from US$75) Birders rave about this lodge, surrounded by 13km of walking trails that provide an excellent chance of spotting the resplendent quetzal during the 6am tours. The scattering of wooden cabins is kept warm by a generous collection of space heaters and woolen blankets. Superior cabins come with Jacuzzis and superb valley views, ideal for canoodling with your sweetie.

San Isidro de El General

With a population of around 45,000, San Isidro de El General is the fastest-growing urban area outside the capital. Little more than a sprawling, utilitarian market town at the crossroads between some of Costa Rica's

prime destinations, it's a place where few travelers choose to linger.

'El General' (often referred to as Pérez Zeledón, the name of the municipality) is the region's largest population center and major transportation hub. If you're traveling to the southern Pacific beaches or Chirripó, a brief stop is inevitable. Some accommodations options just outside the town environs are worthy destinations in their own right.

And – a curious footnote – the women of San Isidro de El General are widely regarded as Costa Rica's finest. Perhaps it's the fresh mountain air and strong coffee?

The heart of San Isidro is the network of narrow streets clustered around the Parque Central.

🎊 Festivals & Events

★Agricultural Festival CULTURAL
(☉1st week of Feb) This fair is a chance for local farmers to strut their stuff – and that they do, by taking over the agricultural show grounds 4km south of the city with regional culinary delights. There are also bullfights (well, bull-teasing), horsemanship events, an orchid exhibition, livestock competitions and concerts in the evening.

🛏 Sleeping

Hotel Chirripó HOTEL $
(☑ 2771-0529; Av 2 btwn Calles Central & 1; r with/without bathroom US$57/41; P🅿🛜) Let's put it bluntly: if you're traveling through town, weary and cash-poor, this is *the* choice. Popular with discerning budget travelers, this centrally located hotel is a two-minute stroll from the bus station and filled with bare, whitewashed rooms that are barren but utterly dirt- and grime-free.

Talari Mountain Lodge LODGE $$
(☑ 2771-0341; www.talari.co.cr; Rivas; s/d incl breakfast US$59/84; P🛜🏊) This secluded mountain lodge is a bird-watcher's haven, with over 200 species of bird spotted along the three well-maintained trails on the riverside property. Accommodations are in simple wooden cabins hemmed in by the forest. To get here from San Isidro, follow the road to San Gerardo de Rivas for 7km; the driveway will be on the right.

Best Western Hotel Zima HOTEL $$
(☑ 2770-1114; www.hotelzima.net; Interamericana; r US$80-115; P🅿🛜🏊) This latest addition to the Best Western stable benefits from a

central location yet is far enough from the main highway to avoid the traffic noise. The rooms are of a standard, not hugely memorable business variety, but comfortable and very clean, and the staff are friendly and eager to please.

★**Hacienda AltaGracia** BOUTIQUE HOTEL **$$$**
(☎815-812-2212; http://altagracia.aubergeresorts.com; r US$350-625; P❄🌐♨) Overlooking the green and lush Valle de General, this hillside boutique hacienda consists of self-contained *casitas* and suites, their decor stylish and understated (neutral shades, dark leather), surrounded by 350 hectares – ideal for hiking, horseback riding and observing from the air from one of the resort's own ultra-lights. Dining focuses on the farm-to-table concept. Detailed directions on website.

✖ Eating

★**Urban Farm Cafe** INTERNATIONAL **$**
(☎2771-2442; Calle Central; mains US$5-7; ☺7am-7pm Mon-Sat; 🌐) With its 'from farm to table' motto, this delightful cafe singlehandedly pushes San Isidro's dining scene up a big notch. Breakfast options range from 'Hawaiian-style' macadamia pancakes with banana to veggie omelettes and bacon wraps, while their lunchtime wraps and salads are just overflowing with fresh vegetables. Wash it down with a delectable fruit smoothie.

Farmers' Market MARKET **$**
(off Calle 3) The largest *feria* in the region, this farmers' market starts early Thursday morning and usually winds down by early afternoon on Friday; organic produce, prepared foods and goods are bountiful.

La Casa del Marisco SEAFOOD **$**
(☎8366-1880, 2772-2862; Calle Central; mains US$5-12; ☺10am-10pm Mon-Sat) Since this unpretentious seafood spot is usually slammed at lunchtime, it's best to come during off hours for its several daily varieties of *ceviche,* fresh fish or shrimp prepared as you like it (plus pastas, burgers, salads and soups). The crowd of local clientele not-so-subtly hints at the choice sustenance served here.

Kafe de la Casa CAFE **$**
(☎2770-4816; Av 3 btwn Calles 2 & 4; meals US$7-14; ☺7am-8pm Mon-Sat, 7am-3pm Sun; 🌐) Set in an old Tico house, this bohemian cafe features eclectic artwork, an open kitchen

San Isidro de El General

San Isidro de El General

and breezy garden seating. The menu has excellent breakfasts, light lunches, gourmet dinners and plenty of coffee drinks. Veggie options include salads and sandwiches.

Supermercados Coopeagri SUPERMARKET **$**
(☎2785-0227; Av 6 btwn Calles Central & 2; ☺7am-9pm Mon-Sat, 8am-4pm Sun) Self-caterers can shop at this large, reasonably well-stocked supermarket.

BUSES FROM SAN ISIDRO DE EL GENERAL

Buses from Terminal Tracopa

You will find **Terminal Tracopa** (☏2771-0468) on the Interamericana, just southwest of Av Central. If heading for Paso Canoas, Golfito or Palmar Norte, try to catch a bus that originates from San Isidro, or risk standing room only.

DESTINATION	COST (US$)	DURATION (HR)	FREQUENCY (DAILY)
Golfito	8.60	3	3-4
Neily	8.60	4	4:45am, 7am, 12:30pm, 3pm
Palmar Norte	6.30	2	4
Paso Canoas	9.25	4½	8am, 10:40am, 4:10pm, 6:30pm, 9:30pm
San José	7.10	3	13 daily 8:35am-8:30pm
San Vito	7.75	3½	5:30am, 9am, 11am, 2pm, 7pm

Buses from Terminal Quepos

Terminal Quepos (☏2771-4744) is on the side street west of the Interamericana.

DESTINATION	COST (US$)	DURATION (HR)	FREQUENCY (DAILY)
Dominical	3.20	1½	7am, 9am, 11:30am, 3:30pm, 4pm
Puerto Jiménez (via Palmar Norte)	10	5	6:30am, 11am, 3pm
Quepos	5.20	3	7am, 11:30am, 3:30pm
Uvita	3.60	2	9am, 4pm

❶ Getting There & Away

AIR

There are flights between San José and San Isidro with **Sansa** (www.flysansa.com) on Sunday, Tuesday and Friday, from US$70 one way.

BUS

In San Isidro the **local bus terminal** (☏), known as Mercado, is on Av 6 and serves nearby villages. The bus to San Gerardo de Rivas (for Parque Nacional Chirripó; US$3; 1½ hours) departs from the local terminal five times daily from 5:30am.

Local buses from **Terminal Gafeso** (☏2771-1523) serve Buenos Aires, with onward connections to Reserva Biológica Dúrika.

Long-distance buses leave from points near the Interamericana and are frequently packed, so buy tickets early. Note that buses heading south to Golfito or Ciudad Neily will go through Palmar Norte.

San Gerardo de Rivas

If you have plans to climb Chirripó, you're in the right place – the tiny, tranquil, spread-out town of San Gerardo de Rivas is at the doorstep of the national park. This is a place to get supplies, a good night's rest and a hot shower before and after the trek.

Given how the park authorities have made it very difficult to obtain hiking permits (almost impossible for walk-ins), San Gerardo is doing its best to promote other activities, and its bird-filled alpine scenery makes it a beautiful place to linger. Those who don't have the time or energy to summit Chirripó can go on lovely, less difficult hikes in its two private nature reserves, and there's rural tourism aplenty, from the local trout farm to local cheese- and chocolate-makers in nearby Canaán.

The road to San Gerardo de Rivas winds its way 22km up the valley of the Río Chirripó from San Isidro.

◉ Sights & Activities

Jardines Secretos   GARDENS
(☏2742 5086; www.sangerardocostarica.com; admission US$5; ☺9am-5pm) These not-so-secret gardens, lovingly reared by an expat German and his Costa Rican colleague, make for a tranquil pre- or post-Chirripó pastime as the owners talk you through their collection of orchids and other tropical plants. Find the turnoff just before the ranger station.

★ Cloudbridge
Nature Reserve   NATURE RESERVE

(☑in USA 917-494-5408; www.cloudbridge.org; admission by donation; ☺sunrise-sunset) About 2km past the trailhead to Cerro Chirripó you will find the entrance to the mystical, magical Cloudbridge Nature Reserve. Covering 182 hectares on the side of Cerro Chirripó, this private reserve is an ongoing reforestation and preservation project spearheaded by New Yorkers Ian and Genevieve Giddy. A network of trails traverses the property, which is easy to explore independently. Even if you don't get far past the entrance, you'll find two waterfalls, including the magnificent Catarata Pacifica. The trails range from the gentle Sendero Catarata Pacifica, leading to the waterfalls, to the steep uphill Sendero Montaña that joins the main trail up Cerro Chirripó.

Volunteer reforestation and conservation opportunities are listed on the reserve's website.

Talamanca Reserve   NATURE RESERVE

(www.talamancareserve.com) With over 4000 acres of primary and secondary cloud forest, this private reserve has numerous hiking trails, the longest being a seven-hour trek, and another leading to its 10 waterfalls. Talamanca is doing its best to promote itself as an alternative to Parque Nacional Chirripó, and non-guests are welcome to hike its trails for a day fee of US$25. ATV tours are available both to guests and non-guests.

Cocolisos Truchero   FISHING, FOOD

(☑2742-5023; ☺8am-6pm Sat & Sun, & by appointment) Down the left fork road just before the Quebrada Chispa bridge, uphill from the ranger station, is this lovely family-run trout farm. Catch your own fish from the trout pools or take in the celebrated orchid collection. Naturally, the fish is the best part; matronly Garita puts together a homemade feast of trout and home-cooked sides for US$7.

⚜ Festivals & Events

Carrera Chirripó   SPORTS

(www.carrerachirripo.com) This grueling race from San Gerardo de Rivas to Crestones Base Lodge and back (34km) takes place at the end of February, with up to 225 participants. If you're trekking up the mountain you may be disheartened to know that the fastest man and woman have covered the distance in three hours, four minutes and four hours, 19 minutes, respectively.

🛏 Sleeping

★ Casa Mariposa   HOSTEL $

(☑2742-5037; www.hotelcasamariposa.net; dm US$16, d US$40-60; ℗@) ✐ Just 50m from the park entrance, this adorable hostel is built into the side of the mountain and is characterized by the warmth and knowledge of owners John and Jill. Traveler-oriented benefits – warm clothes to borrow for the hike, laundry service, assistance with booking the Chirripó lodge and tips on alternative activities in the area – make it ideal.

In the evening, guests gather around the wood stove in the communal living room to read, plan hikes and welcome weary hikers returning from the summit. There's a tidy kitchen, a lookout with hammocks on the roof and a stone soaking tub. There's only space for 15 guests, so advance booking is recommended.

Casa Hostel Chirripó   HOSTEL $

(☑2742-5020; www.casachirripo.com; dm US$15, r with/without bathroom US$40/35; ☎) Near the football field, this colorful new hostel offers its guests a free shuttle to the park entrance at 5am, gives them a space to cook and socialize, and post-hike provides cozy rooms and dorms to lay down their weary heads.

El Urán Hotel y Restaurante   HOSTEL $

(☑2742-5003; www.hoteluran.com; r per person without bathroom US$22, d US$57, all incl breakfast; ℗☎) Just 70m below the trailhead, these no-nonsense budget digs are a longtime mecca for hikers heading to/from Chirripó. Budget-friendly rooms are fine for a restful snooze, while the on-site restaurant, grocery store and laundry facility all cater to the shoestring set. Note that it's possible to buy beer here (the *pulpería* doesn't sell alcohol).

★ Talamanca Reserve   HOTEL $$

(☑2742-5080; www.talamancareserve.com; r & ste US$79-100; ℗☎) ✐ Set within the private Talamanca Reserve, uphill from the ranger station, is a scattering of appealing garden and river cabins – all with terraces and beautifully embellished wood and tile interiors. There's a good on-site restaurant, but the biggest attraction is access to the reserve's many trails. There is also a remote guesthouse with budget rooms (US$45; no wi-fi). The accommodations and hiking tours are managed by the friendly, bilingual Kenneth, who was born and raised on the reserve, and whose family still maintains the gardens, fruit trees, trails and a reforestation project here.

★ **Casa de los Celtas**   B&B **$$**
(☎ 8707-2921, 2770-3524; www.casaceltas.com; r US$60; **P** 🐾) Overlooking four acres of native greenery and brightened by Sheelagh's orchid collection, this delightful B&B is run by two retired British travelers, whose genuine warmth and knowledge of the area greatly enhances your stay. Choose between a twin room or a compact, self-contained cottage and feast on Sheelagh's gourmet cooking (three-course dinner US$19). Extensive breakfasts feature plenty of fresh fruit.

Hotel de Montaña El Pelícano   HOTEL **$$**
(☎ 2742-5050; www.hotelpelicano.net; r US$60-70, ste US$98; **P** 🐾🍴🏊) 🐾 About 300m below the ranger station, steeply uphill from the main road, this simple, functional lodge, surrounded by gorgeous vegetation, has a collection of spartan but spotless rooms that overlook the river valley. The highlight of the property is the gallery of the owner, a late-blooming artist who sculpts whimsical wood pieces.

★ **Monte Azul**   BOUTIQUE HOTEL **$$$**
(☎ 2742-5222, in USA 415-967-4300; www.monteazulcr.com; s/d incl 2 meals from US$399/499; **P** 🐾🍴) 🐾 The elegant and carbon-neutral Monte Azul, set on a private 125-hectare reserve, is a retreat for artists and gourmands. The four individually decorated, luxury riverfront suites have tasteful contemporary art, small kitchens and custom-designed furniture. The gourmet restaurant offers international fusions using organic produce from the garden. There are private walking trails. It's between Rivas and San Gerardo de Rivas.

Río Chirripó Retreat   HOTEL **$$$**
(☎ 2742-5109; www.riochirripo.com; d/cabin/casita incl breakfast US$100/129/250; **P** 🐾🍴🏊) This upscale lodge, 1.5km from San Gerardo, in Canaán, is centered on a yoga studio overlooking the river, and an open-air, Santa Fe–style communal area. You can hear the rush of the river from eight secluded cabins, where woven blankets and stenciled walls evoke the southwest USA. On the grounds are hiking trails, a heated swimming pool and a hot tub.

Restaurante Rios   PIZZA **$**
(mains from US$8; ⊙ 11am-9pm; 🐾) Not far from the soccer field, this new place serves surprisingly good pizzas; we particularly like the one topped with imported meats. Generous portions, and several pizza options are meat-free.

❶ Information

Consorcio Aguas Eternas (Consortium Office; ☎ 2742-5097; infochirriposervicios@gmail. com; ⊙ 8am-noon & 1:30-4:30pm) Right by the soccer field, this is the office responsible for the Crestones Base Lodge bookings. If you've had a third party reserve your space for you, you still need to check in here the day before your hike; otherwise, you may only reserve your space via phone or email with a prior reservation code from the park ranger's office.

Ranger Station (Sinac; ☎ 2742-5348; ⊙ 6:30am-noon & 1-4:30pm) The Chirripó ranger station is 1km below the soccer field, at the entrance to San Gerardo de Rivas. If you've made reservations at Crestones Base Lodge and to hike up Cerro Chirripó, you must stop by the day before to confirm your permit. If you haven't booked your park permit in advance, there's a very slim chance of next-day availability.

❶ Getting There & Away

Arriving via public transportation requires a connection through San Isidro. Buses to San Isidro depart from the soccer field six times daily (three daily on Sunday) between 5:15am and 9pm (US$2, 1½ hours).

Driving from San Isidro, head south on the Interamericana and cross Río San Isidro south of town. About 500m further on, cross the unsigned Río Jilguero and take the first, steep turn up to the left, about 300m beyond the Jilguero. Note that this turnoff is not marked (if you miss the turn, it is signed from the northbound side).

The ranger station is about 18km up this road from the Interamericana. The road passes through Rivas village and is paved as far as the entrance to San Gerardo de Rivas now. It is passable for ordinary cars, but a 4WD is recommended if you are driving to Albergue Urán or to Cloudbridge Nature Reserve, as the unpaved road is steep and hideous.

Parque Nacional Chirripó

Costa Rica's mountainous spine runs the length of the country in four distinct mountain ranges, of which the Cordillera de Talamanca is the highest, longest and most remote. The cordillera's highlight and the focus of the high-altitude **Parque Nacional Chirripó** (☎ 2742-5083; park fee per day US$20; ⊙ closed 2nd half of May & all of Oct) is Costa Rica's highest peak, Cerro Chirripó (3820m).

The only way up Chirripó is on foot. Although the trekking routes are challenging, watching the sunrise from such lofty heights is one of the country's undeniable highlights.

Parque Nacional Chirripó is a welcome respite from lowland heat. Above 3400m, the landscape is *páramo,* comprising scrubby trees and grasslands. Rocky outposts punctuate the otherwise barren hills, and feed a series of glacial lakes that earned the park its iconic name: Chirripó means 'eternal waters.'

The bare *páramo* contrasts with the lush cloud forest, which dominates the hillsides between 2500m and 3400m. Oak trees tower over the dense undergrowth and the evergreen canopy.

Activities

Wildlife-Watching

The varying altitude means an amazing diversity of fauna in Parque Nacional Chirripó. Particularly famous for its extensive birdlife, the national park is home to several endangered species, including the harpy eagle (the largest, most powerful raptor in the Americas) and the resplendent quetzal (especially visible between March and May). Even besides these highlights, you might see highland birds including the three-wattled bellbird, black guan and tinamou. The Andean-like *páramo* guarantees volcano junco, sooty robin, slaty finch, large-footed finch and the endemic volcano hummingbird, which is found only in Costa Rica's highlands.

In addition to the prolific birdlife, the park is home to some unusual high-altitude reptiles, such as the green spiny lizard and the highland alligator lizard. Mammals include puma, Baird's tapir, spider monkey, capuchin and – at higher elevations – Dice's rabbit and the coyotes that feed on them.

Although spotting rarer animals is never a guaranteed proposition, here are a few tips to maximize your chances: pumas stick to the savanna areas and use the trails at dawn and dusk to move about; Baird's tapirs gravitate to various highland lagoons, mainly in the rainy season, so stake out the muddy edges at dawn or dusk if you see recent tracks; and at nighttime, coyotes can be seen feeding at the rubbish bins near Crestones Base Lodge.

Climbing Chirripó

The park entrance is at San Gerardo de Rivas, which lies 1219m above sea level; the altitude at the summit is 3820m, which makes it 2.6km straight up! A well-marked 19.6km trail leads all the way to the top, with trail markers every kilometer, and no technical climbing is required. It would be nearly impossible to get lost.

Altitude sickness can be an issue as you get higher up. Watch out for nausea, shortness of breath, headaches and exhaustion. If you start feeling unwell, rest for a little while; if the symptoms persist, descend immediately.

The amount of time it takes to get up varies greatly – it can take as little as five and as many as 12 hours to cover the 14.5km from the start of the trail to the Crestones Base Lodge, depending on how fit you are; bank on at least seven hours. From the lodge it's another 5.1km to the summit, which takes around 1½ hours one way.

Most hikers start the hike between 5am or 6am, though there's nothing to stop you from leaving earlier. Technically, you're not supposed to be inside the park before 5am,

---

ⓘ DAY HIKING CHIRRIPÓ

The masochistically inclined and the superfit may be thrilled to know that it's feasible to summit Chirripó and return to town in a single day. But whatever you do, don't underestimate the mountain.

It's a 39.2km round trip that involves a climb of 2000m into high-altitude territory and is an exhausting uphill slog most of the way. The summit is more likely to be cloudy in the afternoons than early in the morning, meaning you probably won't get much of a view, and summiting and returning on the same day almost invariably means descending at least part of the way in the dark.

But if you're determined to do it, make sure you take food, water, a flashlight with spare batteries and warm clothes. And start early – around 1am or 2am. That way you can get to Crestones Base Lodge mid-morning, have time to rest, summit, and then head back down again in the afternoon. Walking part of the way in the dark is not a problem, since the trail is clearly marked and it's almost impossible to get lost. But if you have any doubts about your fitness, consider a long day hike in the Cloudbridge Nature Reserve (p415) instead.

ⓘ ADVANCE PLANNING

Hiking up Chirripó requires advance planning, especially as the park authorities have made it very difficult to secure a park permit and reservation at Crestones Base Lodge (base camp for the summit push) from outside Costa Rica, and it's equally difficult to acquire them by simply turning up at the ranger station in San Gerardo de Rivas; Crestones Base Lodge no longer sets aside 10 spaces daily for walk-ins, so you have to arrange both the permit and accommodations on the mountain in advance.

Though the park will supposedly implement an online booking system for park permits sometime in 2016, at research time the only way to reserve your park permit/accommodations was to phone the ranger station in San Gerardo. Since the only ranger answering the phone also deals with clients who come to register their permits, continents may drift before you get an answer.

If you do get through on the phone, you may reserve spaces for up to four hikers. A name and passport number for each hiker is required when you call. Park permits are non-transferable and non-refundable. You will be issued a reservation code, the park's bank account number and the payment amount, as you can no longer pay for the park permit or the accommodations at the ranger station. Payment has to be made in advance into the designated local bank account. The nearest bank is in San Isidro, so if you're a walk-in client and by some miracle you succeed in securing a park permit for the following day, you then have to speed down to San Isidro to pay for it and come back in time to register your permit back at the ranger station (the permit must be registered the day before the hike). So if you're banking on securing a park permit by turning up at the ranger station, you'd better have several days to spare and only try this in low season. You can see why hikers lose the will to live while trying to secure a Chirripó permit...

The only way to secure a park permit and reservation at Crestones Base Lodge from abroad is to go through a third party. Talamanca Reserve (p415) offers this service to its guests free of charge. Casa Mariposa (p415) is always up to date on the latest rules and it recommends seeking out the services of Jane & Fraser Tyrell, who can help you secure your permit.

The dry season (from late December to April) is the most popular time to visit Chirripó. February and March are the driest months with the clearest skies, though it may still rain. On weekends, and especially during holidays, the trails can get a bit crowded with Tico hiking groups. The park is closed in May and October, but the early months of the rainy season are still good for climbing as it usually doesn't rain in the morning.

In any season, temperatures can drop below freezing at night, so warm clothes (including hat and gloves) and rainwear are necessary. Wear sturdy boots and bring good second-skin blister plasters. In exposed areas, high winds seem even colder. The ranger station in San Gerardo de Rivas is a good place to check on the weather conditions.

Chirripó's trails are well marked and do not require maps.

---

but the actual entrance to the park is 4km from the start of the trail in San Gerardo and no one staffs the park entrance.

The trailhead lies 70m beyond Hotel Urán in San Gerardo de Rivas (about 4km from the ranger station).

The first 6km or so are mostly uphill, over uneven, rocky ground, with some relatively flat stretches. You pass through dense cloud forest, so keep an eye out for quetzals.

Then there's a gentle descent toward the shelter at **Llano Bonito** (7.5km), which is a good place for a break. Here you can stock up on drinking water, use the flushing toilets and buy snacks and even aspirin. This place is intended for emergency use, not overnight stays, however.

Just beyond begins the **Cuesta de los Arrepentidos** ('Hill of the Repentants') and boy, will you repent! (At this point, try not to think about the long-distance runners who run from San Gerardo to Crestones and back again in around four hours.) It's a steep uphill slog until you reach the top of **Monte Sin Fe** (which translates as 'Mountain Without Faith'), a preliminary crest that reaches 3200m at around Km 10. By then you're on exposed ground, flanked by stunted tree growth, with gorgeous mountain views around you. The trail then descends gently for around 1.5km, making you grind your teeth, since what goes down must come up! The last section is an interminable, steep ascent before you see the green roofs of the Crestones Base Lodge just downhill from you; breathe a sigh of relief before descending to 3400m.

Reaching the lodge is the hardest part. From here the hike to the summit is 5.1km on relatively flatter terrain (although the last 100m is very steep). Carry a warm jacket, rain gear, water, snacks and a flashlight just in case, but leave anything you don't need at the lodge. From the summit on a clear day, the vista stretches to both the Caribbean Sea and the Pacific Ocean. The deep-blue lakes and the plush-green hills carpet the Valle de las Morenas in the foreground.

Most hikers reach the lodge around lunchtime and spend the rest of the day recuperating before leaving for the summit at around 3am to arrive in time to watch the sunrise – a spectacular experience.

For most people, a minimum of two days is needed to climb from the ranger station in San Gerardo to the summit and back, leaving no time for exploration. During peak season you're allowed to book a maximum of two nights at the lodge, which gives you an extra day to explore the trails around the summit and/or the Base Lodge.

Hiking Other Trails

There are several attractive destinations that are accessible by trails from the Crestones Base Lodge. These will require at least another day and real topographical maps. An alternative, longer route between the Base Lodge and the summit goes via Cerro Terbi (3760m), as well as Los Crestones, the moon-like rock formations that adorn many postcards. If you are hanging around for a few days, the glorious, grassy Sabana de los Leones is a popular destination that offers a stark contrast to the otherwise alpine scenery. Peak-baggers will want to visit Cerro Ventisqueros (3812m), which is also within a day's walk of Crestones. These trails are fairly well maintained, but it's worth inquiring about conditions before setting out.

For hard-core adventurers, an alternative route is to take a guided three- or five-day loop trek that begins in the nearby village of Herradura and spends a day or two traversing cloud forest and *páramo* on the slopes of Fila Urán. Hikers ascend Cerro Urán (3600m) before the final ascent of Chirripó and then descend through San Gerardo. This trip requires bush camping and car-

rying a tent. Costa Rica Trekking Adventures (☎ 2771-4582; www.chirripo.com) can make arrangements for this tour.

🛏 Sleeping & Eating

Crestones Base Lodge (dm US$39; 🛜) is the only accommodations in Parque Nacional Chirripó, with room for up to 54 people in dorm-style bunks.

Space is at a premium during holiday periods and on weekends during the dry season. Your chances of getting a last-minute place are best when you have days to spare or come in low season.

Camping is allowed only at a special designated area near Cerro Urán – not at Crestones or anywhere else in the park.

There's a good cafeteria serving three meals per day (US$10 to US$13 per meal) at Crestones Base Lodge.

ℹ Information

It is essential that you stop at the ranger station (p416) in San Gerardo de Rivas at least one day before you intend to climb Chirripó to register your park permit (bring your reservation and payment confirmation). After you've done that, you have to confirm your Crestones Base Lodge reservation at the consortium office. Park fees are now US$20 per day.

You can also make arrangements at the ranger station to hire a porter (a fixed fee of US$100 for up to 15kg of luggage), though it's now less necessary than ever. Since Crestones offers meals and includes bedding in the accommodations price, you can travel light, without cooking gear or sleeping bag.

Jane & Fraser Tyrell (☎ 2556-8664, UK 0800 612 8718, US & Canada 888-434-0076; chirripo@costaricarios.com) specialize in assisting Chirripó-bound hikers with securing park permits and accommodations reservations for Crestones Base Lodge. They charge US$15 per person to make relevant reservations for one night or US$20 for two nights. You'll still have to register your permit with the ranger office the day before the hike.

ℹ Getting There & Away

Travelers connect to the trails via the mountain village of San Gerardo de Rivas, which is also home to the ranger station. From opposite the ranger station, in front of Cabinas El Bosque, there is free transportation to the trailhead at 5am. Also, several hotels offer early morning trailhead transportation for their guests.

While supplies are brought to Crestones Base Lodge by horse, the only way you can get up and down the mountain is on your own two legs (don't underestimate the challenge).

THE ROAD TO LA AMISTAD

From San Isidro de El General, the Interamericana winds its way southeast through glorious rolling hills and coffee and pineapple plantations backed by striking mountain facades, towering as much as 3350m above. Along this stretch, a series of narrow, steep, dirt roads leads to some of the country's most remote areas – some nearly inaccessible due to the prohibitive presence of the Cordillera de Talamanca. But it's worth enduring the thrilling road for the chance to visit Parque Internacional La Amistad, a true wilderness of epic scale. This part of the country is rich in indigenous culture, and Italian immigrants have left their mark on the mountain town of San Vito, which has the best dining in the area.

Reserva Biológica Dúrika

A perfect example of sustainable tourism in action, the 85-sq-km Reserva Biológica Dúrika is home to a small but thriving community of about 100 Ticos and resident foreigners who are committed to local conservation, natural medicine and the preservation of indigenous culture. Since the late 1980s Dúrika has welcomed travelers interested in its inspiring social experiment, and its beautiful location and community spirit make it an excellent way to connect to this corner of the country, which lies adjacent to Parque Internacional La Amistad.

Originally a 350-hectare piece of cattle-grazed land, the reserve has benefited from over 20 years of reforestation and is a naturalist's paradise. Tours of the farm demonstrate the principles and processes of organic agriculture that Dúrika employs, such as producing organic fertilizer and making cheese from the milk of farm-raised goats.

Those staying in Dúrika can take excellent day hikes to waterfalls (which fuel the community's hydroelectric power) and banana groves. Guests can also arrange short hikes into the reserve, day-long forays to the Cabécar indigenous village of Ujarrás and multiday treks. Volunteer opportunities are available; these require prior arrangement and a commitment of at least five days.

🛏 Sleeping & Eating

Cabinas Dúrika CABINA $$
(☎ 2730-0657; www.durika.org; per person US$70)
Nine comfortable, rustic cabins are available to guests who stay on the farm; cabin rates include guided hikes on the reserve and organic vegetarian meals made from locally grown foods. Reserve with the Fundación Dúrika office.

ℹ Information

The **Fundación Dúrika Office** (☎ 2730-0657; www.durika.org; ⊙ 8am-5pm Mon-Sat) in Buenos Aires can arrange accommodations, provide information on tours and organize transport. Locals can point you to the office; look for the blue-and-white sign: it's 25m south of Banco Nacional.

ℹ Getting There & Away

Driving the 17km gravel road to Dúrika from Buenos Aires in a 4WD takes about 40 minutes. Alternatively, the office in Buenos Aires can arrange transportation to the reserve (one-way transport around US$35) and watch over your car while you're staying at the reserve.

Reserva Indígena Boruca

The picturesque valley of the Río Grande de Térraba cradles several mostly indigenous villages that comprise the reserve of Boruca (Brunka) peoples. At first glance it is difficult to differentiate these towns from typical Tico villages, aside from a few artisans selling their handiwork. These towns hardly cater to the tourist trade, which is one of the main reasons why traditional Boruca life has been able to continue without much distraction. The best way to engage with the community is to come here on a culturally sensitive tour, such as those run by Galería Namu (p95) or Sierpe Azul (☎ 2786-6614), or else contact the community directly to arrange an overnight stay and activities.

Be sensitive when visiting these communities – avoid taking photographs of people without asking permission, and respect the fact that these living communities are struggling to maintain traditional culture amid a changing world.

Marked by an enormous stone sphere out front, the tiny Museo Comunitario Indígena de Boruca (☎ 2730-0045, 2730-2514; ⊙ 9am-4pm) FREE has interpretive exhibits explaining Boruca legends, and displays tools and materials used for making traditional handicrafts. Attached is a shop selling handicrafts made by local artisans.

✨ Festivals & Events

Fiesta de los Diablitos CULTURAL

This raucous three-day festival, held in Boruca (December 30 to January 2) and Curré (February 5 to 8), symbolises the historical struggle between the Spanish and the indigenous population. Villagers wearing wooden devil masks and burlap costumes play the role of the natives in their fight against the Spanish conquerors and the festival culminates in a choreographed battle, which the Spanish lose.

The festival is sometimes called the Danza de los Diablitos, or 'dance of the little devils.' The Spaniards, represented by a man in a bull costume, get whipped by branches at the end of the battle. There's a lot of homemade corn-based alcohol involved.

Fiesta de los Negritos RELIGIOUS

This festival is held during the second week of December to celebrate the Virgin of the Immaculate Conception. Traditional indigenous music (mainly drumming and bamboo flutes) accompanies dancing and costumes.

🛏 Sleeping & Eating

Travelers can find rooms to rent by inquiring locally in Boruca village. Mileni Gonzalez, a local community organizer, can help arrange rustic *cabina* and traditional *rancho* accommodations and also homestays, which are an excellent way to connect with the community and contribute to the local economy.

Galería Namu (p95) in San José can arrange eco-ethno tours of the Boruca area, which include homestays, hiking to waterfalls, handicraft demonstrations and storytelling. These cost US$85 per person per day, and include meals, but not transportation to the village itself, which is relatively simple to work out by bus or taxi via Buenos Aires. Visit the website for more details.

🛍 Shopping

The Boruca are celebrated craftspeople and their traditional art plays a leading role in the survival of their culture. While most make their living from agriculture, some Boruca had begun producing fine handicrafts for tourists around 15 years ago, at the initiative of a female community leader; many carvers are women.

The tribe is most famous for its ornate masks featuring jungle birds and animals as well as devil faces, carved from balsa or cedar, and often colored with natural dyes and acrylics. Boruca women also use pre-Columbian backstrap looms to weave colorful, natural cotton bags, placemats and other textiles. These crafts are available along the Pacific coast, in the Osa Peninsula and the capital, with particularly good selections at Hotel Cristal Ballena (p398) in Uvita, Jagua Arts & Crafts (p448) in Puerto Jiménez, and Galería Namu in San José.

Curré is about 30km south of Buenos Aires, right on the Interamericana. Drivers can stop to visit a small **cooperative** (◷9am-5pm Mon-Fri, 2-5pm Sat) that sells handicrafts. In Boruca, local artisans post signs outside their homes advertising their balsa masks and woven bags, but the best selection of masks and woven goods is found at **Bisha Cra** (🖉2730-0854; www.bishacra.jimdo.com; ◷10am-5pm), near the entrance to the village if you're taking the road south of Curré.

ℹ Information

Mileni Gonzalez (🖉2730-5178; www.boruca. org), the president of La Flor de Boruca artisans' cooperative, is an excellent source of information on the Boruca reserve and can help arrange *cabina* accommodations or homestays – an excellent way to connect with the community and contribute to the local economy.

ℹ Getting There & Away

Buses (US$1.70, one hour) leave the central market in Buenos Aires at noon and 3:30pm daily, traveling to Boruca via a bumpy, partially paved road. The bus returns at 8am and 11am the following morning, which makes an overnight stay necessary if you're relying on public transportation. A taxi from Buenos Aires to Boruca is about US$30.

Drivers will find a better road that leaves the Interamericana about 3km south of Curré – look for the sign to Boruca. This dusty, unpaved route climbs a ridgeline and affords spectacular views of the valleys below. It's about 8km to Boruca from Curré, though the going is slow, and a 4WD is recommended, though not strictly necessary. If you're heading toward San Isidro or Buenos Aires, you can follow this road all the way through the village of Térraba, with more glimpses of indigenous community life along the way.

Palmar

At the intersection of the country's two major highways, this crossroads town serves as a gateway to the Península de Osa and Golfo

Dulce. This functional banana-growing settlement makes a convenient base for exploring the Sierpe area if you have a particular interest in pre-Columbian stone spheres (which the area is newly famous for), and the Festival de la Luz in December is worth stopping for.

Palmar is actually split in two – to get from Palmar Norte to Palmar Sur, take the Interamericana southbound over the Río Grande de Térraba bridge, then take the first right. Most facilities are in Palmar Norte, clustered around the intersection of the Carretera Interamericana and the Costanera Sur – if you're heading to Bahía Drake via Sierpe, this is your last chance to hit an ATM. Palmar Sur is home to the airstrip and a little park with an excellent example of a stone sphere.

✯ Festivals & Events

Festival de la Luz   LIGHT SHOW
Taking place in Palmar over two days in the week before Christmas, the Festival of Light involves lit-up nighttime floats and candles floated down the river.

🛏 Sleeping & Eating

Self-caterers will want to hit the Supermercado BM (☑ 2786-6556; ⏱ 8am-9pm Mon-Sat, 8am-8pm Sun), 200m north of the Interamericana–Costanera intersection, before heading to the Osa, as shopping opportunities are limited in Bahía Drake. The nicest place to eat is the on-site restaurant at Brunka Lodge.

Hotel El Teca   HOTEL $
(☑ 2786-8010, 8810-8481; www.hotelelteca.com; Ruta 2, 25m west of Red Cross bldg; s/d from US$30/35; P❋🛜) Run by a sweet, hospitable local family, this small hotel offers a

clutch of tidy, tiled rooms, complete with coffee makers and mini-fridges. The owners can provide information on the pre-Columbian stone spheres and where best to find them, and also organize trips to Parque Nacional Corcovado, Térraba mangroves and more.

Brunka Lodge   HOTEL $$
(☑ 2786-7489; s/d from US$50/60; P❋🛜🏊) The Brunka Lodge is undoubtedly the most inviting option in Palmar Norte. Sun-filled, clean-swept, brightly painted bungalows are clustered around a swimming pool and a popular, pleasant open-air restaurant, and all rooms have hot-water bathrooms, cable TV and high-speed internet. The suite is particularly nice as it has a private entrance to the pool.

ℹ Getting There & Away

Departing from San José, Sansa (p408) has daily flights to the Palmar airstrip. Prices vary according to season and availability, though you can expect to pay around US$108 to/from San José.

Taxis meet incoming flights and charge up to US$10 to Palmar Norte and US$15 to US$30 to Sierpe. Otherwise, the infrequent Palmar Norte–Sierpe bus goes through Palmar Sur – you can board it if there's space available.

Neily

Although it is southern Costa Rica's second-largest 'city,' Ciudad Neily has retained the friendly atmosphere of a rural town, much like neighboring Palmar. At just 50m above sea level, steamy Neily serves as a regional transportation hub and agricultural center, but is decidedly lacking in tourist appeal.

BUSES FROM PALMAR

Buses to San José and San Isidro stop on the east side of the Interamericana. Other buses leave from in front of the Pirola's Pizza and Seafood restaurant or the Tracopa window across the street. Buses to Sierpe depart from in front of the Gollo store.

DESTINATION	COST (US$)	DURATION (HR)	FREQUENCY (DAILY)
Dominical	2	1½	8:20am, 1:20pm, 3:45pm
Golfito	3.20	1½	11:20am, 12:30pm
Neily	3.20	1½	6 daily 7:30am-5:30pm
Paso Canoas	3.80	2	6 daily 10:30am-8:30pm
San Isidro	6.20	2½	8:30am, noon, 2:45pm, 5pm
San José	11.50	5½	16-19 daily 5:40am-6:30pm
Sierpe	0.75	40min	7 daily 4:30am-5:30pm

BUSES FROM NEILY

Buses leave from **Terminal Tracopa** (☎ 2221-4214), which is attached to a *mercado* with a clutch of busy *sodas,* two blocks east of Hwy 237.

DESTINATION	COST (US$)	DURATION (HR)	FREQUENCY (DAILY)
Golfito	2.90	1½	hourly 6:30am-7:30pm
Palmar	3.20	1½	6 daily 6am-5pm
Paso Canoas	0.85	30min	every 30min
San Isidro	9	4	10 daily
San José	14.80	7	10 daily
San Vito	1.50	1½	8 daily 5am-6pm

There is a **Banco Coopealianza** (⊙8am-3pm Mon-Fri), just southwest of the *mercado* (market), with a 24-hour ATM.

Hotel Andrea   HOTEL **$**
(☎ 2783-3784; www.hotelandreacr.com; r with/without air-con US$60/40; [P][⊙][✽][🖥]) At Hotel Andrea, paths of terracotta tiles are brightly scrubbed, leading guests through the maze of yellow buildings to cool, whitewashed rooms. The heavy-handed Romanesque columns might look a bit like Caesars Palace (the Las Vegas one), but the rooms are good value and very secure. The on-site restaurant, one of Neily's best, serves *comida típica* (from around $8).

Paso Canoas

The main port of entry between Costa Rica and Panama is hectic, slightly seedy and completely devoid of charm. Fortunately, the border crossing itself is straightforward. As you might imagine, most travelers leave Paso Canoas with little more than a passing glance at their passport stamp.

There's little reason to stay in the most insalubrious accommodations in this border town. If crossing the border into Costa Rica, head on down the road to Neily, 30 minutes' drive away. If heading to Panama, continue to David.

❶ Information

Banco Nacional (⊙ATM 5am-10pm) Bank with ATM.

Báncredito (⊙8am-4:30pm) Bank with ATM.

BCR (Banco de Costa Rica; ☎ 2732-2613; ⊙9am-4pm Mon-Sat, 9am-1pm Sun) Bank with ATM.

Instituto Panameño de Turismo (☎ 2727-6524; ⊙6:30am-9:30pm) In the Panamanian immigration post, this office has basic information on travel to Panama.

Migración & Aduana (☎ 2299-8007, 2732-2150; ⊙6am-10pm) Immigration and customs office, next to the Tracopa bus terminal.

❶ Transport

Tracopa buses leave for San José (US$15.40, 7½ hours) at 3:30am, 8am, 11am and 4:30pm. The **Tracopa bus terminal** (☎ 2221-4214; ⊙7am-4pm), a window really, is north of the border post, on the east side of the main road. Sunday-afternoon buses are full of weekend shoppers, so buy tickets as early as possible. Buses for Neily (US$0.85, 30 minutes) leave from in front of the post office at least once an hour from 5:30am to 6:30pm. Taxis to Neily cost about US$10.

Just across the border, buses run to David, the nearest city in Panama, from where there are onward connections to Panama City and elsewhere.

San Vito

Although the Italian immigrants who founded little San Vito in the 1850s are long gone, this hillside village proudly bears traces of their legacy in linguistic, cultural and culinary echoes. As such, the town serves as a base for travelers in need of a steaming plate of pasta and a good night's sleep.

The proximity of the town to the Reserva Indígena Guaymí de Coto Brus means that indigenous peoples pass through this region (groups of Ngöbe – also known as Guaymí – move back and forth across the border with Panama). You might spot women in traditional clothing – long, solid-colored *nagua* dresses trimmed in contrasting hues – riding the bus or strolling the streets.

Tucked in between the Cordillera de Talamanca and the Fila Costeña, the Valle de Coto Brus offers some glorious geography, featuring the green, rolling hills of coffee plantations backed by striking mountain facades.

⊙ Sights

★ Wilson Botanical Garden GARDENS

(☑ 2773-4004; www.ots.ac.cr/lascruces; admission US$8, half-/full-day guided tours US$39/54; ⊙ 7am-5pm Mon-Fri, 8am-5pm Sat & Sun) Covering 12 hectares and surrounded by 254 hectares of natural forest, world-class Wilson Botanical Garden, established by Robert and Catherine Wilson in 1963 and thereafter becoming internationally known for its collection, lies 6km south of San Vito.

A trail map is available for self-guided walks amid exotic species such as orchids, bromeliads and medicinal plants; birdwatchers can look for rare birds here.

Buses between San Vito and Neily (via Agua Buena not Cañas Gordas) pass the entrance to the gardens.

In 1973 the area came under the auspices of the Organization for Tropical Studies (OTS) and today the well-maintained garden – part of Las Cruces Biological Station – holds more than 1000 genera of plants from about 200 families and over 2000 native Costa Rican species. Species threatened with extinction are preserved here for possible reforestation in the future.

The botanical gardens are a choice spot for birders, as it draws hundreds of Costa Rican and migrating species, as well numerous butterfly species.

If you want to stay overnight at the botanical gardens, make reservations well in advance: facilities often fill with researchers. Accommodations are in comfortable cabins (singles/doubles including meals US$95/185) in the midst of the gorgeous grounds. The rooms are simple, but they each have a balcony with an amazing view.

Finca Cántaros PARK

(☑ 2773-3760, 2773-5530; www.fincacantaros.com; adult/12-17yr $6/3; ⊙ 7am-5pm) About 3km south of San Vito, Finca Cántaros is a recreation center and reforestation project. Over 18 acres of grounds – formerly coffee plantations and pasture land – are now a lovely nature reserve with trails, picnic areas and a dramatic lookout over the city. Especially interesting are the pre-Columbian cemetery and a large petroglyph that was discovered on the property in 2009. Though its meaning and age are unclear, the petroglyph is estimated to be about 1600 years old.

Another point of interest, reachable by self-guided hike, is the 3000-year-old Laguna Zoncho – picnic at one of the small shelters and watch for rare birds; if birders wish to visit the *finca* before 7am, arrangements can be made in advance. The reserve's reception contains a small but carefully chosen selection of local and South American crafts.

Camping on the property is allowed (US$8 per person); call ahead if arriving on a Sunday.

🛏 Sleeping & Eating

★ Casa Botania B&B $$

(☑ 2773-4217; www.casabotania.com; s/d incl breakfast US$62/73; ❄ 🐾) ☑ The freshest B&B in the region is exquisitely run by a sweet young Belgian-Tico couple. It hits every note with pitch-perfect elegance, from the modern, beautifully adorned rooms with stellar views, to the library of bird-watching guides, to the gourmet vegetarian meals, served on a polished deck overlooking the lush foliage of the valley below. It's 5km south of San Vito.

If you don't stay, book a dinner reservation; the three-course, locally sourced, ever-changing menu of smart European-touched vegetarian Costa Rican fare wins raves.

Cascata del Bosco BUNGALOW $$

(☑ 2773-3208; www.cascatadelbosco.com; camping US$10, d US$85; 🅿 🐾) The four round cabins at Cascata del Bosco overlook the

---

BUSES FROM SAN VITO

The main **Tracopa bus terminal** (☑ 2773-3410) is about 150m down the road to Sabalito from downtown.

DESTINATION	COST (US$)	DURATION (HR)	FREQUENCY (DAILY)
San Isidro	7.85	3	6:45am, 1:30pm
San José	14.60	7	4am, 7am, 10am, 1:30pm, 3pm

A local bus terminal at the northwest end of town runs buses to Neily (US$1.75, 1½ hours, eight daily) and other destinations.

PARADISE TROPICAL GARDEN

If you'd like to learn about indigenous rainforest medicine, pay a visit to the **Paradise Tropical Garden** (📞2789-8746; http://paradise-garden.tripod.com; Río Claro; admission by donation; ⏰6am-5pm with 1 day's advance notice), where Robert and Ella Beatham have created a sensual introduction to tropical fruits and rainforest remedies that they call the 'Tropical Fruit See, Smell, Taste & Touch Experience.' The gardens are located west of the town of Río Claro – follow the Interamericana for 1km, cross the Río Lagarto and turn right after the bridge. From here, the garden is just 200m beyond.

Besides this interactive display, visitors learn about the production of African palm oil and how it came to be the dominant crop of this region following the collapse of the banana industry. Robert and Ella are wonderful hosts, but you should call a day in advance if you want their full attention.

forested valley below and enclose guests in treehouse-like comfort. Each cabin has a terrace, skylight, kitchenette and bamboo-and-tile interior. Several nature trails wind through the property, and the roadside restaurant is a convivial gathering spot for locals and expats serving delicious BBQ. Located 200m north of Wilson Botanical Garden.

⭐ **Sarambo Tapas Bar**   TAPAS $
(Ruta 613; tapas from US$7; ⏰5-11pm; 🛜) This excellent new addition to San Vito's dining scene is a hard-to-pigeonhole bar with Italian tapas and a rock theme, courtesy of Beatles, Jimi and Clapton photos and Cranberries on the stereo. Expect subdued lighting, local craft beers and Italian wines, generous tapas portions that make use of imported Italian ingredients, large servings of homemade pasta and attentive staff.

ℹ Getting There & Away

The drive north from Neily is a scenic one, with superb views of the lowlands dropping away as the road winds up the hillside. The paved road is steep, narrow and full of hairpin turns. You can also get to San Vito from San Isidro via the Valle de Coto Brus – an incredibly scenic and less-used route with fantastic views of the Cordillera de Talamanca to the north and the lower Fila Costeña to the south.

Parque Internacional La Amistad

The 4070-sq-km Parque Internacional La Amistad – by far the largest protected area in Costa Rica – is an enormous patch of green sprawling across the borders of Panama and Costa Rica (hence its Spanish name La Amistad – 'Friendship'). Standing as a testament to the possibilities of international cooperation and environmental conservation, the park was established in 1982 and declared a Unesco World Heritage Site in 1990. It then became part of the greater Mesoamerican Biological Corridor, which protects a great variety of endangered habitats and animals. Its cultural importance is also significant as it includes several scattered indigenous reserves.

The largest chunk of the park is high up in the Cordillera de Talamanca, and remains virtually inaccessible. There's very little tourist infrastructure within the park, although hard-core exploration of some of the country's most rugged terrain is possible with an experienced guide.

🏃 Activities

Hiking

Except for the specialized guided hikes, park visitors are pretty much limited to the two trails that leave from the Altamira ranger station: Sendero Gigantes del Bosque (p426) and Sendero Valle del Silencio.

Contact the association of guides, AsoProLA (p427), to inquire about arrangements for guided hikes. Rates vary depending on the size of your party and your intended course.

Sendero Valle del Silencio   HIKING
This 20km-long trail (eight to 12 hours round trip) winds its way through pristine and hilly primary forest before ascending to a camping area and refuge at the base of Cerro Kamuk (3549m). It's a challenging, terrific hike that traverses one of the most isolated areas in all of Costa Rica, but a local guide is required; inquire at the Altamira ranger station.

BIOLLEY

Below the wilderness of Parque Internacional La Amistad, a network of rural villages is signposted by Gaudíesque mosaic navigation markers made by a local artist. These farming villages went about their business mostly unperturbed by tourists until 1997, when an enterprising group of local women in the village of Biolley (pronounced *bee-oh-lay*; named for a Swiss biologist who settled here) set up a cooperative, **Asomobi** (Asociación de Mujeres Organizadas de Biolley; ☑ 8916-4638, 2200-4250; www.asomobi-costarica.com). It has 30 members and is designed to promote rural tourism in the area and to generate funds for the cooperative's various sustainable projects, such as organic coffee growing.

Asomobi organizes coffee tours that let you visit the *beneficio* (processing plant) in Biolley that processes delicious locally grown coffee. It uses ecofriendly methods that conserve water and compost organic waste for use as fertilizer. If you arrive independently, you can buy beans at the *beneficio*.

Other tours are on offer, from birding outings and hot-springs tours to hiking the Valle del Silencio in Parque Internacional La Amistad. Arrange in advance.

Sleeping

Asomobi can arrange inexpensive accommodations in a Biolley homestay with a friendly local family. The cooperative was dealt a huge blow when their hotel, Posada Cerro Biolley, was tragically destroyed in a fire in 2012. They are currently working in partnership with **Hotel Finca Palo Alto** (☑ 2743-1063, 2743-1062; www.hotelfincapaloalto.com; Biolley; r US$57; Ⓟ).

Getting There & Away

Biolley is 6km west of the crossroads in Altamira village, but the way there zigzags and is poorly signed; get detailed directions at AsoProLA or by calling Asomobi if traveling independently.

Sendero Gigantes del Bosque   HIKING

Sendero Gigantes del Bosque is a 3km circuit (two hours) named for the ancient 40m trees along the way. Signposts in Spanish provide simple explanations of some of the flora, and the trail passes two lookout towers, good for bird-watching: one on the edge of the primary forest and the other overlooking the rural landscape outside the park.

Wildlife-Watching

Although most of Parque Internacional La Amistad is inaccessible terrain high up in the Talamanca, the park is home to a recorded 90 mammal species and more than 400 bird species. The park has the nation's largest population of Baird's tapirs, as well as giant anteaters, all six species of neotropical (and endangered) cats – jaguar, puma (mountain lion), margay, ocelot, oncilla (tiger cat) and jaguarundi – and many more common mammals.

Bird species (49 unique) that have been sighted – more than half of the total in Costa Rica – include the majestic but extremely rare harpy eagle, now feared extinct in the country. In addition, the park protects 115 species of fish, 215 different reptiles and amphibians, as well as innumerable insect species.

🛏 Sleeping

AsoProLA Lodge   LODGE $

(☑ 2290-7514; www.asoprolacr.es.tl; r from US$40; Ⓟ) The AsoProLA guiding association runs a simple lodge and restaurant in the village of Altamira and can make arrangements for lodging in local homes in Altamira and Santa Elena de Pittier for US$15 to US$20 per person. Homestays are a great way to get an intimate look at the lives of people living on the fringes of the rainforest.

Estación Altamira   CAMPGROUND $

(☑ 2200-5355; dm per person US$6) This ranger station offers camping facilities and no-frills dorm beds, with drinking water, cold-water showers, toilets and electricity. All food and supplies must be packed in and out.

❶ Information

The primary jumping-off point by which visitors lauch into the deepest parts of the park is the tiny mountain town of Altamira, 25km northwest of San Vito. There are four other official entrances to the park: one near Buenos Aires, one near

Helechales, and two near San Vito. But Estación Altamira is the only year-round, staffed facility, and the other entrances are accessed by horrifically bad roads.

To make reservations to camp, call the park headquarters at Estación Altamira directly. This is the best-developed area of the park, with a camping area, showers, drinking water, electricity and a lookout tower.

Altamira Ranger Station (⚡2200-5355; park fee per person per day US$10; ⊗8am-4pm) Collects entrance fees and provides information on the park.

AsoProLA (⚡2743-1294, 2743-1184, in Canada 877-206-4642, in USA 866-393-5889; www.asoprolacr.es.tl; Altamira; ⊗7am-8pm) Guiding association that can arrange guided hikes within Parque Internacional La Amistad.

❶ Getting There & Away

To reach Altamira, you can take any bus that runs between San Isidro and San Vito and get off in the town of Guácimo (often called Las Tablas). From Guácimo buses generally depart at noon and 5pm for El Carmen; if the road conditions permit, they continue 4km to the village of Altamira. From the village of Altamira, follow the Minae sign (near the church) leading to the steep 2km hike to the ranger station.

It's considerably more convenient to explore the area by 4WD rather than with public transportation; the roads are rough and bumpy and the buses are not hugely reliable. The turnoff for the park is signposted after the town of Guácimo if you're driving from San Vito. The park entrance at Altamira is 21km (around an hour's drive) along the unpaved, bone-jarring road from Hwy 237.

PENÍNSULA DE OSA

On the western side of the Península de Osa, the Bahía Drake route is one of two principal ways to reach Parque Nacional Corcovado. The route starts in the town of Sierpe in the Valle de Diquís, at the northern base of the peninsula, from where the Río Sierpe flows out to Bahía Drake. Most travelers opt for the exhilarating boat ride through the mangroves between Sierpe, Drake and Corcovado, with a potential detour via the Humedal Nacional Térraba-Sierpe. Alternatively, there's a rough road to Drake via the former gold-mining settlement of Rancho Quemado, which allows for a spot of *agroturismo* along the way. Either way, the Bahía Drake route offers a chance to experience rural Tico life and also a greater share of creature comforts in the many wilderness lodges.

Of the two principal overland routes to Parque Nacional Corcovado, the Puerto Jiménez route on the eastern side of the peninsula is much more 'developed.' Of course, as this is Osa, development doesn't amount to much more than a single road and a sprinkling of villages along the coast of Golfo Dulce. The landscape is cattle pastures and palm-oil plantations, while the Reserva Forestal Golfo Dulce protects much of the inland area and encompasses the former gold-mining community of Dos Brazos, now the newest entrance to Corcovado and *agroturismo* epicenter.

The largest settlement in the area is the town of Puerto Jiménez, which has transitioned from a boomtown for gold miners to an ecotourism hot spot. South of Jiménez, the surfer haven of Cabo Matapalo and the jungle lodges of Carate beckon travelers in search of nature and solitude.

Sierpe

This sleepy village on the Río Sierpe is the gateway to Bahía Drake, and if you've made a reservation with any of the jungle lodges further down the coast, you will be picked up here by boat. Beyond its function as a transit point, there is little reason to spend any more time here than necessary, though it's well worth taking a peek at one of the celebrated pre-Columbian stone spheres in the main square. If you're visiting the excellent **Sitio Arqueológico Finca 6** (⚡2100-6000; finca6@museocostarica.go.cr; 4km north of Sierpe; admission US$6; ⊗8am-4pm Tue-Sun) near Sierpe, it's worth stopping here for lunch. Mangrove cruises can also be arranged here.

Hotel Oleaje Sereno   HOTEL $$
(⚡2788-1111; s/d incl breakfast from US$35/55; 🅿❋🛜) If you get stuck in Sierpe overnight, the dockside Hotel Oleaje Sereno is the pick of Sierpe's limited accommodations (though it's not much of a horse race). This motel overlooking the Río Sierpe has rather unloved, dusty rooms with wooden floors, sturdy furniture and a restaurant popular with boat-catching gringos. Wi-fi comes and goes like a stray cat.

❶ Information

La Perla del Sur (⚡2788-1082, 2788-1071; info@perladelsur.net; ⊗8am-5pm; 🛜) This info center and open-air restaurant next to the boat dock is the hub of Sierpe – arrange your

SIERPE SPHERES

The Diquís Delta is believed to have been the most developed and historically significant part of Costa Rica, heavily populated in pre-Columbian times and playing an important role as a trading post between the other important cultures in Latin America (the Incas to the south and the Maya to the north) – jade and gold artifacts found in the Delta and created elsewhere suggest that this was so. But while other pre-Columbian cultures left behind vast pyramid-like monuments, unparalleled stonework and sophisticated languages, the Diquís left behind immense stone spheres and little else.

It is known that the civilization invested great efforts in their creation (over 300 spheres have been found in the Diquís Delta), crafting them out of sandstone, limestone, gabbro and granodiorite from the Costeña coastal range using nothing but stone tools, and transporting them great distances, including over water (some have been found on Isla del Caño). Their function remains unclear, though theories suggest that those spheres found in sets or alignments may represent celestial phenomena or function as solar calendars, while others have been interpreted as territorial markers or symbols of an individual's power (the bigger the sphere, the more powerful the individual). Spheres range from a few centimeters to 2.54m in diameter; the largest and heaviest found at the El Silencio site weighs a staggering 24 tons. Smaller spheres have been found in some graves, presumed to be of particularly important chiefs.

In 2014 the Diquís spheres were included on Unesco's list of World Heritage Sites, and efforts are under way to excavate other significant sites in the Diquís Delta and to educate both visitors and the local population about the region's unique history. Communities also hope that this Unesco endorsement will bring more tourism to the Delta and revitalize the area.

While a number of spheres were whisked away from the area in the past to be used as decorative elements in people's gardens, and the most important archaeological finds grace San José museums, there are a few excellent examples of these spheres that can easily be seen in parks in Palmar Sur and Sierpe.

Sitio Arqueológico Finca 6 (p427) offers the best opportunity to view these mysterious spheres, created by the Diquís civilization between 300 BC and 1500 AD, in their originally discovered locale, near culturally significant mounds 20m and 30m in diameter. Walking around you can really appreciate their size and perfect sphericity.

The on-site museum screens a terrific video on the spheres' significance and purpose. The museum displays other fascinating artifacts discovered here, such as stone sculptures unique to the Diquís and *metates* (grain-grinding stones).

The site on which the Finca 6 museum is located is thought to have been a large settlement in pre-Columbian times, with trade links throughout the region. The two mounds are believed to have been next to the houses in which the settlement's most powerful individuals resided, with the largest stone spheres placed by the access ramps to the dwellings to signify the individuals' importance.

long-term parking (US$6 per night), book a tour and take advantage of the free wi-fi before catching your boat to Drake. The food is hit and miss, though.

❶ Getting There & Away

Scheduled flights and charters fly into Palmar Sur, 14km north of Sierpe. If you are heading to Bahía Drake, most upmarket lodges will arrange the boat transfer. Should things go awry or if you're traveling independently, there's no shortage of water taxis milling about – be prepared to negotiate a fair price. Regularly scheduled

colectivo (shared) boats depart Sierpe for Drake at 11:30am (US$15) and 4:30pm (US$20).

Buses to Palmar Norte (US$0.70, 40 minutes) depart from in front of Pulpería Fenix at 5:30am, 8:30am, 10:30am, 12:30pm, 3:30pm and 6pm. A taxi to Palmar costs about US$28.

Humedal Nacional Térraba-Sierpe

The Ríos Térraba and Sierpe begin on the southern slopes of the Talamanca mountains and, nearing the Pacific Ocean, they form a network of channels and waterways that weave around the country's largest mangrove swamp. This river delta comprises the Humedal Nacional Térraba-Sierpe, which protects approximately 330 sq km of wetland and is home to red, black and tea mangrove species. The reserve also protects a plethora of birdlife, especially waterbirds such as herons, egrets and cormorants, and larger denizens of the murky waters and tangled vegetation such as caimans and boas. An exploration of this watery world by boat gives you a unique insight into this very special and fragile ecosystem.

The Térraba-Sierpe reserve is only accessible by a boat tour.

Tours

The Térraba-Sierpe reserve has no facilities for visitors, though lodges and tour companies can organize tours to help you explore the wetlands. Bahía Aventuras (p397) in Uvita offers half-day boat trips (US$85 per person) in the mangroves, as does Corcovado Expeditions (p431; US$110 per person) in Bahía Drake.

Sleeping

Veragua River House B&B $$

(☏ 2788-1460; www.hotelveragua.com/en; s/d incl breakfast US$55/65; P ❄ ☎) Run by an accommodating Italian-Tico couple, this memorable B&B is set on a pair of riverside gardens lovingly planted with fruit trees and tropical flowers. Guests stay in the four garden bungalows, built in a uniquely Costa Rican Victorian architectural style. The B&B is located 3km north of Sierpe. Lunch and dinner (US$15 to US$20) are also available with prior notice.

Bahía Drake

One of Costa Rica's most isolated destinations, Bahía Drake (drah-kay) is a veritable Lost World, bordered by Parque Nacional Corcovado to the south. In the rainforest canopy, howlers greet the rising sun with their haunting bellows, while pairs of macaws soar between the treetops, filling the air with their cacophonous squawking. Offshore in the bay itself, pods of migrating dolphins flit through turquoise waters near the beautiful Isla del Caño marine reserve.

One of the reasons why Bahía Drake is brimming with wildlife is that it remains largely cut off from the rest of the country.

Life is centered around the sedate village of Agujitas, the area's transport hub, which attracts increasing numbers of backpackers and nature lovers with inexpensive digs and plenty of snorkeling, diving and wildlife-watching opportunities. The more remote corners of Bahía Drake are home to some of Costa Rica's best (and priciest) wilderness lodges.

Activities

Swimming & Snorkeling

About 20km west of Agujitas, Isla del Caño (p438) is considered the best place for snorkeling in this area. Lodges offer day trips to the island (from US$80 per person), usually including the park fee, snorkeling equipment and lunch on Playa San Josecito. The clarity of the ocean and the variety of the fish fluctuate according to water and weather conditions: it's worth inquiring before booking.

Along the coast between Agujitas and Corcovado, Playa San Josecito (p438) and Playa Caletas (p438) attract many tropical fish, while Playa Cocalito (p435), a small, pretty beach near Agujitas, is pleasant for swimming and sunbathing.

Hiking & Wildlife-Watching

All of the lodges and most tour companies offer tours to Parque Nacional Corcovado, usually a full-day trip to San Pedrillo or Sirena ranger stations (from US$85 to US$150 per person), including boat transportation, lunch and guided hikes. Some travelers, however, come away from these tours disappointed. The trails around Sirena attract many groups of people, which inhibit animal sightings. Furthermore, most tours arrive at the park well after sunrise, when activity in the rainforest has already quietened down, so overnighting in the park is a better bet if you have your heart set on seeing wildlife.

All park visitors are now required to be accompanied by a guide certified by the ICT (Costa Rica Tourism Board), so exploring the beaches and jungles with an eagle-eyed guide will reveal much more than you would likely discover on your own.

If you'd prefer to hike independently, the easiest and most obvious route is the 17km coastal trail from Agujitas to San Pedrillo (p438). A determined, reasonably fit hiker could make it all the way to San Pedrillo ranger station in six to seven hours (though visitors intending to enter or spend the night

FLOATING FOREST

As many as seven different species of *manglar* (mangrove) thrive in Costa Rica. Comprising the vast majority of tropical coastline, mangroves play a crucial role in protecting it from erosion. Mangroves also serve as a refuge for countless species of animals, especially fish, crab, shrimp and mollusks, and as a sanctuary for roosting birds seeking protection from terrestrial predators.

Mangroves are unique among plants in that they have distinct methods for aeration (getting oxygen into the system) and desalination (getting rid of the salt that is absorbed with the water). Red mangroves, which are the most common species in Costa Rica, use their web of above-ground prop roots for aerating the plant's sap system. Other species, such as the black mangrove, have vertical roots that stick out above the mud, while buttonwood mangroves have elaborate buttresses.

The most amazing feature of the mangrove is its tolerance for salt, which enables the plant to thrive in brackish and saltwater habitats. Some species, such as the Pacific coast black mangrove, absorb the salinated water, then excrete the salt through their leaves and roots, leaving behind visible crystals. Other species filter the water as it is absorbed – the mangrove root system is so effective as a filter that the water from a cut root is drinkable!

Despite their ecological importance, mangrove habitats the world over are being increasingly threatened by expanding human habitats. Furthermore, mangrove wood is an easily exploitable source of fuel and tannin (used in processing leather), which has also hastened their destruction. Fortunately in the Humedal Nacional Térraba-Sierpe, this fragile yet vitally important ecosystem is receiving the respect and protection that it deserves.

in the park must have secured reservations in advance and be accompanied by a guide). An alternative is getting a tour company to drop you off by boat near San Pedrillo and then hiking back to Agujitas; remember that sunset descends swiftly at around 5:30pm. You don't have to hike the entire trail – there are plenty of beaches along the way.

Canoeing & Kayaking

Río Agujitas attracts a huge variety of birdlife and lots of scaly reptiles. The river conveniently empties out into the bay, which is surrounded by hidden coves and sandy beaches ideal for exploring in a sea kayak, best done at high tide. Some accommodations have kayaks and canoes for rent for a small fee; they can also be rented on Agujitas beach, along with paddleboards.

Tours

Adventure Tours

★ Pacheco Tours   WILDLIFE WATCHING
(☑ 8906-2002; www.pachecotours.com) Very competent all-rounder organizing snorkeling tours to Isla del Caño, day trips to Corcovado, day-long tours combining jungle trekking with waterfall swimming (US$55), and whale-watching excursions.

Bird-Watching & Wildlife-Watching

With almost 400 species recorded in the area, Bahía Drake and nearby Corcovado are hands-down the best places to spot Costa Rica's Pacific lowland rainforest species that include such feathered beauties as scarlet macaws, chestnut-mandibled toucans, honeycreepers, hawk-eagles and the black-cheeked ant tanager (endemic to the Osa Peninsula). All upscale lodges organize birding walks, as do the bay's independent tour operators and specialist birding guides.

★ Tracie the Bug Lady   WILDLIFE WATCHING
(☑ 8701-7356, 8701-7462; www.thenighttour.com; tours US$40; ☉ 7:30-10pm) Tracie the 'Bug Lady' has created quite a name for herself with this fascinating nighttime walk in the jungle that takes in bugs, reptiles and birds. Tracie is a walking encyclopedia on bug facts – one of her fields of research is the military use of insects! Her Tico naturalist-photographer husband Gian also leads the night tours; reserve in advance.

Carlos González   BIRD-WATCHING
(clgonzalez08@gmail.com; birding tours from US$70) Highly recommended bird-watching guide with many years' experience, who can tailor excursions to suit your needs. He also conducts excellent mangrove tours.

Corcovado Info Center WILDLIFE WATCHING
(📞2775-0916, 8846-4734; www.corcovadoinfo
center.com; whale-watching/Corcovado day tours
US$110/90) Leading tours into Corcovado and
Isla del Caño, all guides with this outfit are
local, bilingual and ICT-certified. They're at
the beach end of the main road in Agujitas.

Corcovado Expeditions TOUR
(📞2775-0916, 8846-4734; www.corcovadoexpedi
tions.net; tours US$45-85) Offers competitively
priced tours to Corcovado and Isla del Caño,
as well as a wide variety of specialty hikes
including unique excursions to look for rare
tropical birds and poison-dart frogs. The office
is located between the clinic and the school.

Dolphin- & Whale-Watching

Bahía Drake is rife with marine life, including more than 20 species of dolphin and
whale that pass through on their migrations
throughout the year. This area is unique-
ly suited for whale-watching: humpback
whales come from both the northern and
the southern hemispheres to calve, resulting in the longest humpback whale season
in the world. Humpbacks can be spotted in
Bahía Drake from December to March, and
then from July until October.

Several of the lodges are involved with programs that protect and preserve marine life
in Bahía Drake, and offer tourists a chance
for a close encounter, as do independent,
knowledgeable operators in Agujitas. Tours
generally cost about US$100 per person.

★**Divine Dolphin** WILDLIFE WATCHING
(www.divinedolphin.com; adult/under 11yr US$115/
75) Sierra Goodman is the experienced
original tour operator who introduced
whale-watching to Drake Bay and she's also
deeply involved in conservation projects.
Half-day tours depart at 8am and the on-
board hydrophone lets you hear the whale
and dolphin sounds.

Sportfishing

Bahía Drake claims more than 40 fishing
records, including sailfish, marlin, yellowfin
tuna, wahoo, cubera snapper, mackerel and
roosterfish. Fishing is excellent year-round,
although the catch may vary according to
the season. The peak season for tuna and
marlin is from August to December. Sailfish are caught year-round, but experience a
slowdown in May and June. Dorado and wahoo peak between May and August. Other
species are abundant year-round, so you are
virtually assured of reeling in something.

Many lodges can arrange fishing excursions,
but you need to be prepared to pay for the
experience – half-/full-day excursions cost
around US$650/1200.

Diving

Isla del Caño (p438) is one of Costa Rica's
top spots for diving, with attractions including intricate rock and coral formations and
an amazing array of underwater life. Divers
report that the schools of fish swimming
overhead are often so dense that they block
the sunlight from filtering down.

Bajo del Diablo (Devil's Rock) – one of the
best dive sites in the bay – is an astonish-
ing formation of submerged mountains that
attracts an incredible variety of fish species,
including jack, snapper, barracuda, puffer,
parrotfish, moray eel and shark.

A two-tank dive runs from US$120 to
US$150 depending on the site. Several up-
scale lodges have on-site dive centers, and
there are several dive centers in Agujitas.

Drake Divers DIVING
(📞2775-1818; www.drakediverscr.com; ⏰7am-7pm)
This outfit specializes in diving at Isla del
Caño, charging US$135/180 for two-/three-
tank dives. Snorkelers are welcome to come
along (US$80). The equipment is not the new-
est and the boat is not a purpose-built diving
boat, but the divemasters are experienced.

Osa Divers DIVING
(📞8994-9309; www.osadivers.com) Competitively priced, recommended diving outfit
whisking divers (and snorkelers) off for underwater adventures around Isla del Caño.
Snorkeling tours cost US$80; two-/three-
tank dives are US$120/160. Equipment
could be newer, though, and the divemasters
don't have too much patience with novices.

🛏 Sleeping

This area is off the grid, so a few places
do not have 24/7 electricity. Reservations
are recommended in the dry season (mid-
December to mid-April).

Agujitas has an ever-growing number of
budget and midrange options, though Bahía
Drake accommodations are skewed toward
the top end.

All of the midrange and top-end accommodations provide transportation from
Agujitas or the airstrip in Drake with prior
arrangements. For more accommodations
check out the stretch of coastline from Bahía
Drake to Corcovado.

Bahía Drake & Around

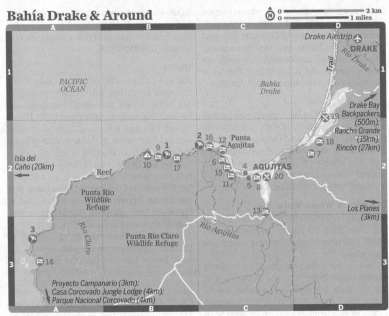

Bahía Drake & Around

★ **Martina's Place** GUESTHOUSE **$**
(☑ 8720-0801; www.puravidadrakebay.com; dm/s/d from US$11/25/35; ☏) With a few fan-cooled dorms and rooms inside, this budget spot also provides access to a clean, thoroughly equipped communal kitchen and an on-site cafe serving German meatballs! This friendly, economical place in the middle of Agujitas is an excellent spot to meet other budget travelers, tap into Martina's wealth of Corcovado intel and arrange a variety of local tours.

Drake Bay Backpackers HOSTEL **$**
(☑ 2775-0726; www.drakebaybackpackers.com; camping per person US$5, dm/s/d from US$13/25/30; ℗ ❋ ☏) This excellent nonprofit, off-the-beaten-track hostel is a boon for budget travelers wanting to connect with the local community. Competitively priced local tours can be arranged, there's a nice hangout area, a BBQ patio and even a volleyball court, and homestays (US$30) can be arranged. It's in the village of El Progreso, near the airstrip, straight after the river crossing.

★ Casita Corcovado
B&B $$

(📞2775-0627, 8996-8987; www.casitacorcovado.com; s/d incl breakfast US$57/80; ⊜ ❋ 🕏) Jamie and Craig's lovely little oceanfront home has three rooms, all sharing a bathroom and with super-comfortable orthopedic beds. Guests have access to two breezy patios and plenty of hammocks, with the amenities of the village at the doorstep, but it's the warmth and helpfulness of your hosts that sets this place apart. Delicious, home-cooked meals are also available.

If you rent the whole house, children of all ages are welcome. If you go for the B&B option, day care is available on request.

★ Finca Maresia
BUNGALOW $$

(📞8888-1625, 2775-0279; www.fincamaresia.com; Camino a Los Planes; incl breakfast s US$30-75, d US$40-90) The globe-trotting owners have created this absolute gem of a *finca* hotel that stretches across a series of hills. Budget travelers are drawn by the excellent value-to-price ratio and superb wildlife-watching opportunities. All rooms and the open-air communal area are exposed to an audio track of jungle sounds, and manager Juan is a phenomenal host.

Beyond the show-stopping natural setting, the good taste of the owners is evident as you walk from room to room and view the transition from modernist glass walls to Japanese-style sliding rice-paper doors.

Cabinas El Mirador
CABINA $$

(📞2775-2727; www.miradordrakebay.com; per person incl breakfast/3 meals from US$26/46; 🅿🕏) High on a hill at the northern end of Agujitas, El Mirador (Lookout Point) offers spectacular views of the bay from its eight cozy cabins – catch the sunset from the balcony or climb to the lookout that perches above. The warm welcome from the hospitable Vargas family and the hearty, home-cooked Costa Rican fare make this a great pick.

Sunset Lodge
CABIN $$

(📞8744-7469, 7102-3058; www.drakebaysunset-lodge.com; cabin US$70-80; 🅿) Comprising just two wooden cabins up a punishingly steep flight of steps on the hillside, this new spot is run by a young, enthusiastic Tico owner whose family were some of the original pioneers who came to settle in Bahía Drake. The views of said bay from the terraces are absolutely stellar and we're assured that wi-fi is coming.

★ Drake Bay
Gateway Resort
BOUTIQUE HOTEL $$$

(📞6003-7253; www.drakebaygateway.com; s/d US$400/570; 🅿🕏) ✿ The five luxurious cabins in this glorious bluff-top location catch the breeze and expansive views of Drake Bay from their private decks. The chef uses organic produce from the property's gardens to serve each guest individually crafted dishes, never repeating himself once during your stay. The service is wonderfully attentive and a full range of tours of the area is available.

Hotel Jinetes de Osa
HOTEL $$$

(📞2231-5806, in USA 866-553-7073; www.jinetesdeosa.com; s/d from US$103/110, ste US$180, all incl breakfast; 🕏) Ideal for divers, the reasonably priced Jinetes de Osa boasts a choice bayside location that is literally steps from the ocean. Jinetes also has a canopy tour, as well as one of the peninsula's top PADI dive facilities. Just outside of Agujitas, this sweet collection of rooms strikes the perfect balance between village and jungle.

Aguila de Osa Inn
LODGE $$$

(📞2296-2190, toll-free in USA 866-924-8452; www.aguiladeosa.com; s/d 2-night package incl all meals from US$521/886; 🅿❋🕏) On the east side of the Río Agujitas, this swanky lodge consists of roomy quarters with cathedral ceilings and private decks with expansive ocean views. Diving and sportfishing charters are available to guests, and the dedicated staff and knowledgeable wildlife guides are the icing on the cake. Rates include an Isla del Caño tour and a Corcovado tour.

Family Adventure packages are on offer, with night tours, horseback riding, canopy and other tours suitable for older children.

La Paloma Lodge
LODGE $$$

(📞2775-1684, 2293-7502; www.lapalomalodge.com; 3-/4-/5-day package per person from US$1025/1285/1545; ❋🕏🏊) This hillside lodge provides guests with an incredible panorama of ocean and forest, all from the comfort of the sumptuous, stylish quarters. Rooms feature queen-sized orthopedic beds and ocean-view balconies, while shoulder-high walls in the bathrooms offer rainforest views. Popular with vacationing families. Three-day minimum; rates include a tour to both Isla del Caño and Corcovado.

Drake Bay Wilderness Resort
CABIN $$$

(📞2775-1715; www.drakebay.com; 4-day package per person US$865; ❋🕏🏊) Sitting pretty

> ### SIR FRANCIS DRAKE SLEPT HERE
>
> The bay is named for Sir Francis Drake himself, who visited this area in March 1579, during his circumnavigation in the *Golden Hind*. History has it that he stopped on the nearby Isla del Caño, but locals speculate that he probably landed on the continent as well. A monument at Punta Agujitas, located on the grounds of the Drake Bay Wilderness Resort, states as much.

on Punta Agujitas, Drake's oldest resort comprises comfortable cabins with mural-painted walls and ocean-view terraces, more functional than luxurious. Naturalists will be won over by the lovely landscaping, from flowering trees to the rocky oceanfront outcroppings, while history buffs will appreciate the memorial to Drake's landing. The views are terrific but some guests have been underwhelmed by the food.

Eating

Drake's Kitchen   COSTA RICAN $
(☑ 2775-1405; mains from US$7; ⊘ noon-9pm; P)
Excellent, small local restaurant along the main dirt road from Agujitas to the airstrip. The *casados,* such as catch-of-the-day with fried plantains and avocado, are clearly prepared by a capable chef, the fresh juices are stellar and the ambience mellow.

★ Gringo Curt's   INTERNATIONAL $$
(☑ 6198-5899; mains US$10; ⊘ noon-9pm) Gringo Curt offers just three things: fish tacos, noodles tossed with vegetables (and sometimes garnished with catch-of-the-day) and super-fresh fish steamed in a banana leaf (serves two). This one-man operation is hugely popular with visitors, and the portions are very generous. Curt's a great source of local info, too, and runs nature tours along with Tico Esteban.

Margarita's Marisquería   SEAFOOD $$
(☑ 2775-1905; mains US$7-12; ⊘ 11:30am-9:30pm)
Right near the beach, this open-air eatery serves up mostly fishy delights, from garlic shrimp spaghetti and *ceviche* to generous helpings of freshly grilled fish, fish tacos and *arroz con mariscos* (seafood-fried rice). The food is great, but the service lives by Zen time and it's best to double-check the bill.

ⓘ Getting There & Away

AIR

Departing from San José, NatureAir (p97) and Sansa (p97) have daily flights to the Drake airstrip, which is 2km north of Agujitas. Prices vary according to season and availability, though you can expect to pay around US$105 one-way.

Alfa Romeo Aero Taxi (☑ 8632-8150; www.alfa romeoair.com) offers charter flights connecting Drake to Puerto Jiménez (US$430), Carate (US$450) and Sirena (US$420). Flights are best booked at the airport in person; if there are several of you, one-way fares are typically less than US$100.

Most lodges provide transportation to/from the airport or Sierpe, which involves a jeep or a boat or both, but advance reservation is necessary.

BOAT

An exhilarating boat ride from Sierpe is one of the true thrills of visiting the area. Boats travel along the river through the rainforest and the mangrove estuary. Captains then pilot boats through tidal currents and surf the river mouth into the ocean. All of the hotels offer boat transfers between Sierpe and Bahía Drake with prior arrangements. Most hotels in Drake have beach landings, so wear appropriate footwear.

If you have not made advance arrangements with your lodge for a pick-up, two *colectivo* boats depart daily from Sierpe at 11:30am and 4:30pm, and from Bahía Drake back to Sierpe at 7:15am (US$15) and 2:30pm (US$20).

BUS

A bus to La Palma (where you can connect to a bus to Puerto Jiménez) picks passengers up along the beach road and in front of the supermarkets at around 4am and 1:30pm (US$5, two hours). The return journey from La Palma is at 11am and 4:45pm. Double-check departure times locally.

CAR

Rincón, on the main road between Puerto Jiménez and the Interamericana, is linked to Agujitas in Bahía Drake by a decent dirt road, although a 4WD is absolutely necessary for this route, which can be impassable during the rainy season as there are several river crossings. The most hazardous crossing is the Río Drake – locals fish many a water-logged vehicle out of the river. Even high-clearance 4WD vehicles have difficulty after it's been raining. If in doubt, wait until a local car appears, watch where it crosses and follow its lead. The construction of a bridge has been approved, but it may be some years yet until it's actually built.

Between Rincón and Rancho Quemado there's also a very narrow bridge with no safety railings; proceed with caution.

Fill up your tank before driving to Drake; there is no gas station here.

Once in Agujitas, you will likely have to abandon your car as most places are accessible only by boat or by foot. Park your car in a secure place, such as a guesthouse. There are several small supermarkets where the management will be happy to watch over your 4WD for a nice tip.

Rancho Quemado

For much of its existence, this small village, founded by gold miners in the 1940s some 15km east of Bahía Drake, has relied on farming and cattle raising for its existence, especially when the gold ran out (though some gold-panning still goes on in the nearby rivers). As production prices fell, bringing unemployment and associated problems – poaching, illegal deforestation – the community began to look at rural tourism as an alternative means of making a living, and for protecting the natural environment at the same time. Part of the Caminos de Osa project (p450), these locals enthusiastically welcome visitors, who come here to learn about gold-panning and farming, or to just enjoy some terrific rural hospitality and hearty Tico food, en route to or from Bahía Drake.

Sights & Activities

By calling Rancho Quemado Information visitors can arrange sugarcane farm tours, gold-panning tours, horseback riding, visiting several farms and more.

Trapiche Don Carmen   FARM

(8455-9742; tours per person US$25) Jholly and his family show visitors around their sugarcane mill. You get to see (and taste) the fresh sugarcane juice when the stalks pass through the grinder, watch Jholly boil the juice and cool it down in special molds, and then behold the finished product – delicious cane sugar.

Mariposario Metamorfosis   NATURE RESERVE

(admission US$8) This small butterfly farm is due to open to visitors in the second half of 2016. It will feature three or four butterfly species native to the Osa Peninsula, with visitors able to learn about the metamorphosis process and tour the small botanical garden.

Artisanal Gold Tour   CULTURAL TOUR

(8731-2882; adult/under 12yr US$25/12) During this two-hour tour, visitors hike to a creek where they are shown how to pan for gold, and they get to try their luck at this time-honored profession, too.

Sleeping & Eating

Rancho Verde   CABIN $

(8646-5431; per person US$15) Right by the road winding through Rancho Quemado, this welcoming little place has a couple of tidy guest cabins, and the friendly proprietress cooks up monumental portions of grilled pork or fish with rice, beans and plantains (meals US$6).

ℹ Information

Rancho Quemado Information (Jessica 8667-2535, Mark 8948-2348; www.visitrancho quemado.com) If you want to book any activities or lodgings in Rancho Quemado in advance, it's best to call either Jessica (Spanish only) or Mark (English and Spanish) to make arrangements.

ℹ Getting There & Away

Twice-daily buses leave La Palma for Rancho Quemado and Bahía Drake at 11:30am and 4:30pm Monday to Saturday (US$2.60, one hour). If you're driving, you'll need a 4WD to get here as there are a couple of shallow rivers to cross.

Bahía Drake to Corcovado

This craggy stretch of coastline is home to sandy inlets that disappear at high tide, leaving only the rocky outcroppings and luxuriant rainforest. Virtually uninhabited and undeveloped beyond a few tourist lodges, the setting here is magnificent and wild. If you're looking to spend a bit more time along the shores of Bahía Drake before penetrating the depths of Parque Nacional Corcovado, consider a night or two in some of the country's most remote accommodations, with plenty of wildlife sightings in the surrounding jungle.

The only way to get around the area is by boat or by foot, which means that travelers are more or less dependent on their lodges unless they're close to Agujitas.

Sights

Playa Cocalito   BEACH

Just west of Punta Agujitas, a short detour off the main trail leads to the picturesque Playa Cocalito, a secluded cove perfect for sunning, swimming and body surfing.

NTCO / GETTY IMAGES ©

1. Cloud forest, Parque Internacional La Amistad (p425)
This 4070-sq-km park is the largest protected area in Costa Rica and crosses into Panama.

2. Harpy eagles (p426)
Sightings of this majestic species are extremely rare.

3. Parque Internacional La Amistad (p425)
Wildlife abounds in this pristine park, with more than 400 bird species and 90 mammal species.

4. Cerro Chirripó (p416)
Costa Rica's highest peak rises 3820m above sea level.

WORTH A TRIP

RESERVA BIOLÓGICA ISLA DEL CAÑO

The centerpiece of Reserva Biológica Isla del Caño (admission US$10, US$4 charge for divers, incl in tour price) is a 326-hectare island – the tip of numerous underwater rock formations. Some 15 different species of coral are here, as well as threatened species including the Panulirus lobster and giant conch. The sheer numbers of fish attract dolphins and whales, as well as hammerhead sharks, manta rays and sea turtles.

The only way to access the island is via snorkeling (US$80) and diving tours (two tanks, US$135), arranged in Bahía Drake.

On the island, at about 110m above sea level, the evergreen trees consist primarily of milk trees (also called 'cow trees' after the drinkable white latex they exude), believed to be the remains of an orchard planted by pre-Columbian indigenous inhabitants. Near the top of the ridge, there are two pre-Columbian granite spheres; the rest have been removed. Archaeologists speculate that the island may have been a ceremonial or burial site for the same indigenous tribes.

To preserve the ecology of the island, recreational visitors have been prohibited from venturing beyond the boat-landing beach since the end of 2013.

Playa Caletas   BEACH

This is one of the recommended spots for snorkeling. It is situated just in front of the Corcovado Adventures Tent Camp.

Playa San Josecito   BEACH

South of Río Claro, Playa San Josecito is the longest stretch of white-sand beach on this side of the Península de Osa. It is popular with swimmers, snorkelers and sunbathers, though you'll only find it crowded at lunchtime since it's the favorite post-snorkeling picnic spot for tour companies coming back from Isla del Caño. Watch out for capuchin monkeys!

🏃 Activities

★**Agujitas–Corcovado Trail**   HIKING

This 17km public trail follows the coastline from Agujitas to the San Pedrillo ranger station for the entire spectacular stretch, and it's excellent for wildlife-spotting (particularly early in the morning), beach-hopping and canoe tours with Río Claro Tours. Tour operators can drop you off by boat at a point of your choosing and you can walk back to Agujitas.

★**Río Claro Tours**   CANOEING

(per person US$15) A 20-minute hike toward Agujitas from Playa San Josecito, a hermit called Ricardo ('Clavito') lives by the Río Claro and runs hugely entertaining canoeing tours that start with a rope-swing plunge and continue to some waterfalls with refreshing plunge pools. Various tour operators can drop you off by boat, leaving you to walk back to Agujitas afterward.

🛏 Sleeping

Reservations are recommended in the dry season (mid-December to mid-April). Some places in this area don't have 24-hour electricity (pack a flashlight) or hot water.

With prior arrangements, accommodations provide transportation (free or for a charge) from Agujitas, Sierpe or the airstrip in Drake.

★**Las Caletas Lodge**   LODGE $$

(☏ 8863-9631, 8826-1460, 2560-6602; www.caletas.cr; Playa Caletas; tent/r per person from US$75/90; @ 🛜) 🍃 This adorable lodge consists of cozy wooden cabins and safari tents perched above the picturesque beach of the same name. The Swiss and Tico owners are warm hosts who established this convivial spot before there was phone access or electricity (now mostly solar- and hydro-powered). The food is delicious and bountiful, the staff friendly and the environment beautifully chill.

Some of the rooms are geared toward families and there's a 50% discount for four- to 11-year-olds.

★**Casa Corcovado Jungle Lodge**   LODGE $$$

(☏ 2256-3181, in USA 888-896-6097; www.casacorcovado.com; s/d 4-day package from US$1515/2790; 🛜🐾) 🍃 A spine-tingling boat ride takes you to this luxurious lodge on 175 hectares of rainforest bordering the national park. Each bungalow is tucked away in its own private tropical garden, and artistic details include antique Mexican tiles and handmade stained-glass windows. Guests can stretch their legs on the lodge's extensive network of trails, which pass a number of watering holes.

On-site, the Margarita Sunset Bar lives up to its name, serving up margaritas and great sunset views over the Pacific. Discounts are available for longer stays.

★**Copa de Arbol** LODGE $$$
(☑ 8935-1212, in USA 831-246-4265; www.copadearbol.com; Playa Caletas; s/d from US$380/600; ✳ 🌐 🏊) Though they look a bit rustic from the outside with their thatch roofs and stilts, these 10 hillside *cabinas* are gorgeously outfitted inside – built with sustainably grown wood and recycled materials, and each with private terrace. The lodge, steps from the beach, is laid-back luxury with an infinity pool, and run smoothly by super-friendly staff. Paddleboards and kayaks are free for guests.

★**Proyecto Campanario** CAMPGROUND $$$
(☑ 2289-8694, 2289-8708; www.campanario.org; 4-day package per person US$502) 🏊 This biological reserve is an education center rather than a tourist facility, aimed at those wanting to learn about the importance of various tropical ecosystems, as evidenced by the dormitory, library and field station. Ecology courses and conservation camps are scheduled throughout the year, attracting individuals passionate about these issues, from university students and field biologists to concerned tourists.

★**Corcovado**
Adventures Tent Camp CAMPGROUND $$$
(☑ 8386-2296, in USA 866-498-0824; www.corcovado.com; 2-day package per person from US$299; 🏊) Less than an hour's walk from Agujitas brings you to this rugged spot run by longtime expat Larry. Spacious safari tents with beds are set up on covered platforms, 20 hectares of rainforest offer plenty of opportunity for exploration, and the beachfront setting is excellent for kayaking, snorkeling and boogie-boarding (equipment use is free). Backpacker digs are in the works.

Guaria de Osa LODGE $$$
(☑ 2235-4313, in USA 510-235-4313; www.guariadeosa.com; per person r incl full board US$150; 🏊) Cultivating a New Age ambience, this Asian-style retreat center offers yoga, tai chi and 'Sentient Experiential' events, along with the more typical rainforest activities. The lovely grounds include an ethnobotanical garden, which features exotic local species. The architecture of this place is unique: the centerpiece is the Lapa Lapa Lounge, a spacious multistory pagoda built entirely from reclaimed hardwood. Three-night minimum.

Parque Nacional Corcovado

This national park takes up 40% of the Osa Peninsula and is the last great original tract of tropical rainforest in Pacific Central America. The bastion of biological diversity is home to *half* of Costa Rica's species, including the largest population of scarlet macaws, as well as countless other endangered species, including Baird's tapir, the giant anteater and the world's largest bird of prey, the harpy eagle.

Corcovado's amazing biodiversity as well as the park's demanding, multiday hiking trails have long attracted a devoted stream of visitors who descend from Bahía Drake and Puerto Jiménez to see the wildlife and experience a bona fide jungle adventure.

🏃 Activities

Hiking
There are three main trails in the park that are open to visitors, as well as shorter trails around the ranger stations. Trails are primitive and the hiking is hot, humid and insect-ridden, but the challenge of the trek and the interaction with wildlife at Corcovado are thrilling. Carry plenty of food, water and insect repellent.

The most popular route traverses the park from Los Patos to Sirena, then exits the park at La Leona (or vice versa). This allows hikers to begin and end their journey in or near Puerto Jiménez, offering easy access to La Leona and Los Patos.

The most popular trail, however, is still La Leona to Sirena (p440), with an additional trail section running parallel to the beach trail for those who don't want to expose themselves to the relentless sun. The toughest day trek is from La Tarde to Sirena via Los Patos – a whopping 30km.

A new El Tigre trail loop (p441) has been added that starts in Dos Brazos and dips into the park but doesn't join up with the rest of the trail network; you still have to pay the full park fee to hike it, though.

Hiking is best in the dry season (from December to April), when there is still regular rain but all of the trails are open. It remains muddy, but you won't sink quite as deep.

Hiking in Parque Nacional Corcovado

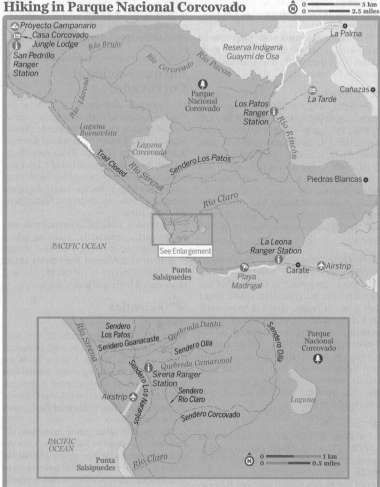

La Leona to Sirena

HIKING

The largely flat 16km hike (five to seven hours) follows the shoreline through coastal forest and along deserted beaches. Take plenty of water, a hat and sunscreen. It involves one major river crossing at Río Claro, just south of Sirena, and there's an excellent chance of seeing monkeys, tapirs and scarlet macaws en route. La Leona is an additional 3.5km to Carate.

A new trail running parallel to this trail allows you to avoid the sizzling tramp along the beach.

Sirena to Los Patos

HIKING

This trail goes 18km through the heart of Corcovado, passing through primary and secondary forest, and is relatively flat for the first 12km. After you wade through two river tributaries before reaching the Laguna Corcovado, the route undulates steeply (mostly uphill!) for the remaining 6km. It's less punishing to do this trek in the opposite direction.

The largest herds of peccary are reportedly on this trail. Local guides advise that peccary sense fear, but they will back off if you act aggressively. Alternatively, if you climb up a tree – about 2m off the ground – you'll avoid being bitten or trampled in the event of running into a surly bunch. Fun fact: peccary herds emit a strong smell of onions, so you usually have a bit of a heads-up before they come crashing through the bush.

Sendero El Tigre
HIKING

Part of this new 8km loop trail passes through Parque Nacional Corcovado, so a guide is mandatory. It's a fairly rugged trail, part of which passes through an ancient indigenous burial ground; be prepared to spend the best part of a day hiking it. It's doable as a day trip yet gives you a good taste of the park.

Wildlife-Watching

Corcovado is home to a staggering 370 species of birds, 140 species of mammals and thousands of insect species, with more still waiting to be discovered. The best wildlife-watching in Corcovado is around Sirena, but the coastal trails have two advantages: they are more open, and the constant crashing of waves covers the sound of noisy walkers. White-faced capuchin, red-tailed squirrel, collared peccary, white-nosed coati, tapir and northern tamandua are regularly seen on both of the following trails.

The coastal trail from Carate to Sirena produces an endless pageant of birds. Sightings of scarlet macaws are guaranteed, as the tropical almond trees lining the coast are a favorite food. The sections along the beach shelter mangrove black hawk by the dozens and numerous waterbird species.

The Los Patos–Sirena trail attracts lowland rainforest birds such as great curassow, chestnut-mandibled toucan, fiery-billed aracari and rufous piha. Encounters with mixed flocks are common. Mammals are similar to those near coastal trails, but Los Patos is better for primates and white-lipped peccary. If you spend a night at La Tarde before hiking to Los Patos, it's an excellent place to see snakes and frogs.

For wildlife-watchers frustrated by the difficulty of seeing rainforest mammals, a stay at Sirena ranger station is a must. Baird's tapirs are practically assured – a statement that can be made at few other places in the world. This endangered and distant relative of the rhinoceros is frequently spotted grazing along the airstrip after dusk. Sirena is excellent for other herbivores, particularly red brocket (especially on the Los Patos–Sirena trail) and both species of peccary. Agouti and tayra are also common.

Jaguars are spotted extremely rarely, as their population in the Osa is suspected to be in the single digits. At night look for kinkajou and crab-eating skunk (especially at the mouth of the Río Sirena). Ocelot represent your best chance for observing a cat, but again, don't get your hopes up.

Corcovado is the only national park in Costa Rica with all four of the country's primate species. Spider monkey, mantled howler and white-faced capuchin can be encountered anywhere, while the Los Patos–Sirena trail is best for the fourth and most endangered species, the Central American squirrel monkey. Sirena also has fair chances for the extremely hard-to-find silky anteater, a nocturnal animal that frequents the beachside forests between the Río Claro and the station.

The Río Sirena is a popular spot for American crocodile, three-toed sloth and bull shark.

Tours

All visitors to Corcovado must be accompanied by an ICT-certified guide. Besides their intimate knowledge of the trails, local guides are amazingly informed about flora and fauna, including the best places to spot various species. Most guides also carry telescopes, allowing for up-close views of wildlife.

Guides are most often hired through the Área de Conservación Osa park office (p449) in Puerto Jiménez, or through hotels and tour operators. Two recommended local offices are the super-reliable, locally run Osa Wild (p445) in Puerto Jiménez and Corcovado Info Center (p431) in Bahía Drake. Prices vary considerably depending on the season, availability, size of your party and type of expedition you want to arrange. In any case, you will need to negotiate a price that includes park fees, meals and transportation.

Sleeping & Eating

Camping costs US$6 per person per day at the Sirena, La Leona and San Pedrillo ranger stations; facilities include potable water and latrines. Remember to bring a flashlight or a headlamp, as the campsites are pitch black at night. Camping is not permitted anywhere other than the three ranger stations; there are no accommodations at Los Patos.

All visitors are required to pack out all of their trash.

Sirena ranger station serves meals (US$20 to US$25 per meal) by advance reservation only and there are no cooking facilities. All other ranger stations have drinking water, but you have to bring your own provisions.

⭐ **La Tarde**　　　　　　　　　　LODGE **$$**
(☏ 2200-9617; www.ecoturisticolatarde.com; per person incl 3 meals US$70; 🕎) ✎ This wonderful, farm-based rural-tourism project is run by Eduardo and his hospitable family. There are various nature trails on the property, and it's a great place to stay if you're looking to hike to Sirena in Parque Nacional Corcovado. Accommodations are either in a dorm, rustic cabins or a brand-new en suite cabin (no electricity).

A resident herpetologist leads excellent night tours (US$20) in search of rare frogs and fer-de-lance snakes.

ℹ Information

Information and maps are available at the office of Área de Conservación Osa (p449) in Puerto Jiménez where you also have to pay your park entry fee of US$15 per day. If you hire a guide through a tour agency, the agency will make all the arrangements for you and include the required fees in the package price. If you hire a guide independently, you may have to make the reservations for lodging and meals yourself. Be sure to make these arrangements a few days in advance, especially in dry season, as there's a daily limit to the number of visitors allowed in the park and facilities often hit their maximum capacity.

Park headquarters are at Sirena ranger station on the coast in the middle of the park. Other ranger stations are located on the park boundaries: San Pedrillo station in the northwest corner on the coast; and La Leona station in the southeast corner on the coast (near the village of Carate). There's a new ranger station in Dos Brazos village, and the rebuilt Los Patos ranger station is actually just outside the park boundary, closest to La Tarde.

ℹ Getting There & Away

AIR

Alfa Romeo Aero Taxi (www.alfaromeoair. com) offers charter flights connecting Puerto Jiménez, Drake and Golfito to Carate and Sirena. Sample flights from Puerto Jiménez or Carate to Sirena cost US$390, but if a pilot is dropping passengers off in Sirena and leaving empty, and you're too exhausted to hike out, there's certainly room for negotiation, and if there's a group of you, it works out more

reasonably. Note that long-term parking is not available at any of these locations, so it's best to make prior arrangements if you need to leave your car somewhere.

FROM BAHÍA DRAKE

From Bahía Drake, you can walk the coastal trail that leads to San Pedrillo station (about seven hours from Agujitas). Many lodges and tour companies run day tours here, with a boat ride to San Pedrillo (30 minutes to an hour, depending on the departure point) or Sirena (one to 1½ hours). You can make camping reservations at San Pedrillo or Sirena stations.

FROM CARATE

In the southeast, the closest point of access is Carate, from where La Leona station is a one-hour, 3.5km hike west along the beach.

Carate is accessible from Puerto Jiménez via a poorly maintained, 45km dirt road. This journey is an adventure in itself, and often allows for some good wildlife-spotting along the way. A 4WD *colectivo* travels this route twice daily for US$9, departing Carate at 8:15am and 3:45pm. Otherwise you can hire a 4WD taxi for around US$90.

If you have your own car, the *pulpería* in Carate is a safe place to park for a few days, though you'll have some extra peace of mind if you tip the manager before setting out.

FROM LA PALMA

From the north, the closest point of access is the town of La Palma, from where you can catch a bus or taxi south to Puerto Jiménez or north to San José.

Heading to Los Patos station, you might be able to find a taxi to take you partway; however, the road is only passable to 4WD vehicles (and not always), so be prepared to hike the 14km to the ranger station. The road crosses the river about 20 times in the last 6km, so not only do you need a rugged vehicle, but you have to be experienced at driving through rivers.

A far more sensible option is to drive to La Tarde (where the road divides, the branch going uphill leads to La Tarde, whereas the lower branch leads to Los Patos) and hike to Los Patos from there, especially since there's nowhere to stay at Los Patos and you have to either limit yourself to a day hike or walk all the way to Sirena.

If you have a car, it's best to leave it with a hotel or lodge in La Palma.

FROM DOS BRAZOS

Dos Brazos is a short drive from Puerto Jiménez; it's 10km to the El Tigre turnoff from where Dos Brazos is signposted along a dirt road. The trailhead is signposted in the Dos Brazos village.

Carate

If you make it all the way here, congratulations. A bone-rattling 45km south of Puerto Jiménez, this is where the dirt road rounds the peninsula and comes to an abrupt dead end. There's literally nothing more than an airstrip, a long strip of wild beach and a *pulpería*. Carate is not a destination in itself, but it is the southwestern gateway for anyone hiking into Sirena ranger station in Parque Nacional Corcovado.

A handful of well-designed wilderness lodges in the area make a good night's rest for travelers heading to/from Corcovado or those in search of a quiet retreat surrounded by jungle. The ride from Puerto Jiménez to Carate is also its own adventure as the narrow, bumpy dirt road winds its way around dense rainforest, through gushing rivers and across windswept beaches. Birds and other wildlife are prolific along this stretch: keep your eyes peeled and hang on tight.

🛏 Sleeping & Eating

Some places in Carate don't have 24-hour electricity or hot water. Reservations are recommended in the dry season – communication is often through Puerto Jiménez, so messages may not be retrieved every day. For shoestringers, the best option is to camp in the yard in front of the *pulpería;* the Canadian owner will charge you about US$5 a day to camp in his yard.

West of Carate is the national park, so if you're planning on hiking into Corcovado, you must be self-sufficient from here on. The *pulpería* is the last chance you have to stock up on food and water.

★ **Luna Lodge**   LODGE **$$$**
(✆2206-5859, in USA & Canada 888-760-0760; www.lunalodge.com; bungalow per person incl all meals US$235; [P][🛏][≋]) 🍴 A steep road crisscrosses the Río Carate and up the valley to this enchanting mountain retreat on the border of Parque Nacional Corcovado. Accommodations range from tent cabins to thatched bungalows with open-air garden showers and private terraces, all with stunning views of the pristine jungle rolling down to the ocean. This is the furthest of Carate's accommodations.

The open-air restaurant is a marvelous place to indulge in the expansive views, while an open-air yoga studio provides an even higher vantage point. Lana, the founder

and owner of the lodge, is passionate about conservation and sustainability and has made the lodge a working practice in both. There are accommodations discounts for under-12s.

Lookout Inn   GUESTHOUSE **$$$**
(✆2735-5431; www.lookout-inn.com; r per person from US$120; [P][@][≋]) Perched up the side of a steep hillside overlooking the ocean, Lookout Inn attracts younger travelers with its comfortable, open-air quarters with mural-painted walls and unbeatable views. Accommodations are accessible by a wooden walkway winding through the trees. The 'Stairway to Heaven' (360 steps) leads up to four observation platforms and a waterfall trail. Lookout is near the airstrip.

More traditional rooms are available in the main building. Interesting gimmick: if you don't spot a scarlet macaw during your stay, your lodging is free!

La Leona Eco-Lodge   LODGE **$$$**
(✆2735-5704; www.laleonaecolodge.com; per person tent half-/full board from US$89/99 ; [≋]) 🍴 On the edge of Parque Nacional Corcovado, this friendly lodge offers all the thrills of camping, without the hassles. The 16 fully screened forest-green tents with beds are nestled between palm trees, with decks facing the beach and allowing frequent wildlife sightings. Solar power provides electricity in the restaurant. All guests must hike the 2.5km in from the Carate airstrip.

❶ Getting There & Away

AIR

Alfa Romeo Aero Taxi (✆8632-8150; www.alfaromeoair.com) offers charter flights from Puerto Jiménez (US$185). Prices are dependent on the number of passengers, so if you're with others, the rate can be as low as US$60 per person.

BUS

The *colectivo* (US$9) departs Puerto Jiménez for Carate at 5:30am and 1:30pm, returning at 8:15am and 3:45pm. Note that it often fills up on its return trip to Puerto Jiménez, especially during the dry season. Arrive at least 30 minutes ahead of time or you might find yourself stranded. Alternatively, catch a taxi from Puerto Jiménez (US$90).

CAR

If you're driving you'll need a 4WD, even in the dry season, as there are several streams to ford, as well as a river. Assuming you don't have valuables in sight, you can leave your car at the *pulpería* (per night US$5) or at any of the tented camps along the road (with prior arrangements), and hike to La Leona station (1½ hours).

Cabo Matapalo

If you didn't know that it was here, you would hardly suspect that the jungle-obscured community of Matapalo existed. There isn't much to the southern tip of the Osa Península save some surfing digs and homes at the entrance to the Golfo Dulce. Matapalo lies just 17km south of Puerto Jiménez, but this heavily forested and beach-fringed cape is a vastly different world. A network of trails traverses the foothills, uninhabited except for migrating wildlife from the Reserva Forestal Golfo Dulce. Along the coastline, miles of beaches are virtually empty, except for handfuls of surfers in the know.

Cabo Matapalo is home to wilderness lodges that cater to travelers searching for seclusion and wildlife. Scarlet macaws, brown pelicans and herons are frequently sighted on the beaches, while all four species of Costa Rican monkey, several wildcat species, sloth, coati, agouti and anteater roam the woods.

🏃 Activities & Tours

★ Psycho Tours   ADVENTURE TOUR
(Everyday Adventures; ☑ 8353-8619; www.psychotours.com; tours US$45-120) Witty, energetic naturalist Andy Pruter runs Psycho Tours, which offers high-adrenaline adventures in Cabo Matapalo. His signature tour is tree climbing (US$65 per person): scaling a 60m ficus tree, aptly named 'Cathedral.' Also popular – and definitely adrenaline inducing – is waterfall rappelling (US$95) down cascades ranging from 15m to 30m. The best one? The tree-climbing/waterfall combo tour (US$130).

For the tamer of heart, excellent three- to four-hour guided nature walks (US$55) tap into the extensive knowledge base of Andy and his staff members.

Playa Matapalo   SURFING
There are three excellent right point breaks off this beach, not far from Encanta La Vida. If there's a south or west swell this is the best time to hit the waves.

Playa Pan Dulce   SURFING
Good for beginners and intermediate surfers, Pan Dulce gets some nice longboard waves most days. You can also go swimming here, but be careful of rip tides.

🛏 Sleeping

This area is off the grid, so some places do not have electricity around the clock or hot water; top-end lodges have their own generators. Advance reservations are highly recommended in the dry season (mid-December to mid-April); many places close for the month of October.

Ojo del Mar   BUNGALOW $$
(☑ 8378-5246; www.ojodelmar.com; road to Carate, Km 16; s/d from US$100/150, tents s/d US$70/90, all incl breakfast; 🅿🛜) 🍃 Tucked in amid a good surfing beach and lush jungle, the six beautifully handcrafted, thatch-roofed bamboo bungalows are entirely open-air, allowing for all the natural sounds and scents to seep in. Surfers chill in palm-strung hammocks and rates include breakfast, with Nico – co-owner and cook – also serving an excellent, all-organic dinner. Yoga classes (US$15) are offered every morning.

★ Lapa Ríos   LODGE $$$
(☑ 2735-5130; www.laparios.com; road to Carate, Km 17; per person r incl 3 meals US$470; 🅿🏊) 🍃 One of Costa Rica's best all-inclusive wilderness lodges, Lapa Ríos combines luxury with a rustic, tropical ambience. It comprises 16 spacious, thatched bungalows, all decked out with queen-sized beds, bamboo furniture, garden showers and private decks with panoramic views (no wi-fi/TV). An extensive trail system allows exploration of the 400-hectare reserve, while swimming, snorkeling and surfing are within easy reach.

★ Blue Osa
Yoga Retreat   BOUTIQUE HOTEL $$$
(☑ in USA 917-400-9797; www.blueosa.com; r from US$269; 🅿🍴🏊🛜🏊) 🍃 With an emphasis on rejuvenation, this intimate oceanfront ecoresort attracts those looking to unwind, through yoga, swimming in the chemical-free pool or getting pampered in the solar-powered eco-spa. Meals comprise organic produce from their own garden, the lodgings are harmonious, with rustic furnishings and screened windows, and there's a definite camaraderie among guests. Halfway between Puerto Jiménez and Matapalo.

Many guests come here on week-long packages.

★**Encanta La Vida**   LODGE **$$$**
(☑8376-3209, 2735-5678; www.encantalavida.
com; Cabo Matapalo; cabins per person US$130-
185 ; P🖈🛜❄) The enchanted life, indeed.
Gorgeous breeze-cooled, wood-beamed
structures – from round treehouses to ro-
mantic, freestanding *casitas* – are scattered
at the foot of a jungle-clad backdrop. The
food is brilliant and the location a perfect
base for exploring the cape. An ocean-view
yoga terrace is available, there are surf-
boards for rent, and tours can be arranged
by the accommodating staff.

Howlers and spider monkeys regularly
travel the treetops, while pairs of great cu-
rassows stroll shyly below.

El Remanso Lodge   LODGE **$$$**
(☑2735-5569; www.elremanso.com; road to Car-
ate, Km 18; s/d from US$275/360; P🖈🛜❄) 🖈 Set
on 56 hectares of rainforest, this bluff-top
lodge is run by the daughter of Greenpeace
activists. Constructed entirely from fallen
tropical hardwoods, the secluded, spacious
and sumptuous cabins have mesh instead of
glass, and guests are taken on birding and
nature hikes by knowledgeable guides. Miles
of private trails lead through jungle to the
beach, a waterfall and tide pools.

Ranchos Almendros   CABINA **$$$**
(Kapu's Place; ☑2735-5531; http://home.earth-
link.net/~kapu; Cabo Matapalo; r per person with/
without meals from US$80/50; P🖈🛜) This is the
end of the line on Cabo Matapalo, where
the road stops pretending and turns into
a sandy beach path. The property includes
three cozy *cabañas* equipped with solar
power, large screened windows, full kitchens
and garden showers. Well suited to surfers
and self-sufficient types, these *cabañas* are
practically steps from the beach and allow
for self-catering.

❶ Getting There & Away

If you are driving, a 4WD is essential even in the
dry season, as roads frequently get washed out.
There are several streams and a river to cross
on the way here. From the Puerto Jiménez–
Carate road, the poorly marked turnoff for Cabo
Matapalo is on the left-hand side, then through
a crumbling cement gate (called 'El Portón
Blanco').

Otherwise, the *colectivo* (US$6) will drop you
here; it passes by at about 7:15am and 2:45pm
heading to Carate, and 9:15am and 4:15pm
heading back to Jiménez. A taxi will come here
from Puerto Jiménez for about US$55.

Puerto Jiménez

Sliced in half by the swampy, overgrown
Quebrada Cacao, and flanked on one side by
the emerald waters of the Golfo Dulce, the
vaguely Wild West outpost of Puerto Jimén-
ez is shared equally by local residents and
wildlife. While walking through the dusty
streets of Jiménez (as it's known to locals),
it's not unusual to spot scarlet macaws
roosting on the soccer field, or white-faced
capuchins traversing the treetops adjacent
to the main street.

On the edge of Parque Nacional Corco-
vado, Jiménez is the preferred jumping-off
point for travelers heading to the famed Si-
rena ranger station, and a great place to or-
ganize an expedition, stock up on supplies,
eat a hot meal and get a good night's rest
before hitting the trails.

Despite the region's largest and most
diverse offering of hotels, restaurants and
other tourist services, this is very much a
close-knit Tico community at its core.

◉ Sights

**Herrera Gardens
& Conservation Project**   GARDENS
(☑2735-5267; admission US$7, 2hr guided tour
US$40; ⊙6am-5pm) 🖈 The Herrera Gardens
& Conservation Project is a 250-acre reserve
with beautiful botanical gardens. This inno-
vative, long-term reforestation project offers
an ecologically and economically sustain-
able alternative to cattle-grazing. Visitors can
explore the 5km of garden trails or 15km of
well-marked forest trails, where you're likely
to see capuchin monkeys and macaws. It's
located 400m east of the airstrip. Guided
tours focus on birding, botany or even tree
climbing. Jagua Arts & Crafts (p448) sells
map and arranges tours.

Playa Platanares   BEACH
About 5km east of town, the long, secluded –
and often deserted – Playa Platanares is ex-
cellent for swimming, sunning and recover-
ing from too much adventure. The nearby
mangroves of Río Platanares are a paradise
for kayaking and bird-watching. Take the
road that runs parallel to the airstrip.

☞ Tours

★**Osa Wild**   TOUR
(☑8709-1083, 8376-1152, 2735-5848; www.osa
wildtravel.com; Rte 245, downtown Puerto Jiménez;
tours from US$30, 1-day Corcovado tour US$85;

Puerto Jiménez

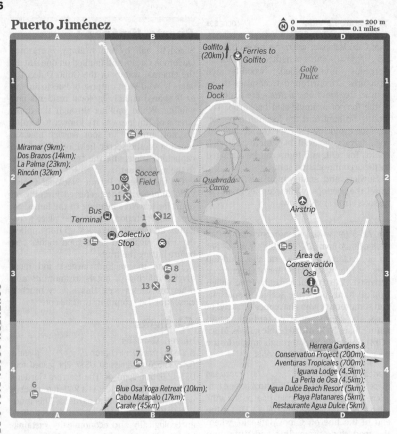

Puerto Jiménez

⊙ 8:30am-noon & 2:30-7pm) 🖉 Osa Wild is *the* way to connect with Corcovado park and Osa. It's just what the area so desperately needed: a resource for travelers to connect with community-oriented initiatives that go to the heart of the real Osa through homestays, farm tours and sustainable cultural exchanges. It also offers more typical stuff like kayaking tours and guided trips through Corcovado.

Run by university-trained biologist Ifi and her husband Daniel, Osa Wild's focus on sustainability, environmental protection and community development put it in a league of its own. It also sets up volunteer programs and rents tents and stoves for trips into the park.

Osa Aventura
ADVENTURE TOUR

(☑8372-6135, 2735-5670; www.osaaventura.com)
🕊 Run by Mike Boston, a biologist with a real passion for nature, Osa Aventura aims to introduce travelers to the beauty of rainforest life and to raise awareness of the need to preserve Corcovado's unique environment. Adventures vary from three-day treks through Corcovado to a new tour that focuses on Golfo Dulce's rural communities. Custom tours also available.

Surcos Tours
TOUR

(☑8603-2387, 2227-1484; www.surcostours.com)
🕊 A trio of excellent guides make Surcos the best company tours into Osa that focus on wildlife and bird-watching. Tours vary from day hikes in Corcovado and Matapalo to multiday experiences in Corcovado and specialized birding tours. Arrangements for tours are made through its website.

Osa Corcovado
ADVENTURE TOUR

(☑8632-8150; www.soldeosa.com; Hwy 245; ⊙8am-noon & 2-5pm) Newish operator offering anything from three-day Corcovado hikes to kayaking in the mangroves, sunset kayak dolphin-watching tours on the Golfo Dulce (US$45) and Matapalo day hikes.

Aventuras Tropicales
ADVENTURE TOUR

(☑2735-5195;   www.aventurastropicales.com)
Aventuras Tropicales is a professional, Tico-run operation that offers all sorts of active adventures. Some of its most popular excursions include kayaking tours of the mangroves, which cost US$45 per person, and their 'intense adventure' day trip (US$90). Located 2km east on the road to Platanares.

🛏 Sleeping

Cabinas Back Packer
GUESTHOUSE $

(☑2735-5181; s/d with air-con US$30/40, without air-con US$17/30; ❄🛜) One of the better budget digs – it's squeaky clean, relatively quiet as it's a couple of blocks from the main street, and comes with a front garden strung with hammocks. Rooms share clean bathrooms and there are bicycles for guest use. It also rents tents and camping gear and there's even a brightly tiled kitchen, available for a US$5 fee.

Lunas Hostel
HOSTEL $

(☑2735-6007; www.lunashostel.com; dm/d US$12/24; ❄🛜) A backpacker haven presided over by friendly and helpful owner Alex, who's been a guardian angel to more than

one traveler in distress. While the fan-cooled dorms and rooms are can't-swing-a-cat size, the handmade furniture and excellent mattresses are a boon. Shared bathrooms only. Alex can arrange Corcovado tours, though there have been mixed reports about the guide he works with.

Oro Verde Hostel
HOSTEL $

(☑2735-5241; www.oroverdehostel.com; dm/s/d US$10/15/24; ❄🛜) This super-central, rambling hostel offers spacious, spartan and rather anonymous rooms and dorms. However, the hot water is reliable, there's a guest kitchen, and the friendly couple who own the place go out of their way to be helpful. Light sleepers: try to avoid the rooms facing the main drag.

★Cabinas Jiménez
CABINA $$

(☑2735-5090; www.cabinasjimenez.com; s/d from US$45/60, cabinas US$80-120; 🅿❄🛜💦) Cabinas Jiménez is hands-down the nicest place to stay in Jiménez proper. All of the rooms come with fridges and jungle scenes painted on the walls, and poolside rooms come with chill-out patios. Pricier *cabinas* have kitchenettes and fantastic views of the lagoon. Bikes and kayaks are free for guests' use, and the bilingual staff is friendly and helpful.

Cabinas Tropicales
CABINA $$

(☑8997-1445, 2735-5298; www.cabinas-tropicales.com; s/d from US$45/50; 🅿❄🛜) Six tidy rooms at Cabinas Tropicales range from simple standards to roomy lofts and a deluxe suite, some of which have lovely outdoor showers. Each is unique, but they all have sturdy furniture, air-con and access to the gorgeous gardens and well-stocked open-air kitchen. Your host, Mark, is both personable and knowledgeable. One of the best-value options in town.

Agua Dulce Beach Resort
RESORT $$

(☑8599-9499, 8310-6304; www.aguadulceresort.com; r/ste/bungalow incl breakfast from US$89/119/299; 🅿❄🛜💦) Literally a stone's throw from Playa Platanares, this resort is centered on a pool and has an appealing open-air restaurant that specializes in excellent pasta dishes. The spacious beachfront bungalows benefit from views of the Golfo Dulce, and even the cheapest garden rooms are sizable and come with private decks. Monkeys and macaws haunt the jungle around the hotel.

Cacao Monkeys
CABINA $$

(2735-5248; www.cacaomonkeys.com; s/d incl breakfast from US$40/60; P) On the fringes of downtown on a cacao farm, this jungle joint has a set of five brightly painted wooden *cabinas* – one with a kitchen and two geared toward families. There's an excellent riverside cafe (meals from US$8). It's removed from town noise, feels jungle-like, and monkeys and iguanas stop by for a visit. One of the bungalows is specially furnished to accommodate a family with two kids.

★ Iguana Lodge
HOTEL $$$

(8848-0752, in USA & Canada 800-259-9123; www.iguanalodge.com; d incl breakfast US$180, casitas per person incl 2 meals from US$220, villa US$650; P) This luxurious lodge fronting Playa Platanares has the most architecturally alluring cabins in the area: four two-story bungalows with breezy decks, bamboo furniture, orthopedic beds draped in mosquito netting, and lovely stone bathrooms with garden showers. The three-story beach house is ideal for families, and there's a spa and exclusive on-site restaurant serving three delectable meals a day.

The restaurant, with a daily changing menu, is open to non-guests with prior reservations. On the premises there's also the more casual Pearl of the Osa eatery.

✖ Eating

★ Jardín Dulce
FRENCH $

(mains US$6-8; 7am-9pm Tue-Sat;) Just across from the soccer field, this delightful garden cafe that doubles as a florist is French-run and serves delicious homemade food. Half the dishes are vegetarian, but you'll also find the likes of quiche lorraine, *croque monsieur* and Lebanese-style chicken. Whatever you do, don't skip the homemade sweets: the fame of its truffles has spead far and wide.

★ Restaurante Monka
COSTA RICAN $

(2735-5051; mains US$5-6; 6am-10pm;) Bright and airy and the best breakfast spot in town, Monka does excellent smoothies and extensive breakfast platters, from American-style, involving bacon and pancakes, to Mexican-style huevos rancheros. The rest of the day you can fill up on good, inexpensive *casados*. Several breakfast options and *casados* are vegetarian.

Soda Valeria
COSTA RICAN $

(mains US$4-8; 10am-8pm Mon-Sat) Clean, cute and smack-dab in the middle of town, this *soda* is a dream – the kind of place you know is good because the local government workers all pile in at lunch. The heaping, fresh *casados* change daily and are delivered with fresh, homemade tortillas and sided with fresh fruit. Considerate, quick service is an extra boon.

BM Corcovado
SUPERMARKET $

(2735-5009; 7am-9pm Mon-Sat, 8am-8pm Sun) The best-stocked supermarket in town.

Restaurante Agua Dulce
INTERNATIONAL $$

(www.aguadulceresort.com; Agua Dulce Beach Resort; mains from US$8; 7am-10pm;) This breezy restaurant, on the premises of Agua Dulce Beach Resort on Playa Platanares, is a trusty spot for imaginative pasta dishes, grilled fish and ample breakfasts, although the service is positively languid. There are various vegetarian pasta dishes and salads.

La Perla de Osa
INTERNATIONAL $$

(8829-5865; mains US$10-17; 11am-8:30pm; P) On the grounds of Iguana Lodge, this jungle-fringed restaurant/bar is locally (and justifiably) famous for its cocktails, accompanied by such delectable nibbles as pulled-pork tacos, grilled Asian-style tuna and shrimp plates. Skip the spicy gazpacho, though. There are vegetarian soups, salads and meat-free pasta mains. Very popular with locals on weekends.

Pizzamail.it
PIZZA $$

(pizzas US$10-20; 4-10:30pm;) While this pizzeria's name sounds more like a website, all doubts will be cast aside when a server at Pizzamail.it brings out the pie: a thin-crust, wood-fired piece of Italy in the middle of the jungle. From its small patio diners can watch squawking macaws in the trees over the soccer pitch. Several pizza options·are meat-free. *Bellissimo!*

🔒 Shopping

★ Jagua Arts & Crafts
ARTS, CRAFTS

(2735-5267; 6:30am-5pm) A terrific, well-stocked crafts shop, featuring local art and jewelry, a wonderful collection of high-quality, colorful Boruca masks and black-and-ocher Guaitil pottery, as well as woven goods by the Emberá and Wounaan people. Kuna weavings technically belong across the border in Panama, but they make excellent gifts.

ℹ️ Information

Área de Conservación Osa (ACOSA; Osa Conservation Area Headquarters; ☎2735-5036; Corcovado park fee per person per day US$15; ⊘8am-noon & 1-4pm Mon-Fri) Information about Parque Nacional Corcovado, Isla del Caño, Parque Nacional Marino Ballena and Golfito parks and reserves.

Banco Nacional (☎2735-5020; ⊘8:30am-3:45pm Mon-Fri) It has an ATM.

BCR (Banco de Costa Rica; ☎2735-5260; ⊘9am-4pm Mon-Fri) Across from the church; it has an ATM.

Police Police.

Post Office (⊘8am-5pm Mon-Sat) Postal services.

ℹ️ Getting There & Away

AIR

The airstrip is to the east of town.

NatureAir (☎2735-5428; www.natureair.com; ⊘6am-2pm) and **Sansa** (☎2735-5890; www.flysansa.com) have flights to/from San José (50 minutes, up to four daily); one-way flights are approximately US$130. NatureAir also does the puddle jumper to Golfito (10 minutes, daily).

Alfa Romeo Aero Taxi (p443) has light aircraft (for three and five passengers) for charter flights to Golfito, Carate, Drake, Sirena, Palmar Sur, Quepos and Limón. Prices are dependent on the number of passengers, so it's best to try to organize a larger group if you're considering this option. Sometimes, if there's already a trip planned into the park, the cost can be as low as US$60 per person.

BOAT

Several fast **ferries** (☎8632-8672, 8656-0926, 8722-3828) travel to Golfito (US$6, 30 minutes), departing at 6am, 8:45am, 11:30am, 2pm and 4:20pm daily. Double-check current schedules, as they change often and without notice.

Alternatively, you could opt to hire a private water taxi to shuttle you across to Golfito or Zancudo. You will have to negotiate, but prices are generally reasonable, especially considering that you set the schedule. Osa Corcovado (p447) has a list of private boat operators.

CAR

Puerto Jiménez is now connected to the rest of the country by a beautifully paved road. You can rent a vehicle from **Solid Car Rental** (☎2735-5777; www.solidcarrental.com; ⊘7am-5pm). If you're driving to Carate or Matapalo, you'll need a 4WD; be sure to fill up at the gas station in Jiménez.

TAXI

The *colectivo* runs daily to Cabo Matapalo (1½ hours, US$9) and Carate (2½ hours, US$19) on the southern tip of the national park. **Departures** (☎8837-3120, 8832-8680) are from Soda Deya at 6am and 1:30pm, returning at 8:30am and 4pm.

Otherwise, you can call and hire a 4WD taxi from the **Central Taxi Center** (☎2735-5481). Taxis usually charge from US$60 for the ride to Carate and from US$70 for the ride to Matapalo, and more than US$120 for the overland trek to Drake.

Dos Brazos

Clustered along two branches of Río Tigre (which gives the village its full name: Dos Brazos de Río Tigre), this appealing village that lives on 'Tico time' is surrounded by secondary forest near the edge of Parque Nacional Corcovado. In the 1970s there was a gold rush here, with miners coming from all over to seek their fortune. But while small-scale gold-panning still goes on, Dos Brazos is now looking toward rural tourism and ecotourism as the way forward for its close-knit community, and is part of the Caminos de Osa project (p450).

🏃 Activities & Tours

A new, rugged 8km trail loop that passes through part of Corcovado, Sendero El Tigre (p441), opened in early 2015, bringing with it new visitors, and all profits are invested in

---

BUSES FROM PUERTO JIMÉNEZ

Most buses arrive at the peach-colored terminal on the west side of town. All of these pass La Palma (23km away) for the eastern entry into Corcovado.

DESTINATION	COST (US$)	DURATION (HR)	FREQUENCY (DAILY)
Neily	4.60	3	5:30am, 2pm
La Palma	2.60	1	at least once hourly
San Isidro de General	10	5½	5am, 9am, 1pm
San José	13	8	5am, 9am

CAMINOS DE OSA

Developed in response to the overcrowding of Parque Nacional Corcovado by a cooperation of private, public, academic and non-profit sectors, the **Caminos de Osa** (Osa Trails; www.caminosdeosa.com), when completed, will take visitors along three different routes bisecting the Osa Peninsula. Passing close to the park, they'll allow visitors to commune with wildlife, while also introducing them to the rural communities that call Osa home.

The **Oro trail** will skirt Corcovado and pass through the former gold-mining villages of Rancho Quemado and Dos Brazos, where visitors will be able to participate in a host of rural activities, from gold-panning to horseback riding, before finishing in Carate.

Passing through the Sierpe mangroves by boat, the **Agua trail** will deposit visitors at San Pedrillo ranger station, also bordering Corcovado, from where they'll be able to hike into Bahía Drake and eventually take the boat back to Sierpe.

Finally, the **Selva trail** will explore the southeastern part of the peninsula, connecting Dos Brazos to Puerto Jiménez and La Palma.

The trails were still in the making at the time of research, but the Caminos de Osa are actively working together with the communities of Dos Brazos, Rancho Quemado and La Palma, which visitors can easily visit – their rural tourism infrastructure is developed and the communities are eager to share their way of life with visitors.

the local community. It's probably the least expensive way of experiencing the national park (US$150 for two people) and is the only part of Corcovado that can be easily seen on a day trip.

The well-organized tourist office, Dos Brazos Oficina de Turismo, also arranges night tours, horseback-riding tours (half-day US$64 for two people) and gold-panning tours, with local gold-seekers showing you how it's done. The local community is brimming with ideas, with birding tours, guided hikes to a local waterfall and botany hikes in the works.

Sleeping

⭐ **Bolita Rainforest Hostel** HOSTEL **$**
(www.bolita.org; dm/cabinas US$12/35) For total immersion in rural life, stay at this semi-sustainable rustic farmhouse in the midst of 61 acres of rainforest. There's no electricity, so you'll be up with the howler monkeys and eating dinner by candlelight. Rooms come with mosquito nets and there are 15km of walking trails (and waterfalls) to explore. The office in the village provides walking directions.

Los Mineros Guesthouse GUESTHOUSE **$**
(☑ 8721-8087; www.losminerosguesthouse.com; per person hut/cabina US$16/21) This is the most characterful place to stay in the village, with a historical bar frequented by miners during the gold rush. The *cabinas*? Most were part of the village brothel; one was the town jail. Or you can bed down in one of the rustic bamboo-and-corrugated-iron huts with a strangely Alpine feel. The multilingual owners can provide meals (US$8 to US$15).

⭐ **Bosque del Río Tigre** LODGE **$$$**
(☑ 8705-3729; www.osaadventures.com; s/d US$195/330, 4-day package per person US$640; ℗) 🦋 In the midst of a 13-hectare private reserve, this ecolodge is a bird-watcher's paradise; guests can opt for unlimited birding and herping packages. Liz and Abraham are effusive hosts, the food is outstanding and wildlife comes up to your door. Four well-appointed guest rooms and one private cabin have huge windows for wildlife-watching. Getting here involves driving through a river.

Amazonita BUNGALOW **$$$**
(☑ 8891-6103; www.osarainforestrentals.com; house US$100) A five-minute walk from the Sendero El Tigre trailhead, on a steep hillside, Amazonita consists of two houses (up to four people) open to the wilderness and dwarfed by towering trees. Mosquito nets protect the beds and the kitchens are fully equipped. Nearby there are 14km of walking trails, or you can just swing in your hammock in beautiful tropical isolation.

ℹ Information

Dos Brazos Oficina de Turismo (☑ 8323-8695; info@dosbrazosderiotigre.com; ⊙ 6am-5pm) Helpful tourist office near the entrance to the village. Here visitors can book various tours, pay the park entry fee (US$15) if they wish to hike the Sendero El Tigre, and book a guide – mandatory for hiking inside the national park.

❶ Getting There & Away

A minibus runs from Puerto Jiménez to Dos Brazos twice daily on weekdays at 11am and 4pm (US$2, 40 minutes); it departs from in front of the Grupo Materiales hardware store. If driving, Río Tigre is well signposted off the main highway, around 10km north of Puerto Jiménez.

Reserva Forestal Golfo Dulce

The northern shore of the Golfo Dulce is home to this vast forest reserve, which links Parque Nacional Corcovado to the Parque Nacional Piedras Blancas. This connecting corridor plays an important role in preserving the biodiversity of the peninsula, and in allowing the wildlife to migrate to the mainland. Although much of the reserve is not easily accessible, there are several lodges in the area doing their part to preserve this natural resource by protecting their own little pieces of this wildlife wonderland.

Not far from the town of La Palma, Playa Blanca is a fairly low-key local scene, with some inexpensive budget digs and sea-kayaking opportunities.

◉ Sights

Finca Köbö   FARM
(🖉 8398-7604; www.fincakobo.com; 3hr tour US$32; 🅿) 🖉 About 8km south of La Palma, Finca Köbö is a chocolate-lover's dream come true (in fact *köbö* means 'dream' in Ngöbere). The 20-hectare *finca* (farm) is dedicated to the organic cultivation of fruits and vegetables and – the product of choice – cacao. Tours in English give a comprehensive overview of the life cycle of cacao plants and the production of chocolate (with degustation!). More than half of the territory is dedicated to protecting and reforesting natural ecosystems.

To really experience the beauty and vision of this *finca,* you can stay in simple, comfortable teak cabins (singles/doubles US$35/66, meals US$8 to US$13), with lovely open-air bathrooms and quality linens. Those who stay longer can hike the surrounding forest trails and speak with local farmers. The onsite gift store sells toasted cocoa nibs – great for energy! – and locally produced organic honey.

🏃 Activities & Tours

Wildlife-Watching

Most travelers skip the northern part of the peninsula and beeline for Puerto Jiménez to make arrangements to get into Parque Nacional Corcovado. If you have time to dawdle, there's lots of DIY wildlife-watching to be had. About 9km southeast of Rincón, the town of La Palma is the origin of the rough road that turns into the trail to Corcovado's Los Patos ranger station. If you're through-hiking Corcovado, this will likely be the start or end point of your trek.

Río Nuevo is a hamlet reachable via a 16km unpaved road from a turnoff just before entering Puerto Jiménez. A good trail network leads to spectacular mountain viewpoints, some with views of the gulf. Bird-watching is excellent in this area: you can expect to see the many species that you would find in Corcovado. Nearby lodges offer excursions in this area.

Kayaking

Playa Blanca, the beautiful sand-and-coral beach at the east end of La Palma, is a low-key scene popular with Ticos and an excellent place to go sea kayaking. The owner of Lapamar (p452) also arranges independent sea-kayaking outings, and this ecolodge is an overnight stop for participants in multiday kayaking trips run by Tropical Sea Kayaking.

Tropical Sea Kayaking   KAYAKING
(🖉 2249-0666, in the USA 719-581-9891; www.tropicalseakayaking.com; 5/8 days from US$999/1699) This experienced, reliable operator organizes in-depth sea-kayaking adventures on the Golfo Dulce, looking for wildlife in the mangroves and dolphin-spotting along the way, stopping on tiny islands and Playa Blanca, and seeking out secret spots that few visitors get to see. Prices include accommodations, meals, kayaking, domestic flights and more.

Cultural Tours

Reserva Indígena Guaymí de Osa   CULTURAL TOUR
The Reserva Indígena Guaymí de Osa is southwest of La Palma town, on the border of Parque Nacional Corcovado. If you're interested in learning more about the indigenous culture, it's possible to arrange a homestay with a Ngöbe family, who will meet you in La Palma for the journey into the reserve.

KNOWING THE NGÖBE

The earliest inhabitants of Costa Rica's far southern corner were the Ngöbe, historically referred to as the Guaymí. The name Guaymí was a Spanish transliteration of what another indigenous group had dubbed the Ngöbe – and while 'Guaymí' is not considered offensive, necessarily, the Ngöbe rightly prefer the name that they call themselves.

Having migrated over generations from neighboring Panama, the Ngöbe now inhabit indigenous reserves in the Valle de Coto Brus, the Península de Osa and southern Golfo Dulce; however, they retain some seminomadic ways and are legally allowed to pass freely over the border into Panama. This occurs frequently during the coffee-harvesting season, when many travel to work on plantations.

The Ngöbe have been able to preserve – to some degree – their customs and culture, and it is not unusual to see women wearing the traditional brightly colored, ankle-length *nagua* dress. Unlike other indigenous groups, the Ngöbe still speak Ngöbere, their native language, and teach it in local schools.

One reason the culture has been able to preserve its traditional ways is that the Ngöbe reserves are largely inaccessible. But as tourism filters into the furthest reaches of the country, the growing interest in indigenous traditions and handicrafts may actually encourage their preservation, so long as it is managed with community participation and visitor respect.

The easiest way to visit a Ngöbe reserve is to head to the visitor center at La Casona or the community museum (open 8am to 5pm) at Villa Palacios in the Coto Brus reserve, about 8km north of San Vito and another 8km off the Interamericana (the turnoff is marked by a hard-to-miss statue of a woman in Ngöbe dress).

To get the full-on immersion experience (and fully off the beaten track), stay for a few nights at Tamandu Lodge on the northern Osa Península. This unique lodge is run by the Carreras, a Ngöbe family, and provides a rare chance for a firsthand experience of the Ngöbe lifestyle. This is hands-on stuff: gather crabs and fish with palm rods; harvest palmito and yucca; and learn how to prepare these specialties over an open fire. Accommodations are in rustic, wooden houses, built on stilts with thatch roofs. Make reservations and find out details about the journey (around 7km from La Palma) on the website.

Sleeping

Lapamar   CABINA $$
(2735-3047; r per person incl breakfast US$30; P) The owner of this ecolodge on Playa Blanca runs excellent sea-kayaking tours (US$25 per person) and is very knowledgeable about local wildlife. Scarlet macaw sightings are a guarantee as they nest in the tree above the basic but comfy guest cabins. If you call ahead when arriving by bus you can get picked up from the Playa Blanca turnoff.

Manglares del Golfo   CABIN $
(8811-5178; tent US$5, cabin per person US$13) Fronting Playa Blanca, its quirky restaurant decorated with nautical flotsam and jetsam, this friendly place has two types of shoestringer digs: mosquito-mesh tents with beds inside, or simple wooden cabins. The proprietress cooks up some wonderfully fresh fish.

Suital Lodge   LODGE $$
(8826-0342; www.suital.com; s/d US$51/71) Lots of love has gone into this tiny clutch of *cabinas* on the northern shores of Golfo Dulce. It's situated 15km northeast of Rincón on 30 hectares of hilly, forested property (not a single tree has been felled). Guests can take advantage of a network of bird-watching trails that winds through the property and down to the beach.

Tamandu Lodge   LODGE $$
(8821-4525; www.tamandu-lodge.com; r per person incl meals US$65) This unique lodge on the Ngöbe reserve provides a rare chance for a firsthand experience of the Ngöbe lifestyle, with the Carreras family (spoken Spanish is a boon). This is hands-on stuff: gather crabs and fish with palm rods; harvest palmito and yucca; and prepare these specialties over an open fire. Accommodations are in rustic, wooden stilt-houses. Reservation and travel details on the website.

★ Danta Corcovado Lodge   LODGE $$$
(2735-1111; www.dantalodge.com; r/bungalow incl breakfast US$108/137; P) Midway between the Los Patos ranger station and La

Palma, this low-key lodge offers tours and activities, including day trips to Corcovado. Winding through this family-run property are 4km of trails, and its delightful room and bungalow designs are dreamed up by the staff, from comfortable wood cabins to a funky concrete dome, with open-air, hot-water bathrooms.

Tours to Los Patos are conducted in a special high-clearance, open-air contraption with benches that's attached to a tractor – the best way to navigate the rough road crisscrossed by a river and ideal for wildlife-viewing.

❶ Getting There & Away

The easiest way to travel on the eastern coast of the peninsula is by car. Otherwise, frequent buses ply the sole road between La Palma and Puerto Jiménez (US$2.60, 30 minutes).

GOLFO DULCE

While the Golfo Dulce is certainly less celebrated than the Península de Osa, an increasing number of travelers are making the arduous journey in search of one of the world's longest left-hand breaks, at Pavones. The region is also home to Parque Nacional Piedras Blancas, a stunning tract of rainforest that used to be part of Corcovado, and still protects the same amazing biodiversity, with some wonderful wilderness lodges on its outskirts. This far corner of Costa Rica is also home to significantly large indigenous populations, which live in the Reserva Indígena Guaymí de Conte Burica near Pavones.

Golfito

With a long and sordid history, spread-out Golfito is a rough-around-the-edges port that stretches out along the Golfo Dulce. The town was built on bananas – the United Fruit Company moved its regional headquarters here in the '30s. In the 1980s, declining markets, rising taxes, worker unrest and banana diseases forced the company's departure.

In an attempt to boost the region's economy, the federal government built the duty-free Zona Americana in Golfito. The surreal shopping mall Depósito Libre (☉8am-9pm) attracts Ticos and expats from around the country, who descend on the otherwise decaying town for 24-hour shopping sprees. There are a few other attractions, but Golfito is largely a transportation hub for hikers heading to Corcovado, surfers heading to Pavones and sportfishers.

◉ Sights

Playa Cacao   BEACH
Just a quick trip across the bay, this small beach offers a prime view of Golfito, with the rainforest as a backdrop. If you get stuck in Golfito, Playa Cacao is probably the most pleasant spot to spend the day. To reach the beach, catch a water taxi from Golfito for around US$6 per person. You can also get to Playa Cacao by taking the 6km dirt road west and then south from the airport – a 4WD is recommended.

Refugio Nacional de
Vida Silvestre Golfito   NATURE RESERVE
(✔Sinac office in Golfito 2775 2620; park fee US$10; ☉8am-4pm) This small, 28-sq-km reserve encompasses most of the steep hills surrounding Golfito, though it's easy to miss. There are no facilities for visitors, save some poorly maintained trails. About 2km south of the center of Golfito, a gravel road heads inland, past a soccer field, and winds 7km up to some radio towers (Las Torres) 486m above sea level. A very steep hiking trail (two hours), almost opposite the Samoa del Sur hotel, brings you out near the radio towers.

The reserve was originally created to protect the town's watershed, though it also protects a number of rare and interesting plant species and attracts a variety of tropical birds, four species of monkeys and several small mammals. It is also home to several cycads, which are 'living fossils,' and are regarded as the most primitive of plants.

★**Fundacíon Santuario**
Silvestre de Osa   WILDLIFE RESERVE
(Osa Wildlife Sanctuary; ✔8888-3803, 8861-1309; www.osawildlife.org; Caña Blanca; minimum donation US$25; ☉8am-noon) Run by Earl and Carol Crews, who began with a lodge that became a bird sanctuary, which then turned into a sanctuary for injured and orphaned animals of all kinds, this nonprofit reserve now rehabilitates and releases all manner of local wildlife. Those that can't be reintroduced into the wild – like the resident spider and howler monkeys – remain at the sanctuary, where visitors can get up close and personal with them.

In a remote spot about 25km from Golfito, the sanctuary can arrange boat transportation for up to six visitors. Lodges in both Golfito and Puerto Jiménez can also arrange tours.

Activities

Golfito is home to several full-service marinas that attract coastal-cruising yachters. If you didn't bring your own boat, you can hire local sailors for tours of the gulf at any of the docks. You can fish year-round, but the best season for the sought-after Pacific sailfish is from November to May.

Banana Bay Marina FISHING
(☑2775-0255; www.bananabaymarinagolfito.com) Charters can be arranged, and a full day of all-inclusive fishing starts at around US$800.

🛏 Sleeping

Note that the area around the soccer field in town (not far east of the Muellecito) is Golfito's red-light district. Domestic tax-free shoppers are required to spend the night in Golfito, so hotel rooms can be in short supply on weekends and during holiday periods. There are some lovely ecolodges along the nearby coastline that pick up guests from Golfito, and are far nicer places to stay than in the town itself.

★**Hostal Del Mar** HOSTEL $
(☑4700-0510; www.hostaldelmargolfito.com; r per person US$20-25 ; P❋🕾) This labyrinthine house, directly overlooking the Golfo Dulce, is run by a sweet young proprietress who is happy to arrange local paddleboating tours and horseback riding in Parque Nacional Piedras Blancas. There's an open-air kitchen for guests and simple, fan-cooled rooms. From the main Hwy 14 into Golfito, take a left turn along the unpaved road right by Hotel Las Gaviotas.

**Cabinas y Marisquería
Princesa de Golfito** CABINA $
(☑2775-0442; s/d US$21/36; P❋🕾) If you're watching your budget, this cozy little red-roofed house is the best option. The rooms aren't too fancy – they have fans and tile floors, firm beds and mismatched linens – but it is safe, homey and secure. The *cabinas* are located in the southern part of town, on Rte 14. They're on the bay side, opposite the Banco Nacional.

Samoa del Sur HOTEL $$
(☑2775-0233; www.samoadelsur.com; s/d incl breakfast US$79/85; P❋🕾🏊) This orange, hard-to-miss French-owned facility offers dated rooms outfitted with tiled floors, wood furniture and thick towels. The bar, with its huge dome ceiling, is a popular spot in the evenings, and the restaurant serves typical Tico fare as well as French specialties like mussels Provençal. Taxi boats to Zancudo leave from the Samoa dock.

🍴 Eating

The small, walkable district of the Pueblo Civil has about a dozen *sodas* of reputable quality. Banana Bay Marina serves the sport-fishing set (with gringo prices to match), but is a great spot to have a beer on the bay and shoot some pool. The restaurant at the Samoa del Sur hotel is also a good standby.

★**Restaurante Buenos Días** COSTA RICAN $
(☑2775-1124; meals US$6-10; ☺6am-10pm; P❋🖉) Rare is the visitor who passes through Golfito without stopping at this cheerful spot opposite the Muellecito (Small Dock). Brightly colored booths, bilingual menus and a super-convenient location ensure a constant stream of guests – whether for an ample early breakfast, a typical Tico *casado* or a good old-fashioned burger, accompanied by tamarind and other fresh juices.

BUSES FROM GOLFITO

Most buses stop at the depot opposite the small park in the southern part of town. Tracopa buses depart from the stop in front of Muelle Bananero.

DESTINATION	COST (US$)	DURATION (HR)	FREQUENCY (DAILY)
Neily	2.90	1½	hourly 6am-7pm
Pavones	3.80	2½	10am & 3pm
San José, via San Isidro de El General (Tracopa)	14.70	7	5am & 1:30pm
Zancudo	3.80	3	10am & 3pm

ℹ Orientation

The southern part of town is where you'll find most of the bars and businesses, including a seedy red-light district. Nearby is the so-called Muellecito, from where the daily ferry to Puerto Jiménez departs. The northern part of town was the old United Fruit Company headquarters, and it retains a languid air with its large, veranda-decked homes. Now, the Zona Americana is home to the airport and the duty-free zone.

ℹ Getting There & Away

AIR

The airport is 4km north of the town center near the duty-free zone. NatureAir and **Sansa** (www.flysansa.com) have daily flights to/from San José. One-way tickets can be as little as US$50. Alfa Romeo Aero Taxi (p443) does the charter puddle-jumper from Puerto Jiménez.

BOAT

There are two main boat docks for passenger service: the Muellecito is the main dock in the southern part of town. There is a smaller dock north of the Muelle Bananero (opposite the ICE building) where you'll find the **Asociación de Boteros** (Abocap; ☑ 2775-0357), an association of water taxis that can provide services anywhere in the Golfo Dulce area.

Fast ferries travel to Puerto Jiménez from the Muellecito (US$6, 30 minutes), departing at 6am, 8:45am, 11:30am, 2pm and 4:20pm daily. This schedule is subject to change, so it's best to check for current times at the dock; in any event, show up early to ensure a spot.

You can also take a private water taxi to Puerto Jiménez. You'll have to negotiate, but prices are usually between US$25 and US$30 per person (sometimes with a US$60 minimum).

At research time there was no scheduled shared *lancha* (small motorboat) to Zancudo, but you can negotiate with loitering boatmen to run you over for around US$30 per person. If you're staying at a coastal lodge north of Golfito and you've made prior arrangements for transportation, the lodge will pick you up at the docks.

Parque Nacional Piedras Blancas

One of the last remaining stretches of lowland rainforest on the Pacific, Piedras Blancas is home to a mindboggling array of flora and fauna, including many of Costa Rica's most exciting animals: pumas, jaguars, monkeys, two-toed sloths and numerous species of bats. Dozens of species of migrating birds stop by here also. According to a study conducted at the biological station at Gamba, the biodiversity of trees in Piedras Blancas is the densest in all of Costa Rica, even surpassing Corcovado.

Consisting of parcels of land purchased by benefactors as diverse as the Nature Conservancy and the Austrian government, this national park was established in 1992 as an extension of Parque Nacional Corcovado, though it's now an independent entity. Piedras Blancas has 120 sq km of undisturbed tropical primary rainforest, as well as 20 sq km of secondary forests, pasture land, coastal cliffs and beaches.

⌂ Sleeping

★ **Esquinas Rainforest Lodge**   LODGE $$$
(☑ 2741-8001; www.esquinaslodge.com; s/d incl meals US$146/260; Ⓟ🛜⛱) 🌿 Esquinas consists of 14 spacious, high-ceilinged, fan-cooled cabins with indigenous textiles on the walls. The lodge's extensive grounds comprise a network of well-marked trails and a stream-fed pool. It was founded by the nonprofit Rainforest of the Austrians, vital in the establishment of Piedras Blancas as a national park. It's in Gamba, 7km west of Km 37 on the Interamericana.

Surrounded by the primary rainforest of the park, Esquinas is integrally connected with the community of Gamba, employing local workers and reinvesting profits in community projects. By offsetting development with tree planting, it has become 100% carbon neutral.

ℹ Getting There & Away

Piedras Blancas is best accessed from the Esquinas Rainforest Lodge, which has an extensive trail network on-site and can easily arrange guided hikes deeper into the park. If you don't have your own transportation, any bus heading north from Golfito can drop you off at the lodge.

If you're staying at any of the coastal lodges north of Golfito, you can inquire about transportation to/from the park as well as guided hikes into the interior.

Zancudo

Occupying a slender finger of land that juts into the Golfo Dulce, the tiny village of Zancudo is about as laid-back a beach destination as you'll find in Costa Rica. On the west side of town, gentle, warm Pacific waters lap onto black sands, and seeing more than a

PLAYAS SAN JOSECITO, NICUESA & CATIVO

Idyllic deserted beaches, backed by the pristine rainforest of Parque Nacional Piedras Blancas, define the northeastern shore of the Golfo Dulce. The appeal of this area is only enhanced by its inaccessibility: part of the charm is that very few people make it to this untouched corner of Costa Rica. If you're looking for a romantic retreat or a secluded getaway, all of the lodges along this stretch of coastline are completely isolated and serve as perfect spots for quiet reflection.

If you're planning on staying at the lodges we've listed, advance reservations via the internet are strongly recommended, especially since it can be difficult to contact them by phone. The lodges are extremely isolated and are accessible only by boat – you can expect a beach landing, so make sure you're wearing appropriate shoes. Prices include boat transportation to/from either Golfito or Puerto Jiménez.

Playa Nicuesa Rainforest Lodge (✆ 2258-8250, in USA 866-504-8116; www.nicuesa lodge.com; Playa Nicuesa; s/d from US$295/470; ☎) Nestled into a 65-hectare private reserve, this place is part-remote-retreat, part-activity-center. The rustic accommodations come with canopied beds, indigenous textile spreads and garden showers. Meals are served in a thatched *rancho* and owners Michael and Donna have activities for all the family, from sportfishing to rainforest adventures. Two-night minimum stay. The lodge is closed October and the first half of November.

Dolphin Quest (✆ 8811-2099, 2775-8630; www.dolphinquestcostarica.com; Playa San Josecito; s/d campsite US$30/55, cabin US$60/100, house US$70/120; P☎) This jungle lodge offers a mile of beach and 750 secluded acres of mountainous rainforest, with accommodations in round, thatched-roof cabins. Meals – featuring organic ingredients from the garden – are served in an open-air pavilion near the shore. Beachcombing, horseback riding, snorkeling and fishing are on offer, and there's a real timelessness to the place. The hotel is only reachable by private boat.

handful of people on the beach means it's crowded. On the east side, a tangle of mangrove swamps attracts birds, crocodiles and plenty of fish, which in turn attract fishers hoping to reel them in. Unlike nearby Pavones, an emerging surf destination, Zancudo is content to remain a far-flung village in a far-flung corner of Costa Rica.

 Activities

The main activities at Zancudo are undoubtedly swinging on hammocks, strolling on the beach and swimming in the aqua-blue waters of the Golfo Dulce. Here, the surf is gentle, and at night the water sometimes sparkles with bioluminescence – tiny phosphorescent marine plants and plankton that light up if you sweep a hand through the water. The effect is like underwater fireflies.

Kayaking

The mangrove swamps offer plenty of opportunities for exploration: birdlife is prolific, while other animals such as crocodile, caiman, monkey and sloth are also frequently spotted. The boat ride from Golfito gives a glimpse of these waters, but you can also paddle them yourself: rent kayaks from any of our accommodations listings.

Fishing

Zancudo is a base for inshore and offshore fishing, river fishing (mangrove snapper, snook and corvina) and fly-fishing. The best sportfishing is from December to May for sailfish and May to September for snook, though many species bite year-round. Trips can be arranged through any of the local accommodations.

Sleeping

Be aware that life goes into hibernation mode in low season – accommodations are discounted up to 50% and there's even less going on than usual. Those seeking solitude and a little self-sufficiency will find Zancudo to be just the thing.

Sol y Mar CABINA $
(✆ 2776-0014; www.zancudo.com; cabins US$37-56; P@☎) This popular hangout offers various lodging options, from smallish cheapies further from the water to private deluxe units with fancy tile showers and

unobstructed ocean views. Even if you're not staying here, the open-air restaurant serving fishburgers and chicken *cordon bleu* (mains US$3 to US$12) and thatched bar are Zancudo favorites. Sportfishing and mangrove boat trips arranged.

Cabinas Coloso Del Mar CABINA $

(☑2776-0050; www.colosodelmar.com; s/d from US$40/45; [P][☎]) It's the little touches that make Coloso stand out – matching sheets, shiny hardwood floors and coffeemakers. Bigger-picture attractions include its ideal location steps from the surf, a cute cafe, JC the stellar manager, Edwin who mixes a mean cocktail, and friendly dogs underfoot.

Au Coeur du Soleil CABINA $$

(☑2776-0112; www.aucoeurdusoleil.com; cabins US$50-70; [P][☎]) These four brightly painted, lovingly maintained cabins have fans, fridges, big windows and a central BBQ – some have kitchenettes and all have a homey charm. Young French hosts Joanne and Daniel are warm and gregarious, and offer guests the use of bikes for cruising around Zancudo and boogie boards for hitting the waves.

Cabinas Los Cocos CABINA $$

(☑2776-0012; www.loscocos.com; cabins US$75; [P]) Los Cocos, run by the ever-helpful Andrew and Susan, is home to two historical cabins that used to be banana-company homes in Palmar but were transported to Zancudo and completely restored. The other two more spacious *rancho* cabins are also charming, with hardwood floors and loft sleeping areas under palm-frond roofs. Boat taxi to Golfito (US$60) can be arranged.

★**Zancudo Lodge** LODGE $$$

(☑2776-0008; www.zancudolodge.com; r/ste US$277/620; [P][✹][☎][≋]) The most luxurious retreat in Zancudo by a long shot, this 16-room lodge sits amid landscaped grounds, complete with trickling water features, bamboo stockades, and spacious, tranquil rooms fitted out with fine linens and other creature comforts. The open-sided gourmet restaurant (open to non-guests) is known for its devotion to ultra-fresh produce. Sportfishing outings and boat pickup from Golfito arranged.

✖ **Eating**

El Coquito COSTA RICAN $

(☑2776-0000; meals US$7-8; ☉7am-8pm Sun-Wed, to late Thu-Sat) Bright, cheerful and right in the middle of Zancudo's main drag, this *soda* is a charmer. It offers a filling *casado* (around US$7) of fresh fish, rice and fruit, and the *licuado* (smoothies) are magically refreshing after the long, dusty ride into town. On weekends the adjoining space transforms into a nightclub, with booming music and dancing.

★**Gamefisher Restaurant** INTERNATIONAL $$

(mains US$10-25; ☉11am-10pm; [☎][✎]) This terrific open-sided restaurant inside the Zancudo Lodge prides itself on its commitment to super-fresh produce and creativity, and it shows – in the best fish tacos for miles around, the tuna smoked in-house and the fine dining experience in the evenings that makes the most of locally available ingredients.

ℹ **Orientation & Information**

Zancudo consists of one dirt road, which leads from the boat dock in the north, past the lodges that are strung along the shore, and out of town south toward Pavones.

There is no bank in town and very few places accept credit cards, so bring plenty of cash.

ℹ **Getting There & Away**

The turnoff to Zancudo is well signposted from the main road leading south from Golfito to Laurel. The main road is partially paved; the 30km of minor road that leads to Zancudo is not. There are two ways of getting from Zancudo to Pavones: the bumpy coastal road that requires a 4WD as it crosses several creeks, and the main unpaved road (retrace your steps to the fork in the road). It takes around 1¼ hours to drive from Golfito and about 45 minutes to drive to Pavones.

A bus to Neily leaves from the *pulpería* near the dock at 5am and noon (US$4.50, two hours). The bus for Golfito (US$4.60) leaves at 5am (2½ hours). Service is erratic in the wet season, so inquire before setting out.

Pavones

Home to the second-longest left-hand surf break on the planet, Pavones is a legendary destination for surfers the world over. As this is Costa Rica's southernmost point, you'll need to work hard to get down here. However, the journey is an adventure in its own right, especially since the best months for surfing coincide with the rainy season.

The village remains relatively off the beaten path, and though both foreigners and Ticos are transforming Pavones from its days as a relative backwater, Pavones' few streets are still unpaved, the pace of life is slow and the overall atmosphere is tranquil and New Agey.

🏃 Activities

Surfing

⭐ **Surfing**   SURFING

Pavones is legendary among surfers for the second-longest left in the world (the longest is the 2km-long break in Chicama, Peru); on the best days, your ride can last over two minutes! Conditions are best with a southern swell, usually during the rainy season from April to October. When the surf's up, this tiny beach town attracts hordes of international elite. During the rest of the year, conditions are ideal for beginners.

When Pavones has nothing (or when it's too crowded), head south to Punta Banco, a reef break with decent rights and lefts. The best conditions are at mid- or high tide, especially with swells from the south or west.

Sea Kings Surf Shop   SURFING

(☑️2776-2015; ⊙9am-5pm Mon-Sat) Sea Kings has plenty of boards for rent (US$15 per day) and can arrange surfing lessons with some local instructors (US$40 to US$60 per person for a two-hour lesson). From the crossroads with the two supermarkets, take the road toward the beach and follow it round to the left.

Yoga

Surfing goes hand in hand with yoga, and there are several yoga studios in Pavones where you can stretch your knotted limbs.

Shooting Star Studio   YOGA

(☑️2776-2107, 8829-2409; www.yogapavones.com; drop-in classes US$15) Only 30m from the beach, this yoga studio is open-air and offers several classes per week, including a specialized 'Yoga for Surfers.' To get here, you have to go all the way to Punta Banco, and then take the steep road uphill (best walked).

Pavones Yoga Center   YOGA

(☑️8723-9240, 2776-2120; www.pavonesyogacenter. com; Calle Altamira; drop-in class US$15) Classes at this teacher-training facility tend to be Vinyasa yoga, and also offer 'Surfers' Therapeutic Yoga' to help you unwind after long sessions in the water; find the class schedule on its website. It's 800m along Calle Altamira – the steep, unpaved road going uphill from the Río Claro grocery store crossroads; if driving, you need a 4WD.

🛏 Sleeping

Accommodations are scattered along the main road in Playa Río Claro and along the coastal road to Punta Banco. Some budget places tend to operate on a first-come, first-served basis. Some shoestringers and locals camp along the coastal road to Punta Banco.

🛏 Playa Río Claro

Cabinas Mira Olas   CABINA $

(☑️2776-2006, 8393-7742; www.miraolas.com; d/tr from US$38/48; P🐾🛜) This 4.5-hectare farm is full of wildlife and fruit trees, with a lookout at the top of a hill. A sweet duplex with comfortable tiled cabins has a terrace in front, while the 'Jungle Deluxe' is a beautiful, open-air lodging with a huge balcony, kitchen and elegant cathedral ceiling. It's signposted off the Río Claro road, before the bridge.

Cabinas & Café de la Suerte   GUESTHOUSE $

(☑️2776-2388; www.cafedelasuerte.com; r US$35-70; 🌐🛜) Run by a friendly surfer couple (who also run the vegetarian restaurant on the premises), this colorful three-room guesthouse is located just 50m from the beach and comes with a hammock-hung terrace shared by the upstairs rooms and a secluded garden corner for the downstairs one. Rooms have fridges. From the supermarket crossroads, follow the beach road to the left.

Riviera Riverside Villas   VILLA $$$

(☑️2776-2396; www.pavonesriviera.com; s/d US$95/105; P🌐🛜) This clutch of upmarket *cabinas* in Pavones proper offers fully equipped kitchens, cool tile floors and attractive hardwood ceilings. Big shady porches overlook the landscaped fruit gardens, which are visited by birds and monkeys and offer a degree of intimacy and privacy found at few other places in town. Owners Sean and Jamie have boards for rent.

🛏 Punta Banco

⭐ **Rancho Burica**   LODGE $

(☑️2776-2223; www.ranchoburica.com; dm/r per person US$15/40; P🌐🛜) This legendary Dutch-run outpost is literally the end of the road in Punta Banco, and it's where surfers and like-minded spirits gather to socialize in the evenings. All fan-cooled rooms are en suite, hammocks are interspersed around the property, which has convivial common areas, a restaurant and a trail to a romantic jungle lookout. The owners are involved in turtle conservation, too.

★ **Lanzas de Fuego**

Surf & Adventure Lodge LODGE **$$**
(☏ 2776-2014, 8634-0739; www.lanzasdefuego.com; r per person US$45; ❀ 🛜) Run by cheerful South African owner Rainy, this hillside lodge organizes multiday surfing, birding and sportfishing packages, with its own boat to whisk surfers to the best hot spots. It's an intimate, friendly place, with three cabins to accommodate eight guests, a huge thatched-roofed hangout space and a restaurant serving wholesome Tico meals. Cross the bridge and carry on until the signpost.

Yoga Farm LODGE **$$**
(www.yogafarmcostarica.org; dm/r/cabin incl meals & yoga US$43/50/65) 🍃 This tranquil retreat has simple rooms and dorms, three vegetarian meals prepared with ingredients from the organic garden, and daily yoga classes in an open-air studio overlooking the ocean. It's an uphill 15-minute walk from road's end in Punta Banco: take the uphill road and go through the first gate on the left. No wi-fi or phones; rejuvenation is key.

★ **Tiskita Jungle Lodge** LODGE **$$$**
(☏ 2296-8125; www.tiskita.com; r per adult/child for 3 nights US$627/407; 🅿 🛜 ☀) Set amid extensive gardens and orchards, this lodge is arguably the most beautiful and intimate in all of Golfo Dulce. Accommodations are in various stunning wooden cabins accented by stone garden showers that allow you to freshen up while bird-watching. Rates include all meals. Guided birding walks, horseback riding, night tours and surfing lessons are available. Advance reservations required; three-night minimum.

★ **Castillo de Pavones** BOUTIQUE HOTEL **$$$**
(☏ 2776-2191; www.castillodepavones.com; ste US$125-150, villa US$400; 🅿 ❀ 🛜) This hillside stone mansion with a wrought-iron staircase overlooks the Pavones point break from its lofty perch. Cross the bridge and follow the rough road until the signpost. Accommodations are in four individually decorated and furnished suites and a self-contained four-bedroom villa; our favorite suite is the split-level Aves. Fantastic food, revitalising packages, sportfishing and surfing are on offer, too.

ⓘ **MUST-HAVES: CASH & GAS**

We cannot stress this enough: Pavones has no bank or gas station, so make sure you have plenty of money and gas prior to arrival. Very few places accept credit cards and the nearest ATM and gas station are in Laurel, an hour's drive away.

Cabinas La Ponderosa CABINA **$$$**
(☏ 2776-2076; www.cabinaslaponderosa.com; r US$95-150, houses US$240-275; 🅿 ❀ 🛜 ☀) Housed on six lovely landscaped hectares midway to Punta Banco, these cozy cabins are tenderly cared for by Marshall and Angela McCarthy. The common lounge offers all kinds of entertainment, including a table-tennis table and a massive video library, and there's an on-site walking trail, but the real appeal of staying here is the warm hospitality of the McCarthys.

✕ **Eating**

Café de la Suerte CAFE **$**
(☏ 2776-2388; meals US$4-9; ⊙ 7am-5pm Mon-Sat; 🛜📶) Filling breakfasts, omelettes and veggie dishes dominate the menu, the chef makes her own hummus, and there's usually a daily special (veggie burgers, lasagna) – all to be washed down with a tropical-fruit smoothie. If you have a sweet tooth, there are gooey brownies on offer.

Soda Doña Dora COSTA RICAN **$**
(☏ 2776-2021; meals US$4-8; ⊙ 6:30am-9:30pm; 🛜) This long-standing family-run spot serves up huge breakfasts of *gallo pinto,* eggs and toast; banana pancakes; *casados* with fresh seafood; burgers and fries; and cheap beer. Look for the Bar La Plaza sign just inland from the football field; the *soda* and bar share this space. If driving, take the beach road from the supermarket crossroads.

★ **La Bruschetta** ITALIAN **$$**
(☏ 2776-2174; mains US$7-12; ⊙ 10am-10pm; 🛜📶) A couple of kilometers along the beach road to Punta Banco, this cheerful place decked out with fairy lights is the most happenin' spot in town. The lovely owner serves you ample portions of homemade pasta, wood-fired pizza and a range of Italian desserts, all made with love and authentic ingredients. Confusingly, the sign says 'La Piña,' despite the name change.

❶ Orientation

The name Pavones is used to refer to both Playa Río Claro de Pavones and Punta Banco, which is 6km south.

The road into Pavones first arrives at Río Claro, where you'll find a crossroads with two small supermarkets. One road leads straight to the beach, with a couple of eateries and a surf rental shop. The road leading to the left crosses a bridge and carries straight on; Playa Río Claro's accommodations are located along and off this road. Straight after the bridge, another road heads right and runs parallel to the waterfront for 6km to Punta Banco where, as the locals say, 'the bad road ends and the good life begins' – the rest of the accommodations are spread out along this coastal road.

❶ Getting There & Away

AIR

NatureAir (p449) and Alfa Romeo Aero Taxi (p443) offer charter flights. Prices are dependent on the number of passengers, so it's best to try to organize a larger group if you're considering this option.

BUS

Two daily buses go to Golfito (US$3.80, two hours). The first leaves at 5:15am, departing from the end of the road in Punta Banco and stopping by the two supermarkets. The second leaves at 12:30pm from the school. You can also pick up the early bus in Pavones; check locally for the current bus stops.

CAR

The turnoff to Pavones and Zancudo is well signposted from the main road leading south from Golfito to Laurel. The main road is partially paved; the 32km of minor road that leads to Pavones is not. There's a rough coastal road connecting Pavones to Zancudo that requires a 4WD as it crosses several creeks; alternatively, retrace your steps to the fork in the road. It takes around 1¼ hours to drive from Golfito and about 45 minutes to drive to Zancudo.

TAXI

A 4WD taxi will charge about US$80 from Golfito, and US$70 from Paso Canoas. One of the locals used to operate a shared-van service to Paso Canoas and Golfito on demand for US$16 per person; ask around if he's back in business.

Understand
Costa Rica

Costa Rica Today

Elation over Costa Rica reaching the 2014 World Cup's quarterfinals having worn off, public discontent has grown over the presidency of Luis Guillermo Solís due to growing unemployment and continuing economic woes. And while Costa Rica has emerged the victor in the long-standing border dispute with Nicaragua, relations between the two countries have worsened due to the Cuban immigrant crisis.

Best on Film

El Regreso (The Return; 2011) Featuring a realistic, contemporary plot, this is the first Tico film to earn international acclaim; Hernán Jiménez wrote, directed, starred in and crowdfunded it.

Agua Fría de Mar (Cold Ocean Water; 2010) Directed by Paz Fábrega, this social commentary unfolds at a paradisiacal Pacific beach; the film won several international awards.

Caribe (Caribbean; 2004) The first Costa Rican film ever to be submitted for Oscar consideration; drama set in Limón.

Best in Print

Tropical Nature: Life and Death in the Rain Forests of Central and South America (Adrian Forsyth and Ken Miyata; 1987) Easy-to-digest natural-history essays on rainforest phenomena, written by two biologists.

There Never Was a Once Upon a Time (Carmen Naranjo; 1989) Ten stories, narrated by children and adolescents, by Costa Rica's most widely translated novelist.

Costa Rica: A Traveler's Literary Companion (Barbara Ras, foreword by Óscar Arias; 1994) Collection of stories reflecting distinct regions of Costa Rica.

Changing of the Guard

Costa Rica acquired a new president after a runoff election (the second in history) in April 2014. Following the departure of the country's first female president, Laura Chinchilla, who termed out, the runoff between Johnny Araya and Luis Guillermo Solís was a formality, as Araya stopped campaigning in March 2014 after it became clear that Solís was overwhelmingly likely to prevail.

With Solís in power, Costa Rica's political landscape hasn't changed dramatically, and it's too soon to say whether his win has signaled a sea change for the National Liberation Party (PLN), which has dominated Costa Rican politics for more than half a century. Araya, a member of the PLN, had attempted to distance himself during his campaign from Chinchilla's PLN administration, which was dogged by corruption scandals.

Solís, affiliated with the center-left Citizens' Action Party (PAC), ran on promises to fight corruption and to address the country's social and economic inequality. As a scholar of Latin American studies, Solís was formerly a professor at the University of Costa Rica and a published writer specializing in Latin American politics and social issues. As such, he is still considered somewhat of a political outsider, despite serving as an advisor to Óscar Arias as a foreign-ministry official.

It seems that many Costa Ricans viewed Solís as an agent of much-needed but not-too-radical change when they voted him in, but his government continues to face substantial problems inherited from past administrations: namely, the growing rate of inflation, growing unemployment and severe income inequality. While past administrations avoided taxing large companies and high-income earners, Solís' government is enforcing taxation of the above to address these issues.

Solís has expressed his support for increased rights for the LBGT community, flying a rainbow flag over the Presidential House on International Day Against Homophobia & Transphobia.

Carbon Neutrality

Costa Rica has long had a reputation for being green, but, to paraphrase Kermit: it ain't easy. Back in 2009, then-president Óscar Arias set an ambitious goal – that Costa Rica achieve carbon neutrality by the year 2021. Meeting this goal would have made Costa Rica the first carbon-neutral country in the world and would coincide auspiciously with the country's bicentennial.

Some measures have not yet been implemented as scheduled, and the numbers suggest that the 2021 target may have been overly ambitious. The first phase – as yet incomplete – addresses energy and agriculture, both major contributors to carbon-dioxide emissions. Proposed changes for the energy sector, for example, include transitioning buses and taxis to natural-gas, electric and hybrid vehicles, and imposing stricter emissions regulations on these companies. Agricultural changes include government-sponsored training programs for smaller farms, teaching them to implement organic methods such as composting, using biochar and creating biodigester systems to trap methane gases and use them as on-site fuel. For larger-scale agriculture, such as the country's sprawling banana plantations, government incentives encourage reforestation and conservation of existing rainforest in order to offset carbon-dioxide emissions (most of which are generated from overseas shipping).

One of the proposals announced by president Luis Guillermo Solís during his electoral campaign was an extension of the carbon-neutrality goal to 2025, yet when Costa Rica submitted its INDC (Intended Nationally Determined Contribution) with regards to the UN Framework Convention on Climate Change, it announced its long-term goal of becoming carbon-neutral by 2085. This was unexpected, especially given the Costa Rican government's recent announcement that it has already reached 81% of its carbon neutral target.

The Río San Juan Flows On

Forming the eastern stretch of the border between Nicaragua and Costa Rica is the Río San Juan, a silty river studded with small marshy islands and floating rafts of water lettuce. This quiet waterway has been the source of much discord between the two countries, to the extent that the International Court of Justice in The Hague has had to preside over several legal disputes in the last 20 years as both countries attempt to lay claim to territory.

The border area is complicated, not only because the river flows from Lago de Nicaragua to the Caribbean Sea and is therefore an evolving geographical entity. The 1858 Cañas-Jerez Treaty asserts that Nicaragua owns the Río San Juan but that Costa Rica retains navigation rights on its side of the river. Though spats have arisen over the years, mostly over the territory on the eastern half, both countries have kept these tensions in relative check. But they've been bubbling over recently.

POPULATION: **4.87 MILLION**

AREA: **51,100 SQ KM**

ADULT LITERACY: **96.3%**

POPULATION BELOW POVERTY LINE: **21.7%**

CARBON DIOXIDE EMISSIONS: **1.7 METRIC TONS PER PERSON PER YEAR**

if Costa Rica were 100 people

94 would be white & *mestizo*
3 would be black
1 would be Chinese
1 would be indigenous
1 would be other

belief systems
(% of population)

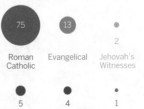

75	13	2
Roman Catholic	Evangelical	Jehovah's Witnesses
5	4	1
Other	None	other Protestant

population per sq km

COSTA RICA   MEXICO   USA

♦ ≈ 6 people

Gringo Media

The Tico Times (www.ticotimes.net) Costa Rica's biggest English-language newspaper is high quality, though news and views are often geared toward the expat community.
Radio Dos Broadcasting across the country on 99.5, Radio 2 spins an amazing selection of US Top 40 music spanning several decades; probably most appealing to Gen X and older.
Costa Rican Times (www.costarican times.com) This online, English-language newcomer focuses on Costa Rica happenings but also features international news.

Tico Travel Tips

La hora Tica Don't be put off if your local host views an appointment as more of a ballpark suggestion of when to meet.
Directo, directo When asking directions, it's a good idea to ask several people along the way, as some locals will – out of an abundance of politeness – want to say something helpful even if they're not sure how to get there.

The latest flap started with Nicaragua dredging Isla Calero's river delta in late 2010. This involved trees being felled and earth being dumped into the river. With Nicaraguan soldiers present during the process, the Costa Rican government decided that this was reason enough to claim invasion, and the situation deteriorated from there. In March 2011, when the International Court of Justice considered the case and reiterated the validity of the Cañas-Jerez Treaty, both sides interpreted the language as a win.

Subsequently, then-president of Costa Rica Laura Chinchilla called for emergency funds to begin construction of a road along the Costa Rican bank of the river, without proper environmental or engineering reviews. This caused consternation not only in Nicaragua but also on Costa Rican soil about the road's environmental and political impact. Nicaraguan president Daniel Ortega, for his part, has proposed the construction of a trans-oceanic canal in the Río San Juan.

Ortega had previously hinted that he wishes to extend an olive branch across the river to Costa Rica's current president, Luis Guillermo Solís. In December 2015 the International Court of Justice ruled that Costa Rica has sovereignty over the 3km patch of wetlands in Río San Juan, and Nicaragua promised to abide by the ruling.

However, there was a new escalation of tensions between the two countries in late 2015 over Cuban immigrants, hundreds of whom have taken to trying to cross Central America in a bid to reach the US, fearing that the thawing of relations between the two countries will soon mean an end to their right to asylum in the US. Costa Rica has been granting Cubans short-term visas, only for them to be turned back at the Nicaraguan border in spite of appeals from the Costa Rican government that the Cubans be granted a 'humanitarian corridor' through the region. As of early 2016, talks with Nicaragua broke down so now Cuban immigrants are being flown from Costa Rica into Mexico and from there they have to make their way to the US border.

History

Like other Central American countries, Costa Rica's history remains a loose sketch during the reign of its pre-Columbian tribes, and European 'discovery' of the New World was followed by the subjugation and evangelization of Costa Rica's indigenous peoples. But in the mid-20th century Costa Rica radically departed from the standard Central American playbook by abolishing its army, diversifying its economy and brokering peace in the region, paving the way for today's stable and environmentally friendly nation.

Lost Worlds of Ancient Costa Rica

The coastlines and rainforests of Central America have been inhabited by humans for at least 10,000 years, but ancient civilizations in Costa Rica are largely the subject of speculation. It is thought that the area was something of a backwater straddling the two great ancient civilizations of the Andes and Mesoamerica, with the exception of the Diquís Valley along the Pacific coast, where archaeological finds suggest that a great deal of trading took place with their more powerful neighbors. On the eve of European discovery some 500 years ago, an estimated 400,000 people were living in today's Costa Rica, though sadly our knowledge about these pre-Columbian cultures is scant.

Unlike the massive pyramid complexes found throughout other parts of Latin America, the ancient towns and cities of Costa Rica (with the exception of Guayabo) were loosely organized and had no centralized government or ceremonial centers. The settlements fought among each other, but for the purpose of getting slaves rather than to extend their land territory. Not known for building edifices that would stand the test of time, Costa Rica's early inhabitants did, however, leave behind mysterious relics: enormous stone spheres, liberally scattered around the Diquís Valley.

Pre-Columbian Sites

Monumento Nacional Arqueológico Guayabo (Turrialba)

Hacienda Barú (Dominical)

Sitio Arqueológico Finca 6 (Sierpe)

Finca Cántaros (San Vito)

Heirs of Columbus

On his fourth and final voyage to the New World in 1502, Christopher Columbus was forced to drop anchor near present-day Puerto Limón after a hurricane damaged his ship. While waiting for repairs, Columbus ventured into the verdant terrain and exchanged gifts with hospitable

TIMELINE	11,000 BC	1000 BC	100 BC
	The first humans occupy Costa Rica and populations quickly flourish due to the rich land and marine resources found along both coastlines.	The Huetar power base in the Central Valley is solidified following the construction and habitation of the ancient city of Guayabo, continuously inhabited until its mysterious abandonment in AD 1400.	Costa Rica becomes part of an extensive trade network that moves gold and other goods and extends from present-day Mexico down through to the Andean empires.

and welcoming chieftains. He returned from this encounter claiming to have seen 'more gold in two days than in four years in Española.' Columbus dubbed the stretch of shoreline from Honduras to Panama 'Veraguas,' but it was his excited descriptions of *costa rica* (the 'rich coast') that gave the region its lasting name. At least that's how the popular story goes.

Anxious to claim its bounty, Columbus petitioned the Spanish Crown to have himself appointed governor. But by the time he returned to Seville, his royal patron Queen Isabella was on her deathbed, which prompted King Ferdinand to award the prize to Columbus' rival, Diego de Nicuesa. Although Columbus became a very wealthy man, he never returned to the New World. He died in 1506 after being worn down by ill health and court politics.

PRE-COLUMBIAN COSTA RICA

The early inhabitants of Costa Rica were part of an extensive trading zone that extended as far south as Peru and as far north as Mexico. The region hosted roughly 20 small tribes, organized into chiefdoms with a *cacique* (permanent leader), who sat atop a hierarchical society that included shamans, warriors, toilers and slaves.

Adept at seafaring, the Carib dominated the Atlantic coastal lowlands and served as a conduit of trade with the South American mainland. In the northwest, several tribes were connected to the great Mesoamerican cultures. Aztec religious practices and Maya jade and craftsmanship are in evidence in the Península de Nicoya, while Costa Rican quetzal feathers and golden trinkets have turned up in Mexico. In the southwest, three chiefdoms showed such influence of Andean indigenous cultures as coca leaves, yucca and sweet potatoes.

There is also evidence that the language of the Central Valley, Huetar, was known by all of Costa Rica's indigenous groups, which may be an indication of their power and influence. The Central Valley is home to Guayabo, the only major archaeological site uncovered in Costa Rica thus far.

Thought to be an ancient ceremonial center, Guayabo once featured paved streets, an aqueduct and decorative gold. Here archaeologists uncovered exquisite gold ornaments and unusual life-size stone statues of human figures, as well as distinctive types of pottery and *metates* (stone platforms that were used for grinding corn). Today the site consists of little more than ancient hewed rock and stone, though Guayabo continues to stand as testament to a once-great civilization of the New World.

Still a puzzle, however, are the hundreds of hand-sculpted, monolithic stone spheres that dot the landscape of the Diquís Valley in Palmar and the Isla del Caño. Weighing up to 16 tons and ranging in size from a baseball to a Volkswagen, the spheres have inspired many theories: an ancient calendar, symbols of power, extraterrestrial meddling or pieces of a giant game.

1522	1562	1563	1737
Spanish settlement develops in Costa Rica, though it will be several decades before the colonists can get a sturdy foothold on the land.	Spanish conquistador Juan Vásquez de Coronado arrives in Costa Rica under the title of governor, determined to move the fringe communities of Spanish settlers to the more hospitable Central Valley.	The first permanent Spanish colonial settlement in Costa Rica is established in Cartago by Juan Vásquez de Coronado, who chooses the site based on its rich and fertile volcanic soils.	The future capital of San José is established, sparking a rivalry with neighboring Cartago that will culminate in a civil war between the two dominant cities.

To the disappointment of his conquistador heirs, Columbus' tales of gold were mostly lies and the locals were considerably less than affable. Nicuesa's first colony in present-day Panama was abruptly abandoned when tropical disease and warring tribes decimated its ranks. Successive expeditions launched from the Caribbean coast also failed as pestilent swamps, oppressive jungles and volcanoes made Columbus' paradise seem more like a tropical hell.

A bright moment in Spanish exploration came in 1513 when Vasco Núñez de Balboa heard rumors about a large sea and a wealthy, gold-producing civilization across the mountains of the isthmus – these almost certainly referred to the Inca empire of present-day Peru. Driven by equal parts ambition and greed, Balboa scaled the continental divide, and on September 26, 1513, he became the first European to set eyes upon the Pacific Ocean. Keeping up with the European fashion of the day, Balboa immediately proceeded to claim the ocean and all the lands it touched for the king of Spain.

The thrill of discovery aside, the conquistadors now controlled a strategic western beachhead from which to launch their conquest of Costa Rica. In the name of God and king, aristocratic adventurers plundered indigenous villages, executed resisters and enslaved survivors throughout the Península de Nicoya. However, none of these bloodstained campaigns led to a permanent presence as intercontinental germ warfare caused outbreaks of feverish death on both sides. The indigenous people mounted a fierce resistance to the invaders, which included guerrilla warfare, destroying their own villages and killing their own children rather than let them fall into Spanish hands.

British explorer, government-sponsored pirate and slaver Sir Francis Drake is believed to have anchored in Bahía Drake in 1579. Rumor has it that he buried some of his plundered treasure here, but the only solid memorial to the man is a monument that looks out to his namesake bay.

New World Order

It was not until the 1560s that a Spanish colony was firmly established in Costa Rica. Hoping to cultivate the rich volcanic soil of the Central Valley, the Spanish founded the village of Cartago on the banks of the Río Reventazón. Although the fledgling colony was extremely isolated, it miraculously survived under the leadership of its first governor, Juan Vásquez de Coronado. Some of Costa Rica's demilitarized present was presaged in its early colonial government: preferring diplomacy over firearms to counter the indigenous threat, Coronado used Cartago as a base to survey the lands south to Panama and west to the Pacific, and secured deed and title over the colony.

Though Coronado was later lost in a shipwreck, his legacy endured. Costa Rica was an officially recognized province of the Viceroyalty of New Spain (Virreinato de Nueva España), which was the name given to the viceroy-ruled territories of the Spanish empire in North America, Central America, the Caribbean and Asia.

1821	April 1823	1824	1856
Following a unanimous declaration by Mexico on behalf of all of Central America, Costa Rica finally gains its independence from Spain after centuries of colonial occupation.	The Costa Rican capital officially moves to San José after intense skirmishes with the conservative residents of Cartago, who take issue with the more liberal longings of the power-hungry *josefinos*.	The Nicoya-Guanacaste region votes to secede from Nicaragua and become a part of Costa Rica, though the region's longing for independence from both countries continues to this day.	Costa Rica quashes the expansionist aims of the war hawks in the USA by defeating William Walker and his invading army at the epic Battle of Santa Rosa.

For roughly three centuries, the Captaincy General of Guatemala (also known as the Kingdom of Guatemala), which included Costa Rica, Nicaragua, Honduras, El Salvador, Guatemala and the Mexican state of Chiapas, was a loosely administered colony in the vast Spanish empire. Since the political and military headquarters of the kingdom were in Guatemala, Costa Rica became a minor provincial outpost that had little if any strategic significance or exploitable riches.

As a result of its status as a swampy, largely useless backwater, Costa Rica's colonial path diverged from the typical pattern in that a powerful landholding elite and slave-based economy never gained prominence. Instead of large estates, mining operations and coastal cities, modest-sized villages of smallholders developed in the interior Central Valley. According to national lore, the stoic, self-sufficient farmer provided the backbone for 'rural democracy' as Costa Rica emerged as one of the only egalitarian corners of the Spanish empire.

Equal rights and opportunities were not extended to the indigenous groups, and as Spanish settlement expanded, the local population decreased dramatically. From 400,000 at the time Columbus first sailed, the population was reduced to 20,000 a century later, and to 8000 a century after that. While disease was the main cause of death, the Spanish were relentless in their effort to exploit the natives as an economic resource by establishing the *encomienda* system that applied to indigenous males and gave the Spaniards the right to demand free labor, with many worked to death. Central Valley groups were the first to fall, though outside the valley several tribes managed to survive a bit longer under forest cover, staging occasional raids. However, as in the rest of Latin America, repeated military campaigns eventually forced them into submission and slavery, though throughout that period, many clergymen protested the brutal treatment of indigenous subjects and implored the Spanish Crown to protect them.

The indigenous people of Costa Rica make up only about 1% of the population, and represent several ethnic groups (the Boruca, Bribrí, Cabécar, Chorotega, Huetar, Këköldi, Maleku, Ngöbe and Térraba) and six surviving languages.

Fall of an Empire

Spain's costly Peninsular War with France from 1808 to 1814 – and the political turmoil, unrest and power vacuums that it caused – led Spain to lose all its colonial possessions in the first third of the 19th century.

In 1821 the Americas wriggled free of Spain's imperial grip following Mexico's declaration of independence for itself as well as the whole of Central America. Of course, the Central American provinces weren't too keen on having another foreign power reign over them and subsequently declared independence from Mexico. However, all of these events hardly disturbed Costa Rica, which learned of its liberation a month after the fact.

1889	1890	1900	1914
Costa Rica's first democratic elections are held, a monumental event given the long history of colonial occupation, though blacks and women are prohibited by law to vote.	The construction of the railroad between San José and Puerto Limón is finally completed despite years of hardships and countless deaths due to accidents, malaria and yellow fever.	The population of Costa Rica reaches 50,000 as the country begins to develop and prosper due to the increasingly lucrative international coffee and banana trades.	Costa Rica is given an economic boost following the opening of the Panama Canal. The canal was forged by 75,000 laborers, many thousands of whom died during construction.

THE LITTLE DRUMMER BOY

During your travels through the countryside, you may notice statues of a drummer boy from Alajuela named Juan Santamaría. He is one of Costa Rica's most beloved national heroes.

In April 1856 the North American mercenary William Walker and his ragtag army attempted to invade Costa Rica during an ultimately unsuccessful campaign to conquer all of Central America. Walker had already managed to seize control of Nicaragua, taking advantage of the civil war that was raging there. It didn't take him long after that to decide to march on Costa Rica, though Costa Rican president Juan Rafael Mora Porras guessed Walker's intentions and managed to recruit a volunteer army of 9000 civilians. They surrounded Walker's army as they lay waiting in an old *hacienda* (estate) in present-day Parque Nacional Santa Rosa. The Costa Ricans won the battle and Walker was forever expelled from Costa Rican soil. During the fighting, Santamaría was killed while daringly setting fire to Walker's defenses – and a national legend was born.

The newly liberated colonies pondered their fate: stay together in a United States of Central America or go their separate national ways. At first they came up with something in between, namely the Central American Federation (CAF), though it could neither field an army nor collect taxes. Accustomed to being at the center of things, Guatemala also attempted to dominate the CAF, alienating smaller colonies and hastening its demise. Future attempts to unite the region would likewise fail.

Meanwhile, an independent Costa Rica was taking shape under Juan Mora Fernández, the first head of state (1824–33). He tended toward nation building, and organized new towns, built roads, published a newspaper and coined a currency. His wife even partook in the effort by designing the country's flag.

Life returned to normal, unlike in the rest of the region, where post-independence civil wars raged on. In 1824 the Nicoya-Guanacaste region seceded from Nicaragua and joined its more easygoing southern neighbor, defining the territorial borders. In 1852 Costa Rica received its first diplomatic emissaries from the USA and Great Britain.

Coffee Rica

In the 19th century the riches that Costa Rica had long promised were uncovered when it was realized that the soil and climate of the Central Valley highlands were ideal for coffee cultivation. Costa Rica led Central America in introducing the caffeinated bean, which transformed the impoverished country into the wealthiest in the region.

1919	1940	1940s	1948
Federico Tinoco Granados is ousted as the dictator of Costa Rica in one of the few episodes of brief violence in an otherwise peaceful political history.	Rafael Ángel Calderón Guardia is elected president and proceeds to improve working conditions in Costa Rica by enacting minimum-wage laws as well as an eight-hour day.	José Figueres Ferrer becomes involved in national politics and opposes the ruling conservatives. Figueres' social-democratic policies and criticism of the government angers the Costa Rican elite and President Calderón.	Conservative and liberal forces clash, resulting in a six-week civil war that leaves 2000 Costa Ricans dead and many more wounded and destroys much of the country's fledgling infrastructure.

When an export market was discovered, the government actively promoted coffee to farmers by providing free saplings. At first Costa Rican producers exported their crop to nearby South Americans, who processed the beans and re-exported the product to Europe. By the 1840s, however, local merchants had already built up domestic capacity and learned to scope out their own overseas markets. Their big break came when they persuaded the captain of HMS *Monarch* to transport several hundred sacks of Costa Rican coffee to London, percolating the beginning of a beautiful friendship.

The Costa Rican coffee boom was on. The drink's quick fix made it popular among working-class consumers in the industrializing north. The aroma of riches lured a wave of enterprising German immigrants, enhancing technical and financial skills in the business sector. By century's end, more than one-third of the Central Valley was dedicated to coffee cultivation, and coffee accounted for more than 90% of all exports and 80% of foreign-currency earnings.

The coffee industry in Costa Rica developed differently from those in the rest of Central America. As elsewhere, there arose a group of coffee barons, elites that reaped the rewards for the export bonanza. But Costa Rican coffee barons lacked the land and labor to cultivate the crop. Coffee production is labor intensive, with a long and painstaking harvest season. The small farmers became the principal planters. The coffee barons, instead, monopolized processing, marketing and financing. The coffee economy in Costa Rica created a wide network of high-end traders and small-scale growers, whereas in the rest of Central America a narrow elite controlled large estates worked by tenant laborers.

Coffee wealth became a power resource in politics. Costa Rica's traditional aristocratic families were at the forefront of the enterprise. At mid-century, three-quarters of the coffee barons were descended from just two colonial families. The country's leading coffee exporter at this time was President Juan Rafael Mora Porras (1849–59), whose lineage went back to the colony's founder, Juan Vásquez de Coronado. Mora was overthrown by his brother-in-law after the president proposed to form a national bank independent of the coffee barons. The economic interests of the coffee elite would thereafter become a priority in Costa Rican politics.

The coffee-processing cooperative Coopedota, located in Costa Rica's Valley of the Saints (famous for growing delicious highland coffee), launched the country's first carbon-neutral coffee in 2011, certified to the British Standards Institution's PAS2060 specifications for carbon neutrality.

Banana Empire

The coffee trade unintentionally gave rise to Costa Rica's next export boom – bananas. Getting coffee out to world markets necessitated a rail link from the central highlands to the coast, and Limón's deep harbor made an ideal port. Inland was dense jungle and insect-infested swamps, which prompted the government to contract the task to Minor Keith, nephew of an American railroad tycoon.

1949	1963	1977	1987
Hoping to heal old wounds and look forward, the temporary government enacts a new constitution abolishing the army, desegregating the country, and granting women and blacks the right to vote.	Reserva Natura Absoluta Cabo Blanco at the tip of the Península de Nicoya becomes Costa Rica's first federally protected conservation area through the efforts of Swedish and Danish conservationists.	The Indigenous Law of 1977 is passed, protecting indigenous communities' right to ownership of their territories.	President Óscar Arias Sánchez wins the Nobel Peace Prize for his work on the Central American peace accords, which brought about greater political freedom throughout the region.

The project was a disaster. Malaria and accidents churned through workers as Tico recruits gave way to US convicts and Chinese indentured servants, who were in turn replaced by freed Jamaican slaves. To entice Keith to continue, the government turned over 3200 sq km of land along the route and provided a 99-year lease to run the railroad. In 1890 the line was finally completed and running at a loss.

Keith had begun to grow banana plants along the tracks as a cheap food source for the workers. Desperate to recoup his investment, he shipped some bananas to New Orleans in the hope of starting a side venture. He struck gold, or rather yellow. Consumers went crazy for the elongated finger fruit. By the early 20th century, bananas surpassed coffee as Costa Rica's most lucrative export and the country became the world's leading banana exporter. Unlike in the coffee industry, the profits were exported along with the bananas.

Costa Rica was transformed by the rise of Keith's banana empire. He joined another American importer to found the infamous United Fruit Company, known locally as Yunai, and soon the largest employer in Central America. To the locals, it was known as *el pulpo* (the octopus) – its tentacles stretched across the region, becoming entangled with the local economy and politics. United Fruit owned huge swaths of lush lowlands, much of the transportation and communication infrastructure and bunches of bureaucrats. The company drew a wave of migrant laborers from Jamaica, changing the country's ethnic complexion and provoking racial tensions. In its various incarnations as the United Brands Company and, later, Chiquita, Yunai was virulently anti-union and maintained control over its workforces by paying them in redeemable scrip rather than cash for many years. Amazingly, the marks that *el pulpo* left on Costa Rica are still present, including the rusting train tracks and a locomotive engine in Palmares.

For details on the role of Minor Keith and the United Fruit Company in lobbying for a CIA-led coup in Guatemala, pick up a copy of the highly readable *Bitter Fruit* by Stephen Schlesinger and Stephen Kinzer.

Birth of a Nation

The inequality of the early 20th century led to the rise of José Figueres Ferrer, a self-described farmer-philosopher and the father of Costa Rica's unarmed democracy. The son of Catalan immigrant coffee planters, Figueres excelled in school and went to Boston's MIT to study engineering. Upon returning to Costa Rica to set up his own coffee plantation, he organized the hundreds of laborers on his farm into a utopian socialist community and appropriately named the property La Luz Sin Fin (The Struggle Without End).

In the 1940s Figueres became involved in national politics as an outspoken critic of President Calderón. In the midst of a radio interview in which he badmouthed the president, police broke into the studio and arrested Figueres. He was accused of having fascist sympathies and was

1994	2000	2006	2007
The indigenous people of Costa Rica are finally granted the right to vote.	The population of Costa Rica tops four million, though many believe the number is far greater due to burgeoning illegal settlements on the fringes of the capital.	Óscar Arias Sánchez is elected president for the second time in his political career on a pro-Cafta (Central American Free Trade Agreement) platform, though he wins by an extremely narrow margin.	A national referendum narrowly passes Cafta. Opinion remains divided as to whether opening up trade with the USA will be beneficial for Costa Rica in the long run.

banished to Mexico. While in exile he formed the Caribbean League, a collection of students and democratic agitators from all over Central America who pledged to bring down the region's military dictators. When he returned to Costa Rica, the Caribbean League, now 700 men strong, went with him and helped protest against the powers that be.

When government troops descended on the farm with the intention of arresting Figueres and disarming the Caribbean League, it touched off a civil war. The moment had arrived: the diminutive farmer-philosopher now played the man on horseback. Figueres emerged victorious from the brief conflict and seized the opportunity to put into place his vision of Costa Rican social democracy. After dissolving the country's military, Figueres quoted HG Wells: 'The future of mankind cannot include the armed forces'.

As head of a temporary junta government, Figueres enacted nearly a thousand decrees. He taxed the wealthy, nationalized the banks and built a modern welfare state. His 1949 constitution granted full citizenship and voting rights to women, African-Americans, indigenous groups and Chinese minorities. Today Figueres' revolutionary regime is regarded as the foundation of Costa Rica's unarmed democracy.

The American Empire

Thirty-three out of 44 Costa Rican presidents prior to 1970 were descended from just three original colonizing families.

Throughout the 1970s and '80s, the sovereignty of the small nations of Central America was limited by their northern neighbor, the USA. Big sticks, gunboats and dollar diplomacy were instruments of a Yankee policy to curtail socialist politics, especially the military oligarchies of Guatemala, El Salvador and Nicaragua.

In 1979 the rebellious Sandinistas toppled the American-backed Somoza dictatorship in Nicaragua. Alarmed by the Sandinistas' Soviet and Cuban ties, fervently anticommunist president Ronald Reagan decided it was time to intervene. Just like that, the Cold War arrived in the hot tropics.

The organizational details of the counterrevolution were delegated to Oliver North, an eager-to-please junior officer working out of the White House basement. North's can-do creativity helped to prop up the famed Contra rebels to incite civil war in Nicaragua. While both sides invoked the rhetoric of freedom and democracy, the war was really a turf battle between left-wing and right-wing forces.

Under intense US pressure, Costa Rica was reluctantly dragged in. The Contras set up camp in northern Costa Rica, from where they staged guerrilla raids. Not-so-clandestine CIA operatives and US military advisors were dispatched to assist the effort. A secret jungle airstrip was built near the border to fly in weapons and supplies. To raise cash for the

2010	2010	2011	2013
Costa Rica elects its first female president, National Liberation Party candidate Laura Chinchilla.	Volcán Arenal, the country's most active volcano for over four decades, stops spitting lava and enters a resting phase.	Central American drug wars encroach on Costa Rica's borders, and the country is listed among the USA's major drug-trafficking centers.	The murder of 26-year-old environmentalist Jairo Mora Sandoval in Limón Province brings international attention to the dangers and lack of police protection that conservationists face on the Caribbean coast.

rebels, North allegedly used his covert supply network to traffic illegal narcotics through the region.

The war polarized Costa Rica. From conservative quarters came a loud call to re-establish the military and join the anticommunist crusade, which was largely underwritten by the US Pentagon. In May 1984 more than 20,000 demonstrators marched through San José to give peace a chance, though the debate didn't climax until the 1986 presidential election. The victor was 44-year-old Óscar Arias Sánchez, who, despite being born into coffee wealth, was an intellectual reformer in the mold of Figueres, his political patron.

Once in office, Arias affirmed his commitment to a negotiated resolution and reasserted Costa Rican national independence. He vowed to uphold his country's pledge of neutrality and to vanquish the Contras from the territory. The sudden resignation of the US ambassador around this time was suspected to be a result of Arias' strong stance. In a public ceremony, Costa Rican schoolchildren planted trees on top of the CIA's secret airfield. Most notably, Arias became the driving force in uniting Central America around a peace plan, which ended the Nicaraguan war and earned him the Nobel Peace Prize in 1987.

Prior to his re-election, Óscar Arias Sánchez founded the Arias Foundation for Peace and Human Progress (www. arias.or.cr).

In 2006 Arias once again returned to the presidential office, winning the popular election by a 1.2% margin and subsequently ratifying the controversial Central American Free Trade Agreement (Cafta), which Costa Rica entered in 2009.

When Laura Chinchilla became the first female president of Costa Rica in 2010, she promised to continue with Arias' free-market policies, in spite of the divisive Cafta agreement (the referendum in 2007 barely resulted in a 'yes' vote at 51%). She also pledged to tackle the rise of violent crime and drug trafficking, on the rise due to Costa Rica being used as a halfway house by Colombian and Mexican cartels. Ironically, a month after discussing the drug cartel problem with US President Barack Obama during his visit to Costa Rica, Chinchilla herself became embroiled in a drug-related scandal over the use of a private jet belonging to a man under investigation by Costa Rican intelligence for possible links to international drug cartels.

2014	2014	2015	2015
Costa Rica advances to the quarterfinals of the 2014 FIFA (Fédération Internationale de Football Association) World Cup in Brazil.	Luis Guillermo Solís is elected president by default when his opponent withdraws from the race.	A Costa Rican judge grants a common-law marriage to a same-sex couple; a first in Costa Rica and in Central America.	The International Criminal Court in The Hague settles the long-standing land dispute between Costa Rica and Nicaragua in Costa Rica's favor.

The Tico Way of Life

Blessed with natural beauty and a peaceful, army-less society, it's no wonder that Costa Rica has long been known as the Switzerland of Central America. While nowadays the country is certainly challenged by its lofty eco-conscious goals, modern intercontinental maladies such as drug trafficking and a disparity in wealth between the haves and have-nots, the Tico attitude remains sunny and family-centered, with a good balance between work and quality of life.

Pura Vida

The expression *matando la culebra* (meaning 'to be idle,' literally 'killing the snake') originates with *peones* (expendable laborers) from banana plantations. When foremen would ask what they were doing, the response would be *'¡Matando la culebra!'*

Pura vida – pure life – is more than just a slogan that rolls off the tongues of Ticos (Costa Ricans) and emblazons souvenirs; in the laid-back tone in which it is constantly uttered, the phrase is a bona fide mantra for the Costa Rican way of life. Perhaps the essence of the pure life is something better lived than explained, but hearing *'pura vida'* again and again while traveling across this beautiful country – as a greeting, a stand-in for goodbye, 'cool,' and an acknowledgement of thanks – makes it evident that the concept lives deep within the DNA of this country.

The living seems particularly pure when Costa Rica is compared with its Central American neighbors such as Nicaragua and Honduras; there's little poverty, illiteracy or political tumult, the country is crowded with ecological jewels, and the standard of living is high. What's more, Costa Rica has flourished without an army for the past 60 years. The sum of the parts is a country that's an oasis of calm in a corner of the world that has been continuously degraded by warfare. And though the Costa Rican people are justifiably proud hosts, a compliment to the country is likely to be met simply with a warm smile and an enigmatic two-word reply: *pura vida.*

Daily Life

With its lack of war, long life expectancy and relatively sturdy economy, Costa Rica enjoys the highest standard of living in Central America. For the most part, Costa Ricans live fairly affluent and comfortable lives, even by North American standards.

As in many places in Latin America, the family unit in Costa Rica remains the nucleus of life. Families socialize together and extended families often live near each other. When it's time to party it's also largely a family affair; celebrations, vacations and weddings are a social outlet for rich and poor alike, and those with relatives in positions of power – nominal or otherwise – don't hesitate to turn to them for support.

Given this mutually cooperative environment, it's no surprise that life expectancy in Costa Rica is slightly higher than in the US. In fact, most Costa Ricans are more likely to die of heart disease or cancer as opposed to the childhood diseases that plague many developing nations. A comprehensive socialized health-care system and excellent sanitation systems account for these positive statistics, as do a generally stress-free lifestyle, tropical weather and a healthy and varied diet – the *pura vida.*

Still, the divide between rich and poor is broad. The middle and upper classes largely reside in San José, as well as in the major cities of the Central Valley highlands (Heredia, Alajuela and Cartago), and enjoy a level of comfort similar to their economic brethren in Europe and the US. City dwellers are likely to have a maid and a car or two, and the lucky few have a second home on the beach or in the mountains.

The home of an average Tico is a one-story construction built from concrete blocks, wood or a combination of both. In the poorer lowland areas, people often live in windowless houses made of *caña brava* (a local cane). For the vast majority of *campesinos* (farmers) and *indígenas* (people of indigenous origin), life is harder than in the cities, poverty levels are higher and standards of living are lower than in the rest of the country. This is especially true along the Caribbean coast, where the descendants of Jamaican immigrants have long suffered from lack of attention by the federal government, and in indigenous reservations. However, although poor families have few possessions and little financial security, every member assists with working the land or contributing to the household, which creates a strong safety net.

As in the rest of the world, globalization is having a dramatic effect on Costa Ricans, who are increasingly mobile, international and intertwined in the global economy – for better or for worse. These days, society is increasingly geographically mobile – the Tico who was born in Puntarenas

THE TICO WAY OF LIFE DAILY LIFE

NICA VS TICO

Ticos have a well-deserved reputation for friendliness, and it's rare for travelers of any sex, race or creed to experience prejudice in Costa Rica. However, it's unfortunate and at times upsetting that the mere mention of anything related to Nicaragua is enough to turn an average Tico into a stereotype-spewing anti-Nica (note that though the term 'Nica' is used colloquially by Nicaraguans, it is used by some Ticos in a somewhat derogatory manner – when in doubt, err on the side of *'nicaragüense'* to refer to a Nicaraguan person). Despite commonalities in language, culture, history and tradition, Nica-versus-Tico relations are at an all-time low, and rhetoric (on both sides) of *la frontera* (the border) isn't likely to improve any time soon.

Why is there so much hostility between Nicaraguans and Ticos? The answer is as much a product of history as it is of misunderstanding, though economic disparities between the countries are largely to blame.

Though Nicaragua was wealthier than Costa Rica as recently as 25 years ago, decades of civil war and a US embargo quickly bankrupted it, and today Nicaragua is the second-poorest country in the western hemisphere (after Haiti). For example, the 2014 CIA World Factbook lists the GDP per capita purchasing-power parity of Costa Rica as US$14,900, while Nicaragua's is only US$4800. The main problem facing Nicaragua is its heavy external debt, though debt-relief programs implemented by the International Monetary Fund (IMF) and the free-trade zone created by the Central American Free Trade Agreement (Cafta) are both promising signs.

In the meantime, however, Nicaraguan families are crossing the border in record numbers, drawn to Costa Rica by its growing economy and impressive education and health systems. However, immigration laws in Costa Rica make it difficult for Nicaraguans to find work, and the majority end up living in shantytowns and doing poorly paid manual labor. Also, crime is on the rise throughout Costa Rica, and though it's difficult to say what percentage is actually attributable to Nicaraguan immigrants, some Ticos are quick to point the finger in their direction.

Costa Rica is currently at loggerheads with Nicaragua over the Cuban immigrant crisis, since Nicaragua refuses to grant Cubans passage to the US after they have been granted temporary Costa Rican visas. Nicaragua, on the other hand, has also passed a law requiring all visiting Ticos to be in possession of a valid visa. As with all instances of deep-rooted prejudice, the solution is anything but clear.

MARRIAGE EQUALITY

Since 1998 there have been laws on the books to protect 'sexual option,' and discrimination is generally prohibited in most facets of society, including employment. However, though the country is becoming increasingly more gay friendly, this traditional culture has not always been quick to adopt equal protection.

Legal recognition of same-sex partnerships has been a hot topic since 2006 and was a major point of contention in the 2010 presidential race. In January 2012 Costa Rica's primary newspaper *La Nación* conducted a poll in which 55% of the respondents believed that same-sex couples should have the same rights as heterosexual couples. Then in July 2013 the Costa Rican legislature 'accidentally' passed a law legalizing gay marriage, due to a small change in the bill's wording. In 2015 a Costa Rican judge granted a same-sex common-law marriage, making it the first country in Central America to recognize gay relationships. The current president, Luis Guillermo Solís, has expressed support for gay rights, and even flew the rainbow flag at the presidential house.

might end up managing a lodge on the Península de Osa. And, with the advent of better-paved roads, cell coverage, and the increasing presence of North American and European expats (and the accompanying malls and big box stores), the Tico family unit is subject to the changing tides of a global society.

Women in Costa Rica

By the letter of the law, Costa Rica's progressive stance on women's issues makes the country stand out among its Central American neighbors. A 1974 family code stipulated equal duties and rights for men and women. Additionally, women can draw up contracts, assume loans and inherit property. Sexual harassment and sex discrimination are also against the law, and in 1996 Costa Rica passed a landmark law against domestic violence that was one of the most progressive in Latin America. With women holding more and more roles in political, legal, scientific and medical fields, Costa Rica has been home to some historic firsts: in 1998 both vice presidents (Costa Rica has two) were women, and in February 2010 Arias Sánchez' former vice president, Laura Chinchilla, became the first female president.

In conjunction with two indigenous women, Paula Palmer wrote *Taking Care of Sibö's Gifts,* an inspiring account of the intersection between the spiritual and environmental values of the Bribrí.

Still, the picture of sexual equality is much more complicated than the country's bragging rights might suggest. A thriving legal prostitution trade has fueled illicit underground activities such as child prostitution and the trafficking of women. Despite the cultural reverence for the matriarch (Mother's Day is a national holiday), traditional Latin American machismo is hardly a thing of the past and anti-discrimination laws are rarely enforced. Particularly in the countryside, many women maintain traditional societal roles: raising children, cooking and running the home.

Sports

From the scrappy little matches that take over the village pitch to the breathless exclamations of 'Goal!' that erupt from San José bars on the day of a big game, no Costa Rican sporting venture can compare with *fútbol* (soccer). Every town has a soccer field (which usually serves as the most conspicuous landmark) where neighborhood aficionados play in heated matches.

The *selección nacional* (national selection) team is known affectionately as La Sele. Legions of rabid Tico fans still recall La Sele's most memorable moments, including an unlikely showing in the quarterfinals at the 1990 World Cup in Italy and a solid (if not long-lasting) performance in the 2002 World Cup. More recently, La Sele's failure to qualify for the 2010 World Cup led to a top-down change in leadership and the reinstatement of one-time coach Jorge Luis Pinto, a Colombian coach who has had mixed results on the international stage. In general, Pinto seems to be a good fit for the team's ferocious young leaders such as record-setting scorer Álvaro Saborío, goalkeeper Keylor Navas and forward Bryan Ruiz. And in fact, Pinto led the team to qualify for the 2014 World Cup in Brazil, where the team reached the quarterfinals, making them national heroes.

With such perfect waves, surfing has steadily grown in popularity among Ticos, especially those who grow up shredding in surf towns. Costa Rica hosts numerous national and international competitions annually that are widely covered by local media, as well as holding regular local competitions such as the weekly contest at Playa Hermosa (south of Jacó).

Bullfighting is also popular, particularly in the Guanacaste region, though the bull isn't killed in the Costa Rican version of the sport. More aptly described, bullfighting is really a ceremonial opportunity to watch an often tipsy cowboy run around with a bull.

Arts

Literature

Costa Rica has a relatively young literary history and few works of Costa Rican writers or novelists are available in translation. Carlos Luis Fallas (1909–66) is widely known for *Mamita Yunai* (1940), an influential 'proletarian' novel that took the banana companies to task for their labor practices, and he remains very popular among the Latin American left.

Carmen Naranjo (1928–2012) is one of the few contemporary Costa Rican writers who have risen to international acclaim. She was a novelist, poet and short-story writer who also served as ambassador to India in the 1970s, and a few years later as minister of culture. In 1996 she was awarded the prestigious Gabriela Mistral medal by the Chilean government. Her collection of short stories, *There Never Was a Once Upon a Time,* is widely available in English. Two of her stories can also be found in *Costa Rica: A Traveler's Literary Companion.*

José León Sánchez (1929–) is an internationally renowned memoirist of Huetar descent from the border of Costa Rica and Nicaragua. After being convicted for stealing from the famous Basílica de Nuestra Señora de Los Ángeles in Cartago, he was sentenced to serve his term at Isla San Lucas, one of Latin America's most notorious jails. Illiterate when he was incarcerated, Sánchez taught himself how to read and write, and clandestinely authored one of the continent's most poignant books: *La isla de los hombres solos* (called *God Was Looking the Other Way* in the translated version).

Music & Dance

Although there are other Latin American musical hotbeds of more renown, Costa Rica's central geographical location and colonial history have resulted in a varied musical culture that incorporates elements from North and South America and the Caribbean islands.

San José features a regular lineup of domestic and international rock, folk and hip-hop artists, but you'll find that the regional sounds also survive, each with their own special rhythms, instruments and styles. For instance, the Península de Nicoya has a rich musical history, most of it made with guitars, maracas and marimbas. The traditional sound on the Caribbean coast is calypso, which has roots in Afro-Caribbean slave culture.

Popular dance music includes Latin dances, such as salsa, merengue, bolero and *cumbia.* Guanacaste is also the birthplace of many traditional

Get player statistics and game schedules and find out everything you ever needed to know about La Sele, the Costa Rican national soccer team, at www.fede futbol.com.

Little of his work is translated but poet Alfonso Chase is a Fulbright scholar and a contemporary literary hero. In 2000 he won the nation's highest literary award, the Premio Magón.

dances, most of which depict courtship rituals between country folk. The most famous dance – sometimes considered the national dance – is the *punto guanacasteco*. What keeps it lively is the *bomba,* a funny (and usually racy) rhymed verse shouted by the male dancers during the musical interlude.

The most comprehensive and complete book on Costa Rican history and culture is *The Ticos: Culture and Social Change in Costa Rica* by Mavis, Richard and Karen Biesanz.

Visual Arts

The visual arts in Costa Rica first took on a national character in the 1920s, when Teodórico Quirós, Fausto Pacheco and their contemporaries began painting landscapes that differed from traditional European styles, depicting the rolling hills and lush forest of the Costa Rican countryside, often sprinkled with characteristic adobe houses.

The contemporary scene is more varied and it is difficult to define a unique Tico style. Several individual artists have garnered acclaim for their work, including the magical realism of Isidro Con Wong, the surreal paintings and primitive engravings of Francisco Amighetti and the mystical female figures painted by Rafa Fernández. The Museo de Arte y Diseño Contemporáneo in San José is the top place to see this type of work, and its permanent collection is a great primer.

Many art galleries are geared toward tourists and specialize in 'tropical art' (for lack of an official description): brightly colored, whimsical folk paintings depicting flora and fauna that evoke the work of French artist Henri Rousseau.

Folk art and handicrafts are not as widely produced or readily available here as in other Central American countries. However, the dedicated souvenir hunter will have no problem finding the colorful Sarchí oxcarts that have become a symbol of Costa Rica. Indigenous crafts, which include intricately carved and painted masks made by the Boruca, as well as handwoven bags and linens and colorful Chorotega pottery, can also be found in San José and more readily along Costa Rica's Pacific coast.

Film

Artistically, while film is not a new medium in Costa Rica, young filmmakers have been upping the country's ante in this arena. Over the last decade or so, a handful of Costa Rican filmmakers have submitted their work for Oscar consideration, and many others have received critical acclaim for their pictures nationally and internationally. These films range from adaptations of Gabriel García Márquez' magical-realism novel *Del amor y otro demonios* (Of Love and Other Demons, 2009), directed by Hilda Hidalgo, and a comedic coming-of-age story of young Ticos on the cusp of adulthood in contemporary Costa Rica in *El cielo rojo* (The Red Sky, 2008), written and directed by Miguel Alejandro Gomez, to a light-hearted story of a Costa Rican farmer who embarks on the journey to Europe to raise money to avoid losing his farm in *Maikol Yordan de viaje perdido* (Maikol Yordan Traveling Lost, 2014), also directed by Gomez.

A film-festival calendar has also been blossoming in Costa Rica, though dates vary year on year. Sponsored by the Ministerio de Cultura y Juventud, the Costa Rica Festival Internacional de Cine (www.costaricacinefest.go.cr) takes place in San José (check the website for current dates) and features international films fitting the year's theme. The longer-running Costa Rica International Film Festival (CRIFF; www.filmfestivallife.com) hits Montezuma in early June, with an associated documentary film festival the week following.

Above La Paz Waterfall Gardens (p112)

Landscapes & Ecology

Despite its diminutive size – at 51,000 sq km it is slightly smaller than the USA's West Virginia – Costa Rica's land is an astounding collection of different habitats. On one coast are the breezy skies and big waves of the Pacific, while only 119km away lie the languid shores of the Caribbean. In between there are active volcanoes, alpine peaks and crisp high-elevation forest. Few places on earth can compare with this little country's spectacular interaction of natural, geological and climactic forces.

The Land
Pacific Coast

Two major peninsulas hook out into the ocean along the 1016km-long Pacific coast: Nicoya in the north and Osa in the south. Although they look relatively similar from space, on the ground they could hardly be more different. Nicoya is one of the driest places in the country and holds some of Costa Rica's most developed tourist infrastructure; Osa is wet and rugged, run through by wild, seasonal rivers and rough dirt roads that are always under threat from the creeping jungle.

Just inland from the coast, the landscapes of the Pacific lowlands are a narrow strip of land backed by mountains. This area is equally dynamic, ranging from dry deciduous forests and open cattle country in the north to misty, mysterious tropical rainforests in the south.

Central Costa Rica

Costa Rica's national tree is the guanacaste, commonly found on the lowlands of the Pacific slope.

Move a bit inland from the Pacific coast and you immediately ascend the jagged spine of the country: the majestic Cordillera Central in the north and the rugged, largely unexplored Cordillera de Talamanca in the south. Continually being revised by tectonic activity, these mountains are part of the majestic Sierra Madre chain that runs north through Mexico.

A land of active volcanoes, clear trout-filled streams and ethereal cloud forest, these mountain ranges generally follow a northwest to southeast line, with the highest and most dramatic peaks in the south near the Panamanian border. The highest in the country is the windswept 3820m peak of Cerro Chirripó.

In the midst of this powerful landscape, surrounded on all sides by mountains, are the highlands of the Meseta Central – the Central Valley. This fertile central plain, some 1000m above sea level, is the agricultural heart of the nation and enjoys abundant rainfall and mild temperatures. It includes San José and cradles three more of Costa Rica's five largest cities, accounting for more than half of the country's population.

Caribbean Coast

Tales of the green turtle's resurgence in Tortuguero are told by Archie Carr in *The Windward Road: Adventures of a Naturalist on Remote Caribbean Shores*.

Cross the mountains and drop down the eastern slope and you'll reach the elegant line of the Caribbean coastline – a long, straight 212km along low plains, brackish lagoons and waterlogged forests. A lack of strong tides allows plants to grow right over the water's edge along coastal sloughs. Eventually, these create the walls of vegetation along the narrow, murky waters that characterize much of the region. As if taking cues from the slow-paced, Caribbean-influenced culture, the rivers that rush out of the central mountains take on a languid pace here, curving through broad plains toward the sea.

Compared with the smoothly paved roads and popular beaches of the Pacific coast, much of the land here is still largely inaccessible except by boat or plane.

Geology

If all this wildly diverse beauty makes Costa Rica feel like the crossroads between vastly different worlds, that's because it is. Part of the thin strip of land that separates two continents with hugely divergent wildlife and topographical character and right in the middle of the world's two largest oceans, it's little wonder that Costa Rica boasts such a colorful collision of climates, landscapes and wildlife.

DON'T DISTURB THE DOLPHINS

Swimming with dolphins has been illegal since 2006, although shady tour operators out for a quick buck may encourage it. Research indicates that in some heavily touristed areas, dolphins are leaving their natural habitat in search of calmer seas. When your boat comes across these amazing creatures of the sea, avoid the temptation to jump in with them – you can still have an awe-inspiring experience peacefully observing them without disturbing them.

Playa Blanca (p170)

The country's geological history began when the Cocos Plate, a tectonic plate that lies below the Pacific, crashed headlong into the Caribbean Plate, which is off the isthmus' east coast. Since the plates travel about 10cm every year, the collision might seem slow by human measure, but it was a violent wreck by geological standards, creating the area's subduction zone. The plates continue to collide, with the Cocos Plate pushing the Caribbean Plate toward the heavens and making the area prone to earthquakes and ongoing volcanic activity.

Despite all the violence underfoot, these forces have blessed the country with some of the world's most beautiful and varied tropical landscapes.

Out on a Reef

Compared with the rest of the Caribbean, the coral reefs of Costa Rica are not a banner attraction. Heavy surf and shifting sands along most of the Caribbean coast produce conditions that are unbearable to corals. The exceptions are two beautiful patches of reef in the south that are protected on the rocky headlands of Parque Nacional Cahuita and Refugio Nacional de Vida Silvestre Gandoca-Manzanillo. These diminutive but vibrant reefs are home to more than 100 species of fish and many types of coral and make for decent snorkeling and diving.

Unfortunately, the reefs themselves are in danger due to sediment washing downriver from logging operations and toxic chemicals that wash out of nearby agricultural fields. Although curbed by the government, these factors persist. Also, a major earthquake in 1991 lifted the reefs as much as 1.5m, stranding and killing large portions of this fragile ecosystem. More recently, climate change has led to warmer water in the Caribbean, which puts the reefs at the greatest peril – scientists released a report in 2008 that found that over half of Caribbean reefs were dead due to increased temperatures.

The world-famous Organization for Tropical Studies (www.ots.ac.cr) runs three field stations and offers numerous classes for students seriously interested in tropical ecology.

Owl butterfly, Parque Nacional Tortuguero (p152)

Biodiversity

Nowhere else are so many types of habitats squeezed into such a tiny area, and species from different continents have been commingling here for millennia. Costa Rica has the world's largest number of species per 10,000 sq km: 615, compared with wildlife-rich Rwanda's 596 and the comparatively impoverished USA's 104. This simple fact alone makes Costa Rica the premier destination for nature lovers.

The large number of species here is also due to the country's relatively recent appearance. Roughly three million years ago Costa Rica rose from the ocean, and formed a land bridge between North and South America. As species from these two vast biological provinces started to mingle, the number of species essentially doubled in the area where Costa Rica now sits.

The National Bio-diversity Institute (www.inbio.ac.cr) is a clearinghouse of information on both biodiversity and efforts to conserve it.

Flora

Simply put, Costa Rica's floral biodiversity is mind-blowing – close to 12,000 species of vascular plants have been described, and the list gets more and more crowded each year. Orchids alone account for about 1400 species. The diversity of habitats created when this many species mix is a wonder to behold.

Rainforest

The humid, vibrant mystery of the tropical rainforest connects acutely with a traveler's sense of adventure. These forests, far more dense with plant life than any other environment on the planet, are leftover scraps of the prehistoric jungles that once covered the continents. Standing in the midst of it and trying to take it all in can be overwhelming: tropical rainforests contain over half of the earth's known living organisms.

Naturally, this riotous pile-on of life requires lots of water – it typically gets between 5m and 6m of rainfall annually (yes, that's *meters*!).

Classic rainforest habitats are well represented in the parks of southwestern Costa Rica or in the mid-elevation portions of the central mountains. Here you will find towering trees that block out the sky, long, looping vines and many overlapping layers of vegetation. Large trees often show buttresses – wing-like ribs that extend from their trunks for added structural support. And plants climb atop other plants, fighting for a bit of sunlight. The most impressive areas of primary forest – a term designating completely untouched land that has never been disturbed by humans – exist on the Península de Osa.

Cloud Forest

Visiting the unearthly terrain of a cloud forest is a highlight for many visitors; there are amazing swaths of it in Monteverde, along the Cerro de la Muerte and below the peaks of Chirripó. In these regions, fog-drenched trees are so thickly coated in mosses, ferns, bromeliads and orchids that you can hardly discern their true shapes. These forests are created when humid trade winds off the Caribbean blow up into the highlands, cool and condense to form thick, low-hanging clouds. With constant exposure to wind, rain and sun, the trees here are crooked and stunted.

Cloud forests are widespread at high elevations throughout Costa Rica and any of them warrant a visit. Be forewarned, however, that in these habitats the term 'rainy season' has little meaning because it's always dripping wet from the fog – humidity in a cloud forest often hovers around 100%.

Tropical Dry Forest

Along Costa Rica's northwest coast lies the country's largest concentration of tropical dry forest – a stunningly different scene to the country's wet rainforests and cloud forests. During the dry season many trees drop their foliage, creating carpets of crackling, sun-drenched leaves and a sense of openness that is largely absent in other Costa Rican habitats. The large trees here, such as Costa Rica's national tree, the guanacaste, have broad, umbrella-like canopies, while spiny shrubs and vines or cacti dominate the understory. At times, large numbers of trees erupt into spectacular displays of flowers, and at the beginning of the rainy season everything is transformed with a wonderful flush of new, green foliage.

This type of forest was native to Guanacaste and the Península de Nicoya, though it suffered generations of destruction for its commercially valuable lumber. Most was clear-cut or burned to make space for ranching. Guanacaste and Santa Rosa national parks are good examples of the dry forest and host some of the country's most accessible nature hiking.

Mangroves

Along brackish stretches of both coasts, mangrove swamps are a world unto themselves. Growing on stilts out of muddy tidal flats, five species of trees crowd together so densely that no boats and few animals can penetrate. Striking in their adaptations for dealing with salt, mangrove trees thrive where no other land plant dares tread and are among the world's most relentless colonizers. The mangrove seeds are heavy and fleshy, blooming into flowers in the spring before falling off to give way to fruit. By the time the fruit falls, it is covered with spiky seedlings that anchor in the soft mud of low tides. In only 10 years, a seedling has the potential to mature into an entire new colony.

Above Kayakers crossing a suspension bridge, Parque Nacional Manuel Antonio (p383)
Left Mangroves, Manuel Antonio area (p375)

Parque Nacional Volcán Poás (p111)

Mangrove swamps play extremely important roles in the ecosystem. Not only do they buffer coastlines from the erosive power of waves, they also have high levels of productivity because they trap nutrient-rich sediment and serve as spawning and nursery areas for innumerable species of fish and invertebrates. The brown waters of mangrove channels – rich with nutrients and filled with algae, shrimp, crustaceans and caimans – form tight links in the marine food chain and are best explored in a kayak, early in the morning.

There are miles of mangrove channels along the Caribbean coast, and a vast mangrove swamp on the Pacific, near Bahía Drake.

Fauna

Though tropical in nature – with a substantial number of tropical animals such as poison-dart frogs and spider monkeys – Costa Rica is also the winter home for more than 200 species of migrating bird that arrive from as far away as Alaska and Australia. Don't be surprised to see one of your familiar backyard birds feeding alongside trogons and toucans. Birds are one of the primary attractions for naturalists, who scan endlessly for birds of every color, from strawberry-red scarlet macaws to the iridescent jewels called violet sabrewing (a type of hummingbird). Because many birds in Costa Rica have restricted ranges, you are guaranteed to find different species everywhere you travel.

Visitors will almost certainly see one of Costa Rica's four types of monkey or two types of sloth, but there are an additional 230 types of mammal awaiting the patient observer. More exotic sightings might include the amazing four-eyed opossum or silky anteater, while a lucky few might spot the elusive tapir, or have a jaguarundi cross their path. The extensive network of national parks, wildlife refuges and other protected areas are prime places to spot wildlife.

> Mangroves can survive in highly saline environments by secreting salt via the surface of their leaves, filtering it at the root level and accumulating it in bark and leaves that eventually fall off.

Sloth

If you are serious about observing birds and animals, the value of a knowledgeable guide cannot be underestimated. Their keen eyes are trained to notice the slightest movement in the forest, and they recognize the many exotic sounds. Most professional bird guides are proficient in the dialects of local birds, greatly improving your chances of hearing or seeing these species.

No season is a bad one for exploring Costa Rica's natural environment, though most visitors arrive during the peak dry season, when trails are less muddy and more accessible. An added bonus of visiting between December and February is that many of the wintering migrant birds are still hanging around. A trip after the peak season means fewer birds, but this is a stupendous time to see dried forests transform into vibrant greens and it's also when resident birds begin nesting.

Endangered Species

Excellent, contemplative books on birds by the esteemed Dr Alexander Skutch include *A Naturalist in Costa Rica* and *The Minds of Birds*.

As expected in a country with unique habitats and widespread logging, there are numerous species whose populations are declining or in danger of extinction. Currently, the number-one threat to most of Costa Rica's endangered species is habitat destruction, followed closely by hunting and trapping.

Costa Rica's four species of sea turtle – olive ridley, leatherback, green and hawksbill – deservedly get a lot of attention. All four species are classified as endangered or critically endangered, meaning they face an imminent threat of extinction. While populations of some species are increasing, thanks to various protection programs along both coasts, the risk for these *tortugas* (turtles) is still very real.

Destruction of habitat is a huge problem. With the exception of the leatherbacks, all of these species return to their natal beach to nest, which means that the ecological state of the beach directly affects that turtle's ability to reproduce. All of the species prefer dark, undisturbed beaches, and any sort of development or artificial lighting (including flashlights) will inhibit nesting.

Hunting and harvesting eggs are two major causes of declining populations. Green turtles are hunted for their meat. Leatherbacks and olive ridleys are not killed for meat, but their eggs are considered a delicacy – an aphrodisiac, no less. Hawksbill turtles are hunted for their unusual shells, which are sometimes used to make jewelry and hair ornaments. Of course, any trade in tortoiseshell products and turtle eggs and meat is illegal, but a significant black market exists.

The ultra-rare harpy eagle and the legendary quetzal – the birds at the top of every naturalist's must-see list – teeter precariously as their home forests are felled at an alarming rate. Seeing a noisy scarlet macaw could be a bird-watching highlight in Costa Rica, but trapping for the pet trade has extirpated these magnificent birds from much of their former range. Although populations are thriving on the Península de Osa, the scarlet macaw is now extinct over most of Central America, including the entire Caribbean coast.

A number of Costa Rica's mammals are highly endangered, including the elusive jaguar and the squirrel monkey, both due to destruction of habitat. The two survive in the depths of Parque Nacional Corcovado, with the latter also found in some numbers in Parque Nacional Manuel Antonio.

Harassment and intimidation of conservationists in Costa Rica is nothing new, and although the brutal murder (p150) of 26-year-old environmentalist Jairo Mora Sandoval in Limón Province in 2013 brought the issue to international attention, those accused of his murder were acquitted. Since 1989, 10 murders of conservationists have gone unsolved.

National Parks & Protected Areas

The national-park system began in the 1960s, and has since been expanded into a National Conservation Areas System with an astounding 186 protected areas, including 27 national parks, eight biological reserves, 32 protected zones, 13 forest reserves and 58 wildlife refuges. At least 10% of the land is strictly protected and another 17% is included in various multiple-use preserves. Costa Rican authorities enjoy their claim that more than 27% of the country has been set aside for conservation, but multiple-use zones still allow farming, logging and other exploitation, so the environment within them is not totally protected. The smallest number might be the most amazing of all: Costa Rica's parks are a safe haven to approximately 5% of the world's wildlife species.

In addition to the system of national preserves, there are hundreds of small, privately owned lodges, reserves and haciendas (estates) that have been set up to protect the land. Many belong to longtime Costa Rican expats who decided that this country was the last stop in their journey along the 'gringo trail' in the 1970s and '80s. The abundance of foreign-owned protected areas is a bit of a contentious issue with Ticos. Although these are largely nonprofit organizations with keen interests in conservation, they are private and often cost money to enter. There's also a number of animal rescue and rehabilitation centers (also largely set up by expats), where injured and orphaned animals and illegal pets are rehabilitated and released into the wild, or looked after for life if they cannot be released.

Although the national-park system appears glamorous on paper, national conservation body the Sistema Nacional de Areas de Conservación (Sinac) still sees much work to be done. A report from several years ago amplified the fact that much of the protected area is, in fact, at risk. The

The eight species of poison-dart frog in Costa Rica are beautiful but have skin secretions of varying toxicity that cause paralysis and death if they get into your bloodstream.

Parque Nacional Volcán Poás (p111)

government doesn't own all of this land – almost half of the areas are in private hands – and there isn't the budget to buy it. Technically, the private lands are protected from development, but there have been reports that many landowners are finding loopholes in the restrictions and selling or developing their properties, or taking bribes from poachers and illegal loggers in exchange for access.

On the plus side is a project by Sinac that links national parks and reserves, private reserves and national forests into 13 conservation areas. This strategy has two major effects. First, these 'megaparks' allow greater numbers of individual plants and animals to exist. Second, the administration of the national parks is delegated to regional offices, allowing a more individualized management approach. Each conservation area has regional and subregional offices charged with providing effective education, enforcement, research and management, although some regional offices play what appear to be only obscure bureaucratic roles.

In general, support for land preservation remains high in Costa Rica because it provides income and jobs to so many people, plus important opportunities for scientific investigation.

For maps and descriptions of the national parks, visit www. costarica-national parks.com.

Environmental Issues

No other tropical country has made such a concerted effort to protect its environment, and a study published by Yale and Columbia Universities in 2012 ranked Costa Rica in the top five nations for its overall environmental performance. At the same time, as the global leader in the burgeoning ecotourism economy, Costa Rica is proving to be a case study in the pitfalls and benefits of this kind of tourism. The pressures of overpopulation, global climate change and dwindling natural resources have also made it a key illustration of the urgency of environmental protection.

Catarata de Río Celeste (p218), Parque Nacional Volcán Tenorio

Deforestation

Sometimes, when the traffic jams up around the endless San José sprawl, it is hard to keep in mind that this place was once covered in a lush, unending tropical forest. Tragically, after more than a century of clearing for plantations, agriculture and logging, Costa Rica lost about 80% of its forest cover before the government stepped in with a plan to protect what was left. Through its many programs of forest protection and reforestation, 52.8% of the country is forested once again – a stunning accomplishment.

Despite protection for two-thirds of the remaining forests, cutting trees is still a major problem for Costa Rica, especially on private lands that are being cleared by wealthy landowners and multinational corporations. Even within national parks, some of the more remote areas are being logged illegally because there is not enough money for law enforcement.

Apart from the direct loss of tropical forests and the plants and animals that depend on them, deforestation leads directly or indirectly to a number of other severe environmental problems. Forests protect the soil beneath them from the ravages of tropical rainstorms. After deforestation, much of the topsoil is washed away, lowering the productivity of the land and silting up watersheds and downstream coral reefs.

Cleared lands are frequently planted with a variety of crops, including acres of bananas, the production of which entails the use of pesticides as well as blue plastic bags to protect the fruit. Both the pesticides and the plastic end up polluting the environment. Cattle ranching has been another historical motivator for clear-cutting. It intensified during the 1970s, when Costa Rican coffee exports were waning in the global market.

Because deforestation plays a role in global warming, there is much interest in rewarding countries such as Costa Rica for taking the lead in protecting their forests. The US has forgiven millions of dollars of Costa Rica's debt in exchange for increased efforts to preserve rainforests. The Costa Rican government itself sponsors a program that pays landowners for each hectare of forest they set aside, and has petitioned the UN for a global program that would pay tropical countries for their conservation efforts. Travelers interested in taking part in projects that can help protect Costa Rica's trees should look to volunteer opportunities in conservation and forestry.

Tourism

The other great environmental issue facing Costa Rica comes from the country being loved to death, directly through the passage of more than two million foreign tourists a year, and less directly through the development of extensive infrastructure to support this influx. For years resort hotels and lodges continued to pop up, most notably on formerly pristine beaches or in the middle of intact rainforest. Too many of these projects were poorly planned, and they necessitate additional support systems, including roads and countless vehicle trips, with much of this activity unregulated and largely unmonitored.

The number-one reason for forest clearing in Central America is to graze cattle, mostly for export. Can't give up eating beef? Consider going for more environmentally friendly domestic (US or Canadian) grass-fed beef.

As tourism continues to become a larger piece of the Costa Rican economy, the bonanza invites more and more development. Taking advantage of Costa Rica's reputation as a green destination, developers promote mass tourism by building large hotels and package tours that, in turn, drive away wildlife, hasten erosion and strain local sewer and water systems. The irony is painful: they threaten to ruin the very environment that they're selling.

It's worth noting that many private lodges and reserves are also doing some of the best conservation work in the country, and it's heartening to run across the ever-increasing homespun efforts to protect Costa Rica's environment, spearheaded by hardworking families or small organizations tucked away in some quiet corner of the country. These include projects to boost rural economies by raising native medicinal plants, efforts by villagers to document their local biodiversity, and resourceful fundraising campaigns to purchase endangered lands.

Sustainable Travel

Costa Rica's visitors presently account for the largest sector of the national economy and thus have unprecedented power to protect this country. How? By spending wisely, asking probing questions about sustainability claims and simply avoiding businesses that threaten Costa Rica's future.

Due to deforestation it is best to avoid products made from tropical hardwoods if you're uncertain of the origin.

In its purest form, sustainable tourism simply means striking the ideal balance between the traveler and their surrounding environment. This often includes being conscientious about energy and water consumption, and treading lightly on local environments and communities. Sustainable tourism initiatives support their communities by hiring local people for decent wages, furthering women's and civil rights, and supporting local schools, artists and food producers.

On the road, engage with the local economy as much as possible: for example, if a local artisan's handiwork catches your eye, make the purchase – every dollar infuses the micro-economy in the most direct (and rewarding) way.

Eco-Friendly Credentials

Interpreting the jargon – 'green,' 'sustainable,' 'low carbon footprint,' 'ecofriendly' etc – can be confusing when every souvenir stall and ATV tour operator claims to be ecofriendly.

Top Hanging bridge, Monteverde (p193)
Bottom Green basilisk lizard

TOM BOYDEN / GETTY IMAGES ©

Farmer harvesting coffee beans

Since sustainable travel has no universal guidelines, here are some things to look for:

➡ For hotels and restaurants: obvious recycling programs, effective management of waste water and pollutants, and alternative energy systems and natural illumination, at a bare minimum.

➡ A high rating from a legitimate sustainability index. In Costa Rica, the government-sanctioned Certificado para la Sostenibilidad Turística (CST; www. turismo-sostenible.co.cr) offers a 'five-leaf' rating system. Factors considered by the CST include physical-biological parameters, infrastructure and services, and socioeconomic environment, including interaction with local communities. Its website has a complete directory.

➡ Partnership with environmental conservation programs, education initiatives, or regional or local organizations that work on solving environmental problems.

➡ Grassroots connections: sourcing a majority of employees from the local population, associating with locally owned businesses, providing places where local handicrafts can be displayed for sale, serving foods that support local markets, and using local materials and products in order to maintain the health of the local economy.

BRANDON ALMS / SHUTTERSTOCK ©

Costa Rica Wildlife Guide

Costa Rica's reputation as a veritable Eden precedes it – with its iconic blue morpho butterflies, four species each of monkey and sea turtle, scarlet and great green macaws, two- and three-toed sloths, a rainbow of poison-dart frogs, mysterious tapirs and cute coatis.

Contents

➡ **Birds**
➡ **Reptiles & Amphibians**
➡ **Marine Animals**
➡ **Land Mammals**
➡ **Insects & Arachnids**

Above Red-eyed tree frog

1. Keel-billed toucan 2. Resplendent quetzal 3. Summer tanager
4. Green violetear hummingbirds

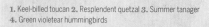

Birds

Toucan

Six species of this classic rainforest bird are found in Costa Rica. Huge bills and vibrant plumage make the commonly sighted chestnut-mandibled toucan and keel-billed toucan hard to miss. Listen for the keel-billed's song: a repetitious 'carrrick!'

Scarlet Macaw

Of the 16 parrot species in Costa Rica, none is as spectacular as the scarlet macaw. Unmistakable for its large size, bright-red body and ear-splitting squawk, it's common in Parque Nacional Carara and the Península de Osa. Macaws have long, monogamous relationships and can live 50 years.

Resplendent Quetzal

The most dazzling bird in Central America, the quetzal once held great ceremonial significance for the Aztecs and the Maya. Look for its iridescent-green body, red breast and long green tail at high elevations and near Parque Nacional Los Quetzales.

Roseate Spoonbill

This wading bird has a white head and a distinctive spoon-shaped bill, and feeds by touch. Common around the Península de Nicoya, Pacific lowlands and on the Caribbean side at the Refugio Nacional de Vida Silvestre Caño Negro.

Tanager

There are 42 species of tanager in the country – many are brightly colored and all have bodies about the size of an adult fist. Look for them everywhere except at high elevation. Their common name in Costa Rica is *viuda* (meaning widow).

Hummingbird

More than 50 species of hummingbird have been recorded – and most live at high elevations. The largest is the violet sabrewing, with a striking violet head and body and dark-green wings.

1. Red-eyed tree frog 2. Green iguana 3. Strawberry poison-dart frog 4. Eyelash pit viper

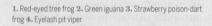

PANORAMIC IMAGES / GETTY IMAGES ©

Reptiles & Amphibians

Green Iguana

The stocky green iguana is regularly seen draping its 2m-long body along a branch. Despite their enormous bulk, iguanas are incessant vegetarians, and prefer to eat young shoots and leaves. You'll see them just about everywhere in Costa Rica – in fact, if you're driving, beware of iguanas sunning on or skittering across the roads.

Red-Eyed Tree Frog

The unofficial symbol of Costa Rica, the red-eyed tree frog has red eyes, a green body, yellow and blue side stripes, and orange feet. Despite this vibrant coloration, they're well camouflaged in the rainforest and rather difficult to spot. They are widespread apart from on the Península de Nicoya, which is too dry for them. You'll have a particularly good chance of seeing them at Estación Biológica La Selva.

Poison-Dart Frog

Among the several species found in Costa Rica, the blue-jeans or strawberry poison-dart frog is the most commonly spotted, from Arenal to the Caribbean coast. These colorful, wildly patterned frogs' toxic excretions were once used to poison indigenous arrowheads. The Golfo Dulce poison-dart frog is endemic to Costa Rica.

Crocodile

Impressive specimens can be seen from Crocodile Bridge on the central Pacific coast or in a more natural setting on boat trips along the Tortuguero canals.

Viper

Three serpents you'll want to avoid are the fer-de-lance pit viper, which lives in agricultural areas of the Pacific and Caribbean slopes, the black-headed bushmaster (endemic to Costa Rica) and the beautiful eyelash pit viper, which lives in low-elevation rainforest. To avoid serious or fatal bites, watch your step and look before you grab onto any vines when hiking.

498

1. Whale shark 2. Bottlenose dolphins 3. Manta ray
4. Hammerhead shark

PHOTOBOTOS IMAGE / GETTY IMAGES ©

2

Marine Animals

Olive Ridley Turtle

The smallest of Costa Rica's sea turtles, the olive ridley is easy to love – it has a heart-shaped shell. Between September and October they arrive to nest at Ostional beach in Guanacaste Province and near Ojochal on the Pacific coast.

Leatherback Turtle

The gigantic 360kg leatherback sea turtle is much, much bigger than the olive ridley, and is distinguished by its soft, leathery carapace, which has seven ridges. It nests on the Pacific beaches of the Osa and Nicoya peninsulas.

Whale

Migrating whales, which arrive from both the northern and southern hemispheres, include orca, blue and sperm whales and several species of relatively unknown beaked whale. Humpback whales are commonly spotted along the Pacific coast and off the Península de Osa.

Bottlenose Dolphin

These charismatic, intelligent cetaceans are commonly sighted, year-round residents of Costa Rica. Keep a lookout for them on the boat ride to Bahía Drake.

Whale Shark

Divers may encounter this gentle giant in the waters off Reserva Biológica Isla del Caño, the Golfo Dulce or Isla del Coco. The world's biggest fish, whale sharks can reach 6m long and over 2000kg in weight.

Manta Ray

With wings that can reach 7m, the elegant manta ray is common in warm Pacific waters, especially off the coast of Guanacaste and around the Bat and Catalina islands.

Hammerhead Shark

The intimidating hammerhead has a unique cephalofoil that enables it to maneuver with incredible speed and precision. Divers can see enormous schools of hammerheads around the remote Isla del Coco.

4

500

1. Coati 2. Sloth 3. Jaguar 4. Squirrel monkeys

JONATHAN PIFE / GETTY IMAGES ©

Land Mammals

Sloth

Costa Rica is home to the brown-throated, three-toed sloth and Hoffman's two-toed sloth. Both species tend to hang seemingly motionless from branches, their coats growing moss. Look for them in Parque Nacional Manuel Antonio.

Howler Monkey

The loud vocalizations of a male mantled howler monkey can carry for more than 1km even in dense rainforest, and echoes through many of the nation's national parks.

White-Faced Capuchin

The small and inquisitive white-faced capuchin has a prehensile tail that is typically carried with the tip coiled – one is likely to steal your lunch near Volcán Arenal or Parque Nacional Manuel Antonio.

Squirrel Monkey

The adorable, diminutive squirrel monkey travels in small- to medium-sized groups during the day, in search of insects and fruit. They live only along the Pacific coast and are common in Parque Nacional Manuel Antonio and on the Península de Nicoya.

Jaguar

The king of Costa Rica's big cats, the jaguar is extremely rare, shy and well camouflaged, so the chance of seeing one is virtually nonexistent (but the best chance is in Parque Nacional Corcovado).

White-Nosed Coati

A frequently seen member of the raccoon family, with a longer, slimmer and lighter body than your average raccoon. It has a distinctive pointy, whitish snout and a perky striped tail.

Baird's Tapir

A large browsing mammal related to the rhinoceros, the tapir has a characteristic prehensile snout and lives deep in forests ranging from the Península de Osa to Parque Nacional Santa Rosa.

Blue morpho butterfly

Insects & Arachnids

Blue Morpho Butterfly

The blue morpho butterfly flutters along tropical rivers and through openings in the forests. When it lands, the electric-blue upper wings close, and only the mottled brown underwings become visible, an instantaneous change from outrageous display to modest camouflage.

Tarantula

Easily identified by its enormous size and hairy appendages, the Costa Rican red tarantula is an intimidating arachnid that can take down a mouse, but it is completely harmless to humans. They are most active at night while foraging and seeking mates.

Hercules Beetle

Turn on your flashlight while visiting one of Costa Rica's old-growth forests and you might draw out the Hercules beetle, one of the largest bugs in the world, a terrifying-looking but utterly harmless scarab beetle that can be as big as a cake plate. Fun fact: it can carry over 100 times its own body weight.

Leaf-Cutter Ant

Long processions of busy leaf-cutter ants traverse the forest floors and trails of Costa Rica, appearing like slow-moving rivulets of green leaf fragments. Leaf-cutter ants are actually fungus farmers – in their underground colonies, the ants chew the harvested leaves into a pulp to precipitate the growth of fungus, which feeds the colonies. Don't confuse them with the predatory army ants!

Survival Guide

Directory A–Z

Accommodations

Accommodations come at every price and comfort level: from luxurious ecolodges and sparkling all-inclusive resorts and backpacker palaces to spartan rooms with little more than a bed and four cinder-block walls. The variety and number of rooms on offer means that advance booking is not usually mandatory.

The term *cabina* (cabin) is a catch-all that can define a wide range of prices and amenities – from very rustic to very expensive.

Booking Services

➡ **Costa Rica Innkeepers Association** (www.costaricainnkeepers.com) A nonprofit association of B&Bs, small hotels, lodges and inns.

➡ **Escape Villas** (www.villascostarica.com) High-end accommodations across Costa Rica, most near Parque Nacional Manuel Antonio, which are suitable for families and honeymooners looking for luxury.

➡ **Lonely Planet** (www.lonelyplanet.com/costa-rica/hotels) Recommendations and bookings.

Apartments & Villas

The network of long-term rentals has grown dramatically in recent years. These can be an excellent option for families, as they typically include a kitchen and several bedrooms. In many beach towns, vacation villas and apartments of varying quality are rented by the week, month or longer, and some come with resort access, beach toys and other amenities.

B&Bs

Generally speaking, B&Bs in Costa Rica tend to be midrange to top-end affairs, often run by resident European and North American expats. You can find B&Bs listed in the *Tico Times*.

Camping

➡ Camping on Costa Rica's coasts is not legal but is widely tolerated. Many local families camp at the beach during the holidays.

➡ Most major tourist destinations have at least one campsite and most budget hotels outside San José accommodate campers on their grounds. Although these usually include toilets, cold showers and basic self-catering facilities (sink and BBQ pit), they can be crowded and noisy.

➡ In most national parks, campsites are usually of excellent quality and rigorously cleaned and maintained by staff. As a general rule, you will need to carry in all of your food and supplies, and carry out all of your trash.

➡ Theft is a major concern; don't leave anything in your tent unattended. Camp in a group if possible.

➡ Don't camp near riverbanks, which are prone to flooding and home to snakes.

➡ Mosquito nets and repellent with DEET are often essential.

Hostels

Although there is still a handful of Hostelling International (HI) hostels left in Costa Rica, the backpacker scene has gone increasingly upmarket. Compared to other destinations in Central America, hostels in Costa Rica tend to be fairly expensive, though the quality of service and accommodations is unequaled.

Expect to pay between US$10 to US$15 for a dorm bed.

Hotels

It is always advisable to ask to see a room – and a bathroom – before committing to a stay, especially in budget lodgings. Rooms within a single hotel can vary greatly.

➡ Some pricier hotels will require confirmation of a reservation with a credit card. Before doing so, note that some top-end hotels require a 50% to 100% deposit upfront when you reserve. This rule is not always clearly communicated.

➡ In most cases advance reservations can be canceled and refunded with enough notice. Ask the hotel about its cancellation policy before booking. It is often easier to make the reservation than to unmake it.

➡ Many hotels charge a hefty service fee for credit-card use.

➡ Have the hotel fax or email you a confirmation. Hotels often get overbooked, and if you don't have a confirmation, you could be out of a room.

Prices & Accommodations

Rates provided are for the high (dry) season, generally between December to April. Many lodgings lower their prices during the low (rainy) season, from May to November. Prices change quickly and many hotels charge per person rather than per room – read rates carefully and always check ahead. Expect to pay a premium during Christmas, New Year and Easter week (Semana Santa).

US dollars is the preferred currency for listing

> ### SLEEPING PRICE RANGES
>
> The following price ranges refer to a standard double room with bathroom in high season. Unless otherwise stated a combined tourism and sales tax of 13% is included in the price.
>
> **$** less than US$50
>
> **$$** US$50–100
>
> **$$$** more than US$100

---

rates in Costa Rica. However, colones are accepted everywhere and are usually exchanged at current rates without an additional fee. Paying with a credit card sometimes incurs a surcharge.

BUDGET

➡ Budget accommodations in the most popular regions of the country are competitive and need to be booked well in advance during the high season.

➡ The cheapest places generally have shared bathrooms, but it's still possible to get a double with a bathroom for US$25 in towns off the tourist trail.

➡ At the top end of the budget scale, rooms will frequently include a fan and a bathroom with hot water.

➡ Hot water in showers is often supplied by electric showerheads, which will dispense hot water if the pressure is kept low.

➡ Most budget hotels also have a few midrange options with more amenities, including air-con and TV.

➡ Wi-fi is increasingly available at budget accommodations, particularly in popular tourist destinations.

MIDRANGE

➡ Midrange rooms will be more comfortable than budget options, and will generally include a bathroom with gas-heated hot water, a choice between

fans and air-con, and cable or satellite TV.

➡ Most midrange hotels have wi-fi, though it is sometimes limited to the area near reception or the office.

➡ Many midrange places offer tour services, and will have an on-site restaurant or bar and a swimming pool or Jacuzzi.

➡ Hotels in this price range often offer kitchenettes or even full kitchens.

TOP END

➡ Top-end accommodations include many ecolodges, all-inclusive resorts, and business and chain hotels, in addition to a strong network of intimate boutique hotels, remote jungle camps and upmarket B&Bs.

➡ Costa Rica's top-end lodgings adhere to the same standards of quality and service as similarly priced accommodations in North America and Europe.

➡ Staff will likely speak English.

➡ Many top-end lodgings include amenities such as hot-water bath tubs, private decks, satellite TV and air-con, as well as concierge, tour and spa services.

➡ A typical breakfast is usually *gallo pinto* (literally 'spotted rooster'), a stir-fry of rice and beans. This national breakfast dish is usually served with eggs, cheese or *natilla* (sour cream). Tropical-style continental breakfasts are also offered.

Climate

San José

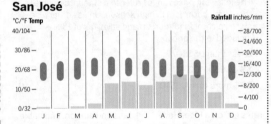

Puerto Limón

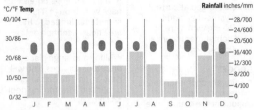

Puntarenas

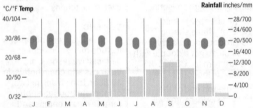

→ **International Student Exchange** (ISE; www.isecard.com; US$25) Discounts on museums and tour fees for full-time students between 12 and 26 years old.

Electricity

Costa Rica uses a power system that is compatible with North American devices. Note that power surges and fluctuation are frequent.

120V/60Hz

120V/60Hz

Customs Regulations

→ All travelers over the age of 18 are allowed to enter the country with 5L of wine or spirits and 500g of processed tobacco (400 cigarettes or 50 cigars).

→ Camera gear, binoculars, and camping, snorkeling and other sporting equipment are readily allowed into the country.

→ Dogs and cats are permitted entry providing they have obtained both general health and rabies vaccination certificates.

→ Pornography and illicit drugs are prohibited.

Discount Cards

Note that discount cards are not universally accepted at museums and parks.

→ **Costa Rica Discount+** (http://costaricadiscount.com; from US$50 for six days) Discounts on car rental, activities and hotels of up to 20%. Cards are valid for six to 60 days. One card is valid for up to eight people and one vehicle. Buy it online and print it.

→ **International Student Identity Card** (ISIC; www.isic.org; around US$25 depending on country of origin) Discounts on museum and tour fees for any full-time student.

Embassies & Consulates

Australia and New Zealand do not have consular representation in Costa Rica; their closest embassies are in Mexico City. Most countries are represented in San José. Mornings are the best time to go to embassies and consulates.

Canadian Embassy (☑2242-4400; www.costarica.gc.ca; Oficentro Ejecutivo La Sabana, 3rd fl, Edificio 5, Sabana Sur; ⊙7:30am-4pm Mon-Thu, to 1pm Fri) Behind La Contraloría.

Dutch Embassy (☑2296-1490; costarica.nlambassade.org; 3rd fl, Oficentro La Sabana, Edificio 3, Sabana Sur; ⊙7:30am-4:30pm Mon-Thu, to 12:30pm Fri)

French Embassy (☑2234-4167; www.ambafrance-cr.org; Curridabat; ⊙7:30am-12:30pm Mon-Fri) On the road to Curridabat, 200m south and 50m west of the Mitsubishi agency.

German Embassy (☑2290-9091; www.san-jose.diplo.de; 8th fl, Edificio Torre Sabana, Sabana Norte; ⊙8am-noon Mon-Fri) Two blocks west of the ICE building.

Guatemalan Embassy (☑2291-6172, 2220-1297; www.minex.gob.gt; Sabana Sur; ⊙9am-1pm Mon-Fri) Situated 100m south and 50m west of Gimnasio Fitsimons.

Honduran Embassy (☑2291-5145, 2232-9506; www.embajadahonduras.co.cr; Blvr Rohrmoser; ⊙9am-noon & 1:30-5pm Mon-Fri)

Israeli Embassy (☑2221-6444; embassies.gov.il; 11th fl, Edificio Colón, Paseo Colón btwn Calles 38 & 40; ⊙9am-noon Mon-Fri)

Italian Embassy (☑2234-2326, 2224-6574; www.ambsanjose.esteri.it; Los Yoses; ⊙9am-noon Mon-Fri) In Los Yoses.

Mexican Embassy (☑2257-0633; embamex.sre.gob.mx/costarica; Av 7 btwn Calles 13 & 15; ⊙9am-6pm Mon-Fri) About 250m south of the Subaru dealership, Los Yoses.

Nicaraguan Embassy (☑2221-2884, 2221-2957; www.cancilleria.gob.ni/embajadas; Av Central 2540 btwn Calles 25 & 27; ⊙9am-5pm Mon-Fri) In Barrio La California.

Panamanian Embassy (☑2281-2442; www.embajadadepanamaencostarica.org; Barrio La Granja; ⊙9am-3pm Mon-Fri) In San Pedro.

Spanish Embassy (☑2222-5745, 2222-1933; www.exteriores.gob.es; Calle 32 btwn Paseo Colón & Av 2; ⊙8am-noon Mon-Fri)

Swiss Embassy (☑2221-4829; www.eda.admin.ch/sanjose; 10th fl, Edificio Centro Colón, Paseo Colón btwn Calles 38 & 40; ⊙8am-4pm Mon-Thu, to noon Fri)

UK Embassy (☑2258-2025; www.gov.uk/government/world/organisations/british-embassy-in-costa-rica; 11th fl, Edificio Centro Colón, Paseo Colón btwn Calles 38 & 40; ⊙8:30am-4:15pm Mon-Thu, to 1pm Fri)

US Embassy (☑2519-2590, 2519-2000; costarica.usembassy.gov; cnr Avenida Central & Calle 120; ⊙8am-noon & 1-4pm Mon-Fri) Opposite Centro Comercial del Oeste in Pavas.

GLBT Travelers

In Costa Rica the situation facing gay and lesbian travelers is better than in most Central American countries and some areas of the country – particularly Quepos and Parque Nacional Manuel Antonio – have been gay vacation destinations for two decades. Homosexual acts are legal, and in 2015 Costa Rica became the first country in Central America to recognize gay relationships. Still, most Costa Ricans are tolerant of homosexuality only at a 'don't ask, don't tell' level. Same-sex couples are unlikely to be the subject of harassment, though public displays of affection might attract unwanted attention.

The undisputed gay and lesbian capital of Costa Rica is Manuel Antonio; while there, look for the gay magazine *Playita*. The monthly newspaper *Gayness* and the magazine *Gente 10* (in Spanish) are both available at gay bars in San José.

➡ **Agua Buena Human Rights Association** (☑2280-3548; www.aguabuena.org) This noteworthy nonprofit organization has campaigned steadily for fairness in medical treatment for people living with HIV/AIDS in Costa Rica.

➡ **Center of Investigation & Promotion of Human Rights in Central America** (CIPAC; ☑2280-7821; www.cipacdh.org) The leading gay activist organization in Costa Rica.

➡ **Toto Tours** (☑800-565-1241, in USA 773-274-8686; www.tototours.com) Gay-travel specialists who organize regular trips to Costa Rica, among other destinations.

Health

Travelers to Central America need to be vigilant about food- and mosquito-borne infections. Most of these illnesses are not life-threatening, but they can certainly ruin your trip.

PRACTICALITIES

Newspapers

➜ **La Nación** (www.nacion.com) General purpose daily newspaper.

➜ **La Prensa Libre** (www.laprensalibre.cr) Oldest continually published daily newspaper in Costa Rica.

➜ **The Tico Times** (www.ticotimes.net) Costa Rica's biggest English-language newspaper is high quality, though news and views are often geared toward the expat community.

➜ **Costa Rican Times** (www.costaricantimes.com) This online, English-language newcomer focuses on Costa Rica happenings but also features international news.

➜ **DVDs** In Costa Rica DVDs are region 4.

Weights & Measures

Costa Ricans use the metric system for weights, distances and measures.

Besides getting the proper vaccinations, it's important to use a good insect repellent and exercise care in what you eat and drink.

Before You Go
HEALTH INSURANCE

Should you wish to take part in high-risk adventure activities or water sports such as diving, make sure you pay for the appropriate level of insurance coverage. Some insurance companies may cover basic activities, such as hiking, but not zip lining or surfing; if diving, some companies may only cover you up to a certain depth. If in doubt, check with your insurance company before setting off on your trip.

A list of medical evacuation and travel insurance companies can be found on the **US State Department** (www.travel.state.gov) website under the 'Before You Go' tab.

VACCINATIONS

➜ Get necessary vaccinations four to eight weeks before departure.

➜ Ask your doctor for an International Certificate of Vaccination (otherwise known as the 'yellow booklet'), which will list all the vaccinations you've received. This is mandatory for countries that require proof of yellow-fever vaccination upon entry. (Costa Rica only requires such proof if you are entering from a country that carries a risk of yellow fever.)

In Costa Rica
AVAILABILITY & COST OF HEALTH CARE

➜ Good medical care is available in most major cities but may be limited in rural areas.

➜ For an extensive list of physicians, dentists and hospitals visit http://costarica.usembassy.gov and look under 'U.S. Citizen Services/Lawyers and Doctors/Medical Practitioners List.'

➜ Most pharmacies are well supplied and a handful are open 24 hours. Pharmacists are licensed to prescribe medication. If you're taking any medication on a regular basis, make sure you know its generic (scientific) name, since many pharmaceuticals go under different names in Costa Rica.

ENVIRONMENTAL HAZARDS

➜ **Animal bites** Do not attempt to pet, handle or feed any animal. Any bite or scratch by a mammal, including bats, should be promptly and thoroughly cleansed with large amounts of soap and water, and an antiseptic such as iodine or alcohol should be applied. Contact a local health authority in the event of such an injury.

➜ **Insect bites** No matter how much you safeguard yourself, getting bitten by mosquitoes is part of every traveler's experience here. The best prevention is to stay covered up – wear long pants, long sleeves, a hat, and shoes, not sandals. Invest in a good insect repellent, preferably one containing DEET. Apply to exposed skin and clothing (but not to eyes, mouth, cuts, wounds or irritated skin). Compounds containing DEET should not be used on children under the age of two and should be used sparingly on children under 12. Invest in a bug net to hang over beds (along with a few thumbtacks or nails with which to hang it). Many hotels in Costa Rica don't have windows (or screens), and a cheap little net will save you plenty of nighttime aggravation. The mesh size should be less than 1.5mm. Dusk is the worst time for mosquitoes, so take extra precautions.

➜ **Sun** Stay out of the midday sun, wear sunglasses and a wide-brimmed hat, and apply sunblock with SPF 15 or higher, with both UVA and UVB protection. Drink plenty of fluids and avoid strenuous exercise when the temperature is high.

INFECTIOUS DISEASES

➜ **Dengue fever (breakbone fever)** Dengue is transmitted by *Aedes aegypti* mosquitoes, which often bite during the daytime and are usually found close to human habitations, often indoors. Dengue is especially common in densely populated urban environments. It usually causes flu-like symptoms including fever, muscle aches, joint pains, headaches, nausea and vomiting, often followed by a rash. Most cases resolve uneventfully in a few days. There is no treatment for dengue fever except taking analgesics such as acetaminophen/ paracetamol (Tylenol) and drinking plenty of fluids. Severe cases may require hospitalization for intravenous fluids and supportive care. There is no vaccine. The key to prevention is taking insect-protection measures.

➡ **Hepatitis A** The second most common travel-related infection (after traveler's diarrhea). It's a viral infection of the liver that is usually acquired by ingestion of contaminated water, food or ice, though it may also be acquired by direct contact with infected persons. Symptoms may include fever, malaise, jaundice, nausea, vomiting and abdominal pain. Most cases resolve without complications, though hepatitis A occasionally causes severe liver damage. There is no treatment. The vaccine for hepatitis A is extremely safe and highly effective.

➡ **Leishmaniasis** This is transmitted by sand flies. Most cases occur in newly cleared forest or areas of secondary growth; the highest incidence is in Talamanca. It causes slow-growing ulcers over exposed parts of the body. There is no vaccine. To protect yourself from sand flies, follow the same precautions as for mosquitoes.

➡ **Malaria** Malaria is very rare in Costa Rica, occurring only occasionally in rural parts of Limón Province. It's transmitted by mosquito bites, usually between dusk and dawn. Taking malaria pills is not necessary unless you are making a long stay in the province of Limón (not Puerto Limón). Protection against mosquito bites is most effective.

➡ **Traveler's diarrhea** Tap water is safe and of high quality in Costa Rica, but when you're far off the beaten path it's best to avoid tap water unless it has been boiled, filtered or chemically disinfected (with iodine tablets). To prevent diarrhea, be wary of dairy products that might contain unpasteurized milk and be highly selective when eating food from street vendors. If you develop diarrhea, be sure to drink plenty of fluids, preferably with an oral rehydration solution containing lots of salt and sugar. If diarrhea is bloody or persists for more than 72 hours, or is accompanied by fever, shaking chills or severe abdominal pain, seek medical attention.

➡ **Typhoid** Caused by ingestion of food or water contaminated by a species of salmonella known as *Salmonella typhi*. Fever occurs in virtually all cases. Other symptoms may include headache, malaise, muscle aches, dizziness, loss of appetite, nausea and abdominal pain. Possible complications include intestinal perforation, intestinal bleeding, confusion, delirium or (rarely) coma. A pretrip vaccination is recommended.

➡ **Zika virus** At the time of research, pregnant women are advised against traveling to Costa Rica, as the virus may be linked to microcephaly, a birth defect that affects a baby's brain development. Zika is primarily transmitted by mosquitoes, but it can also be transmitted by a man to his sex partner or by a woman to her fetus. Be aware that symptoms are usually mild in adults, and many people may not realize that they are infected.

TAP WATER

➡ It's generally safe to drink tap water in Costa Rica, except in the most rural and undeveloped parts of the country. However, if you prefer to be cautious, buying bottled water is your best bet.

➡ If you have the means, vigorous boiling for one minute is the most effective means of water purification. At altitudes greater than 2000m, boil for three minutes.

➡ Another option is to disinfect water with iodine pills: add 2% tincture of iodine to 1L of water (five drops to clear water, 10 drops to cloudy water) and let stand for 30 minutes. If the water is cold, longer times may be required.

➡ Alternatively, carry a SteriPen that destroys most bacteria, viruses and protozoa with UV light.

Insurance

It is vital that travelers purchase the right type of travel insurance before coming to Costa Rica. Basic insurance tends to cover medical expenses, baggage loss, trip cancelation, accidents and personal liability, but it's worth spending extra to make sure you're covered in the event of natural disasters. If you intend to take part in adventure sports, make sure that those particular sports are covered by your policy; for divers, some policies only cover you up to a certain depth.

Worldwide travel insurance is available at www.lonelyplanet.com/travel-insurance. You can buy, extend and claim online anytime – even if you're already on the road.

Internet Access

➜ The number of internet cafes in Costa Rica has greatly decreased with the advent of smartphones and wi-fi in restaurants and cafes.

➜ Expect to pay US$1 to US$2 per hour in San José and tourist towns.

➜ Wi-fi is common in all midrange and top-end hotels, and in the vast majority of budget hotels and hostels. Some hostels still have computers for guest use and/or wi-fi.

Language Courses

➜ Spanish-language schools operate all over Costa Rica and charge by the hour for instruction.

➜ Many courses can be found in central San José and the suburb of San Pedro, and the Central Valley.

➜ It is best to arrange classes in advance. A good clearinghouse is the **Institute for Spanish Language Studies** (ISLS; ☑ in USA 866-391-0394, in USA 505-404-0736; www.isls.com), which has eight schools in Costa Rica.

Legal Matters

➜ If you are arrested your embassy can offer limited assistance. Embassy officials will not bail you out and you are subject to Costa Rican laws, not the laws of your own country.

➜ The use of recreational substances, other than tobacco and alcohol, is illegal in Costa Rica and punishable by imprisonment.

➜ In Costa Rica the legal age for driving and voting is 18 years.

➜ Keep in mind that travelers may be subject to the laws of their own country in regard to sexual relations.

Maps

Unfortunately, detailed maps are hard to come by in Costa Rica, so it's best to purchase one online before your trip.

➜ The excellent, water-resistant 1:350,000 *Costa Rica Adventure Map* published by National Geographic also has an inset map of San José. Available online or in various book and gift shops in San José.

➜ Another quality option is the 1:330,000 Costa

Rica sheet produced by International Travel Map, which is waterproof and includes a San José inset.

➜ The **Fundación Neotrópica** (☑2253-2130; www.neotropica.org) publishes a 1:500,000 map showing national parks and other protected areas; available online and in San José bookstores.

➜ The ICT (Instituto Costarricense de Turismo) publishes a 1:700,000 Costa Rica map with a 1:12,500 Central San José map on the reverse; it's free at the ICT office in San José.

➜ **Maptak** (www.maptak. com) has maps of Costa Rica's seven provinces and their capitals.

➜ Few national-park offices or ranger stations have maps for hikers. Topographical maps are available for purchase from **Instituto Geográfico Nacional** (IGN; ☑2257-7798; Calle 9 btwn Avs 20 & 22, San José; ☺7:30am-noon & 1-3pm Mon-Fri).

➜ The *Mapa-Guía de la Naturaleza Costa Rica* is an atlas no longer published by Incafo that included 1:200,000 topographical sheets, as well as English and Spanish descriptions of Costa Rica's natural areas. Out-of-print used copies can be purchased online.

Money

ATMs

ATMs are ubiquitous, typically dispensing colones or US dollars. They are not easily found in rural and remote areas.

Bargaining

➜ A high standard of living along with a steady stream of international tourist traffic means that the Latin American tradition of haggling is uncommon in Costa Rica.

➡ Do not try to bargain for hotel room rates as this is very uncommon.

➡ Negotiating prices at outdoor markets is acceptable, and bargaining is accepted when hiring long-distance taxis.

Cash & Currency

➡ The Costa Rican currency is the colón (plural colones), named after Cristóbal Colón (Christopher Columbus).

➡ Bills come in 1000, 2000, 5000, 10,000, 20,000 and 50,000 notes, while coins come in denominations of five, 10, 20, 25, 50, 100 and 500.

➡ Paying for things in US dollars is common, and at times is encouraged, since the currency is viewed as being more stable than colones.

➡ In US-dollar transactions the change will usually be given in colones.

➡ Newer US dollars (ie big heads) are preferred throughout Costa Rica.

➡ When paying in US dollars at a local restaurant, bar or shop the exchange rate can be unfavorable.

Credit Cards

➡ Cards are widely accepted at midrange and top-end hotels, as well as at top-end restaurants and some travel agencies; they are less likely to be accepted in small towns and remote areas.

➡ A transaction fee (around 3% to 5%) on all international credit-card purchases is often added.

➡ Holders of credit and debit cards can buy colones in some banks, though expect to pay a high transaction fee.

➡ All car-rental agencies require drivers to have a credit card. It's possible to hire a car with just a debit card, but only on the condition that you pay for full insurance.

Exchanging Money

All banks will exchange US dollars, and some will exchange euros and British pounds; other currencies are more difficult. Most banks have excruciatingly long lines, especially at the state-run institutions (Banco Nacional, Banco de Costa Rica, Banco Popular), though they don't charge commission on cash exchanges. Private banks (Banex, Banco Interfin, Scotiabank) tend to be faster. Make sure the bills you want to exchange are in good condition or they may be refused.

Taxes

Travelers will notice a 13% sales tax at hotels and restaurants, although many smaller budget and midrange businesses waive the tax (shhh) if you pay in cash.

Tipping

➡ **Restaurants** Your bill at many restaurants will usually include a 10% service charge. If not, you might leave a small tip to show your appreciation, but it is not required.

➡ **Hotels** It is customary to tip the bellhop/porter (US$1 to US$5 per service) and the housekeeper (US$1 to US$2 per day) in top-end hotels, less in budget places.

➡ **Taxis** Taxi drivers are not usually tipped unless some special service is provided.

➡ **Guides** On guided tours, tip the guide US$5 to US$15 per person per day. Tip the tour driver about half of what you tip the guide. Naturally, tips depend upon quality of service.

Traveler's Checks

With the popularity of ATMs and credit cards, traveler's checks are increasingly uncommon in Costa Rica and difficult to exchange outside big cities. They can be exchanged at banks, typically only for US dollars or Costa Rican colones.

Opening Hours

Opening hours vary throughout the year. The following are high-season opening hours; hours will generally decrease in the shoulder and low seasons. Unless otherwise stated, count on sights, activities and restaurants to be open daily.

➡ **Banks** 9am to 4pm Monday to Friday, sometimes 9am to noon Saturday.

➡ **Bars & clubs** 8pm to 2am.

➡ **Government offices** 8am and 5pm Monday to Friday. Often closed between 11:30am and 1:30pm.

➡ **Restaurants** 7am to 9pm. Upscale places may open only for dinner. In remote areas, even the small *sodas* (inexpensive eateries) might open only at specific meal times.

➡ **Shops** 8am to 6pm Monday to Saturday.

Photography

➡ Always ask permission to take someone's photo.

➡ With the prominence of digital cameras, it is increasingly difficult to purchase high-quality film in Costa Rica.

Post

➡ Mailing smaller parcels (less than 2kg) internationally is quite reliable; for example, a 1kg package costs around US$30 to ship to North America and takes one to two weeks to arrive.

➡ EMS (Express Mail Service) courier service costs a bit more but includes tracking and is speedier.

Public Holidays

Días feriados (national holidays) are taken seriously in Costa Rica. Banks, public offices and many stores close. During these times, public transport is tight and hotels are heavily booked. Many festivals coincide with public holidays.

➡ **New Year's Day** January 1

➡ **Semana Santa** (Holy Week; March or April) The Thursday and Friday before Easter Sunday is the official holiday, though most businesses shut down for the whole week. From Thursday to Sunday bars are closed and alcohol sales are prohibited; on Thursday and Friday buses stop running.

➡ **Día de Juan Santamaría** (April 11) Honors the national hero who died fighting William Walker in 1856; major events are held in Alajuela, his hometown.

➡ **Labor Day** May 1

➡ **Día de la Madre** (Mother's Day; August 15) Coincides with the annual Catholic Feast of the Assumption.

➡ **Independence Day** September 15

➡ **Día de la Raza** (Columbus Day; October 12)

➡ **Christmas Day** (December 25) Christmas Eve is also an unofficial holiday.

➡ **Last week in December** The week between Christmas and New Year is an unofficial holiday; businesses close and beach hotels are crowded.

Safe Travel

Costa Rica is a largely safe country but petty crime (bag snatchings, car break-ins etc) is common and muggings do occur, so it's important to be vigilant. Many of Costa Rica's dangers are nature-related: riptides, earthquakes and volcanic eruptions are among them. Predatory and venomous wildlife can also pose a threat, so a wildlife guide is essential if trekking in the jungle.

Earthquakes & Volcanic Eruptions

Costa Rica lies on the edge of active tectonic plates, so it is decidedly earthquake-prone. Recent major quakes occurred in 1990 (7.1 on the Richter scale), 1991 (7.4) and 2012 (7.6). Smaller quakes and tremors happen quite often – particularly on the Península de Nicoya – cracking roads and knocking down telephone lines.

The volcanoes in Costa Rica are not really dangerous, though, as long as you stay on designated trails and don't try to peer into the crater of an active volcano. As a precaution, always check with park rangers before setting out in the vicinity of active volcanoes.

Hiking Hazards

Hikers setting out into the wilderness should be adequately prepared for their trips.

➡ Know your limits and don't set out to do a hike you can't reasonably complete.

➡ Carry plenty of water, even on very short trips.

➡ Carry maps, extra food and a compass.

➡ Let someone know where you are going, so they can narrow the search area in the event of an emergency.

➡ Be aware that Costa Rica's wildlife can pose a threat to hikers, particularly in Parque Nacional Corcovado.

Riptides

Each year Costa Rican waters see approximately 200 drownings, 90% of which are caused by riptides (strong currents that pull the swimmer out to sea). Many deaths in riptides are caused by pan-

---

GOVERNMENT TRAVEL ADVICE

The following government websites offer travel advisories and information on Costa Rica.

Australian Department of Foreign Affairs (www.smarttraveller.gov.au)

Canadian Department of Foreign Affairs (www.dfait-maeci.gc.ca)

US State Department (www.travel.state.gov)

UK Foreign & Commonwealth Office (www.fco.gov.uk)

Exit the baggage claim at the international airport in San José and you'll be welcomed by a sign that reads 'In Costa Rica sex with children under 18 is a serious crime. Should you engage in it we will drive you to jail.' For decades, travelers have arrived in Costa Rica in search of sandy beaches and lush mountainscapes; unfortunately, an unknown percentage of them also come in search of sex – not all of it legal.

Prostitution by men and women over the age of 18 is legal. But the tourist juggernaut of the last few decades has fueled illicit activities at its fringes – namely child prostitution and, to a lesser degree, human trafficking. Sex with a minor in Costa Rica is illegal, carrying a penalty of up to 10 years in jail, but child prostitution has nonetheless flourished. In fact, a number of aid groups, along with the country's national child-welfare agency (Patronato Nacional de la Infancia; PANI), estimate that there may be over 3000 child prostitutes in San José alone. In turn, this has led to women and children being trafficked for the purpose of sexual exploitation, as documented in a 2008 report issued by the US Department of State.

Alarm over the problem has increased steadily since 1999, when the UN Committee on Human Rights issued a statement saying that it was 'deeply concerned' about child-sex tourism in Costa Rica. Since then, the government has established national task forces to combat the problem, trained the police force in how to deal with issues of child exploitation and formed a coalition against human trafficking. But enforcement remains weak – largely due to lack of personnel and lack of funding. Meanwhile the USA – the principal source of sex tourists to Costa Rica – has made it a prosecutable crime for Americans to have sex with minors anywhere in the world.

Along with Thailand and Cambodia, Costa Rica is one of the most notorious sex-tourism destinations in the world, according to Ecpat International, a nonprofit dedicated to ending child prostitution. The phenomenon has been magnified by the internet: entire sex-tourism websites chronicle – in detail – where and how to find sex. In all of these, Costa Rica figures prominently.

Various organizations fight the sexual exploitation of children in Costa Rica. See the websites of **Ecpat International** (www.ecpat.org) and **Cybertipline** (www.cybertipline.com) to learn more about the problem or to report any incidents you encounter.

icked swimmers struggling to the point of exhaustion. If you are caught in a riptide, do not struggle. Simply float and let the tide carry you out beyond the breakers, after which the riptide will dissipate, then swim parallel to the beach and allow the surf to carry you back in.

Theft

The biggest danger that most travelers face is theft, primarily from pickpockets, but also when personal possessions are left in parked cars. There is a lot of petty crime in Costa Rica, so keep your wits about you at all times.

Telephone

➡ Mobile service now covers most of the country and nearly all of the country that is accessible to tourists.

➡ Public phones are found all over Costa Rica, and chip or Colibrí phonecards are available in 1000-, 2000- and 3000-colón denominations.

➡ Chip cards are inserted into the phone and scanned. Colibrí cards (more common) require you to dial a toll-free number (☑199) and enter an access code. Instructions are provided in English or Spanish.

➡ The cheapest international calls from Costa Rica are direct-dialed using a phonecard. To make international calls, dial '☑00' followed by the country code and number.

➡ Pay phones cannot receive international calls.

➡ To call Costa Rica from abroad, use the country code (☑506) before the eight-digit number.

➡ Due to the widespread popularity of voice-over IP services such as Skype, and more reliable ethernet connections, traveling with a smartphone or tablet can be the cheapest and easiest way to call internationally.

Time

Costa Rica is six hours behind GMT, so Costa Rican time is equivalent to Central Time in North America. There is no daylight-saving time.

Toilets

➡ Public restrooms are rare, but most restaurants and cafes will let you use their facilities, sometimes for a small charge – never more than 500 colones.

⇒ Bus terminals and other major public buildings usually have toilets, also at a charge.

⇒ Don't flush your toilet paper. Costa Rican plumbing is often poor and has very low pressure.

⇒ Dispose of toilet paper in the rubbish bin inside the bathroom.

Tourist Information

⇒ The government-run tourism board, the **ICT** (ICT; Map p70; ☎2222-1090, in USA & Canada 866-267-8274; www.visitcostarica.com; Edificio de las Academias, Av Central btwn Calles 1 & 3; ⊕8am-5pm Mon-Fri), has an office in the capital; English is spoken.

⇒ The ICT can provide you with free maps, a master bus schedule, information on road conditions in the hinterlands, and a helpful brochure with up-to-date emergency numbers for every region.

⇒ Consult the ICT's English-language website for information.

⇒ From the USA call the ICT's toll-free number for brochures and information.

Travelers with Disabilities

Independent travel in Costa Rica is difficult for anyone with mobility constraints. Although Costa Rica has an equal-opportunity law, the law applies only to new or newly remodeled business-es and is loosely enforced. Therefore, very few hotels and restaurants have features specifically suited to wheelchair use. Many don't have ramps, and room or bathroom doors are rarely wide enough to accommodate a wheelchair.

Streets and sidewalks are potholed and poorly paved, making wheelchair use

frustrating at best. Public buses don't have provisions to carry wheelchairs, and most national parks and outdoor tourist attractions don't have trails suited to wheelchair use. Notable exceptions include **Parque Nacional Volcán Poás** (☎2482-1226; admission US$15; ⊕8am-3:30pm), **INBioparque** (☎2507-8107; www.inbioparque.com/en; Santo Domingo; adult/student/child US$25/19/15, serpentarium admission adult/child US$3/2; ⊕9am-3pm Fri, 9am-4pm Sat & Sun) ⌨ and the **Rainforest Aerial Tram** (☎2257-5961, in USA 1-866-759-8726; www.rainforestadventure.com; adult/student & child tram US$60/30, zip line US$50/35).

Download Lonely Planet's free Accessible Travel guide from http://lptravel.to/AccessibleTravel.

Visas

Passport-carrying nationals of the following countries are allowed 90 days' stay with no visa: Argentina, Australia, Canada, Chile, Iceland, Ireland, Israel, Japan, Mexico, New Zealand, Panama, South Africa, the US and most Western European countries.

Most other visitors require a visa from a Costa Rican embassy or consulate.

For the latest info on visas, check the websites of the **ICT** (ICT; Map p70; ☎2222-1090, in USA & Canada 866-267-8274; www.visitcostarica.com; Edificio de las Academias, Av Central btwn Calles 1 & 3; ⊕8am-5pm Mon-Fri) or the **Costa Rican Embassy** (www.costarica-embassy.org).

Extensions

⇒ Extending your stay beyond the authorized 30 or 90 days is time-consuming; it's easier to leave the country for 72 hours and then re-enter.

⇒ Extensions can be handled by the **migración** (Immigration; ☎2220-0355; ⊕8am-4pm) in San José,

opposite Channel 6, about 4km north of Parque La Sabana.

⇒ Requirements for extensions change, so allow several working days.

Volunteering

Costa Rica offers a huge number of volunteer opportunities. Word of mouth is a powerful influence on future volunteers, so a majority of programs in Costa Rica are very conscientious about pleasing their volunteers. Almost all placements require a commitment of two weeks or more.

Teaching English

Amerispan Study Abroad (www.amerispan.com) Offers a variety of educational travel programs in specialized areas.

Sustainable Horizon (www.sustainablehorizon.com) Arranges volunteering trips such as guest-teaching spots.

Forestry Management

Cloudbridge Nature Reserve (www.cloudbridge.org) Trail building, construction, tree planting and projects monitoring the recovery of the cloud forest are offered to volunteers, who pay for their own housing with a local family. Preference is given to biology students, but all enthusiastic volunteers can apply.

Tropical Science Center (www.cct.or.cr) This long-standing NGO offers volunteer placement at Reserva Biológica Bosque Nuboso Monteverde. Projects can include trail maintenance and conservation work.

Fundación Corcovado (www.corcovadofoundation.org) An impressive network of people and organizations committed to preserving Parque Nacional Corcovado.

Monteverde Institute (www.monteverde-institute.org) A nonprofit educational institute offering training in tropical biology, conservation and sustainable development.

Organic Farming

WWOOF Costa Rica (www.wwoofcostarica.org) This loose network of farms is part of the large international network of Willing Workers on Organic Farms (WWOOF). Placements are incredibly varied. WWOOF Mexico, Costa Rica, Guatemala and Belize have a joint US$33 membership, which gives potential volunteers access to all placement listings.

Reserva Biológica Dúrika (www.durika.org) A sustainable community on an 8500-hectare biological reserve.

Finca La Flor de Paraíso (www.la-flor.org) Offers programs in a variety of disciplines from animal husbandry to medicinal-herb cultivation.

Punta Mona (www.puntamona.org) An organic farm and retreat center that is centered on organic permaculture and sustainable living.

Rancho Margot (www.rancho margot.com) This self-proclaimed life-skills university offers a natural education emphasizing organic farming and animal husbandry.

Wildlife Conservation

Be aware that conservationists in Costa Rica occasionally face harassment or worse from local poachers and that police are pretty ineffectual in following up incidents.

Earthwatch (www.earthwatch.org) This broadly recognized international volunteer organization works in sea-turtle conservation in Costa Rica.

Sea Turtle Conservancy (www.conserveturtles.org) From March to October, this Puerto Limón organization hosts 'eco-volunteer adventures' working with sea turtles and birds.

Profelis (www.grafischer.com/profelis) A feline conservation program that takes care of confiscated wild cats, both big and small.

Reserva Playa Tortuga (www.reservaplayatortuga.org) Assist with olive ridley turtle conservation efforts near Ojochal.

Women Travelers

Most female travelers experience little more than a *'mi amor'* ('my love') or an appreciative hiss from the local men. But, in general, Costa Rican men consider foreign women to have looser morals and to be easier conquests than Ticas (female Costa Ricans). Men will often make flirtatious comments to single women, particularly blondes, and women traveling together are not exempt. The best response is to do what Ticas do: ignore it entirely. Women who firmly resist unwanted verbal advances from men are normally treated with respect.

➡ In small highland towns, dress is usually conservative. Women rarely wear shorts, but belly-baring tops are all the rage. On the beach, skimpy bathing suits are OK, but topless and nude bathing are not.

➡ Solo women travelers should avoid hitchhiking.

➡ Do not take unlicensed 'pirate' taxis (licensed taxis are red and have medallions) as there have been reports of assaults on women by unlicensed drivers.

➡ Birth-control pills are available at most pharmacies without a prescription.

➡ Sanitary products can be found at any pharmacy.

Work

It is difficult for foreigners to find work in Costa Rica. The only foreigners legally employed in Costa Rica are those who work for their own businesses, possess skills not found in the country, or work for companies that have special agreements with the government.

Getting a bona fide job necessitates obtaining a work permit, which can be a time-consuming and difficult process. The most likely source of paid employment is as an English teacher at one of the language institutes, or working in the hospitality industry in a hotel or resort. Naturalists or river guides may also be able to find work with either private lodges or adventure-travel operators, though you shouldn't expect to make more than survival wages.

Transportation

GETTING THERE & AWAY

Costa Rica can be reached via freqent, direct international flights from the US, Canada and other Central American countries. You can also cross a land border into Costa Rica from Panama or Nicaragua. Flights, cars and tours can be booked online at lonelyplanet.com/bookings.

Entering the Country

➡ Entering Costa Rica is mostly free of hassle, with the exception of some long queues at the airport.

➡ The vast majority of travelers enter the country by plane, and most international flights arrive at Aeropuerto Internacional Juan Santamaría, outside San José.

➡ Liberia is a growing destination for international flights; it is in the Guanacaste Province and serves travelers heading to the Península de Nicoya.

➡ Overland border crossings are straightforward and travelers can move freely between Panama to the south and Nicaragua to the north.

➡ Some foreign nationals will require a visa. Be aware that you cannot get a visa at the border.

Passports

➡ Citizens of all nations are required to have a passport that is valid for at least six months beyond the dates of their trip.

➡ The law requires that you carry your passport at all times; if you're driving, you must have your passport handy, but otherwise the law is seldom enforced.

Onward Ticket

➡ Officially, travelers are required to have a ticket out of Costa Rica before they are allowed to enter. This is rarely and erratically enforced.

➡ Those arriving overland with no onward ticket can purchase one from international bus companies in Managua (Nicaragua) and Panama City (Panama).

Air

Costa Rica is well connected by air to other Central and South American countries, as well as the USA.

Airports & Airlines

➡ **Aeropuerto Internacional Juan Santamaría** (☎2437-2400; fly2sanjose.com) International flights arrive here, 17km northwest of San José, in the town of Alajuela.

➡ **Aeropuerto Internacional Daniel Oduber Quirós** (LIR; www.liberiacostaricaairport. net) This airport in Liberia also receives international flights from the USA, the Americas and Canada. It serves a number of American

---

CLIMATE CHANGE & TRAVEL

Every form of transport that relies on carbon-based fuel generates CO_2, the main cause of human-induced climate change. Modern travel is dependent on airplanes, which might use less fuel per kilometer per person than most cars but travel much greater distances. The altitude at which aircraft emit gases (including CO_2) and particles also contributes to their climate change impact. Many websites offer 'carbon calculators' that allow people to estimate the carbon emissions generated by their journey and, for those who wish to do so, to offset the impact of the greenhouse gases emitted with contributions to port-folios of climate-friendly initiatives throughout the world. Lonely Planet offsets the carbon footprint of all staff and author travel.

and Canadian airlines and some charters from London, as well as regional flights from Panama and Nicaragua.

➡ **Avianca** (part of the Central American airline consortium Grupo TACA; www.avianca.com) The national airline flies to the USA and Latin America, including Cuba.

➡ The US Federal Aviation Administration has assessed Costa Rica's aviation authorities to be in compliance with international safety standards.

Tickets

Airline fares are usually more expensive during the Costa Rican high season (from December through April); December and January are the most expensive months to travel.

TO/FROM CENTRAL AMERICA

➡ **American Airlines** (www. aa.com), **Delta** (www.delta. com), **United** (www.united. com) and **US Airways** (www.usairways.com) have connections to Costa Rica from many Central and Latin American countries. Grupo TACA usually offers the most flights on these routes.

➡ **Nature Air** (www. natureair.com) flies from Liberia to Managua (Nicaragua). Note that rates vary considerably according to season and availability.

➡ Grupo TACA offers daily direct flights to Caracas (Venezuela), Guatemala City (Guatemala) and San Salvador (El Salvador). TACA and Mexicana have daily flights to Mexico City, while both TACA and COPA have several flights a day to Panama City. Rates vary considerably according to season and availability.

TO/FROM OTHER COUNTRIES

➡ Flights from Houston, Miami or New York are most common.

➡ From Canada, most travelers to Costa Rica connect through US gateway cities, though Air Canada has direct flights from Toronto.

➡ From the UK, Costa Rica is served by British Airways and Virgin, typically with at least one stop.

➡ Flights from the UK and Europe connect either in the USA, Mexico City or Toronto. High-season fares may still apply during the northern summer, even though this is the beginning of the Costa Rican rainy season.

➡ From Australia and New Zealand, travel routes usually go through the USA or Mexico. Fares are highest in June and July, even though this is the beginning of the rainy season in Costa Rica.

Land
Border Crossings

Costa Rica shares land borders with Nicaragua and Panama. There is no fee for travelers to enter Costa Rica; however, there have been several reports of towns recently adding their own entry and exit fees, usually US$1.

NICARAGUA

There is a brand new border crossing at **Los Chiles–Las Tablillas**, thanks to the new bridge that crosses the Río San Juan just north of the Nicaraguan border.

➡ The Los Chiles–Las Tablillas border crossing is open from 8am to 4pm daily.

➡ Hourly buses connect Los Chiles and Las Tablillas (US$1, 15 minutes). There are also direct buses from San José and Ciudad Quesada (San Carlos).

➡ A Costa Rica land exit fee of US$7 is payable at immigration by credit or debit card only (no cash).

➡ After walking across the border, you'll go through Nicaraguan immigration. The entrance fee is US$12, payable in US dollars or cordobas.

➡ After exiting immigration, you can catch a boat up the river or hop on a bus or a *collectivo* (shared transport) to San Carlos (US$2.20, 30 minutes).

➡ If you are entering Costa Rica from Nicaragua, you can take an hourly bus to Los Chiles or Ciudad Quesada, or catch the direct bus to San José, which departs at 2:30pm.

➡ It's also still possible to cross this border by boat, which is a slower but more pleasant way of doing it. There is only one round trip per day (US$10 to US$12, departing Los Chiles 1pm or when there's sufficient demand). You'll avoid the Costa Rica land exit fee, but you'll still have to pay US$12 to enter Nicaragua.

Situated on the Interamericana, **Sapoá–Peñas Blancas** is the most heavily trafficked border station between Nicaragua and Costa Rica.

➡ The Sapoá–Peñas Blancas border crossing is open from 6am to 10pm Monday to Saturday, and until 8pm Sunday.

➡ This is the only official border between Nicaragua and Costa Rica that you can drive across.

➡ Waiting times at this border can be several hours. Plan on at least an hour's wait.

➡ **Tica Bus** (☎ in Managua 222-6094, in Panama City 262 2084), **Nica Bus** (☎ in Managua 228-1374) and **TransNica** (Map p66; ☎ 2223-4242; www.transnica.com; Calle 22 btwn Avs 3 & 5) all have daily buses that serve points north and south. Regular buses depart Peñas Blancas, on the Costa Rican side, for La Cruz, Liberia and San José.

➡ Note that Peñas Blancas is only a border post, not a town, so there is nowhere to stay.

PANAMA
Note that Panama is GMT minus five hours, one hour ahead of Costa Rica.

At the time of writing, entry to Panama required proof of US$500 (per person), proof of onward travel from Panama and two photocopies of your passport. Travelers have reported being turned away from Panamanian border crossings even with onward bus tickets, so our tip is to reserve an airline ticket online (for a flight originating in Panama), print the itinerary, and let the reservation expire without actually booking it.

The Carretera Interamericana (Pan-American Hwy) at **Paso Canoas** is by far the most frequently used entry and exit point with Panama, and is open 6am to 10pm Monday to Friday, and to 8pm on weekends.

➡ The border crossing in either direction is generally straightforward, if slow.

➡ Get an exit stamp from Costa Rica at the immigration office before entering Panama; do the same on the Panamanian side when entering Costa Rica.

➡ There is no charge for entering Costa Rica. Entry to Panama costs US$1.

➡ Northbound buses usually stop running at 6pm. Travelers without a private vehicle should arrive during the day.

➡ Those with a private vehicle are likely to encounter long lines.

➡ Tica Bus travels from Panama City to San José (US$42 to US$58, 15 hours) daily and crosses this border post. In David, Tracopa has one bus daily from the main terminal to San José (nine hours). In David you'll also find frequent buses to the border at Paso Canoas (US$2.60, 1½ hours) that leave every 10 minutes from 4am to 8pm.

Situated on the Caribbean coast, **Guabito–Sixaola** is a fairly tranquil and hassle-free border crossing.

➡ If you are coming from Bocas del Toro, you first have to take the frequent boat to Almirante (US$2), then a public bus or shuttle to Changuinola (40 minutes), from where you can take a quick taxi to the border or to the bus station (US$5).

➡ One daily bus travels between Changuinola and San José at 10am (US$16, eight hours). Otherwise, you can walk over the border and catch one of the hourly buses that go up the coast from Sixaola.

Río Sereno–San Vito is a rarely used crossing in the Cordillera de Talamanca. The border is open 8am to 4pm on the Costa Rican side and 9am to 5pm on the Panamanian side. The small village of Río Sereno on the Panamanian side has a hotel and a place to eat; there are no facilities on the Costa Rican side.

➡ Regular buses depart Concepción and David in Panama for Río Sereno. Local buses (US$1.60, 40 minutes, 11 daily) and taxis (US$30) go from the border to San Vito.

➡ For travelers departing Costa Rica, there is a US$7 exit tax, payable at a kiosk at the border crossing.

Bus
➡ If crossing a border by bus, note that international buses may cost slightly more than taking a local bus to the border, then another local bus onward from the border, but they're worth it. These companies are familiar with border procedures and will tell you what's needed to cross efficiently.

➡ There will be no problems crossing borders provided your papers are in order. If you are on an international bus, you'll have to exit the bus and proceed through both border stations. Bus drivers will wait for everyone to be processed before heading on.

➡ If you choose to take local buses, it's advisable to get to border stations early in the day to allow time for waiting in line and processing. Note that onward buses tend to wind down by the afternoon.

➡ International buses go from San José to Changuinola (Bocas del Toro), David and Panama City in Panama; Guatemala City in Guatemala; Managua in Nicaragua; San Salvador in El Salvador; and Tegucigalpa in Honduras.

Car & Motorcycle
The cost of insurance, fuel and border permits makes a car journey significantly more expensive than buying an airline ticket. To enter Costa Rica by car, you'll need the following items:

→ valid registration and proof of ownership

→ valid driver's license or International Driving Permit

→ valid license plates

→ recent inspection certificate

→ passport

→ multiple photocopies of all these documents in case the originals get lost.

Before departing, check that the following elements are present and in working order:

→ blinkers and head- and taillights

→ spare tire

→ jerry can for extra gas

→ well-stocked toolbox including parts, such as belts, that are harder to find in Central America

→ emergency flares and roadside triangles.

Insurance from foreign countries isn't recognized in Costa Rica, so you'll have to buy a policy locally. At the border it will cost about US$12 a month. In addition, you'll have to pay a US$4.50 fumigation fee.

You are not allowed to sell the car in Costa Rica. If you need to leave the country without the car, it must be left in a customs warehouse in San José.

Sea

Cruise ships stop in Costa Rican ports and enable passengers to make a quick foray into the country. Typi-

cally, ships dock at either the Pacific ports of Caldera, Puntarenas, Quepos and Bahía Drake, or the Caribbean port of Puerto Limón.

It is also possible to arrive in Costa Rica by private yacht.

GETTING AROUND

Air

Charters

→ Travelers on a larger budget or in a larger party should consider chartering a private plane, which is by far the quickest way to travel around the country.

Domestic Air Routes

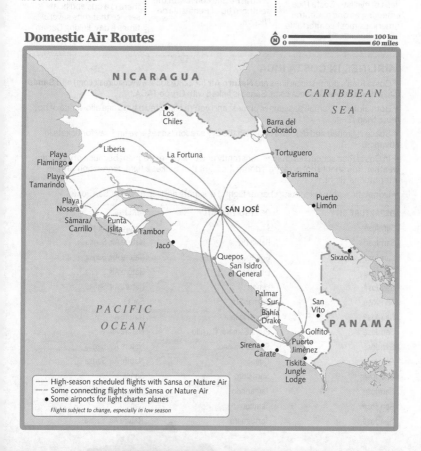

High-season scheduled flights with Sansa or Nature Air
Some connecting flights with Sansa or Nature Air
● Some airports for light charter planes
Flights subject to change, especially in low season

→ It takes under 90 minutes to fly to most destinations, though weather conditions can significantly speed up or delay travel time.

→ The two most reputable charters in the country are **Nature Air** (☎2220-3054; www.natureair.com) and **Alfa Romeo Aero Taxi** (☎2735-5353; www.alfaromeoair.com). Both can be booked directly through the company, a tour agency or some high-end accommodations.

→ Luggage space on charters is extremely limited.

Bicycle

With an increasingly large network of paved secondary roads and heightened awareness of cyclists, Costa Rica is emerging as one of Central America's most comfortable cycle-touring destinations. That said, many roads are narrow and winding and there are no designated cycle lanes, so there's an element of risk involved.

Mountain bikes and beach cruisers can be rented in towns with a significant tourist presence, for US$10 to US$20 per day. A few companies organize bike tours around Costa Rica.

Boat

→ In Costa Rica there are some regular coastal services and safety standards are generally good.

→ Ferries cross the Golfo de Nicoya, connecting the central Pacific coast with the southern tip of Península de Nicoya.

→ The **Coonatramar Ferry** (☎2661-1069; www.coonatramar.com; adult/child/bicycle/motorcycle/car US$2/1/4/6/18) links the port of Puntarenas with Playa Naranjo four times daily. The **Ferry Naviera Tambor** (☎2661-2084; www.navieratambor.com; adult/child/bicycle/motorcycle/car US$1.65/1/4.50/7/23) travels between Puntarenas and Paquera every two hours, for a bus connection to Montezuma.

→ On the Golfo Dulce a daily passenger ferry links Golfito with Puerto Jiménez on the Península de Osa. On the other side of the Península de Osa, water taxis connect Bahía Drake with Sierpe.

→ On the Caribbean coast there is a bus and boat service that runs several times a day, linking Cariari

---

AIRLINES IN COSTA RICA

→ Costa Rica's domestic airlines are **Nature Air** (☎2220-3054; www.natureair.com) and **Sansa** (☎2290-4100; www.flysansa.com). Sansa is linked with Grupo TACA.

→ Both airlines fly small passenger planes, and you're allocated a baggage allowance of no more than 12kg.

→ Space is limited and demand is high in the dry season, so reserve and pay for tickets in advance.

→ In Costa Rica schedules change constantly and delays are frequent because of inclement weather. You should not arrange a domestic flight that makes a tight connection with an international flight.

→ Domestic flights (excepting charter flights) originate and terminate at San José.

DEPARTURE CITY	DESTINATION CITY	AIRLINE
San José	Arenal	Nature Air, Sansa
San José	Bahía Drake	Nature Air, Sansa
San José	Golfito	Nature Air, Sansa
San José	Liberia	Nature Air, Sansa
San José	Limón	Nature Air, Sansa
San José	Palmar Sur	Sansa
San José	Playa Nosara	Nature Air
San José	Playa Sámara/Carrillo	Nature Air
San José	Puerto Jiménez	Nature Air, Sansa
San José	Quepos	Nature Air, Sansa
San José	San Isidro	Sansa
San José	Tamarindo	Nature Air, Sansa
San José	Tambor	Sansa
San José	Tortuguero	Nature Air, Sansa

and Tortuguero via La Pavona, while another links Parismina and Siquirres (transfer in Caño Blanco).

➡ Boats ply the canals that run along the coast from Moín to Tortuguero, although no regular service exists. A weekly water taxi connects Puerto Viejo de Sarapiquí with Trinidad on the Río San Juan on Tuesday afternoons. The San Juan is Nicaraguan territory, so take your passport. You can try to arrange boat transportation for Barra del Colorado in any of these towns.

Bus
Local Buses
➡ Local buses are a cheap and reliable way of getting around Costa Rica. The longest domestic journey out of San José costs less than US$20.

➡ San José is the transportation center for the country, though there is no central terminal. Bus offices are scattered around the city: some large bus companies have big terminals that sell tickets in advance, while others have little more than a stop – sometimes unmarked.

➡ Buses can be very crowded but don't usually pass up passengers on account of being too full. Note that there are no buses from Thursday to Saturday before Easter Sunday.

➡ There are two types of bus: *directo* and *colectivo*. The *directo* buses should go from one destination to the next with few stops; the *colectivos* make more stops and are very slow going.

➡ Trips longer than four hours usually include a rest stop as buses do not have toilets.

➡ Space is limited on board, so if you have to check luggage be watchful. Theft from overhead racks is

rampant, though it's much less common than in other Central American countries.

➡ Bus schedules fluctuate wildly, so always confirm the time when you buy your ticket. If you are catching a bus that picks you up somewhere along a road, get to the roadside early.

➡ For information on departures from San José, pay a visit to the **ICT** (ICT; Map p70; ☎2222-1090, in USA & Canada 866-267-8274; www.visitcostarica.com; Edificio de las Academias, Av Central btwn Calles 1 & 3; ☺8am-5pm Mon-Fri) office to pick up the reasonably up-to-date copy of the master schedule, which is also available on its website.

Shuttle Buses
The tourist-van shuttle services (aka gringo buses) are a pricier alternative to the standard intercity buses. Shuttles are provided by **Gray Line** (www.grayline-costarica.com), **Easy Ride** (www.easyridecr.com), **Monkey Ride** (www.monkeyride-cr.com) and **Interbus** (www.interbusonline.com).

➡ All four companies run overland transportation from San José to the most popular destinations, as well as directly between other destinations (see the websites for the comprehensive list).

➡ These services will pick you up at your hotel, and reservations can be made online, or through local travel agencies and hotel owners.

➡ Popular destinations they serve include Quepos, Monteverde/Santa Elena, Manuel Antonio, Jacó, Dominical, Uvita, Puerto Jiménez, Arenal, Montezuma and Mal País.

➡ Easy Ride offers international services directly from Jacó, Tamarindo and Liberia to Granada and Managua in Nicaragua and from Monteverde to Managua.

Car & Motorcycle
➡ Drivers in Costa Rica are required to have a valid driver's license from their home country. Many places will also accept an International Driving Permit (IDP), issued by the automobile association in your country of origin. After 90 days, however, you will need to get a Costa Rican driver's license.

➡ Gasoline (petrol) and diesel are widely available, and 24-hour service stations are along the Interamericana. At the time of research, fuel prices averaged US$1.01 per liter.

➡ In more remote areas, fuel will be more expensive and might be sold at the neighborhood *pulpería* (corner store).

→ Spare parts may be hard to find, especially for vehicles with sophisticated electronics and emissions-control systems.

Hire & Insurance

→ There are car-rental agencies in San José and in popular tourist destinations on the Pacific coast.

→ All of the major international car-rental agencies have outlets in Costa Rica, though you can sometimes get better deals from local companies.

→ Due to road conditions, it is necessary to invest in a 4WD unless travel is limited only to the Interamericana.

→ Many agencies will insist on 4WD in the rainy season, when driving through rivers is a matter of course.

→ To rent a car you need a valid driver's license, a major credit card and a passport. The minimum age for car rental is 21 years. It's possible to rent with a debit card, but only if you agree to pay full insurance.

→ Carefully inspect rented cars for minor damage and make sure that any damage is noted on the rental agreement. If your car breaks down, call the rental company. Don't attempt to get the car fixed yourself – most companies won't reimburse expenses without prior authorization.

→ Prices vary considerably; on average you can expect to pay over US$200 per week for a standard SUV, including *kilometraje libre* (unlimited mileage). Economy cars are much cheaper, as little as US$80 a week. The price of mandatory insurance makes this more expensive, often doubling the rate.

→ Costa Rican insurance is mandatory, even if you have insurance at home. Expect to pay about US$12 to US$25 per day. Many rental companies won't rent you a car without it. The basic insurance that all drivers must buy is from a government monopoly, the Instituto Nacional de Seguros. This insurance does not cover your rental car at all, only damages to other people, their cars, or property. It is legal to drive only with this insurance, but it can be difficult to negotiate with a rental agency to allow you to drive away with only this minimum standard. Full insurance through the rental agency can be up to US$50 a day.

→ Some roads in Costa Rica are rough and rugged, meaning that minor accidents or car damage are common.

→ Note that if you pay basic insurance with a gold or platinum credit card, the card company will usually take responsibility for damages to the car, in which case you can forgo the cost of the full insurance. Make sure you verify this with your credit-card company ahead of time.

→ Most insurance policies do not cover damage caused by flooding or driving through

DRIVING THROUGH RIVERS

Driving in Costa Rica will likely necessitate a river crossing at some point. Unfortunately, too many travelers have picked up their off-road skills from watching TV, and every season Ticos get a good chuckle out of the number of dead vehicles they help wayward travelers fish out of waterways.

If you're driving through water, follow the rules below:

→ **Only do this in a 4WD** Don't drive through a river in a car. (It may seem ridiculous to have to say this, but it's done all the time.) Getting out of a steep, gravel riverbed requires a 4WD. Besides, car engines flood very easily.

→ **Check the depth of the water before driving through** To accommodate an average rental 4WD, the water should be no deeper than above the knee. In a sturdier vehicle (Toyota 4Runner or equivalent), water can be waist deep. If you're nervous, wait for a local car to come along, and follow their lead.

→ **The water should be calm** If the river is gushing so that there are white crests on the water, do not try to cross. Not only will the force of the water flood the engine, it could sweep the car away.

→ **Drive very, very slowly** The pressure of driving through a river too quickly will send the water right into the engine and will impair the electrical system. Keep steady pressure on the accelerator so that the tailpipe doesn't fill with water, but go slowly; if driving stick shift, go in first gear.

→ **Err on the side of caution** Car-rental agencies in Costa Rica do not insure for water damage, so ruining a car in a river can come at an extremely high cost.

a river, so be aware of the extent of your policy.

→ Rental rates fluctuate wildly, so shop around. Some agencies offer discounts for extended rentals. Note that rental offices at the airport charge a 12% fee in addition to regular rates.

→ Thieves can easily recognize rental cars. Never leave anything in sight in a parked car – nothing! – and remove all luggage from the trunk overnight. If possible, park the car in a guarded parking lot rather than on the street.

→ Motorcycles (including Harleys) can be rented in San José and Escazú.

Road Conditions & Hazards

→ The quality of roads varies, from the quite smoothly paved Interamericana to the barely passable, bumpy, potholed, rural back roads. Any can suffer from landslides, sudden flooding and fog.

→ Most roads are single-lane and winding, lacking hard shoulders; others are dirt-and-mud affairs that climb mountains and traverse rivers.

→ Drive defensively and expect a variety of obstructions in the roadway, from cyclists and pedestrians to broken-down cars and cattle. Unsigned speed bumps are placed on some stretches of road without warning.

→ Roads around major tourist areas are adequately marked; all others are not.

→ Always ask about road conditions before setting out, especially in the rainy season when a number of roads become impassable.

Road Rules

→ There are speed limits of 100km/h or less on all primary roads and 60km/h or less on secondary roads.

FLAT TIRE SCAM

For years Aeropuerto Internacional Juan Santamaría has suffered from a scam involving sudden flat tires on rental cars. Though it is commonly reported, it continues to happen.

It goes like this: after you pick up a rental car and drive out of the city, the car gets a flat; as you pull over to fix it, the disabled vehicle is approached by a group of locals, ostensibly to help. There is inevitably some confusion with the changing of the tire, and in the commotion you are relieved of your wallet, luggage or other valuables.

This incident has happened enough times to suggest that travelers should be very wary – and aware – if somebody pulls over to help after they get a flat on a recently rented car. Keep your wallet and passport on your person whenever you get out of a car.

→ Traffic police use radar, and speed limits are sometimes enforced with speeding tickets.

→ Tickets are issued to drivers operating vehicles without a seat belt.

→ It's illegal to stop in an intersection or make a right turn on a red.

→ At unmarked intersections, yield to the car on your right.

→ Drive on the right. Passing is allowed only on the left.

→ If you are issued with a ticket, you have to pay the fine at a bank; instructions are given on the ticket. If you are driving a rental car, the rental company may be able to arrange your payment for you – the amount of the fine should be on the ticket. A portion of the money from these fines goes to a children's charity.

→ Police have no right to ask for money, and they shouldn't confiscate a car, unless the driver cannot produce a license and ownership papers, the car lacks license plates, the driver is drunk or the driver has been involved in an accident causing serious injury.

→ If you are driving and see oncoming cars with headlights flashing, it often means that there is a road problem or a radar speed trap ahead. Slow down immediately.

Hitchhiking

Hitchhiking is never entirely safe, and we don't recommend it. Travelers who hitchhike should understand that they are taking a small but potentially serious risk. People who do hitchhike will be safer if they travel in pairs and let someone know where they are planning to go. Solo women should use even greater caution.

Hitchhiking in Costa Rica is unusual on main roads that have frequent buses. On minor rural roads, hitchhiking is more common. To get picked up, most locals wave down passing cars. If you get a ride, offer to pay when you arrive by saying '¿Cuánto le debo?' (How much do I owe you?). Your offer may be waved aside, or you may be asked to help with money for gas.

Local Transport

Bus

Local buses operate chiefly in San José, Puntarenas, San Isidro de El General, Golfito and Puerto Limón, connecting urban and suburban areas. Most local buses pick up passengers on the street and on main roads. For years, these buses were converted school buses imported from the USA, but they have slowly been upgraded and now include coaches.

Taxi

In San José taxis have *marías* (meters) and it is illegal for a driver not to use it. Outside San José, however, most taxis don't have meters and fares tend to be agreed upon in advance. Bargaining is quite acceptable.

In some towns there are *colectivos* (taxis that several passengers are able to share). Although *colectivos* are becoming increasingly difficult to find, the basic principle is that the driver charges a flat fee (usually about US$0.50) to take passengers from one end of town to the other.

In rural areas, 4WDs are often used as taxis and are a popular means for surfers (and their boards) to travel from their accommodations to the break. Prices vary wildly depending on how touristy the area is, though generally speaking a 10-minute ride costs between US$5 and US$15.

Taxi drivers are not normally tipped unless they assist with your luggage or have provided an above-average service.

Language

Spanish pronunciation is easy, as most sounds have equivalents in English. Also, Spanish spelling is phonetically consistent, meaning that there's a clear and consistent relationship between what you see in writing and how it's pronounced. If you read our colored pronunciation guides as if they were English, you'll be understood. Note that kh is a throaty sound (like the 'ch' in the Scottish *loch*), v and b are like a soft English 'v' (between a 'v' and a 'b'), and r is strongly rolled. The stressed syllables are in italics in our pronunciation guides.

The polite form is used in this chapter; where both polite and informal options are given, they are indicated by the abbreviations 'pol' and 'inf'. Where necessary, both masculine and feminine forms of words are included, separated by a slash and with the masculine form first, eg *perdido/a* (m/f).

BASICS

Hello.	*Hola.*	o·la
Goodbye.	*Adiós.*	a·dyos
How are you?	*¿Cómo va?* (pol)	ko·mo va
	¿Cómo vas? (inf)	ko·mo vas
Fine, thanks.	*Bien, gracias.*	byen gra·syas
Excuse me.	*Con permiso.*	kon per·mee·so
Sorry.	*Perdón.*	per·don
Please.	*Por favor.*	por fa·vor

WANT MORE?

For in-depth language information and handy phrases, check out Lonely Planet's *Latin American Spanish Phrasebook*. You'll find it at **shop.lonelyplanet.com**, or you can buy Lonely Planet's iPhone phrasebooks at the Apple App Store.

Thank you.	*Gracias.*	gra·syas
You're welcome.	*Con mucho gusto.*	kon moo·cho goo·sto
Yes.	*Sí.*	see
No.	*No.*	no

My name is ...
Me llamo ...   me ya·mo ...

What's your name?
¿Cómo se llama Usted?   ko·mo se ya·ma oo·ste (pol)
¿Cómo te llamas?   ko·mo te ya·mas (inf)

Do you speak English?
¿Habla inglés?   a·bla een·gles (pol)
¿Hablas inglés?   a·blas een·gles (inf)

I don't understand.
Yo no entiendo.   yo no en·tyen·do

ACCOMMODATIONS

Do you have a ... room?	*Tiene una habitación ...?*	tye·ne oo·na a·bee·ta·syon ...
single	*sencilla*	sen·see·ya
double	*doble*	do·ble

How much is it per night/person?
¿Cuánto es por noche/persona?   kwan·to es por no·che/per·so·na

Is breakfast included?
¿Incluye el desayuno?   een·kloo·ye el de·sa·yoo·no

campsite	*área para acampar*	a·re·a pa·ra a·kam·par
hotel	*hotel*	o·tel
hostel	*hospedaje*	os·pe·da·khe
guesthouse	*casa de huéspedes*	ka·sa de wes·pe·des
youth hostel	*albergue juvenil*	al·ber·ge khoo·ve·neel

TIQUISMOS

These colloquialisms and slang terms (*tiquismos*) are frequently heard, and are for the most part used only in Costa Rica.

¡Adiós! – Hi! (used when passing a friend in the street, or anyone in remote rural areas; also means 'Farewell!' but only when leaving for a long time)

bomba – gas station

buena nota – OK/excellent (literally 'good note')

chapulines – a gang, usually of young thieves

chunche – thing (can refer to almost anything)

cien metros – one city block

¿Hay campo? – Is there space? (on a bus)

machita – blonde woman (slang)

mae – buddy (pronounced 'ma' as in 'mat' followed with a quick 'eh'; it's mainly used by boys and young men)

mi amor – my love (used as a familiar form of address by both men and women)

pulpería – corner grocery store

¡Pura vida! – Super! (literally 'pure life,' also an expression of approval or even a greeting)

sabanero – cowboy, especially one who hails from Guanacaste Province

salado – too bad; tough luck

soda – cafe or lunch counter

¡Tuanis! – Cool!

¡Upe! – Is anybody home? (used mainly in rural areas at people's homes, instead of knocking)

vos – you (singular and informal, same as *tú*)

air-con	aire acondi- cionado	ai·re a·kon·dee· syo·na·do
bathroom	baño	ba·nyo
bed	cama	ka·ma
window	ventana	ven·ta·na

DIRECTIONS

Where's ...?
¿Adónde está ...?   a·don·de es·ta ...

What's the address?
¿Cuál es la dirección?   kwal es la dee·rek·syon

Could you please write it down?
¿Podría escribirlo?   po·dree·a es·kree·beer·lo

Can you show me (on the map)?
¿Me puede enseñar (en el mapa)?   me pwe·de en·se·nyar (en el ma·pa)

at the corner	en la esquina	en la es·kee·na
at the traffic lights	en el semáforo	en el se·ma·fo·ro
behind ...	detrás de ...	de·tras de ...
far	lejos	le·khos
in front of ...	en frente de ...	en fren·te de ...
left	a la izquierda	a la ees·kyer·da
near	cerca	ser·ka
next to ...	a la par de ...	a la par de ...
opposite ...	opuesto a ...	o·pwes·to a ...
right	a la derecha	a la de·re·cha
straight ahead	aquí directo	a·kee dee·rek·to

EATING & DRINKING

Can I see the menu, please?
¿Puedo ver el menú, por favor?   pwe·do ver el me·noo por fa·vor

What would you recommend?
¿Qué me recomienda?   ke me re·ko·myen·da

Do you have vegetarian food?
¿Tienen comida vegetariana?   tye·nen ko·mee·da ve·khe·ta·rya·na

I don't eat (red meat).
No como (carne roja).   no ko·mo (kar·ne ro·kha)

That was delicious!
¡Estuvo delicioso!   es·too·vo de·lee·syo·so

Cheers!
¡Salud!   sa·lood

The bill, please.
La cuenta, por favor.   la kwen·ta por fa·vor

I'd like a table for ...	Quisiera una mesa para ...	kee·sye·ra oo·na me·sa pa·ra ...
(eight) o'clock	las (ocho)	las (o·cho)
(two) people	(dos) personas	(dos) per·so·nas

Key Words

appetisers	aperitivos	a·pe·ree·tee·vos
bar	bar	bar
bottle	botella	bo·te·ya
bowl	plato hondo	pla·to on·do
breakfast	desayuno	de·sa·yoo·no
cafe	café	ka·fe
(too) cold	(muy) frío	(mooy) free·o
dinner	cena	se·na

food	comida	ko·mee·da
fork	tenedor	te·ne·dor
glass	vaso	va·so
hot (warm)	caliente	kal·yen·te
knife	cuchillo	koo·chee·yo
lunch	almuerzo	al·mwer·so
main course	plato fuerte	pla·to fwer·te
market	mercado	mer·ka·do
menu	menú	me·noo
plate	plato	pla·to
restaurant	restaurante	res·tow·ran·te
spoon	cuchara	koo·cha·ra
supermarket	supermercado	soo·per·mer·ka·do
with/without	con/sin	kon/seen

Meat & Fish

beef	carne de vaca	kar·ne de va·ka
chicken	pollo	po·yo
duck	pato	pa·to
fish	pescado	pes·ka·do
lamb	cordero	kor·de·ro
pork	cerdo	ser·do
turkey	pavo	pa·vo
veal	ternera	ter·ne·ra

Fruit & Vegetables

apple	manzana	man·sa·na
apricot	albaricoque	al·ba·ree·ko·ke
asparagus	espárragos	es·pa·ra·gos
banana	banano	ba·na·no
bean	frijol	free·khol
cabbage	repollo	re·po·yo
carrot	zanahoria	sa·na·o·rya
cherry	cereza	se·re·sa
corn	maíz	ma·ees
cucumber	pepino	pe·pee·no
fruit	fruta	froo·ta
grapes	uvas	oo·vas
lemon	limón	lee·mon
lentils	lentejas	len·te·khas
lettuce	lechuga	le·choo·ga
mushroom	hongo	on·go
nuts	nueces	nwe·ses
onion	cebolla	se·bo·ya
orange	naranja	na·ran·kha
peach	melocotón	me·lo·ko·ton
pea	petipoa	pe·tee·po·a

pepper (bell)	pimentón	pee·men·ton
pineapple	piña	pee·nya
plum	ciruela	seer·we·la
potato	papa	pa·pa
pumpkin	calabaza	ka·la·ba·sa
spinach	espinaca	es·pee·na·ka
strawberry	fresa	fre·sa
tomato	tomate	to·ma·te
vegetable	vegetal	ve·khe·tal
watermelon	sandía	san·dee·a

Other

bread	pan	pan
butter	mantequilla	man·te·kee·ya
cheese	queso	ke·so
egg	huevo	we·vo
honey	miel	myel
jam	jalea	kha·le·a
oil	aceite	a·sey·te
pastry	pastel	pas·tel
pepper	pimienta	pee·myen·ta
rice	arroz	a·ros
salt	sal	sal
sugar	azúcar	a·soo·kar
vinegar	vinagre	vee·na·gre

Drinks

beer	cerveza	ser·ve·sa
coffee	café	ka·fe
(orange) juice	jugo (de naranja)	khoo·go (de na·ran·kha)
milk	leche	le·che
tea	té	te
(mineral) water	agua (mineral)	a·gwa (mee·ne·ral)
(red/white) wine	vino (tinto/ blanco)	vee·no (teen·to/ blan·ko)

SIGNS	
Abierto	Open
Cerrado	Closed
Entrada	Entrance
Hombres/Varones	Men
Mujeres/Damas	Women
Prohibido	Prohibited
Salida	Exit
Servicios/Baños	Toilets

EMERGENCIES

Help!	*¡Socorro!*	so·ko·ro
Go away!	*¡Váyase!*	va·ya·se

Call ...!	*¡Llame a ...!*	ya·me a ...
a doctor	*un doctor*	oon dok·tor
the police	*la policía*	la po·lee·see·a

I'm lost.
Estoy perdido/a.   es·toy per·dee·do/a (m/f)

I'm ill.
Estoy enfermo/a.   es·toy en·fer·mo/a (m/f)

It hurts here.
Me duele aquí.   me dwe·le a·kee

I'm allergic to (antibiotics).
Soy alérgico/a a   soy a·ler·khee·ko/a a
(los antibióticos).   (los an·tee·byo·tee·kos) (m/f)

Where are the toilets?
¿Dónde está el   don·de es·ta el
baño?   ba·nyo

SHOPPING & SERVICES

I'd like to buy ...
Quiero comprar ...   kye·ro kom·prar ...

I'm just looking.
Sólo estoy viendo.   so·lo es·toy vyen·do

Can I look at it?
¿Lo puedo ver?   lo pwe·do ver

How much is it?
¿Cuánto cuesta?   kwan·to kwes·ta

That's too expensive.
Está muy caro.   es·ta mooy ka·ro

Can you lower the price?
¿Podría bajarle   po·dree·a ba·khar·le
el precio?   el pre·syo

There's a mistake in the bill.
Hay un error   ai oon e·ror
en la cuenta.   en la kwen·ta

ATM	*cajero*	ka·khe·ro
	automático	ow·to·ma·tee·ko
credit card	*tarjeta de*	tar·khe·ta de
	crédito	kre·dee·to

QUESTION WORDS

How?	*¿Cómo?*	ko·mo
What?	*¿Qué?*	ke
When?	*¿Cuándo?*	kwan·do
Where?	*¿Dónde?*	don·de
Who?	*¿Quién?*	kyen
Why?	*¿Por qué?*	por ke

market	*mercado*	mer·ka·do
post office	*correo*	ko·re·o
tourist office	*oficina*	o·fee·see·na
	de turismo	de too·rees·mo

TIME & DATES

What time is it?	*¿Qué hora es?*	ke o·ra es
It's (10) o'clock.	*Son (las diez).*	son (las dyes)
It's half past (one).	*Es (la una) y media.*	es (la oo·na) ee me·dya

morning	*mañana*	ma·nya·na
afternoon	*tarde*	tar·de
evening	*noche*	no·che
yesterday	*ayer*	a·yer
today	*hoy*	oy
tomorrow	*mañana*	ma·nya·na

Monday	*lunes*	loo·nes
Tuesday	*martes*	mar·tes
Wednesday	*miércoles*	myer·ko·les
Thursday	*jueves*	khwe·ves
Friday	*viernes*	vyer·nes
Saturday	*sábado*	sa·ba·do
Sunday	*domingo*	do·meen·go

January	*enero*	e·ne·ro
February	*febrero*	fe·bre·ro
March	*marzo*	mar·so
April	*abril*	a·breel
May	*mayo*	ma·yo
June	*junio*	khoon·yo
July	*julio*	khool·yo
August	*agosto*	a·gos·to
September	*septiembre*	sep·tyem·bre
October	*octubre*	ok·too·bre
November	*noviembre*	no·vyem·bre
December	*diciembre*	dee·syem·bre

TRANSPORTATION

boat	*barco*	bar·ko
bus	*bús*	boos
plane	*avión*	a·vyon
train	*tren*	tren

first	*primero*	pree·me·ro
last	*último*	ool·tee·mo
next	*próximo*	prok·see·mo

A ... ticket, please.	*Un pasaje de ..., por favor.*	oon pa·*sa*·khe de ... por fa·*vor*
1st-class	*primera clase*	pree·*me*·ra *kla*·se
2nd-class	*segunda clase*	se·*goon*·da *kla*·se
one-way	*ida*	*ee*·da
return	*ida y vuelta*	*ee*·da ee *vwel*·ta

I want to go to ...
Quisiera ir a ...   kee·*sye*·ra eer a ...

Does it stop at ...?
¿Hace parada en ...?   a·se pa·*ra*·da en ...

What stop is this?
¿Cuál es esta parada?   kwal es *es*·ta pa·*ra*·da

What time does it arrive/leave?
¿A qué hora llega/ sale?   a ke o·ra ye·ga/ *sa*·le

Please tell me when we get to ...
Por favor, avíseme cuando lleguemos a ...   por fa·*vor* a·*vee*·se·me *kwan*·do ye·*ge*·mos a ...

I want to get off here.
Quiero bajarme aquí.   kye·ro ba·*khar*·me a·*kee*

airport	*aeropuerto*	a·e·ro·*pwer*·to
aisle seat	*asiento de pasillo*	a·*syen*·to de pa·*see*·yo
bus stop	*parada de autobuses*	pa·*ra*·da de ow·to·*boo*·ses
cancelled	*cancelado*	kan·se·*la*·do
delayed	*atrasado*	a·tra·*sa*·do
platform	*plataforma*	pla·ta·*for*·ma
ticket office	*taquilla*	ta·*kee*·ya
timetable	*horario*	o·*ra*·ryo
train station	*estación de trenes*	es·ta·*syon* de *tre*·nes
window seat	*asiento junto a la ventana*	a·*syen*·to *khoon*·to a la ven·*ta*·na

I'd like to hire a ...	*Quiero alquilar ...*	kye·ro al·kee·*lar* ...
4WD	*un cuatro por cuatro*	oon *kwa*·tro por *kwa*·tro
bicycle	*una bicicleta*	*oo*·na bee·see·*kle*·ta
car	*un carro*	oon *ka*·ro
motorcycle	*una moto- cicleta*	*oo*·na mo·to- see·*kle*·ta

NUMBERS

1	*uno*	*oo*·no
2	*dos*	dos
3	*tres*	tres
4	*cuatro*	*kwa*·tro
5	*cinco*	*seen*·ko
6	*seis*	seys
7	*siete*	*sye*·te
8	*ocho*	*o*·cho
9	*nueve*	*nwe*·ve
10	*diez*	dyes
20	*veinte*	*veyn*·te
30	*treinta*	*treyn*·ta
40	*cuarenta*	kwa·*ren*·ta
50	*cincuenta*	seen·*kwen*·ta
60	*sesenta*	se·*sen*·ta
70	*setenta*	se·*ten*·ta
80	*ochenta*	o·*chen*·ta
90	*noventa*	no·*ven*·ta
100	*cien*	syen
1000	*mil*	meel

child seat	*asiento de seguridad para niños*	a·*syen*·to de se·goo·ree·*da* pa·ra nee·nyos
diesel	*diesel*	dee·*sel*
helmet	*casco*	*kas*·ko
mechanic	*mecánico*	me·*ka*·nee·ko
petrol/gas	*gasolina*	ga·so·*lee*·na
service station	*bomba*	*bom*·ba
truck	*camión*	ka·*myon*

Is this the road to ...?
¿Por aquí se va a ...?   por a·*kee* se va a ...

(How long) Can I park here?
¿(Cuánto tiempo) Puedo parquear aquí?   (*kwan*·to *tyem*·po) *pwe*·do par·ke·*ar* a·*kee*

The car has broken down (at ...).
El carro se varó en ...   el *ka*·ro se va·ro en ...

I've had an accident.
Tuve un accidente.   *too*·ve oon ak·see·*den*·te

I've run out of petrol.
Me quedé sin gasolina.   me ke·*de* seen ga·so·*lee*·na

I have a flat tyre.
Se me estalló una llanta.   se me es·ta·yo *oo*·na *yan*·ta

GLOSSARY

adiós – means 'goodbye' universally, but used as a greeting in rural Costa Rica

alquiler de automóviles – car rental

apartado – post-office box (abbreviated 'Apdo')

artesanía – handicrafts

ATH – *a toda hora* (open all hours); used to denote ATMs

automóvil – car

avenida – avenue

avión – airplane

bahía – bay

barrio – district or neighborhood

biblioteca – library

bomba – short, funny verse; also means 'gas station' and 'bomb'

bosque – forest

bosque nuboso – cloud forest

buena nota – excellent, OK; literally 'good note'

caballo – horse

cabaña – cabin; see also *cabina*

cabina – cabin; see also *cabaña*

cajero automático – ATM

calle – street

cama, cama matrimonial – bed, double bed

campesino – peasant, farmer or person who works in agriculture

carreta – colorfully painted wooden oxcart, now a form of folk art

carretera – road

casado – inexpensive set meal; also means 'married'

casita – cottage or apartment

catedral – cathedral

caverna – cave; see also *cueva*

cerro – mountain or hill

Chepe – affectionate nickname for José; also used when referring to San José

cine – cinema

ciudad – city

cocina – kitchen or cooking

colectivo – bus, minivan or car operating as shared taxi

colibrí – hummingbird

colina – hill

colón – Costa Rican unit of currency; plural colones

cordillera – mountain range

correo – mail service

Costarricense – Costa Rican; see also Tico/a

cruce – crossing

cruda – often used to describe a hangover; literally 'raw'

cueva – cave; see also *caverna*

culebra – snake; see also *serpiente*

Dios – God

directo – direct; refers to long-distance bus with few stops

edificio – building

estación – station, eg ranger station or bus station; also means 'season'

farmacia – pharmacy

fauna silvestre – wildlife

fiesta – party or festival

finca – farm or plantation

floresta – forest

frontera – border

fútbol – soccer (football)

garza – cattle egret

gasolina – gas (petrol)

gracias – thanks

gringo/a (m/f) – US or European visitor; can be affectionate or insulting, depending on the tone used

hacienda – rural estate

hielo – ice

ICT – Instituto Costarricense de Turismo; Costa Rica Tourism Board

iglesia – church

indígena – indigenous

Interamericana – Pan-American Hwy; the nearly continuous highway running from Alaska to Chile (it breaks at the Darién Gap between Panama and Colombia)

invierno – winter; the rainy season in Costa Rica

isla – island

jardín – garden

josefino/a (m/f) – resident of San José

lago – lake

lavandería – laundry facility, usually offering dry-cleaning services

librería – bookstore

llanura – tropical plain

machismo – an exaggerated sense of masculine pride

macho – literally 'male'; figuratively also 'masculine,' 'tough.' In Costa Rica *macho/a* (m/f) also means 'blonde.'

maría – local name for taxi meter

mercado – market

mercado central – central town market

Meseta Central – Central Valley or central plateau

mestizo/a (m/f) – person of mixed descent, usually Spanish and indigenous

metate – flat stone platform, used by Costa Rica's pre-Columbian populations to grind corn

migración – immigration

Minae – Ministerio de Ambiente y Energía; Ministry of Environment and Energy, in charge of the national park system

mirador – lookout point

mole – rich chocolate sauce

mono – monkey

mono tití – squirrel monkey

motocicleta – motorcycle

muelle – dock

museo – museum

niño – child

normal – refers to long-distance bus with many stops

obeah – sorcery rituals of African origin

ola(s) – wave(s)

OTS – Organization for Tropical Studies

pájaro – bird

palapa – shelter with a thatched, palm-leaf roof and open sides

palenque – indigenous settlement

páramo – habitat with highland shrub and tussock grass

parque – park

parque central – central town square or plaza

parque nacional – national park

perezoso – sloth

perico – mealy parrot

playa – beach

posada – country-style inn or guesthouse

puente – bridge

puerto – port

pulpería – corner grocery store

punta – point

pura vida – super; literally 'pure life'

quebrada – stream

rana – frog or toad

rancho – small house or house-like building

río – river

sabanero – cowboy from Guanacaste

selva – jungle

Semana Santa – the Christian Holy Week that precedes Easter

sendero – trail or path

serpiente – snake

Sinac – Sistema Nacional de Areas de Conservación; National System of Conservation Areas

supermercado – supermarket

telenovela – Spanish-language soap opera

Tico/a (m/f) – Costa Rican; see also *Costarricense*

tienda – store

tiquismos – typical Costa Rican expressions or slang

tortuga – turtle

valle – valley

verano – summer; the dry season in Costa Rica

volcán – volcano

zoológico – zoo

Food Glossary

a la plancha – grilled or pan-fried

agua – water

agua de sapo – literally 'toad water,' a lemonade made with fresh ginger and brown sugar

agua dulce – sugarcane juice

aguacate – avocado

almuerzo – lunch

almuerzo ejecutivo – literally 'executive lunch'; a more expensive version of a set meal or *casado*

arroz – rice

batido – fruit shake made with milk or water

bocas – small savory dishes served in bars; tapas

café – coffee

camaron – shrimp

carambola – starfruit

cas – a type of tart guava

casado – inexpensive set meal; also means 'married'

cena – dinner

cerveza – beer; also known as birra

ceviche – seafood marinated in lemon or lime juice, garlic and seasonings

chan – drink made from chia seeds

chuleta – pork chop

comida típica – typical local food

desayuno – breakfast

dorado – mahi-mahi

empanada – savory turnover stuffed with meat or cheese

ensalada – salad

frito – fried

gallo pinto – stir-fry of rice and beans

guanabana – soursop or cherimoya

guaro – local firewater made from sugarcane

leche – milk

linaza – drink made from flaxseeds

lomito – fillet; tenderloin

macrobiótica – health-food store

maracuya – passion fruit

mariscos – seafood

melón – cantaloupe

mora – blackberry

natilla – sour cream

olla de carne – beef stew

palmito – heart of palm

pargo – red snapper

pan – bread

pan tostada – toast

panadería – bakery

pastelería – pastry shop

patacones – twice-fried green plantains

patí – Caribbean version of empanada

pescado – fish

piña – pineapple

pipa – young green coconut; harvested for refreshing coconut water

plátanos maduros – ripe plantain cut in slices lengthwise and baked or broiled with butter, brown sugar and cinnamon

pollo – chicken

queso – cheese

resbladera – sweet barley and rice drink

ron – rum

rondón – seafood gumbo

Salsa Lizano – Costa Rican version of Worcestershire sauce; a key ingredient in *gallo pinto*

sandía – watermelon

soda – informal lunch counter or inexpensive eatery

tamarindo – fruit of the tamarind tree

tapa de dulce – brown sugar

vino – wine

Behind the Scenes

SEND US YOUR FEEDBACK

We love to hear from travelers – your comments keep us on our toes and help make our books better. Our well-traveled team reads every word on what you loved or loathed about this book. Although we cannot reply individually to your submissions, we always guarantee that your feedback goes straight to the appropriate authors, in time for the next edition. Each person who sends us information is thanked in the next edition – the most useful submissions are rewarded with a selection of digital PDF chapters.

Visit **lonelyplanet.com/contact** to submit your updates and suggestions or to ask for help. Our award-winning website also features inspirational travel stories, news and discussions.

Note: We may edit, reproduce and incorporate your comments in Lonely Planet products such as guidebooks, websites and digital products, so let us know if you don't want your comments reproduced or your name acknowledged. For a copy of our privacy policy visit lonelyplanet.com/privacy.

OUR READERS

Many thanks to the travelers who used the last edition and wrote to us with helpful hints, useful advice and interesting anecdotes:

Margot Besson, Denton Brown, Lucie Brunelle, Melissa Buich, Romana Bur, Robert Cotter, Cris Currie, Laura Daly, Martin Davies, Ellie Davis, Pieter Decolvenaer, Daan Esch, Annelie Forbriger, Alisha Frank, John Jones, Petra Kaika, Nikolaos Karadimas, Wouter Kroes, Ilona Kumar, Åsa Lidmark, Matt Lubejko, Vanessa MacDougal, Louisa Mackenzie, Jane Mason, Andrew Moncrieff, Kath Norgrove, Roger Oldfield, Marion Owen, Lidija Pohar, Sharon Ranch, Alejandra Rodríguez, René Saitenmacher, Kathi Schmid, Darren Shore, Hugh and Meryl Skipper, Judith Smit, Catriona Smith, Willy Stroobants, Charles Sullivan, Laura Wallman, John Welch, Margaret Wiedeman

AUTHOR THANKS

Mara Vorhees

Muchas gracias to my co-authors, Anna and Ashley, for their cooperation and collaboration on this title. While I got plenty of help from countless amigos along the way, I am especially grateful to Meghan Casey and Davis Azofeifa at the Chilamate Rainforest Eco Retreat – and the three kiddos – for their generous spirits, their in-depth knowledge of the Sarapiquí region and their passion for what they do. So much gratitude to my adventurous parents and to my three favorite traveling companions for accompanying me on this wild and wonderful journey.

Ashley Harrell

This guidebook came together with the support of friends, family, colleagues and so many kind people I met along the way. Stacey Auch, Zach Dyer, Lindsay Fendt, Genna Robustelli, Colin Brownlee and Amy Benziger: thanks for your assistance and ever-amusing company. Anna Kaminski, Mara Vorhees, Bailey Johnson and Gregor Clark: thanks for fielding my anxiety-laden emails. And a huge thanks to my family (and dog-sitting team), including Mack and Ronni Harrell, Claudia Dawson, and all the Lavenders, especially Andy.

Anna Kaminski

I would like to thank Bailey for entrusting me with a chunk of Costa Rica, my fellow scribes – Mara and Ashley – and everyone who helped me around the way. In particular: Steve from Villas Jacquelina, the Paddle 9 crew for everything, Luís Daniel of Osa Wild for the terrific Corcovado hike, John and Jill in San Gerardo for Chirripó tips and looking after me after my trek, Sheelagh for the hospitality and terrific advice, Julieta for introducing me to the Caminos de Osa, Hadas and Ran in Pavones and the Cristal Ballena team for all the information.

ACKNOWLEDGEMENTS

Climate map data adapted from Peel MC, Finlayson BL & McMahon TA (2007) 'Updated World Map of the Köppen-Geiger Climate Classification', *Hydrology and Earth System Sciences*, 11, pp1633–44.

Cover photograph: Scarlet macaw in flight, Parque Nacional Corcovado, Marco Simoni/ AWL ©

THIS BOOK

This 12th edition of Lonely Planet's *Costa Rica* guidebook was researched and written by Mara Vorhees, Ashley Harrell and Anna Kaminski. Wendy Yanagihara, Gregor Clark and Mara Vorhees wrote and re-searched the previous edition. This guidebook was produced by the following:

Destination Editor
Bailey Johnson
Product Editors Carolyn Boicos, Kate Chapman
Senior Cartographer Mark Griffiths
Book Designer Michael Buick
Assisting Editors Imogen Bannister, Nigel Chin, Katie Connolly, Carly Hall, Gabrielle Innes, Anne Mulvaney

Cartographer Michael Garrett
Assisting Book Designers Lauren Egan, Kerrianne Jenkins
Cover Researcher Naomi Parker
Thanks to Joel Cotterell, Andi Jones, Catherine Naghten, Karyn Noble, Kirsten Rawlings, Tony Wheeler

Index

Map Legend

Sights

- Beach
- Bird Sanctuary
- Buddhist
- Castle/Palace
- Christian
- Confucian
- Hindu
- Islamic
- Jain
- Jewish
- Monument
- Museum/Gallery/Historic Building
- Ruin
- Shinto
- Sikh
- Taoist
- Winery/Vineyard
- Zoo/Wildlife Sanctuary
- Other Sight

Activities, Courses & Tours

- Bodysurfing
- Diving
- Canoeing/Kayaking
- Course/Tour
- Sento Hot Baths/Onsen
- Skiing
- Snorkeling
- Surfing
- Swimming/Pool
- Walking
- Windsurfing
- Other Activity

Sleeping

- Sleeping
- Camping

Eating

- Eating

Drinking & Nightlife

- Drinking & Nightlife
- Cafe

Entertainment

- Entertainment

Shopping

- Shopping

Information

- Bank
- Embassy/Consulate
- Hospital/Medical
- Internet
- Police
- Post Office
- Telephone
- Toilet
- Tourist Information
- Other Information

Geographic

- Beach
- Gate
- Hut/Shelter
- Lighthouse
- Lookout
- Mountain/Volcano
- Oasis
- Park
- Pass
- Picnic Area
- Waterfall

Population

- Capital (National)
- Capital (State/Province)
- City/Large Town
- Town/Village

Transport

- Airport
- Border crossing
- Bus
- Cable car/Funicular
- Cycling
- Ferry
- Metro station
- Monorail
- Parking
- Petrol station
- Subway/Subte station
- Taxi
- Train station/Railway
- Tram
- Underground station
- Other Transport

Note: Not all symbols displayed above appear on the maps in this book

Routes

- Tollway
- Freeway
- Primary
- Secondary
- Tertiary
- Lane
- Unsealed road
- Road under construction
- Plaza/Mall
- Steps
- Tunnel
- Pedestrian overpass
- Walking Tour
- Walking Tour detour
- Path/Walking Trail

Boundaries

- International
- State/Province
- Disputed
- Regional/Suburb
- Marine Park
- Cliff
- Wall

Hydrography

- River, Creek
- Intermittent River
- Canal
- Water
- Dry/Salt/Intermittent Lake
- Reef

Areas

- Airport/Runway
- Beach/Desert
- Cemetery (Christian)
- Cemetery (Other)
- Glacier
- Mudflat
- Park/Forest
- Sight (Building)
- Sportsground
- Swamp/Mangrove

OUR STORY

A beat-up old car, a few dollars in the pocket and a sense of adventure. In 1972 that's all Tony and Maureen Wheeler needed for the trip of a lifetime – across Europe and Asia overland to Australia. It took several months, and at the end – broke but inspired – they sat at their kitchen table writing and stapling together their first travel guide, *Across Asia on the Cheap*. Within a week they'd sold 1500 copies. Lonely Planet was born.

Today, Lonely Planet has offices in Dublin, Franklin, London, Melbourne, Oakland, Beijing and Delhi, with more than 600 staff and writers. We share Tony's belief that 'a great guidebook should do three things: inform, educate and amuse'.

OUR WRITERS

Mara Vorhees

Coordinating Author, Northwestern Costa Rica, Arenal & Northern Lowlands, Península de Nicoya In 20 years of travel to Costa Rica, Mara has spotted 162 species of birds, all four New-World monkeys, anteaters, sloths, tapirs, peccaries, coatis, agoutis, a kinkajou and a jaguarundi. None of it, she attests, is quite as wild as her 5-year-old twins, who accompanied her while hiking, swimming, snorkeling, surfing, zipping, rafting, birding and horseback riding around Costa Rica. Mara has written many guidebooks for Lonely Planet, including *Central America on a Shoestring* and *Belize*. When not spying on sloths, she lives in Somerville, Massachusetts, with her husband, two kiddies and two kitties. Follow her adventures at www.havetwinswilltravel.com.

Ashley Harrell

San José, Central Valley & Highlands, Caribbean Coast When Ashley was 12, her dad took her on a medical mission to León, Nicaragua, where she remembers diving into a muddy swimming hole, devouring whole fried fish (eyeballs included) and downing her first beer. Twenty years and thousands of beers later, Central America enticed her again, and she moved to Costa Rica to be closer to sloths and work as a journalist, eventually enlisting with Lonely Planet. The 'research' for this guidebook involved sampling the capital's new farm-to-table restaurants, befriending a crocodile whisperer and exploring far-flung corners of the Caribbean, where she spotted a great jacamar and broke her flip-flops. Ashley also wrote the Plan Your Trip section.

Anna Kaminski

Central Pacific Coast, Southern Costa Rica & Península de Osa This was Anna's second research trip to Costa Rica and on this occasion she was lucky enough to tackle the southern part of the country – with the best dining scene, most rugged mountain and jungle trekking and the best opportunities to delve into indigenous culture. With a university background in the history and culture of Latin America, Anna has been traveling all over this part of the world for nearly 15 years. She tweets at @ACKaminski. Anna also wrote the Understand Costa Rica and Survival Guide sections.

Published by Lonely Planet Global Limited
CRN 554153
12th edition – October 2016
ISBN 978 1 78657 112 0
© Lonely Planet 2016   Photographs © as indicated 2016
10 9 8 7 6 5 4 3 2
Printed in Singapore